Career Guide to Industries

2000-2001 Edition

A Companion Reference to the *Occupational Outlook Handbook*

U.S. Department of Labor
Alexis M. Herman, Secretary

Bureau of Labor Statistics
Katharine G. Abraham, Commissioner

Bulletin 2523

> Published by JIST, this book's industry descriptions are a complete reprint of the *Career Guide to Industries* as produced by our friends at the U.S. Department of Labor.

For other industry- and career-related materials, turn to the back of this book. Some of JIST's many publications are described there. Among the many JIST-published occupational references are the following:

- *Occupational Outlook Handbook*
- *The O*NET Dictionary of Occupational Titles™*
- *Best Jobs for the 21st Century™*
- *Best Jobs for the 21st Century™ for College Graduates*
- *Best Jobs for the 21st Century™ Through Work Experience and On-the-Job Training*
- *The Enhanced Occupational Outlook Handbook*
- *Young Person's Occupational Outlook Handbook*
- *Dictionary of Occupational Titles*
- *Dictionary of Instructional Programs and Careers*
- *The Quick Internet Guide to Career and Education Information*
- *Health-Care Careers for the 21st Century*
- *The College Majors Handbook*
- *NAICS Desk Reference: The North American Industry Classification System Desk Reference*
- *North American Industry Classification System* (the original manual)
- *America's Top 300 Jobs*
- *America's Fastest Growing Jobs*
- *America's Top Jobs for People Without a Four-Year Degree*
- *America's Top Jobs for College Graduates*
- *America's Top Medical, Education, & Human Services Jobs*
- *America's Top White-Collar Jobs*
- *America's Top Military Careers*

Software

- JIST's Multimedia Occupational Outlook Handbook CD-ROM
- Young Person's Electronic Occupational Outlook Handbook
- JIST's Electronic O*NET Dictionary of Occupational Titles
- CareerExplorer™ CD-ROM
- Mike Farr's Get a Job Workshop on CD-ROM

JIST Works

Career Guide to Industries
2000-2001 Edition

A Companion Reference to the *Occupational Outlook Handbook*

© 2000 by JIST Publishing, Inc.

Published by JIST Works, an imprint of JIST Publishing, Inc.
8902 Otis Avenue
Indianapolis, IN 46216-1033

Phone: 1-800-648-JIST   Fax: 1-800-JIST-FAX
E-mail: editorial@jist.com   Web site: www.jist.com

About Career Materials Published by JIST

For the best information on occupations, many people—including experienced career professionals—rely on JIST. JIST has published information about careers and job search since the 1970s. JIST offers occupational references plus hundreds of other books, videos, assessment devices, and software.

Quantity discounts are available for this and other JIST books. Please call the JIST sales staff at 1-800-648-JIST weekdays for details.

Visit www.jist.com to find out about other JIST products, get free book chapters, and link to other career-related sites. You can also learn more about JIST authors and JIST training available to professionals.

A free catalog is available to professionals at schools, institutions, and other programs. It presents hundreds of helpful publications on career, job search, self-help, and business topics from JIST and other publishers. Please call 1-800-648-JIST to request the JIST catalog.

Thanks! We send you our best wishes from sunny Indianapolis.

Printed in the United States of America

02 01 00   9 8 7 6 5 4 3 2 1

The industry information contained in the *Career Guide* presents a general, composite description of firms and jobs and cannot be expected to reflect work situations in specific establishments or localities. The *Career Guide*, therefore, is not intended and should not be used as a guide for determining wages, hours, the right of a particular union to represent workers, appropriate bargaining units, or formal job evaluation systems. Nor should earnings data in the *Career Guide* be used to compute future loss of earnings in adjudication proceedings involving work injuries or accidental deaths.

Credits. This book is a complete reprint of the original, published by the good people at the Bureau of Labor Statistics, U.S. Department of Labor. Here is the text, from the original, providing credits to the many people who worked on this:

The *Career Guide to Industries* was produced in the Bureau of Labor Statistics under the general guidance and direction of Neal H. Rosenthal, Associate Commissioner for Employment Projections, and Mike Pilot, Chief of the Division of Occupational Outlook. Jon Sargent and Chester C. Levine, Managers, Occupational Outlook Studies, were responsible for planning and day-to-day direction.

Supervisors overseeing the research and preparation of material were Theresa Cosca, Mark Mittelhauser, Kristina Shelley, and Carolyn M. Veneri. Analysts who contributed material were Hall Dillon, Arlene K. Dohm, Eric B. Figueroa, Chad Fleetwood, Jeffrey C. Gruenert, Jonathan W. Kelinson, R. Sean Kirby, T. Alan Lacey, Kevin M. McCarron, Andrew J. Nelson, Erik A. Savisaar, Terry Schau, Jill S. Silver, Gary Steinberg, Tiffany T. Stringer, and Patricia Tate. Cover and other artwork (for the original) were designed by Keith Tapscott. Word processing support was provided by Beverly A. Williams.

ISBN 1-56370-804-3

About This Book

Helpful Career Planning Information on 42 Major Industries Employing 75% of the Workforce

Most people, when planning their careers, think mainly about the job they want and the education or training needed to get it. Unfortunately, they often overlook the enormous importance of the industry where they work. This book is designed to help.

The *Career Guide to Industries* provides information on employment trends and opportunities in industries. It is a companion to another book, also published by the U.S. Department of Labor, titled the *Occupational Outlook Handbook (OOH)*. These books fulfill a Labor Department mission to provide useful information for career planning and job seeking.

While the *OOH* provides information on jobs, the *Career Guide to Industries* gives details on the industries where people hold these jobs. JIST suggests you use both of these important references in your career planning.

The *Career Guide to Industries* Is Easy-to-Use!

This book was developed to provide, in a readable and useful format, information to assist you in making good career decisions. Use the table of contents to identify industries that interest you, and then find out more about them by turning to the page where each industry is described. You can also get a good overview on major employment trends from reading the short section titled "Major Trends in Industries and Employment."

Table of Contents

Quick Summary of Major Sections

Information Provided in the *Career Guide to Industries*: A quick review of the information elements provided in each industry description in this book. *Begins on page v.*

Major Trends in Industries and Employment: An excellent (and short!) overview of trends within related groupings of industries and jobs. *Begins on page 1.*

The Industry Descriptions: This is the major section of the book, providing detailed descriptions of 42 industries that employ about 75 percent of the workforce. Use the list on this page titled "Industries Described in This Book" to locate industries that interest you—and learn more about them by reading their descriptions beginning on the page number indicated. *Begins on page 9.*

Sources of State and Local Job Outlook Information: State-by-state sources of additional information, including Internet addresses. *Begins on page 229.*

Industries Described in This Book

Information Provided in the Career Guide to Industries

What kinds of workers are employed by a particular industry, and what jobs are you qualified for right now? What jobs require special education or training? And what advancement opportunities do these jobs offer in the long run? The *Career Guide to Industries* addresses these and other questions for 42 diverse industries. These industries, when combined, account for nearly 3 out of 4 wage and salary jobs in 1998.

As a companion to the *Occupational Outlook Handbook (OOH)*, the *Career Guide* discusses careers from an industry perspective. Why? Because many career-minded people think in terms of industries rather than occupations. Your personal circumstances or choice of lifestyle may compel you to remain in your area, limiting prospective jobs to those offered by the distinctive mix of industries in your state or community. Or, you may be attracted to a particular industry for other reasons—the glamour and travel associated with the air transportation industry, the potential for high earnings in the securities and commodities industry, the appeal of using advanced technology in aerospace manufacturing, the opportunity to work with children offered by the educational services industry, or the stability of jobs in the federal government, to name a few. By focusing on industries, the *Career Guide* provides information that the *Occupational Outlook Handbook* does not. Furthermore, some occupations are unique to a particular industry, and are not discussed in the *OOH*. In addition, some industries offer specific paths of career advancement that are not addressed in the *OOH*.

For each industry, the *Career Guide* includes a section with information on each of the following topics, although the information presented within each section varies slightly from industry to industry:

Industry Title

This is the name the industry is most commonly called.

SIC Number

To the right of the industry title you will see, in parentheses, the SIC code number. These are the Standard Industrial Classification (SIC) codes. They are from a reference titled the *Standard Industrial Classification Manual*, a publication of the Federal Office of Management and Budget that defines and names industries and establishes a structure for relating industries to one another. Readers interested in obtaining more detailed definitions of the industries in the *Career Guide* should consult the *SIC Manual*, which is available in the reference section of many libraries. The *SIC Manual* may also be consulted on the Internet at http://www.osha.gov/oshstats/sicser.html.

Significant Points

One or more key information items are presented at the beginning of each industry description.

Nature of the Industry

- Description of the goods produced or the services provided.
- Description of individual segments of the industry.
- Description of production processes.
- Changes in technology or business practices taking place.

Working Conditions

- Description of the physical environment in which workers perform their duties.
- Hours of work, including frequency of night or weekend work, or split shifts.
- Physical activities essential to successful job performance.
- Proportion of part-time workers.
- Rate of job-related injury and illness.
- Extent and frequency of travel.

Employment

- Number of wage and salary jobs in the industry.

- Number of self-employed persons in the industry, where significant.
- Data on the age of workers, where significant.
- Number of establishments and concentration of industry employment by state.
- Distribution of establishments and employment in the industry by employment-size class.
- Data on other unusual characteristics of industry workers, where significant.

Occupations in the Industry
- Description of the various jobs in the industry and how each fits into the process of producing goods or delivering services to consumers.
- Current and projected wage and salary jobs by occupation.

Training and Advancement
- Qualifications required or preferred for key occupations.
- Types of formal education and other training that employers in the industry generally require or prefer.
- Discussion of how experience, on-the-job training, formal employer training, and continuing education enable workers to advance in this industry.
- Paths of career advancement for key types of workers.
- Opportunities for self-employment.

Earnings
- Average weekly earnings in the industry.
- Earnings of key occupations in the industry.
- Employee benefits that are often offered in the industry but that are uncommon in other industries.
- Principal unions representing workers in the industry.
- The proportion of workers who belong to unions or who are covered by union contracts.

Outlook
- Rate at which jobs in the industry are projected to grow or decline.
- The projected rate of job growth compared to that of the economy as a whole.
- Factors expected to influence employment growth in the industry, such as new technology, changing business practices, and demographics.
- Occupations expected to grow or decline.
- Ease or difficulty of acquiring a job in the industry may be discussed.

Sources of Additional Information
This section includes organizations providing additional information via the Internet or by mail on the industry and its job opportunities. It also lists jobs described in the *Occupational Outlook Handbook* that are typically found in the industry.

A great many trade associations, professional societies, unions, industrial organizations, and government agencies provide career information that is valuable to counselors and job seekers. For the convenience of *Career Guide* users, some of these organizations and their Internet addresses are listed at the end of each industry statement. Although these references were carefully compiled, the Bureau of Labor Statistics has neither authority nor facilities for investigating the organizations or the information or publications that may be sent in response to a request and cannot guarantee the accuracy of such information. The listing of an organization, therefore, does not constitute in any way an endorsement or recommendation by the Bureau either of the organization and its activities or of the information it may supply. Each organization has sole responsibility for whatever information it may issue.

Information Tables
Unless otherwise indicated, the Bureau of Labor Statistics is the source of data presented in the various tables.

Major Trends in Industries and Employment

You have many factors to consider in targeting one industry over another when making job and career choices. Some industries pay more than others, are growing more rapidly, have more openings, fit your interests, or have other advantages.

This section will give you a quick overview of the major employment trends in various occupations and industries in the U.S. economy.

The U.S. economy is comprised of industries with diverse characteristics. For each industry covered in the *Career Guide* detailed information is provided about specific characteristics: the nature of the industry, working conditions, employment, occupational composition, training and advancement requirements, earnings, and job outlook. This chapter provides an overview of these characteristics for the economy as a whole.

Nature of the Industry

Industries are defined by the goods and services the industry provides. Because workers in the United States produce such a wide variety of products and services, industries in the U.S. economy range widely, from aerospace manufacturing to motion picture production. Although many of these industries are related, each industry contains a unique combination of occupations, production techniques, and business characteristics. Understanding the nature of the industry is important, because it is this unique combination that determines working conditions, educational requirements, and the job outlook for each of the industries discussed in the *Career Guide.*

Industries are comprised of many different places of work, called *establishments*, which range from large factories and office complexes employing thousands of workers to small businesses employing only a few workers. Not to be confused with "companies," which are legal entities, establishments are physical locations where people work, such as the branch office of a bank. Establishments that produce similar goods or services are grouped together into *industries*. Industries that produce related types of goods or services are, in turn, grouped together into *major industry divisions*. These are further grouped into the *goods-producing sector* (agriculture, forestry, and fishing; mining; construction; and manufacturing) or the *service-producing sector* (transportation, communications, and public utilities; wholesale and retail trade; finance, insurance, and real estate; services; and government).

Distinctions within industries are also varied. Each industry is comprised of a number of subdivisions, which are determined largely by differences in production processes. An easily recognized example of these distinctions is in the food processing industry, which is made up of subdivisions that produce meat products, preserved fruits and vegetables, bakery items, beverages, and dairy products, among others. Each of these subdivisions requires workers with varying skills and employ unique production techniques. Another example of these distinctions is in public utilities, which employs workers in establishments that provide electricity, sanitary services, water, and natural gas. Working conditions and establishment characteristics often differ widely in each of these smaller subdivisions.

There were nearly 7 million business establishments in the United States in 1997. The average size of these establishments varies widely across industries. Among industry divisions,

manufacturing included many industries having among the highest employment per establishment in 1997. For example, the aerospace, motor vehicle, and steel manufacturing industries each averaged 150 or more employees per establishment.

Most establishments in the wholesale and retail trade, finance, and services industries are small, averaging fewer than 20 employees per establishment. Exceptions are the air transportation industry with 62 employees and educational services with 44. In addition, wide differences within industries can exist. Hospitals, for example, employ an average of 716 employees, while doctor's offices employ an average of 9. Similarly, despite an average of 14 employees per establishment for all of retail trade, department stores employ an average of 183 people.

Establishments in the United States are predominantly small; 55 percent of all establishments employed fewer than five workers in 1997. The medium to large establishments, however, employ a greater proportion of all workers. For example, establishments that employed 50 or more workers accounted for only 5 percent of all establishments, yet employed 58 percent of all workers. The large establishments—those with more than 500 workers—accounted for only 0.3 percent of all establishments, but employed 20 percent of all workers. Table 1 presents the percent distribution of employment according to establishment size.

Establishment size can play a role in the characteristics of each job. Large establishments generally offer workers greater occupational mobility and advancement potential, whereas small establishments may provide their employees with broader experience by requiring them to assume a wider range of responsibilities. Also, small establishments are distributed throughout the nation; every locality has a few small businesses. Large establishments, in contrast, employ more workers and are less common, but they play a much more prominent role in the economies of the areas in which they are located.

Table 1. Percent distribution of establishments and employment in all industries by establishment size, 1997

Establishment size (number of workers)	Establishments	Employment
Total	100.0	100.0
1-4	54.5	6.1
5-9	19.6	8.5
10-19	12.4	10.9
20-49	8.3	16.4
50-99	2.8	12.7
100-249	1.7	16.2
250-499	0.4	9.4
500-999	0.2	7.0
1,000 or more	0.1	12.7

SOURCE: Department of Commerce, County Business Patterns, 1997

Working Conditions

Just as the goods and services of each industry are different, working conditions in industries can vary significantly. In some industries, the work setting is quiet, temperature-controlled, and virtually hazard free. Other industries are characterized by noisy, uncomfortable, and sometimes dangerous work environments. Some industries require long workweeks and shift work; in many industries, standard 35-to 40-hour workweeks are common. Still other industries can be seasonal, requiring long hours during busy periods and abbreviated schedules during slower months. These varying conditions usually are determined by production processes, establishment size, and the physical location of work.

One of the most telling indicators of working conditions is an industry's injury and illness rate. Overexertion, being struck by an object, and falls on the same level, were among the most common incidents causing injury or illness. In 1997, approximately 6.1 million nonfatal injuries and illnesses were reported throughout private industry. Among major industry divisions, manufacturing had the highest rate of injury and illness—10.3 cases for every 100 full-time workers—while finance, insurance, and real estate had the lowest rate—2.2 cases. About 6,000 work-related fatalities were reported in 1998; transportation accidents, violent acts, contact with objects and equipment, falls, and exposure to harmful substances or environments were among the most common events resulting in fatal injuries. Table 2 presents industries with the highest and lowest rates of nonfatal injury and illness.

Table 2. Nonfatal injury and illness rates of selected industries, 1997

Industry	Cases per 100 full-time employees
All industries	7.1
High rates	
Motor vehicle manufacturing	25.5
Air transportation	16.4
Nursing and personal care facilities	16.2
Food processing	14.5
Trucking and warehousing	10.0
Low rates	
Insurance	1.9
Banking	1.8
Radio and TV broadcasting	1.8
Computer and data processing	0.8
Securities and commodities	0.7

Work schedules are another important reflection of working conditions, and the operational requirements of each industry lead to large differences in hours worked and part-time versus full-time status. The contrast in an average workweek was notable between retail trade and manufacturing—29.1 hours and 41.7 hours, respectively, in 1998. More than 30 percent of workers in retail trade work part time (1 to 34 hours per week), compared to only 5 percent in manufacturing. Table 3 presents industries having relatively high and low percentages of part-time workers.

Table 3. Percent of part-time workers in selected industries, 1998

Industry	Percent part-time
All industries	15.9
Many part-time workers	
Apparel and accessory stores	38.6
Eating and drinking places	38.0
Department stores	33.0
Grocery stores	32.5
Child-care services	29.7
Few part-time workers	
Public utilities	3.0
Chemical manufacturing, except drugs	2.9
Textile mill products manufacturing	2.5
Motor vehicle and equipment manufacturing	1.8
Steel manufacturing	1.7

The low proportion of part-time workers in some manufacturing industries often reflects the continuity of the production processes and the specificity of skills. Once begun, it is costly to halt these processes; machinery and materials must be tended and moved continuously. For example, the chemical manufacturing industry produces many different chemical products through controlled chemical reactions. These processes require chemical operators to monitor and adjust the flow of materials into and out of the line of production. Production may continue 24 hours a day, 7 days a week under the watchful eyes of chemical operators who work in shifts.

Retail trade and service industries, on the other hand, have seasonal cycles marked by various events, such as school openings or important holidays, that affect the hours worked. During busy times of the year, longer hours are common, whereas slack periods lead to cutbacks and shorter workweeks. Jobs in these industries are generally appealing to students and others who desire flexible, part-time schedules.

Employment

The number of wage and salary worker jobs in the United States totaled nearly 128 million in 1998, and it is projected to reach almost 148 million by 2008 (See Table 4). In addition to these workers, the U.S. economy also provided employment for nearly 12 million self-employed workers and about 182,000 unpaid family workers.

As shown in table 4, employment is not evenly divided among the various industries. The services major industry division is the largest source of employment, with over 47 million workers, followed by wholesale and retail trade and manufacturing major industry divisions. Among the industries covered in the *Career Guide*, wage and salary employment ranged from 181,000 in cable and other pay television services to 11.2 million in educational services. Three industries—educational services, health services, and eating and drinking places—together accounted for about 30 million jobs, or nearly a quarter of the Nation's employment.

3

Table 4. Wage and salary employment in selected industries, 1998 and projected change, 1998 to 2008

(Employment in thousands)

Industry	1998 Employment	Percent distribution	2008 Employment	1998-2008 Employment change	Percent change
All Industries	128,008	100.0	147,543	19,535	15.3
Goods-producing industries	27,506	21.5	27,951	445	1.6
Agriculture, forestry, and fishing	2,159	1.7	2,257	98	4.6
Agricultural services	1,005	0.8	1,251	246	24.5
Agricultural production	1,106	0.9	968	-138	-12.5
Mining	590	0.5	475	-115	-19.4
Oil and gas extraction	339	0.3	283	-56	-16.7
Mining and quarrying	251	0.2	192	-59	-23.2
Construction	5,985	4.7	6,535	550	9.2
Manufacturing	18,772	14.7	18,684	-88	-0.5
Electronics manufacturing	1,564	1.2	1,701	137	8.8
Food processing	1,686	1.3	1,721	35	2.1
Printing and publishing	1,564	1.2	1,545	-19	-1.3
Motor vehicle and equipment manufacturing	990	0.7	940	-50	-5.0
Chemicals manufacturing, except drugs	764	0.6	734	-30	-3.9
Apparel and other textile products manufacturing ..	763	0.6	586	-178	-23.3
Textile mill products manufacturing	598	0.5	501	-97	-16.2
Aerospace manufacturing	524	0.4	656	132	25.2
Drug manufacturing	279	0.2	308	29	10.7
Steel manufacturing	232	0.2	177	-55	-23.7
Service-producing industries	100,501	78.5	119,590	19,089	19.0
Transportation, communications, and public utilities ...	6,600	5.2	7,540	940	14.3
Trucking and warehousing	1,745	1.4	1,944	199	11.4
Air transportation	1,183	0.9	1,400	217	18.3
Telecommunications	1,042	0.8	1,285	244	23.4
Public utilities	855	0.7	822	-33	-3.8
Radio and television broadcasting	247	0.1	253	6	2.5
Cable and other pay TV services	181	0.1	230	49	27.0
Wholesale and retail trade	29,128	22.8	32,693	3,565	12.2
Eating and drinking places	7,760	6.1	9,082	1,322	17.0
Wholesale trade	6,831	5.3	7,330	499	7.3
Department, clothing, and variety stores	3,872	3.0	4,101	228	5.9
Grocery stores	3,066	2.4	3,240	174	5.7
Motor vehicle dealers	1,145	0.9	1,277	132	11.6
Finance, insurance, and real estate	7,407	5.8	8,367	960	13.0
Insurance	2,344	1.8	2,576	233	9.9
Banking	2,042	1.6	2,100	58	2.8
Securities and commodities	645	0.5	900	255	39.6
Services	47,528	37.1	60,445	12,917	27.2
Educational services	11,175	8.7	12,885	1,680	15.3
Health services	10,829	8.5	13,614	2,785	25.7
Personnel supply services	3,230	2.5	4,623	1,393	43.1
Social services	2,039	1.6	2,878	839	41.1
Hotels and other lodging places	1,776	1.4	2,088	312	17.6
Amusement and recreation services	1,601	1.3	2,108	507	31.7
Computer and data processing services	1,599	1.2	3,471	1,872	117.1
Management and public relations services	1,034	0.8	1,500	466	45.1
Child-care services	605	0.5	800	196	32.3
Motion picture production and distribution	270	0.2	316	46	16.9
Advertising	268	0.2	323	55	20.5
Government	9,838	7.7	10,545	707	7.2
State and local government	7,152	5.6	7,996	844	11.8
Federal Government	1,819	1.4	1,655	-164	-9.0

Although workers of all ages are employed in each industry, certain industries tend to possess workers of distinct age groups. For the reasons mentioned above, retail trade employs a relatively high proportion of younger workers to fill part-time and temporary positions. The manufacturing sector, on the other hand, has a relatively high median age because many jobs in the sector require a number of years to learn and rely on skills that do not easily transfer to other firms. Also, manufacturing employment has been declining, providing fewer opportunities for younger workers to get jobs. As a result, almost one-third of the workers in retail trade were 24 years of age or younger, whereas only 10 percent of workers in manufacturing were 24 or younger. Table 5 contrasts the age distribution of workers in all industries with the distributions in retail trade and manufacturing.

Table 5. Percent distribution of industry sector employment by age group, 1998

Age group	All industries	Retail trade	Manufacturing
Total	100.0	100.0	100.0
16-24	15.0	32.5	9.9
25-54	72.3	56.9	78.2
55 and older	12.7	10.6	11.8

Employment in some industries is concentrated in one region of the country, and job opportunities in these industries should be best in the States in which their establishments are located. Such industries are often located near a source of raw materials upon which the industries rely. For example, oil and gas extraction jobs are concentrated in Texas, Louisiana, and Oklahoma; many textile mill products manufacturing jobs are found in North Carolina, Georgia, and South Carolina; and a significant proportion of motor vehicle and equipment manufacturing jobs are located in Michigan. On the other hand, some industries—such as grocery stores and educational services—have jobs distributed throughout the Nation, reflecting population density in different areas.

Occupations in the Industry
As mentioned above, the occupations found in each industry depend on the types of services provided or goods produced. For example, construction companies require skilled trades workers to build and renovate buildings, so these companies employ a large number of carpenters, electricians, plumbers, painters, and sheet metal workers. Other occupations common to the construction sector include construction equipment operators and mechanics, installers, and repairers. Retail trade, on the other hand, displays and sells manufactured goods to consumers, so this sector hires numerous sales clerks and other workers, including nearly 5 out of 6 cashiers. Table 6 shows the major industry divisions and the occupational groups which predominate in the division.

Table 6. Industry divisions and largest occupational concentration, 1998

Industry division	Largest occupational group	Percent of wage and salary jobs
Agriculture, forestry, and fishing	Agriculture and related	78.8
Mining	Precision production	44.0
Construction	Precision production	55.5
Manufacturing	Operators, fabricators, and laborers	45.0
Transportation, communications, and public utilities	Operators, fabricators, and laborers	33.0
Wholesale and retail trade	Marketing and sales	32.7
Finance, insurance, and real estate	Administrative support	44.8
Services	Professional specialty	28.4
Government	Administrative support	26.1

The Nation's occupational distribution clearly is influenced by its industrial structure, yet there are many occupations, such as general manager or secretary, which are found in all industries. In fact, some of the largest occupations in the U.S. economy are dispersed across many industries. Because nearly every industry relies on administrative support, for example, this occupational group is the largest in the Nation (see table 7). Other large occupational groups include service occupations, professional specialty workers, and operators, fabricators, and laborers.

Table 7. Total employment in broad occupational groups, 1998 and projected change, 1998-2008

(Employment in thousands)

Occupational group	1998 Employment	1998-2008 Percent change
Total, all occupations	140,514	14.4
Executive, administrative, and managerial	14,770	16.4
Professional specialty	19,802	27.0
Technicians and related support	4,949	22.2
Marketing and sales	15,341	14.9
Administrative support, including clerical	24,461	9.0
Services	22,548	17.1
Agriculture, forestry, fishing, and related	4,435	1.6
Precision production, craft, and repair	15,619	8.0
Operators, fabricators, and laborers	18,588	9.4

Table 8. Percent distribution of highest grade completed or degree received by industry division, 1998

Industry division	Bachelor's degree or higher	Some college or associate degree	High school graduate of equivalent	Less than 12 years or no diploma
Agriculture, forestry, and fishing	13	20	34	33
Mining	24	22	39	15
Construction	10	25	44	21
Manufacturing	21	24	40	15
Transportation, communications, and public utilities	20	33	38	9
Wholesale and retail trade	14	29	37	20
Finance, insurance, and real estate	37	32	27	4
Services	39	24	28	9
Government, public administration	37	36	25	2

Training and Advancement

Workers prepare for employment in many ways, but the most fundamental form of job training in the United States is a high school education. Fully 87 percent of the Nation's workforce possessed a high school diploma or its equivalent in 1998. As the premium placed on education in today's economy increases, workers are responding by pursuing additional training. In 1998, 28 percent of the Nation's workforce had some college or an associate's degree, while an additional 27 percent continued in their studies and attained a bachelor's degree or higher. In addition to these types of formal education, other sources of qualifying training include formal company training, informal on-the-job training, correspondence courses, the Armed Forces, and friends, relatives, and other nonwork-related training.

The unique combination of training required to succeed in each industry is determined largely by the industry's occupational composition. For example, machine operators in manufacturing generally need little formal education after high school, but sometimes complete considerable on-the-job training. These requirements by major industry division are clearly demonstrated in table 8. Workers with no more than a high school diploma comprised about 67 percent of all workers in agriculture, forestry, and fishing; 65 percent in construction; 55 percent in manufacturing; and 57 percent in wholesale and retail trade. On the other hand, workers who had acquired at least some training at the college level comprised 73 percent of all workers in government; 69 percent in finance, insurance, and real estate; and 63 percent in services. Tables 9 and 10 provide further illustration of how greatly industries vary in their training requirements, which show industries having the highest percentages of college graduates and workers without education beyond high school.

Table 9. Industries with the highest percentage of workers who have a bachelor's degree or higher, 1998

Industry	Percent
Management and public relations services	68.6
Securities and commodities	64.9
Elementary and secondary schools	62.8
Legal services	62.5
Accounting and auditing services	62.3

Education and training are also important factors in the variety of advancement paths found in different industries. In general, workers who complete additional on-the-job training or education help their chances of being promoted. In much of the manufacturing sector, for example, production workers who receive training in management and computer skills increase their likelihood of being promoted to supervisors. Other factors which may figure prominently in the industries covered in the *Career Guide* include the size of the establishment or company, institutionalized career tracks, and the skills and aptitude of each worker. Each industry has some unique advancement paths, so persons who seek jobs in particular industries should be aware of how these paths may later shape their careers.

Table 10. Industries with the highest percentage of workers who have 12 years or less of schooling or no diploma, 1998

Industry	Percent
Meat products processing	79.5
Apparel and other finished textile products manufacturing	74.4
Private households	74.4
Lumber and wood products manufacturing	74.2
Services to dwellings and other buildings	73.2
Agricultural production, crops	73.1

Earnings

Like other characteristics, earnings differ from industry to industry, the result of a highly complicated process that relies on a number of factors. For example, earnings may vary due to the occupations in the industry, average hours worked, geographical location, industry profits, union affiliation, and educational requirements. In general, wages are highest in metropolitan areas to compensate for the higher cost of living. And, as would be expected, industries that employ relatively few unskilled minimum-wage or part-time workers tend to have higher earnings.

A good illustration of these differences is shown by the earnings of production and nonsupervisory workers in coal mining, which averaged $858 a week in 1998, and those in eating and drinking places, where the weekly average was $162. These differences are so large because the coal mining industry employs a relatively highly-skilled, highly-unionized workforce, while eating and drinking places employ many relatively lower-skilled, part-time workers, few of whom belong to unions. In addition, many workers in eating and drinking places are able to supplement their low wages with money they receive as tips, which are not included in the industry wages data. Table 11 highlights the industries with the highest and lowest average weekly earnings. Because these data exclude supervisors, they generally are lower than the average earnings for all workers in a given industry.

Table 11. Average weekly earnings of nongovernment production or nonsupervisory workers in selected industries, 1998

Industry	Earnings
All industries	$442
Industries with high earnings	
Coal mining	858
Railroad transportation	845
Aerospace manufacturing	845
Public utilities	843
Steel manufacturing	822
Computer and data processing services	815
Engineering services	810
Securities and commodities	800
Motion picture production and services	789
Motor vehicle production	780
Industries with low earnings	
Help supply services	330
Nursing and personal care services	318
Apparel and other textile products manufacturing	318
Hotels and other lodging places	279
Grocery stores	276
Amusement and recreation services	258
General merchandise stores	256
Child care services	237
Apparel and accessory stores	226
Eating and drinking places	162

Employee benefits, once a minor addition to wages and salaries, continue to grow in diversity and cost. In addition to traditional benefits—including paid vacations, life and health insurance, and pensions—many employers now offer various benefits to accommodate the needs of a changing labor force. Such benefits are child care, employee assistance programs that provide counseling for personal problems, and wellness programs that encourage exercise, stress management, and self-improvement. Benefits vary among occupational groups, full and part-time workers, public and private sector workers, regions, unionized and nonunionized workers, and small and large establishments. Data indicate that full-time workers and those in medium-size and large establishments—those with 100 or more workers—receive better benefits than part-time workers and those in smaller establishments.

Table 12. Percent of workers who are union members or covered by union contracts by industry division, 1998

Industry division	Union members or covered by union contracts
Total, all industries	15.4
Government, public administration	37.5
Transportation, communications, and public utilities	33.7
Construction	19.8
Manufacturing	16.8
Services	15.4
Mining	13.6
Wholesale and retail trade	5.8
Finance, insurance, and real estate	3.4
Agriculture, forestry, and fishing	2.3

Union affiliation may also play a role in earnings and benefits. In 1998, about 15 percent of workers throughout the Nation were union members or covered by union contracts. As table 12 demonstrates, union affiliation of workers varies widely by industry. Over a third of the workers in government and transportation, communications, and public utilities are union members or are covered by union contracts, compared to less than 4 percent in finance, insurance, and real estate and agriculture, forestry, and fishing.

Outlook

Total employment in the United States is projected to increase about 15 percent over the 1998-2008 period. Employment growth, however, is only one source of job openings; the total number of openings provided by any industry depends on its current employment level, its growth rate, and its need to replace workers who leave their jobs. Throughout the economy, in fact, replacement needs will create more job openings than employment growth. Employment size is a major determinant of job openings—larger industries generally provide more openings. The occupational composition of an industry is another factor. Industries with a high concentration of professional, technical, and other jobs that require more formal education—occupations in which workers tend to leave their jobs less frequently—generally have fewer openings resulting from replacement needs. On the other hand, industries with a high concentration of service, laborer, and other jobs that require little formal education and have lower wages generally have more replacement openings because these workers are more likely to leave their occupations.

Employment growth is determined largely by changes in the demand for the goods and services produced by an industry, worker productivity, and foreign competition. Each industry is affected by a different set of variables that impacts the number and composition of jobs that will be available. Even within an industry, employment in different occupations may grow at different rates. For example, changes in technology, production methods, and business practices in an industry might eliminate some jobs, while creating others. Some industries may be growing rapidly overall, yet opportunities for workers in occupations that are adversely affected by technological change could be stagnant. Similarly, employment of some occupations may be declining in the economy as a whole, yet may be increasing in a rapidly growing industry.

As shown in table 4, employment growth rates over the next decade will vary widely among industries. Employment in goods-producing industries will increase slightly, as growth in construction and agriculture, forestry, and fishing is expected to be offset by declining employment in mining and manufacturing. Growth in construction employment will be driven by new factory construction as existing facilities are modernized; by new school construction, reflecting growth in the school-age population; and by infrastructure improvements, such as road and bridge construction. Overall employment in agriculture, forestry, and fishing will grow more slowly than average, with almost all new jobs occurring in the rapidly growing agricultural services industry—which includes landscaping, farm management, veterinary, soil preparation, and crop services. Employment in mining is expected to decline, due to the spread of labor-saving technology and increasing reliance on foreign sources of energy. Manufacturing employment also will decline slightly, as improvements in production technology and rising imports eliminate many production occupations. Apparel manufacturing is projected to lose about 178,000 jobs over the 1998-2008 period—more than any other manufacturing industry—due primarily to increasing imports. Some manufacturing industries with strong domestic markets and export potential, however, are expected to experience increases in employment. The drug manufacturing and aerospace manufacturing industries are two examples. Sales of drugs are expected to increase with the rise in the population, particularly the elderly, and the availability of new drugs on the market. An increase in air traffic, coupled with the need to replace aging aircraft will generate strong sales for commercial aircraft. Both industries have large export markets.

Growth in overall employment will result primarily from growth in service-producing industries over the 1998-2008 period, almost all of which are expected to witness increasing employment. Rising employment in these industries will be driven by services industries—the largest and fastest growing major industry sector—which is projected to provide more than 2 out of 3 new jobs across the Nation. Health, education, and business services will account for almost 9 million of these new jobs. In addition, employment in the Nation's fastest growing industry—computer and data processing services—is expected to more than double, adding another 1.8 million jobs. Job growth in the services sector will result from overall population growth, the rise in the elderly and school age population, and the trend toward contracting out for computer, personnel, and other business services.

Wholesale and retail trade is expected to add an additional 3.6 million jobs over the coming decade. Nearly 500,000 of these jobs will arise in wholesale trade, driven mostly by growth in trade and the overall economy. Retail trade is expected to add 3 million jobs over the 1998-2008 period, resulting largely from a greater population and increased personal income levels. Although most retail stores are expected to add employees, nonstore retailers will experience the fastest growth rate—55 percent—as electronic commerce and mail order sales account for an increasing portion of retail sales. Eating and drinking places will have the largest number of openings, over 1.3 million.

Employment in transportation, communications, and public utilities is projected to increase by nearly 940,000 new jobs. The telecommunications industry will have the biggest increase—244,000 jobs. Strong demand for new telecommunications services, such as Internet and wireless communications, will lead to an expansion of the telecommunications infrastructure and provide strong employment growth. Trucking and air transportation are expected to generate over 400,000 jobs. Trucking industry growth will be fueled by growth in the volume of goods that need to be shipped as the economy expands. Air transportation will expand as consumer and business demand increases, reflecting a rising population and increased business activity. Finally, while radio and television broadcasting will show little employment growth due to consolidations in the industry, cable and other pay television companies will increase by 27 percent as they upgrade their systems to deliver a wider array of communication and programming services.

Overall employment growth in finance, insurance, and real estate is expected to be around 13 percent, with close to 1 million jobs added by 2008. Securities and commodities will be the fastest growing industry in this sector, adding over 250,000 jobs. A growing interest in investing and the rising popularity of 401(k) and other pension plans are fueling increases in this industry. In contrast, the largest industry in this sector, banking, will grow by only 2.8 percent, or 58,000 jobs, as technological advances and the increasing use of electronic banking reduce the need for large administrative support staffs. Nondepository institutions—including personal and business credit institutions, as well as mortgage banks—are expected to grow at a rapid rate, and insurance will also expand, increasing by 232,000 jobs.

All 707,000 new government jobs are expected to arise in State and local government, reflecting growth in the population and its demand for public services. In contrast, the Federal Government is expected to lose more than 160,000 jobs over the 1998-2008 period, as efforts continue to cut costs by contracting out services and giving States more responsibility for administering Federally funded programs.

In sum, recent changes in the economy are having far-reaching and complex effects on employment in each of the industries covered in the *Career Guide*. Jobseekers should be aware of these changes, keeping alert for developments that can affect job opportunities in industries and the variety of occupations which are found in each industry. For more detailed information on specific occupations, consult the 2000-2001 Edition of the *Occupational Outlook Handbook*, which provides information on 250 occupations.

The Industry Descriptions

This is the book's major part, which describes 42 major industries. Look in the table of contents for a complete list of the industries, arranged into these seven clusters:

- Agriculture, mining, and construction
- Manufacturing
- Transportation, communications, and public utilities
- Wholesale and retail trade
- Finance and insurance
- Services
- Government

Agriculture, Mining, and Construction

Agricultural Production

SIGNIFICANT POINTS

- Commercial farms make up about one-fourth of all agricultural establishments, yet generate approximately 90 percent of total agricultural output.

- Self-employed workers—mostly farmers—account for more than half of the industry's workforce.

- Employment in agricultural production is expected to continue its long-term decline.

Nature of the Industry

Agricultural production, or farming and ranching, has long been a mainstay of the Nation's economy, successfully feeding and clothing the domestic population as well as exporting agricultural goods around the world. Once a labor intensive industry, providing jobs for at least 12 percent of the workforce as late as 1950, both agricultural employment and the number of farms have dropped significantly in recent decades because of mechanization and other technological improvements. Although approximately one-third the number of farms exists today as compared to 50 years ago, output has more than doubled, exports of agricultural goods continue to contribute positively to the trade balance, and agricultural production remains one of the Nation's top 10 industries in terms of total employment.

Thanks to generally temperate climates, rich soil, and a variety of growing conditions, the agricultural sector produces an abundance and wide selection of goods. The industry is roughly divided into two major segments: livestock production, including animal specialties; and crop production. *Livestock production* includes establishments that raise livestock, such as beef cattle, sheep, and hogs; dairy farms; poultry and egg farms; and farms, such as apiaries (bee farms) and aquaculture, that raise animal specialties. *Crop production* includes the growing of cash grains, such as wheat, corn, and barley; field crops, such as cotton and tobacco; vegetables and melons; fruits and nuts; and horticultural specialties, such as flowers and ornamental plants.

About 2.2 million establishments make up the agricultural production industry. According to the U.S. Department of Agriculture, an establishment must sell at least $1,000 worth of produce per year to qualify as a farm. Establishments selling between $1,000 and $50,000 are known as *noncommercial farms*, while those selling more than $50,000 are identified as *commercial farms*. Noncommercial farms account for about three-fourths of all farms, many of which are individually owned family farms. Commercial farms, though substantially fewer in number, are much larger in size and generate about 90 percent of total agricultural sales.

Production of some types of crops and livestock tend to be concentrated in particular regions of the country, based on the growing conditions and the topography. For example, the warm climates of Florida and Southern California are best suited for citrus fruit production. The Southern States are the major growers of tobacco, cotton, rice, and peanuts. In the Northeast, from Maine to New Jersey, blueberries, maple syrup, and apples are major agricultural products. Cranberry bogs are mainly found in Massachusetts and Wisconsin. Hogs, grains, potatoes, and range-fed cattle are major products in the Plains States. In the Southwest and West, ranchers raise beef cattle. In Washington State, apples are an important crop; in California grapes for wine are prominent, as well as most vegetables and fruits. Poultry and dairy farms tend to be found in most areas of the country.

The nature of the work in the agricultural production industry varies depending on the type of product. Consumption of, and demand for, cash grains tend to be strong and steady, and they comprise a substantial part of agricultural output. They are generally grown in large-scale operations in several areas in the Nation, but particularly the Midwest. During the planting, growing, and harvesting seasons, workers are busy for long hours plowing, disking, harrowing, seeding, fertilizing, and harvesting. Fieldwork on large farms consisting of hundreds, sometimes thousands, of acres is often done using massive, climate-controlled tractors and other modern agricultural equipment. In some cases, "teams" of operators with tractors, combines, or other agricultural equipment travel from one farm to another during harvest time in a practice known as "custom harvesting."

Small-scale establishments are more common in the Northeast as compared to the larger establishments elsewhere in the country, particularly the Southwest and West. However, these small farms in States with limited growing seasons cannot provide produce for markets during the months of late fall, winter, and early spring. Therefore, the majority of fresh vegetables is grown on large farms in California, and shipped throughout the country. Vegetables are generally still harvested manually by groups of migrant farm workers, although new machines have been developed to replace manual labor for some fruit crops. Vegetable growers on large farms of approximately 100 acres or more usually practice "monoculture," large-scale cultivation of one crop on each division of land.

Dairy farms provide the nation with a variety of products, including milk, cheese, butter, and ice cream. Dairy farming requires outdoor, as well as indoor, work. Farmers, farm managers, and farm workers must feed cows, heifers, and calves, clean their stalls, and take them outside to pastures for exercise and grazing. Workers may also plant, harvest, and store several crops to feed the cattle through the cold of winter or the drought of summer.

Though the nature of the work on large ranches in the West and Southwest still entails the kind of activities—such as branding and herding—often seen in cowboy movies, the use of modern equipment and technology has changed the way the work is done. Branding and vaccinating of herds, for example, are largely mechanized. The work on such establishments still tends to be seasonal and to take place largely outdoors. Common activities include raising feed crops, rotating cattle from one pasture to another, and keeping fences in good repair. But the use of trucks, portable communications gear, and geopositioning equipment is now common and saves valuable time for livestock ranchers.

Poultry and egg farms are, for the most part, large operations resembling production lines. With the exception of free-range farms, where fowl are allowed some time outside during the day for exercise and sunlight, poultry production involves mainly indoor work, with workers performing a limited number of specific tasks repeatedly. Because of increased mechanization, poultry growers can raise chickens by the hundreds—sometimes the thousands—under one roof. Eggs still are collected manually in some small-scale hatcheries, but in larger hatcheries eggs tumble down onto conveyor belts. Machines then wash, sort, and pack the eggs into individual cartons. From there, workers place the cartons into boxes and stack the boxes onto pallets.

On aquaculture farms, farmers raise fish and shellfish in salt, brackish, or fresh water—depending on the requirements of the particular species—usually in ponds, floating net pens, raceways, or recirculating systems. They stock, feed, protect, and otherwise manage aquatic life sold for consumption or used for recreational fishing. Horticulture farms raise ornamental plants, bulbs, shrubbery, sod, and flowers. Although much of the work takes place outdoors, in seasonal climates much production also takes place in greenhouses or hothouses.

Some agricultural establishments cater directly to the public. For example, some fruit and vegetable growers use the marketing strategy of "pick-your-own" produce, or set up roadside stands. Nurseries and greenhouses, which grow everything from seedlings to sod, also provide products directly to individual consumers as well as to retail establishments and other industries.

Working Conditions

Agricultural production attracts people who enjoy an independent lifestyle and working with animals or outdoors on the land. For many, the wide-open physical expanse, the variability of day-to-day work, and the rural setting provide benefits that offset the sometimes hard labor, the danger that unseasonable or extreme weather may stunt or ruin crops, and the risk that unfavorable commodity prices may lower income.

Although the working conditions vary by occupation and setting, there are some characteristics common to most agricultural jobs. Hours are generally uneven and oftentimes long; work can't be delayed when crops must be planted and harvested, or when animals must be sheltered and fed. Weekend work is common, and farmers, farm managers, crew leaders, farm equipment operators, and farm workers may work a 6- or 7-day week during planting and harvesting seasons. More than 1 out of 4 employees in this industry work variable schedules compared to less than 1 in 10 workers in all industries combined. Since much of the work is seasonal in nature, many farm workers must cope with the difficulty in obtaining year-round, full-time employment. Migrant farm workers, who move from location to location as crops ripen, live an unsettled lifestyle, which can be stressful.

Much farm and ranch work takes place outdoors in all kinds of weather and is physical in nature. Harvesting vegetables, in particular, requires manual labor, and workers do much bending, stooping, and lifting. Some field workers may lack adequate sanitation facilities, and their drinking water may be limited. The year-round nature of much livestock production work means that ranch workers must be out in the heat of summer, as well as the cold of winter. Those who work directly with animals risk being bitten or kicked.

Farmers and farm workers in crop production risk exposure to pesticides and other potentially hazardous chemicals that are sprayed on crops or plants. Those who work on mechanized farms must take precautions when working with tools and heavy equipment to avoid injury. Farmwork has long had one of the highest incidences of illnesses and injuries of any industry. In 1997, crop production had 9.1 injuries and illnesses per 100 full-time workers compared to an average of 7.1 throughout private industry.

Employment

In 1998, agricultural production employed a total of about 2.5 million workers, making it one of the largest industries in the Nation. This industry is unusual in that self-employed workers account for a slight majority of its workforce. Among all occupations, just over half—about 1.3 million—are self-employed; nearly 1.2 million wage and salary workers and 35,000 unpaid family workers make up the remainder.

For wage and salary workers, the single most common occupation was that of farm workers, who made up nearly 25 percent of the overall workforce. The majority of self-employed workers were farmers, accounting for approximately 52 percent of total employment in this industry. Agricultural production is one of the few remaining areas of the economy where unpaid family workers remain a significant part of the workforce. Most unpaid family workers on farms assist with the farm work, but a small number do bookkeeping and accounting or act as farmers.

Employment is fairly evenly distributed between livestock production and crop production, with livestock-producing establishments employing about 55 percent of all workers and crop-producing establishments employing 45 percent. Establishments specializing in ornamental nursery products employed the largest number of workers in 1997, followed by vegetable and melon producing farms and fruit orchards. Crop farms, dairy farms, and vineyards also employed a significant number of workers. Most individual agricultural production establishments, however, employ fewer than 10 workers (chart).

Workers in agricultural production tend to be slightly older than the workers in other industries. In livestock production, for example, about half of the workers are over the age of 44, compared to about one-third, on average, in all industries. In agricultural production, the median age was significantly higher, 43, than for workers in all other industries, 39, probably reflecting the strong attachment that self-employed farmers have to their occupation.

11

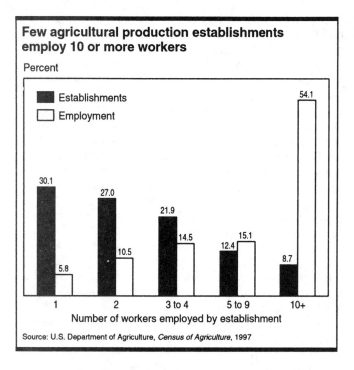

Few agricultural production establishments employ 10 or more workers

Percent

- ■ Establishments
- □ Employment

Number of workers employed by establishment	Establishments	Employment
1	30.1	5.8
2	27.0	10.5
3 to 4	21.9	14.5
5 to 9	12.4	15.1
10+	8.7	54.1

Source: U.S. Department of Agriculture, *Census of Agriculture*, 1997

Occupations in the Industry

It takes several kinds of occupational specialties—from book-keepers, accountants, and auditors to mechanics and repairers—to keep the industry functioning (table 1). However, despite upgrades in technology, new forms of machinery, and the complex financial records that must be kept, three occupations still compose the overwhelming majority of workers in agricultural production: Farmers, farm managers, and farm workers.

Farmers are the self-employed owner-operators of establishments that produce agricultural output. Their work encompasses numerous tasks. They keep records of their animals' health, crop rotation, operating expenses, major purchases, bills paid and income due, as well as pay bills and file taxes. Computer literacy has become as necessary for farmers as it has for many other occupations.

Farmers must have additional skills to keep a farm operating day-in and day-out. A basic understanding and working knowledge of mechanics, carpentry, plumbing, and electricity are all helpful, if not essential, for running a farm. The ability to maintain and repair equipment and facilities is important to keep costs down and the farm running smoothly.

Farmers who work large commercial farms for cash crops make decisions as much as a year in advance about which crop to grow. Therefore, a farmer must be aware of prices in national and international markets to use for guidance, while tracking the costs associated with each particular crop. When dealing in hundreds or thousands of acres of one crop, even small errors in judgment are magnified, so the impact can be substantial. Thus, large-scale farmers strive to keep costs to a minimum in every phase of the operation. Furthermore, risk management of portfolios—the practice of juggling stocks, buying and selling futures, and engaging in other paper deals like bond trading—is now becoming more important for farmers of large commercial farms.

Farm managers operate the farm on a daily basis for the owners. Large commercial farms may have a manager for different operations within the establishment. On smaller farms, farm managers oversee all operations. They purchase the inputs used in the farm's production: Machinery, seed, fertilizers, herbicides and pesticides, fuel, and labor. They must be aware of any laws that govern the use of such inputs in the farm's locality. Additionally, they may hire and oversee other farm employees as they plow, disk, harrow, plant, fertilize, harvest, and care for livestock. Farm managers must be knowledgeable about crop rotation, soil testing, and various types of capital improvements necessary to maximize crop yields.

Farm managers perform many of the functions of farmers themselves, with the added tasks of managing the schedules and work of the employees. They assign, monitor and assess individuals' performances day-in and day-out. They may keep in order all the paperwork needed to satisfy legal requirements, including keeping payroll records and state and Federal tax records.

Farm workers perform the whole spectrum of daily chores involved in crop or livestock production. On nurseries they plant seedlings, transplant saplings, and water and trim plants. On crop farms they may manually plant, cultivate, and harvest vegetables, fruits, nuts, and field crops using hand tools such as shovels, trowels, hoes, tampers, pruning hooks, shears, and knives. Among their duties are tilling soil and applying fertilizers; transplanting, weeding, thinning, or pruning crops; applying fungicides, herbicides, or pesticides; and packing and loading harvested products. They also may repair fences and farm buildings, or keep irrigation equipment functioning. Some farm workers attend to farm or ranch animals such as sheep, cattle, goats, hogs, and poultry. They clean and maintain animal housing areas; feed, water, herd, brand, weigh, and load animals; shear wool from sheep; collect eggs from hatcheries; tend dairy milking machines; and shoe animals.

Farm equipment operators handle the tractors and equipment used for plowing, sowing, and harvesting on large-scale establishments. Teams of such operators may travel throughout the Plains States during harvest time, working long hours each day in order to reap as quickly as possible while the nutrients in the grains are at their fullest. On establishments of smaller scale, farm equipment operators handle field work of different types using machinery such as fertilizer spreaders, haybines, raking equipment, balers, combines, and threshers.

Training and Advancement

The agricultural production industry is characterized by a large number of workers with low levels of educational attainment. More than one-third of this industry's workforce does not have a high school diploma, compared to only 13 percent of all workers in other industries. The proportion of workers without a high school diploma is particularly high in the crop production sector, where there are more labor-intensive establishments employing migrant farm workers.

Training and education requirements for general farm workers are few. Some experience in farm or ranch work is beneficial, but most tasks require manual labor and are learned fairly quickly on-the-job. Advancement for farm workers is limited. Motivated and experienced farm workers may become crew leaders or farm labor contractors. Farm workers who wish to become independent farmers first must buy or rent a plot of land.

Table 1. Employment of wage and salary workers in agricultural production by occupation, 1998 and projected change, 1998-2008

(Employment in thousands)

Occupation	1998 Employment Number	1998 Employment Percent	1998-2008 Percent change
All occupations	1,163	100.0	-11.2
Agriculture, forestry, and fishing	1,030	88.5	-10.9
Farm workers	606	52.1	-14.3
Farm managers	164	14.1	-0.1
Landscaping, groundskeeping, nursery, greenhouse, and lawn service occupations	54	4.6	-9.6
Supervisors, farming, forestry, and agricultural related occupations	28	2.4	-14.5
Operators, fabricators, and laborers	40	3.4	-9.1
Truckdrivers	18	1.6	-8.6
Machine setters, set-up operators, operators, and tenders	8	0.7	-7.2
Helpers, laborers, and material movers, hand	5	0.5	-12.3
Hand workers, including assemblers and fabricators	5	0.4	-10.3
Administrative support, including clerical	33	2.8	-18.9
Bookkeeping, accounting and auditing clerks	13	1.1	-19.5
Secretaries	8	0.7	-25.9
Precision, production, craft and repair	22	1.9	-14.2
Mechanics, installers and repairers	14	1.2	-13.8
Executive, administrative, and managerial	14	1.2	-12.7
Service	11	0.9	-18.1
All other occupations	14	1.2	-8.8

Becoming a farmer generally does not require formal training or credentials. However, knowledge and expertise about agricultural production are essential to success for prospective farmers. The traditional method for acquiring such knowledge is through growing up on a farm. This method is becoming less and less common as the percentage of the U.S. population raised on farms continues to dwindle. But even with a farming background, a person considering farming would benefit from the formal schooling offered by land-grant universities in each State. Programs usually incorporate hands-on training into curricula that complements the academic subjects. Typical coursework covers the agricultural sciences (crop, dairy, and animal) and business subjects such as accounting and marketing.

Experience and some formal education are necessary for farm managers. A bachelor's degree in business with a concentration in agriculture provides a good background. Work experience in the different aspects of farm operations enhances knowledge and develops decision-making skills, which further qualifies prospective farm managers. The experience of having performed routines on other farming establishments in the capacity of a farm worker may save managers valuable time in forming daily or monthly workplans and in avoiding pitfalls that could result in finañcial burdens for the farm.

Whether gained through experience or formal education, both farmers and farm managers need enough technical knowledge of crops, growing conditions, and plant diseases to make sound scientific and financial decisions. A rudimentary knowledge of veterinary science, as well as animal husbandry, is important for dairy and livestock farmers and farm managers.

It also is crucial for farmers and farm managers to stay abreast of the latest developments in agricultural production. They may do this by reviewing agricultural journals that publish information about new cost-cutting procedures, new forms of marketing, or good results with new techniques. County cooperative extension agencies serve as a link between university and government research programs and farmers and farm managers, providing the latest information on numerous agricultural-related subjects. County cooperative extension agents may demonstrate new animal breeding techniques, or more environmentally safe methods of fertilizing, for example. Other organizations provide information—through journals, newsletters, and the Internet—on agricultural research and the results of implementing innovative methods and ideas.

Some private organizations are helping to make farmland affordable for new farmers through a variety of institutional innovations. The Land Link program, run by the Center for Rural Affairs, matches old farmers up with young. In the matching process, farmers approaching retirement arrange to pass along their land to young farmers wishing to keep the land under cultivation. The Center for Rural Affairs also operates a private loan program for first-time buyers, as well as a program, the Rural Investment Corporation, designed to give beginning farmers an equal opportunity for farm credit.

Earnings

In 1998, median earnings for workers in agricultural production were $299 per week, substantially lower than the median of $523 for all workers in private industry. In fact, only the highest 10 percent of workers in agricultural production earned more than $582. Lower than average earnings are due in part to the low level of skill required for many of the jobs in the industry and the seasonal nature of the work.

Farm income can vary substantially, depending on a number of factors, including: the type of crop or livestock being raised, price fluctuations for various agricultural products, and weather conditions that affect yield. For many farmers, particularly those working non-commercial farms, crop or livestock production is not their major occupation or source of income.

Outlook

The expanding world population should lead to a rise in demand for food and fiber. Demand for U.S. agricultural exports is expected to grow in the long run as developing nations improve their economies and personal incomes. However, increasing productivity in the highly efficient U.S. agricultural production industry is expected to meet domestic consumption needs and export requirements with fewer farms and less farm labor than in the past. Furthermore, market pressures may continue to lead to the consolidation of many farms. The trend toward fewer and larger farms is expected to continue through the 1998-2008 period, result-

13

ing in an 18 percent decline of overall employment in agricultural production. The decline will be fastest, at 24 percent, among self-employed workers, most of whom are farmers. Employment of wage and salary workers will decline half as slowly as the self-employed.

In recent decades, new technology in the form of larger and more efficient farm machinery, computerization of farm equipment and financial systems, and biotechnology methods have resulted in higher yields and increased productivity. Further technological improvements will continue to boost output between 1998 and 2008.

Federal Government subsidy payments traditionally have shielded many agricultural producers from the ups and downs of the market. Currently, both domestic and international official policy is to open up the industry to competitive forces. As European producers face the loss of price supports in the marketplace, prices of European agricultural goods should drop, meaning increased competition for U.S. farmers. In the United States, the 1996 Federal Agriculture Improvement and Reform Act (also known as the 1996 Farm Act) phases out price supports for agricultural produce such as wheat, corn, grain sorghum, barley, oats, rice, and upland cotton. Farm establishments that grow such crops may experience heavy fluctuations in incomes as they deal with the adverse affects of climate and price changes. Dairy farming also will be affected by the 1996 Farm Act. Starting in the year 2000, government price supports for milk will disappear and milk prices will be determined by market forces. Under these conditions, the larger and more financially sound farms will be best able to cope with international and competitive forces. Owners of farms that do not have sufficient funds to withstand the changes in the marketplace and still cover all operating costs may eventually be forced to consolidate with larger operations or leave agricultural production altogether. However, the initial effects of the 1996 Farm Act may lead to reconsideration of Federal agricultural policies, and some aspects of the 1996 legislation may eventually be revised.

Employment on many farms will most likely continue to be characterized by low wages and lack of benefits. This, combined with continuously rising agricultural productivity, should translate into a further reduction in the workforce. Employment of farmers, farm managers and farm workers are all projected to decrease.

Employment declines resulting from growing productivity and consolidations might be counterbalanced somewhat by other changes taking place in the agricultural production industry. Dairy and other farms may increasingly turn to programs conducted by State and local governments that allow farmers to sell the development rights to their property. This immediately lowers the market value of the land and the property taxes along with it, making farming more affordable. New developments in marketing milk and other agricultural produce through farmer-owned and operated cooperatives hold out promise for many in the agricultural production industry. Also, demand for organic farm produce is increasing as consumers become more conscious about the pesticides and fertilizers used in conventional agriculture, allowing farms of small acreage—which only 10 years ago appeared to have almost no future as working farms—to remain economically viable.

Sources of Additional Information

For general information about academic programs and aquaculture, contact:

➢ The Alternative Farming Systems Information Center (AFSIC), 10301 Baltimore Ave., Room 304, Beltsville, MD 20705-2351. Internet: **http://www.nal.usda.gov/afsic**

For information about Community Supported Agriculture and internships in organic farming, contact:

➢ The Biodynamic Farming and Gardening Association, Inc., Building 1002B, Thoreau Center, The Presdio, P.O. Box 29135, San Francisco, CA 94129-0135. Internet: **http://www.biodynamics.com**
➢ Appropriate Technology Transfer for Rural Areas, P.O. Box 3657, Fayetteville, AR, 72702. Internet: **http://www.attra.org/attra-pub/atmatlst.html#resource**

For information on a career as a farm manager, contact:

➢ American Society of Farm Managers and Rural Appraisers, 950 South Cherry St., #508, Denver, CO 80222. Internet: **http://www.agri-associations.org/asfmra**

For information on the Land Link Program, contact:

➢ Center for Rural Affairs, P.O. Box 46, Walthill, NE 68067.

For information about State agencies that are involved in the purchases of development rights of farmland, contact:

➢ American Farmland Trust, 1200 18th Street, NW., Washington, DC 20036. Internet: **http://www.farmland.org**

Information on the following occupations may be found in the 2000-01 *Occupational Outlook Handbook*:

● Farmers and farm managers
● Landscaping, groundskeeping, nursery, greenhouse, and lawn service occupations
● Bookkeeping, accounting, and auditing clerks

Agricultural Services

SIGNIFICANT POINTS

- About 40 percent of all agricultural service workers are employed in California, Florida, and Texas.

- Entry-level jobs that can be learned on the job in less than a week—including animal caretakers, farm workers, and landscaping, groundskeeping, and nursery laborers—account for a substantial portion of employment.

Nature of the Industry

The agricultural services industry is made up of several diverse segments that provide services to an equally diverse clientele. Groups using services from the industry range from agricultural producers seeking stronger financial returns to their farmland through skilled farm management, to individual urban dwellers needing veterinary care for their pets, and urban and suburban businesses wishing to boost "curb appeal" of their establishments through professional landscaping. Many of the jobs in this industry require agricultural knowledge or skills, but only about 30 percent of wage and salary employment is directly related to the production of crops or the raising of livestock.

Landscape and horticultural services, employing more than 1 in 10 wage and salary workers in this industry, provide landscape planning and installation, landscape architecture, lawn care, and grounds maintenance services. Customers range from individual homeowners to large corporations and Federal, State, and local governments.

Landscape architecture firms plan and design the development of land for projects such as parks and other recreational facilities, airports, highways, and commercial and residential buildings. They prepare site plans showing landscape features, locations of structures, and roads, walks, and parking areas, as well as specifications and cost estimates for land development. *Landscape contracting firms* actually carry out the plans designed by landscape architecture establishments. They develop a budget for the project in consultation with the client, hire the manual laborers and provide any equipment needed, and obtain the plants to be installed.

Landscaping, lawn maintenance, and groundskeeping firms establish and maintain grounds, lawns, and gardens for homeowners as well as governments, colleges and universities, real estate and land developers, and other private businesses. These firms are responsible for planting, mulching, watering, fertilizing, mowing, and seeding lawns and grounds; applying pesticides; installing turf and sod; and pruning plants and trees. They also rake leaves, clear outdoor areas of debris, remove snow, and maintain outdoor amenities and decorative features such as pools, fountains, benches, and planters.

Veterinary services employ 1 in 5 wage and salary workers in this industry and provide medical care for household pets, horses, livestock, and zoo and sporting animals. The majority of veterinary practices treat companion animals, such as dogs and cats; some practices also treat pigs, goats, sheep, and some nondomestic animals. Veterinarians in such practices diagnose animal health problems, vaccinate against diseases such as distemper and rabies, medicate animals with infections or illnesses, treat and dress wounds, set fractures, perform surgery, and advise owners about feeding, behavior, and breeding. A smaller number of veterinary practices focus exclusively on large animals such as horses or cows, but may care for all kinds of food animals. Large animal veterinarians drive to farms or ranches to provide health services, with an emphasis on preventive care, for herds or individual animals. They test for and vaccinate against diseases, and consult with farm or ranch owners and managers on production, feeding, and housing issues. They also treat and dress wounds, set fractures, perform surgery—including cesarean sections on birthing animals.

Farm labor and management services is nearly equal in employment size to veterinary services. *Farm labor contractors or crew leaders* provide and manage temporary farm laborers—often migrant workers—who usually work during peak harvesting times. Contractors may place bids with farmers to harvest labor-intensive crops such as fruit, nuts, or vegetables, or perform other short-term tasks. Once the bid is accepted, the contractor, or crew leader, organizes and supervises the laborers as they harvest, load, move, and store the crops. *Farm management services* establishments guide and assist farm and ranch land owners, farmers, and ranchers in maximizing the financial returns to their land by managing the day-to-day activities necessary to run a farming operation. Farm management services usually negotiate with the landowner to receive a percentage of any profit resulting from agricultural production on the land. They may employ or contract with a tenant farmer to oversee the actual crop or livestock production.

Companies that provide *soil preparation* and *crop services* plant, cultivate, and harvest crops by machine, employing just over 12 percent of agricultural services workers. Because some types of farm machinery are highly specialized and very expensive, farms that do not want to invest in machinery often contract with these specialized firms to perform planting, harvesting, or other tasks. For example, farmers or farm managers might contract with crop services firms to do aerial dusting and spraying of pesticides over a large number of acres. Establishments in crop services also perform tasks to prepare crops for market, including shelling, fumigating, cleaning, grading, grinding, and packaging agricultural products.

Animal specialty services, except veterinary is the smallest segment of the agricultural services industry, accounting for

15

just 5 percent of wage and salary employment. It is divided into those establishments that provide livestock services and those that provide services for pets, horses, and other animal specialties. *Nonfarm animal services* include animal shelters, boarding dog kennels and horse stables, dog grooming, and animal training. *Livestock services* include firms that assist in breeding and artificial insemination, do sheep dipping and shearing, and provide herd improvement advice. Breeding services usually monitor herd condition and nutrition; evaluate the quality and quantity of forage; recommend adjustments to feeding when necessary; identify the best cattle or other livestock for breeding and calving; advise on livestock pedigrees; inseminate cattle artificially; and feed and care for sires.

Working Conditions

The agricultural services industry is attractive to people who enjoy working outdoors or with animals. However, many people in this industry work long hours, and farm operators, managers, crew leaders, farm equipment operators, and farm workers may work a 6- or 7-day week during the planting and harvesting seasons. Workers in these establishments also routinely perform tasks that involve much physical exertion, often requiring strength and manual dexterity, and operate heavy machinery.

Workers in veterinary and animal specialty services may have to lift, hold, or restrain animals of all sizes, and risk being bitten, kicked, or scratched. Evening, night, and weekend or holiday work is common, and some of the tasks of animal caretakers, such as cleaning cages and lifting heavy supplies, may be unpleasant and physically demanding. Many of the jobs in landscape and horticultural services are also physically demanding and repetitive. Laborers do much bending, kneeling, and shoveling, and lift and move supplies as they plant shrubs, trees, flowers, and grass and install decorative features.

Many workers in all segments of the agricultural services industry risk exposure to insecticides, germicides, and other potentially hazardous chemicals that are sprayed on crops and plants or used to treat flea infestation or other conditions in animals.

Also, much of the work in this industry is performed outdoors in all kinds of weather, and adequate sanitation facilities, including drinking water, may not always be available to employees. Some farm workers and landscaping laborers must also cope with the difficulty in obtaining year-round, full-time employment because of the short-term or seasonal nature of the work. They often must string together as many jobs as possible. Workers also run the risk of injury when working with planting and harvesting equipment, such as combines, chain saws, and electric clippers. In 1997, the rate of injury and illness in agricultural services was 7.9 per 100 full-time workers, compared to 7.1 for all private industry.

Employment

In 1998, the rapidly growing agricultural services industry comprised just over 1 million wage and salary workers, and about 450,000 self-employed workers. The following tabulation shows the distribution of wage and salary employment by industry segment:

Landscape and horticultural services	460,000
Veterinary services	196,000
Animal services, except veterinary	53,000
Agricultural services, not elsewhere classified	296,000

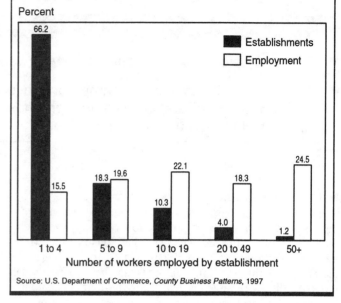

Few agricultural services establishments employ 20 workers or more

Source: U.S. Department of Commerce, *County Business Patterns*, 1997

About 111,000 establishments employed these wage and salary workers in 1997. Agricultural services establishments are smaller than average—about 85 percent of the establishments employed 9 or fewer workers, compared to about 75 percent of the establishments in all industries combined. In addition, relatively few agricultural services firms employ 50 or more workers (chart).

The median age of agricultural services workers is 35, nearly 4 years younger than the median for workers in all industries. This industry provides employment for many new entrants to the labor market. In 1998, almost 23 percent of the industry's workers were between 16 and 24 years old. Nearly 50 percent were under age 35, compared to 39 percent of workers in all industries combined—reflecting the high proportion of seasonal and part-time job opportunities (table 1).

Nearly 40 percent of all agricultural services workers are employed in California, Florida, and Texas. Other States with a large number of agricultural services workers include Arizona, Illinois, Pennsylvania, Ohio, and New York.

Table 1. Percent distribution of employment in the agricultural services industry by age group, 1998

Age group	Agricultural services	All industries
Total	100.0	100.0
16-19	9.3	5.4
20-24	13.7	9.5
25-34	27.2	23.8
35-44	26.9	27.5
45-54	15.2	21.0
55-64	6.0	9.8
65 and older	1.8	2.9

Occupations in the Industry

The agricultural services industry offers jobs in many occupations requiring specialized skills or the ability to operate agricultural and horticultural equipment (table 2).

Workers in the *landscaping, groundskeeping, nursery, greenhouse, and lawn service* occupations, employed largely in landscape and horticultural services establishments, account for 34 percent of industry employment. Nursery and greenhouse workers help to cultivate the plants used in landscaping projects by preparing nursery acreage or greenhouse beds for planting, and watering, weeding, and spraying trees, shrubs, and plants. They also prepare sod, trees, and other plants for transport to landscaping sites. Landscape contractors coordinate and oversee the installation of trees, flowers, shrubs, sod, benches, and other ornamental features. They implement construction plans at the site, which may involve grading the property, installing lighting or sprinkler systems, and building walkways, terraces, patios, and fountains. Landscaping laborers install and maintain landscaped areas by transporting and planting new vegetation; transplanting, mulching, fertilizing, watering, and pruning plants; and mowing and watering lawns. Some landscaping laborers, called pruners, specialize in pruning, trimming, and shaping ornamental trees and shrubs, and others, called lawn service workers, specialize in maintaining lawns and shrubs. Groundskeeping laborers perform many of the same tasks as landscaping laborers, but their duties are usually more varied, and encompass snow, leaf, and debris removal, and upkeep and repair of sidewalks, equipment, pools, fences, and benches.

Landscape architects, also concentrated in the landscape and horticultural services segment, plan and design the arrangement of flowers, shrubs, trees, walkways, fountains and other decorative features for parks, shopping centers, golf courses, private residences, and industrial parks. They also perform environmental impact studies.

Veterinarians provide health care, ranging from preventive medicine to diagnosis and treatment of diseases or injuries, for pets and farm or other animals. They also advise pet owners about feeding, behavior, and breeding, and consult with farm or ranch owners and managers on production, feeding, disease prevention and eradication. Some inspect livestock at public stockyards and at points of entry into the United States to keep diseased animals out of the country or administer tests for animal diseases, and conduct programs for disease control. *Veterinary technologists* and *technicians* usually work under the supervision of a veterinarian and assist in providing medical care to animals. They may prepare and administer injections and medications; dress wounds; take vital signs; prepare animals and instruments for surgery; and perform laboratory tests. *Veterinary assistants* also aid veterinarians, but are more involved in the basic care of animals, cleaning cages and examining areas, feeding, changing water dishes, and monitoring animals recovering from surgery.

Animal caretakers also provide basic care for animals, and feed, water, bathe, groom, and exercise those under their charge. Their duties may vary depending on the type of establishment in which they work. For example, animal caretakers employed in shelters keep records of the animals received and discharged, answer questions from the public, and euthanize seriously ill or unwanted animals, in addition to providing basic care. Animal caretakers in stables saddle and unsaddle horses, give them rubdowns, polish saddles, and store supplies and feed.

Animal breeders use their knowledge of genetics to select and breed animals, either for show or improved performance or productivity. Responsibilities typically include the feeding,

watering, and housing of breeding animals, and maintaining weight, diet, and pedigree records.

Table 2. Employment of wage and salary workers in agricultural services by occupation, 1998 and projected change, 1998-2008

(Employment in thousands)

Occupation	1998 Employment Number	1998 Employment Percent	1998-2008 Percent change
All occupations	1,005	100.0	24.5
Agriculture, forestry, and fishing	691	68.7	26.5
Landscaping, groundskeeping, nursery, greenhouse, and lawn service occupations	337	33.5	32.0
Farm workers	178	17.7	22.0
Animal caretakers, except farm	52	5.2	25.4
Veterinary assistants	44	4.4	28.7
Supervisors, farming, forestry, and agricultural-related occupations	27	2.7	27.3
Administrative support, including clerical	96	9.6	20.1
Receptionists and information clerks	35	3.5	35.0
Secretaries	15	1.5	2.7
General office clerks	16	1.6	27.2
Bookkeeping, accounting, and auditing clerks	16	1.6	3.8
Operators, fabricators, and laborers	56	5.6	10.6
Helpers, laborers, and material movers, hand	28	2.8	6.5
Truck drivers	12	1.2	16.5
Professional specialty	44	4.4	34.0
Veterinarians	34	3.4	36.4
Executive, administrative, and managerial	37	3.6	21.3
General managers and top executives	28	2.8	22.0
Technicians and related support	35	3.5	16.2
Veterinary technologists and technicians	31	3.1	17.2
Precision production, craft, and repair	21	2.1	15.7
Mechanics, installers, and repairers	11	1.1	15.9
Marketing and sales	17	1.7	29.6
Service	8	0.8	13.2

Farm workers perform the manual labor required to plant, cultivate, and harvest crops. Their duties vary with the season. Before seeding, they may prepare the soil by tilling and fertilizing. Once the crops are partially grown, they may return to farms to cultivate fields, transplant, weed, or prune. Often, they spray crops to control weeds, harmful insects, and fungi. Some farms, such as those producing fruit or vegetables, need large numbers of workers to harvest crops. After the harvest, workers are needed to prepare produce for shipment. *Farm equipment operators* drive the heavy machinery used to mechanically harvest and combine crops.

Many of the farm workers in agricultural services contract for employment with *farm labor contractors,* or *crew leaders.* Crew leaders contract with farms to provide workers to perform what are often short-term, labor-intensive farm jobs, such as manually harvesting, loading, and moving vegetables. The crew leader is also responsible for transporting the hired workers to the fields or orchards, and for meeting Federal and State regulations regarding the hiring of transient workers, including paying a guaranteed minimum wage, payment for overtime work, and collecting Social Security taxes. Crew leaders, like the workers they hire and supervise, may practice "follow-the-crop" migration, typically recruiting a crew in the southern States, then moving north in a set pattern as crops ripen. Others remain in a single locality.

Farm managers use their knowledge of agriculture and business to make farming management decisions for landowners. Managers may employ a farm operator or contract with a tenant farmer to run the day-to-day activities involved in crop or livestock production. Farm managers help select the type and mix of crops; select practices for tillage and soil conservation as well as methods of irrigation; purchase seed, pesticides, and fertilizers; determine crop transportation and storage requirements; market the crops or livestock; oversee maintenance of the property and equipment; recommend capital improvements; and monitor operating expenses. Farm managers may also hire and assign workers when needed, contract with other firms for specialized services such as chemical spraying of crops, and advise land owners about the purchase or sale of additional farm lands. Managing an agricultural production operation is a sophisticated business, and farm managers use computers extensively. Some also use cutting-edge technologies, such as the Global Positioning System and remote sensing.

Training and Advancement

The skills needed by workers in the agricultural services industry differ widely by occupation. The industry is characterized by an unusually high proportion of workers who have not finished high school. These workers qualify for entry-level positions as animal caretakers, farm laborers, and landscaping, groundskeeping, and nursery laborers, which require little or no prior training or experience. The basic tasks associated with many of these jobs usually can be learned in less than a week, and most newly hired workers are trained on the job. Training often is given under the close supervision of an experienced employee or supervisor.

For jobs such as veterinarian, farm manager, and landscape architect, a minimum of 4 years of formal postsecondary training are needed. Aspiring veterinarians generally complete 4 years of preveterinary study, including biology, chemistry, physics, and calculus, before embarking on 4 years of veterinary medical school. They must graduate with a Doctor of Veterinary Medicine degree and obtain a license to practice. Prospective landscape architects must complete a professional program in landscape architecture, and be registered or licensed before they may practice in most States. Farm managers usually obtain a bachelor's degree in a business-related field with a concentration in agriculture. A degree in an agriculture-related discipline with an emphasis on business courses, such as marketing and finance, is also good preparation. Many States require farm managers to carry a real estate license. Although accreditation is not mandatory, farm managers may, after several years of experience and meeting established standards, obtain the designation Accredited Farm Manager through the American Society of Farm Managers and Rural Appraisers. College training and professional licensing may also be required for many other jobs in agricultural services,

such as grounds manager and landscape contractor. Schools of agriculture are found at many State universities and all State land grant colleges. They offer a variety of programs at the bachelor's, master's, and doctoral levels.

Community colleges and vocational schools also offer an array of programs for people interested in various agricultural services occupations—for example, animal breeder and farm equipment operator. Many employers prefer previous work experience, combined with vocational certification or a 2-year degree. Many States have licensing requirements for veterinary technologists, which include 2 years of college-level study in an accredited veterinary technology program culminating in an Associate in Applied Science or related degree, and passing an examination before being allowed to fully assist veterinarians.

Opportunities for advancement for agricultural services workers vary by occupation. Farm workers have limited opportunities for advancement, but experienced and highly motivated laborers may move into positions as farm labor contractors or crew leaders. Likewise, landscaping, lawn service, and groundskeeping laborers may advance to supervisory positions after gaining experience, or become a manager of a lawn service firm. Some become self-employed landscape or lawn service contractors, but such positions often require additional formal training. Although many top-level managerial and professional jobs—especially in small companies—are filled by promotion from within, technological innovations in agronomy and animal husbandry have made postsecondary education advantageous for career advancement in agricultural services.

Earnings

Average earnings in the agricultural services industry are relatively low—nonsupervisory workers averaged $9.95 an hour in 1998, compared to $12.77 an hour for workers throughout private industry. Nonsupervisory workers in landscape and horticultural services earned somewhat more than other agricultural services workers.

Earnings can vary greatly during the year, depending on the season. Many workers in this industry find work only in the growing or harvesting seasons and are unemployed or work in other jobs during the rest of the year. Nearly 18 percent worked part-time in 1998, compared to the industry average of 15.9 percent. Part-time workers are less likely to receive employer-provided benefits. Earnings in selected occupations in agricultural services in 1997 appear in table 3.

According to a survey by the American Veterinary Medical Association, veterinarians in private clinical practice earned an average income of $76,360 in 1997, and first-year veterinary school graduates entering private clinical practice had average starting salaries of $36,724.

Union membership in the agricultural services industry is far below the average for all industries. In 1998, less than 2 percent of all agricultural services workers were union members or were covered by union contracts, compared to 15.4 percent of workers in all industries.

Outlook

Wage and salary jobs in agricultural services are projected to increase 25 percent through the year 2008. In addition, numerous job openings will arise from the need to replace workers who leave the industry every year. Much of the work in entry-level jobs, which account for a substantial portion of all jobs in the industry, is physically demanding and low paying, making it unattractive for workers over the long term. Turnover is very high among landscaping and groundskeeping laborers, nonfarm animal caretakers, and farm workers, reflecting the seasonal and part-time nature of the work as well as the low pay and high physical demands.

Table 3. Median hourly earnings of the largest occupations in agricultural services, 1997

Occupation	Agricultural services	All industries
Veterinarians and veterinary inspectors	$23.56	$23.97
General managers and top executives	17.91	26.05
First line supervisors and mangers/ supervisors-agricultural, forestry, fishing, and related workers	12.02	12.94
Veterinary technicians and technologists	9.23	9.27
Receptionists and information clerks	7.70	8.69
Laborers, landscaping and groundskeeping	7.69	8.08
Veterinary assistants	7.57	7.57
Animal caretakers, except farm	6.57	6.97
Graders and sorters, agricultural products	5.70	6.20
Farmworkers, food and fiber crops	5.65	5.66

The agricultural services industry grew very rapidly during the 1980s and first half of the 1990s, with all segments of the industry experiencing employment increases. Job growth was fueled by especially strong increases in two of the largest segments—landscaping and horticultural services, and veterinary services. Although demand for agricultural services is expected to remain strong, the rate of employment growth is expected to slow over the 1998-2008 period.

Employment gains in landscaping and horticultural services are tied, in part, to the level of new construction. Construction activity tends to vary depending on the health of the overall economy. Over the long run, the construction industry is expected to grow, though at a slower rate than over the previous 10-year period. Federal, State, and local government budget constraints may also limit demand for services to beautify and care for grounds surrounding public buildings. Nevertheless, employment outlook should remain bright. Individuals and businesses are expected to increasingly recognize the value of maintaining and renovating existing landscaping and grounds. As businesses compete to attract customers, enhancing curb appeal by investing in landscaping and lawn services will become an increasingly important marketing method. A growing number of homeowners continue to use lawn maintenance and landscaping services to enhance the beauty of their property and to conserve leisure time. Additionally, many land developers and builders who face complex environmental regulations and land-use zoning issues are turning to landscape architecture firms for help in planning sites and integrating buildings and other structures into the natural environment. Overall concern about environmental issues and a growing appreciation for nature will add to the desire for more professional landscaping and horticultural services.

Employment gains in veterinary services, partially attributable to increases in the number of pet owners, are also expected to slow slightly as the pet population grows more slowly during the projection period. Slowdowns will be tempered as new technology and better marketing of nontraditional pet medical services, such as preventive dental care, expand the treatment provided for individual animals.

Nonfarm animal services, except veterinary, should also be affected by slowing trends in pet population growth. However, pet owners are expected to increasingly take advantage of grooming services and daily and overnight boarding services.

Expect slower employment growth of the farm-related agricultural services—crop services, soil preparation services, farm labor and management services, and livestock services—that are linked to the health of the agricultural production industry. When agricultural producers face difficult times, such as the recent economic downturns in some Asian countries that reduced the demand for exports of agricultural products from the United States, the demand for farm-related agricultural services also drop. Over the long-run, however, overall employment should slowly increase. Growth in the animal population, emphasis on scientific methods of breeding and raising livestock and poultry, and continued support for public health and disease control programs, will contribute to the demand for farm-related veterinary and livestock animal services. Agricultural producers and farm managers should continue to turn to farm labor contracting services to ease their responsibility for meeting labor requirements for workers who are only needed on a temporary basis. Mechanization of the industry is largely in place and food needs will continue to grow as the population increases. However, agricultural producers are expected to continue to produce more with less labor. The dominance of large producers, food companies, and agribusiness, along with farms that are growing in average size, allows the use of state-of-the-art, more efficient farming practices and technologies, leading to slower demand for contracting services.

Sources of Additional Information

For general information about agricultural and farming occupations, contact:

➤   National Association of State University and Land Grant Colleges, One Dupont Circle NW., Suite 710, Washington, DC 20036-1191.

For information on careers in landscaping and horticulture, contact:

➤   Associated Landscape Contractors of America, Inc., 150 Eldon St., Suite 270, Herndon, VA 20170.
➤   American Society of Landscape Architects, 4401 Connecticut Ave. NW., Suite 500, Washington, DC 20008. Internet: **http://www.asla.org/asla**
➤   Professional Grounds Management Society, 120 Cockeysville Rd., Suite 104, Hunt Valley, MD 21030.

For information on careers in veterinary science, send a self-addressed, stamped envelope to:

➤   American Veterinary Medical Association, 1931 N. Meacham Rd., Suite 100, Schaumburg, IL 60173-4360.

For information on careers in animal specialty services, contact:

➤   National Association of Animal Breeders, 401 Bernadette Dr., P.O. Box 1033, Columbia, MO 65205-1033. Internet: **http://www.naab-css.org**

For a list of State-licensed dog grooming schools, send a self-addressed, stamped envelope to:

➤ National Dog Groomers Association of America, P.O. Box 101, Clark, PA 16113.

For information on careers in farm management, contact:

➤ American Society of Farm Managers and Rural Appraisers, 950 S. Cherry St., Suite 508, Denver, CO 80222. Internet: **http://www.agri-associations.org**

Information on these occupations may be found in the 2000-01 *Occupational Outlook Handbook*:

● Farmers and farm managers
● Landscape architects
● Landscaping, groundskeeping, nursery, greenhouse, and lawn service occupations
● Veterinarians
● Veterinary assistants and nonfarm animal caretakers

Construction

SIGNIFICANT POINTS

- Construction is one of the economy's largest industries.

- Over 8 out of 10 establishments employ fewer than 10 people.

- Construction has a very large number of self-employed workers.

- Job prospects for construction workers are expected to be good.

- Workers in construction have relatively high hourly earnings.

Nature of the Industry

Houses, apartments, factories, offices, schools, roads, and bridges are only some of the products of the construction industry. This industry's activities include work on new structures as well as additions, alterations, and repairs. (Some government establishments do the same work and employ a significant number of people, but information about them is not included in this statement. Information concerning government construction is included in the *Career Guide* statements on Federal Government and State and local government, excluding education and hospitals.)

The construction industry is divided into three major segments: General building contractors, heavy construction contractors, and special trade contractors. *General building contractors* build residential, industrial, commercial, and other buildings. *Heavy construction contractors* build sewers, roads, highways, bridges, tunnels, and other projects. *Special trade contractors* are engaged in specialized activities such as carpentry, painting, plumbing, and electrical work.

Construction is usually done or coordinated by *general contractors*, who specialize in one type of construction such as residential or commercial building. They take full responsibility for the complete job, except for specified portions of the work that may be omitted from the general contract. Although general contractors may do a portion of the work with their own crews, they often subcontract most of the work of the construction to heavy construction or special trade contractors.

Special trade contractors usually do the work of only one trade, such as painting, carpentry, electrical work, or two or more closely related trades, such as plumbing and heating or plastering and lathing. Beyond fitting their work to that of the other trades, they have no responsibility for the structure as a whole. They obtain orders for their work from general contractors, architects, or property owners. Repair work is almost always done on direct order from owners, occupants, architects, or rental agents.

Working Conditions

Most workers in this industry work full time, many over 40 hours a week. In 1998, more than 1 in 5 wage and salary construction workers worked 45 hours or more a week; over half of self-employed individuals worked over 45 hours a week. Construction craftsworkers may sometimes work evenings, weekends, and holidays to finish a job or take care of an emergency.

Construction workers need sufficient physical stamina because work frequently requires prolonged standing, bending, stooping, and working in cramped quarters. Exposure to weather is common because much of the work is done outside or in partially enclosed structures.

Construction workers often work with potentially dangerous tools and equipment amidst a clutter of building materials; some work on temporary scaffolding and in bad weather. Consequently, they are more prone to injuries than workers in other jobs. In 1997, cases of work-related injury and illness were 9.5 per 100 full-time workers, which is significantly higher than the 7.1 rate for the entire private sector. Workers who do roofing, masonry, stonework, and plastering experienced the highest injury rates. In response, employers increasingly emphasize safe working conditions and work habits that reduce the risk of injuries.

Employment

Construction, with 6 million wage and salary and 1.6 million self-employed nongovernment jobs in 1998, was one of the Nation's largest industries.

About 1 out of 5 jobs were with special trade contractors, primarily plumbing, electrical, and masonry contractors. Almost 2 out of 3 jobs were with general building contractors, mostly in residential and nonresidential construction. The rest were with road and other heavy construction contractors (table 1). Employment in this industry is distributed geographically in much the same way as the Nation's population; the concentration of employment is generally in industrialized and highly populated areas.

There were about 667,000 construction companies in the United States in 1997: 197,091 were general contractors and operative builders; 37,701 were heavy construction or highway contractors; and 431,877 were specialty trade contractors. Most of these establishments tend to be small, the majority employing fewer than 10 workers (chart). About 8 out of 10 workers are employed by small contractors.

Construction offers more opportunities than most other industries for individuals who desire to own and run their own business. The 1.5 million self-employed and unpaid family workers in 1998 performed work directly for property owners or acted as contractors on small jobs, such as additions, remodeling, and maintenance projects. The large majority of self-employed work in the construction trades. The rate of self-employment varies greatly by individual occupation in the construction trades (see chart on next page).

Table 1. Nongovernment wage and salary employment in construction, 1998

(Employment in thousands)

	1998 Employment	1998-2008 Percent change
Total	5,985	9.2
General building contractors	1,372	7.6
Residential building construction	700	11.3
Operative builders	27	-3.7
Nonresidential building construction	646	4.1
Heavy construction contractors	838	4.9
Highway and street construction	253	10.2
Heavy construction, except highways	585	2.6
Special trade contractors	3,774	10.7
Plumbing, heating, and air-conditioning	827	10.2
Painting and paper hanging	204	8.9
Electrical work	727	12.2
Masonry, stonework, and plastering	499	9.3
Carpentering and floor work	274	9.7
Roofing, siding, and sheet metal work	250	12.3
Concrete work	327	7.7
Water well drilling	23	13.5
Miscellaneous special trade	644	12.7

Occupations in the Industry

Work in construction offers a great variety of career opportunities. People with many different talents and educational backgrounds—managers, clerical workers, skilled craftsworkers, semiskilled workers, and laborers—find job opportunities in construction and related activities (table 2).

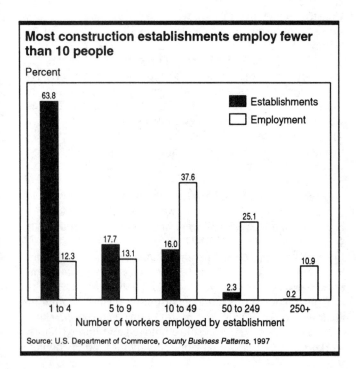

Most construction establishments employ fewer than 10 people

Percent

Source: U.S. Department of Commerce, *County Business Patterns*, 1997

Table 2. Employment of nongovernment wage and salary workers in construction by occupation, 1998 and projected change, 1998-2008

(Employment in thousands)

Occupation	1998 Employment Number	Percent	1998-2008 Percent change
All occupations	5,985	100.0	9.2
Precision production, craft, and repair	3,319	55.5	11.5
Carpenters	567	9.5	7.8
Electricians	387	6.5	14.4
Blue collar worker supervisors	293	4.9	16.0
Plumbers, pipefitters, and steamfitters	254	4.3	6.5
Construction equipment operators	185	3.1	9.7
Painters and paperhangers	173	2.9	12.5
Heating, air conditioning, and refrigeration mechanics and installers	144	2.4	18.3
Cement masons, concrete finishers, and terrazzo workers	126	2.1	7.0
Sheet metal workers and duct installers	122	2.0	25.9
Drywall installers and finishers	118	2.0	9.2
Bricklayers and stone masons	110	1.8	16.9
Roofers	107	1.8	6.9
Machinery mechanics, installers, and repairers	82	1.4	7.4
Structural and reinforcing metal workers	77	1.3	7.7
Insulation workers	58	1.0	8.4
Operators, fabricators, and laborers	1,142	19.1	6.7
Helpers, construction trades	537	9.0	7.5
All other helpers, laborers, and material movers, hand	289	4.8	-1.0
Truck drivers	136	2.3	10.6
Excavation and loading machine operators	75	1.3	22.6
Executive, managerial, and administrative	636	10.6	9.6
General managers and top executives	257	4.3	7.7
Construction managers	188	3.2	12.4
Cost estimators	89	1.5	12.9
Financial managers	41	0.7	4.1
Administrative support, including clerical	536	9.0	-1.5
General office clerks	152	2.6	12.0
Secretaries	145	2.4	-11.7
Bookkeeping, accounting, and auditing clerks	132	2.2	-9.6
Agriculture, forestry, fishing, and related	144	2.4	10.1
Laborers, landscaping and groundskeeping	143	2.4	10.1
Marketing and sales	97	1.6	13.3
All other occupations	111	1.9	9.8

Most of the workers in construction are skilled craftsworkers or laborers, helpers, and apprentices who assist the more skilled workers. These groups represent 75 percent of the industry's employment; over 56 percent are construction craftsworkers. *Construction craftsworkers* are generally classified as either structural, finishing, or mechanical workers. *Structural workers* include carpenters, operating engineers (construction machinery operators), bricklayers, cement masons, stonemasons, and reinforcing metal

Many construction occupations have a substantial percentage of self-employed workers

Occupation	Percent of total employment
Insulation workers	4.1
Electricians	10.5
Glaziers	12.9
Plasterers and stucco masons	16.9
Plumbers, pipefitters, and steamfitters	19.5
Drywall installers	25.6
Bricklayers, blockmasons, and stonemasons	27.6
Roofers	31.9
Carpenters	32.1
Tile setters, hard	39.0
Painters and paperhangers	43.7
Carpet installers	64.0

workers. *Finishing workers* include lathers, plasterers, marble setters, terrazzo workers, carpenters, ceiling installers, drywall workers, painters, glaziers, roofers, floor covering installers, and insulation workers. *Mechanical workers* include plumbers, pipefitters, construction electricians, sheet metal workers, and heating, air-conditioning, and refrigeration technicians.

The greatest number of construction craftsworkers worked as carpenters, electricians, plumbers, pipefitters, painters, concrete and terrazzo workers, bricklayers, and drywall installers. The construction industry employs nearly all of the workers in some construction craft occupations—such as plasterers, roofers, structural metal workers, and drywall installers. In other construction crafts occupations—for example, electricians, painters and paperhangers, plumbers, and carpet installers—large numbers also work in other industries (table 3). Other industries employing large numbers of construction craftsworkers include transportation equipment manufacturing, transportation and public utilities, wholesale and retail trade, educational services, and State and local government.

Many persons enter the construction crafts through apprenticeship programs. These programs offer on-the-job training under the close supervision of a craftsperson, as well as some formal classroom instruction. Depending on the trade, apprentices learn a variety of skills, ranging from laying brick to putting together steel beams.

Many persons advance to construction craft occupations from related, less skilled jobs as *helpers* or *laborers*. They acquire skills while they work. They are first hired as laborers or helpers, performing a variety of unskilled tasks and providing much of the routine physical labor needed in construction. They erect and dismantle scaffolding, clean up debris, help unload and carry materials and machinery, and operate simple equipment. They work alongside experienced craftsworkers, learning the basic skills of a particular craft. After acquiring experience and skill in various phases of the craft, they may become skilled journey level craftworkers.

To develop their skills further after training, construction craftsworkers may work on many different projects, such as housing developments, office and industrial buildings, or highways, bridges, and dams. Flexibility and a willingness to adopt new techniques, as well as the ability to get along with people, are essential for advancement. Those skilled in all facets of the trade and who show good leadership qualities may be promoted to *supervisor*. As supervisors, they oversee craftsworkers and helpers and insure work is done well. They plan the job and solve problems as they arise. Those with good organizational skills and exceptional supervisory ability may advance to *superintendent*. Superintendents are responsible for getting a project completed on schedule by working with the architect's plans, making sure materials are delivered on time, assigning work, overseeing craft supervisors, and making sure every phase of the project is completed properly and expeditiously. They also resolve problems and see to it that work proceeds without interruptions. Superintendents may advance to large projects as general managers and top executives. Some go into business for themselves as contractors.

Table 3. Percent of wage and salary workers in construction craft occupations employed in the construction industry, 1998

Occupation	Employed
Roofers	99.6
Drywall installers and finishers	97.2
Bricklayers and stone masons	96.8
Plasterers and stucco masons	96.6
Cement masons, concrete finishers, and terrazzo workers	95.6
Insulation workers	90.2
Carpenters	78.4
Plumbers, pipefitters, and steamfitters	74.1
Carpet, floor, and tile installers and repairers	73.8
Structural and reinforcing metal workers	69.8
Electricians	65.8
Glaziers	64.7
Painters and paperhangers	64.6

Other workers in the construction industry operate material-moving machines and other construction equipment. Such workers include operating engineers; grader, bulldozer, and scraper operators; and paving, surfacing, and tamping equipment operators. They move construction debris, earth, and other heavy materials, and apply asphalt and concrete to roads and other substructures. They may also set up and inspect equipment, make adjustments, and perform minor repairs.

Training and Advancement

Persons may enter most jobs in the construction industry without any formal classroom training after high school. Laborers can learn their job in a few days, but the skills required for many jobs are substantial, although they can usually be learned on the job. Skilled workers such as carpenters, bricklayers, plumbers, and other construction trade specialists either need several years of informal on-the-job experience, or apprenticeship training. Workers pick up skills by working alongside more experienced workers, and through instruction provided by their employers. As they demonstrate their ability to perform tasks they are assigned, they move to progressively more challenging work. As they broaden their skills, they are allowed to work more independently, and responsibilities and earnings increase. They may qualify for jobs in related, more highly skilled, occupations. For example, after several years of experience painters' helpers may become journey level painters.

Apprenticeships administered by local employers, trade associations, and trade unions provide the most thorough training. Apprenticeships usually last between 3 and 5 years and consist of on-the-job training and 144 hours or more of related classroom instruction. A number of apprenticeship programs are beginning to use competency standards instead of just time requirements. This allows a more competent person to complete the program in a shorter amount of time. Those who enroll in apprenticeship programs usually are least 18 years old and in good physical condition.

Persons can enter the construction industry with a variety of educational backgrounds. Those entering construction right out of high school start as laborers, helpers, or apprentices. Those who enter construction from technical or vocational schools may also go through apprenticeship training; however, they progress at a somewhat faster pace because they already have had courses such as mathematics, mechanical drawing, and woodworking. Skilled craftsworkers may advance to supervisor or superintendent positions, or may transfer to jobs as construction building inspector, purchasing agent, sales representative for building supply companies, contractor, and technical or vocational school instructor.

Executive, administrative, and managerial personnel usually have a college degree or considerable experience in their specialty. Individuals who enter construction with college degrees usually start as management trainees or construction managers' assistants. Those who receive degrees in construction science often start as field engineers, schedulers, or cost estimators. College graduates may advance to positions as assistant manager, construction manager, general superintendent, cost estimator, construction building inspector, general manager or top executive, contractor, or consultant. Although a college education is not always required, administrative jobs are usually filled by people with degrees in business administration, finance, accounting, or similar fields.

Opportunities for workers to form their own firms are better in construction than in many other industries. Construction workers need only a moderate financial investment to become contractors and they can run their businesses from their homes, hiring additional construction workers only as needed for specific projects. The contract construction field, however, is very competitive, and the rate of business failure is high.

Earnings

Earnings in construction are significantly higher than the average for all industries (table 4). In 1998, production or nonsupervisory workers in construction averaged $16.56 an hour, or about $643 a week. Average earnings of workers in the special trade contractors segment were somewhat higher than those working for building or heavy construction contractors.

Earnings of workers in the construction industry vary largely depending on education and experience of the worker, type of work, the size and nature of the construction project, its geographic location, and economic conditions. Earnings of construction trade workers are also often affected by poor weather. Traditionally, winter is the slack period for construction activity, especially in colder parts of the country. Some workers, such as laborers or roofers, may not work for several months. Heavy rain may also slow or even stop work on a construction project. Because construction trades are dependent on one another—especially on large projects—work delays in one trade delay or stop the work in another. Earnings in selected occupations in construction in 1997 appear in table 5.

Table 4. Average weekly and hourly earnings by nongovernment construction industry sector, 1998

Industry segment	Weekly	Hourly
Total, private industry	$442	$12.77
Construction industry	643	16.56
General building contractors	602	15.87
Residential building contractors	543	14.83
Operative builders	573	15.17
Nonresidential building contractors	665	16.91
Heavy construction, except building	683	16.15
Highway and street construction	696	16.22
Heavy construction, except highway	679	16.12
Special trade contractors	646	16.90
Plumbing, heating, and air conditioning	674	17.16
Painting and paper hanging	562	15.22
Electrical work	732	18.40
Masonry, stonework, and plastering	601	16.73
Carpentry and floor work	596	16.46
Roofing, siding, and sheet metal work	509	14.74

About 20 percent of all workers were union members or were covered by union contracts, compared to 15.4 percent of workers throughout private industry. Many different unions represent the various construction trades and form joint apprenticeship committees with local employers to supervise apprenticeship programs.

Outlook

Employment of wage and salary jobs in the construction industry is expected to grow about 9 percent through the year 2008, slower than the average for all industries. Over the 1998-2008 period, employment growth is projected to add about 550,000 new jobs in construction. Many openings will also result each year from the need to replace experienced workers who leave jobs in the industry.

Employment in this industry depends primarily on the level of construction and remodeling activity. New construction is usually cut back during periods when the economy is not expanding, and the number of job openings in construction fluctuates greatly from year to year. Employment growth in the various segments of the construction industry varies somewhat, depending on the projected demand for what the industry is hired to construct.

Employment in residential construction is expected to grow slowly because the anticipated slowing of population growth and household formation will reduce the demand for new housing units. The aging of the population will reduce the demand for larger single-family homes. In addition, higher home prices will make ownership less affordable. Slow employment growth is also expected in nonresidential construction, because the demand for commercial buildings will be lessened by technological trends favoring telecommuting, electronic shopping, home offices, teleconferencing, and globalization of information services, as well as business management practices in downsizing, temporary workforces, and inventory reduction. Industrial construction, however, is expected to be stronger because exports by the manufacturing sector of the economy are expected to increase. Replacement of many industrial plants has been delayed for years, and a large number of structures will have to be replaced or remodeled. Construction of nursing, convalescent homes, and other extended care institutions will also increase for several reasons: The aging of the population, the increasing use of high technology medical treatment facilities, and the need for more drug treatment clinics. Construction of schools will also increase to accommodate the children of the "baby-boom" generation.

Table 5. Median hourly earnings of the largest occupations in construction, 1997

Occupation	General building contractors	Heavy construction, except buildings	Special trade contractors	All industries
General managers and top executives	$28.12	$30.33	$24.18	$26.05
Construction managers ..	21.13	22.27	21.44	21.95
First-line supervisors and managers/supervisors-construction trades and extractive occupations	18.32	18.28	17.77	18.28
Electricians	14.42	16.97	16.10	16.54
Plumbers, pipefitters, and steamfitters	14.67	15.55	16.02	16.14
Carpenters	13.21	15.49	14.33	13.38
Secretaries, except legal and medical..............	10.17	10.27	9.41	11.00
Helpers, carpenters and related workers	8.92	9.35	9.36	9.16
General office clerks	8.88	9.06	8.80	9.10
Painters and paperhangers, construction and maintenance	10.94	—	11.59	11.59

Employment in heavy construction is projected to increase about as fast as the industry average. Growth is expected in highway, bridge, and street construction, as well as repairs to prevent further deterioration of the Nation's highways and bridges. Bridge construction is expected to increase the fastest due to the serious need to repair or replace structures before they become unsafe. Poor highway conditions will also result in increased demand for highway maintenance and repair. Congress recently passed a six-year public works bill designed to provide money for such construction projects, including building mass transit systems.

Employment in special trades contracting, the largest segment of the industry, should grow a little faster than the entire construction industry. Demand for special trades subcontractors in building and heavy construction is rising, and at the same time, more workers will be needed to repair and remodel existing homes. Home improvement and repair construction is expected to continue to grow faster than new home construction. Remodeling should be the fastest growing sector of the housing industry because of a growing stock of old residential and non-residential buildings. Many "starter" units will be remodeled to appeal to more affluent, space and amenity hungry buyers. Also, some of the trade-up market may result in remodeling and additions rather than new larger homes. Remodeling tends to be more labor-intensive than new construction.

Employment growth will differ among various occupations in the construction industry. Employment of construction managers is expected to grow as a result of advances in building materials and construction methods, as well as a proliferation of laws dealing with building construction, worker safety, and environmental issues. Construction managers with a bachelor's degree in construction science with an emphasis on construction management, and who acquire work experience in construction management services firms, should have an especially favorable job outlook. Administrative support occupations are expected to decline due to increased office automation.

Although employment in construction trades is expected to grow about as fast as the industry average, the rate of growth will vary among the various trades. Employment of bricklayers, electricians, sheet metal workers and duct installers, painters, and heating, air-conditioning, and refrigeration technicians should grow faster than the industry average because technological changes are not expected to offset employment demand as construction activity grows. Employment of carpenters; cement masons, concrete finishers, and terrazzo workers; plumbers; and structural metal workers is expected to grow somewhat more slowly than average because the demand for these workers is expected to be offset by a greater use of new materials and equipment. For example, increasing use of prefabricated components in residential construction is expected to reduce the demand for carpenters.

Many industry sources feel job opportunities are excellent in most construction crafts because there are shortages of skilled workers and adequate training programs. The shortage situation may worsen between 1998 and 2008 because the pool of young workers available to enter training programs will be increasing slowly, and many in that group are reluctant to seek training for jobs that may be strenuous and have uncomfortable working conditions.

Sources of Additional Information

Information about apprenticeships and training can be obtained from local construction firms and employer associations, the local office of the State employment service or State apprenticeship agency, or the local office of the Bureau of Apprenticeship and Training, U.S. Department of Labor.

For additional information on jobs in the construction industry, contact:

➢ Associated Builders and Contractors, 1300 North 17th St. NW., Rosslyn, VA 22209.
➢ Associated General Contractors of America, Inc., 1957 E St. NW., Washington, DC 20005.
➢ National Association of Home Builders, 15th and M Sts. NW., Washington, DC 20005.

Additional information on occupations in construction may be found in the 2000-01 *Occupational Outlook Handbook*:

- Bricklayers and stonemasons
- Carpenters
- Carpet, floor, and tile installers and finishers
- Cement masons, concrete finishers, and terrazzo workers
- Construction and building inspectors
- Construction equipment operators
- Construction managers
- Drywall installers and finishers
- Electricians
- Glaziers
- Handlers, equipment cleaners, helpers, and laborers
- Heating, air-conditioning, and refrigeration mechanics and installers
- Insulation workers
- Material moving and equipment operators
- Painters and paperhangers
- Plasterers and stucco masons
- Plumbers, pipefitters and steamfitters
- Roofers
- Sheet metal workers and duct installers
- Structural and reinforcing metal workers

Mining and Quarrying

SIC 10, 12 and 14

SIGNIFICANT POINTS

- Technological innovations, environmental regulations, and international competition will continue to reduce employment in mining and quarrying.

- Most production jobs require little or no formal education or training beyond high school.

- Earnings are higher than average.

Nature of the Industry

Throughout history, mining has played an important part in the development of the United States. In the past, the discovery of minerals such as gold and silver has resulted in population shifts and economic growth. Extraction of minerals, such as coal and copper, continues to provide the foundation for the local economy in some parts of the country. Products of this industry are used as inputs for products, processes, and services provided by all other industries, including agriculture, manufacturing, transportation, communications, and construction. Such uses include coal for energy, copper for wiring, gold in satellites and sophisticated electronic components, and a variety of other minerals used as ingredients in medicines and household products.

Besides the mining and quarrying of coal and metallic and nonmetallic minerals, employers in this industry explore for minerals and develop new mines and quarries. *Metallic minerals* include ores, such as bauxite—from which aluminum is extracted—copper, gold, iron, lead, silver, and zinc. *Nonmetallic minerals* include stone, sand, gravel, clay, and other minerals such as lime and soda ash used as chemicals and fertilizers. This industry also includes initial mineral processing and preparation activities, because processing plants usually operate together with mines or quarries as part of the extraction process. A separate section in the *Career Guide* covers careers in oil and gas extraction.

Mining is the process of digging into the earth to extract naturally occurring minerals. There are two kinds of mining, *surface mining* and *underground mining*. Surface mining, also called open pit mining or strip mining, is undertaken if the mineral is near the earth's surface. This method is usually more cost efficient and requires fewer workers to produce the same quantity of ore as underground mining. In surface mining, after blasting with explosives, huge earthmoving equipment, such as power shovels or draglines, scoops off the layers of soil and rock covering the mineral bed. Once the mineral is exposed, smaller shovels lift it from the ground and load it into trucks. The mineral can also be broken up using explosives, if necessary. In quarrying operations, workers use machines to extract stone for use primarily as building material. Stone, such as marble, granite, limestone and sandstone, is quarried by splitting blocks of rock from a massive rock surface.

Underground mining is employed when the mineral deposit lies deep below the surface of the earth. When developing an underground mine, miners first must dig two or more openings, or tunnels, deep into the earth near the place where they believe coal or minerals are located. Depending on where the vein of ore is in relation to the surface, tunnels may be vertical, horizontal, or sloping. One opening allows the miners to move in and out of the mine with their tools, and also serves as an opening to transport the mined rock by small railroad cars or by conveyor belt to the surface. The other opening is used for ventilation. Miners remove the mineral from the bed, load it on the railroad cars or conveyor belts, and then haul it out of the mine through the other opening, or tunnel.

Entries are constructed so that miners and equipment can get to the ore and carry it out, while allowing fresh air to enter the mine. Once underground at the proper depth, a mine's tunnels interconnect with a network of passageways going in many directions. Long steel bolts and pillars of unmined ore support the roof of the tunnel. Using the room-and-pillar method, miners remove half of the ore as they work the ore seams from the tunnel entrance to the edge of the mine property, leaving columns of ore to support the ceiling. This process is then reversed, and the remainder of the ore is extracted, as the miners work their way back out. In the case of longwall mining of coal, self-advancing roof supports, made of hydraulic jacks and metal plates, are moved ahead, allowing the ceiling in the mined area to cave in as the miners work back towards the tunnel entrance.

During the 1980s and early 1990s, production of both metal and nonmetallic minerals increased. Given its more volatile price, metal production fluctuated more than that of nonmetallics. However, employment in both sectors declined significantly, as new technology and more sophisticated mining techniques increased productivity, allowing growth in output while employing fewer workers.

During this period, production of coal also increased, mainly as a result of increasing electric utility demand. Coal accounts for about one-third of overall domestic energy production and over half of U.S. electrical power was generated by burning coal in 1996. However, technological advancements in the U.S. coal industry, including larger, more powerful machinery and equipment; the use of new mining techniques; and the development of large surface mines, continue to reduce employment in coal mines.

Working Conditions

The average worker in the mining and quarrying industry worked 44 hours a week in 1998. Work environments vary by occupation. Scientists and technicians work in office buildings and laboratories, miners and mining engineers spend much of their time in the mine.

27

Working conditions in mines and quarries can be unusual and sometimes dangerous. Underground mines are damp and dark, and some can be very hot. At times, several inches of water may cover tunnel floors. Although underground mines have electric lights, only the lights on miners' caps illuminate many areas. Workers in mines with very low roofs may have to work on their hands and knees, backs, or stomachs in confined spaces. In underground mining operations, dangers include the possibility of an explosion or cave-in, electric shock, or exposure to harmful gas.

Workers in surface mines and quarries are subject to rugged outdoor work in all kinds of weather and climates. Physical strength and stamina are necessary, because the work involves lifting, stooping, and climbing. Surface mining, however, usually is less hazardous than underground mining.

In 1997, the rate of work-related injury and illness was 4.9 per 100 full-time workers in metal mining, 4.7 in nonmetallic minerals, and 7.8 in coal mining, compared with 7.1 for the entire private sector. Although mine health and safety conditions have improved dramatically over the years, dust generated by drilling in mines still places miners at risk of developing either of two serious lung diseases: pneumoconiosis, called "black lung disease," from coal dust, or silicosis from rock dust. The Federal Coal Mine Health and Safety Act of 1969 regulates dust concentrations in coal mines, and respirable dust levels are closely monitored. Dust concentrations in mines have declined as a result. Underground miners are now required to have their lungs x rayed when starting a job, with a mandatory follow-up x ray 3 years later, in order to monitor any development of respiratory illness. Additional x rays are given every 5 years on a voluntary basis. Workers who develop black lung disease or silicosis may be eligible for Federal aid.

Employment
There were approximately 251,000 wage and salary jobs in the mining and quarrying industry in 1998; around 92,000 in coal mining; 50,000 in metal mining; and 109,000 in nonmetallic mineral mining. According to the Energy Information Administration, there were around 1,800 coal mining operations in 25 States in 1997. Over half of U.S. coal is produced in three states: Kentucky, Wyoming, and West Virginia. Metal mining is more prevalent in the West and Southwest, particularly in Arizona, Colorado, Nevada, New Mexico, and Utah. Nonmetallic mineral mining is the most widespread, as quarrying of nonmetallic minerals, such as stone, clay, sand, and gravel, is done in nearly every State. About 50 percent of mining and quarrying establishments employ fewer than 10 workers (chart).

Occupations in the Industry
The mining and quarrying industry requires many kinds of workers. In 1998, almost 4 out of 5 workers were in *precision production, craft, and repair* or *operator, fabricator, and laborer* occupations (table 1).

Mining occupations. The majority of jobs in the mining and quarrying industry are in equipment operation and skilled craft and repair occupations. Though most of these jobs can be entered directly from high school, or after acquiring some experience and on-the-job training in an entry-level position,

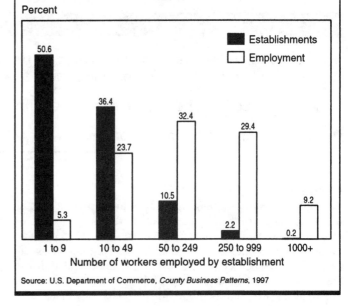

About 50 percent of mining and quarrying establishments employ fewer than 10 workers

Percent

Source: U.S. Department of Commerce, *County Business Patterns*, 1997

the increasing sophistication of equipment and machinery used in mining means a higher level of technical skill may now be required for many positions.

Underground mining primarily includes three methods: Conventional, continuous, and longwall mining. Conventional mining, which is being phased out, is the oldest method, requiring the most workers and procedures. In this method, a strip or "kerf" is cut underneath the ore seam to control the direction in which the ore falls after it has been blasted. *Cutting machine operators* use a huge electric chain saw with a cutter from 6 to 15 feet long to cut the kerf. Next, *drilling machine operators* drill holes in the ore where the *shot firers* place explosives. This potentially dangerous work requires workers to follow safety procedures, such as making sure everyone is clear of the area before the explosives are detonated. After the blast, *loading machine operators* scoop up the material and dump it into small rubber-tired cars run by *shuttle car operators*, who bring the coal or ore to a central location for transportation to the surface.

The continuous mining method eliminates the drilling and blasting operations of conventional mining by using a machine called a continuous miner. Traditionally, a *continuous mining machine operator* sits or lies in a machine's cab and operates levers that cut or rip out ore and load it directly onto a conveyor or shuttle car. However, the use of remote-controlled continuous mining machines—which have increased safety considerably—now allows an operator to control the machine from a distance.

In longwall mining, which is similar to continuous mining, *longwall machine operators* run large machines with rotating drums that automatically shear and load ore on a conveyor. At the same time, hydraulic jacks reinforce the roof of the tunnel. As ore is cut, the jacks are hydraulically winched forward, supporting the roof as they move along.

Many other workers are needed to operate safe and efficient underground mines. Before miners are allowed underground, a *mine safety inspector* checks the work area for such hazards as loose roofs, dangerous gases, and inadequate ventilation. If safety standards are not met, the inspector prohibits the mine from producing until conditions are made safe. *Rock-dust machine operators* spray the mine walls and floor to hold down dust which can interfere with breathing.

Roof bolters operate the machines that automatically install roof support bolts to prevent roof cave-ins, the biggest cause of mining injuries. *Brattice builders* construct doors, walls, and partitions in tunnel passageways to force air into the work areas. *Shift bosses*, or *blue-collar worker supervisors*, oversee all operations at the work site.

In surface mining, most miners operate huge machines that either remove the earth above the ore deposit, or dig and load the ore onto trucks. The number of workers required to operate a surface mine depends on the amount of overburden, or earth, above the ore seam. In many surface mines, the overburden is first drilled and blasted. *Overburden stripping operators* or *dragline operators* then scoop the earth away to expose the coal or metal ore. Some draglines are among the largest land machines on earth.

Next, *loading machine operators* rip the exposed ore from the seam and dump it into trucks to be driven to the preparation plant. *Tractor operators* use bulldozers to move earth and ore and to remove boulders or other obstructions. *Truckdrivers* haul ore to railroad sidings or to preparation plants, and transport supplies to mines.

Craft and *repair occupations*. Other workers, who are not directly involved in the extraction process, work in and around mines and quarries. For example, skilled *mechanics* are needed to repair and maintain the wide variety of mining machinery, and skilled *electricians* are needed to check and install electrical wiring. Mechanical and electrical repair work has become increasingly complex, as machinery and other equipment have become computerized. *Carpenters* construct and maintain benches, bins, and stoppings (barricades to prevent air flow through a tunnel). These workers generally need specialized training to work under the unusual conditions in mines. Mechanics, for example, may have to repair machines while on their knees with only their headlamps to illuminate the working area.

Quarrying occupations. Workers at quarries have duties similar to miners. Using jackhammers and wedges, *rock splitters* remove pieces of stone from a rock mass. *Dredge operators* and *dipper tenders* operate power-driven dredges, or dipper sticks of dredges, to mine sand, gravel, and other materials from beneath the surface of lakes, rivers, and streams. Using power-driven cranes with dragline buckets, *dragline operators* excavate or move sand, gravel, and other materials.

Processing plant occupations. Processing plants often are located next to mines or quarries. In these plants, rocks and other impurities are removed from the ore, which is then washed, crushed, sized, or blended to meet buyer specifications. Methods for physically separating the ore from surrounding material also include more complex processes, such as leaching—mixing the ore with chemical solutions or other liquids in order to separate materials. Most processing plants are highly mechanized and require only a few workers for the washing, separating and crushing operations. *Processing plant supervisors* oversee all operations. In plants that are not heavily

mechanized, *wash box attendants* operate equipment that sizes and separates impurities from ore, and *shake tenders* monitor machinery that further cleans and sizes ore with a vibrating screen. Most jobs in the processing plant are repetitive and, as a result of highly computerized mechanization, are becoming more automated.

Table 1. Employment of wage and salary workers in mining and quarrying by occupation, 1998 and projected change, 1998-2008

(Employment in thousands)

Occupation	1998 Employment Number	1998 Employment Percent	1998-2008 Percent change
All occupations	250	100.0	-23.2
Precision production, craft, and repair	111	44.4	-25.1
Mining, quarrying, and tunneling occupations	22	8.8	-19.5
Blue-collar worker supervisors	17	6.6	-26.6
Industrial machinery mechanics	15	5.8	-25.8
All other extraction and related workers	14	5.4	-25.2
Grader, bulldozer, and scraper operators	11	4.5	-29.2
Mobile heavy equipment mechanics	6	2.5	-24.8
Maintenance repairers, general utility	5	2.1	-25.9
Electricians	4	1.8	-30.0
Operating engineers	2	1.0	-20.9
Operators, fabricators, and laborers	87	34.7	-19.3
Truckdrivers	22	8.7	-18.4
Helpers, laborers, and material movers, hand	15	5.6	-25.4
All other material moving equipment operators	12	4.6	-25.8
Excavation and loading machine operators	11	4.5	-13.8
Crushing, grinding, mixing, and blending machine operators and tenders	9	3.5	4.6
Welders and cutters	4	1.6	-25.0
Industrial truck and tractor operators	3	1.3	-21.3
Separating, filtering, clarifying, precipitating, and still machine operators and tenders	2	0.7	-25.0
Administrative support, including clerical	19	7.6	-25.6
General office clerks	4	1.4	-16.1
Bookkeeping, accounting, and auditing clerks	3	1.1	-33.6
Secretaries	3	1.0	-37.2
Weighers, measurers, checkers, and samplers, recordkeeping	2	0.9	-18.1
Executive, administrative, and managerial	19	7.6	-26.3
General managers and top executives	6	2.2	-22.2
Management support occupations	4	1.7	-27.4
Professional specialty	7	2.7	-24.3
Engineers		1.5	-25.5
Geologists, geophysicists, and oceanographers	1	0.4	-28.6
Technicians and related support	4	1.7	-28.6
Engineering and science technicians	4	1.5	-27.4
All other occupations	4	1.4	-23.0

29

Managerial, professional, technical, and *administrative support occupations.* Administrative workers include *general managers* and *top executives,* who are responsible for making policy decisions. Staff specialists (such as *accountants, attorneys,* and *market researchers*) provide information and advice for policymakers.

Professional and technical workers in mining and quarrying include engineering, scientific, and technical personnel. *Geologists* and *geophysicists* search for locations likely to yield coal or mineral ores in sufficient quantity to warrant extraction costs. *Mining engineers* examine seams for depth and purity, determine the type of mine to build, and supervise the construction, maintenance, and operation of mines. *Mechanical engineers* oversee the installation of equipment, such as heat and water systems; *electrical engineers* oversee the installation and maintenance of electrical equipment; *civil engineers* oversee the building and construction of mine sites, plants, roads, and other infrastructure; and *safety engineers* direct health and safety programs. Using sophisticated technologies and equipment, such as the Global Positioning System (GPS)—a satellite system that locates points on the earth using radio signals transmitted by satellites—*surveyors* help map areas for mining.

Environmental engineers and *scientists* play an increasingly important role in mining and quarrying, given environmental concerns and stringent Federal, State, and local regulations imposed on all operations. Restrictions imposed by environmental regulations make obtaining permits for new mine development projects increasingly difficult. Mine owners and operators face substantial penalties should they fail to abide by current regulations. In addition, both State laws and Federal regulations, such as the Surface Mining Control and Reclamation Act (SMCRA), require that land reclamation be part of the mining process. Reclamation plans must usually be approved by both government officials and local interest groups. When a mining operation is closed, the land must be restored to its pre-mine condition, which can include anything from leveling soil and removing waste to replanting vegetation.

Exploration, mine design, impact assessment, and restoration efforts can depend on computer analysis. In addition, rapid technological advancements, particularly in processing plant operations, are the result of increased computerization. This has led to a growing reliance on professionals with computer skills, such as *systems analysts* and *computer scientists.*

Training and Advancement

Workers in mining and quarrying production occupations must be at least 18 years old, in good physical condition, and able to work in confined spaces. A high school diploma is not necessarily required. Most workers start as helpers to experienced workers and learn skills on the job; however, formal training is becoming more important, as more technologically advanced machinery and mining methods are used. Some employers prefer to hire recent graduates of high school vocational programs in mining or graduates of junior college or technical school programs in mine technology. Such programs usually are only found at schools in mining areas.

Mining companies may also offer formal training in either classrooms or training mines for a few weeks before new miners actually begin work. At mines covered by contracts with the United Mine Workers of America (UMWA),

workers receive employer-sponsored pre-service instruction and annual retraining sessions in subjects such as machine operation, first aid, and health and safety regulations. All miners receive annual retraining instruction in all aspects of their job concerning health and safety. The U.S. Mine Safety and Health Administration conducts classes on health, safety, and mining methods; and some mining machinery manufacturers also offer courses in machine operation and maintenance.

As production workers gain more experience, they can advance to higher-paying jobs requiring greater skill. A mining machine operator's helper, for example, may become an operator. When vacancies occur, announcements are posted and all qualified workers can bid for the job. Positions are filled on the basis of seniority and ability. Miners with significant experience or special training can also become mine safety inspectors. According to the U.S. Mine Safety and Health Administration, an inspector needs, in general, at least 5 years experience as a miner, or a degree in mining engineering.

For professional and managerial positions in mining and quarrying, a bachelor's degree in engineering, one of the physical sciences, or business administration is preferred. A number of colleges and universities have mining schools or departments and programs in mining or minerals. Environmental positions require regulatory knowledge and a strong natural science background, or a background in a technical field, such as environmental engineering or hydrology. To date, most environmental professionals have been drawn from the ranks of engineers and scientists who have had experience in the mining and quarrying industry.

Universities and mining schools have introduced more environmental course work into their programs, and mining and quarrying firms are hiring professionals from existing environment-related disciplines and training them to their companies' needs. Additionally, specialized mine technology programs are available from a few colleges. Enrollment in these programs can lead to a certificate in mine technology after 1 year, an associate degree after 2 years, or a bachelor's degree after 4 years. Courses cover areas such as mine ventilation, roof bolting, and machinery repairs.

Earnings

Average earnings in mining and quarrying were significantly higher than the average for all industries. In 1998, production workers in coal mining averaged $19.16 an hour; workers in metal mining averaged $18.25 an hour; and workers in nonmetallic minerals mining averaged $14.72 an hour (table 2). Workers in underground mines spend time traveling from the mine entrance to their working areas, so their paid workday is slightly longer than that of surface mine workers, 8 hours versus 7-1/4-hour shifts. Workers in underground mines also tend to earn more per hour than miners on the surface. Earnings in selected occupations in selected mining and quarrying industries appear in table 3.

Table 2. Average earnings of nonsupervisory workers in mining and quarrying, 1998

Industry segment	Weekly	Hourly
Total, private industry	$442	$12.77
Coal mining	858	19.16
Metal mining	812	18.25
Nonmetallic mineral mining	683	14.72

Around 26 percent of mine workers are union members or are covered by union contracts, compared to about 15 percent of workers throughout private industry. About 30 percent of workers in coal and metal mining were union members in 1998, compared to about 22 percent of workers in nonmetallic mineral mining. Union coal miners are primarily represented by the UMWA. The United Steelworkers of America, the International Union of Operating Engineers, and other unions also represent miners.

Workers covered by UMWA contracts receive 11 paid holidays, 14 days of paid vacation each year, and 5 days of personal or sick leave; however, coal miners generally must take their vacations during one of three regular vacation periods, to assure a continuous supply of coal. As length of service increases, UMWA miners get up to 13 extra vacation days after 18 years of continuous employment. Union workers also receive benefits from a welfare and retirement fund.

Table 3. Median hourly earnings of the largest occupations in coal mining and nonmetallic minerals, except fuels, 1997

Occupation	Coal mining	Nonmetallic minerals, except fuels	All industries
Grader, bulldozer, and scraper operators	$16.87	—	$12.62
Excavating and loading machine operators	—	$11.58	12.77
Crushing, grinding, mixing, and blending machine operators and tenders	—	11.36	10.85
Truck drivers, heavy or tractor-trailer	—	10.95	13.08

Outlook

Employment in mining and quarrying is expected to decline by about 23 percent through the year 2008. This continuing long-term decline is due, in part, to increased productivity, resulting from technological changes in mining operations, as well as factors such as stringent environmental regulations and international competition.

Declining employment will be led by a decline in the coal mining sector. The products of the coal mining industry are used to produce electricity and steel products. Although production of coal is expected to increase, employment should continue to decline, as more efficient and automated production operations require less labor. Advances in longwall and surface mining, which are less labor-intensive, have increased productivity, as have improvements in transportation and processing. Additionally, innovations such as roof bolting, self-advancing roof supports, and continuous mining machinery have led to safer, more efficient operations.

The long-term outlook for coal also depends on how electric utility companies—the major consumers of coal—respond to provisions of the Clean Air Act Amendments of 1990, which attempt to limit the emission of sulfur dioxide and other harmful pollutants. Phase I of the Amendments, which took affect in 1995, requires reductions in sulfur emissions from coal combustion. Compliance involves the installation of costly cleaning and monitoring equipment or increased use of low-sulfur coal. Already, low transportation costs and rising demand for cleaner-burning coal have resulted in regional shifts in coal production and markets. Because of this, lower-sulfur Western coal now accounts for an increasing share of output. Improvements in clean coal technologies may help the industry cope with increasingly restrictive regulations through projects like the Integrated Gasification Combined Cycle (IGCC). This technology combines traditional coal gasification with gas turbine and steam power to generate electricity more efficiently and reduce carbon and sulfur dioxide emissions. Additional options include switching to other fossil fuels, or trading or selling "emission credits" among companies trying to meet standards. Though coal remains an abundant energy source, the coal mining industry will have to contend with environmental issues as all aspects of the production, processing, and use of coal come under stricter regulation.

Like coal mining, continuing productivity increases are expected to cause employment in the metal mining industry to decline through 2008. The metal mining industry produces iron ore and ferroalloy ores, such as manganese, tungsten, cobalt, and molybdenum; copper ores; and lead; zinc; gold; silver; aluminum; and uranium, as well as other ores. These materials are used mainly to produce primary nonferrous metals, steel, and industrial chemicals. Metals, such as copper and gold, for example, are used throughout the economy in products such as wire or electrical connectors and contact pads, which are vital to the communications and electronics industries. Nonresidential construction also consumes a large portion of the output of metal mining, as do the automotive and appliance industries. The ability of U.S. mines to remain internationally competitive will influence the long-term outlook. Currently, U.S. mines are among the most technologically advanced in the world; however, mining operations in other countries have lower labor costs and are subject to fewer government regulations. In addition, pending reform of the Mining Law of 1872, which involves issues such as access to public lands and the payment of royalties, is of particular concern to this sector of the mining industry. Changes in policies could have significant long term implications; and uncertainty over restrictions, regulations, and the future of this law could serve to focus more exploration and investment opportunities elsewhere.

The nonmetallic mineral industry produces stone such as limestone or granite, gravel, sulfur, and other nonmetallic minerals. These minerals are used to make concrete and agricultural chemicals and as materials in residential, non-residential, and maintenance construction. Production of most nonmetallic minerals rose almost continuously from 1961 to 1994. Although demand for minerals remains strong, technological changes will continue to increase productivity, limiting the need for workers, so employment in this sector of the industry is expected to decline through 2008.

Sources of Additional Information

For additional information about careers and training in the mining and quarrying industry, write to:

➤ Mine Safety and Health Administration, 4015 Wilson Blvd., Arlington, VA 22203.
Internet: **http://www.msha.gov**

➤ National Mining Association, 1130 17th St. NW., Washington, DC 20036. Internet: **http://www.nma.org**

➤ Society for Mining, Metallurgy and Exploration, Inc., P.O. Box 625002, Littleton, CO 80162.
Internet: **http://www.smenet.org**

➤ United Mine Workers of America, 900 15th St. NW., Washington, DC 20005.

Information on the following occupations in mining and quarrying may be found in the 2000-01 *Occupational Outlook Handbook*:

- Blue-collar worker supervisors
- Chemical engineers
- Electrical and electronics engineers
- Electricians
- Geologists, geophysicists, and oceanographers
- Materials engineers
- Mining engineers, including mine safety engineers
- Petroleum engineers
- Surveyors, cartographers, photogrammetrists, and surveying technicians
- Truckdrivers

Oil and Gas Extraction

SIGNIFICANT POINTS

- Most establishments employ fewer than 10 workers.

- About 60 percent of the industry's workforce is concentrated in 4 States.

- Although technological innovations have expanded exploration and development worldwide, employment is expected to decline.

Nature of the Industry

Petroleum, or oil as it is more commonly referred to, is a natural fuel formed from the decay of plants and animals buried beneath the ground for millions of years under tremendous heat and pressure. Formed by a similar process, natural gas often is found in separate deposits and sometimes mixed with oil. Because oil and gas are difficult to locate, exploration and drilling are key activities in the oil and gas extraction industry. Oil and natural gas furnish about three-fourths of our energy needs, fueling our homes, workplaces, factories, and transportation systems. In addition, they provide the raw materials for plastics, chemicals, medicines, fertilizers, and synthetic fibers.

Using a variety of methods, on land and at sea, small crews of specialized workers search for geologic formations that are likely to contain oil and gas. Sophisticated equipment and advances in computer technology have increased the productivity of exploration. Maps of potential deposits are now made using remote sensing satellites. Seismic prospecting—a technique based on measuring the time it takes sound waves to travel through underground formations and return to the surface—has revolutionized oil and gas exploration. Computers and advanced software analyze seismic data to provide 3-dimensional models of subsurface rock formations. This technique lowers the risk involved in exploring by allowing scientists to locate and identify structural oil and gas reservoirs and the best locations to drill. 4-D or "time-lapsed" seismic technology tracks the movement of fluids over time and enhances production performance even further. Another method of searching for oil and gas is based on collecting and analyzing core samples of rock, clay, and sand in the earth's layers.

After scientific studies indicate the possible presence of oil, an oil company selects a well site and installs a derrick—a tower-like steel structure—to support the drilling equipment. A hole is drilled deep in the earth until oil or gas is found, or the company abandons the effort. Similar techniques are employed in offshore drilling, except the drilling equipment is part of a steel platform that either sits on the ocean floor, or floats on the surface and is anchored to the ocean floor. Although some large oil companies do their own drilling, most land and offshore drilling is done by contractors.

In rotary drilling, a rotating bit attached to a length of hollow drill pipe bores a hole in the ground by chipping and cutting rock. As the bit cuts deeper, more pipe is added. A stream of drilling "mud"—a mixture of clay, chemicals, and water—is continuously pumped through the drill pipe and through holes in the drill bit. Its purpose is to cool the drill bit, plaster the walls of the hole to prevent cave-ins, carry crushed rock to the surface, and prevent "blowouts" by equalizing pressure inside the hole. When a drill bit wears out, all drill pipe must be removed from the hole a section at a time, the bit replaced, and the pipe returned to the hole. New materials and better designs have advanced drill bit technology, enabling faster, more cost effective drilling, for longer lengths of time.

Advancements in directional or horizontal drilling techniques, which allow increased access to potential reserves, have had a significant impact on drilling capabilities. Drilling begins vertically, but the drill bit can be turned so drilling can continue at an angle of up to 90 degrees. This technique extends the reach, enabling a drill to reach separate pockets of oil or gas. Because constructing new platforms is costly, this technique is commonly employed by offshore drilling operations.

When oil or gas is found, the drill pipe and bit are pulled from the well, and metal pipe (casing) is lowered into the hole and cemented in place. The casing's upper end is fastened to a system of pipes and valves called a wellhead, or "Christmas Tree," through which natural pressure forces the oil or gas into separation and storage tanks. If natural pressure is not great enough to force the oil to the surface, pumps may be used. In some cases, water, steam, or gas may be injected into the oil-producing formation to improve recovery.

Crude oil is transported to refineries by pipeline, ship, barge, truck, or railroad. Natural gas is usually transported to processing plants by pipeline. While oil refineries may be many thousands of miles away from the producing fields, gas processing plants usually are near the fields, so impurities—water, sulfur, and natural gas liquids—can be removed, before the gas is piped to customers. The oil refining industry is considered a separate industry and its activities are not covered here, even though many oil companies both extract and refine oil.

The oil and gas extraction industry has experienced both "boom" and "bust" in recent years. During the 1970s and early 1980s, the price of crude oil rose sharply, stimulating domestic exploration and production. Between 1970 and 1982—the year industry employment peaked—this industry created 438,000 jobs, a percentage increase that was more than four times greater than that of the economy as a whole. Employment rose twice as fast in the oil and gas field services segment than in crude petroleum, natural gas, and natural gas liquids segment, reflecting the fact that most exploration and drilling is done on a contract basis.

Starting in 1982, oil-producing countries around the world began yielding much larger volumes of crude oil, driving prices down, culminating in the collapse of oil prices in the mid-1980s. During this time, the industry experienced a sharp decline in domestic exploration and production and an extended period of downsizing and restructuring, losing almost 390,000 jobs from 1982 to 1995. As was the case during the boom period, employment in oil and gas field services changed more than employment in crude petroleum and natural gas production.

Working Conditions

Working conditions in this industry vary significantly by occupation. Jobs as roustabouts and other production workers may involve rugged outdoor work in remote areas in all kinds of weather. For these jobs, physical strength and stamina are necessary. This work involves standing for long periods of time, lifting moderately heavy objects, and climbing and stooping to work with tools that are often oily and dirty. Executives generally work in office settings, as do most administrators and clerical workers. Geologists, engineers, and managers may split their time between the office and the job sites, particularly while involved in exploration work.

Only 1 employee in 20 works fewer than 35 hours a week, reflecting few opportunities for part-time work. In fact, a higher percentage of workers in this industry work overtime than in all industries combined. The average nonsupervisory worker worked 42.7 hours per week in 1998, compared to 34.6 hours for all workers.

Oil and gas well drilling and servicing can be hazardous. However, in 1997, the rate of work-related injury and illness in the oil and gas extraction industry, as a whole, was 5.9 per 100 full-time workers, somewhat lower than the 7.1 for the entire private sector. The rate for workers in oil and gas field services, 8.7 per 100 full-time workers, was nearly five times higher than for workers in crude petroleum and natural gas, which was only 2.0.

Drilling rigs operate continuously. On land, drilling crews usually work 6 days, 8 hours a day, and then have a few days off. In offshore operations, workers can work 14 days, 12 hours a day, and then have 14 days off. If the offshore rig is located far from the coast, drilling crew members live on ships anchored nearby or in facilities on the platform itself. Workers on offshore rigs are always evacuated in the event of a storm. Most workers in oil and gas well operations and maintenance or in natural gas processing work 8 hours a day, 5 days a week.

Many oil field workers are away from home for weeks or months at a time. Exploration field personnel and drilling workers frequently move from place to place as work at a particular field is completed. In contrast, well operation and maintenance workers and natural gas processing workers usually remain in the same location for extended periods of time.

Employment

The oil and gas extraction industry, with about 339,000 wage and salary jobs in 1998, is the largest industry in the mining division, accounting for more than one-half of employment. The workforce is divided between two segments: crude petroleum, natural gas, and natural gas liquids, with about 143,000 jobs, and oil and gas field services, with about 196,000 jobs.

Although onshore oil and gas extraction establishments are found in 48 States, about 60 percent of the industry's workers in 1999 were located in just 4 States—California, Louisiana, Oklahoma, and Texas. While most workers are employed on land, many work at offshore sites. Although they are not included in employment figures for this industry, many Americans are employed by oil companies at locations in Africa, the North Sea, the Far East, the Middle East, South America, and countries of the former Soviet Union.

More than 7 out of 10 establishments employ fewer than 10 workers, although more than half of all workers in this industry work in establishments with 50 or more workers (chart).

Relatively few oil and gas extraction workers are in their teens or early 20s. Over 65 percent of the workers in this industry are between 35 and 54 years of age.

Occupations in the Industry

People with many different skills are needed to explore for oil and gas, drill new wells, maintain existing wells, and process natural gas. The largest group is production workers, accounting for nearly 44 percent of industry employment. Executive, managerial, and professional workers account for about 14 percent of employment; while clerical and administrative support workers account for about 11 percent (table 1).

A *petroleum geologist* or a *geophysicist*, who is responsible for analyzing and interpreting the information gathered, usually heads exploration operations. Other geological specialists, such as *paleontologists*, who study fossil remains to locate oil; *mineralogists*, who study physical and chemical properties of mineral and rock samples; *stratigraphers*, who determine the rock layers most likely to contain oil and natural gas; and *photogeologists*, who examine and interpret aerial photographs of land surfaces, may also be involved in exploration activities. Additionally, exploration parties may include *surveyors* and *drafters*, who assist in surveying and mapping activities.

Some geologists and geophysicists work in district offices of oil companies or contract exploration firms, where they prepare and study geological maps and analyze seismic data. These scientists may also analyze samples from test drillings.

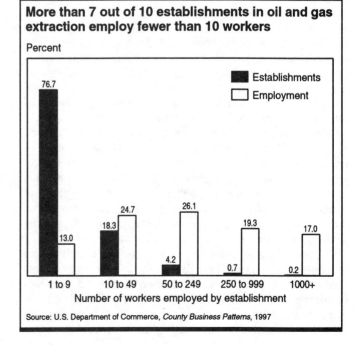

More than 7 out of 10 establishments in oil and gas extraction employ fewer than 10 workers

Percent

Number of workers employed by establishment

Source: U.S. Department of Commerce, *County Business Patterns*, 1997

Other workers involved in exploration are *geophysical prospectors*. They lead crews consisting of *gravity* and *seismic prospecting observers*, who operate and maintain electronic seismic equipment; *scouts*, who investigate the exploration, drilling, and leasing activities of other companies to identify promising areas to explore and lease; and *lease buyers*, who make business arrangements to obtain the use of the land with owners of land or mineral rights.

Table 1. Employment of wage and salary workers in oil and gas extraction by occupation, 1998 and projected change, 1998-2008

(Employment in thousands)

Occupation	1998 Employment Number	1998 Employment Percent	1998-2008 Percent change
All occupations	339	100.0	-16.7
Precision production, craft, and repair	148	43.7	-9.2
All other oil and gas extraction occupations	39	11.6	-.1
Roustabouts, oil and gas	29	8.6	-21.6
Blue-collar worker supervisors	20	5.8	-13.4
All other extraction and related workers	14	4.1	4.1
Gas and petroleum plant and systems occupations	12	3.4	-8.9
Construction trades	9	2.6	-1.8
Industrial machinery mechanics	6	1.9	-13.7
Maintenance repairers, general utility	4	1.1	-27.7
Operators, fabricators, and laborers	58	17.1	-2.6
Material moving equipment operators	17	4.9	-22.7
Helpers, laborers, and material movers, hand	15	4.3	11.2
Hand workers, including assemblers and fabricators	13	3.9	5.9
Truck drivers	9	2.6	2.9
Executive, managerial, and administrative	46	13.6	-31.6
General managers and top executives	11	3.3	-20.4
Accountants and auditors	7	2.2	-44.0
All other managers and administrators	5	1.4	-28.9
Financial managers	3	0.8	-30.2
Administrative support, including clerical	36	10.8	-32.9
Secretaries	8	2.4	-42.3
General office clerks	9	2.8	-28.7
Bookkeeping, accounting, and auditing clerks	6	1.8	-41.9
Material recording, scheduling, dispatching, and distributing occupations	4	1.1	-14.8
Professional specialty	29	8.6	-32.0
Petroleum engineers	6	1.9	-21.6
Geologists, geophysicists, and oceanographers	6	1.8	-46.5
Computer systems analysts, engineers, and scientists	4	1.2	-7.1
Technicians and related support	14	4.1	-32.0
Science and mathematics technicians	7	2.0	-32.1
Engineering technicians	3	0.8	-21.7
Marketing and sales occupations	5	1.4	-7.9
All other occupations	2	0.8	-24.1

Petroleum engineers are responsible for planning and supervising the actual drilling operation, once a potential drill site has been located. These engineers develop and implement the most efficient recovery method, in order to achieve maximum profitable recovery. They also plan and supervise well operation and maintenance. *Drilling superintendents* serve as supervisors of drilling crews, supervising one or more drilling rigs.

Rotary drilling crews usually consist of four or five workers. *Rotary drillers* supervise the crew and operate machinery that controls drilling speed and pressure. *Rotary-rig engine operators* are in charge of engines that provide the power for drilling and hoisting. Second in charge, *derrick operators* work on small platforms high on rigs to help run pipe in and out of well holes and operate the pumps that circulate mud through the pipe. *Rotary-driller helpers*, also known as *roughnecks*, guide the lower ends of pipe to well openings and connect pipe joints and drill bits.

Though not necessarily part of the drilling crew, *roustabouts*, or general laborers, do general oil field maintenance and construction work, such as cleaning tanks and building roads.

Pumpers and their helpers operate and maintain motors, pumps, and other surface equipment that force oil from wells and regulate the flow, according to a schedule set up by petroleum engineers and production supervisors. In fields where oil flows under natural pressure and does not require pumping, *switchers* open and close valves to regulate the flow. *Gaugers* measure and record the flow, taking samples to check quality. *Treaters* test the oil for water and sediment and remove these impurities by opening a drain or using special equipment. In most fields, pumping, switching, gauging, and treating operations are automatic.

Other skilled oil field workers include *oil well cementers*, who mix and pump cement into the space between the casing and well walls to prevent cave-ins; *acidizers*, who pump acid down the well and into the producing formation to increase oil flow; *perforator operators*, who use subsurface "guns" to pierce holes in the casing to make openings for oil to flow into the well bore; *sample-taker operators*, who take samples of soil and rock formations from wells to help geologists determine the presence of oil; and *well pullers*, who remove pipes, pumps, and other subsurface devices from wells for cleaning, repairing, and salvaging.

Many other skilled workers—such as welders, pipefitters, electricians, and machinists—are also employed in maintenance operations to install and repair pumps, gauges, pipes, and other equipment.

In addition to the types of workers required for onshore drilling, crews at offshore locations also need radio operators, cooks, ships' officers, sailors, and pilots. These workers make up the support personnel who work on or operate drilling platforms, crewboats, barges, and helicopters.

Most workers involved in gas processing are operators. *Gas treaters* tend automatically controlled treating units that remove water and other impurities from natural gas. *Gas-pumping-station operators* tend compressors that raise the pressure of gas for transmission in pipelines. Both types of workers can be assisted by *gas-compressor operators*.

Many employees in large natural gas processing plants—*welders*, *electricians*, *instrument repairers*, and *laborers*, for example—perform maintenance activities. In contrast, many small plants are automated and are checked at periodic intervals by maintenance workers or operators, or monitored by instruments that alert operators if trouble develops. In non-automated plants, workers usually combine the skills of both operators and maintenance workers.

Training and Advancement

Workers can enter the oil and gas extraction industry with a variety of educational backgrounds. The most common entry-level field jobs are as roustabouts or roughnecks, jobs that usually require little or no previous training or experience. Applicants for these routine laborer jobs must be physically fit and able to pass a physical examination. Companies also may administer aptitude tests and screen prospective employees for drug use. Basic skills can usually be learned over a period of days through on-the-job training. However, previous work experience or formal training in petroleum technology—that provides knowledge of oil field operations and familiarity with computers and other automated equipment—can be beneficial. In fact, given the increasing complexity of operations and the sophisticated nature of technology used today, employers now demand a higher level of skill and adaptability, including the ability to work with computers and other sophisticated equipment.

Other entry-level positions, such as engineering technician, usually require at least a 2-year technical school certificate. Professional jobs, such as geologist, geophysicist, or petroleum engineer, require at least a bachelor's degree and often a specialized graduate degree.

For well operation and maintenance jobs, companies generally prefer applicants who live nearby, have mechanical ability, and possess knowledge of oil field processes. Because this work offers the advantage of a fixed locale, members of drilling crews or exploration parties who prefer not to travel may transfer to well operation and maintenance jobs. Training is acquired on the job.

Promotion opportunities for some jobs may be limited due to the general decline of the domestic petroleum industry. Advancement opportunities for oil field workers remain best for those with skill and experience. For example, roustabouts may move up to switchers, gaugers, and pumpers. More experienced roughnecks may advance to derrick operators and, after several years, to drillers. Drillers may advance to tool pushers. There should continue to be some opportunities for entry-level field crew workers to acquire the skills that qualify them for higher level jobs within the industry. Due to the critical nature of the work, offshore crews, even at the entry level, generally are more experienced than land crews. Many companies will not employ someone who has no knowledge of oil field operations to work on an offshore rig, so workers who have gained experience as part of a land crew might advance to offshore operations.

As workers gain knowledge and experience, U.S. or foreign companies operating in other countries also may hire them. Although this can be a lucrative and exciting experience, it may not be suitable for everyone, because it usually means leaving family and friends and adapting to different customs and living standards.

Experience gained in many oil and gas extraction jobs also has application in other industries. For example, roustabouts can move to construction jobs, while machinery operators and repairers can transfer to other industries with similar machinery. Geologists and engineers may become involved with environmental activities, especially those related to this industry.

Earnings

Average earnings in the oil and gas extraction industry were significantly higher than the average for all industries (table 2). Due to the working conditions, employees at offshore operations generally earn higher wages than workers at onshore oil fields. College-educated workers and technical school graduates in professional and technical occupations usually earn the most. Earnings in selected occupations in oil and gas extraction appear in table 3.

Table 2. Average earnings of nonsupervisory workers in oil and gas extraction, 1998

Industry segment	Weekly	Hourly
Total, private industry	$442	$12.77
Total, oil and gas extraction	719	16.83
Crude petroleum and natural gas	945	22.66
Oil and gas field services	600	13.91

Few industry workers belong to unions. In fact, only about 4 percent of workers were union members or covered by union contracts in 1998, compared to about 15 percent of all workers throughout private industry.

Table 3. Median hourly earnings of the largest occupations in oil and gas extraction, 1997

Occupation	Oil and gas extraction	All industries
General managers and top executives	$34.74	$26.05
Accountants and auditors	22.73	17.66
First-line supervisors and supervisor/managers-construction trade and extractive workers	21.70	18.28
Rotary drill operators, oil and gas extraction	14.44	14.41
Secretaries, except legal and medical	11.87	11.00
Derrick operators, oil and gas extraction	11.35	11.36
General office clerks	10.87	9.10
Service unit operators	10.28	10.31
Truck drivers, heavy or tractor-trailer	9.82	13.08
Roustabouts	8.73	8.75

Outlook

The level of future crude petroleum and natural gas exploration and development, and therefore, employment opportunities, remain contingent upon a number of uncertainties—most importantly, the future price of oil and gas. Sharply higher prices mean companies, seeking greater profits, can be expected to implement new technologies, expand domestic exploration and production, and increase employment. Substantially lower prices, on the other hand, could make domestic exploration and continued production from many existing wells unprofitable, resulting in reduced employment opportunities.

In addition, environmental concerns, accompanied by strict regulation and limited access to protected Federal lands, continue to have a major impact on the industry. For example, environmental constraints, especially restrictions on drilling in environmentally sensitive areas, should continue to limit exploration and development, both onshore and offshore.

Overall employment in the oil and gas extraction industry is expected to decline 17 percent through the year 2008, even though worldwide demand for oil and gas is expected to remain strong. Employment in the crude petroleum, natural gas, and natural gas liquids segment of the industry is expected to decline about 46 percent, while employment in oil and gas field services—which includes all contract exploration and drilling services—is expected to increase by 5 percent.

While some new oil and gas deposits are being found in this country, especially in coastal waters, companies are increasingly moving to more lucrative foreign locations. As companies expand into other areas around the globe, the need for employees in the United States is reduced. However, advances in technology have increased the proportion of exploratory wells that yield oil and gas, enhanced offshore exploration and drilling capabilities, and extended the production of existing wells. As a result, more exploration and development ventures are profitable and provide employment opportunities that otherwise would have been lost.

Technological innovations, coupled with the declining cost of implementing such technologies, have reduced employment in many areas. Because overall employment is expected to decline, the need to replace workers who transfer to other industries, retire, or leave the workforce will be the sole source of job openings. Nevertheless, there is demand for qualified professionals and production workers who have significant experience in oil field operations and who can work with these new technologies. Employment opportunities will be best for those with previous experience and with strong technical skills. As employers develop and implement new technologies—such as 3-D and 4-D seismic exploration methods, horizontal and directional drilling techniques, and deepwater and subsea technologies—more workers capable of using sophisticated equipment will be needed.

Sources of Additional Information

Information on training and career opportunities for petroleum engineers or geologists is available from:

➤ Society of Petroleum Engineers, 222 Palisades Creek Dr., Richardson, TX. Internet: **http://www.spe.org**
➤ American Association of Petroleum Geologists, Communications Department, P.O. Box 979, Tulsa, OK 74101.

Information on some occupations in the oil and gas extraction industry may be found in the 2000-01 *Occupational Outlook Handbook*:

● Blue-collar worker supervisors
● Geologists geophysicists, and oceanographers
● Material moving equipment operators
● Petroleum engineers
● Truckdrivers

Manufacturing

Aerospace Manufacturing

(SIC 372, 376)

SIGNIFICANT POINTS

- Skilled production, professional specialty, and technician jobs comprise the bulk of employment.

- Increased employment opportunities will stem primarily from continued growth in the commercial aircraft sector.

- Earnings are substantially higher, on average, than in most other manufacturing industries.

Nature of the Industry

The aerospace industry is comprised of companies producing aircraft, guided missiles, space vehicles, aircraft engines, propulsion units, and related parts. Aircraft repair and modification, and aerospace research and development are also included. The combination of advanced production processes, a highly trained workforce, and significant research and development has allowed U.S. industry to remain dominant in the international market.

The aerospace industry can be divided into two large segments: firms producing aircraft, engines, and parts; and firms producing guided missiles and space vehicles, propulsion units, and parts. The larger employer of the two segments—firms producing aircraft, engines, and parts—can be further divided according to what they produce: civil aircraft or military aircraft.

Firms producing civil transport aircraft comprise the largest segment of civil aircraft. Civil transport aircraft are produced for air transit businesses such as airlines and cargo transportation companies. These craft range from small turboprops to jumbo jets and are used to move people and goods all over the world. Another segment of civil aircraft is general aviation aircraft. These aircraft are produced for private individuals and corporations. General aviation aircraft range from the small two-seaters designed for leisure use to corporate jets designed for business transport. The last segment of civil aircraft, civil helicopters, are commonly used by police departments, emergency medical services, and businesses such as oil and mining companies that need to transport people to remote work sites.

Military aircraft and helicopters are purchased by governments to meet national defense needs, such as delivering weapons to military targets and to transporting troops and equipment around the globe. Some of these aircraft are specifically designed to deliver a powerful array of weaponry to military targets with tremendous maneuverability and low detectability. Research into the materials, electronics, and manufacturing methods used to produce military aircraft has resulted in a vast number of commercial applications. Aircraft engines used in civil and military aircraft are not produced by the aircraft manufacturers but by aircraft engine manufacturers. These manufacturers design and build engines that match the thrust of the engine to the size and flight characteristics of the aircraft. Aircraft manufacturers may use engines produced by different companies on one model aircraft, depending on the initial design of the aircraft.

The smaller segment of the aerospace industry includes firms producing guided missiles and spacecraft. Firms producing guided missiles and missile propulsion units are supported primarily by military and government demands. Although missiles are predominantly viewed as offensive weapons, improved guidance systems have led to their increased use as defensive systems. Applications of missile propulsion units also include their use in launching satellites into orbit.

Space vehicles are predominantly satellites. Firms producing space vehicles also produce craft for space flight and interplanetary scientific exploration. Consumers of spacecraft include the National Aeronautics and Space Administration (NASA), the Department of Defense (DOD), telecommunications companies, television networks, and news organizations. Satellites, in addition to military uses, observe weather and the Earth in general, monitor and explore the cosmos, aid in search and navigation, and enable many communications services. The businesses that build satellites are usually separate from the businesses that operate them once they are in orbit.

About 1,828 establishments make up the aerospace industry. Most are concentrated in the aircraft and parts sector, which has about 1,726 establishments, compared to 102 in the guided missiles and space vehicles sector. In the aircraft and parts industry, most establishments are subcontractors that manufacture parts and employ fewer than 50 workers (table 1). In contrast, almost 16 percent of the guided missile and spacecraft establishments employ over 1,000 workers each, compared to less than 3 percent of the aircraft and parts firms. Nevertheless, over 70 percent of the jobs in both aircraft and parts and guided missiles and spacecraft are in large establishments that employ 1,000 or more workers (chart).

Table 1. Percent distribution of establishments in aerospace manufacturing by establishment size, 1997

Establishment size (number of workers)	Aerospace manufacturing	Aircraft and parts	Guided missiles and space vehicles
Total	100.0	100.0	1 00.0
1-9	39.8	41.0	19.6
10-49	29.7	29.8	28.4
50-249	18.9	18.7	21.6
250-999	8.0	7.6	14.7
1,000 or more	3.6	2.9	15.7

SOURCE: U.S. Department of Commerce, *County Business Patterns*, 1997

Percent

■ Establishments
☐ Employment

	1 to 9	10 to 49	50 to 249	250 to 999	1000+
Establishments	39.8	29.7	18.9	8.0	3.6
Employment	0.5	2.6	8.6	14.7	73.6

Number of workers employed by establishment

Source: U.S. Department of Commerce, *County Business Patterns*, 1997

The Federal Government traditionally has been the biggest customer of the aerospace industry, accounting for more than half of industry sales for many years. As defense purchases have declined substantially in recent years, the value of sales to the Government now accounts for about two-fifths of total industry sales. The vast majority of Government contracts to purchase aerospace equipment are awarded by DOD. NASA also is a major purchaser of the industry's products and services, mainly for space vehicles and satellites. The decline in defense purchases has increased the importance of civil aviation customers, who now are the dominant customer segment.

The aerospace industry is dominated by a few large firms that contract to produce aircraft with Government and private businesses, usually airline and cargo transportation companies. These large firms, in turn, subcontract with smaller firms to produce specific systems and parts for their vehicles. Government purchases are largely related to defense. Typically, DOD announces its need for military aircraft, satellites, or missile systems, specifying a multitude of requirements. Large firms specializing in defense products subsequently submit bids, detailing proposed technical solutions and designs, along with cost estimates, hoping to contract this new business. Firms may also research and develop materials, electronics, and components relating to their bid, often at their own expense, in order to enhance their chance of winning the contract. Following a negotiation phase, a manufacturer is selected and a prototype vehicle is developed and built, and then tested and evaluated. If approved by DOD, the aircraft is put into production.

Commercial airlines and private businesses typically identify their needs for a particular model of new aircraft based on a number of factors, including the routes they fly. After specifying requirements such as range, size, cargo capacity, and seating arrangements, the airlines invite manufacturers of civil aircraft to submit bids. Selection is ultimately based on a manufacturer's ability to deliver reliable aircraft that best fit the purchaser's stated market needs at the lowest cost and at favorable financing terms.

The way in which commercial and military aircraft are designed, developed, and produced is undergoing significant change in response to the need to cut costs, product development time, and manufacturing time. Firms producing commercial aircraft have reduced development time drastically through computer-aided design (CAD), which allows firms to design an entire aircraft, including the individual parts. The electronic drawings of these parts are sent to subcontractors, who use them to program their machinery. Recently, product development teams are increasingly being used through every phase of development, teaming customers, engineers, and production workers together to make decisions concerning the aircraft. Additionally, the military has changed its design philosophy, using available commercial off-the-shelf technology when appropriate, rather than developing new customized components.

Working Conditions

The average aerospace production employee worked about 44 hours a week in 1998, compared to less than 42 hours a week throughout manufacturing and less than 35 hours a week across all industries.

Working conditions in aerospace manufacturing facilities vary. Many new factories are spacious, well lit, and modern, in contrast to older facilities. Work environments usually depend on the occupation. Engineers, scientists, and technicians frequently work in office settings or laboratories, although production engineers may spend much of their time with production workers on the factory floor. Production workers, such as welders and other assemblers, may have to cope with high noise levels. Oil, grease, and grime are often present, and some workers may face exposure to volatile organic compounds found in solvents, paints, and coatings. Heavy lifting is required for many production jobs.

Cases of work-related injury and illness in the aircraft and parts sector were approximately 8.7 per 100 full-time workers in 1998, higher than 3.2 per 100 workers in the guided missiles sector. In comparison, cases of work-related injury and illness throughout the private sector averaged 7.1 per 100 workers.

Employment

Aerospace manufacturing provided over 615,000 wage and salary jobs in 1998—nearly 524,000 of them in the aircraft and parts sector and nearly 92,000 in the guided missiles, space vehicles, and parts sector. According to the most recent data available from the Aerospace Industries Association, more than 4 out of 10 industry employees worked on civil aircraft, nearly 3 out of 10 worked on military aircraft, and another 3 out of 10 worked on guided missiles and space vehicles.

The largest numbers of aerospace jobs are in California, although many are also located in Washington, Texas, Connecticut, Kansas, Florida, and Arizona.

Occupations in the Industry

The design and manufacture of the technologically sophisticated products of the aerospace industry require the input and skills of various workers. Skilled production, professional specialty, and technician jobs comprise the bulk of employment. A significant number of employees are employed in managerial and administrative support occupations, stemming from the need to manage the design process and factory operations, coordinate the hundreds of thousands of parts that are assembled into an aircraft, and ensure compliance with Federal recordkeeping regulations. A larger proportion of workers in the aerospace industry has education beyond high school than the average for all industries.

The aerospace industry is on the leading edge of technology and is constantly striving to create new products and improve existing ones. The industry invests a great amount of time and money on research and development, and much of the work is performed by professionals and technicians—who make up 29 percent of the aerospace workforce (table 2). A bachelor's degree in a specialized field, such as engineering, is required for many of these jobs; and a master's or doctoral degree is preferred for a few. Two years of technical training after high school is favored for many technician occupations.

Professionals and technicians develop new designs and advances to existing designs. Some also do basic aeronautical research. *Aerospace engineers* are integral members of the teams that research, design, test, and produce aerospace vehicles. Some specialize in areas such as structural design, guidance, navigation and control, and instrumentation and communication. Electrical and electronics, industrial, and mechanical engineers also contribute to the research, development, and production of aerospace products. For example, *mechanical engineers* help design mechanical components and develop the specific tools and machines needed to produce aircraft, missile, and space vehicle parts, or they may design jet and rocket engines. *Electrical* and *electronics engineers* specialize in electronic equipment used in aerospace products, such as radar and other transmission and communication equipment. *Engineering technicians* assist engineers, both in the research and development laboratory, and on the manufacturing floor. They may help build prototype versions of newly designed products, run tests and experiments, and perform a variety of other technical tasks. One of the earliest users of computer-aided design software, the aerospace industry continues to use the latest computer technology. *Computer scientists, computer engineers, computer programmers,* and *systems analysts* are responsible for the design, testing, evaluation, and set-up of computer systems that are used throughout the industry for design and manufacturing purposes. A multitude of computer and electronic systems are central to the function of aerospace products, and computer professionals work to integrate the vast array of data these systems provide into a cohesive set of information useful to pilots.

Managers and administrators accounted for nearly 18 percent of industry employment. Most persons advance to these jobs from professional occupations. Many managers in the aerospace industry have a technical or engineering background and supervise teams of engineers in activities such as testing and research and development. *Industrial production managers* oversee all workers and lower-level managers in a factory. They also coordinate all activities that relate to production. In addition to technical and production managers, *financial managers, purchasing agents, cost estimators,* and *accountants* are needed to negotiate with customers and subcontractors and track costs.

Of all aerospace workers, 42 percent are employed in production-related jobs in precision production, craft, and repair occupations, and operator, fabricator, and laborer occupations. Many of these jobs are not specific to aerospace and can be found in other manufacturing industries. Many production jobs are open to persons with only a high school education; however, special vocational training after high school is preferred for some of the more highly skilled jobs.

Precision production occupations make up a large part of production jobs. *Precision assemblers* usually specialize in one assembly task; hundreds of different assemblers may work at various times on producing a single aircraft. Assemblers may put together parts of airplanes, such as wings or landing gear, or install parts and equipment into the airplane itself. Those involved in assembling aircraft or systems must be skilled in reading and interpreting engineering specifications and instructions.

Table 2. Employment of wage and salary workers in aerospace manufacturing by occupation, 1998 and projected change, 1998-2008

(Employment in thousands)

Occupation	1998 Employment Number	1998 Employment Percent	1998-2008 Percent change
All occupations	615	100.0	21.9
Precision production, craft and repair	174	28.2	19.4
Machinists	29	4.7	32.0
Inspectors, testers, and graders, precision	25	4.0	8.0
Blue-collar worker supervisors	22	3.6	26.3
Aircraft mechanics and service technicians	19	3.1	11.2
Aircraft assemblers, precision	16	2.7	19.5
Electrical and electronic equipment assemblers	11	1.8	23.8
Professional specialty	137	22.3	26.7
Aerospace engineers	25	4.1	11.8
Mechanical engineers	15	2.5	27.4
Industrial engineers	14	2.4	31.2
Computer engineers and scientists	15	2.4	28.9
Electrical and electronics engineers	10	1.7	41.7
Systems analysts	7	1.2	85.9
Executive, administrative, and managerial	112	18.1	25.1
Engineering, mathematical, and natural science managers	10	1.6	43.0
Purchasing agents	8	1.3	25.0
General managers and top executives	7	1.1	19.8
Operators, fabricators, and laborers	87	14.2	23.6
Machine setters, setup operators, and tenders	41	6.7	24.2
Hand workers, including assemblers and fabricators	33	5.4	23.6
Helpers, laborers, and material movers, hand	10	1.6	20.6
Administrative support, including clerical	54	8.9	11.9
Production planning and expediting clerks	11	1.8	11.9
General office clerks	8	1.3	26.1
Secretaries	7	1.2	-3.1
Technicians and related	40	6.4	18.2
Engineering technicians	29	4.7	23.4
Service	8	1.3	15.3
All other occupations	4	0.6	26.0

Machinists make parts when there are too few needed to be mass-produced. They follow blueprints and specifications and are highly skilled with machine tools and metalworking. *Sheet metal workers* study blueprints to determine specifications for the pieces they are shaping. They cut or punch out pieces they need and finish by fastening the seams with bolts, rivets, or other devices. *Tool* and *die makers* possess highly developed skills. They are responsible for constructing precision tools and metal forms, called dies, which are used to shape metal. Increasingly, as individual components are designed electronically, these skilled craft workers must be able to read electronic blueprints and set up and operate computer-controlled machines.

Inspectors, testers, and *graders* are responsible for performing numerous quality and control and safety checks on aerospace parts, from the beginning stages through the final production. Their work is vital to ensure the safety of the aircraft.

The remaining jobs in the industry were in administrative support, clerical, and service occupations. Most of these jobs can be entered without education beyond high school. Workers in administrative support and clerical jobs help coordinate the flow of materials to the worksite, draw up orders for supplies, keep records, and help with all of the other paperwork associated with keeping a business functioning. Those in service occupations were mostly employed as guards, janitors, and food service workers.

Training and Advancement

Industry support of education and training is substantial. Due to the constantly changing and advancing technology in the aerospace industry, employers are interested in well-informed, knowledgeable employees, who possess the skills needed to keep up with advancements in the industry. Firms provide on-site, job-related training to upgrade the skills of technicians, production workers, and engineers. Classes featuring computer skills and blueprint reading are common. Some firms reimburse employees for educational expenses at colleges and universities, emphasizing 4-year degrees and post-graduate studies.

Professionals, such as engineers and scientists, require a bachelor's degree in a specialized field. For some jobs, particularly in research and development, a master's or doctoral degree may be preferred.

Production workers may enter the aerospace industry with minimal skills. Mechanical aptitude and good hand-eye coordination are usually necessary. A high school diploma is preferred, but not required, and some vocational training in electronics or mechanics is also favored.

Unskilled production workers typically start by being shown how to perform a simple assembly task. Through experience, on-the-job instruction provided by other workers, and brief, formal training sessions, they expand their skills. Their pay increases as they advance into more highly skilled or responsible jobs. For example, machinists may take additional training to become tool programmers or tool and die or instrument makers. Inspectors are usually promoted from assembly, machine operation, and mechanical occupations.

Due to the increasing reliance on computers and computer-operated equipment, classes in computer skills are becoming more common. With training, production workers may be able to advance to supervisory or technician jobs.

To enter some of the more highly skilled production occupations, workers must go through a formal apprenticeship before they can become fully qualified for their positions. Machinists, sheetmetal workers, and electricians go through apprenticeships that can last up to 4 years. Apprenticeships usually include classroom instruction and shop training.

Entry level positions for technicians usually require a degree from a technical school or junior college. Companies sometimes retrain technicians to upgrade their skills or to teach different specialties. They are often taught traditional as well as new production technology skills, such as computer-aided design and manufacturing and statistical process control methods.

Earnings

Production workers in the aerospace industry earn higher pay than the average for all industries. Weekly earnings for production workers in aerospace manufacturing averaged about $844 in 1998, compared to $563 in all manufacturing, and $442 in all private industry. Above average earnings are due in part to the high levels of skill required by the industry, the high cost of aerospace products, and the need to motivate workers to concentrate on maintaining high quality standards in their work. Non-production workers, such as engineering managers, engineers, and computer specialists, generally command higher pay due to their advanced education and training.

Earnings in selected occupations in aerospace manufacturing appear in table 3.

Table 3. Median hourly earnings of the largest occupations in aircraft and parts manufacturing, 1997

Occupation	Aircraft and parts	All industries
Aeronautical and astronautical engineers	$34.69	$32.95
Mechanical engineers	24.89	24.33
First-line supervisors and managers/ supervisors-production and operating workers	20.70	16.62
Aircraft structure, surfaces, rigging, and systems assemblers, precision	19.65	16.63
Mechanical engineering technicians and technologists	18.52	18.17
Precision inspectors, testers, and graders	17.03	12.74
Machinists	15.48	13.38
Aircraft mechanics	15.23	17.80
Production inspectors, testers, graders, sorters, samplers and weighers	14.41	10.15
Assemblers and fabricators, except machine, electrical, electronic, and precision	11.39	9.25

In 1998, 30 percent of all workers in the aircraft and parts sector and 13 percent of workers in the guided missiles and space vehicles sector were union members or were covered by union contracts, compared to 15.4 percent of all workers throughout private industry. Some of the major aerospace unions include the International Association of Machinists and Aerospace Workers; the United Automobile, Aerospace, and Agricultural Implement Workers of America; and the International Union of Allied Industrial Workers of America.

Outlook

Employment in the aerospace industry is expected to increase by 22 percent over the 1998-2008 period, compared to the 15 percent growth projected for all industries combined. In the large aircraft and parts sector of the industry, employment is projected to grow by 25 percent, whereas employment in the smaller guided missiles and space vehicles sector is expected to increase by about 3 percent. Factors affecting the employment outlook in the aerospace industry include Federal defense expenditures, commercial aircraft sales, the growth of telecommunications, and exports.

Federal defense expenditures on the products of the aerospace industry have fallen dramatically since the late 1980s. During most of the 1980s, large defense purchases of aircraft and missiles, together with support of research to develop new military aerospace equipment, kept employment and output at a high level. Large cuts in Federal defense spending have caused an ongoing restructuring of the defense aerospace industry, and significant declines in employment, as firms adjust to the new, lower spending levels. Some companies are selling their defense-oriented business and others are merging. Although the aerospace industry is less dependent on defense spending than in the past, defense purchases still support a significant number of aerospace workers. Defense spending, although not expected to decline further, is not expected to return to previous levels (chart).

Although new employment opportunities will be limited in the defense-related sector of the aerospace industry, they should be much better in the sector supported by civilian aviation. Employment growth is expected in the production of commercial aircraft for both domestic and export purposes. Air passenger traffic is expected to increase at a healthy pace over the projection period. Also, aging aircraft may have trouble meeting worldwide and domestic fuel emissions and noise standards, requiring replacement or modification.

Commercial aircraft sales have been strong and they are expected to remain strong through 2008. Air travel has been rapidly growing over the years. In addition, environmental and safety concerns have highlighted the benefits of newer aircraft. As a result, airlines are purchasing more planes to meet the increased demand and to upgrade their fleets.

The expanded use of the Internet, direct broadcasting, and wireless communications services, such as cellular telephones and pagers, have increased the need for telecommunications equipment. Because satellites are widely used in telecommunications, this trend should spur further growth in the aerospace manufacturing industry.

Commercial exports have been rising strongly for years, reflecting the growth in overseas markets. Collaboration between domestic and foreign companies is becoming increasingly common as manufacturers seek to win sales in these growing markets and to share the substantial risks and costs of developing and producing new aerospace products. In addition to commercial exports, foreign military sales are also expected to bolster defense contractors, as countries around the world meet their defense needs with U.S. jet fighters, transports, and helicopters.

The continuing focus on advanced technology in aerospace manufacturing will lead to significant employment growth among professional specialty workers. Employment of engineers, for example, is expected to grow by 24 percent over the 1998-2008 period. Replacement needs also will be significant because large numbers of engineers who entered the industry in the 1960s are approaching retirement. Demand for computer engineers, computer scientists, and systems analysts is also expected to be very strong. Overall, professionals in the aerospace industry usually enjoy more employment stability than other workers. During slowdowns in production, companies prefer to keep technical teams intact to continue research and product development activities, in anticipation of new business. Production workers, on the other hand, are particularly vulnerable to layoffs during downturns in the economy when aircraft orders decline.

Sources of Additional Information

For additional information about the aerospace industry write to:

➢ Aerospace Industries Association of America, Communications Department, 1250 Eye St. NW., Washington, DC 20005. Internet: **http://www.aia-aerospace.org**
➢ American Institute of Aeronautics and Astronautics, Inc., Suite 500, 1801 Alexander Bell Dr., Reston, VA 20191-4344. Internet: **http://www.aiaa.org**

Information on the following occupations may be found in the 2000-01 *Occupational Outlook Handbook*.

- Aerospace engineers
- Aircraft mechanics and service technicians
- Blue-collar worker supervisors
- Computer engineers and scientists
- Computer systems analysts
- Electrical and electronics engineers
- Engineering technicians
- Machinists and numerical tool and process control programmers
- Mechanical engineers
- Metalworking and plastics-working machine operators
- Precision assemblers
- Tool and die makers
- Welders, cutters, and welding machine operators

Employment in aerospace manufacturing is projected to grow more slowly than in the late 1980s

Employment (thousands)

Apparel and Other Textile Products

(SIC 23)

SIGNIFICANT POINTS

● Nearly half of all workers are sewing machine operators.

● Primarily due to increased imports and new technology, apparel manufacturing is projected to lose 178,000 jobs—more than almost any other industry—over the 1998-2008 period.

● Average earnings are below those of other manufacturing industries.

Nature of the Industry

The range of apparel and other textile products is as broad as their uses—suits, rainwear, fur coats, purses, and curtains are just a few examples. Workers in the apparel industry transform fabrics produced by textile manufacturers into these finished goods and many others that fill the Nation's retail stores. By cutting and sewing fabrics or other materials, such as leather, rubberized fabrics, plastics, and furs, workers in this industry help to keep us warm, dry, and in style.

As in other industries, technological advances, globalization, and changing business practices are affecting the apparel industry. One significant change is the increased emphasis on quick response to customer demand. This ability is vital in an industry that sells its products in an ever-changing, fashion-conscious market. Quick response capability links apparel producers more closely to related firms in the textile and retail sectors of the economy. Aided by communications technology, such as electronic data interchange, point of sale terminals, and bar codes, information is instantaneously communicated to and received from firms in these industries.

Other technologies affecting the apparel industry include computerized equipment and material transport systems. Computers and computer-controlled equipment aid in many functions, such as design, marking, and cutting. Overhead conveyor systems transport material between sewing machine operators and between processes. Despite these changes, however, the apparel industry—especially its sewing function—has remained significantly less automated than many other manufacturing industries.

The apparel industry traditionally has consisted of production workers who perform a specific function in an assembly line. This organizational philosophy increasingly is being replaced by a team concept, in which garments are made by a group of sewing machine operators organized into production "modules." Each operator in a module is trained to perform nearly all of the functions required to assemble a garment. Each team is responsible for its own performance, and individuals usually receive compensation based on the team's performance. These changes have greatly altered the atmosphere and responsibilities from those of the traditional assembly line.

Fierce competition from abroad has prompted these changes in work structure and technology. Apparel firms also have responded to growing competition by merging and employing workers in other countries to perform some production functions. Workers in lower-wage countries are increasingly being hired to assemble garments—the most labor-intensive step in the production process—whereas U.S. workers now perform a greater share of the pre-assembly functions and coordinate the process. Such changes in the nature of the domestic apparel industry will certainly continue as globalization proceeds.

Working Conditions

Working conditions depend on the age of the facility, the equipment used, and company policies. Sewing machine operators and other production workers work an average of 37.3 hours weekly, but overtime is common during periods of peak production. Some firms in the industry operate several shifts and may require employees to work nights or weekends. As more expensive machinery is introduced, companies may add shifts to keep expensive machines from being idle.

Factories are generally clean, well lit, and well ventilated, but sewing areas may be noisy. Operators often sit for long periods of time and lean over machines. New ergonomically designed chairs and machines that allow workers to stand during operation are some ways that firms seek to minimize discomfort for production workers. Another concern for workers is injuries caused by repetitive motions. The implementation of modular units and specially designed equipment reduces potential health problems by lessening the stress of repetitive motions. In 1997, cases of work-related injury and illness in the apparel industry averaged 7.0 per 100 workers, lower than the 10.3 average in all manufacturing industries, and about the same as the 7.1 rate for all industries.

The movement away from traditional piecework systems often results in a significant change in working conditions. Modular manufacturing involves teamwork, increased responsibility, and greater interaction among coworkers than traditional assembly lines.

Employment

The apparel industry provided about 763,000 wage and salary jobs in 1998. As shown in table 1, employment is concentrated in three segments of the industry. Women's and misses' outerwear accounts for about 28 percent of the industry's employment; men's and boys' furnishings, 25 percent; and miscellaneous fabricated textile products, 29 percent. Together, these segments employ 4 out of every 5 workers in the industry.

Most jobs are found in eight States: Alabama, California, Georgia, New York, North Carolina, Pennsylvania, Tennessee, and Texas. The industry had about 24,000 establishments in 1998, with employment concentrated in large firms. Three out of four jobs are in establishments with 50 or more workers (chart).

Table 1. Percent distribution of establishments and employment in apparel and other textile products, 1997

Industry segment	Establishments	Employment
Total	100.0	100.0
Miscellaneous fabricated textile products	42.0	28.8
Women's and misses', outerwear	36.9	27.9
Men's and boys' furnishings	9.3	25.3
Girl's and children's outerwear	2.5	4.1
Women's and children's undergarments	1.6	3.9
Men's and boys' suits and coats	1.2	3.9
Miscellaneous apparel and accessories	3.9	3.7
Hats, caps, and millinery	1.7	2.4
Fur goods	0.5	0.1

SOURCE: U. S. Department of Commerce, *County Business Patterns*, 1997

Occupations in the Industry

Although a variety of workers are needed to produce apparel and other textile products, operators, fabricators, and laborers account for about 70 percent of total employment in the industry. About half of all workers are sewing machine operators (table 2).

Fashion designers are the artists of the apparel industry. They create ideas for a range of products including coats, dresses, hats, handbags, and underwear. Some are self-employed and work with individual clients, while others cater to fashion specialty stores or high-fashion department stores. Most fashion designers work for apparel manufacturers or retailers, adapting fashion trends for specific markets.

Before sewing can begin, pattern pieces must be made, layouts determined, and fabric cut. *Patternmakers* create the "blueprint" or pattern pieces for a particular apparel design. This often involves "grading," or adjusting the pieces

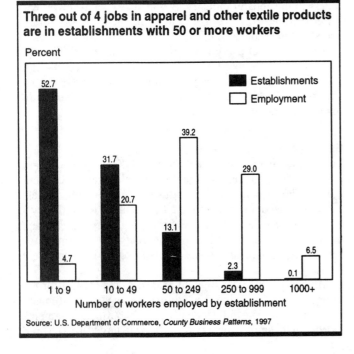

Three out of 4 jobs in apparel and other textile products are in establishments with 50 or more workers

Percent

■ Establishments
□ Employment

| 1 to 9 | 10 to 49 | 50 to 249 | 250 to 999 | 1000+ |
52.7 / 4.7 · 31.7 / 20.7 · 13.1 / 39.2 · 2.3 / 29.0 · 0.1 / 6.5

Number of workers employed by establishment

Source: U.S. Department of Commerce, *County Business Patterns*, 1997

for different sized garments. Grading once was a time-consuming job, but now it is quickly completed with the aid of a computer. *Markers* determine the best arrangement of pattern pieces to minimize wasted fabric. Traditionally, markers judged the best arrangement of pieces by eye; today, computers quickly help determine the best layout.

Table 2. Employment of wage and salary workers in apparel and other textile products by occupation, 1998 and projected change, 1998-2008

(Employment in thousands)

Occupation	1998 Employment Number	1998 Employment Percent	1998-2008 Percent change
All occupations	763	100.0	-23.3
Operators, fabricators, and laborers	533	69.8	-24.9
Sewing machine operators, garment	287	37.5	-36.2
Sewing machine operators, non-garment	63	8.2	0.1
All other assemblers, fabricators, and hand workers	35	4.5	-6.5
Hand packers and packagers	22	2.8	-14.6
Textile draw-out and winding machine operators	20	2.6	-15.5
Pressing machine operators and tenders, textile, garment, and related materials	13	1.7	-42.5
Freight, stock, and material movers, hand	13	1.7	-31.7
Cutters and trimmers, hand	12	1.6	-27.1
All other helpers laborers and material movers, hand	11	1.4	-10.7
Cutting and slicing machine setters, operators, and tenders	10	1.3	-17.6
Screen printing machine setters	7	1.0	4.9
Precision production, craft, and repair	89	11.7	-18.5
Blue-collar worker supervisors	26	3.4	-16.9
Inspectors, testers, and graders	24	3.1	-31.7
Patternmakers and layout workers, fabric and apparel	12	1.5	-4.5
Industrial machinery mechanics	10	1.3	-15.0
Administrative support, including clerical	69	9.0	-25.1
Shipping, receiving, and traffic clerks	17	2.2	-26.6
Financial records processing occupations	12	1.6	-31.9
General office clerks	9	1.2	-16.6
Executive, administrative, and managerial	35	4.6	-17.1
General managers and top executives	14	1.9	-14.1
Marketing and sales	17	2.2	-15.9
Professional specialty	11	1.5	2.7
All other occupations	9	1.2	-27.5

The layout arrangement is then given to *cutters*. In less automated companies, cutters may use electric knives or cutting machines to cut pattern pieces. In more automated facilities, markers electronically send the layout to a computer-controlled cutting machine, and the cutter monitors the machine's work. As a result, computer-controlled machine operators are replacing many cutters.

46

Sewing machine operators assemble or finish clothes or other goods such as curtains and purses. Most sewing functions are specialized and require the operator to receive specific training. Although operators specialize in one function, the trend toward cross-training requires them to broaden their skills.

Cutters, trimmers, inspectors and *pressers* receive a garment after it has been assembled. Cutters, trimmers, and inspectors finish the product by trimming loose threads. Pressers eliminate wrinkles and give shape to finished products. Most pressers use specially formed, foot-controlled pressing machines to perform their duties. Some pressing machines now have the steam and pressure controlled by computers.

Training and Advancement

Most production workers are trained on the job. Although a high school diploma is not required, some employers prefer it. Basic math and computer skills are important for computer-controlled machine operators.

Cutters and pressers are trained on the job, while patternmakers and markers usually have technical or trade school training. All of these workers must understand textile characteristics and have a good sense of three-dimensional space. Traditional cutters need exceptional hand-eye coordination. Computers are becoming a standard tool for these occupations as patternmakers and markers increasingly design pattern pieces and layouts on a computer screen, so new entrants will help themselves by learning computer skills. Those running automatic cutting machines could need technical training, which is available from vocational schools.

Sewing machine operators must have good hand-eye coordination and dexterity, as well as an understanding of textile fabrics. They normally are trained on the job for a period of several weeks to several months, depending on their previous experience and the function for which they are training. Setting a sleeve, for example, is more complicated and requires more training than sewing a side seam. In general, though, new machinery greatly reduces the required skill level and training needed to perform many functions.

Modular manufacturing requires operators to perform more than one function, so they are usually trained to perform several duties. In addition to this functional training, workers in a modular system may also be offered courses in the interpersonal and communication skills necessary to work as part of a team. Further, the added responsibility of self-managing their modules may lead these workers to receive training in problem solving and management.

Designers need a good sense of color, texture, and style. In addition, they must understand the construction and characteristics of specific fabrics, such as durability and stiffness. This specialized training usually is obtained through a university or design school that offers 4-year or 2-year degrees.

Those interested in engineering or production management need a bachelor's degree. Degrees in mechanical, chemical, or industrial engineering are common, but related studies may also be accepted. A few programs offer concentrations in apparel and textile production that focus on the unique characteristics and issues associated with apparel production. Universities offering these specializations are generally found in the South and Northeast.

Earnings

Average weekly earnings for production workers were $318 in 1998, significantly lower than the overall $563 per week in manufacturing and $442 in the entire private sector. Table 3 shows average weekly and hourly earnings in various segments of the apparel industry.

Table 3. Average earnings of nonsupervisory workers in the apparel and other textile products industry, 1998

Industry segment	Weekly	Hourly
Total, private industry	$442	$12.77
Apparel and other textile products	318	8.52
Miscellaneous fabricated textile products	368	9.39
Men's and boy's suits and coats	324	8.69
Miscellaneous apparel and accessories	300	8.15
Women's and children's undergarments	300	8.14
Women's and misses' outerwear	297	8.18
Girl's and children's outerwear	295	8.07
Men's and boy's furnishings	292	7.98

Earnings in selected occupations in apparel and other textile products appear in table 4. Traditionally, sewing machine operators are paid on a piecework basis determined by the quantity of goods they produce. Many companies are changing to incentive systems based on group performance that consider both the quantity and quality of the goods produced. A few companies pay production workers a salary.

Table 4. Median hourly earnings of the largest occupations in apparel and other textile products, 1997

Occupation	Apparel and other textile products	All industries
General managers and top executives	$26.01	$26.05
First-line supervisors and supervisor/managers-production and operating workers	11.38	16.62
Assemblers and fabricators, except machine, electrical, electronic, and precision	9.02	9.25
Shipping, receiving, and traffic clerks	8.02	10.29
Textile machine operators and tenders, winding, twisting, knitting, weaving, and cutting	7.88	9.03
Sewing machine, non-garment	7.57	7.91
Production inspectors, testers, graders, sorters, samplers, and weighers	7.56	10.15
Pressing machine operators and tenders, textile, garment, and related materials	7.45	7.09
Hand packers and packagers	6.83	6.90
Sewing machine operators, garment	6.69	6.92

The apparel industry has a relatively low unionization rate; about 8.5 percent of apparel workers are union members or are covered by a union contract, compared with 15.4 percent for the economy as a whole. The major union in the apparel industry is the Union of Needletrades, Industrial, and Textile Employees (UNITE), which was formed in 1995 from the International Ladies' Garment Workers Union and the Amalgamated Clothing and Textile Workers Union.

Outlook

Wage and salary employment in the apparel industry is expected to decline 23 percent through 2008, while employment throughout the economy is projected to increase 15 percent. The expected decline translates into 178,000 lost jobs over the period—greater than almost any other industry. Declining employment will be caused by growing imports, new automation, and fierce cost-cutting pressures imposed by retailers and international competition. Nevertheless, some job openings will arise as experienced workers transfer to other industries, retire, or leave the workforce.

Changing trade regulations are the single most important factor influencing future employment patterns. Because the apparel industry is labor-intensive, it is especially vulnerable to import competition from nations in which workers receive lower wages. The protection provided to the domestic apparel industry over the past two decades will be significantly reduced in coming years, enabling more apparel imports. Because many U.S. firms will continue to move their assembly operations to low-wage countries, this trend is likely impact lower-skilled machine operators most severely. It will not, however, have as adverse an effect on the demand for some of the pre-sewing functions, such as designing and cutting, because much of the apparel will still be designed and cut in the United States.

New technology will increase the apparel industry's productivity, but unlike other industries, the apparel industry is likely to remain labor-intensive. The variability of cloth and the intricate cuts and seams of the assembly process have been difficult to automate. Machine operators, therefore, will continue to perform most sewing tasks, and automated sewing will be limited to simple functions. In some cases, however, computerized sewing machines will increase the productivity of operators and reduce required training time.

Technology also is increasing the productivity of workers who perform other functions such as designing, marking, cutting, and pressing. Computers and automated machinery will continue to lift productivity and reduce the demand for workers in these areas, but the growth in demand for their services generated by offshore assembly sites will help to moderate this decline. These workers also will benefit from the increasing rate at which fashions change, which will produce greater demand for workers who are employed in firms in the United States that have quick response capabilities.

Cost-cutting pressures will be applied to all workers in the apparel and textile industries by continuing changes in the market for apparel goods. As consumers become more price-conscious, retailers gain bargaining power over apparel producers, and increasing competition limits the ability of producers to pass on costs to consumers, apparel firms are likely to respond by relying more on foreign production and boosting productivity through investments in technology and new work structures. These responses will adversely affect employment of American apparel workers.

Sources of Additional Information

Information about job opportunities in technical and design occupations can be obtained from colleges offering programs in textile and apparel engineering, production, and design. For information about career opportunities, trade developments, and technology, contact:

➢ American Apparel Manufacturing Association, 2500 Wilson Blvd., Suite 301, Arlington, VA 22201.
  Internet: **http://www.americanapparel.org**

Information on many occupations in apparel manufacturing, including those listed below, appears in the 2000-01 *Occupational Outlook Handbook*:

● Apparel workers
● Designers
● Engineers
● Textile machinery operators

Chemicals Manufacturing, Except Drugs

(SIC 28, except 283)

SIGNIFICANT POINTS

● Employment is projected to decline.

● Most jobs in research and development require substantial technical education after high school, but opportunities exist for persons with degrees ranging from a 2-year associate degree up to a doctorate.

● Production workers earn more than in most industries.

Nature of the Industry

Passing a large chemical plant, one might see a large maze of tanks, pressure vessels, and twisting pipes, but most of us do not realize that goods produced by chemical plants account for over six percent of the total value of manufacturing in the United States. Although some chemical manufacturers produce and sell consumer products such as soap, bleach, and cosmetics, most chemical products are used as intermediate products for other goods.

Chemical manufacturing is divided into eight segments, seven of which are covered here. These industry segments include plastics materials, cleaning preparations, inorganic chemicals, organic chemicals, miscellaneous chemicals, agricultural chemicals, and drug manufacturing. The eighth segment, drug manufacturing, is covered in a separate *Career Guide* statement.

The largest employer of the segments included here is the plastics materials and synthetics industry, which produces a wide variety of finished products as well as raw materials. Some of these include polypropylene, polyvinyl chloride (PVC), and polystyrene, which can be made into products such as loudspeakers, PVC pipes, and beverage bottles; the automotive manufacturers are particularly large users of these products. Another segment of the industry includes firms making soaps, detergents, and cleaning preparations. Cosmetics and toiletries are also included in this segment. Households and businesses use these products in many ways, cleaning everything from babies to bridges. This is the only segment of the chemical industry in which much of the production is geared directly toward consumers.

The industrial organic chemicals segment produces chemicals that contain carbon and are made primarily from petroleum and natural gas, and are often referred to as petrochemicals. Although organic chemicals are used to make dyes, plastics, and pharmaceutical products, most of these chemicals are used in the production of other chemicals.

Industrial inorganic chemicals are usually made from salts, other minerals, and metal compounds. This segment also includes industrial gases such as oxygen, nitrogen, and helium. Inorganic chemicals are often used by businesses as reaction aids. Other chemical companies are the largest single customer of this segment.

The fifth largest employer in the chemical industry is the miscellaneous chemical product sector. This segment manufactures adhesives, explosives and fireworks, inks, and many other products used by consumers or in the manufacture of other products.

The paints and allied products segment includes paints, varnishes, lacquers, putties, paint removers, sealers, and stains. The construction and furniture industries are large customers of this segment. Other customers range from individuals refurbishing their homes to businesses that need anti-corrosive paints that can withstand high temperatures.

Finally, the segment employing the fewest number of workers in the chemical industry is agricultural chemicals. This segment supplies farmers and home gardeners with fertilizers, herbicides, pesticides, and other agricultural chemicals.

Chemicals are generally classified into two groups—commodity chemicals and specialty chemicals. Commodity chemical manufacturers produce large quantities of basic and relatively inexpensive compounds using large plants often built specifically to make one chemical. Specialty chemical manufacturers commonly produce smaller quantities of more expensive chemicals that are used less frequently. Specialty manufacturers often supply larger chemical companies on a contract basis. Many traditionally commodity chemical manufacturers are becoming specialty chemical manufacturers to better compete.

Table 1. Distribution of employment in chemicals and allied products, 1998

Industry	Employment	Percent
Total, all industries	763,800	100.0
Plastics materials and synthetics	157,000	20.6
Soaps, cleaners, and toilet goods	155,500	20.4
Industrial organic chemicals	137,700	18.0
Industrial inorganic chemicals	115,400	15.1
Miscellaneous chemicals	93,900	12.3
Paints and allied products	52,300	6.8
Agricultural chemicals	52,000	6.8

The diversity of products produced by the chemical industry also is reflected in the establishments that comprise it. For example, firms producing plastics materials operated relatively large plants in 1997. This segment had 8 percent of the reporting establishments, yet employed almost 21 percent of those working in the chemical manufacturing industry. On the other hand, manufacturers of paints and allied products had a greater number of establishments, each employing a much smaller number of workers. This segment comprised over 14 percent of the establishments in the chemical industry, yet employed only 8 percent of all workers. The average workplace in the chemical industry ranged from 138 workers in the plastics materials segment to 35 workers in the soaps and cosmetics segment.

The chemical industry segments vary in the degree to which their workers are involved in production activities, administration and management, or research and development. Industries that make products such as cosmetics or paint that are ready for sale to the final consumer employ more administrative and marketing personnel. Industries that market their products mostly to industrial customers generally employ a greater proportion of precision production workers and a lower proportion of unskilled labor.

Chemical firms are concentrated in areas abundant with other manufacturing businesses, such as in the Great Lakes region near the automotive industry, or on the West Coast near the electronics industry. Chemical plants are also located near the petroleum and natural gas production centers of the South. Because chemical production processes often use water and chemicals are exported all over the world, primarily by ship, major industrial ports are another common location of chemical plants. California, Illinois, New Jersey, New York, Ohio, Pennsylvania, South Carolina, Tennessee, and Texas had about 50 percent of the establishments in the industry.

Working Conditions

Manufacturing chemicals usually is a continuous process; this means that once a process has begun, it cannot be stopped when it is time for workers to go home. Split, weekend, and night shifts are common, and workers on such schedules are usually compensated with higher rates of pay. As a result, the average workweek in the chemical industry was over 43 hours in 1998, over 2 hours longer than the average for nondurable manufacturing industries, and over 8 hours longer than the average for all private industries. The industry employs relatively few part-time workers.

The plants usually are clean, although the continually running machines sometimes are loud. Hardhats and safety goggles are worn throughout the plant.

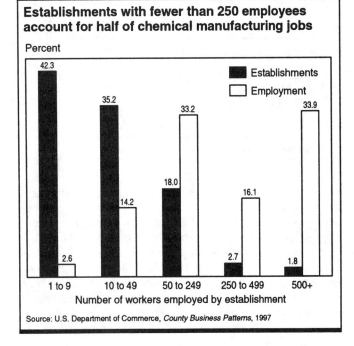

Establishments with fewer than 250 employees account for half of chemical manufacturing jobs

Percent

- Establishments
- Employment

	1 to 9	10 to 49	50 to 249	250 to 499	500+
Establishments	42.3	35.2	18.0	2.7	1.8
Employment	2.6	14.2	33.2	16.1	33.9

Number of workers employed by establishment

Source: U.S. Department of Commerce, *County Business Patterns*, 1997

Hazards in the chemical industry can be substantial, but they are generally avoided through strict safety procedures. Workers require protective gear and extensive knowledge of the dangers associated with the chemicals being handled. Body suits with breathing devices designed to filter out any harmful fumes are mandatory for work in dangerous environments.

In spite of the hazards of working with chemicals, extensive worker training on handling hazardous chemicals and chemical company safety measures have resulted in injury and illness rates for some segments of the chemical industry that are much lower than the average for the manufacturing sector. The chemical industry reported just 4.8 cases per 100 workers of work-related injury or illness, compared to an average of 10.3 cases for all manufacturing industries in 1997.

Employment

The chemical and allied products industry employed about 763,800 wage and salary workers in 1998, about 4.1 percent of the total number employed in manufacturing and over 10 percent of the total number employed in nondurable goods manufacturing . Most segments of the industry had substantial numbers of jobs, as shown in table 1. Employment in the chemical industry has declined recently as chemical companies have increased productivity and reduced costs by eliminating all but the most essential personnel.

Occupations in the Industry

Over half of those employed in the industry work in precision production, craft, and repair and operator, fabricator, and laborer occupations. Another one-quarter work in executive, managerial, and administrative occupations. The third largest group, with about one-fifth of chemical industry employment, are in professional specialty, technical, and marketing occupations. The remaining workers are in service and related occupations (table 2).

Production. Workers in production occupations operate and fix plant machinery, transport raw materials, and monitor the production process. Improvements in technology gradually are increasing the level of plant automation, reducing the number of jobs in production occupations. Although high school graduates qualify for most entry level production jobs, advancement into better paying jobs, requiring higher skills or more responsibility, is possible with on-the-job training and work experience or through additional vocational training at a 2-year technical college.

Chemical plant and system operators monitor the entire production process. From chemical ingredient ratios to chemical reaction rates, the operator is responsible for the efficient operation of the chemical plant. Chemical plant operators advance to these positions generally from among the most experienced production workers, usually after having acquired extensive experience and technical training in chemical production processes. Experienced operators sometimes advance to senior supervisory positions.

Chemical equipment controllers monitor the flow and mix ratios of chemicals moving through production equipment. Experienced workers advance to controller positions after demonstrating their ability to handle more responsibility in lower skilled jobs. Sometimes new engineers in training are temporarily assigned to controller positions to learn the production process first-hand. Undergraduate engineering students in cooperative education programs also may work in these positions temporarily as a means of gaining hands-on experience in their field before graduating from college.

Table 2. Employment of wage and salary workers in chemical and allied products by occupation, 1998 and projected change, 1998-2008

(Employment in thousands)

Occupation	1998 Employment Number	1998 Employment Percent	1998-2008 Percent change
All occupations	764	100.0	-3.9
Operators, fabricators, and laborers	274	35.9	1.6
Chemical equipment controllers	50	6.5	16.2
Helpers, laborers, and material movers, hand	43	5.6	-5.0
Packaging and filling machine operators	31	4.0	11.4
Crushing, grinding, mixing and blending machine operators	28	3.7	-3.1
Hand workers, including assemblers and fabricators	25	3.2	1.7
Truck drivers	13	1.8	-7.0
Extruding and forming machine operators, synthetic or glass fibers	13	1.8	7.7
Industrial truck and tractor operators	8	1.1	-3.2
Textile draw-out and winding machine operators	9	1.2	-22.5
Precision production, craft, and repair	170	22.2	-4.6
Blue-collar worker supervisors	42	5.4	-5.9
Chemical plant and system operators	36	4.7	10.6
Maintenance repairers, general utility	19	2.5	-15.0
Industrial machinery mechanics	21	2.8	-4.3
Inspectors, testers, and graders	11	1.5	-18.2
Administrative support, including clerical	86	11.2	-13.8
Secretaries	16	2.1	-24.4
Shipping, receiving, and traffic clerks	11	1.4	-11.2
General office clerks	10	1.4	-3.8
Bookkeeping, accounting, and auditing clerks	8	1.1	-21.8
Executive, managerial, and administrative	88	11.5	-6.1
Management support occupations	26	3.5	-7.4
General managers and top executives	16	2.1	-6.9
Industrial production managers	11	1.5	-6.9
Engineering, science, and computer and information systems managers	6	0.8	11.8
Marketing, advertising, and public relations managers	8	1.0	-2.1
Professional specialty	65	8.6	-2.2
Chemists	17	2.2	-10.6
Chemical engineers	17	2.2	7.1
Computer systems analysts, engineers, and scientists	6	0.8	31.0
Technicians and related	41	5.4	-13.6
Science and mathematics technicians	30	4.0	-14.3
Engineering technicians	8	1.1	-8.3
Marketing and sales	31	4.1	-3.2
Service	7	0.9	-12.3

Mechanics, installers, and repairers repair equipment, install machines, or practice preventive maintenance in the plant. Workers advance to these jobs either through apprenticeships, formal vocational training, or by completing in-house training courses.

Inspectors, testers, and graders assure that the production process runs efficiently and that products are of acceptable quality. They refer problems to plant operators or management.

Packaging and filling operators wrap products and fill boxes to prepare the final product for shipment or sale to the wholesaler or consumer. Over half of these jobs are in the soap and cosmetics industry, due to the amount of packaging needed for this industry's consumer products.

Transportation and material moving workers move materials around the plant using industrial trucks or deliver finished products to customers by truck. For these jobs, employers seek experienced workers with knowledge of chemical hazards, safety procedures, and regulations governing the transport of hazardous chemicals. Operation of industrial trucks and tractors can be learned with on-the-job training, but previous experience driving a truck and a commercial driver's license generally are required to operate a tractor trailer carrying chemicals.

Helper, laborer, and material mover jobs usually are open to workers without experience. These workers move raw materials and finished products through the chemical plant and assist motor vehicle operators in loading and unloading raw materials and chemicals. They learn safe ways to handle chemicals on the job and develop skills that enable them to advance to other occupations.

Research, development, and technical. Most workers in research and development have college degrees, and many have advanced degrees. Engineers, scientists, and technicians comprise a growing portion of industry employment.

Chemists conduct chemical research, analyze compounds, and experiment with liquids and gases. They try to develop new chemicals for specific applications and new applications for existing chemicals. The most senior chemists sometimes advance to management positions. Although chemical companies hire chemists with bachelor's degrees, a master's or doctoral degree is becoming more important for chemist jobs.

Chemical engineers design equipment and develop processes for manufacturing chemicals on a large scale. Chemical research engineers design and conduct experiments to learn how processes behave and conduct research for potential new chemical products and processes. A bachelor's degree is essential for these jobs, and a master's degree may be preferred or required for some jobs.

Engineering and science technicians assist chemists and engineers in research activities and may conduct some research independently. Those with bachelor's degrees in chemistry or graduates of 2-year technical institutes usually fill these positions. Some graduates of engineering programs start as technicians until an opportunity to advance into an engineering position arises.

Administration and management. Most managers need a 4-year college degree in addition to experience in the industry. As in other highly technical industries, top managerial positions often are held by those with substantial technical experience. Employment in administrative support and managerial occupations is expected to decline as companies merge and consolidate operations.

Engineering and *science managers* conduct cost estimations, perform plant design feasibility studies, and coordinate daily operations. These jobs require a college degree in a technical discipline such as chemistry or chemical engineering and experience in the industry. Some employees advance from research and development positions to management positions.

Marketing and *sales* workers promote sales of chemical products by informing customers of company products and services. A bachelor's degree in marketing, chemistry, or chemical engineering usually is required for these jobs.

Administrative support workers perform office functions such as secretarial duties, bookkeeping, material records processing, and other clerical duties. Training beyond high school and familiarity with computers is preferred for these occupations.

Training and Advancement

The chemical industry has a wide variety of companies and products, which creates career opportunities for persons with varying levels of experience and education. Training and advancement differ for the three major categories of occupations in the chemical industry.

Production workers may start as laborers or in other unskilled jobs and, with experience and training, advance into better paying positions that require greater skills or have greater responsibility. Substantial advancement is possible even within a single occupation. For example, chemical plant operators may move up through several levels of responsibility until they reach the highest paying operator job. Advancement in production occupations usually requires mastery of advanced skills. Such skills usually are a combination of on-the-job-training and formal training provided by the employer. Some workers advance into supervisory positions.

Most jobs in research and development require substantial technical education after high school, but opportunities exist for persons with degrees ranging from a 2-year associate degree up to a doctorate. Development of new products and the award of patents bring increases in pay and prestige, but after a point advancement requires moving from research and development into management. Researchers usually are familiar with company objectives and production methods which, combined with college education, equips them with many of the tools necessary for management positions.

Managerial jobs usually require a 4-year college degree, though some may require only a 2-year technical degree. Managers can usually advance into higher level jobs without additional formal training outside the workplace, although competition is keen. In general, advancement into the highest management ranks depends on experience and proven ability to handle responsibility in several functional areas. Among larger worldwide firms, international experience is important for career advancement. Also, recent industry restructuring has left fewer layers of management, increasing competition for promotions.

Earnings

Wages of workers in the chemical industry vary according to occupation, the specific industry segment, and size of the production plant. Earnings by major occupation group are shown in table 3 and earnings for the largest occupations in selected industries are shown in table 4.

Table 3. Median weekly earnings of full-time workers in chemical manufacturing, except drugs by occupation group, 1998

Occupation group	Median earnings
Professional specialty	$1,044
Executive, administrative, and managerial	959
Technicians	739
Precision production, craft, and repair	673
Administrative support	535
Machine operators	501
Transportation and material moving	454
Handlers, equpment cleaners, and laborers	415

Earnings also vary by industry within the chemical industry. Median weekly earnings for production workers were highest in industrial organic chemicals, $917, and lowest in soaps and cosmetics, $577.

Table 4. Median hourly earnings of the largest occupations in selected chemicals manufacturing industries, 1997

Occupation	Industrial inorganic chemicals	Plastics materials and synthetics	Soaps, cleaners and toilet goods	Industrial organic chemicals	All industries
First-line supervisors and managers/ supervisors-production and operating workers	—	$20.06	—	$23.50	$16.62
Chemical plant and system operators	$18.21	18.81	—	19.09	18.27
Chemical equipment controllers and operators	16.90	17.75	—	17.29	15.25
Chemical technicians and technologists, except health	—	—	—	16.97	14.89
Packaging and filling machine operators and tenders	—	—	$10.72	—	9.38
Assemblers and fabricators, except machine, electrical, electronic, and precision	—	—	9.10	—	9.25
Hand packers and packagers	—	—	8.01	—	6.90

Earnings in the chemical industry are higher than average. The weekly earnings for all production workers in chemical manufacturing averaged $740 in 1998, compared to $563 in all manufacturing industries and $442 throughout private industry. This was due, in part, to more overtime and weekend work, which command higher hourly rates.

The principal unions representing chemical workers are the Oil, Chemical, and Atomic Workers Union and the International Chemical Workers Union. Fifteen percent of chemical manufacturing workers are union members or are covered by union contracts, compared to 15.4 percent of all workers in private industry.

Outlook

Although the chemical industry's output is expected to grow, employment in the chemical and allied products industry, excluding drugs, is projected to decline by 4 percent over the 1998-2008 period, compared to 15 percent growth expected for the entire economy. The expected decline in chemical manufacturing can be attributed to trends affecting the U.S. and global economies. More efficient production processes and increased plant automation, company mergers and consolidation, increased foreign competition, outsourcing of production, growth of environmental health and safety concerns and legislation, precision farming techniques, and an emphasis on specialty chemicals will influence chemical industry employment.

Improvements in production technology have reduced the need for workers in precision production, craft, and repair and operator, fabricator, and laborer occupations, which comprise over half of the jobs in the chemical industry. The growing application of computerized controls in standard production, and the growing manufacture of specialty chemicals requiring precise, computer-controlled production methods, will reduce the need for workers to monitor or directly operate equipment.

Foreign competition has been intensifying in most industries, and the chemical industry is no exception. Although the U.S. chemical industry has enjoyed a favorable trade balance for quite some time—a trend expected to continue—growing global trade and rapidly expanding foreign production capabilities should increase competition. Pressure to reduce costs and streamline production will result in the continuing mergers and consolidation of companies both within the United States and abroad. Mergers and consolidations are allowing chemical companies to increase profits by eliminating duplicate departments and shifting operations where costs are lowest. U.S. companies are expected to continue investing heavily in overseas production plants, taking advantage of expanding markets in some developing countries, East Asia and Latin America. Domestic production activities that are less automated will be affected by this shift of production abroad. Lower skilled production occupations should decline as a result.

To satisfy growing public environmental concerns, and comply with the many Government regulations, the chemical industry invests billions of dollars yearly in technology to reduce pollution and clean up existing waste sites. Growing concerns about chemicals and the environment will spur producers to create chemicals with fewer, less dangerous, or useable by-products that can be recycled or disposed of cleanly. This will require greater investment in research and development. As a result, occupations related to environmental compliance, improving product visibility, and promoting consumer confidence should grow slowly.

Precision farming techniques have reduced the demand for agricultural chemicals in this country as farmers use computer technology to determine what chemicals need to be applied in different areas of the farm, rather than simply fertilizing the whole farm. However, this reduced demand will be partially offset by the increase in global demand for agricultural chemicals as other countries become more sophisticated in their farming techniques.

Another trend in the chemical industry is the rising demand for specialty chemicals. Chemical companies are finding that in order to remain competitive, they must differentiate their products and produce specialty chemicals, such as advanced polymers and plastics designed for specific uses—for example, a durable body panel on an automobile. Because advanced processes often produce specialty chemicals, this trend should increase employment opportunities for highly trained research and development and production-oriented chemists, chemical engineers, technicians, and production personnel. In these small to medium-size firms, responsiveness to customers' chemical needs is imperative, so opportunities for marketing staff such as sales engineers should also be available.

The factors affecting employment in the chemical manufacturing industry will impact different segments of the industry in varying degrees. The two segments projected to add jobs are miscellaneous chemical products, with an increase of about 4,100 jobs, and soap, cleaners, and toilet goods, with an increase of around 9,500 jobs. The two largest losers of jobs are plastics materials and synthetics, with about 16,000 fewer jobs projected, and industrial inorganic chemicals, with a projected loss of about 14,000 jobs.

In terms of specific occupations, employment opportunities in the chemical industry can be divided into production and nonproduction occupations. Jobs in production are expected to decline; the outlook is somewhat brighter for certain professional specialty jobs, such as chemical engineers and computer engineers and scientists. Employment in production occupations should continue to decline as the increasing automation of the chemical industry improves efficiency. The market shift to specialty chemicals, together with increasing competition, will give rise to more jobs in marketing and sales occupations, as companies differentiate their products and compete more heavily in the world marketplace. However, this rise in employment will likely be offset by the elimination of personnel as a result of company restructuring and mergers. In general, persons with technical and advanced degrees will have the best opportunities in the chemical industry.

Sources of Additional Information
Additional information on the chemical and allied products industry is available from:

> American Chemical Society, 1155 16th St. NW., Washington, DC 20036. Internet: **http://www.acs.org**
> American Institute of Chemical Engineers, 3 Park Ave., New York, NY 10016-5901. Internet: **http//www.aiche.org**

Detailed information on many occupations in the chemical industry, including the following, may be found in the 2000-01 edition of the *Occupational Outlook Handbook.*

- Blue-collar worker supervisors
- Chemical engineers
- Chemists
- Computer programmers
- Computer systems analysts, engineers, and scientists
- Engineering technicians
- Industrial production managers
- Material moving equipment operators

Drug Manufacturing

SIGNIFICANT POINTS

- Over half of all workers have a bachelor's, graduate, professional, or Ph.D. degree—roughly double the proportion for all industries combined.

- Forty-one percent of all jobs are in large establishments employing more than 1,000 workers.

- Earnings in drug manufacturing are much higher than those in other manufacturing industries.

- Drug manufacturing is projected to be one of the faster growing manufacturing industries.

Nature of the Industry

The drug manufacturing industry has produced a variety of medicinal and other health-related products undreamed of by even the most imaginative apothecaries of the past. These drugs have saved the lives of millions of people from various diseases, and they permit many ill people to lead reasonably normal lives.

Thousands of medications are available today for diagnostic, preventive, and therapeutic uses. These medicines aid in the control of venereal disease, tuberculosis, influenza, cardiovascular disease, malaria, pneumonia, diabetes, and some forms of cancer. New drugs do much to reduce the severity of mental illness. Vaccines have dramatically reduced the toll of polio, whooping cough, and measles. Discoveries in veterinary drugs have increased animal productivity and controlled various diseases, some of which are transmissible to humans.

The drug industry is comprised of about 1,700 places of employment, which are located throughout the country. These include establishments that make pharmaceutical preparations or finished drugs; biological products, such as serums and vaccines; bulk chemicals and botanicals used in making finished drugs; and diagnostic substances such as pregnancy and blood glucose kits. Pharmaceutical manufacturing firms make up the majority of establishments and employ 60 percent of the workers in this industry.

The American drug industry has achieved worldwide prominence through its research and development of new drugs, and spends a higher proportion of its funds for research than any other industry in the United States. Each year the drug industry tests many thousands of new substances, which may eventually yield only 10 to 20 new prescription medicines.

For the majority of firms in this industry, the actual manufacture of drugs is the last stage in a lengthy process that begins with scientific research to discover new products, and to improve or modify existing ones. The research and development (R&D) departments in drug manufacturing firms start this process by seeking new chemical compounds which have the potential to prevent, combat, or alleviate symptoms of diseases or other health problems. Scientists use sophisticated tools, such as computer simulation and combinatorial chemistry, to hasten and simplify the discovery of potentially useful new compounds. Most firms devote a substantial portion of their R&D budgets to applied research, with the purpose of obtaining and using scientific knowledge to develop a drug targeted to a specific use. For example, an R&D unit may focus on developing a compound that will effectively slow the advance of breast cancer. If the discovery phase yields promising compounds, technical teams then attempt to develop a safe and effective product based on the discoveries. For testing new products in development, a research method called "screening" is used. To screen an antibiotic, for example, a sample is first placed in a bacterial culture. If the antibiotic is effective, it is next tested on infected laboratory animals. Each year, researchers study the effects of potential new medicines on millions of animals, including mice, rats, chickens, and guinea pigs, for evidence of useful—and harmful—effects. A new drug is selected for testing in humans only if it promises to have therapeutic advantages over drugs already in use, or if it offers the possibility of having fewer side effects.

After laboratory screening, firms conduct clinical investigations, or "trials," of the drug on human patients. Human clinical trials normally take place in three phases. First, medical scientists administer the drug to a small group of healthy volunteers in order to determine and adjust dosage levels, and monitor for side effects. If a drug appears useful and safe, additional tests are conducted in two more phases, each phase using a successively larger group of volunteers or carefully selected patients.

Once a drug has successfully passed animal and clinical tests, the Food and Drug Administration (FDA) must review the drug's performance on human patients, the results of which have been carefully documented, before approving the substance for commercial use. The entire process, from the first discovery of a promising new compound to FDA approval, can take up to 15 years, but scientific and information technology advances will shorten that process considerably for many drugs. After FDA approval, problems of production methods and costs must be worked out before manufacturing begins. If the original laboratory process of preparing and compounding the ingredients is complex and too expensive, pharmacists, chemists, chemical engineers, packaging engineers, and production specialists are assigned to develop a process economically adaptable to mass production.

In many production operations, drug manufacturers have developed a high degree of automation. Milling and micronizing machines, which pulverize substances into extremely fine particles, are used to reduce bulk chemicals to the required size. These finished chemicals are combined and processed further in mixing machines. The mixed ingredients may then be mechanically capsulated, pressed into tablets, or made into solutions. One type of machine, for example, automatically fills, seals, and stamps capsules. Other machines fill bottles with capsules, tablets, or liquids, and seal, label, and package the bottles.

Quality control is vital in this industry. Many production workers are assigned full time to quality assurance functions, whereas other employees may devote part of their time to these functions. For example, although pharmaceutical company sales representatives, called detailers, primarily work in marketing, they engage in quality control when they assist pharmacists in checking for outdated products.

Working Conditions

Working conditions in drug plants are better than in most other manufacturing plants. Much emphasis is placed on keeping equipment and work areas clean because of the danger of contamination. Plants usually are air-conditioned, well lighted, and quiet. Ventilation systems protect workers from dust, fumes, and disagreeable odors. Special precautions are taken to protect the relatively small number of employees who work with infectious cultures and poisonous chemicals. With the exception of work performed by material handlers and maintenance workers, most jobs require little physical effort. In 1997, the incidence of work-related injury and illness was 4.1 cases per 100 full-time workers, compared to 10.3 per 100 for all manufacturing industries and 7.1 per 100 for the entire private sector.

Only 6.5 percent of the workers in the drug manufacturing industry are union members or are covered by a union contract, compared to 15.4 percent of workers throughout private industry.

Employment

In 1998, there were 279,000 wage and salary jobs in the drug industry. Three out of 5 jobs were in establishments that made pharmaceutical preparations (finished drugs), such as tranquilizers, antiseptics, and antibiotics. The remaining jobs were in establishments that made biological products, such as serums, vaccines, toxins, plasmas, and bulk medicinal chemicals and botanicals used in making finished drugs, and for firms making diagnostic substances.

Drug manufacturing establishments typically employ many workers. Over 40 percent of this industry's employees work for firms with more than 1,000 workers (chart). Most jobs were in New Jersey, California, Pennsylvania, New York, North Carolina, Illinois, and Indiana.

Occupations in the Industry

About 22 percent of all jobs in the drug industry are in professional and technical occupations (mostly scientists and science technicians), and about 25 percent are in executive and managerial, administrative support, and sales occupations. Over 51 percent of the jobs in the drug industry are in production occupations; these include less skilled operator, fabricator, and laborer occupations and more skilled precision production occupations. The remaining jobs are in service occupations (table 1).

Scientists, engineers, and technicians conduct research to develop new drugs. Others work to streamline production methods and improve environmental and quality control. Life scientists comprise the largest occupation among this industry's scientific and technical workers. Most of these scientists are *biological scientists* who use biotechnology to recombine the genetic material of animals or plants, thus producing new drugs. Biological scientists normally specialize in a particular area. *Biologists* and *bacteriologists* study the effect of chemical agents on infected animals. *Biochemists* study the action of drugs on body processes, by studying the chemical combination and reactions involved in metabolism, reproduction, and heredity. *Microbiologists* grow strains of microorganisms that produce antibiotics. *Physiologists* investigate the effect of drugs on body functions and vital processes. *Pharmacologists* and *zoologists* study the effect of drugs on animals. *Virologists* grow viruses, develop vaccines, and test them in animals. *Botanists*, with their special knowledge of plant life, contribute to the discovery of botanical ingredients for drugs. Other biological scientists include *pathologists*, who study normal and abnormal cells or tissues, and *toxicologists*, who are concerned with the safety, dosage levels, and compatibility of different drugs. Drug manufacturers also employ *medical scientists*, who may also be physicians, to do research, test products, and oversee human clinical trials.

Physical scientists, particularly *chemists*, are also important in the research and development of new drugs. *Organic chemists* combine new compounds for biological testing. *Physical chemists* separate and identify substances, determine molecular structure, help create new compounds, and improve manufacturing processes. *Radiochemists* trace the course of drugs through body organs and tissues. *Pharmaceutical chemists* set standards and specifications for the form of products and for storage conditions; they also see that drug labeling and literature meet the requirements of State and Federal laws. *Analytical chemists* test raw and intermediate materials and finished products for quality.

Science technicians play an important part in both the research for, and the product development of, new medicines. They set up, operate, and maintain laboratory equipment, monitor experiments, analyze data, and record and interpret results. Science technicians usually work under the supervision of scientists or engineers.

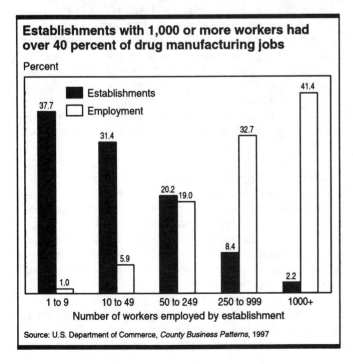

Establishments with 1,000 or more workers had over 40 percent of drug manufacturing jobs

Percent

- ■ Establishments
- □ Employment

Number of workers employed by establishment	Establishments	Employment
1 to 9	37.7	1.0
10 to 49	31.4	5.9
50 to 249	20.2	19.0
250 to 999	8.4	32.7
1000+	2.2	41.4

Source: U.S. Department of Commerce, *County Business Patterns,* 1997

Although engineers account for a small fraction of scientific and technical workers, they make significant contributions toward improving quality control and production efficiency. *Chemical engineers* design equipment and devise manufacturing processes. *Bioprocess engineers*, who are similar to chemical engineers, design fermentation vats and various bioreactors for microorganisms that will produce a given product. *Industrial engineers* plan equipment layout and workflow to maintain efficient use of plant facilities. *Mechanical engineers* coordinate the installation and maintenance of sterilizing, heating, cooling, humidifying, and ventilating equipment.

Table 1. Employment of wage and salary workers in drug manufacturing by occupation, 1998 and projected change, 1998-2008

(Employment in thousands)

Occupation	1998 Employment Number	1998 Employment Percent	1998-2008 Percent change
All occupations	279	100.0	10.7
Operators, fabricators, and laborers	97	34.7	7.8
Packaging and filling machine operators	29	10.2	-9.7
Chemical equipment controllers, operators and tenders	24	8.8	12.8
Helpers, laborers, and material movers, hand	14	4.9	9.1
Crushing, grinding, mixing and blending machine operators	8	2.8	35.5
Hand workers, including assemblers and fabricators	6	2.2	12.9
Precision production, craft, and repair	47	16.7	11.3
Blue-collar worker supervisors	15	5.5	12.9
Industrial machinery mechanics	8	2.7	16.2
Inspectors, testers, and graders	7	2.5	-2.2
Maintenance repairers, general utility	4	1.4	2.6
Chemical plant and systems operators	3	0.9	30.9
Professional specialty	41	14.8	22.9
Chemists	14	4.9	12.9
Engineers	8	2.8	17.6
Biological scientists	8	2.7	35.5
Computer systems analysts, engineers, and scientists	4	1.4	58.4
Executive, administrative, and managerial	34	12.3	13.8
Management support occupations	12	4.1	11.7
General managers and top executives	5	1.7	9.6
Engineering, natural science, and computer and information systems managers	4	1.4	32.1
Industrial production managers	4	1.4	20.6
Administrative support, including clerical	28	10.1	1.3
Secretaries	6	2.3	-10.1
Records processing occupations	4	1.4	-4.0
Shipping, receiving, and traffic clerks	3	1.1	3.8
General office clerks	3	1.0	14.0
Technicians and related support	19	6.9	6.2
Science and mathematics technicians	15	5.5	5.8
Marketing and sales	6	2.2	12.9
Service	6	2.0	4.7
Janitors and cleaners	3	1.1	1.6
All other occupations	1	0.3	12.5

At the top of the managerial group are executives who make policy decisions concerning matters of finance, marketing, and research. Other executive, administrative, and managerial workers include *engineering, natural science,* and *computer and information systems managers*; *industrial managers*; and *advertising, marketing, promotions, public relations,* and *sales managers*.

Administrative support employees include *secretaries, general office clerks*, and others who keep records on personnel, payroll, raw materials, sales, and shipments.

Pharmaceutical sales representatives, often called pharmaceutical detailers, describe their company's products to physicians, pharmacists, dentists, and health services administrators. These sales representatives serve as lines of communication between their companies and clients.

Most plant workers can be divided into three occupational groups: Production or processing workers, who operate the drug-producing equipment and inspect the products; maintenance workers, who install, maintain, and repair production equipment; and packers, truckdrivers, and material handlers, who package and transport the drugs.

Many different types of chemical operators are involved in the production of pharmaceutical preparations and biological products. *Pharmaceutical operators* control machines that produce tablets, capsules, ointments, and medical solutions. *Granulator machine operators* tend milling and grinding machines that reduce mixtures to particles of designated sizes. *Compounders* tend tanks and kettles in which solutions are mixed and compounded to make up creams, ointments, liquid medications, and powders. *Compressors* operate machines that compress ingredients into tablets. *Pill* and *tablet coaters*, often called capsule coaters, control a battery of machines that apply coatings to tablets, which flavor, color, preserve, add medication, or control disintegration time. *Tablet testers* inspect tablets for hardness, chipping, and weight to assure conformity with specifications. *Ampoule fillers* operate machines that fill small glass containers with measured doses of liquid drug products. *Ampoule examiners* examine ampoules for discoloration, foreign particles, and flaws in the glass.

After the drug is prepared and inspected, it is bottled or otherwise packaged. Semiskilled workers do most of the packaging and bottle filling with machines that measure exact amounts of the product and seal containers.

Plant workers who do not operate or maintain equipment perform a variety of other tasks. Some drive trucks to make deliveries to other parts of the plant; some load and unload trucks and railroad cars; others keep inventory records. The industry also employs service workers, such as guards and janitors.

Training and Advancement

Training requirements for jobs in the drug industry range from a few hours of on-the-job training to years of formal education, plus job experience; about half of all workers have a bachelor's or graduate degree—roughly double the proportion for all industries combined. The drug industry places a heavy emphasis on continuing education for employees, and many firms provide classroom training in safety, environmental and quality control, and technological advances.

For production and maintenance occupations, drug manufacturers usually hire inexperienced workers and train them on the job; high school graduates are generally preferred.

Beginners in production jobs assist experienced workers and learn to operate processing equipment. With experience, employees may advance to more skilled jobs in their departments.

Many companies encourage production and maintenance workers to take courses related to their jobs in local schools and technical institutes or to enroll in correspondence courses. College courses in chemistry and related areas are particularly encouraged for highly skilled production workers who operate sophisticated equipment. Some companies reimburse workers for part, or all, of their tuition. Skilled production and maintenance workers with leadership ability may advance to supervisory positions.

For science technicians in the drug industry, most companies prefer to hire graduates of technical institutes or junior colleges or those who have completed college courses in chemistry, biology, mathematics, or engineering. Some companies, however, require science technicians to hold a bachelor's degree in a biological or chemical science. In many firms, newly hired workers begin as laboratory helpers or aides, performing routine jobs, such as cleaning and arranging bottles, test tubes, and other equipment.

The experience required for higher-level technician jobs varies from company to company. Usually, employees advance over a number of years from assistant technician, to technician, to senior technician, and then to technical associate, or supervisory technician.

For most scientific and engineering jobs, a bachelor of science degree is the minimum requirement. Scientists who are involved in research and development usually have a master's or doctoral degree. A doctoral degree is generally the minimum requirement for medical scientists, and those who administer drug or gene therapy to patients in clinical trials must have a medical degree. Because biotechnology is not one discipline, but the interaction of several disciplines, the best preparation for work in biotechnology is training in a traditional biological science, such as genetics, molecular biology, biochemistry, virology, biochemical engineering, plant pathology, or botany. Individuals with a scientific background and several years of industrial experience may eventually advance to managerial positions. Some companies offer training programs to help scientists and engineers keep abreast of new developments in their fields and to develop administrative skills. These programs may include meetings and seminars with consultants from various fields. Many companies encourage scientists and engineers to further their education; some companies provide financial assistance for this purpose. Publication of scientific papers also is encouraged.

Drug manufacturing companies prefer to hire college graduates, particularly those with strong scientific backgrounds, as pharmaceutical detailers. Newly employed pharmaceutical representatives complete rigorous formal training programs revolving around their company's product lines.

Earnings

Earnings of workers in the drug industry are higher than the average for all manufacturing industries. In 1998, production or nonsupervisory workers in the drug industry averaged $717 a week, while those in all manufacturing industries averaged $563 a week. Earnings in selected occupations in drug manufacturing in 1997 appear in table 2.

Some employees work in plants that operate around the clock—three shifts a day, 7 days a week. In most plants,

workers receive extra pay when assigned to the second or third shift. Because drug production is subject to little seasonal variation, work is steady.

Table 2. Median hourly earnings of the largest occupations in drug manufacturing, 1997

Occupation	Drug manufacturing	All industries
Biological scientists	$22.26	$21.01
Chemists, except biochemists	20.84	21.14
First line supervisors and managers/ supervisors, production and operating workers	20.27	16.62
Chemical technicians and technologists, except health	15.34	14.89
Chemical equipment controllers and operators	14.99	15.25
Secretaries, except legal and medical	14.22	11.00
Production inspectors, testers, graders, sorters, samplers, and weighers	10.78	10.15
Crushing, grinding, mixing, and blending machine operators and tenders	10.77	10.85
Packaging and filling machine operators and tenders	10.52	9.38
Assemblers and fabricators, except machine, electrical, electronic and precision	7.73	9.25

Outlook

Wage and salary jobs in drug manufacturing are expected to increase by about 11 percent over the 1998-2008 period, making it among the faster growing manufacturing industries. Demand for this industry's products is expected to remain strong. Even during times of fluctuating economic conditions, there will be a market for over-the-counter and prescription drugs, including the diagnostics used in hospitals, laboratories, and homes; the vaccines used routinely on infants and children; analgesics and other symptom-easing drugs; and antibiotics and "miracle" drugs for life-threatening diseases. Although the use of drugs, particularly antibiotics and vaccines, has contributed towards eradicating or limiting a number of deadly diseases, many others, such as cancer, Alzheimer's, and heart disease, continue to elude cures. On-going research and the manufacture of new products to combat these diseases will continue to contribute to employment growth. Because so many of the drug industry's products are related to preventive or routine health care, rather than just illness, demand is expected to increase as the population expands. Demand will be further stimulated by the growing number of older people who will require more health care services and by the growth of both public and private health insurance programs, which increasingly cover the cost of drugs and medicine. Other factors expected to increase the demand for drugs include greater personal income and the rising health consciousness and expectations of the general public. Biotechnological research continues to offer possibilities for the development of new drugs and products to combat illnesses and diseases which have previously been unresponsive to treatments derived by traditional chemical processes. Scientists will also use biotechnology to develop new antibiotics for use against increasingly drug-resistant bacteria.

Drug producers and buyers are expected to place more emphasis on cost-effectiveness, due to concerns about the cost of health care, including prescription drugs. Growing competition from the producers of generic drugs may also exert cost pressures on many firms in this industry. These factors, combined with continuing improvements in manufacturing processes, are expected to result in slower employment growth over the 1998-2008 period than occurred during the previous 10-year period.

Faster than average growth is anticipated for professional specialty occupations—especially the biological and medical scientists engaged in research and development, the backbone of the drug industry, and computer systems analysts, engineers, and scientists. Slower than average overall growth is projected for operators, fabricators, and laborers. Average growth is projected for skilled mechanics, who service the growing amount of automatic processing and control equipment. Employment of administrative support and clerical workers is expected to experience little or no change, as companies streamline operations and increasingly rely on computers.

Unlike many other manufacturing industries, drug industry employment is not highly sensitive to changes in economic conditions. Even during periods of high unemployment, work is likely to be relatively stable in this industry.

Sources of Additional Information

For additional information about careers in drug manufacturing and the industry in general, write to the personnel departments of individual drug manufacturing companies.

For information about careers in biotechnology, contact:

➢ Biotechnology Industry Organization, Suite 1100, 1625 K St. NW., Washington, DC 20006. Internet: **http://www.bio.org**

Information on these key drug manufacturing occupations may be found in the 2000-01 *Occupational Outlook Handbook*:

- Biological and medical scientists
- Chemists
- Computer scientists, computer engineers, and systems analysts
- Engineers
- Inspectors, testers, and graders
- Science technicians

Electronic Equipment Manufacturing

SIGNIFICANT POINTS

- Rapid technological change and intense competition make research and development efforts the key to success.

- Employment prospects are good for highly skilled technical personnel, but employment of production workers will grow slowly.

Nature of the Industry

The electronic equipment manufacturing industry produces computers, television sets, and audio equipment, as well as a wide range of goods used for both commercial and military purposes. In addition, many electronics products or components are incorporated into other industries' products, such as cars, toys, watches, appliances, and a variety of electronic gadgets.

Technological innovation characterizes this industry almost unlike any other and, in fact, drives much of the industries' production. On the horizon are many products, including loudspeakers that can be heard but not seen, photographs stored on (and viewed from) CDs, and computers that can recognize voices.

Products currently being manufactured in this industry include computers and computer storage devices such as disk drives and computer peripheral equipment such as printers and scanners. The industry also produces calculating and accounting machines such as automated teller machines (ATM's); communications equipment such as telephone switching equipment and cellular telephones; consumer electronics, such as television and stereo sets; and military electronics such as radar, sonar, missile guidance systems, and electronic warfare equipment. This industry also includes the manufacture of semiconductors—silicon or computer "chips," or integrated circuits—which are the heart of computers and many other advanced electronic products. Two of the most significant types of computer chips are microprocessors, which comprise the central processing system of computers, and memory chips, which store information.

This industry differs from other manufacturing industries in that production workers account for a much lower proportion of all workers. The unusually rapid pace of innovation and technological advancement requires a high proportion of engineering and technical workers to continually develop and produce new products. American companies manufacture and assemble many products abroad because of lower production costs and new trade agreements. However, the growing complexity of some of the most highly technical production processes—in semiconductor and electronic component manufacturing in particular—is leading to increased demand for a more highly skilled workforce in the United States.

Companies producing components, intermediate, and finished goods frequently cluster near each other because it allows easier access to recent innovations. Electronic products contain many components—and sometimes even major parts, such as integrated circuits—which often are purchased from other manufacturers. As a result of having the skilled workforce that fosters product improvement, some areas of the country have become centers of the electronics industry. The most prominent of these centers is "Silicon Valley," a concentration of integrated circuit and computer firms in California's Santa Clara valley near San Jose. Other emerging centers are in Texas, Massachusetts, and more recently Oregon. There are, however, electronics manufacturing plants throughout the country.

To a large extent, electronics manufacturing has become truly global, and it is difficult to characterize many companies and their products as American or foreign. The movement of foreign companies to manufacture some goods in the United States does not change the fact that many products are being designed in one country, manufactured in another, and assembled in a third. Highly sensitive and sophisticated products such as semiconductors and computers are being designed and manufactured in the United States, for example, but it remains likely that other parts of final products such as the keyboards and outer casings are made somewhere else and shipped to another site for final assembly.

Although some of the companies in this industry are large, most are actually small. The history of innovation in the industry explains the start-up of many small firms. Some companies are involved in design or research and development (R&D), whereas others may simply manufacture components such as computer chips under contract for others. Often an engineer or physicist will have an innovative idea and set up a new company to develop the product. Although electronic products can be very sophisticated, it has been possible to manufacture many electronic products or components (not necessarily finished products) with a relatively small investment. Furthermore, investors often are willing to put their money behind new companies in this industry because of its history of large paybacks from some very successful companies. Such success depends on innovation, and, although investment costs are rising, there should continue to be opportunities to develop good ideas.

The rapid pace of innovation in electronics technology makes for a constant demand for newer and faster products and applications. This demand puts a greater emphasis on research and development (R&D) than is typical in most manufacturing operations. Being the first firm to market a new or better product usually determines the success or failure of the product and often the company. Even for many relatively commonplace items, R&D continues to result in better, cheaper products with more desirable features. For example, a company that develops a new kind of computer chip to be used in many brands of computers can earn millions of dollars in sales until a competitor is able to copy the technology or develop a better chip. Many employees, therefore, are research scientists, engineers, and technicians whose job it is to continually develop and improve products.

The product design process includes not only the initial design, but also development work which ensures that the product functions properly and can be manufactured as inexpensively as possible. When a product is manufactured, the components are assembled, usually by soldering them to a printed circuit board. Often tedious, hand assembly requires both good eyesight and coordination, as many of the parts are very small. However, because of the cost and precision involved, assembly and packaging are becoming highly automated.

Working Conditions

In general, electronics manufacturing enjoys relatively good working conditions, even for production workers. In contrast to many other manufacturing industries, production workers in this industry usually work in clean and relatively noise-free environments. Computer chips are manufactured in "clean rooms," in which the air is filtered and workers wear special garments to prevent any dust from getting into the air. A speck of dust will ruin a computer chip.

In 1997, the rates of work-related injuries and illness per 100 full-time workers were 3.0 per 100 full-time workers in computer and office equipment, 3.7 in communications equipment, 5.0 in electronic components and accessories, 6.9 in household audio and video equipment, and 2.2 in search and navigation equipment. These rates were all lower than the 7.1 average for the private sector. However, some jobs in this industry may have risks. For example, some workers who fabricate integrated circuits and other components may be exposed to potentially hazardous chemicals, and working with small parts may cause eyestrain.

Most employees work regular 40-hour weeks, but pressure to develop new products ahead of competitors may result in some research and development personnel working extensive overtime to meet deadlines. The competitive nature of the industry makes for an exciting, but sometimes stressful, work environment—especially for those in technical and managerial occupations.

Employment

The electronic equipment manufacturing industry employed about 1.6 million wage and salary workers in 1998 (table 1). Few workers were self-employed.

Table 1. Distribution of wage and salary employment in electronic equipment manufacturing by industry segment, 1998

Industry segment	Employment (in thousands)	Percent
Total, electronic equipment manufacturing	1,564	100.0
Electronic components and accessories ...	666	42.6
Computer and office equipment	379	24.2
Communication equipment	282	18.0
Search and navigation equipment...........	162	10.4
Household audio and video equipment ...	82	5.2

The industry comprised about 13,000 establishments in 1997, many of which were small, employing only 1 or a few workers. Large establishments of 250 workers or more employed the majority—70 percent—of the industry's workforce (chart).

Occupations in the Industry

Given the importance of R&D to the industry, it is not surprising that a large proportion—about 1 in 5—of all workers are in professional specialty occupations (table 2). Over 50 percent of these are engineers—mainly *electrical and electronics engineers* and *computer engineers*. These workers develop new products and devise better, more efficient production methods. Engineers may coordinate and lead teams developing new products. Others may work with customers to help them make the best use of the products. A growing number of *computer systems analysts* and *computer scientists* are being employed throughout the industry as both development and production methods become more computerized. Other professionals include *mathematical* and *physical scientists*, and *technical writers*.

About 8 percent of workers are technicians—mostly *engineering technicians* —many of who work closely with engineers. They help develop new products, work in production areas, and sometimes help customers install, maintain and repair equipment. They also may test new products or processes to make sure everything works correctly.

Despite the relatively high proportion of professional and technical workers in electronics manufacturing, more than 4 out of 10 workers are production workers. Many are assemblers, who place and solder components on circuit boards, or assemble and connect the various parts of electronic devices. *Electronic semiconductor processors* initiate and control the many automated steps in the process of manufacturing of integrated circuits or computer chips. *Electrical and electronic assemblers* are responsible for putting together products such as computers and appliances, telecommunications equipment, and even missile control systems. *Precision assemblers* must be able to do accurate work at a rapid

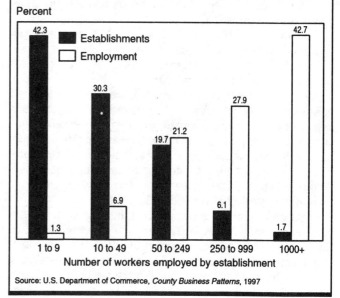

Though most electronics firms are small, employment is concentrated in large establishments

Percent

- Establishments
- Employment

	1 to 9	10 to 49	50 to 249	250 to 999	1000+
Establishments	42.3	30.3	19.7	6.1	1.7
Employment	1.3	6.9	21.2	27.9	42.7

Number of workers employed by establishment

Source: U.S. Department of Commerce, *County Business Patterns*, 1997

pace. Some assemblers are highly skilled and require significant experience and training to assemble major components. A skilled assembler may put together an entire subassembly or even an entire product, especially when products are made in relatively small numbers. Other less skilled assemblers often work on a production line, attaching one or a few parts and continually repeating the same operation. Increasingly, as production work becomes more automated, assemblers and other production workers monitor the machinery which actually does the assembly work. *Precision inspectors, testers,* and *graders* use sophisticated testing machinery to ensure devices operate as designed.

About 14 percent of workers in the industry are in executive, administrative, and managerial occupations. In this industry, top management is much more likely to have a technical background than in other industries, especially in smaller companies, which often are founded by engineers, computer scientists, or other technical professionals.

About 13 percent of workers in this industry hold administrative, clerical, or sales jobs. Sales positions require technical knowledge and abilities, and as a result, engineers and technicians often may find opportunities in sales or sales support.

Training and Advancement

Workers with varying levels of education find employment opportunities in the electronic equipment manufacturing industry. Entry to engineering occupations generally requires at least a bachelor's degree in engineering, although those with 4-year degrees in physical science or computer science or other technical areas can sometimes qualify as well. Some positions, however, may require a master's degree or higher or relevant work experience. Computer systems analysts or scientists usually need a degree in computer science or a related field, and in many cases, they also must have considerable programming experience. Since companies are often founded by professionals with technical backgrounds, opportunities for advancement into executive, administrative, and managerial positions may arise for experienced workers who keep up with rapid changes in technology.

Training for engineering technicians is available from a number of sources. Although most employers prefer graduates of 2-year postsecondary training schools—usually technical institutes or junior colleges—training in the Armed Forces or through proprietary schools may also meet employer requirements. Engineering technicians, like engineers, should have an aptitude for math and science. Entry level technicians may begin working with a more experienced technician or engineer. Advancement opportunities for experienced technicians may include supervisory positions or movement into other production and inspection operations.

Though assembly workers generally need only a high school diploma, assemblers in the electronics industry may need more specialized training or experience than workers in other manufacturing industries. Precision assembly work can be extremely sophisticated and complex, and some precision assembly jobs even may require formal technical training. Again, advancement opportunities depend not only on work experience, but also the level of technical training and the ability to keep up with changing technology.

Table 2. Employment of wage and salary workers in electronic equipment manufacturing by occupation, 1998 and projected change, 1998-2008

(Employment in thousands)

Occupation	1998 Employment Number	1998 Employment Percent	1998-2008 Percent change
All occupations	1,564	100.0	8.8
Operators, fabricators, and laborers	370	23.6	19.1
Electrical and electronic assemblers	124	7.9	18.0
Electronic semiconductor processors	62	4.0	46.3
All other assemblers, fabricators, and hand workers	46	3.0	9.9
Helpers, laborers, and material movers, hand	19	1.2	-2.5
Professional specialty	328	21.0	14.9
Electrical and electronics engineers	102	6.5	14.5
Computer engineers	44	2.8	10.9
Computer support specialists	26	1.7	37.6
Industrial engineers	17	1.1	-1.7
Mechanical engineers	15	1.0	12.2
Precision production, craft, and repair	315	20.1	4.8
Electrical and electronic equipment assemblers, precision	117	7.5	7.7
Inspectors, testers, and graders, precision	57	3.6	-12.9
Mechanics, installers, and repairers	43	2.7	9.6
Blue-collar worker supervisors	43	2.7	10.6
Industrial machinery mechanics	17	1.1	14.7
Metal workers, precision	15	1.0	9.7
Executive, administrative, and managerial	219	14.0	4.4
Engineering, natural science, and computer and information systems managers	28	1.8	22.8
General managers and top executives	27	1.7	3.0
Industrial production managers	18	1.1	1.5
Purchasing agents, except wholesale, retail, and farm products	17	1.1	6.2
Accountants and auditors	16	1.0	-3.8
Administrative support, including clerical	157	10.1	-5.6
Secretaries	28	1.8	-17.2
Production, planning, and expediting clerks	18	1.2	-4.1
Shipping, receiving, and traffic clerks	15	1.0	1.3
General office clerks	14	0.9	7.0
Financial records processing occupations	14	0.9	-12.0
Technicians and related support	122	7.8	-0.5
Electrical and electronics technicians and technologists	61	3.9	2.5
All other engineering technicians and technologists	28	1.8	8.7
Computer programmers	20	1.3	-19.8
Marketing and sales	42	2.7	5.9
All other occupations	12	0.7	0.7

Earnings

In general, earnings in the electronics industry are high, although this is partly because many of the lower wage production jobs have been automated or exported to other countries. Average weekly earnings of all production or nonsupervisory workers in the industry in 1998 were higher than the average of $442 for all industries (table 3).

Table 3. Average earnings of nonsupervisory workers in the electronic equipment manufacturing industry, 1998

Industry segment	Weekly	Hourly
Total, private industry	$442	$12.77
Electronics industry		
Search and navigation equipment	733	17.32
Computer and office equipment	640	15.32
Communications equipment	596	14.02
Electronic components and accessories	549	13.25
Household audio and video equipment	485	11.94

Earnings in selected occupations in several components of the electronic equipment manufacturing in 1997 appear in table 4.

Table 4. Median hourly earnings of the largest occupations in electronic equipment manufacturing, 1997

Occupation	Computer and office equipment	Household audio and video equipment	Comm-unications equipment	Electronic components and accessories
Electrical and electronic engineers	$32.24	—	$28.55	$28.78
Computer engineers	30.63	—	28.41	29.62
Electrical and electronic engineering technicians and technologists	15.88	—	15.30	18.44
Electrical and electronic equipment assemblers, precision	11.24	$9.68	9.94	8.70
Electrical and electronic assemblers	8.85	8.79	8.70	8.24
First-line supervisors and managers/supervisors-production and operating workers	—	—	15.80	16.58
Electronic semiconductor processors	—	—	—	11.73
Precision Inspectors, testers, and graders	—	—	—	10.31
Production inspectors, testers, graders, sorters, samplers, and weighers	—	—	10.78	10.39
Assemblers and fabricators, except machine, electrical, electronic, and precision	8.97	—	—	—

Outlook

The revolutions taking place in computers, semiconductors, and telecommunications should provide workers in many of the industry's occupations with employment opportunities, especially in research and development. Breakthroughs in telephone, navigational, and household audio and video equipment will have a major impact on the workplace and in homes. Products of the electronic equipment manufacturing industry, especially powerful computer chips, will continue to enhance productivity in all areas of the economy. Overall employment is projected to grow by about 9 percent between 1998 and 2008. The industry is expected to continue its rapid productivity growth, so even though output is expected to increase in most segments as global demand for electronics products rises, employment of production workers will not grow as quickly, and is actually expected to decline in some segments.

Expected employment growth varies by industry segment (table 5). Demand for computers should remain strong worldwide, but new technology and automated manufacturing processes should continue to eliminate jobs. This trend is also true in the areas of household audio and video equipment, and to some extent search and navigation equipment; these industry segments are using the same technology to automate production of increasingly sophisticated equipment. In addition, labor-intensive manufacturing, assembly, and packaging operations are still being moved to low-wage countries in the Far East or to Mexico when cost effective, although this strategy grows less attractive as the technical demands of manufacturing become more complex. In addition, the need for manufacturing to be located near the research site may help to moderate the move abroad.

Employment in electronic components and accessories, on the other hand, is expected to grow faster than the average over the projection period, more than offsetting expected declines in other segments. The market for semiconductors is growing tremendously and as a result, the need for skilled labor has been increasing worldwide. As chips become smaller and more powerful and production processes more sophisticated, the size of the U.S. market, coupled with the need for a strong infrastructure and highly skilled workforce, has shifted focus back to the U.S. in this segment of the industry.

Table 5. Projected employment change in electronics manufacturing by industry segment, 1998-2008

Industry segment	Percent change
Total, electronic equipment manufacturing	8.8
Electronic components and accessories	24.2
Communications equipment	7.3
Computer and office equipment	-2.8
Search and navigation equipment	-11.5
Household audio and video equipment	-17.3

Demand for communications equipment, such as cellular phones, should result in employment growth in the industry. Ownership of cellular phones has grown quickly in recent years; continuing improvements in quality and services should lead to even greater growth between 1998 and 2008. As cellular phones change over to digital technology, they will allow users to browse the Internet away from a desk. In addition, a substantial increase in baud speeds for these phones will raise their attractiveness to businesses that have had to rely on desktop PCs with their much faster speeds.

With respect to "wired" communications, the replacement of existing forms of wire—in buildings, airplanes, and underground—with more technologically advanced fiber optics also will contribute to demand for workers in the communications segment of electronic equipment manufacturing.

Much of the employment growth in this industry is expected to be among the professional specialty occupations. Electronic semiconductor processors and electrical and electronic assemblers will also grow faster than the industry average. Highly skilled technical personnel should be able to take advantage of the increasingly sophisticated level of manufacturing technology as industries become more integrated and development and manufacturing processes more advanced. Employment of production workers is expected to grow more slowly than the industry as a whole, as more jobs are lost to technological innovation. Overall, employment of managers is also expected to grow slower than the average while clerical occupations are expected to decline.

The electronics industry is characterized by rapid technological advances and has grown faster than most other industries over the past 30 years, although rising capital costs and the rapid pace of innovation continue to pose challenges. Certain segments and individual companies often are subject to problems. For example, the computer industry occasionally undergoes severe downturns, and individual companies can run into trouble—even those in segments of the industry doing well—because they have not kept up with the latest technological developments or because they have erred in deciding which products to manufacture. Such uncertainties can be expected to continue. In addition, foreign competition and the future role of imports remain difficult to project. Import competition has wiped out major parts of the domestic consumer electronics industry, and future effects of import competition are dependent on trade policies and market forces. The industry is likely to continue to encounter strong competition from imported electronic goods and components, especially from Japan, but also from other countries throughout Asia and Europe.

Sales of military electronics, an important segment of the industry, will likely decline as defense expenditures decrease. On the other hand, it is likely that firms will continue developing new products, creating large new markets as they have in the past. Smaller, more powerful computer chips are continually being developed and incorporated into an even wider array of products, and the semiconductor content of all electronic products will continue to increase. The growth of digital technology, artificial intelligence, and multimedia applications will continue to create new opportunities. Future developments will lead to a much greater convergence of products and technologies with the expansion of the Internet and demand for global information networking.

Sources of Additional Information

For information on the electronics industry, contact:

➤ The Electronic Industries Alliance 2500 Wilson Blvd., Arlington, VA 22201. Internet: **http://www.eia.org**
➤ American Electronics Association, The Center for Workforce Excellence, 5201 Great America Pkwy., Suite 520, Santa Clara, CA 95054. Internet: **http://www.aeanet.org**

For information on careers as an electrical, electronics, or computer engineer, contact:

➤ The Institute of Electrical and Electronics Engineers, Inc., 1828 L Street, NW., Suite 1202, Washington, DC 20036-5104.

For information on careers and training as an electronics technician, contact:

➤ Electronics Technicians Association, 602 North Jackson, Greencastle, IN 46135.

Information on these occupations may by found in the 2000-01 *Occupational Outlook Handbook*:

● Computer systems analysts, engineers, and scientists
● Electrical and electronics engineers
● Electronic semiconductor processors
● Engineering, natural science, and computer and information systems managers
● Engineering technicians
● Precision assemblers

Food Processing

- The industry has a high incidence of injury and illness; meatpacking plants have the highest incidence among all industries.

- Production workers account for 3 out of 4 jobs.

- Most jobs require little formal education or training; many can be learned in a few days.

- Little growth is expected in employment because of increasing automation and productivity.

Nature of the Industry

Workers in the food processing industry link farmers and other agricultural producers with consumers. They do this by processing raw fruits, vegetables, grains, meats, and dairy products into finished goods ready for the grocer or wholesaler to sell to households, restaurants, or institutional food services.

Food processing workers perform tasks as varied as the many foods we eat. For example, they slaughter, dress, and cut meat or poultry; process milk, cheese, and other dairy products; can and preserve fruits, vegetables, and frozen specialties; manufacture flour, cereal, pet foods, and other grain mill products; make bread, cookies, and other bakery products; manufacture sugar, candy, and other confectionery products; process shortening, margarine, and other fats and oils; produce alcoholic and nonalcoholic beverages; prepare packaged fish and seafood, coffee, potato and corn chips, and peanut butter. Although this list is long, it is not exhaustive—food processing workers also play a part in delivering numerous other food products to our tables.

Table 1 shows that about 29 percent of all food processing workers are employed in plants that produce meat products, and another 26 percent work in establishments that make bakery goods and preserved fruits and vegetables. Sugar and confectionery products, the smallest sector of the food processing industry, accounts for only about 6 percent of all jobs.

Table 1. Employment in food processing by industry segment, 1998 and projected change, 1998-2008

(Employment in thousands)

Industry segment	1998 Employment	1998-2008 Percent change
Total employment	1,686	2.1
Meat products	494	15.4
Preserved fruits and vegetables	229	-5.6
Bakery products	206	-4.7
Miscellaneous foods products	178	10.6
Beverages	182	-9.7
Grain mill products and fats and oils	158	0.8
Dairy products	140	-11.6
Sugar and confectionery products	97	-4.0

Working Conditions

Many production jobs in food processing involve repetitive, physically demanding work. Production workers often stand for long periods and may be required to lift heavy objects or use cutting, slicing, grinding, and other potentially dangerous tools and machines. Food processing workers are highly susceptible to repetitive strain injuries to hands, wrists, and elbows. This type of injury is especially common in meatpacking and poultry processing plants. In 1997, there were 14.5 cases of work-related injury or illness per 100 full-time food processing workers, more than double the 7.1 rate for the private sector as a whole. Injury rates vary significantly in specific food processing industries, ranging from a low of 6.8 per 100 workers in wet corn mills to 32.1 in meatpacking plants, the highest rate among all industries.

In an effort to reduce occupational hazards, many plants have redesigned equipment, increased job rotation, allowed longer or more frequent breaks, and developed training programs in safe work practices. Some workers wear protective hats, gloves, aprons, and shoes. In many industries, uniforms and protective clothing are changed daily for sanitary reasons.

Because of the considerable mechanization in this industry, most food processing plants are noisy, with limited opportunities for interaction among workers. In some highly automated plants, "hands-on," manual work has been replaced by monitoring and troubleshooting for many production workers.

Working conditions also depend on the type of food being processed. For example, some bakery employees work at night or on weekends and spend much of their shift near ovens that can be uncomfortably hot. In contrast, workers in dairies and meat processing plants work typical daylight hours and may experience cold and damp conditions. Some plants, such as those producing processed fruits and vegetables, operate on a seasonal basis, so workers are not guaranteed steady, year-around employment and occasionally travel from region to region seeking work. These plants are increasingly rare, however, as the industry continues to diversify, and processing plants produce alternate foods and beverages during otherwise inactive periods.

Employment

The food processing industry provided nearly 1.7 million jobs in 1998. Almost all employees are wage and salary workers, but a few food processing workers are self-employed. In 1997, about 11,900 establishments processed food, over half employing fewer than 20 workers (chart). Nevertheless, establishments employing 100 or more workers accounted for nearly 80 percent of all jobs.

Food processing workers are found in all States, although some sectors of the industry are concentrated in certain parts of the country. For example, Arkansas, Georgia, Iowa, North Carolina, and Texas employ over a third of workers in meat producing industries. Wisconsin has more cheese processing workers than any other State. Similarly, most workers producing chewing gum work in Illinois and Pennsylvania. California accounts for more than 1 in 5 canned, frozen, and preserved fruit, vegetable, and food specialty workers, and together with Illinois, Pennsylvania, and New York, employs a third of all workers who produce bakery products. Employment in raw cane sugar processing is concentrated in Florida, Hawaii, and Louisiana.

Occupations in the Industry

The food processing industry employs many different types of workers. About three-fourths are production workers, including skilled precision workers and less-skilled machine operators and laborers (table 2). Production jobs require manual dexterity, good hand-eye coordination, and in some industries, strength.

Red meat production is the most labor-intensive food processing operation. Because animals are not uniform in size, *slaughterers and meatpackers* must slaughter, skin, eviscerate, and cut each carcass into large pieces. They usually do this work by hand, using large, heavy power saws. They also clean and salt hides and make sausage. *Meatcutters* and *trimmers* use hand tools to break down the large primary cuts into smaller sizes for shipment to wholesalers and retailers. *Poultry trimmers and cutters* use knives and other hand tools to eviscerate, split, and bone chickens and turkeys.

Bakers mix and bake ingredients according to recipes to produce breads, cakes, pastries, and other goods. Bakers produce goods in large quantities, using mixing machines, ovens, and other equipment.

Many food processing workers use their hands or small hand tools to do their jobs. *Cannery workers* perform a variety of routine tasks—such as sorting, grading, washing, trimming, peeling, or slicing—in canning, freezing, or packing food products. *Hand food decorators* apply artistic touches to prepared foods. *Candy molders* and *marzipan shapers* form fancy shapes by hand.

With increasing levels of automation in the food processing industry, a growing number of workers operate machines. For example, *food batchmakers* operate equipment that mixes, blends, or cooks ingredients used in manufacturing various foods, such as cheese, candy, honey, and tomato sauce. *Dairy processing equipment operators* process milk, cream, cheese, and other dairy products. *Cutting* and *slicing machine operators* slice bacon, bread, cheese, and other foods. *Mixing* and *blending machine operators* produce dough batters, fruit juices, or spices. *Crushing* and *grinding machine operators* turn raw grains into cereals, flour, and other milled grain products, and they produce oils from nuts or seeds. *Extruding* and *forming machine operators* produce molded food and candy, and *casing finishers* and *stuffers* make sausage links and similar products. *Bottle packers* and *bottle fillers* operate machines that fill bottles and jars with beverages, preserves, pickles, and other foodstuffs.

Cooking machine operators steam, deep fry, boil, or pressure cook meats, grains, sugar, cheese, or vegetables. *Grain roasters* operate equipment that roasts grains, nuts, or coffee beans, and *drying machine operators* tend ovens, kilns, dryers, and other equipment that removes moisture from macaroni, coffee beans, cocoa, and grain. *Baking equipment operators* tend ovens that bake bread, pastries, and other products. Some foods—ice cream, frozen specialties, and meat, for example—are placed in freezers or refrigerators by *cooling* and *freezing equipment operators*. Other workers tend machines and equipment that clean and wash food or food processing equipment. Some machine operators also clean and maintain machines and perform other duties such as checking the weight of foods.

Many other workers are needed to keep food processing plants and equipment in good working order. *Industrial machinery mechanics* repair and maintain production machines and equipment. *Maintenance repairers* perform routine machinery maintenance, such as changing and lubricating parts. Specialized mechanics include *air-conditioning* and *refrigeration technicians*, *farm equipment mechanics*, and *diesel engine specialists*.

Still other workers directly oversee the quality of the work and of final products. *Blue-collar worker supervisors* direct the activities of production workers. *Graders* and *sorters* of agricultural products, *production inspectors,* and *quality control technicians* evaluate foodstuffs before, during, or after processing.

Food may spoil if not properly packaged and promptly delivered, so packaging and transportation employees play a vital role in the industry. Among these are *freight, stock,* and *material movers*, who manually move materials; *hand packers* and *packagers*, who pack bottles and other items as they come off the production line; and *machine feeders* and *offbearers*, who remove goods from the end of the production line. *Industrial truck* and *tractor operators* drive gasoline or

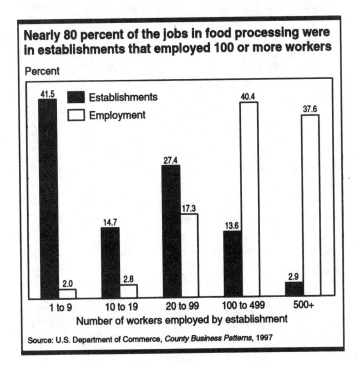

Nearly 80 percent of the jobs in food processing were in establishments that employed 100 or more workers

Percent

- ■ Establishments
- □ Employment

Number of workers employed by establishment	Establishments	Employment
1 to 9	41.5	2.0
10 to 19	14.7	2.8
20 to 99	27.4	17.3
100 to 499	13.6	40.4
500+	2.9	37.6

Source: U.S. Department of Commerce, *County Business Patterns*, 1997

electric-powered vehicles equipped with fork lifts, elevated platforms, or trailer hitches to move goods around a storage facility. *Truckdrivers* transport and deliver livestock, materials, or merchandise, and may load and unload trucks. *Driver/sales workers* drive company vehicles over established routes to deliver and sell goods, such as bakery items, beverages, and vending machine products.

The food processing industry also employs a variety of managerial and professional workers. Managers include *general managers* and *top executives*, who make policy decisions; *industrial production managers*, who organize, direct, and control the operation of the manufacturing plant; and *marketing, advertising,* and *public relations managers*, who direct advertising, sales promotion, and community relations programs.

Engineers, scientists, and technicians are becoming increasingly important as the food processing industry implements new automation. These workers include *industrial engineers,* who plan equipment layout and workflow in manufacturing plants, emphasizing efficiency and safety. Also, *mechanical engineers* plan, design, and oversee the installation of tools, equipment, and machines. *Chemists* perform tests to develop new products and maintain quality of existing products. *Computer programmers* and *systems analysts* develop computer systems and programs to support management and scientific research. Food scientists, such as *food technicians* and *technologists* and *chemical technicians*, work in research laboratories or on production lines to develop new products, test current ones, and control food quality.

Finally, many sales workers, including *manufacturers' representatives* and *demonstrators*, are needed to sell the manufactured goods to wholesale and retail establishments. *Bookkeeping* and *accounting clerks*, *procurement clerks*, and *traffic clerks* keep track of the food products going into and out of the plant. *Janitors* and *cleaners* keep buildings clean and orderly.

Training and Advancement

Most workers in production line food processing jobs require little formal education or training. Graduation from high school is preferred but not always required. In general, inexperienced workers start as helpers to experienced workers and learn skills on the job. Many of these entry-level jobs can be learned in a few days. Typical jobs include operating a bread slicing machine, washing fruits and vegetables before processing begins, hauling carcasses, or packing bottles as they come off the production line. Even though it may not take long to learn to operate a piece of equipment, employees may need several years of experience to enable them to keep the equipment running smoothly, efficiently, and safely.

Some food processing workers receive specialized training. Inspectors and quality control workers, for example, are often trained in food safety and may need a certificate to be employed in a food processing plant. In addition to specialized training, a growing number of workers receive broader training to perform a number of jobs. The need for flexibility in more automated workplaces has meant that many food processing workers are learning new tasks and being trained to effectively work in teams.

Advancement may come in the form of higher earnings or more responsibility. Helpers usually progress to jobs as machine operators, but the speed of this progression can vary considerably. Some workers who perform exceptionally well

on the production line, or those with special training and experience, may advance to supervisory positions. Advancement opportunities may be influenced by plant size and the existence of formal promotion tracks.

Table 2. Employment in food processing by occupation, 1998 and projected change, 1998-2008

Occupation	1998 Employment Number	1998 Employment Percent	1998-2008 Percent change
All occupations	1,686	100.0	2.1
Operators, fabricators, and laborers	903	53.6	4.6
Meat, poultry, and fish cutters and trimmers, hand	140	8.3	24.6
Packaging and filling machine operators and tenders	138	8.2	6.0
Hand packers and packagers	113	6.7	3.5
Truckdrivers	88	5.2	-5.3
Cannery workers	48	2.9	-12.2
Freight, stock, and material movers, hand	41	2.5	-15.2
Crushing and mixing machine operators and tenders	32	1.9	4.1
Industrial truck and tractor operators	29	1.7	0.3
Cooking and roasting machine operators and tenders	28	1.6	-9.1
Dairy processing equipment operators	14	0.8	-18.8
Machine feeders and offbearers	13	0.8	7.7
Precision production, craft, and repair	360	21.4	3.2
Blue-collar worker supervisors	79	4.7	2.0
Butchers and meatcutters	59	3.5	3.2
Industrial machinery mechanics	52	3.1	8.4
Bakers, manufacturing	39	2.3	14.6
Inspectors, testers, and graders, precision	27	1.6	-10.8
Maintenance repairers, general utility	23	1.4	-6.6
Administrative support, including clerical	130	7.7	-8.0
Shipping, receiving, and traffic clerks	23	1.4	-7.9
Financial records processing occupations	22	1.3	-16.3
General office clerks	16	1.0	2.0
Executive, administrative, and managerial	100	5.9	-1.8
General managers and top executives	25	1.5	-1.3
Management support occupations	23	1.4	-1.1
Industrial production managers	16	1.0	-3.5
Marketing and sales	68	4.1	-2.3
Service	60	3.5	-9.5
Janitors and cleaners	33	2.0	-7.3
Agriculture, forestry, fishing, and related	28	1.6	5.1
Technicians and related support	20	1.2	-6.9
Professional specialty	17	1.0	11.7

Requirements for other jobs are similar to requirements in other industries. Employers usually hire high school graduates for secretarial and other clerical work. Graduates of 2-year associate degree or other postsecondary programs often are sought for science technician and related positions. College graduates or highly experienced workers are preferred for middle management or professional jobs in personnel, accounting, marketing, or sales. Some specialized research positions may require a master's or doctoral degree in chemistry, engineering, food science or technology, or a closely related field.

Table 3. Average earnings of production or nonsupervisory workers in food processing by industry segment, 1998

Industry segment	Weekly	Hourly
Total, private industry	$442	$12.77
Total, food processing	482	11.80
Beverages	706	16.11
Grain mill products	680	14.89
Fats and oils	553	12.84
Dairy products	570	13.57
Sugar and confectionery products	539	13.05
Bakery products	520	12.75
Preserved fruits and vegetables	472	11.34
Miscellaneous foods	423	10.67
Meat products	398	9.66

Earnings

Table 3 shows that production workers in food processing averaged $11.80 an hour, compared to $12.77 per hour for all workers in private industry in 1998. Weekly earnings among food processing workers, however, were higher than average, $482 compared to $442, reflecting more hours of work. Food processing workers averaged about 41.7 hours a week, compared to only 34.6 for all workers in the private sector. Weekly earnings ranged from $398 in meat products manufacturing plants to $706 in beverages manufacturing plants. Hours worked play a large part in determining earnings. For example, fats and oils manufacturing workers, who averaged 43.1 hours a week, had lower hourly earnings but higher weekly earnings than bakery products manufacturing workers, who averaged 40.8 hours a week. Earnings in selected occupations in food processing appear in table 4.

In 1998, about 23 percent of workers in the food processing industry belonged to a union or were covered by a union contract, compared to 15.4 percent of all workers in the private sector. Prominent unions in the industry include the United Food and Commercial Workers, Teamsters, Bakery and Confectionery Workers, Grain Millers, and Distillery Workers.

Outlook

Employment in food processing is expected to grow by about 2 percent over the 1998-2008 period, more slowly than the 15 percent growth projected for all industries in the economy. The primary source of this growth will be the rising demand for food products by an increasing population. Growing automation and productivity will moderate the increase somewhat, but the rapid employee turnover in many segments of food processing will create numerous job openings for workers wishing to enter the industry.

Job growth will be concentrated among production workers—the largest group of workers in the industry. Because many of the sorting, cutting, and chopping tasks performed by these workers have proven difficult to automate, employment among hand workers will rise along with the growing demand for food products. One rapidly growing, hand-working occupation is meat, poultry, and fish cutters, whose employment will rise as the consumption of meat, poultry and fish climbs and more processing takes place at the manufacturing level. Indeed, many production workers will benefit from the recent rise in the share of processing that occurs in food processing plants instead of in retail establishments.

Table 4. Median hourly earnings of the largest occupations in food processing, 1997

Occupation	Food processing	All industries
First-line supervisors and supervisors/ managers-production and operating workers	$15.49	$16.62
Machinery maintenance mechanics	13.89	14.72
Truck drivers, heavy or tractor-trailer	12.81	13.08
Bakers, manufacturing	10.28	10.25
Packaging and filling machine operators and tenders	9.69	9.38
Janitors and cleaners, except maids and housekeeping cleaners	8.73	7.44
Slaughterers and butchers	8.69	8.67
Hand packers and packagers	8.30	6.90
Cannery workers	7.56	7.55
Meat, poultry, and fish cutters and trimmers, hand	7.46	7.51

Although automation has had little effect on most hand workers, it is having a broader impact on numerous other occupations in the industry. Fierce competition has led food processing plants to invest in technologically advanced machinery to be more productive. These machines have been applied to tasks as varied as packaging, inspection, and inventory control. As a result, employment has fallen among some machine operators, such as packaging machine operators, but has risen for industrial machinery mechanics who repair and maintain the new machinery. Computers are also being widely implemented throughout the industry, reducing employment levels of some mid-level managers and administrative support workers, but increasing the demand for workers with excellent technical skills. Taken as a whole, automation will continue to have a significant impact on workers in the industry as competition becomes even more intense in coming years.

Food processing firms will be able to use this new automation to better meet the changing demands of the American marketplace. As convenience becomes more important, consumers increasingly demand highly-processed foods such as pre-peeled and cut carrots and microwaveable soups or "ready-to-heat" dinners. Such a shift in consumption will contribute to the demand for food processing workers and will lead to the development of thousands of new processed foods. Domestic producers will also attempt to market these goods abroad as international trade continues to grow. The combination of growing export markets and shifting domestic consumption will help employment among food processing workers to rise slightly over the next decade and will lead to significant changes throughout the food processing industry.

Sources of Additional Information

For information on job opportunities in food processing, contact individual manufacturers, locals of the unions listed above, and State employment service offices. Informational brochures on occupations in the industry are available from:

> United Food and Commercial Workers International Union, 1775 K St. NW., Washington, DC 20006.

Detailed information on many occupations in food processing, including the following, appears in the 2000-2001 *Occupational Outlook Handbook*.

- Butchers and meat, poultry, and fish cutters
- Blue-collar worker supervisors
- Handlers, equipment cleaners, helpers, and laborers
- Industrial production managers
- Material moving equipment operators
- Truckdrivers
- Science and mathematics technicians

Motor Vehicle and Equipment Manufacturing

(SIC 371)

SIGNIFICANT POINTS

- Nearly one-third of all the industry's jobs are located in Michigan.

- Very large establishments dominate the industry.

- Average earnings are very high compared to other industries.

- Employment is expected to decline and is highly sensitive to cyclical swings in the economy.

Nature of the Industry

The motor vehicle is an intricate series of systems, subsystems, and components integrated into a final product. In the process of product design, no system is developed to exist as a separate entity; all systems must interface with others. Motor vehicle and equipment manufacturers, like the systems making up their products, are complex organizations that are constantly evolving to maximize efficiency and remain viable in a highly competitive market.

Motor vehicles play a central role in our society. Most Americans rely on them every day to get to work or school, to go shopping, or to visit family and friends. Businesses depend on motor vehicles to transport people and goods. The United States is the world's largest marketplace for motor vehicles due to the size and affluence of its population. In 1998, over 180 million motor vehicles—over 103 million passenger cars and 77 million trucks—were registered in the United States. The number of light trucks has shown especially steady growth since the mid- to late 1980's.

The motor vehicle and equipment manufacturing industry in the United States has become increasingly integrated into the international economy. American motor vehicle and equipment manufacturers have teamed up with some of their foreign competitors to design, produce, and distribute vehicles and parts, leading to a highly complex system of production. In a move to reduce distribution costs, manufacturers from the United States, Europe, and the Pacific Rim have located production plants in the countries where they plan to sell their vehicles. Foreign motor vehicle and parts makers with production sites in the United States are known as "transplants" and account for a growing share of production and employment in the United States.

Globalization of the industry has boosted competition among U.S. motor vehicle manufacturers, prompting innovations in product design and the manufacturing process. One result of these innovations is a proliferation of rapidly designed and produced new models aimed at niches in the market. Firms must be flexible to quickly implement new types of production. As the nature of the vehicle market in the United States continues to change, production techniques used by U.S. motor vehicle producers change along with it.

The cars we drive are only a small part of the story in motor vehicle and equipment manufacturing. In 1997, about 5,300 establishments manufactured motor vehicles and equipment, ranging from small parts plants with only a few workers to huge assembly plants that employ thousands.

Table 1 shows that nearly 7 out of 10 establishments manufactured motor vehicle parts and accessories—including axles, brakes, camshafts, defrosters, engines, frames, manifolds, radiators, steering mechanisms, transmissions, and windshield wiper systems. Other establishments specialized in assembling finished motor vehicles—passenger cars, sport utility vehicles, pickup trucks and vans, heavy-duty trucks, buses, and special purpose motor vehicles ranging from limousines to garbage trucks. Still others manufacture truck trailers, motor homes, and special bodies placed on separately purchased truck or bus chassis.

Motor vehicle and equipment manufacturers have a major influence on other industries in the economy. They are major consumers of steel, rubber, plastics, glass, and other basic materials, thus creating jobs in industries that produce those materials. The production of motor vehicles also spurs employment growth in other industries, including motor vehicle dealerships, automotive repair shops, gasoline service stations, highway construction companies, and public transit companies.

Table 1. Percent distribution of establishments in motor vehicle and equipment manufacturing by activity, 1997

Manufacturing activity	Establishments
Total	100.0
Motor vehicle parts and accessories	68.5
Truck and bus bodies	13.3
Motor vehicles and car bodies	9.1
Truck trailers	7.4
Motor homes	1.7

SOURCE: U.S. Department of Commerce, *County Business Patterns*, 1997

Working Conditions

In 1998, 37 percent of workers in the motor vehicle and equipment manufacturing industry worked, on average, more than 40 hours per week. Overtime is especially common during periods of peak demand. Most employees, however, typically work an 8-hour shift; either from 7:00 a.m. to 3:30 p.m. or 4:00 p.m. to 12:30 a.m., with two breaks per shift and a half-hour for meals. A third shift often is reserved for maintenance and cleanup.

Although working conditions have improved in recent years, some production workers are still subject to uncomfortable conditions. Heat, fumes, noise, and repetition are not uncommon in this industry. In addition, many workers come into contact with oil and grease and may have to lift and fit heavy objects. Employees also may operate powerful, high-speed machines that can be dangerous. Accidents and injuries usually are avoided when protective equipment and clothing are worn and safety practices are observed.

Newer plants are more automated and have safer, more comfortable conditions. For example, these plants may have ergonomic work areas, designed to accommodate the worker's physical size and eliminate unnecessary reaching and bending. Workers may function as part of a team, doing more than one job and thus reducing the repetitiveness of assembly line work.

Workers in the motor vehicle and equipment manufacturing industry experience higher rates of injury and illness than workers in most other industries. In 1997, cases of work-related injury and illness averaged 19.2 per 100 full-time workers in motor vehicle and equipment manufacturing, compared to 10.3 in all manufacturing industries and 7.1 in the entire private sector.

As in other industries, professional and managerial workers normally have clean, comfortable offices, and are not subject to the hazards of assembly line work. Improved ergonomics help clerical support workers avoid repetitive strain injuries, but employees using computer terminals for long periods may develop eye strain and fatigue.

Employment

Motor vehicle and equipment manufacturing was among the largest of the manufacturing industries in 1998, providing 990,000 jobs. The majority of jobs, 60 percent, are in firms that make motor vehicle parts and accessories. About 29 percent of workers in the industry are employed in firms assembling motor vehicles and car bodies, while 11 percent work in firms producing truck and bus bodies, truck trailers, and motor homes.

Although motor vehicle and equipment manufacturing jobs are scattered throughout the Nation, certain States account for the greatest number of jobs. Michigan, for example, accounts for nearly one-third of all jobs. Combined, Michigan, Ohio, and Indiana include over half of all the jobs in this industry. Other States that account for significant numbers of jobs are California, New York, Illinois, Missouri, North Carolina, Tennessee, and Wisconsin.

Employment is concentrated in a relatively small number of very large establishments. Over 51 percent of motor vehicle and equipment manufacturing jobs are in firms with over 1,000 workers (chart). Motor vehicle and car body manufacturing employment in particular is concentrated in large firms, whereas many motor vehicle parts and accessories jobs are found in small and medium-sized firms.

Compared to other industries, workers in motor vehicle and equipment manufacturing are somewhat older than average. In 1998, the median age was 40.8 years, compared to 39.1 years for all workers.

Occupations in the Industry

Most people know about the assembly line, a concept that originated in the motor vehicle manufacturing industry, but few are aware that production of a part or assembly of a motor vehicle is preceded by extensive design work, engineering, testing, and production planning. These tasks often require years and millions of dollars.

Executives and *managers* establish guidelines to follow in the design of motor vehicles by teams of experts in engineering, design, marketing, sales, finance, and production. From the earliest stages of planning and design, these specialists help assess whether the vehicle will satisfy consumer demand, meet safety and environmental regulations, and prove economically practical to make.

Using artistic talent, computers, and information on product use, marketing, materials, and production methods, *designers* create a design they hope will make the vehicle competitive in the marketplace. Sketches and computer-aided design techniques are used to create computer models of proposed vehicles. Workers may repeatedly modify and redesign the models until they meet the engineering, production, and marketing specifications. Designers working in parts and accessory production increasingly collaborate with manufacturers in the initial design stages to insure that motor vehicle parts and accessories are fully integrated into the design specifications for each vehicle.

Employing computer-aided drafting systems, *drafters* prepare drawings showing the technical specifications of motor vehicles and parts. Once the vehicle's design is established, a fiberglass model of the exterior and perhaps some interior features is made.

Engineers—the largest professional specialty occupation in the industry—play an integral role in all stages of motor vehicle manufacturing. They oversee the building and testing of the engine, transmission, brakes, suspension, and other mechanical and electrical components. Using computers and assorted models, instruments, and tools, engineers simulate various parts of the vehicle to determine whether they meet cost, safety, performance, and quality specifications. *Mechanical engineers* design improvements for engines, transmissions, and other working parts. *Electrical and electronics engineers* design the vehicle's electrical system, including the ignition system and accessories, and industrial robot control systems used to assemble the vehicle.

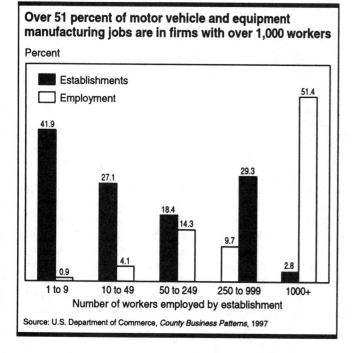

Over 51 percent of motor vehicle and equipment manufacturing jobs are in firms with over 1,000 workers

Percent

- ■ Establishments
- □ Employment

Number of workers employed by establishment	Establishments	Employment
1 to 9	41.9	0.9
10 to 49	27.1	4.1
50 to 249	18.4	14.3
250 to 999	9.7	29.3
1000+	2.8	51.4

Source: U.S. Department of Commerce, *County Business Patterns*, 1997

Engineering technicians are the largest technician occupation in the industry. They prepare specifications for materials, devise and run tests to ensure product quality, and study ways to improve manufacturing efficiency under the direction of engineers. For example, testing may reveal how metal parts perform under heat, cold, and stress, and whether emissions control equipment meets environmental standards. Finally, prototype vehicles incorporating all the components are built and tested on test tracks, road simulators, and in test chambers that can duplicate almost every driving condition, including crashes.

Before full production begins, engineers, technicians, scientists, designers, and others continue to modify the vehicle's interior and exterior design, and they determine the exact materials and parts to be used. *Industrial engineers* concentrate on plant layout, including the arrangement of assembly line stations, material moving equipment, work standards, and other production matters. *Computer programmers* write detailed instructions for computers, and *systems analysts* work with computer systems to improve manufacturing efficiency. When the many details are worked out, the machinery and tools required for assembly line production of the vehicle are set in place. *Purchasing agents and managers* buy the raw materials, machinery, tools, and other equipment required to produce the motor vehicles and parts.

Industrial production managers oversee *blue-collar worker supervisors*. These supervisors oversee skilled craft and repair workers, machine operators, and laborers, and coordinate all production activities—scheduling, staffing, equipment, quality control, and inventory control. A variety of manufacturing processes are used. For example, metal parts are welded; plastic and glass parts are molded and cut; seat cushions are sewn; and many parts are painted. Many manufacturing processes are highly automated; robots, computers, and programmable devices are an integral part of motor vehicle manufacturing. Throughout the manufacturing process, "statistical process control" (team work and quality control) is emphasized. From initial planning and design to final assembly, numerous tests and inspections insure that vehicles meet quality and safety standards.

Production workers and *operators, fabricators, and laborers* account for nearly 3 out of 4 motor vehicle and equipment manufacturing jobs (table 2). Formal educational requirements range from less than high school for unskilled laborers, to a high school diploma for semiskilled machine operators and skilled workers, to vocational school or community college training for some skilled jobs such as welders and cutters or mechanics and repairers. As the industry becomes more complex and the need for unskilled laborers decreases, employers are increasingly looking for candidates with at least a high school education.

Operators, fabricators, and *laborers* comprise over half of industry employment. These workers need physical stamina and coordination, and they must adapt to technological advances. *Assemblers* put together various parts to form subassemblies and then put the subassemblies together to build a complete motor vehicle. Some may perform other routine tasks such as mounting and inflating tires, adjusting brakes, and adding gas, oil, brake fluid, and coolant. *Grinders* and *polishers* work on metal, plastic, and glass parts. Although robots perform most of the welding, *welders* and *cutters* still are needed for some welding and for maintenance and repair duties.

Table 2. Wage and salary employment in motor vehicle and equipment manufacturing by occupation, 1998 and projected change, 1998-2008

(Employment in thousands)

Occupation	1998 Employment Number	1998 Employment Percent	1998-2008 Percent change
All occupations	990	100.0	-5.0
Operators, fabricators, and laborers	523	52.8	-4.9
Hand workers, including assemblers and fabricators	289	29.2	-4.9
Machine setters, operators, and tenders	183	18.5	-3.7
Helpers, laborers, and material movers, hand	31	3.2	-8.7
Transportation and material moving machine and vehicle operators	20	2.0	-10.6
Precision production, craft, and repair	203	20.5	-8.9
Mechanics, installers, and repairers	52	5.3	-5.8
Blue-collar worker supervisors	36	3.6	-13.9
Metal workers, precision	29	2.9	-6.4
Inspectors, testers, and graders	29	2.9	-17.1
Assemblers, precision	24	2.5	-7.3
Electricians	15	1.5	-4.4
Tool and die makers	13	1.3	-13.9
Professional specialty	93	9.4	8.5
Engineers	68	6.8	10.2
Executive, administrative, and managerial	67	6.7	-3.8
Management support occupations	26	2.6	-5.2
Industrial production managers	10	1.1	2.2
Administrative support, including clerical	56	5.7	-12.3
Material recording, scheduling, dispatching, and distributing occupations	25	2.6	-11.3
Technicians and related support	24	2.4	-9.0
Engineering technicians	22	2.2	-8.4
Marketing and sales	12	1.3	-4.4
Service	11	1.2	-4.4

Machine setters, operators, and tenders—who run various machines that produce the array of motor vehicle bodies and parts—account for nearly 1 out of 5 jobs. These workers set up and operate machines and make adjustments according to their instructions. In computer-controlled systems, they monitor computers that control the machine processes and may have little interaction with the machinery or materials. *Machine tool cutting and forming setters, operators, and tenders,* the largest occupation in this group, operate numerous machines from drill presses used to drill holes to lathe machines that cut materials such as rods or crankshafts. Some workers specialize in one type of machine; others operate more than one type.

Among other machine operators, *numerical-control machine-tool operators* use machine tools that can be programmed to manufacture parts of different dimensions automatically. *Welding machine operators* tend laser-beam and other welding machines that join together metal parts. *Painting* and *coating machine operators* paint surfaces of motor vehicles, and *furnace operators* tend heating equipment that performs such operations as baking fiberglass, drying painted products, and fusing glass or enamel to metal products. *Sewing machine operators* sew together pieces of material to form seat covers and other parts.

Keeping the plant running smoothly requires vehicle and mobile equipment operators and manual laborers. *Industrial truck* and *tractor operators* carry materials and equipment around and between factories, warehouses, and outdoor storage areas. *Truckdrivers* carry raw materials to plants, equipment and materials between plants, and finished motor vehicles to dealerships for sale to consumers. Among unskilled laborers, *freight, stock, and material movers* move materials to and from storage areas, loading docks, delivery vehicles, and containers. *Machine feeders* and *offbearers* feed materials into or remove materials from machines or equipment on the assembly line, and *hand packers* manually package or wrap materials. *Vehicle washers* and *equipment cleaners* clean vehicles and machinery using various cleaning equipment and agents.

Precision production, craft, and *repair workers*, the second largest group of production jobs, account for 1 out of 5 jobs in the motor vehicle and equipment manufacturing industry. These skilled workers set up, maintain, and repair equipment and assemble complex components, such as engines. *Electricians* service complex electrical equipment. *Plumbers* and *pipefitters* install and repair piping, valves, pumps, and compressors. *Industrial machinery mechanics* and *maintenance repairers* maintain machinery and equipment to prevent costly breakdowns and, when necessary, perform repairs. *Millwrights* install and move machinery and heavy equipment according to the factory's layout plans. *Vehicle* and *mobile equipment mechanics* repair bodies, engines, and other parts of motor vehicles, industrial trucks, and other mobile heavy equipment.

Precision assemblers assemble engines and perform other assembly work requiring great precision. Throughout the manufacturing process, *inspectors, testers,* and *graders* ensure that motor vehicles and parts meet quality standards. They inspect raw materials, check parts for defects, check the uniformity of subassemblies, and test drive vehicles. *Machinists* produce precision metal parts that are made in numbers too small to produce with automated machinery. *Tool and die makers* produce tools, dies, and special guiding and holding devices used in machines. *Sheet metal workers* cut, bend, and straighten sheet metal suitable for various motor vehicle parts.

Training and Advancement

Faced with technological advances and the continued need to cut costs, manufacturers increasingly emphasize continuing education and cross-train many workers, that is, they train workers to do more than one job. This has led to a change in the profile of the industry's workers. Standards for new hires are much higher now than in the past. Employers increasingly require a minimum of a high school diploma as the number of unskilled jobs declines. The average worker is expected to work with much less supervision than in the past and needs to be self-motivated. Because many plants now emphasize the team approach, employees interact more with co-workers and superiors to determine the best way to get the job done. Therefore, employers look for employees with good communication and math skills, as well as an aptitude for computers, problem solving and critical thinking. However, manual dexterity will continue to be necessary in many production jobs.

Opportunities for training and advancement vary considerably by occupation, plant size, and sector. Training programs in larger auto and light truck assembly plants usually are more extensive than those in smaller parts and accessories, truck trailer, and motor home factories. Production workers receive most of their training on the job or through more formal apprenticeship programs. Training normally takes from a few days to several months and may combine classroom with on-the-job training under the guidance of more experienced workers. Attaining the highest level of skill in some production jobs requires several years, however. Training includes courses in health and safety, teamwork, and quality control. With advanced training and experience, production workers can advance to inspector or more skilled production, craft, or repair jobs.

Skilled precision production workers—such as tool and die makers, millwrights, machinists, pipefitters, and electricians—are normally hired on the basis of previous experience and, in some cases, a competitive examination. Alternatively, the company may train inexperienced workers in apprenticeship programs that last up to 5 years and combine on-the-job training with classroom instruction. Typical courses include mechanical drawing, tool designing and programming, blueprint reading, shop mathematics, hydraulics, and electronics. Training also includes courses on health and safety, teamwork, quality control, computers, and diagnostic equipment. The most highly motivated, experienced workers can advance to blue-collar worker supervisor.

Motor vehicle manufacturers provide training opportunities to all workers, regardless of educational background. Manufacturers offer classes themselves and pay tuition for workers who enroll in colleges, trade schools, or technical institutes. Workers sometimes can get college credit for training received on the job. Company training ranges from courses in communication skills to computer science. Formal educational opportunities range from courses in English and basic mathematics to work-study programs leading to college and graduate degrees in engineering, management, and other fields.

Earnings

Average weekly earnings of production or non-supervisory workers in the motor vehicle and equipment manufacturing industry are relatively high. In 1998, workers in the industry earned $780 per week, compared to $563 for all manufacturing industries, and $442 for the entire private sector. At $933 per week, earnings of production workers in establishments that manufacture complete motor vehicles and car bodies were among the highest in the Nation. Workers in establishments that make motor vehicle parts and accessories averaged $732 weekly; those in truck and bus body manufacturing earned $681; while truck trailer manufacturing workers earned $481. Earnings in selected occupations in motor vehicle and equipment manufacturing appear in table 3.

Table 3. Median hourly earnings of the largest occupations in motor vehicle and equipment manufacturing, 1997

Occupation	Motor vehicle manufacturing	All industries
Industrial engineers, except safety	$28.33	$24.18
Electricians	21.45	16.54
Tool and die makers	20.87	17.37
First line supervisors and managers/ supervisors-production and operating workers	20.13	16.62
Machinery maintenance mechanics	19.81	14.72
Machine tool cutting operators and tenders, metal and plastic	18.87	11.32
Production inspectors, testers, graders, sorters, samplers, and weighers	17.83	10.15
Machine builders and other precision machine assemblers	16.56	13.47
Assemblers and fabricators, except machine, electrical, electronic, and precision	14.10	9.25
Welders and cutters	11.88	11.90

These hourly earnings may increase during overtime or special shifts. Workers generally are paid 1 1/2 times their normal wage rate for working more than 8 hours a day, 40 hours a week, or for working on Saturdays. They may receive double their normal wage rate for working on Sundays and holidays. The largest manufacturers and suppliers often offer other benefits including paid vacations and holidays; life, accident, and health insurance; education allowances; non-wage cash payment plans, such as performance and profit-sharing bonuses; and pension plans. Some laid-off workers in the motor vehicle and equipment manufacturing industry have access to supplemental unemployment benefits, which can provide them with nearly full pay and benefits for up to 3 years, depending on the worker's seniority.

In 1998, 36.9 percent of workers in motor vehicle and equipment production were union members or were covered by union contracts, compared to 15.4 percent of workers throughout private industry. Unionization rates are higher in motor vehicle production than in parts and accessories producers. The primary union in the industry is the United Automobile, Aerospace, and Agricultural Implement Workers of America, also known as the United Auto Workers (UAW). Nearly all production workers in motor vehicle assembly plants and most in motor vehicle parts plants are covered by collective bargaining agreements negotiated by the UAW. Other unions—including the International Association of Machinists and Aerospace Workers of America, the United Steelworkers of America, and the International Brotherhood of Electrical Workers—cover certain plant locations or specified trades in the industry.

Outlook

Employment in the motor vehicle and equipment manufacturing industry is expected to decline 5 percent over the 1998-2008 period. The need to replace workers who transfer to jobs in other industries or retire will be the only source of job openings. However, a substantial number of job openings is expected from this source because over one-third of the motor vehicle manufacturing workforce is over 44 years old and positioned to retire in the near future.

Not all the workers who transfer to other occupations or retire will be replaced. Jobs will be lost due to downsizing and productivity increases. The growing intensity of international and domestic competition has increased cost pressures on manufacturers. In response, they have sought to improve productivity and quality through the application of high technology production techniques, including robots, computers, programmable equipment, and other production techniques. Increasing productivity should more than offset the increasing demand for motor vehicles, resulting in a net loss of jobs. In fact, output in the motor vehicle and equipment manufacturing industry is projected to increase, while employment is expected to decline.

Growth in demand for motor vehicles could be limited by a number of factors. A slowdown in the growth of the driving age population, as the smaller post-baby-boom generation comes of age may slow growth in demand for cars and trucks. Competition from foreign motor vehicle and parts producers will continue to control much of the U.S. market. Other factors that may limit growth of domestic motor vehicle production include improvements in vehicle quality and durability, which extend longevity and more stringent safety and environmental regulations, which increase the cost of producing and operating motor vehicles.

Employment in motor vehicle and equipment manufacturing is highly sensitive to cyclical swings in the economy. Over the 1972-98 period, employment peaked at over 1 million in 1978 and plunged to under 700,000 in 1982, a recession year. A 10-percent change in employment from one year to the next is not unusual, and employment has changed as much as 20 percent in one year (chart). During periods of economic prosperity, consumers are more willing and able to purchase expensive goods such as motor vehicles, which may require large down payments and extended loan payments. During recessions, however, consumers are more likely to delay such purchases. Motor vehicle manufacturers respond to these changes in demand by hiring or laying off workers. As it has become more critical to adopt cost-saving measures, the industry is increasingly turning to contract employees because it is less costly to hire and lay off such workers, and it serves as a screening mechanism as jobs become more complex.

Overall industry employment is expected to decline by 50,000 jobs over the 1998-2008 period. Expanding factory automation, robotics, efficiency gains, and the need to cut costs is driving the downward trend. The movement towards efficiency and automation will force an employment decline in hand worker, precision assembler, and machine setter occupations. Employment of service workers, such as custodians, is expected to continue its decline as firms employ service contractors to perform these duties. Administrative support and clerical workers will absorb some of the decline in industry employment, losing 7,000 jobs to expanding office and warehouse automation. Employment in marketing and sales is also expected to decline.

Automation and continued global competition, however, are expected to produce growth for engineers, industrial production managers, and computer specialists. These workers will increasingly be relied upon for further innovation in reducing costs and enhancing competitive advantage.

73

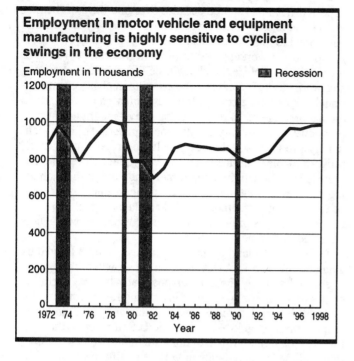

Employment in motor vehicle and equipment manufacturing is highly sensitive to cyclical swings in the economy

Employment in Thousands   ■ Recession

manufacturing firms, and locals of the unions mentioned above.

Detailed information on most occupations in this industry, including the following, appears in the 2000-01 *Occupational Outlook Handbook*.

- Blue-collar worker supervisors
- Designers
- Drafters
- Electricians
- Engineers
- Engineering technicians
- Handlers, equipment cleaners, helpers, and laborers
- Industrial machinery repairers
- Industrial production managers
- Inspectors, testers, and graders
- Machinists and numerical tool and process control programmers
- Maintenance mechanics, general utility
- Material moving equipment operators
- Material recording, scheduling, dispatching, and distributing occupations
- Mechanical engineers
- Metalworking and plastics-working machine operators
- Millwrights
- Painting and coating machine operators
- Precision assemblers
- Tool and die makers
- Welders, cutters, and welding machine operators

Sources of Additional Information

Information on employment and training opportunities in the motor vehicle and equipment manufacturing industry is available from local offices of the State employment service, employment offices of motor vehicle and equipment

Printing and Publishing

(SIC 27)

SIGNIFICANT POINTS

- Over 22 percent of the jobs in the industry were in managerial and professional occupations, a higher proportion than any other manufacturing industry.

- Most firms are small, employing fewer than 10 people.

- Computerization is changing or eliminating occupations.

Nature of the Industry

The printing and publishing industry produces products ranging from newspapers, magazines, and books to brochures, labels, newsletters, postcards, memo pads, business order forms, checks, maps, and even T-shirts.

This industry includes a number of segments (table 1). Commercial printing establishments, which print newspaper inserts, catalogs, pamphlets, and advertisements, make up the largest segment of the industry, accounting for 40 percent of employment and 55 percent of total establishments. Newspapers are the next largest sector, with 26 percent of industry employment. The greeting card segment is the smallest, accounting for only 1.4 percent of employment and 0.2 percent of total establishments.

Printing and publishing is a large industry composed of many shops, varying in size. Almost 7 of every 10 printing shops comprising the industry employ 10 or fewer workers (chart). These small printing shops are often referred to as "job shops," because what they print is determined by the jobs customers need to have printed.

Table 1. Establishments and wage and salary employment in printing and publishing by detailed industry, 1997

	Establishments	Employment
Total	62,577	1,501,714
Printing		
Commercial printing	34,223	597,828
Blankbooks and bookbinding..................	1,712	64,900
Book printing	776	52,709
Manifold business forms	924	44,019
Typesetting	2,057	26,114
Platemaking services	1,301	25,203
Publishing		
Newspapers...	8,749	393,590
Periodicals	6,245	119,607
Book publishing	2,954	88,881
Miscellaneous publishing	3,358	67,365
Greeting cards	156	21,422

SOURCE: U.S. Department of Commerce, *County Business Patterns*, 1997

There are five printing methods that use plates or some other form of image carrier: lithography, letterpress, flexography, gravure, and screen printing. Plateless or nonimpact processes such as electronic, electrostatic, or inkjet printing, are mainly used for copying, duplicating, and specialty printing, usually in quick or in-house print shops.

Lithography, which uses the basic principle that water repels oil, remains the dominant printing process in the industry, accounting for most of it. Lithography lends itself to computer composition and the economical use of color, accounting for its dominance. In the future, flexography and gravure are expected to be more widely used. Flexography produces vibrant colors with little ruboff, qualities valued for newspapers, directories, and books, which are its biggest markets. Gravure's high quality reproduction, flexible pagination and formats, and consistent print quality has won it a significant share of packaging and product printing and a growing share of periodical printing. In response to environmental concerns, printers increasingly use alcohol-free solutions, water-based inks, and recycled paper.

The printing industry, like many other industries, continues undergoing technological change, as computers and technology alter the manner in which work is performed. Many of the processes that were once done by hand are becoming more automated. Technology's influence can be seen in all three stages of printing: *prepress*, preparation of materials for printing; *press*, the actual printing process; and *post-press* or *finishing*, the folding, binding, and trimming of printed sheets into final form. The most notable changes are occurring in the prepress stage. Instead of cutting and pasting articles by hand, it is now common to produce an entire publication on a computer, complete with artwork and graphics. Columns can be displayed and arranged on the computer screen exactly as they will appear in print, and then printed. Nearly all prepress work is expected to be computerized by 2008, and workers will need more training in electronics, computers, and mathematics.

Many segments of the publishing industry produce their products electronically. For example, many periodicals, books, and promotional materials can be found on the Internet, on CD-ROM, and on audio and video tapes. This expansion into nonprint media is expected to continue as the Internet heralds a new era in the printing and publishing industry. Individuals are now designing their own work on the World Wide Web and, consequently, have a reader base of millions. As a result, the market for the design and development of Internet pages and publications is growing significantly.

Working Conditions

The average nonsupervisory worker in the printing industry worked approximately 38.3 hours per week in 1998, compared to 41.7 hours per week across all manufacturing industries. Workers in the industry generally put in an 8-hour day, but overtime often is required to meet publication deadlines. Some

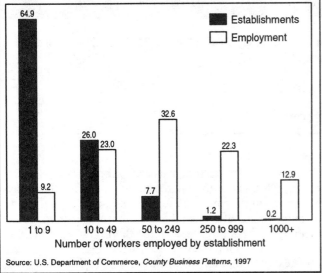

Nearly two-thirds of establishments in printing and publishing employ fewer than 10 workers

Percent

Legend:
- Establishments (filled)
- Employment (open)

Number of workers employed by establishment	Establishments	Employment
1 to 9	64.9	9.2
10 to 49	26.0	23.0
50 to 249	7.7	32.6
250 to 999	1.2	22.3
1000+	0.2	12.9

Source: U.S. Department of Commerce, *County Business Patterns*, 1997

employees, particularly those employed by newspapers, work nights, weekends, and holidays. Larger companies tend to have shift work. There is a fair amount of flexibility with shift schedules and overtime, which is largely based on seniority.

Working conditions vary by occupation. For example, press operators work in noisy environments and often wear ear protectors. On the other hand, typesetters and compositors usually work in quiet, clean, air-conditioned offices. Most printing work involves dealing with fine detail, which can be tiring both mentally and physically. Fortunately, with the advanced technology in machinery, there is not as much strain on the eyes as in the past.

Even with more safety enhanced machinery, some workers are still subject to occupational hazards. Platemakers, for example, may work with toxic chemicals that can cause skin irritations, and press operators work with rapidly moving machinery that can cause injuries. In 1997, work-related injuries and illnesses were 5.7 per 100 full-time workers, much lower than the 10.3 percent rate for manufacturing as a whole. Blankbooks, such as ledgers and notebooks, and bookbinding had the highest incidence of injury and illness, with 7.7 cases per 100 full-time employees. In recent years, however, the working environment has become less hazardous as the industry has become more automated. Also, companies are using fewer chemicals and solutions than in the past and are experiencing fewer equipment-related accidents.

Employment

In 1998, the printing and publishing industry had about 1.6 million wage and salary jobs in addition to 125,000 self-employed workers, ranking it among the largest manufacturing industries. Nearly two-thirds of wage and salary jobs were in establishments emloying less than 10 workers (chart); nearly 70 percent were in the two largest sectors: commercial printing and newspapers (table 1). Printing plants are widely dispersed throughout the country; however, more specialized types of printing tend to be regionally concentrated. For example, financial printing is concentrated in New York City.

Occupations in the Industry

Printing and publishing occupations range from writers, editors, and sales workers to specialized production occupations rarely found in other industries (table 2). The printing sectors that perform press preparation or printing and binding work, such as commercial printing plants, blankbook and bookbinding shops, and printing trade services account for the majority of specialized printing occupations.

Specialized printing occupations comprise 25 percent of industry employment and are located in the prepress, press, and binding or post-press stages of printing. Almost all jobs in the printing industry require at least a high school education. Additional training and cross training is becoming increasingly necessary as the industry continues to automate. It often is beneficial to receive training in mathematics, electronics, and computers.

Prepress printing workers—including *typesetting* and *composing machine operators*, and *photoengraving* and *lithographic machine operators*—prepare material for printing presses. Included among their tasks are composing text, designing page layout, photographing text and pictures, and making printing plates. *Precision compositors* and *typesetters* set up and arrange type by hand or by computer into a galley for printing. *Job printers* set type according to copy, read proof copy for errors and clarity, and correct mistakes. *Desktop publishing specialists*, using a computer screen, call up type and art elements to arrange them into a completed page. The page is then transmitted into film or directly into plates for production.

Camera operators—who are classified as line camera operators, halftone operators, or color separation photographers—start the process of making a lithographic plate by photographing and developing negatives of the material to be printed. *Scanner operators* employ electronic or computerized scanning equipment to produce and screen film separations of photographs or art to use in lithographic printing plates. Operators review all work and adjust the equipment if they need to make corrections to the original. *Lithographic dot etchers* retouch negatives by sharpening or reshaping the images on the negatives. They work by hand, using chemicals, dyes, and special tools. *Film strippers* cut the film to required size and arrange and tape the pieces of negatives onto "flats," or layout sheets, used to make press plates. *Platemakers* produce printing plates by exposing sensitized metal sheets to special light through a photographic negative. Some platemakers operate machines that process the plates automatically. In letterpress and gravure printing, *photoengravers* photograph copy, develop negatives, and prepare photosensitized metal plates for use.

When the material is ready, *printing press operators* install and adjust the printing plate, mix fountain solution, adjust pressure, ink the presses, load paper, and adjust the presses to paper size. Operators must also correct any problems that might occur during a press run.

Technology is rapidly changing the nature of many traditional press and prepress occupations. Manual film handling is quickly becoming the exception rather than the rule. Typesetters, platemakers, paste up workers, and film strippers are being replaced with workers who have mastered desktop publishing and the electronic aspects of the various printing processes. Where a camera negative was used in the past to produce plates of images, those images are increasingly being recorded by computerized photographic devices.

Table 2. Employment of wage and salary workers in printing and publishing by occupation, 1998 and projected change, 1998-2008

(Employment in thousands)

Occupation	1998 Employment Number	1998 Employment Percent	1998-2008 Percent change
All occupations	1,565	100.0	-1.3
Operators, fabricators, and laborers ...	497	31.8	-2.7
Helpers, laborers, and material movers, hand	107	6.8	-0.4
Printing press machine setters, operators and tenders	80	5.1	3.1
Bindery machine operators and set-up operators	72	4.6	6.0
Offset lithographic press operators ...	57	3.6	-16.0
Truck drivers	42	2.7	-5.7
Hand workers, including assemblers and fabricators	32	2.0	2.2
Typesetting and composing machine operators and tenders	13	0.8	-60.1
Letterpress operators	10	0.6	-18.1
Administrative support, including clerical	318	20.3	-8.4
Office clerks, general	35	2.2	2.9
Bookkeeping, accounting, and auditing clerks	29	1.8	-17.4
Office and administrative support supervisors and managers	23	1.5	.4
Shipping, receiving, and traffic clerks..	21	1.4	-3.0
Secretaries	20	1.3	-17.7
Order clerks	19	1.2	-6.3
Adjustment clerks	17	1.1	13.0
Data entry keyers	16	1.0	-18.2
Receptionists and information clerks..	16	1.0	.9
Duplicating, mail, and other office machine operators	16	1.0	-12.6
Precision production, craft, and repair	209	13.3	-1.3
Blue collar worker supervisors	44	2.8	1.8
Desktop publishing specialists	25	1.6	71.0
Film strippers, printing	23	1.4	-33.1
Job printers	16	1.0	3.8
Platemakers	14	0.9	-5.4
Paste-up workers	9	0.6	-51.3
Compositors and typesetters, precision	8	0.5	-40.4
Camera operators	7	0.5	-34.7
Bookbinders	5	0.4	-16.1
Professional specialty	192	12.3	13.4
Writers and editors	70	4.5	19.3
News analysts, reporters and correspondents	38	2.4	-7.1
Artists and commercial artists	32	2.0	22.8
Computer systems analysts, engineers, and specialists	16	1.0	4.1
Marketing and sales	165	10.6	.2
All other sales and related workers ..	141	9.0	9.2
Marketing and sales worker supervisors	21	1.4	-.1
Executive, managerial, and administrative	157	10.1	.2
General managers and top executives	56	3.6	-.5
Management support occupations	32	2.1	3.4
Marketing, advertising, and public relations managers......................	21	1.4	2.3
All other occupations	26	1.6	-13.8

Pre-flight technicians examine and edit the work of desktop publishers. They ensure that the design, format, settings, quality and all other aspects of the automated desktop work are acceptable, and the finished product is completed according to the client's specifications before it is delivered.

During the binding or post-press stage, the printed sheets are transformed into products such as books, catalogs, magazines, or directories. *Bookbinders* assemble books from large, flat, printed sheets of paper. They cut, saw, and glue parts to bind new books and perform other finishing operations, such as decorating and lettering, often using hand tools.

A small number of bookbinders work in hand binderies. These highly skilled workers design original or special bindings for publications with limited editions, or restore and rebind rare books. In many shops, *bindery workers* do much of the work. They fasten sheets or signatures together using a machine stapler and feed signatures into various machines for stitching, folding, or gluing.

In addition to these specialized printing occupations, administrative support workers, including clerical personnel, marketing and sales workers, professional specialty occupations, and managers are also employed in significant numbers in the printing and publishing industry. One occupation becoming more common is customer service representative, who tracks the various processes of production and acts as liaison between clients and technicians. The representative ensures the customer's satisfaction with the timely delivery of a high quality product.

Establishments engaged in publishing newspapers, periodicals, books, and other miscellaneous items employ the greatest numbers of professional specialty occupations, particularly reporters, writers, editors, artists, and marketing and sales occupations These positions usually require a college education.

News analysts, reporters, and correspondents gather information and prepare stories that inform us about local, State, National, and international events. They collect and analyze facts about events by interview, investigation, or observation and write stories for newspapers and magazines. *Writers* develop fiction and nonfiction for books, magazines, trade journals, and newspapers. *Editors* supervise writers and select, plan, and prepare the contents of books, magazines, or newspapers. *Graphic artists* use a variety of print and film media to create and execute art that meets a client's needs. They increasingly use computers to lay out and test various designs, patterns, and colors before printing a final design. Finally, *marketing and sales workers* promote and sell a printer's or publisher's product.

Training and Advancement
Workers enter the industry with various educational backgrounds. In general, job applicants must be high school graduates with mathematical, verbal, and written communication skills, and be computer literate.

Helpers generally have a high school or vocational school background, and management trainees may have a college background. Formal graphic arts programs, offered by community and junior colleges and some 4-year colleges, provide an introduction to the industry. Training in desktop publishing is particularly useful. Bachelor's degree programs in graphic arts prepare persons who may want to enter management, and 2-year programs provide technical skills. A bachelor's degree in journalism, communications, or English provides a good background for those wishing to become reporters or writers. Experience on school newspapers and internships with news organizations are also beneficial.

As the industry continues to become more computerized, most workers will need a working knowledge of computers. Courses in electronics and computers are beneficial for anyone entering the industry, and some employers will offer tuition assistance or continuing education classes.

In the past, apprenticeships were quite common for specialized printing occupations. Now, workers are usually trained informally on the job. Hand bookbinders are one exception. These workers usually need a 4-year apprenticeship to learn the craft of restoring rare books and producing valuable collector items.

The length of on-the-job training needed to learn skills varies by occupation, and shop. For example, press operators begin as helpers and advance to press operators after years of training. Bindery workers begin by doing simple tasks such as moving paper from cutting machines to folding machines. Workers learn how to operate more complicated machinery within a few months. Training often is given under the close supervision of an experienced or senior employee. Through experience and training, workers may advance to more responsible positions. Workers usually begin as helpers, advance to skilled craft jobs, and may eventually be promoted to supervisor. Reporters and writers may advance to editors or supervising reporters.

Opportunities for advancement depend on the specific plant or shop. Technological changes will continue to introduce new types of computerized equipment or dictate new work procedures, and retraining will be essential to careers in printing and publishing.

Earnings

In 1998, average weekly earnings for production workers in the printing and publishing industry were $515, compared to $563 for all production workers in manufacturing. As shown in table 3, weekly wages in the printing and publishing industry ranged from $414 in blankbooks and bookbinding, to $671 in printing trade services.

The principal union in this industry is the Graphic Communications International Union. About 9.8 percent of employees are union members or are covered by a union contract, compared to 15.4 percent of workers throughout the economy, but this proportion varies greatly from city to city.

Outlook

Automation and shifting consumer demand are significantly affecting the printing and publishing industry. Employment is projected to decline 1 percent over the 1998 to 2008 period, compared to the 15 percent growth projected for the economy as a whole. This decline reflects competition from nonprint media, such as the Internet, and increasing use of nontraditional printing technologies. Nonetheless, predictions that computers will one day turn us into a paperless society have not yet come true. The printing industry will continue to supply products for education, business, and leisure for a long time to come. Although technological innovation and automation, mergers and acquisitions of small to medium-size printing firms, and partnering services offered among printing firms will result in fewer jobs, certain sectors of the industry will experience growth.

Table 3. Median hourly earnings of the largest occupations in printing and publishing, 1997

Occupation	Printing and publishing	All industries
General managers and top executives ...	$30.19	$26.05
Sales representatives, except retail and scientific and related products and services	17.38	16.54
Writers and editors	15.07	15.69
Offset lithographic press setters and set-up operators	14.55	14.37
Sales agents, advertising	13.24	14.16
Printing press machine operators and tenders	12.56	12.09
Reporters and correspondents	10.94	11.23
Bindery machine operators and tenders	9.69	9.02
Machine feeders and offbearers	8.80	8.69
Hand packers and packagers	7.37	6.90

Employment in printing trade services is expected to decline because more companies are preparing printing and post-press in-house. Employment in newspapers is also expected to decline as more people choose to receive their news from nonprint sources. Newspapers will also continue to face strong competition for advertising dollars from direct-mail advertising, which targets specific types of consumers in a more cost-effective manner. Many newspapers are responding by featuring specialized products and services for niche markets.

Slow employment growth is expected in periodicals, spurred by increasing interest in professional, scientific, and technical journals, as well as special interest publications, such as health and fitness magazines. Similarly, employment in book publishing and greeting cards should also see slow growth, spurred by an increasing and aging population.

Employment in miscellaneous publishing is expected to grow slowly. The popularity of catalogs and mail order shopping fuel this sector. However, increased paper costs, consumer preferences, and the growth of on-line catalogs will result in fewer jobs than in years past.

Employment growth will differ among the various occupations in the printing and publishing industry, largely due to technological advances. Processes currently performed manually will be automated in the future, causing a shift from craft occupations to related occupations that perform the same function using electronic equipment. For example, employment of desktop publishing specialists is expected to increase much faster than average as the elements of print production, including layout, design, and printing, are increasingly performed electronically. In contrast, demand for workers who perform these tasks manually, including paste-up workers, photoengravers, camera operators, film strippers, and platemakers, is expected to decline.

With increasing use of computers that do typesetting and composing electronically, the number of typesetting and composing machine operators will decline sharply. Declines among precision typesetters and compositors will occur in the newspaper industry, because news analysts and editors can perform these tasks themselves. Of other prepress occupations, job printers, desktop publishers, and other printing workers who perform a variety of printing tasks, are expected to experience growth.

Employment of press operators is expected to decline. Employment of offset press operators and letterpress operators should decrease rapidly. Employment of bookbinders will decline in response to the growth of electronic printing; however, bindery machine operators will increase.

As the industry continues to modernize, a greater diversity of workers will be needed, including engineers, marketing specialists, graphic artists, and computer specialists. New equipment will require workers to update their skills to remain competitive in the job market. For example, paste-up workers will have to learn how to lay out pages using a computer. The concepts and principles behind page layout and design are the same, but the workers will have to learn how to perform their work using different tools. Employment of marketing and sales workers in the printing and publishing industry is expected to experience little to no growth as a result of increased competition from nonprint media and advances in printing technologies.

Sources of Additional Information

Information on apprenticeships and other training opportunities may be obtained from local employers such as newspapers and printing shops, local offices of the Graphic Communications International Union, local affiliates of the Printing Industries of America, or local offices of the State employment service.

For general information on careers and training programs in printing, contact:

➤ Education Council of the Graphic Arts Industry, 1899 Preston White Dr., Reston, VA 20191.
   Internet: **http://www.npes.org**
➤ The Graphic Arts Technical Foundation, 200 Deer Run Rd., Sewickley, PA 15143.
   Internet: **http://www.gatf.org**
➤ Graphic Communications International Union, 1900 L St. NW., Washington, DC 20036.
   Internet: **http://www.gciu.org**
➤ National Association of Printers and Lithographers, 75 W. Century Rd., Paramus, NJ 07652.
   Internet: **http://www.napl.org**
➤ Printing Industries of America, Inc., 100 Dangerfield Rd., Alexandria, VA 22314.
   Internet: **http://www.printing.org**

Information on most occupations in the printing and publishing industry, including the following, may be found in the 2000-01 *Occupational Outlook Handbook*:

- Artists and commercial artists
- Bindery workers
- News analysts, reporters, and correspondents
- Prepress workers
- Printing press operators
- Writers and editors, including technical writers

Steel Manufacturing

SIGNIFICANT POINTS

● Employment is expected to continue to decline.

● Much steel production has shifted to the electric arc furnace, changing many jobs and enhancing opportunities for individuals with technical skills and training.

Nature of the Industry

Few industries in the United States have changed as rapidly in recent years as the steel industry. As a result of new investment in equipment and worker training, this industry has gone from a seemingly moribund one, to one that leads the world in worker productivity and is the low cost producer for some types of steel. The U.S. steel industry still faces stiff competition, and employment is expected to continue to decline; but it is now in a more promising position to meet these challenges.

With new investments have come fundamental changes in the nature of this industry. The most significant change in the American steel industry is the development of the electric arc furnace (EAF), sometimes called the "minimill," which converts scrap metal from many sources—such as bridges, refrigerators, and automobiles—to steel. The term "minimill" originated from the relatively smaller size of these mills when they first appeared, compared with traditional integrated mills. Today, many EAF's or minimills are actually larger than integrated mills producing steel from raw materials. The smaller capital outlay required to start and operate an EAF has helped drive its growth. Moreover, scrap metal is found in all parts of the country, so EAF's are not tied as closely to raw material deposits as integrated mills and can locate closer to consumers. EAF's now comprise almost half of American steel production and their share is expected to continue to grow in coming years.

The growth of EAF's comes partly at the expense of integrated mills. Integrated mills produce iron in blast furnaces, from coal, iron ore, and limestone. The iron is then refined into steel, most commonly in basic oxygen furnaces. The steel produced by integrated mills generally is considered to be of higher quality than steel from EAF's, but because more steps are involved in the production process, it also is more costly. The initial step in the integrated mill process is to prepare coal for use in a blast furnace by converting it to coke. Coal is heated in coke ovens to remove impurities and to reduce it to nearly pure carbon. Because coke production is considered to be one of the dirtiest steps in production, many firms are looking for substitutes for coke in steelmaking.

At the other end of the steel manufacturing process, semifinished steel from either EAF's or integrated mills is converted into finished products. Some of the goods produced in finishing mills are steel wire, pipe, bars, rods, and sheets. Products also may be coated with chemicals, paints, or other metals that give the steel desired characteristics for various industries and consumers. Also involved in steel manufacturing are firms that produce alloys, by adding materials like silicon and manganese to the steel. Varying the amounts of carbon and other elements contained in the final product can produce thousands of different types of steel, each with specific properties suited for a particular use.

Increasing competition from abroad and in the domestic market has caused integrated and EAF producers to modernize. For workers, this often has meant learning new skills to operate sophisticated equipment. Competition also has resulted in increasing specialization of steel production, as various producers attempt to capture different niches in the market. With these changes has come a growing emphasis on flexibility and adaptability for both workers and equipment. As international and domestic competition mounts for U.S. steel producers, the nature of the industry is expected to continue to change in these directions.

Working Conditions

Steel mills evoke images of strenuous, hot, and potentially dangerous work. While many dangerous and difficult jobs remain in the steel industry, modern equipment and facilities have helped to change this. The most strenuous tasks were among the first to be automated. For example, computer-controlled machinery helps to monitor and move iron and steel through the production processes, reducing the need for heavy labor. In some cases, workers now monitor and control the equipment from air-conditioned rooms.

Nevertheless, large machinery and molten metal can be hazardous, unless safety procedures are observed. Hard hats, safety shoes, protective glasses, ear plugs, and protective clothing are required in most production areas.

The expense of plant and machinery and significant production startup costs force most mills to operate around the clock. Workers averaged 44.6 hours per week in 1998, and only about 1.7 percent of workers are employed part time. Night and weekend shifts are common, as is overtime work during peak production periods. In 1998, 33.7 percent of all steel workers put in overtime.

Cases of occupational injury and illness in the industry were 12.0 per 100 full-time workers in 1997, significantly higher than the 7.1 cases per 100 workers for the entire private sector and also higher than the 10.3 cases per 100 for all manufacturing. The highest injury rate in the steel industry—16.3— was found in steel pipes and tubes.

Employment

Employment in the steel industry declined to about 232,000 wage and salary jobs in 1998, less than half its 1980 level. The rate of decline, however, has slowed in recent years. The steel industry traditionally has been located in the eastern and midwestern regions of the country, where iron ore, coal, or one of the other natural resources required for steel are found. Even today, about 50 percent of all steelworkers are employed in Pennsylvania, Ohio, and Indiana. The growth of EAF's, though, has allowed steel-making to spread to virtually all parts of the country. Large firms employ most workers in the steel industry. Over 9 out of 10 work in establishments employing at least 50 workers, and almost half work in establishments employing 1,000 or more persons (chart 1).

Occupations in the Industry

Opportunities exist in a variety of occupations, but the majority of workers—79 percent—are employed in operator, fabricator, and laborer and precision production, craft, and repair occupations (table 1). About 17 percent work in managerial, professional, and administrative support occupations.

At an integrated steel mill, production begins when *material moving equipment operators* load iron ore, coke, and limestone into the top of a blast furnace. As the materials are heated, a chemical reaction frees the iron from other elements in the ore. *Blowers* direct the overall operation of the blast furnace. *Blowers* are responsible for the quality and quantity of the iron produced and for supervising *keepers* and their helpers. *Keepers* operate the equipment used to tap the liquid iron and to remove impurities from the furnace. The molten iron then is ready to be transformed into steel.

Generally, either a basic oxygen or an electric arc furnace is used to make steel. Although the steel making procedure varies with the type of furnace used, the jobs associated with the various processes are similar. *Melters* supervise *furnace operators* and their assistants who control the furnace. *Melters* gather information on the characteristics of the raw materials they will use and the type and quality of steel they are expected to produce. They direct the loading of the furnace with raw materials and supervise the taking of samples, to insure that the steel has the desired qualities. *Melters* also coordinate the loading and melting of raw materials with the steel molding or casting operation to avoid delays in production.

Furnace operators use controls to tilt the furnace to receive the raw materials. Once they have righted the furnace, *furnace operators* use levers and buttons to control the flow of oxygen and other materials into the furnace. During the production process, assistants routinely take samples to be analyzed. Based on this analysis, *operators* determine how much longer they must process the steel or what materials they must add to meet specifications. *Operators* also pay close attention to conditions within the furnace and correct any problems that arise during the production process.

Traditionally, liquid steel was moved from the furnaces into a ladle from which it was poured into ingots. Steel producers now use a process known as "continuous casting" almost exclusively. Continuous casting allows firms to produce steel ready for the next step in processing directly from liquid steel, thus eliminating many of the steps involved in pouring and rolling ingots. *Molding* and *casting machine operators* tend machines that release the molten steel from the ladle into water-cooled molds at a controlled rate. Molded steel is then cut to desired lengths, as it emerges from the rolls. During this process, operators monitor the flow of raw steel and the supply of water to the mold.

The "rolling" method shapes most steel processed in steel mills. In this method, hot steel is squeezed between two cylinders or "rollers," which flatten or shape the steel. *Heaters* monitor equipment that tells when the ingot is uniformly heated to the required temperature. *Rollers* operate equipment that rolls the steel ingots into semifinished product; the quality of the product and the speed at which the ingot is rolled depend on the roller's skills. *Manipulator operators* tend the machinery, which controls the position of the ingot on the roller. Placing the ingot and positioning the rollers are very important, for they control the product's final shape. Improperly adjusted equipment may damage the rollers or gears.

Millwrights are employed to install and maintain much of the sophisticated machinery in steel mills. As the technology becomes more advanced, they work more closely with *electricians*, who help repair and install electrical equipment like computer controls for machine tools.

With more sophisticated technology and demands for specialized products, *scientists*, *engineers*, and *technicians* have a significant role in the steel industry. For example, *engineers* test batches of steel before they are cast, to check for the desired composition. They also may develop new specialized metals as well as new equipment. As in other industries, there also are many managerial and administrative support jobs.

Training and Advancement

As machinery becomes more complex, employers increasingly prefer to hire college graduates for highly skilled operating positions. For some production positions, vocational or community college training may be required.

Once production workers are hired, they receive training on the job. New workers entering the production process as lower-skilled laborers generally assist more experienced workers, beginning with relatively simple tasks. As workers acquire experience, they specialize in a particular process and acquire greater skill in that area. They may progress from second helper to first helper, and then to a skilled position, such as melter or roller. The time required to become a skilled worker depends upon individual abilities, acquired skills, and available job openings. It generally takes at least 4 or 5 years,

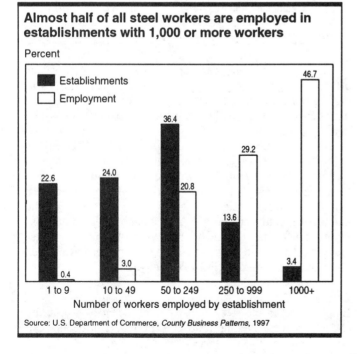

Almost half of all steel workers are employed in establishments with 1,000 or more workers

Percent

Number of workers employed by establishment

Source: U.S. Department of Commerce, *County Business Patterns*, 1997

and sometimes much longer, to advance to a skilled position. At times, workers change their specialization to increase their opportunities for advancement. Especially in EAF's, workers are trained to perform a variety of tasks and provide more flexibility to the firm, as company needs change.

Table 1. Employment of wage and salary workers in steel manufacturing by occupation, 1998 and projected change, 1998-2008

(Employment in thousands)

Occupation	1998 Employment Number	1998 Employment Percent	1998-2008 Percent change
All occupations	232	100.0	-23.7
Operators, fabricators, and laborers	112	48.6	-21.2
Machine tool cutting and forming setters, operators, and tenders, metal and plastic	24	10.4	-13.8
Helpers, laborers, and material movers, hand	18	7.8	-26.8
Other machine setters, operators, and tenders	11	4.8	-20.8
Crane and tower operators	10	4.3	-23.6
All other assemblers, fabricators, and hand workers	9	4.0	-23.6
All other metal and plastic machine setters, operators and related workers	8	3.2	-23.6
Furnace operators and tenders	6	2.4	-16.0
Industrial truck and tractor operators	5	2.1	-23.6
Welders and cutters	4	1.6	-31.3
Heat treating machine operators and tenders	3	1.5	-23.6
Metal fabricating machine operators	3	1.2	-20.9
Precision production, craft, and repair	70	30.0	-26.6
Blue collar worker supervisors	16	7.0	-23.6
Industrial machinery mechanics	11	4.9	-21.4
Inspectors, testers, and graders, precision	6	2.7	-33.8
Electricians	9	3.7	-23.6
Millwrights	5	2.1	-51.5
Maintenance repairers, general utility	3	1.5	-30.6
Machinists	3	1.3	-23.6
Administrative support, including clerical	16	6.9	-30.4
Other clerical and administrative support workers	3	1.5	-25.3
Shipping, receiving, and traffic clerks	2	1.0	-29.8
Financial records processing occupations	2	0.9	-36.6
Executive, administrative, and managerial	15	6.3	-24.9
Management support occupations	5	2.1	-24.9
Industrial production managers	3	1.2	-25.8
General managers and top executives	2	1.0	-25.9
Professional specialty	9	3.7	-13.8
Engineers	5	2.3	-19.2
Technicians and related support	3	1.4	-29.0
Engineering and science technicians and technologists	3	1.2	-27.9
Marketing and sales	4	1.9	-23.6
Service	3	1.2	-29.5

Computers have become important, as companies have modernized. Workers must learn to operate computers and other advanced equipment. Although much of the specific training is done on the job, employers prefer to hire applicants who have completed formal classroom training in a technical school or college.

To work as an engineer, scientist, or in some other technical occupation in the steel industry, a college education is necessary. Many workers in administrative and managerial occupations have degrees in business or possess a combination of technical and business degrees. A master's degree may give an applicant an advantage in getting hired or help an employee advance.

Earnings

Earnings in the steel industry vary by occupation and experience but are higher than average earnings in private industry. Average weekly earnings of nonsupervisory production workers in 1998 were $822 in the steel industry, compared to $563 in all manufacturing and $442 throughout private industry. Weekly earnings in blast furnaces and steel mills, at $907, were significantly higher than those in steel pipes and tubes, at $626. Earnings in selected occupations in steel manufacturing appear in table 2.

Table 2. Median hourly earnings of the largest occupations in steel manufacturing, 1997

Occupation	Steel manufacturing	All industries
First line supervisors and managers/ supervisors-production and operating workers	$20.05	$16.62
Electricians	17.42	16.54
Machinery maintenance mechanics	17.16	14.72
Millwrights	15.88	16.99
Crane and tower operators	14.89	14.04
Furnace operators and tenders	14.89	11.88
Rolling machine setters and set-up operators, metal and plastic	14.35	12.52
Industrial truck and tractor operators	13.73	10.99
Production inspectors, testers, graders, sorters, samplers, and weighers	12.60	10.15
Machine forming operators and tenders, metal and plastic	11.69	9.55

Union membership, geographic location, and plant size affect earnings and benefits of workers. In some firms, earnings or bonuses are linked to output. Workers receive standard benefits, including health insurance, paid vacation, and pension plans.

The iron and steel industry traditionally has been highly unionized. In 1998, 44.3 percent of steel workers were covered by union contracts, compared with 16.8 percent in all of manufacturing and 15.4 percent in all industries. In some instances, companies are closed shops; that is, workers must belong to the union, in order to work there. EAF's, though, typically are non-union. The overall decline of employment in traditional integrated steel mills and the growth of EAF's, together, have caused union membership to decline in recent years.

Outlook

Employment in the steel industry is expected to decline by about 24 percent over the 1998-2008 period. This decline can mostly be attributed to increased use of labor-saving technologies and machinery. Other factors affecting employment in the industry include foreign trade, overall economic conditions, the growth of EAF's, and environmental regulations. Despite the continuing decline in employment, qualified workers still will be needed to replace workers who retire or leave the industry. Opportunities will be best for individuals with the technical skills and training to handle technologically advanced machinery.

Employment levels in coming years will be greatly affected by the ability of steel makers located in the United States to compete with imports from abroad. Worker productivity has increased in U.S. firms in recent years, leaving the domestic steel industry better able to compete with imports. Many American steel producers, however, complain that they face unfair competition from abroad and that foreign producers, subsidized by their governments, are "dumping" steel in the U.S. market. Efforts currently are underway to improve trade relations in steel. If these efforts are successful, increasing trade would almost certainly result, which would foster growth in the most efficient American firms as they take advantages of growing export opportunities. It also would hasten the demise of inefficient plants trying to compete with low-priced imports.

Employment in the steel industry varies with overall economic conditions and the demand for goods produced with steel. For example, as the automotive industry produces more cars and light trucks, it will purchase more steel. In this way, much of the demand for steel is derived from the demand for other products. Other industries that are significant users of steel include structural metal products, motor vehicle parts and equipment, and household appliances. As many of these goods require a large outlay, consumers are more likely to purchase them in good economic times.

Steel companies, like most businesses, have entered the era of sophisticated technology. Taking several forms, this technology has improved both product quality and worker productivity. Computers are essential to most technological advances in steel production, from production scheduling and machine control, to metallurgical analysis. Computerized systems change the nature of many jobs, while they eliminate or reduce the demand for others. For example, computers allow one worker to perform duties that previously took the efforts of several workers. However, computer-controlled equipment often requires operators to have greater skills. Hence, workers who are comfortable with computers and other high-tech equipment—as well as those willing and able to learn—will be more widely sought after by employers. This automation will contribute to better opportunities for engineers and other professional specialty occupations, while causing significant declines for lower-skilled machine operators and inspectors.

Environmental issues also have affected the steel industry. Past decades have seen technological changes spurred by environmental emission regulations. Emission standards, under the present Clean Air Act, will likely result in costly modifications or shutdowns in many coal-processing facilities that employ a dirty, heavily polluting process. Necessary furnace modifications will require major investments and increase the overall cost of production for coke-producing plants. These modifications are, therefore, likely to raise costs in integrated mills that use coke to produce steel.

The emergence of EAF's is perhaps the most important factor in transforming the steel industry. This trend will continue in the foreseeable future, as EAF's dominate the new capacity expected to begin operation in the next few years. Integrated mills are expected to maintain a major share of the market in higher grade steel and are also entering areas like residential construction; but EAF's will continue to account for a larger share of the international steel market. Growth of EAF's is driven by many factors, including relatively low startup costs, flexibility, and the ability to locate close to the consumer. This is especially important in the construction industry. Because the scrap steel they need to operate is widely available, EAF's have provided job opportunities in the steel industry in additional geographic areas. However, since they generally have higher worker productivity, as EAF's capture more of the domestic steel market, fewer workers will be employed to meet the existing demand for steel products.

Sources of Additional Information

For additional information about careers and training in the steel industry, contact:

➢ American Iron and Steel Institute, 1101 17th St. NW., Suite 1300, Washington, DC 20036-4700.
➢ Steel Manufacturers Association, 1730 Rhode Island Ave. NW., Suite 907, Washington, DC 20036-3101.

Information on the following occupations may be found in the 2000-01 *Occupational Outlook Handbook*:

● Blue-collar worker supervisors
● Electricians
● Engineers
● Industrial machinery repairers
● Inspectors, testers, and graders
● Machinists and numerical tool and process control programmers
● Material moving equipment operators
● Metalworking and plastics-working machine operators
● Millwrights

Textile Mill Products

SIGNIFICANT POINTS

- About 3 out of 5 jobs are in three States—North Carolina, South Carolina, and Georgia.

- Production-related workers account for over 4 out of 5 jobs.

- Employment is expected to decline, due to technological advances and an open trading environment.

- Average earnings are low.

Nature of the Industry

Textile mills make yarn and fabric for clothing and many other items that keep us warm, safe, and in style. Although most people associate textiles with cloth for apparel, the industry also manufactures such products as carpeting, towels, cord and twine, automotive upholstery, reinforcing materials, bullet-proof vests, and decorative braids and ribbons.

A textile mill takes natural and synthetic fibers, such as cotton and polyester, and blends them to create yarn and fabric used in the production of finished products like clothing and upholstered furniture. A few products—sheets, towels, and hosiery, for example—are ready for the retail market when they leave the textile mill. Although a large share of textile products are used in the production of apparel, nontraditional uses, such as in highway construction and fire resistant housing panels, are growing rapidly.

Textile mills are classified by the type of product or process. The major processes of textile production include yarn spinning, weaving, knitting, and tufting. Some textiles are "nonwoven" and are produced by fusing fibers with heat or bonding fibers by using a type of glue. Two or more of these processes often can be found in the same facility. For example, one mill may spin yarn and also weave it into fabric.

Yarn and *thread mills* employ about 15 percent of all workers in the industry. Yarns are strands of fibers in a form ready for weaving, knitting, or otherwise intertwining to form a textile fabric. They form the basis for most textile production and are commonly made of cotton, wool, or synthetic fiber. Yarns also can be made of thin strips of plastic, paper, or metal. To produce spun yarn, natural fibers, such as cotton and wool, must first be processed to remove impurities and give products the desired texture and durability, as well as other characteristics. After this initial cleaning stage, the fibers are spun into yarn.

Weaving mills employ about 28 percent of all persons working in the textile industry. Workers in these mills use looms to transform yarns into cloth, a process that has been known for centuries. Looms weave or interlace two yarns, so they cross each other at right angles to form fabric. Although modern looms are complex, automated machinery, the principle remains the same as in ancient times.

Knitting is another method of transforming yarn into fabric. Knitting interlocks a series of loops of one or more yarns to form familiar goods, such as sweaters. However, unlike the knitting done with hand-held needles, knitting in the textile industry is performed on automated machines. Many consumer items, such as socks, panty-hose, and underwear, are produced from knitted fabric. Knitting mills account for 29 percent of employment in the industry.

Tufting, used by carpeting and rug mills, is a process by which a cluster of soft yarns is drawn through a backing fabric. These yarns project from the backing's surface in the form of cut yarns or loops to form the familiar texture of many carpets and rugs. Tufting mills employ about 9 percent of textile workers.

Finally, *nonwoven textile products* are produced by fusing fibers or bonding fibers with a cementing medium or heat. A familiar example of a nonwoven fabric is felt. This segment of the industry is one of the fastest growing, because of its medical and sanitary uses.

Regardless of the process used, mills in the textile industry are rapidly modernizing, as new investments in automation and information technology have been made necessary by growing domestic and international competition. Firms also have responded to competition by developing new products and services. These innovations have had a wide effect across the industry. For example, advanced machinery is boosting productivity levels in textiles, costing some workers their jobs, while fundamentally changing the nature of work for others. New technology also has led to broad and increasingly technical training for workers throughout the industry.

The emphasis in the industry continues to shift from mass production to flexible manufacturing, as textile mills aim to supply customized markets. Firms are concentrating on systems that allow small quantities to be produced with minimum lead time. This flexibility brings consumer goods to retailers significantly faster than before. Information technology allows the retail industry to rapidly assess its needs and communicate them back through the apparel manufacturer to textile firms.

Working Conditions

Working conditions vary greatly. Production workers, including front-line managers and supervisors, spend most of their shift on or near the production floor. Some factories are noisy and can have airborne fibers and odors; but most textile facilities are relatively clean, well lit, and ventilated.

In 1997, work-related injury and illnesses in the textile mill products industry averaged 6.7 per 100 full-time workers, compared to 10.3 percent for all manufacturing and 7.1 percent for the entire private sector. This record has been achieved, in part, by requiring, when appropriate, the use of protective face masks, earplugs, and protective clothing. Also, new machinery is designed with additional protection, such as noise shields. Still, many workers in production occupations are required to stand for long periods of time while bending over machinery, and noise and dust still is a problem in some plants.

Most mills operate around the clock, 7 days a week, so some production workers have weekend and evening schedules. Production workers averaged 41.0 hours per week in 1998, compared to an average of 34.6 hours per week for all production workers in the private sector. Overtime is common for these workers during periods of peak production. Managerial, administrative, and administrative support occupations typically work a 5-day, 40-hour week in an office setting, although some of these employees can work significant overtime.

Employment

Most of the 598,000 wage and salary workers employed in textile mills in 1998 were found in southeastern States. North Carolina accounted for about 30 percent of textile jobs. South Carolina and Georgia combined to provide employment for another 30 percent of the workers in this industry. The remaining jobs were found in the South, California, and the Northeast.

Most textile production is concentrated in large mills. In fact, establishments employing over 250 persons accounted for almost 60 percent of all textile workers in 1997 (chart).

Occupations in the Industry

The textile industry offers employment opportunities in a wide variety of occupations, but precision production, craft, and repair occupations, coupled with operators, fabricators, and laborers, accounted for over 80 percent of all jobs. Some of these occupations are unique to the industry (see table 1). Additional opportunities exist in general management, engineering, and clerical occupations.

Many workers enter the textile industry as *machine setters and operators*, the largest occupational group in the

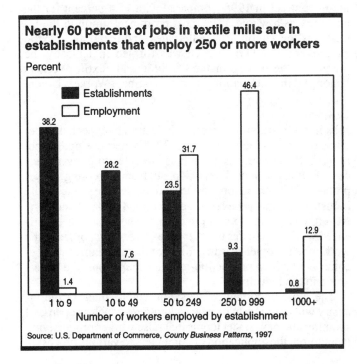

Nearly 60 percent of jobs in textile mills are in establishments that employ 250 or more workers

Percent

Source: U.S. Department of Commerce, *County Business Patterns*, 1997

industry. They are responsible for setting each machine and monitoring its operation. Usually, operators work with one type of less complex machine, but they can advance to jobs operating more sophisticated machinery or several machines simultaneously. For example, experienced operators may work with machinery that processes raw cotton, spins fibers into thread, or weaves fabric. Additionally, they must diagnose problems when the machinery stops and restart it as soon as possible, to reduce costly machine idle time. Traditionally, operators tended a small number of machines; however, as production processes have become more automated, the number of machines each operator monitors has increased.

Production occupations that require extensive training or apprenticeships include those that install and repair machinery. *Industrial machinery mechanics* comprise about 5 percent of employment in the textile industry. Skilled production occupations also include *inspectors*, *testers*, and *graders*, who use precision measuring instruments and complex testing equipment to detect product defects, wear, or deviations from specifications.

Engineers and *engineering technicians*, a vital part of the textile industry, comprise less than 1 percent. Some engineers are *textile engineers*, who specialize in the design of textile machinery, the study of fibers, and textile production. The industry also employs other types of engineers, particularly *industrial* and *mechanical engineers*.

Training and Advancement

As the textile industry becomes increasingly automated, production workers need to be prepared. A high school diploma may be necessary for many entry-level positions, and extensive postsecondary training is required for more technical jobs. This training may be obtained at technical schools and community colleges. More and more often, job applicants are screened through the use of tests, to ensure that they have the necessary skills.

Extensive on-the-job training has become an integral part of working in today's textile mills. This training may be provided by experienced workers at the firm or by outside contractors and vendors. Technical training is designed to help workers understand complex, automated machinery, recognize problems, and restart machinery, when the problem is solved. Precision production workers, such as industrial machinery mechanics, also require extensive training, often through a combination of classroom and apprenticeship programs. Training may help experienced workers advance to supervisory positions.

Increasingly, training is being offered to enable people to work well in a team-oriented environment. Many firms have established training centers or hosted seminars that encourage employee self-direction and responsibility and the development of interpersonal skills. The emphasis on teamwork, combined with few levels of management in modern textile mills, have placed a premium on workers who show initiative and communicate effectively.

Engineering applicants generally need a bachelor's or advanced degree in a field of engineering or production management. Degrees in mechanical or industrial engineering are common, but concentrations in textile-specific areas of engineering are especially useful. Many applicants, for example, take classes in textile engineering, textile technology, textile materials, and design. These specialized programs usually are found in engineering and design schools in the South and Northeast. As in other industries, a technical degree with an advanced degree in business can lead to opportunities in management.

Table 1. Employment of wage and salary workers in textile mill products by occupation, 1998 and projected change, 1998-2008

(Employment in thousands)

Occupation	1998 Employment Number	1998 Employment Percent	1998-2008 Percent change
All occupations	598	100.0	-16.2
Operators, fabricators, and laborers ...	390	65.2	-19.5
Textile draw-out and winding machine operators and tenders	155	26.0	-28.8
Helpers, laborers, and material movers, hand	57	9.6	- 13.9
Sewing machine operators, garment	37	6.1	-30.3
Other machine setters, setup operators, operators, and tenders	35	5.8	-8.8
Textile machine setters and setup operators	24	3.9	-10.2
Textile bleaching and dyeing machine operators and tenders ...	22	3.6	-8.7
Hand workers, including assemblers and fabricators.............................	17	2.8	-11.6
Sewing machine operators, non-garment	11	1.8	-6.0
Extruding and forming machine operators and tenders, synthetic or glass fibers	10	1.7	5.5
Industrial truck and tractor operators	8	1.3	-8.7
Printing, binding, and related workers	6	1.0	-15.4
Precision production, craft, and repair	110	18.4	-6.7
Industrial machinery mechanics........	32	5.3	10.8
Blue-collar worker supervisors	25	4.2	-9.7
Inspectors, testers, and graders, precision	25	4.2	-23.8
Textile, apparel, and furnishings workers, precision	11	1.8	2.1
Maintenance repairers, general utility..	6	1.0	-21.4
Administrative support, including clerical	44	7.3	-17.2
Shipping, receiving, and traffic clerks	8	1.4	-15.4
Financial records processing occupations	6	1.0	-26.0
Executive, administrative, and managerial	26	4.4	-12.2
General managers and top executives	7	1.2	-13.2
Industrial production managers	6	1.0	-11.7
Professional specialty	8	1.4	0.6
Marketing and sales	7	1.2	-7.8
Service	8	1.3	-19.6
All other occupations	5	0.8	-15.4

Earnings

Textile production workers' weekly average earnings were $426 in 1998, compared to $563 for production workers in all manufacturing and $442 for production workers throughout private industry. Wages within the textile industry depend upon skill level and type of mill. At $498, weekly earnings in miscellaneous textile goods were the highest in the industry, whereas workers in knitting mills earned an average of $378 per week, the lowest in the industry. In addition to typical benefits, employees often are eligible for discounts in factory merchandise stores. Earnings in largest occupations in textile mill products appear in table 2.

Table 2. Median hourly earnings of the largest occupations in textile mill products, 1997

Occupation	Textile mill products	All industries
First-line supervisors and managers/ supervisors-production and operating workers	$14.96	$16.62
Machinery maintenance mechanics, textile machines	11.49	11.49
Textile machine setters and set-up operators	10.16	10.13
Textile bleaching and dyeing machine operators and tenders	9.14	9.00
Textile machine operators and tenders, winding, twisting, knitting, weaving, and cutting	9.08	9.03
Production inspectors, testers, graders, sorters, samplers, and weighers	8.92	10.15
Machine feeders and offbearers	8.65	8.69
Sewing machine operators, nongarment	8.33	7.91
Hand packers and packagers	7.68	6.90
Sewing machine operators, garment	7.31	6.92

The industry has a low unionization rate; only 5.7 percent of textile workers were union members or were covered by a union contract in 1998, compared with 15.4 percent for the economy as a whole. The most prominent union in the industry is the Union of Needletrades, Industrial and Textile Employees (UNITE), which was formed in 1995 by the merger of the Amalgamated Clothing and Textile Workers Union and the International Ladies' Garment Workers Union.

Outlook

Jobs in the textile mill products industry are expected to decline by about 16 percent through 2008, whereas employment in the U.S. economy as a whole is projected to grow 15 percent. Employment declines will result from increasing worker productivity, international trade, and the decline of the textile industry's primary buyer—the American apparel industry. Nevertheless, a number of job openings will arise, as experienced workers transfer to other industries, retire, or leave the workforce for other reasons. Most of these openings will become available in production-related occupations, the largest group in the industry.

The most important influence on employment in the industry will continue to be new technologies, such as open-end spinning and new air-jet looms that raise worker productivity. In addition, the application of computers to various processes in textile production will allow workers to increase productivity and expand the textile industry's competitiveness. These technologies will be implemented at a growing rate in coming years, as textile mills merge to consolidate capital and make their operations as efficient as possible. As this happens, demand for many of the low-skilled machine operators and material handlers will continue to decline.

Jobs also will be affected by the relatively open trading environment, resulting from ratification of the North American Free Trade Agreement and the Agreement on Textiles and Clothing of the World Trade Organization. These agreements will open additional markets to textiles made in the United States, but they will also expose U.S. textile producers to increasing competition from abroad. Some segments of the textile industry, like industrial fabrics, carpets, and specialty yarns, are highly automated, innovative, and competitive on a global scale, so they will be able to expand exports, as a result of more open trade. Other sectors, such as fabric for apparel, will be negatively impacted, as a number of textile and apparel manufacturers relocate production to other countries. On balance, textile mills are likely to lose employment, as a result of this open trade, because of its effect on the American apparel industry. The expected increase in apparel imports and the decline in apparel production will adversely affect demand for domestically-produced textiles.

Sources of Additional Information

For additional information concerning career opportunities, technological advances, and legislation in the textile industry, contact:

➤ American Textile Manufacturers Institute, 1130 Connecticut Ave. NW., Suite 1200, Washington, DC 20036-3954. Internet: **http://www.atmi.org**
➤ Institute of Textile Technology, 2551 Ivy Rd., Charlottesville, NC 22903-4614. Internet: **http://www.itt.edu**

Information on the following occupations employed in the textile industry can be found in the 2000-01 *Occupational Outlook Handbook*:

- Apparel workers
- Industrial machinery repairers
- Inspectors, testers, and graders
- Machinists
- Material moving equipment operators
- Textile machinery operators

Transportation, Communications, and Public Utilities

Air Transportation

- Although flight crews—pilots and flight attendants—are the most visible occupations in this industry, over three-fourths of all employees work in ground occupations.

- Senior pilots for major airlines are among the highest paid workers in the Nation.

- Except for pilots, most workers in this industry are trained to do their jobs after they are hired.

- A significant number of workers are unionized.

Nature of the Industry

The rapid development of air transportation has increased the mobility of the population and created thousands of job opportunities. The air transportation industry involves many activities. Most familiar are the major airlines, which provide transportation for passengers and cargo, and airports, which provide the many ground support services required by aircraft, passengers, and cargo. Air taxi companies and commuter airlines also provide commercial transportation, such as passenger and cargo service, often to and from small airports not serviced by the airlines. Other companies provide air courier services—which furnish air delivery for individually addressed letters, parcels, and packages—and helicopter and sightseeing airplane services for tourists. This industry also includes services related to air transportation, such as aircraft repair, cleaning, and storage.

The air transportation industry has been through a period of adjustment and turmoil since the start of Federal deregulation in the late 1970s. Nonetheless, most of the 1980s was a prosperous period for the industry, marked by high earnings and rapid job growth as new carriers entered the industry. The reduction in air travel that accompanied the recession of the early 1990s exposed many companies to problems of overcapacity and high labor costs. Intense competition—including destructive fare cutting—created a great deal of instability, causing many airlines to go out of business and many persons to lose their jobs.

The air transportation industry has recovered from the severe financial losses it suffered during the early 1990s. Smaller regional and commuter airlines, which have lower costs than larger airlines, have emerged in recent years to primarily serve shorter routes. Major airlines are regaining profitability and hope to achieve long-term stability by reducing capacity and distribution and marketing costs, using their aircraft and crews more efficiently, and reducing their labor costs through negotiations with the major labor unions that represent air transportation workers.

Working Conditions

Working conditions vary widely, depending on the occupation. Although most employees work in fairly comfortable surroundings, such as offices, terminals, or airplanes, mechanics and others who service aircraft are subject to noise, dirt, and grease, and sometimes work outside in bad weather.

In 1997, the air transportation industry had 16.4 injuries and illnesses per 100 full-time workers, compared to 7.1 throughout private industry. Virtually all work-related fatalities resulted from transportation accidents.

Because airlines operate flights at all hours of the day and night, some workers often have irregular hours or schedules. Flight and ground personnel may have to work at night, on weekends, or holidays. Flight personnel may be away from their home bases frequently. When they are away from home, the airlines provide hotel accommodations, transportation between the hotel and airport, and an allowance for meals and expenses. Pilots and flight attendants employed outside the major airlines also may have irregular schedules.

Flight crews, especially those on international routes, often suffer jet lag—disorientation and fatigue caused by flying into different time zones. Some personnel may work under pressure to meet flight schedules.

Employment

The air transportation industry provided 1.2 million jobs in 1998. Most employment is found in larger establishments—nearly 9 out of 10 jobs are in establishments with 50 or more workers. However, over half of all establishments employ fewer than 10 workers (chart).

Most air transportation employees work at major airports located close to cities. A substantial proportion of these employees work at airports which serve as central hubs for major airlines, such as New York, Chicago, Los Angeles, Atlanta, San Francisco, Dallas-Fort Worth, and Miami.

Occupations in the Industry

Although pilots and flight attendants are the most visible occupations in this industry, over 80 percent of all employees in air transportation work in ground occupations (table 1). For example, *aircraft mechanics* service, inspect, and repair planes, and *aircraft cleaners* clean aircraft interiors after each flight.

Aircraft mechanics may work on several different types of aircraft, such as jet transports, small propeller-driven airplanes, or helicopters. Many, however, specialize in one section of a particular type of aircraft, such as the engine, hydraulic, or electrical systems. In small, independent repair

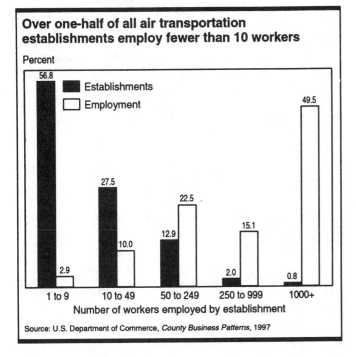

Over one-half of all air transportation establishments employ fewer than 10 workers

Percent

Establishments
Employment

Number of workers employed by establishment	Establishments	Employment
1 to 9	56.8	2.9
10 to 49	27.5	10.0
50 to 249	12.9	22.5
250 to 999	2.0	15.1
1000+	0.8	49.5

Source: U.S. Department of Commerce, *County Business Patterns*, 1997

Table 1. Employment of wage and salary workers in the air transportation industry by occupation, 1998 and projected change, 1998-2008

(Employment in thousands)

Occupation	1998 Employment Number	1998 Employment Percent	1998-2008 Percent change
All occupations	1,183	100.0	18.3
Operators, fabricators, and laborers	401	33.9	25.8
Helpers, laborers, and material movers, hand	171	14.5	21.9
Truckdrivers	155	13.1	23.8
Administrative support, including clerical	298	25.2	7.2
Reservation and transportation ticket agents and travel clerks	160	13.5	-0.1
Material recording, scheduling, dispatching, and distributing occupations	52	4.4	14.7
General office clerks	16	1.4	25.0
Financial records processing occupations	15	1.2	4.3
Adjustment clerks	12	1.1	35.7
Office and administrative support supervisors and managers	17	1.4	20.4
Precision production, craft, and repair	153	12.9	17.0
Aircraft mechanics and service technicians	87	7.3	14.7
Blue-collar worker supervisors	28	2.4	23.9
Machinery mechanics, installers, and repairers	11	1.0	14.1
Precision production occupations	9	0.8	12.8
Service	135	11.4	25.5
Flight attendants	98	8.3	30.0
Technicians and related	92	7.8	6.3
Aircraft pilots and flight engineers	81	6.8	4.1
Executive, administrative, and managerial	62	5.2	21.4
Management support occupations	18	1.5	22.8
Communications, transportation, and utilities operations managers	16	1.4	23.8
General managers and top executives	10	0.8	20.2
Professional specialty	24	2.1	36.1
Marketing and sales	18	1.5	19.9

shops, mechanics usually inspect and repair many different types of aircraft.

Many mechanics specialize in scheduled maintenance required by the Federal Aviation Administration (FAA). Following a schedule based on the number of hours flown, calendar days, cycles of operation, or a combination of these factors, mechanics inspect the engines, landing gear, instruments, and other parts of aircraft and perform necessary maintenance and repairs.

Dispatchers plan flights for airlines' crews, analyze weather conditions, and determine fuel requirements and the maximum weight the aircraft can carry. Before flights, they assist pilots by suggesting routes and altitudes and provide them with information on their flight path, such as terrain and weather peculiarities.

Other employees interact with the public. *Ticket* and *reservation agents* answer telephones, sell tickets, and make reservations for passengers on scheduled airlines. *Customer service representatives* assist passengers, check tickets when passengers board or disembark an airplane, and check luggage at the reception area and insure that it is placed on the proper carrier. They also assist elderly or handicapped persons and unaccompanied children in claiming personal belongings and baggage and getting on and off the plane. They may also provide assistance to passengers who become ill or injured. *Airline security representatives* screen passengers and visitors to ensure that weapons and illegal or forbidden articles are not carried into restricted areas. *Airplane cargo agents* take orders from shippers and arrange for transportation of their goods. *Baggage handlers* are responsible for loading and unloading passengers' baggage. They stack baggage on specified carts or conveyors to ensure it gets to the proper destination, and also return baggage to passengers at airline terminals upon receipt of their claim check. The airline industry also employs many other workers who are found in a wide range of industries, such as lawyers, accountants, managers, secretaries, and general office clerks.

Flight crew members make up the remainder—*about* one-fifth—of air transportation employment and include pilots and flight attendants.

Most *pilots* transport passengers and cargo. Others apply chemicals to crops, spread seed for reforestation, test aircraft, and take photographs. *Helicopter pilots* are involved in firefighting, police work, evacuation and rescue efforts, logging operations, construction work, and weather station operations; some also transport passengers.

Except on small aircraft, two pilots usually make up the cockpit crew. Generally, the most experienced pilot, or captain, is in command and supervises all other crew members. The pilot and copilot split flying and other duties such as communicating with air traffic controllers and monitoring the instruments. Some aircraft have a third pilot in the cockpit—

the flight engineer or second officer—who assists the other pilots by monitoring and operating many of the instruments and systems and watching for other aircraft. Most newer aircraft are designed to be flown without a flight engineer.

Most airline flights have one or more *flight attendants* on board. Their most important function is assisting passengers in the event of an emergency. This may range from reassuring passengers during occasional encounters with strong turbulence, to opening emergency exits and inflating escape chutes. More routinely, flight attendants instruct passengers in the use of safety and emergency equipment. Once in the air, they serve meals and snacks, answer questions about the flight, distribute magazines and pillows, and help care for small children and elderly and handicapped persons. They also may administer first aid to passengers who become ill.

Training and Advancement
The skills and experience needed by workers in the air transportation industry differ by occupation. Some jobs may be entered directly from high school, while others require extensive specialized training. Mechanics and pilots must be certificated by the FAA; skills for many other air transportation occupations can be learned on the job.

Pilots must have a commercial pilot's license with an instrument rating and must be certified to fly the types of aircraft their employer operates. For example, helicopter pilots must hold a commercial pilot's certificate with a helicopter rating. Pilots receive their training from the military or from civilian flying schools. Physical requirements are strict. With or without glasses, pilots must have 20/20 vision, good hearing, and be in excellent health. In addition, airlines generally require 2 years of college and increasingly prefer or require a college degree. Pilots who work for smaller airlines may advance to flying for larger companies. They can also advance from flight engineer to co-pilot to captain and, by becoming certified, to fly larger planes.

Applicants for flight attendant jobs must be in excellent health. Employers prefer those who have completed some college and have experience in dealing with the public. Applicants are trained for their jobs at company schools. Training may include crew resource management, which emphasizes teamwork and safety. Advancement opportunities are limited, although some attendants become customer service directors, instructors, or recruiting representatives.

When hiring aircraft mechanics, employers prefer graduates of aircraft mechanic trade schools who are in good physical condition. Most mechanics remain in the maintenance field, but they may advance to head mechanic, and sometimes to supervisor. Most other workers in ground occupations learn their job through a combination of company classroom and on-the-job training. At least a high school education is required for most jobs.

A good speaking voice and a pleasant personality are essential for reservation agents and customer service representatives. Reservation agents also need some keyboard skills. Airlines prefer applicants with experience in sales or dealing with the public and most require a high school education, but some college is preferred. Some advance to supervisor or other administrative positions.

Some entry-level jobs in this industry, such as baggage handler, aircraft cleaner, cabin-service attendant, and food service worker, require little or no previous training. The basic tasks associated with many of these jobs are learned in less than a week, and most newly hired workers are trained on the job under the guidance of an experienced employee or a manager. However, promotional opportunities for many ground occupations are limited due to the limited scope of the duties and specialized skills of some occupations. Some may advance to supervisor or other administrative positions.

Earnings
Earnings in selected occupations in air transportation appear in table 3.

Table 3. Median hourly earnings of the largest occupations in air transportation, 1997

Occupation	Air transportation	All industries
Aircraft pilots and flight engineers	$39.32	$36.81
Communications, transportation, and utilities operations managers	22.40	24.10
Aircraft mechanics	19.28	17.80
First-line supervisors and managers/ supervisors-clerical and administrative support workers	16.82	14.26
Truck drivers, heavy or tractor-trailer	16.82	13.08
Flight attendants	16.79	16.82
Truck drivers, light, including delivery and route workers	14.06	9.83
Reservation and transportation ticket agents	11.12	10.41
General office clerks	10.64	9.10
Transportation agents	10.56	10.56

Most employees in the air transportation industry receive standard benefits, such as life and health insurance and retirement plans. Some airlines provide allowances to employees for purchasing and cleaning their company uniforms. A unique benefit—free or reduced fare transportation for airline employees and their immediate families—attracts many jobseekers.

In 1998, 40.1 percent of all workers in the air transportation industry were union members or were covered by union contracts, compared to 15.4 percent of all workers throughout the economy.

Outlook
Wage and salary jobs in the air transportation industry are projected to increase by 18 percent over the 1998-2008 period, about as fast as the average for all industries. Passenger and cargo traffic is expected to increase in response to increases in population, income, and business activity. Employment in other air transportation activities is also expected to rise as more aircraft are purchased for business, agricultural, and recreational purposes.

Air travel has become an affordable means of transportation for more and more people. Demographic and income trends indicate favorable conditions for leisure travel in the

United States over the next decade. An aging population, in combination with growing disposable income among the elderly, should increase the demand for air transportation services. On the other hand, the growth in business travel will be restricted as American corporations continue to downsize and automate operations, eliminating many middle management positions and reducing the base of both current and future business travelers. In addition, communication technologies—such as fax machines, computer networks, and teleconferencing—have somewhat reduced the need for business travel.

Besides job openings created by employment growth, many openings also will arise as experienced workers retire or transfer to other industries. Job opportunities may vary from year to year, however, because the demand for air travel—particularly pleasure travel, a discretionary expense—fluctuates with ups and downs in the economy.

New technology is not expected to have any significant effect on air transportation occupations over the 1998-2008 period; most labor-saving technology already has been introduced and should have minimal impact on future employment. Job opportunities in the air transportation industry are expected to vary depending on the occupation. Pilots understandably have a strong attachment to their occupation because it requires a substantial investment in specialized training and offers very high earnings. Low turnover rates mean fewer job openings and more intense competition among applicants. Customer service representatives and ticket and reservation agents also are expected to face keen competition for available positions because they offer reasonably good pay, the opportunity to travel, and require little education after high school.

Job opportunities should be more favorable among flight attendants and aircraft mechanics. Many of the major airlines have instituted a two-tier wage structure lowering the average wages of flight attendants significantly, reducing the supply of people wanting to enter the occupation. As a result, opportunities for flight attendants are expected to be good. There should also be an improved outlook for aircraft mechanics over the next 10 years. The smaller numbers of younger workers aged 21 to 34, coupled with the military downsizing and a large number of retirements, points to favorable opportunities for students just beginning technician training. Opportunities will be somewhat better for mechanics working in general aviation than for commercial airlines; mechanics will face competition for jobs at the commercial airlines because these jobs tend to pay more. Opportunities should be better with rapidly growing commuter and regional airlines and at FAA repair stations.

Opportunities are also expected to be good among unskilled entry-level positions, such as baggage handler, aircraft interior cleaner, and food service worker, because the turnover rate of these jobs is usually high.

Sources of Additional Information

Information about specific job opportunities and qualifications required by a particular airline may be obtained by writing to personnel managers of the airlines.

For information about job opportunities in companies other than airlines, consult the classified section of aviation trade magazines or apply to companies that operate aircraft at local airports.

Information on these key air transportation occupations may be found in the 2000-01 *Occupational Outlook Handbook*:

- Aircraft mechanics and service technicians
- Aircraft pilots
- Flight attendants
- Reservation and transportation ticket agents and travel clerks

Cable and Other Pay Television Services

SIGNIFICANT POINTS

- Administrative support and craft and repair occupations comprise most jobs.

- The majority of jobs are in large establishments.

- The need for employees in a variety of occupations will create openings for both high school and college graduates; opportunities will be best for applicants with technical skills and an understanding of the new telecommunications services provided by this industry.

Nature of the Industry

Establishments in this industry provide television and other services on a subscription or fee basis. These establishments include both cable networks and distributors. Cable networks produce or acquire television programming and deliver it to distributors. The distributors then transmit the programming to customers.

Cable networks produce some original television programs in their studios; however, much of the programming is acquired from the motion picture industry. (See the statement on motion picture production and distribution elsewhere in the *Career Guide*.)

Distributors of pay television services transmit programming through a variety of systems. Cable systems transmit programs over fiber optic and coaxial cables. Fiber optic cables are made of glass strands and can carry more information than conventional coaxial cables, made of wire. Other pay television systems include wireless and satellite systems. Operators of wireless systems transmit programming over the airwaves from transmission towers to customers' television antennas. Direct-to-home (DTH) operators transmit programming from orbiting satellites to customer receivers, known as satellite dishes.

Establishments in this industry generate revenue through subscriptions, special service fees, and advertising sales. Pay television systems charge installation and subscription fees to set up and provide service. They also charge fees for special services, such as the transmission of specialty pay-per-view programs; these are often popular movies or sporting events. Some cable networks sell advertising time during selected programs. Rates paid by advertisers depend on size and characteristics of the program's audience and the time of day the program is shown.

Subscription television services are widely used. In 1998, more than two-thirds of households with television sets received pay television services. Most of these customers subscribed to cable service; however, subscriptions to non-cable services are growing rapidly. The number of national cable networks has also been increasing. Between 1992 and 1998, this number doubled from 87 to 174 networks.

Changes in technology and regulation are transforming the industry. An important change has been the rapid increase in two-way communications capacity. Conventional pay television services only provided communications from the distributor to the customer. These services could not provide effective communications from the customer back to other points in the system, due to signal interference and the limited capacity of conventional cable systems.

Encouraged by the increasing need for communications services, cable operators have implemented new technologies to reduce signal interference. The capacity of distribution systems has also increased, due to the installation of fiber optic cables and improved data compression. As a result, pay television systems now offer two-way telecommunications services, such as telephone service and high-speed Internet access. Cable subscribers can access the Internet by installing cable modems that connect customers' personal computers to the cable system.

The upgraded systems also facilitate the transmission of digital television signals. Digital signals consist of simple electronic code that can carry more information than conventional television signals. Digital transmission creates higher resolution television images, referred to as high definition television. It also allows the transmission of a variety of other information. This includes computer software, telephone directories, electronic newspapers, and any other information that can be translated into digital code.

The Telecommunications Act of 1996 reduced barriers to competition across all communications industries. As a result, operators of pay television systems are competing with telephone companies and public utilities to provide video, telephone, and high-speed Internet services. Consolidations have increased, as companies acquire facilities that allow them to offer their customers multiple services. Such combined offerings are popular with customers seeking to simplify their purchase of communications services. (A statement on telecommunications appears elsewhere in the *Career Guide*.)

Working Conditions

Working conditions in cable and other pay television services vary by occupational group. Most professional, clerical, and sales employees work indoors in comfortable, well-lighted surroundings. However, workers in technical, craft, and repair jobs must travel to various locations to perform installation, maintenance, and repair duties. These responsibilities often require outdoor work under a variety of weather conditions.

Workers who install pay television services travel to the customers' premises to perform the installation. Cable service installers must sometimes climb telephone poles or access underground cables to connect a customer's television set to the cable system. Antenna and satellite dish installers must climb ladders and attach the receiving equipment to rooftops or the sides of houses.

Cable television line installers and repairers travel to locations in the cable system that are malfunctioning. They often travel in vehicles equipped with aerial buckets so they can do repair work on cables carried on telephone poles. Technicians responsible for monitoring signal quality sometimes work on outdoor equipment, such as transmission towers and satellite dishes.

Cases of work-related injury and illness in cable and other pay television services in 1997 were approximately 7.3 per 100 full-time workers, slightly higher than the 7.1 per 100 full-time workers throughout private industry. Rates of injury and illness in this industry were at this level, because many of the positions are craft jobs that pose hazards. These hazards can result in injuries from falls or electric shock from contact with high voltage power lines, for example.

Employment

Cable and other pay television services provided about 181,000 wage and salary jobs in 1998. Most jobs were in establishments that employed more than 50 workers (chart). However, just over half of the establishments in the industry employed fewer than 10 workers. Pay television establishments are found throughout the country, but jobs with large employers are concentrated in large cities.

Occupations in the Industry

Administrative support and craft and repair occupations comprise most jobs. The remaining employees are found in variety of occupations (table 1). In small cable establishments, employees are less specialized and may have a wide range of responsibilities.

Administrative support occupations. About a third of all jobs in this industry are in administrative support occupations. *Customer service representatives* talk with customers by phone or in person and receive orders for installation,

turn-on, discontinuance, or change in services. They often work at a computer, so they can quickly access customer records and authorize the provision of new services. As the industry begins to offer new services—such as telephone and high-speed Internet access—customer service representatives must also respond to technical questions about the operation of these services. Some customer service representatives are expected to sell services and may work on a commission basis.

Other administrative service occupations include *adjustment clerks* and *dispatchers*. *Adjustment clerks* investigate customer questions about pay television services, including billing questions. They determine responsibility for a customer complaint and notify customers of any adjustments, such as refunds or other changes to customers' bills. *Dispatchers* schedule work crews and service vehicles for installation of pay television service. Duties can include transmitting assignments via radio or telephone, and compiling statistics and reports on work progress.

Craft and repair occupations. Craft and repair occupations include about another one-third of the workers in the industry. The largest occupation in this group is *line installers and repairers*. These workers are known by a variety of titles, including *installer*, *line technician*, and *service* or *maintenance technician*. Line installers and repairers lay fiber optic and coaxial cable and install equipment, such as repeaters and amplifiers; this equipment maintains signal strength, as transmissions pass along the network. Maintenance and repair duties include periodic monitoring of the cable system to identify malfunctions. When a problem is detected, the technicians travel to the location of the malfunction and repair or replace the defective cable or equipment. Construction duties related to line installation, such as erecting supports and digging underground trenches, are often contracted to employees working in other industries.

Installers travel to customers' premises to set up pay television service so customers can receive programming. Cable service installers connect a customer's television set to the cable serving the entire neighborhood. Wireless and satellite service installers attach antennas or satellite dishes to the sides of customers' houses. These devices must be positioned to provide clear lines of sight with satellite locations. (Satellite installation may be handled by employees of electronic retail stores that sell satellite dishes. Such workers are not employed by cable and other pay television services.)

Installers check the strength and clarity of the television signal, before completing the installation. They may need to explain to the subscriber how pay television services operate. As these services expand to include telephone and high-speed Internet access, an understanding of the basic technology and an ability to communicate that knowledge are increasingly important.

A new occupation found among cable operators is *cable modem installer*. These workers install cable modems, which allow customers to connect their personal computers to the cable line. Cable modem installers connect the modem to the cable line and configure the modem, so it is compatible with the customer's personal computer.

Other occupations. The remaining employees in this industry, approximately one-third, work in a variety of occupations.

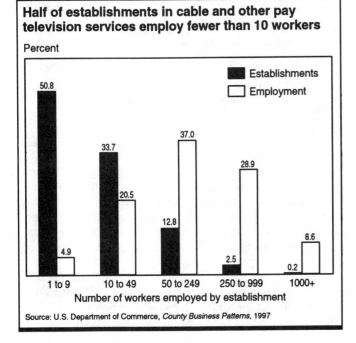

Half of establishments in cable and other pay television services employ fewer than 10 workers

Percent

Legend: ■ Establishments □ Employment

Number of workers employed by establishment	Establishments	Employment
1 to 9	50.8	4.9
10 to 49	33.7	20.5
50 to 249	12.8	37.0
250 to 999	2.5	28.9
1000+	0.2	8.6

Source: U.S. Department of Commerce, *County Business Patterns*, 1997

Many are employed by cable networks that produce television programs, such as news or talk shows. *Camera operators* set up and operate television cameras to photograph scenes for cable television broadcasts. *Producers* plan and develop live or taped productions, determining how the show will look and sound. *Newscasters* analyze, interpret, and broadcast news received from various sources. (The motion picture industry produces many programs seen on cable television. Actors and directors working on these pre-recorded programs are not employed by cable or other pay television services.)

Electrical and *electronics engineers* design cable and wireless distribution systems for pay television services. Engineers determine the physical layout and requirements of the system, test equipment, solve operating problems, and estimate the time and cost of engineering projects. In wireless cable systems, engineers determine where operators need to install repeaters and towers in the distribution systems.

Network administrators set up and maintain systems of computer servers. These servers store customer data for billing and authorization purposes. Network administrators set up connections between servers, so customer service agents and other employees can efficiently access customer data for billing and authorization purposes. Other computer specialists include *computer engineers*, who work with the hardware and software aspects of systems design and development, and *computer support specialists*, who provide assistance and advice to users.

Market researchers and *sales representatives* at cable networks work together to sell advertising time to sponsors. Researchers analyze data about program audiences to identify audience characteristics, such as age and income. Sales representatives present this information to potential sponsors and attempt to sell advertising time.

Technicians and related support occupations include *broadcast and sound technicians*, also known as *cable technicians*. These technicians set up, operate, and maintain the electronic equipment used to transmit television programming. In cable services, they insure that incoming signals from satellites are clearly received and transmitted along cable lines to the customer. *Engineering technicians* assist professional engineers by designing, building, and testing electrical equipment. In cable networks that produce television programming, *master control engineers* ensure that the scheduled program elements—such as on-location feeds, pre-recorded segments, and commercials—are smoothly transmitted.

Training and Advancement

Many jobs in the cable and other pay television services industry do not require a college degree. Applicants with a high school diploma generally qualify for entry-level positions in administrative support or craft and repair occupations. However, a college degree is usually required for managerial and professional specialty jobs.

Customer service representatives require a high school degree and good communication skills. Familiarity with personal computers and a clear speaking voice are helpful. These workers receive on-the-job training to familiarize them with company services.

Installers require a high school degree, mechanical ability, and some technical knowledge. Newly hired installers receive on-the-job training and after several years may advance to line technician positions and work on complex maintenance and installation tasks. Cable modem installers should

have experience working with computers or an associate degree in computer information systems.

Table 1. Employment of wage and salary workers in cable and other pay television services by occupation, 1998 and projected change, 1998-2008

(Employment in thousands)

Occupation	1998 Employment Number	1998 Employment Percent	1998-2008 Percent change
All occupations	181	100.0	27.0
Administrative support, including clerical	65	35.7	24.5
Office and administrative support supervisors and managers	5	2.7	24.0
Dispatchers	5	2.6	36.5
Order clerks	4	2.3	14.8
Adjusters, investigators, and collectors	3	1.9	38.3
Secretaries	3	1.5	1.5
General office clerks	3	1.4	28.7
Bookkeeping, accounting, and auditing clerks	2	1.0	3.9
Precision production, craft, and repair	58	32.1	26.5
Telephone and cable TV line installers and repairers	40	22.0	27.5
Blue collar workers supervisors	5	2.9	27.5
Telecommunications equipment mechanics, installers, and repairers	3	1.5	15.3
Executive, administrative, and managerial	17	9.5	25.1
General managers and top executives	5	2.5	23.8
Management support occupations	4	2.1	24.7
Advertising, marketing, promotions, public relations, and sales managers	2	1.3	27.5
Communication, transportation, and utilities operations managers	2	1.2	27.5
Marketing and sales	17	9.5	27.5
All other sales and related workers	14	7.8	27.5
Marketing and sales worker supervisors	2	1.3	27.5
Professional specialty	14	7.9	43.5
Actors, directors, and producers	4	2.0	53.0
Camera operators, television, motion picture, video	2	1.0	72.2
Technicians and related	8	4.5	24.8
Engineering technicians	4	2.0	27.5
Broadcast and sound technicians	3	1.9	27.5
All other occupations	1	0.7	23.0

Line installers and repairers working on large feeder and trunk lines require several years' experience with cable technology. A two-year associate degree is helpful, as is knowledge of basic electronics and good mathematical aptitude. Experienced line technicians may advance to broadcast technicians, operating and maintaining electronic equipment used to transmit cable programming.

The Society of Cable Telecommunications Engineers (SCTE) offers certification programs for a variety of technician positions. Applicants for certification must be employed in the industry and attend training sessions at local SCTE chapters.

Applicants must pass both written and hands-on exams to receive certification. Similar training for cable technicians is available from private trade schools and organizations.

Professional positions in pay television services normally require a college degree. Employees in program production, such as producers and news analysts, often receive degrees in communications or broadcast journalism. Camera operator positions may only require a vocational school degree or equivalent experience. Competition for program production positions is strongest in large metropolitan areas. As a result, entry-level applicants must often look for work in small markets. Internships while in school are recommended for employment in program production; experience gained at college television stations is also helpful.

Engineering positions require a college degree, usually in electrical and electronic engineering. Useful specializations include communications, radio frequency systems, and signal processing. Positions as computer specialists, such as computer network administrators, also require a college degree. These employees generally need knowledge of the Internet and familiarity with different computer operating systems. Positions as market researchers and sales representatives usually require a degree in business, communications, or related fields. Experience gained through college internships is also useful.

Earnings

Earnings in 1998 averaged $564 a week in cable and other pay television services. This was higher than the average for all private industry; however, it was lower than average for communications industries as a whole (table 2.) Communications industries include telecommunications; radio and television broadcasting; and cable and other pay television services. Earnings in selected occupations in cable and other pay television services appear in table 3.

Table 2. Average earnings of nonsupervisory workers in cable and other pay television services, 1998

Industry segment	Weekly	Hourly
Total, private industry	$442	$12.77
Communications industries	706	17.30
Cable and other pay television services	564	14.14

Table 3. Median hourly earnings of the largest occupations in cable and other pay television services, 1997

Occupation	Cable and other pay TV services	All industries
Sales agents, advertising	$14.21	$14.16
Telephone and cable television line installers and repairers	11.56	15.32
Customer service representatives, utilities	9.83	12.55

Outlook

Employment in cable and other pay television services is expected to increase 27 percent between 1998 and 2008, faster than the 15 percent projected for all industries combined. Job growth will be driven by advances in technology that allow the industry to expand beyond pay television services. The delivery of new telecommunications services—such as high-speed Internet access, telephone communications, and digital television programming—will increase demand for subscriptions to pay television services. Industry employment will grow, as companies expand and upgrade their equipment to efficiently provide these new services, and as they add to their marketing capacity to compete for increased customer demand. The need for employees in a variety of occupations should create openings for both high school and college graduates. Opportunities will be best for those with technical skills and an understanding of the new telecommunications services offered in this industry. Some jobs will be lost, as a result of consolidation in this industry; however, these losses will be more than offset by employment gains stemming from increased customer demand for additional or improved services.

A variety of occupations will experience employment growth. Operators of cable systems will need workers to lay fiber optic cable, deploy new technologies to increase line capacity, and maintain the growing networks of cable lines. As cable systems become more competitive, there may be overbuilding—new companies will lay cables adjacent to existing cables in an attempt to compete for service. These trends should contribute to an increase in the employment of line installers. Operators of wireless systems will increase the number of transmission towers to provide high capacity service to additional customers. To lay out and design these systems, these operators will increase their employment of engineers, especially those with knowledge of radio frequency systems.

Employment of installers who set up service also will increase, as residential and business customers are drawn to high-speed Internet access and telephone services. However, the development of software that allows subscribers to install and configure the modems themselves may eventually reduce the need for cable modem installers.

All distributors of pay television services—cable, wireless, and satellite—will need more customer service representatives. Customers are unfamiliar with the new services offered in this industry and need help understanding their operation. In this increasingly competitive industry, providing easily accessible customer service representatives will be a priority for all distributors.

Finally, the introduction of digital technology, resulting in an increase in the number of cable networks and pay television service providers, will create opportunities in program production occupations, such as producers, newscasters, and camera operators. As distributors of pay television services install networks of computer servers, employment of computer specialists, such as network administrators, will increase. Computer servers will not only track customer information for authorization and billing, but will also house digital information, such as movies that customers can access on demand. With additional networks attempting to sell advertising, the demand for market researchers and sales staff should increase, as well.

Sources of Additional Information

Information on the cable industry is available from:

➤ National Cable Television Association, 1724 Massachusetts Ave. NW., Washington, DC 20036.
Internet: **http://www.ncta.com**

> American Cable Association, One Parkway Center, Suite 212, Pittsburgh, PA 15220. Internet: **http://www.scbateam.org**

For information on training and certification programs in the cable industry, contact:

> Society of Cable Telecommunications Engineers, Certification Department, 140 Philips Rd., Exton, PA 19341. Internet: **http://www.scte.org**

Information on careers in fixed wireless telecommunications is available from:

> Wireless Communications Association International (WCA), 1140 Connecticut Ave. NW., Suite 810, Washington, DC 20036. Internet: **http://www.wcai.com**

For information on satellite television services, contact:

> Satellite Broadcasting & Communications Association, 225 Reinekers Lane, Suite 600, Alexandria, VA 22314. Internet: **http://www.sbca.com**

Information on the following occupations can be found in the 2000-01 *Occupational Outlook Handbook*:

- Actors, directors, and producers
- Broadcast and sound technicians
- Computer systems analysts, engineers, and scientists
- Engineers
- Line installers and repairers
- Photographers and camera operators

Public Utilities

SIGNIFICANT POINTS

- Persons with college training in advanced technology will have the best opportunities.

- Employment growth and opportunities vary among segments of the industry.

- Production workers' earnings are significantly higher than in most other industries.

Nature of the Industry

The simple act of walking into a restroom, turning on the light, and washing your hands, uses the products of perhaps four different utilities. Electricity powers the light, water supply systems provide water for washing and drinking, wastewater treatment plants treat the sewage, and natural gas or electricity heats the water. Some government establishments do the same work and employ a significant number of workers; however, information about them is not included in this statement. Information concerning government employment in public utilities is included in the *Career Guide* statements on Federal Government and State and local government, excluding education and hospitals. Each of the various segments within the public utilities sector is distinctly different.

Electric services. This segment includes firms engaged in the generation, transmission, and distribution of electricity for sale. Electric plants harness highly pressurized steam or some force of nature to spin the blades of a turbine, which is attached to an electric generator. Coal is by far the dominant fuel used to generate steam in electric power plants, followed by nuclear power, natural gas, petroleum, and other energy sources. Hydroelectric generators are powered by the release of the tremendous pressure of water existing at the bottom of a dam or near a waterfall. Scientists are also conducting considerable research into renewable sources of electric power—geothermal, wind, and solar energy. Some municipalities capture combustible gasses or burn waste materials at landfills to generate electricity.

Legislative changes have created new classes of firms that generate and sell electricity. Industrial plants often have their own electricity generation facilities, usually capable of producing more than they require. They are called nonutility generators (NUG) and sell their excess power to utilities or to other industrial plants. A type of NUG, termed an independent power producer, is an electricity generating plant designed to take advantage of both industry deregulation and the latest generating technology to compete directly with utilities for industrial and other wholesale customers.

Transmission or high voltage lines supported by huge towers connect generating plants with industrial customers and substations. At substations, the electricity's voltage is reduced and made available for household and small business use via distribution lines, which are usually carried by telephone poles.

Gas production and transmission. Natural gas, a clear odorless gas, is found underground, often near or associated with crude oil reserves. Exploration and extraction of natural gas is part of the oil and gas extraction industry, covered elsewhere in the *Career Guide*. Once found and brought to the surface, it is transported throughout the United States, Canada, and Mexico by gas transmission companies in pressurized pipelines. Local distribution companies take natural gas from the pipeline, depressurize it, add its odor, and operate the system that delivers the gas from transmission pipelines to industrial, commercial, and residential customers. Nearly half of the natural gas produced is used by industries such as the chemical and paper industries. Households, which use gas for heating and cooking, electric utilities, and commercial businesses—such as hospitals and restaurants—account for most of the rest of the gas consumed.

Combination electric and gas, and other utility services. Utilities are classified as combination utilities when they are involved in both the production of electricity and the distribution of natural gas, or some other utility service. They are considered either electric combined or gas combined services, depending on which service makes up the majority of their business. Combination utilities are usually located in large metropolitan areas.

Water supply. Water utilities provide over 175 gallons of fresh, treated water every day for each person in this country, or about 40 billion gallons per day nationwide. Water is collected from various sources such as rivers, lakes, and wells. After collection, water is filtered, treated, and sold for residential, industrial, commercial, and public use. Depending on the population served by the water system, the utility may be a small plant in a rural area that requires the occasional monitoring of a single operator or a huge system of reservoirs, dams, pipelines, and treatment plants requiring the coordinated efforts of hundreds of people.

Sanitary services. This segment includes sewage systems and refuse systems. Sewage systems collect wastewater from homes and industries, treat it, and return clean water to the surface water supply. Wastewater treatment plants are similar to water treatment plants, but the treatment processes and regulatory requirements are generally more complicated, especially when dealing with industrial wastes.

Refuse systems collect and dispose of household garbage—called municipal solid waste—and refuse from commercial and industrial establishments by processing or destroying it through the operation of waste treatment plants, landfills, recycling plants, and incinerators. An increasing proportion of refuse is either recycled or burned to generate electricity.

Other utilities include steam and air-conditioning supply utilities, which produce and sell steam and cooled air, and irrigation systems, which operate water supply systems primarily for irrigation.

Utilities and the services they provide are so vital to everyday life that they are considered "public goods" and are heavily regulated. Formerly, utility companies operated as "regulated monopolies," meaning that in return for having no competition, they were subject to control by public utility commissions that ensured utilities acted in the public interest and regulated the rates they were allowed to charge. However, recent legislative changes have introduced competition into the utilities industry in an effort to promote efficiency, lower costs to customers, and provide users with an increased amount of service options.

Many utility companies are municipally owned. For example, of the roughly 2,000 gas distribution companies in the United States, about 1,000 are municipally owned. In general, utilities serving large cities have sufficient numbers of customers to justify the large expenditures necessary for building plants, and are run by private, investor-owned companies. In rural areas, where the small number of customers in need of services would not provide an adequate return for private investors, the State or local government funds the plant construction and operates the utility.

The various segments of the utilities industry vary in the degree to which their workers are involved in production activities, administration and management, or research and development. Industries such as water supply that employ relatively few workers employ more production workers and plant operators. On the other hand, electric utilities and combination electric and gas utilities generally operate larger plants using very expensive, high technology equipment, and thus employ more professional and technical personnel.

A unique feature of the utilities industry is that urban areas with many inhabitants generally have relatively few utility companies. For instance, there were about 54,000 community water systems in the United States in 1998 serving roughly 253 million people. The 46,000 small water systems served only 25 million people while the 8,000 largest systems served almost 228 million. Alaska, with a population equaling 10 percent of Massachusetts', had about three times more electric generating plants than Massachusetts in 1998. These examples result from economies of scale in the utilities industry that allow one or two companies to serve large numbers of customers in metropolitan areas more efficiently than many smaller companies.

Unlike most industries, the utilities industry imports and exports only a small portion of its product. In the natural gas industry, this reflects the fact that the country has a sizable, proven resource base that can be used economically to meet the country's needs. This is the result of a National policy that utilities should be self-sufficient, without dependence on imports for the basic services our country requires. However, easing trade restrictions, increased pipeline capacity, and shipping natural gas in liquefied form have made importing and

exporting natural gas more economical. In 1998, about 14 percent of the natural gas consumed was imported, mostly from Canada. A small portion of natural gas is exported in liquefied form, primarily to Japan.

Working Conditions

Electricity, gas, and water are produced and used continuously throughout each day. As a result, split, weekend, and night shifts are common for utility workers. The average workweek in utilities was 42.2 hours in 1998, compared to 34.6 hours for all industries, and 39.5 hours for all transportation and public utilities. Employees often must work overtime to accommodate peaks in demand and to repair damage caused by storms, cold weather, accidents, and other causes. The industry employs relatively few part-time workers.

The hazards of working with electricity, natural gas, treatment chemicals, and wastes can be substantial, but generally are avoided by following rigorous safety procedures. Protective gear such as rubber gloves with long sleeves, non-sparking maintenance equipment, and body suits with breathing devices designed to filter out any harmful fumes are mandatory for work in dangerous environs. Employees also undergo extensive training on working with hazardous materials and utility company safety measures.

In 1997, the electric services and combination utility services industries reported just 5.7 cases of work-related injury or illness per 100 full-time workers, compared to an average of 7.1 cases for all industries, and 10.3 cases for manufacturing industries. Sanitary services, however, had injury and illness rates higher than the average for all industries, with 11.2 cases per 100 full-time workers, reflecting the physically demanding nature of refuse collection and disposal.

Employment

Public utilities employed about 855,000 workers in 1998. Electric services provided over 40 percent of all jobs, as shown in table 1.

Table 1. Distribution of wage and salary employment in nongovernment public utilities, 1998

(Employment in thousands)

Industry	Employment	Percent
Total, all industries	855	100.0
Electric services	364	42.6
Water supply and sanitary services	196	22.9
Combination utility services	159	18.6
Gas production and distribution	136	15.9

Even though electric utilities are among the biggest customers of natural gas utilities, the processes used to produce their services are largely unrelated. This diversity of production processes is reflected in the size of the establishments that comprise the utilities industry. The combination electric and gas utility industry consists of relatively large plants. In 1997, it accounted for 9 percent of the reporting establishments, yet employed an average of over 100 workers per establishment. On the other hand, water supply utilities accounted for 16 percent of workplaces, yet

100

employed only an average of 7 workers per establishment (table 2).

Table 2. Nongovernment establishments in electric, gas, and sanitary services and average employment per establishment, 1997

(Employment in thousands)

Industry	Number of establishments	Employment per establishment
Total, all utilities	22,505	37
Sanitary services	6,288	18
Electric services	6,117	57
Gas production and distribution	3,839	33
Water supply	3,723	7
Combination electric and gas, and other combinations	2,125	107
Irrigation systems....................................	316	4
Steam and air-conditioning supply	85	20

SOURCE: U.S. Department of Commerce, *County Business Patterns*, 1997

Although many establishments are small, almost half of public utilities workers are employed in establishments with 250 or more workers (chart).

Occupations in the Industry

About 49 percent of those employed in the public utilities industry work in precision production or operator, fabricator, or laborer occupations (table 3). About 21 percent work in administrative support occupations; another 27 percent are employed in managerial, professional specialty, and technician occupations; and the remaining workers are in marketing, service, and related occupations.

Workers in production occupations install and maintain pipelines and powerlines, operate and fix plant machinery, and monitor treatment processes. *Line installers* and *repairers* install and repair cables or wires used in electrical power or

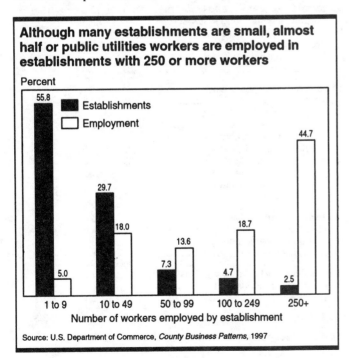

Although many establishments are small, almost half or public utilities workers are employed in establishments with 250 or more workers

Percent

- Establishments
- Employment

Number of workers employed by establishment	Establishments	Employment
1 to 9	55.8	5.0
10 to 49	29.7	18.0
50 to 99	7.3	13.6
100 to 249	4.7	18.7
250+	2.5	44.7

Source: U.S. Department of Commerce, *County Business Patterns*, 1997

distribution systems. They install insulators, wooden poles, and light or heavy-duty transmission towers. *Blue-collar worker supervisors* directly supervise and coordinate the activities of production workers. These supervisors ensure that workers, equipment, and materials are used and maintained properly and efficiently to maximize productivity.

Plant and system occupations include electric power generating plant operators, power reactor operators, power distributors and dispatchers, gas plant operators, and water and wastewater treatment plant operators. *Electric power generating plant operators* control or operate machinery, such as stream-driven turbine generators, to generate electric power, often through the use of control boards or semi-automatic equipment. *Power reactor operators* control nuclear reactors that produce steam for the generation of electric power, coordinate operation of auxiliary equipment, and regularly perform operating tests to ensure all equipment is working properly. *Power distributors* and *dispatchers* coordinate, regulate, or distribute electricity or steam in generating stations, over transmission lines to substations, and over electric power lines. *Gas plant operators* operate gas liquefying-and-regasification equipment, operate compressors to control gas pressure in transmission pipelines, and coordinate injections and withdrawals at storage fields. *Water and wastewater treatment plant operators* control the process of treating water or liquid waste, take samples of water for testing, and may perform maintenance of treatment plants.

Industrial machinery repairers install, repair, and maintain machinery in power generating stations, gas plants, and water treatment plants. They repair and maintain the mechanical components of generators, waterwheels, water-inlet controls, and piping in generating stations; steam boilers, condensers, pumps, compressors, and similar equipment in gas manufacturing plants; and equipment used to process and distribute water for public and industrial uses.

Maintenance mechanics, general utility, perform work involving a variety of maintenance skills to keep machines, mechanical equipment, and the structure of an establishment in repair. Generally found in small establishments, duties may involve pipefitting, boilermaking, electrical work, carpentry, welding, and installing new equipment.

Administrative support occupations account for about one-fifth of the jobs in the utilities industry. *Customer service representatives* interview applicants for water, gas, and electric service. They talk with customers by phone or in person and receive orders for installation, turn-on, discontinuance, or change in service. *General office clerks* may do bookkeeping, typing, stenography, office machine operation, and filing. *Meter readers* read electric, gas, water, or steam consumption meters visually or remotely using radio transmitters and record the volume used by residential and industrial customers. Financial records processing occupations, such as *billing, cost,* and *rate clerks*, compile data, compute fees and charges, and prepare invoices for billing purposes, in addition to the routine calculating, posting, and verifying duties necessary to keep financial records complete.

Operator, fabricator, and laborer occupations include *helpers*, the entry-level occupation in almost all utilities occupations tied to production activities. Other helpers include *refuse collectors*, who collect and dump refuse from containers into a truck. *Material moving equipment operators* distribute refuse around landfills and ensure that the refuse is covered by the necessary amount of soil or cover each day. *Truckdrivers* operate refuse collection trucks that are either self-loading or loaded by refuse collectors.

Executives, managers, and administrators in the utilities industry plan, organize, direct, and coordinate management activities. They are often responsible for maintaining an adequate supply of electricity, gas, water, steam, or sanitation service.

Professional specialty occupations in this industry include engineers and computer systems analysts, engineers, and scientists. *Engineers* develop technologies that allow, for example, utilities to produce and transmit gas and electricity more efficiently and water more cleanly. They may also develop improved methods of landfill or wastewater treatment operations in order to maintain compliance with government regulations. *Computer systems analysts, engineers*, and *scientists* develop computer systems to automate utility processes; provide plant simulators for operator training; and improve operator decision making.

Technicians account for only a small proportion of total employment in this industry. Technician occupations include *Engineering* and *science technicians* who assist engineers in research activities and may conduct some research independently.

Training and Advancement

Public utilities provide career opportunities for persons with varying levels of experience and education. However, because the utilities industry consists of many different companies and products, skills developed in one industry may not be transferable to other industries.

High school graduates qualify for most entry-level production jobs. Production workers may start as laborers or in other unskilled jobs and, by going through an apprenticeship program and gaining on-the-job experience, advance into better paying positions that require greater skills or have greater responsibility. Substantial advancement is possible even within a single occupation. For example, electric power plant operators may move up through several levels of responsibility until they reach the highest paying operator jobs. Advancement in production occupations generally requires mastery of advanced skills on the job, usually with some formal training provided by the employer or through additional vocational training at a 2-year technical college. Additional formal education from an outside source is sometimes needed.

Most computer, engineering, and technician jobs require technical education after high school, although opportunities exist for persons with degrees ranging from an associate degree to a doctorate. These workers are usually familiar with company objectives and production methods which, combined with college education, equips them with many of the tools necessary for advancement to management positions. Graduates of 2-year technical institutes usually fill technician positions. Sometimes graduates of engineering programs will start as technicians until an opportunity to advance into an engineering position arises.

Managerial jobs generally require a 4-year college degree, though a 2-year technical degree may be sufficient in smaller plants. Managers can usually advance into higher-level management jobs without additional formal training outside the workplace. Competition is expected to be keen for management positions, as recent industry restructuring is forcing utility companies to shed excess layers of management to improve productivity and be able to compete in the new deregulated environment.

Table 3. Employment of wage and salary workers in public utilities by occupation, 1998 and projected change, 1998-2008

(Employment in thousands)

Occupation	1998 Employment		1998-2008 Percent change
	Number	Percent	
All occupations	855	100.0	-3.8
Precision production, craft, and repair	312	36.6	-4.9
Electric powerline installers and repairers	61	7.2	-14.6
Blue collar worker supervisors	46	5.4	-6.0
Electric power generating plant operators, distributors, and dispatchers	31	3.7	-2.5
Industrial machinery mechanics	25	3.0	-5.4
Maintenance repairers, general utility	16	1.9	-6.7
Vehicle and mobile equipment mechanics and repairers	14	1.6	8.3
Water and liquid waste treatment plant and system operators	9	1.1	44.3
Construction equipment operators	8	0.9	13.9
Administrative support, including clerical	179	20.9	-9.8
Meter readers, utilities	27	3.1	-11.3
General office clerks	22	2.6	1.0
Financial records processing occupations	20	2.3	-5.3
Office and administrative support supervisors and managers	17	2.0	-4.0
Secretaries	15	1.8	-22.1
Stock clerks and order fillers	8	1.0	-8.9
Adjusters, investigators, and collectors	8	0.9	-.5
Operators, fabricators, and laborers	105	12.3	13.8
Helpers, laborers, and material movers, hand	50	5.8	2.7
Truckdrivers	32	3.7	36.0
Material moving equipment operators	12	1.4	10.2
Executive, managerial, and administrative	114	13.3	-5.5
General managers and top executives	17	2.1	7.5
Communication, transportation, and utilities operations managers	16	1.9	-6.1
Accountants and auditors	10	1.2	-11.9
Engineering, natural science, and computer and information systems managers	7	0.9	15.3
Professional specialty	71	8.3	-2.1
Electrical and electronics engineers	13	1.5	-9.4
Computer systems analysts, engineers, and scientists	11	1.3	22.2
Technicians and related support	43	5.0	-15.7
Engineering technicians	21	2.5	-11.4
Drafters	9	1.1	-27.7
Marketing and sales	17	1.9	3.5
All other occupations	14	1.7	-.4

Earnings

Overall, the industry had average weekly wages of $843 in 1998. Earnings varied by industry segment within public utilities (table 4). Average weekly earnings for production workers were highest in combination utilities ($1,024) and electric services ($878), and lowest in sanitary services ($674).

Table 4. Average earnings and hours of nonsupervisory workers in public utilities by segment of industry, 1998

Industry segment	Earnings Weekly	Earnings Hourly	Weekly hours
Total, private industry	$442	$12.77	34.6
Public utilities	843	19.97	42.2
Combination utility services	1,024	24.30	42.9
Electric services	878	21.01	41.8
Gas production and distribution	783	18.56	42.2
Sanitary services	674	15.70	42.9

Earnings in public utilities are generally higher than earnings in other industries. The hourly earnings for production workers in public utilities averaged $19.97 in 1998, compared to $15.34 in all transportation, communications, and public utilities, and $12.77 in all private industry. This was due in part to more overtime and weekend work—as utility plant operations must be monitored 24 hours a day—which commands higher hourly rates. Earnings in selected occupations in public utilities appear in table 5.

Table 5. Median hourly earnings of the largest occupations in public utilities, 1997

Occupation	Public utilities	All industries
General managers and top executives ...	$34.30	$26.05
First-line supervisors and manager/ supervisors-mechanics, installers, and repairers	24.34	18.17
Electrical Power-Line Installers and Repairers	20.75	19.87
Maintenance mechanics, water or power generation plant	20.26	17.64
First-line supervisors and managers/ supervisors-clerical and administrative support workers	18.60	14.26
Meter readers, utilities	14.10	12.15
Customer service representatives, utilities	13.79	12.55
Truck drivers, heavy or tractor-trailer	13.37	13.08
General office clerks	11.22	9.10
Refuse and recyclable material collector	11.00	10.19

Almost 34 percent of workers in public utilities are union members or are covered by a union contract, more than double the 15.4 percent rate for all industries.

Outlook

Employment in public utilities is expected to decline by 4 percent from 1998 to 2008. Projected employment change, however, varies by industry segment, as shown in table 6. Although electric power and natural gas are essential to everyday life, employment declines will result from improved production methods and technology, energy conservation by consumers and more efficient appliances, and a more competitive regulatory environment.

Table 6. Projected employment growth in public utilities by industry segment, 1998-2008

Industry segment	Percent change
Total, all public utilities	-3.8
Water supply and sanitary services	34.3
Electric services	-14.5
Combination utility services	-17.2
Gas production and distribution	-14.4

Over the past several years, deregulation of electric and gas utilities has increased competition and provided incentives for improved efficiency. For example, non-utility generators of electricity, such as a major industrial plant operating its own power generators, now are allowed to sell their excess electricity to utilities at competitive rates. Independent power producers can now build electric power generating plants for the sole purpose of selling their power to utilities. These producers generally build gas-turbine-generating plants, which have lower construction and environmental costs, fewer employees, and can generally sell electric power more cheaply than the coal-powered steam-turbine generator plants.

In the gas transmission and distribution industry, regulatory changes now allow wholesale buyers to purchase gas at competitive rates from any producer and to use the gas pipeline transmission network to transport the gas. This process is also occurring at the distribution level. These changes caused an increase in gas and electric utility mergers, workforce reductions, and the redesign and reallocation of job duties in a process that will continue through the projection period.

New energy policies also provide for investment tax credits for research and development directed at renewable sources of energy and set standards for the efficiency of the various types of equipment used in electric utilities. As a result, electric utilities will continue to improve the productivity of their plants and workers, resulting in a slowdown in employment opportunities. However, highly trained technical personnel with the education and experience to take advantage of new developments in electric utilities should face good prospects for employment.

In the water supply and sanitary services industries, regulatory changes have had the opposite impact. Regulations in these industries have not been designed to increase competition, but to increase the number of contaminants that must be monitored and treated and to tighten the environmental impact standards of these industries, resulting in increased employment.

Two non-regulatory competing trends affect gas production and distribution utilities. Although natural gas is an increasingly popular choice among homeowners and businesses, the efficiency of natural gas furnaces has increased dramatically, significantly reducing average home consumption. These energy-conserving technologies are expected to decrease the relative use of natural gas by most industries and by individual homes. In addition, utilities in colder climates have begun to automate meter reading and billing procedures. Combined, these developments are projected to result in a decrease in employment in natural gas transmission and distribution services.

Water supply and sanitation services are projected to be the fastest growing sector of public utilities, with employment projected to increase 34 percent from 1998 to 2008. This industry is expected to grow due to an increase in the amount of waste generated per person, an increase in population, increasing disposal requirements for different materials, and an increase in the percentage of refuse that is recycled. Also, newly constructed housing developments are more likely to have community water supplies and wastewater treatment facilities, increasing demand for these services. About 14,000 new jobs in this industry will be created for truckdrivers and operators of material moving equipment, such as landfill bulldozer operators. Despite automation and other improvements in production technology in this industry, expanding hazardous waste regulations and the increase in recycling facilities are expected to contribute to growth in production workers such as hazardous materials removal workers, water and liquid waste treatment plant operators and machinery, equipment, and motor vehicle mechanics.

In general, persons with college training in advanced technology will have the best opportunities in public utilities industries. Computer engineers, scientists, and systems analysts are expected to be among the fastest growing occupations in the professional specialty occupational group. With emphasis on improving plant automation and productivity, employment of these college-educated workers is projected to grow by 22 percent. Marketing and sales workers are expected to increase in number and importance as competition for wholesale customers, who can now buy power from the lowest bidder, increases and utilities begin to rely on their sales staff to expand their customer base. Some administrative support workers, such as meter readers and financial records processing occupations, are among those affected by increasing automation. Technologies including radio-transmitting meter reading and computerized billing procedures are expected to decrease employment.

Sources of Additional Information

General information on the public utilities industry and employment opportunities is often available from local utilities, the unions to which their workers belong, and from:

➢ American Gas Association, 400 N. Capitol St. NW., Washington, DC 20001.
Internet: **http://www.aga.org**
➢ Utility Workers Union of America, 815 16th St. NW., Suite 605, Washington, DC 20006.
➢ American Water Works Association, 6666 West Quincy, Denver, CO 80235.
➢ International Brotherhood of Electrical Workers, 1125 15th St. NW., Washington, DC 20005.

Detailed information on many of the key occupations in the public utilities industry, including the following, may be found in the 2000-01 edition of the *Occupational Outlook Handbook*:

● Blue-collar worker supervisors
● Computer engineers and scientists
● Computer systems analysts
● Electrical and electronics engineers
● Electric power generating plant operators and power distributors and dispatchers
● Engineering technicians
● Handlers, equipment cleaners, helpers, and laborers
● Industrial machinery repairers
● Line installers and repairers
● Maintenance mechanics, general utility
● Material moving equipment operators
● Nuclear engineers
● Water and wastewater treatment plant operators

Radio and Television Broadcasting

SIGNIFICANT POINTS

- Keen competition is expected for many jobs due to the large number of jobseekers attracted by the glamour of this industry.

- Many entry-level positions are at smaller stations, where an employee may perform several different job functions.

- Except for news, relatively few workers in this industry are involved in the production of television programs because most are pre-recorded by the motion picture industry.

Nature of the Industry

This industry consists of radio and television stations that broadcast programs free of charge to the public. Broadcast signals travel over the airwaves from a station's transmission tower to the antennas of television sets and radios; personal computers can also be equipped to receive the transmissions. Anyone in the signal area with a radio, television, or properly equipped personal computer can receive the programming. Television broadcasts carried on cable and other pay television systems are classified in a separate industry. (The statement on cable and other pay television services appears elsewhere in the *Career Guide*.)

Radio and television stations broadcast a variety of programs, such as national and local news, talk shows, music programs, movies, other entertainment, and advertisements. Broadcast stations produce some of these programs in their own studios, notably news programs; however, much of the programming is produced outside the broadcast industry. Establishments which produce programming for radio and television stations—but which do not broadcast the programming—are classified in the amusement and recreation services industry and the motion picture industry. (Statements on amusement and recreation services and motion picture production and distribution appear elsewhere in the *Career Guide*).

Radio and television stations broadcast programs free of charge; owners of radios and television sets do not pay broadcasters to receive programming. Revenue for commercial radio and television stations comes from the sale of advertising time during selected programs. The rates paid by advertisers depend on the size and characteristics of the program's audience, and the time of day the program is broadcast. Revenue for educational and non-commercial stations primarily comes from donations, foundations, government, and corporations. These stations are generally owned and managed by public broadcasting organizations, religious institutions, or school systems.

Changes in government regulation and technology are affecting the broadcast industry. The Telecommunications Act of 1996 relaxed ownership restrictions, resulting in an increased number of consolidations among broadcast stations. The Federal Communications Commission (FCC), the government agency responsible for regulating the broadcast industry, also is encouraging the development of low-powered broadcast stations. These stations are relatively inexpensive to establish, making it easier for community, religious, and educational groups to broadcast in their local areas.

The FCC is also a proponent of digital television (DTV), a technology that uses digital signals to transmit television programs. Digital signals consist of pieces of simple electronic code that can carry more information than conventional signals. A growing number of television stations are implementing digital broadcasting. This allows for the transmission of higher resolution pictures, referred to as high definition television (HDTV).

Broadcasters can use digital technology to transmit a single HDTV broadcast or they can multicast several conventional broadcasts. Multicasting is the transmission of more than one signal on a given channel. For example, a broadcast station could transmit a sporting event from several different camera angles on the same channel. Viewers would then be able to select which view their television set receives.

Digital broadcasting can transmit a variety of information besides television programming. For example, viewers with access to DTV could obtain electronic newspapers, computer software, telephone directories, and any other information that can be translated into digital code.

Working Conditions

Most employees in this industry work in clean, comfortable surroundings in broadcast stations and studios. Some employees work outside the broadcast studio, however, under less favorable conditions.

News teams made up of reporters, camera operators, and technicians travel in electronic news gathering trucks to various locations to cover news stories. Although such location work is exciting, assignments such as reporting on natural disasters may present danger. These assignments may also require outdoor work under adverse weather conditions.

Camera operators working on such news teams must have the physical stamina to carry and set up their equipment. Technicians on electronic news gathering trucks must insure that the mobile unit's antenna is correctly positioned in order to avoid electrocution from power lines. Field service engineers work on outdoor transmitting equipment and may have to climb poles or antenna towers; their work can take place under a variety of weather conditions. Broadcast technicians who maintain and set up equipment may have to do heavy lifting.

News, programming, and engineering employees work under a great deal of pressure in order to meet deadlines. As a result, these workers are more likely to experience varied or erratic work schedules than are sales and administrative workers.

For many people, the excitement of working in broadcasting compensates for the demanding nature of the jobs. Although this industry is noted for its high pressure, the work is not hazardous. The rate of occupational illness and injury in broadcasting is much lower than the average for all industries. In 1997, cases of work-related injury and illness averaged only 1.8 per 100 full-time workers in radio and television broadcasting, significantly lower than the rate of 7.1 per 100 for all private industry.

Employment

The radio and television broadcasting industry provided 247,000 wage and salary jobs in 1998. Of this total, 116,000 were in radio broadcasting, and 131,000 were in television broadcasting. Most jobs were in large establishments; more than 60 percent of the jobs were in establishments with over 50 employees (chart). Radio and television broadcasting establishments are found throughout the country, but jobs in larger stations are concentrated in large cities.

Occupations in the Industry

Occupations at large broadcast stations fall into five general categories: Program production, news-related, technical, sales, and general administration. At small stations, jobs are less specialized and employees often perform several functions. Although on camera or on air positions are the most familiar occupations in broadcasting, the majority of employment opportunities are behind the scenes (table 1).

Program production occupations. Most television programs are produced by the motion picture industry; actors, directors, and producers working on these pre-recorded programs are not employed by the television and radio broadcast industry.

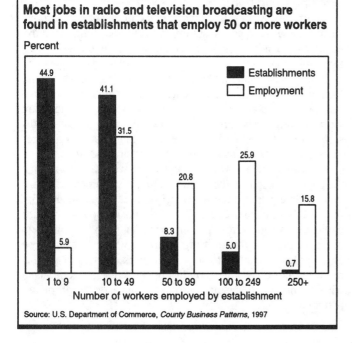

Most jobs in radio and television broadcasting are found in establishments that employ 50 or more workers

Percent

Establishments / Employment

1 to 9: 44.9 / 5.9
10 to 49: 41.1 / 31.5
50 to 99: 8.3 / 20.8
100 to 249: 5.0 / 25.9
250+: 0.7 / 15.8

Number of workers employed by establishment

Source: U.S. Department of Commerce, *County Business Patterns*, 1997

Program production occupations at television and radio stations create programs such as news and talk shows and musical programming.

Production assistants help the producer create the program. They provide clerical and research assistance; assist with the preparation of musical, written, and visual materials; and time the production to make sure it does run over schedule. They may also operate cameras and other audio and video equipment.

Video editors select and assemble pre-taped video, including sound and special effects, to create a finished program. Conventional editing requires assembling pieces of videotape to create a finished product in a linear fashion. The editor first assembles the beginning of the program, and then works sequentially towards the end. Newer computerized editing allows an editor to electronically cut and paste video segments. This technique is known as non-linear editing because the editor is no longer restricted to working sequentially; a segment may be moved at any time to any location in the program.

Producers plan and develop live or taped productions, determining how the show will look and sound. They select the script, talent, sets, props, lighting, and other production elements. They also coordinate the activities of on-air personalities, production staff, and other personnel. *Website* or *Internet producers*, a relatively new occupation in the broadcast industry, plan and develop Internet sites that provide news updates, program schedules, and information about popular shows. The website producer decides what will appear on the site and is responsible for its overall design and maintenance.

Announcers make news announcements and provide other information such as program schedules and station breaks for commercials or public service information. *Disc jockeys* announce recorded music on radio stations and may take requests from listeners, interview guests, and may comment on the music, weather, or traffic. They often select the music to be played and may operate tape machines, CD players, and transmitter equipment, especially in smaller stations. Announcers and disc jockeys need a good speaking voice; disc jockeys also need knowledge of music.

Program directors are in charge of on-air programming in radio stations. Program directors decide what type of music will be played, supervise on-air personnel, and sometimes select the specific songs and order in which they will be played. Considerable experience, usually as a disc jockey, is required, as well as a thorough knowledge of music.

News-related occupations. News, weather, and sports reports are important to many television stations because they attract a large audience. Many radio stations depend on up-to-the-minute news for a major share of their programming. Program production occupations, such as producers and announcers, also work on the production of news programs.

Reporters and *correspondents* gather information from various sources, analyze and prepare news stories, and report on the air. *Correspondents* report on news occurring in the large U.S. and foreign cities where they are stationed. *Newswriters* edit and write the news stories from information collected by reporters; newswriters may advance to positions as reporters or correspondents.

Newscasters, also known as *news analysts* or *news anchors*, analyze, interpret and broadcast news received from various sources. News anchors present news stories and introduce videotaped news or live transmissions from on-the-scene reporters. Newscasters at large stations may specialize in a particular field. *Weathercasters*, also called weather reporters, report current and forecasted weather conditions. They gather information from national satellite weather services, wire services, and local and regional weather bureaus. Some weathercasters are trained *meteorologists* and can develop their own weather forecasts. *Sportscasters* are responsible for reporting sporting events. They usually select, write, and deliver the sports news for each newscast.

Assistant news directors supervise the newsroom; they coordinate wire service reports, tape or film inserts, and stories from individual newswriters and reporters. *Assignment editors* assign stories to news teams, sending them on location if necessary.

News directors have overall responsibility for the news team of reporters, writers, editors, and newscasters as well as studio and mobile unit production crews. This senior administrative position has responsibilities that include determining events to be covered, and how and when they will be presented in a news broadcast.

Technical occupations. Employees in these occupations operate and maintain the electronic equipment that records and transmits radio or television programs. The titles of some of these occupations use the terms "engineer," "technician," and "operator" interchangeably.

Broadcast and *sound technicians* operate equipment that regulates the signal strength, clarity, and range of sounds and colors of broadcasts. *Audio control engineers* operate equipment to regulate volume and sound quality of a broadcast; *video control engineers* regulate brightness, contrast, and visual quality. *Transmitter operators* monitor and log outgoing signals and operate transmitters. *Maintenance technicians* set up and maintain electronic broadcasting equipment. *Field technicians* or *field service engineers* set up, operate, and maintain equipment outside the studio, including portable transmitting equipment and stationary transmitters on towers.

Camera operators set up and operate studio cameras, which are used in the television studio; and electronic news gathering cameras, which are mobile and used outside the studio when a news team is pursuing a story at another location. Camera operators need training in video as well as some experience in television production.

Master control engineers ensure that all of the radio or television station's scheduled program elements, such as on-location feeds, pre-recorded segments, and commercials, are smoothly transmitted. They are also responsible for ensuring that transmissions meet Federal Communications Commission (FCC) requirements.

Technical directors direct the studio and control room technical staff during the production of a program. They need a thorough understanding of both the production and technical aspects of broadcasting, acquired as a lighting director, camera operator, or in another position.

Assistant chief engineers oversee the day-to-day technical operations of the station. *Chief engineers* or *directors of engineering* are responsible for all the station's technical facilities and services. These workers need a bachelors' degree in electrical engineering, technical training in broadcast engineering, and years of broadcast engineering experience acquired in less responsible positions.

Table 1. Employment of wage and salary workers in radio and television broadcasting by occupation, 1998 and projected change, 1998-2008

(Employment in thousands)

Occupation	1998 Employment Number	1998 Employment Percent	1998-2008 Percent change
All occupations	247	100.0	2.5
Professional specialty	123	49.9	5.4
Announcers	44	17.9	-6.7
Actors, directors, producers	22	8.8	19.9
News analysts, reporters and correspondents	19	7.6	4.7
Photographers and camera operators	14	5.8	19.3
Writers and editors, including technical writers	6	2.4	4.7
Marketing and sales	34	13.7	4.7
All other sales and related workers	29	11.7	4.7
Marketing and sales worker supervisors	5	1.9	4.7
Executive, administrative, and managerial	30	12.0	2.4
General managers and top executives	9	3.6	1.6
Advertising, marketing, promotions, public relations, and sales managers	5	2.1	4.7
Management support occupations	5	1.9	3.0
Communication, transportation, and utilities operations managers	3	1.3	4.7
Technicians and related	28	11.3	-4.1
Broadcast and sound technicians	23	9.2	-5.8
Engineering technicians	3	1.4	4.7
Administrative support, including clerical	27	10.8	-5.7
Secretaries	4	1.7	-16.7
General office clerks	4	1.6	5.7
Receptionists and information clerks	3	1.4	4.6
Office and administrative support supervisors and managers	3	1.3	1.8
Bookkeeping, accounting, and auditing clerks	3	1.0	-14.7
Precision production, craft, and repair	3	1.3	-3.5
All other occupations	2	0.9	-2.7

Sales and marketing occupations. Most of the workers in this category are *sales representatives*, sometimes known as *account executives*. They sell advertising time to sponsors, advertising agencies, and other buyers. Sales representatives must have a thorough knowledge of the size and characteristics of their station's audience, including income levels and consumption patterns.

Large stations generally have several workers who spend all of their time handling sales. *Sales managers*, who may handle a few large accounts personally, supervise these workers. If the station is large enough, *researchers* may be employed to collect and analyze statistics and other market information on the community being served. In small stations, part-time sales personnel or announcers often handle sales responsibilities during hours they are not on the air.

General administration. *General managers* or *station managers* coordinate all radio and television station activities. In very small stations, the manager and a bookkeeper may handle all the accounting, purchasing, hiring, and other routine office work. In larger stations, the general administrative staff includes business managers, accountants, lawyers, personnel workers, public relations workers, and others. They are assisted by administrative support workers such as secretaries, typists, bookkeepers, clerks, and messengers.

Training and Advancement

Professional specialty, management, and sales occupations generally require a college degree; technical occupations often do not. It is easier to obtain employment and gain promotions with a degree, especially in larger, more competitive markets. Advanced schooling is generally required for supervisory positions—including technical occupations—having greater responsibility and higher salaries.

Entry-level jobs in news or program production increasingly require a college degree and some broadcast experience. Approximately 450 colleges offer formal programs in journalism and mass communications, including programs in radio and television broadcasting. Some community colleges offer 2-year programs in broadcasting. Broadcast trade schools offer courses which last 6 months to a year and teach radio and television announcing, writing, and production.

Individuals pursuing a career in broadcasting often gain initial experience through work at college radio and television stations or through internships at professional stations. Although these positions are usually unpaid, they sometimes provide college credit or tuition. More importantly, they provide hands-on experience and a competitive edge when applying for jobs. In this highly competitive industry, broadcasters are less willing to provide on-the-job training, and instead seek candidates who can perform the job immediately.

Some technical positions require only a high school diploma. However, many broadcast stations seek individuals with training in broadcast technology, electronics, or engineering from a technical school, community college, or 4-year college. An understanding of computer networks and software will become more important as the industry introduces more digital technology. Supervisory technical positions and jobs in large stations generally require a college degree.

The Society of Broadcast Engineers (SBE) issues certification to technicians who pass a written examination. Several classes of certification are available, requiring increasing levels of experience and knowledge for eligibility. The Telecommunications Act of 1996 mandated that the FCC drop its licensing requirements for transmitter maintenance; SBE certification has filled the void left by the elimination of this license.

Employees in the radio and television broadcasting industry often find their first job in broadcast stations serving smaller markets. Competition for positions in large metropolitan areas is stronger, and these stations usually seek highly experienced personnel. Because many radio and television stations are small, workers in this industry often must change employers to advance. Relocation to communities in other parts of the country is frequently necessary.

Earnings

Weekly earnings in 1998 averaged $633 in radio and television broadcasting, higher than the average of $442 for all private industry. As a common rule, earnings of broadcast personnel are highest in large metropolitan areas. Earnings in selected occupations in radio and television broadcasting for 1997 appear in table 2.

Table 2. **Median hourly earnings of the largest occupations in radio and television broadcasting, 1997**

Occupation	Radio and television broadcasting	All industries
General managers and top executives ...	$33.63	$26.05
Marketing, advertising, and public relations managers	23.88	25.61
Sales agents, advertising	13.66	14.16
Photographers	13.17	9.61
Producers, directors, actors, and other entertainers	13.02	—
Writers and editors	12.66	15.69
Reporters and correspondents	11.18	11.23
Broadcast technicians	10.41	11.21
Announcers, radio and television	8.21	8.34
Camera operators, television and motion picture	8.15	9.50

The principal unions representing employees in radio and TV broadcasting are the National Association of Broadcast Employees and Technicians (NABET), the International Brotherhood of Electrical Workers (IBEW), the International Alliance of Theatrical Stage Employees (IATSE), and the American Federation of Television and Radio Artists (AFTRA).

Outlook

Employment in radio and television broadcasting is expected to increase only 2 percent over the 1998-2008 period, slower than the 15 percent projected for all industries combined. Factors contributing to the slow rate of growth include industry consolidation, introduction of new technologies, greater use of prepared programming, and competition from other media. Keen competition is expected for many jobs due to the large number of jobseekers attracted by the glamour of this industry. Job prospects will be best for applicants with college degrees and technical training.

Consolidation of individual broadcast stations into large networks, especially in the radio sector, has increased due to relaxed ownership regulations. This trend will limit employment growth as networks use workers more efficiently. For example, a network can produce news programming at one station and then use the programming for broadcast from other stations, eliminating the need for multiple news staffs. Similarly, technical workers can be pooled to maintain equipment at several stations simultaneously.

The introduction of new technology is also slowing employment growth. Conventional broadcast equipment used to be relatively specialized; each piece of equipment served a separate function and required an operator with specialized knowledge. Newer computerized equipment often combines the functions of several older pieces of equipment and does not require specialized knowledge for operation. This reduces the need for certain types of workers, including those responsible for editing, recording, and graphics creation. In addition, increased use of remote monitoring equipment allows technical workers in one location to operate and monitor transmissions at a remote station.

Employment growth is also being constrained by the increasing use of radio and television programming created by services outside the broadcasting industry. These establishments provide prepared programming including music, news, weather, sports, and professional announcer services. The services can easily be accessed through satellite hook ups and reduce the need for program production and news staff at radio and television stations.

Finally, employment growth will remain relatively slow because broadcasters anticipate decreasing advertising revenues due to increased competition from cable systems; satellite and other pay television services; and from widespread use of the Internet.

However, broadcasting may experience faster employment growth in the area of data services. The introduction of digital transmission will allow broadcasters to start transmitting data such as electronic publications, software, and interactive educational materials. Although the broadcasters who enter the data services market will face much competition from other industries—such as telecommunications and cable and other pay television services—strong consumer demand could lead to employment growth in this area.

Sources of Additional Information

For a list of schools with accredited programs in broadcast journalism, send a request to:

➤ Accrediting Council on Education in Journalism and Mass Communications, University of Kansas, School of Journalism, Stauffer-Flint Hall, Lawrence, KS 66045. Internet: **http:// www.ukans.edu/~acejmc**

For information on certification of broadcast technicians, contact:

➤ Society of Broadcast Engineers, 8445 Keystone Crossing, Suite 140, Indianapolis, IN 46240. Internet: **http://www.sbe.org**

For career information, contact:

➤ National Association of Broadcast Employees and Technicians, Communications Workers of American (NABET/CWA), International, 501 Third St. NW., Washington, DC 20001. Internet: **http://union.nabetcwa.org/nabet**
➤ National Association of Broadcasters, Career Center, 1771 N St. NW., Washington, DC 20036. Internet: **http://www.nab.org**

For employment and salary information, contact:

➤ National Association of Broadcasters, Research and Planning Department, 1771 N St. NW., Washington, DC 20036. Internet: **http://www.nab.org**

Information on the following occupations may be found in the 2000-01 *Occupational Outlook Handbook*:

- Actors, directors, and producers
- Announcers
- Broadcast and sound technicians
- News analysts, reporters, and correspondents
- Photographers and camera operators
- Writers and editors, including technical writers

Telecommunications

(SIC 481, 482, 489)

SIGNIFICANT POINTS

- Telecommunications are rapidly expanding beyond traditional voice telephone service.

- The demand for greater telecommunications capacity—or bandwidth—will create jobs that require technical skills.

- Average earnings in telecommunications greatly exceed average earnings throughout private industry.

Nature of the Industry

Changes in technology and government regulation continue to transform the telecommunications industry. Whereas voice telephone communication was once the primary service of the industry, the transmission of a variety of materials, including data, graphics, and video is now commonplace. The widespread installation of fiber optic cables, which transmit light signals along glass strands, permits faster, higher capacity transmissions than traditional copper wirelines. In addition, networks of radio towers and satellites are rapidly expanding wireless telecommunications services.

Changes in government regulation have introduced competition into an industry that was once dominated by a single company. Competition from outside the industry will increase as cable companies and public utilities enter the newly deregulated telecommunications market.

The principal sector of the telecommunications industry is telephone communications; establishments in this sector operate both wireline and wireless networks. Wireline networks use wires and cables to connect customers' premises to central offices maintained by telecommunications companies. Central offices contain switching equipment that routes content to its final destination or to another switching center. For example, switching equipment may route local phone calls directly from the central office to their final destination; long distance calls are routed to larger switching centers that determine the most efficient route for the call to take.

Wireless networks are rapidly expanding; they operate through the transmission of signals over networks of radio towers and communications satellites. For example, a wireless cellular telephone transmits radio signals to an antenna located on a radio tower; the signal is then transmitted through the antenna into the wireline network. Other wireless services include beeper, paging, and satellite telephone services. Because these devices require no wireline connection, they are popular with customers who need to communicate as they travel, residents of areas with inadequate wireline service, and those who simply desire the convenience of portable communications.

The wireline and wireless sectors also include resellers of telecommunications services. These resellers lease transmission facilities, such as telephone wirelines, from existing telecommunications networks, and then resell the service to other customers. Other sectors in the industry include message communications services such as e-mail and facsimile services; and operators of other communication services ranging from radar stations to radio networks used by taxicab companies.

Voice telephone communications have long been the predominant service offered by telephone companies. With the rising popularity of the Internet, however, customers increasingly use their telephone service to transmit data and other electronic materials. The transmission of such content relies on digital technologies that use telecommunications networks more efficiently than conventional systems. Digital signals consist of separate pieces of electronic code that can be broken apart during transmission and then reassembled at the destination without losing clarity. Telecommunications providers have built networks of computerized switching equipment, called packet switched networks, to route digital signals. Packet switches break the signals into small segments or "packets" and provide each with the necessary routing information. Segments may take separate paths to their destination, and may share the paths with transmissions from other users. At the destination, the segments are reassembled, and the transmission is complete. Because packet switching considers alternate routes, and allows multiple transmissions to share the same route, it results in a more efficient use of telecommunications capacity.

The transmission of analog voice signals requires relatively small amounts of capacity on telecommunications networks. By contrast, the transmission of data, video, and graphics requires much higher capacity. This transmission capacity is referred to as bandwidth. As the demand increases for high-capacity transmissions—especially with the rising popularity of the Internet—telecommunications companies are continually expanding and upgrading their networks to increase the amount of available bandwidth.

Wireline providers are expanding their networks by laying additional fiber optic cable, which provides higher bandwidth and transmission speed than copper wire. The capacity of fiber optic cables is increasing due to a technology known as wavelength division multiplexing (WDM). WDM divides each glass strand within a cable into different colors of the spectrum; each color can carry a separate stream of data, increasing overall capacity. Providers have also begun offering upgraded service on the copper wirelines that connect most residential customers with the central offices. Technologies such as digital subscriber lines allow these lines to simultaneously transmit voice and data communications at relatively high speeds. Additionally, satellite communications providers are planning the launch of a network of satellites that will compete with wireline providers for high-bandwidth data communication services.

Government deregulation has resulted in an increase in competition in the telecommunications industry. Until the early 1980s, the American Telephone and Telegraph Corporation (AT&T) provided most telephone service in this country and operated under a system of State and Federal regulations. In 1984, efforts by the U.S. courts to break up AT&T's dominance over the telecommunications market led to the breakup of the company. Under the divestiture agreement, AT&T gave up ownership and control of its local telephone companies, which were reorganized into seven independent "Baby Bell" companies that continued to provide local service. The new AT&T became a provider of long distance telephone service, in competition with other companies.

The Telecommunications Act of 1996 allowed competition in all sectors of the communications industry, from local and long-distance telephone services, to cable television and broadcasting. The Act also opened the telecommunications market to sectors outside the industry, such as public utilities. As a result of this latest round of industry deregulation, telecommunications companies are able to compete across traditionally separate markets. For example, a single provider might offer both local and long distance telephone service. Providers from other industries are also entering the telecommunications market, offering cable TV and high-speed Internet access, as well as telephone service. Such convergent services are popular with customers seeking to consolidate their purchase of communication services. To meet this demand for combined services, mergers have begun to take place as companies seek to acquire the services they need to compete in the marketplace.

Working Conditions

The telecommunications industry offers steady, year-round employment. Overtime is sometimes required, especially during emergencies such as floods or hurricanes when workers may need to report to work with little notice.

Line installers and repairers work in a variety of places, both indoors and outdoors, and in all kinds of weather. Their work involves lifting, climbing, reaching, stooping, crouching, and crawling. They must work in high places such as rooftops and telephone poles. Their jobs bring them into proximity with electrical wires and circuits, so they must take precautions to avoid shocks. These workers must wear safety equipment when entering manholes, and test for the presence of gas before going underground.

Telecommunications equipment mechanics, installers, and repairers generally work indoors—most often in a telecommunication company's central office or a customer's place of business. They may have to stand for long periods, climb ladders, and do some reaching, stooping, and light lifting. Adherence to safety precautions is essential to guard against work hazards such as minor burns and electrical shock.

Most communications equipment operators, such as telephone operators, work at video display terminals in pleasant, well-lighted, air-conditioned surroundings. If the work site is not well designed, however, operators may experience eyestrain and back discomfort. The rapid pace of the job and close supervision may cause stress. Some workplaces have introduced innovative practices among their operators to reduce job-related stress.

The number of disabling injuries in telephone communications, the principal sector of the telecommunications industry, has been well below the average in past years. In 1997, cases of work-related injury and illness were 3.0 per 100 full-time workers, significantly lower than the 7.1 for the entire private sector.

Employment

The telecommunications industry provided 1,042,000 wage and salary jobs in 1998. Most jobs were concentrated in telephone communications, which employed 1,007,000 workers. The two remaining sectors of the telecommunications industry—telegraph and other message communications, and communications services, not elsewhere classified—provided 35,000 jobs in 1998.

Most telephone employees work in large establishments. About 77 percent of employment is in establishments with 50 or more employees (chart). With continuing deregulation, however, the number of small contractors has been increasing. Telecommunications jobs are found in almost every community, but most telephone employees work in cities that have large concentrations of industrial and business establishments.

Occupations in the Industry

Although the telecommunications industry employs workers in many different occupations, about 60 percent of all workers are employed in either administrative support or precision production, craft, and repair occupations (table 1).

Telephone craft workers install, repair, and maintain telephone equipment, cables and access lines, and telecommunications systems. These workers can be grouped by the type of work they perform. *Line installers and repairers* connect telephone central offices to customers' telephone systems. They install poles and terminals and place wires and cables that lead to a consumer's premises. They use power-driven equipment to dig holes and set telephone poles. Line installers climb the poles or use truck-mounted buckets (aerial work platforms) and attach the cables using

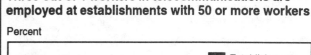

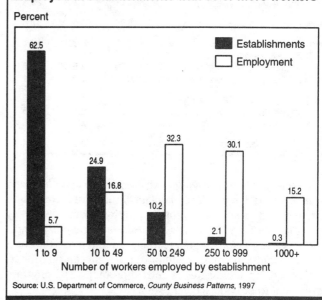

Three out of 4 workers in telecommunications are employed at establishments with 50 or more workers

Percent

- Establishments
- Employment

Number of workers employed by establishment	Establishments	Employment
1 to 9	62.5	5.7
10 to 49	24.9	16.8
50 to 249	10.2	32.3
250 to 999	2.1	30.1
1000+	0.3	15.2

Source: U.S. Department of Commerce, *County Business Patterns*, 1997

various hand tools. After line installers place cables on poles, towers, or in underground conduits and trenches, they complete the line connections.

Table 1. Employment of wage and salary workers in telecommunications by occupation, 1998 and projected change, 1998-2008

(Employment in thousands)

Occupation	1998 Employment		1998-2008 Percent change
	Number	Percent	
All occupations	1,042	100.0	23.4
Administrative support, including clerical	354	34.0	7.9
General office clerks	28	2.7	-23.2
Central office operators	23	2.2	-17.0
Directory assistance operators	22	2.1	-36.3
Office and administrative support supervisors and managers	20	1.9	23.6
Material recording scheduling, dispatching, and distributing occupations	19	1.9	16.0
Adjustment clerks	19	1.8	38.4
Secretaries	14	1.3	1.5
Bookkeeping, accounting, and auditing clerks	9	0.9	3.3
Precision production, craft, and repair	261	25.0	23.0
Telephone and cable TV line installers and repairers	82	7.9	43.0
Central office and PBX installers and repairers	38	3.7	34.9
Station installers and repairers, telephone	23	2.3	-36.2
Blue-collar worker supervisors	22	2.1	2.1
Electrical powerline installers and repairers	9	0.9	27.4
Executive, administrative, and managerial	165	15.9	37.3
Communication, transportation, and utilities operations managers	51	4.9	38.9
Management support occupations	37	3.6	26.0
General managers and top executives	16	1.6	22.5
Advertising, marketing, promotions, public relations, and sales managers	11	1.1	26.8
Marketing and sales	109	10.5	37.6
Professional specialty	95	9.2	46.7
Computer systems analysts, engineers, and scientists	38	3.6	71.5
Electrical and electronics engineers	18	1.8	35.1
Technicians and related support	47	4.5	13.6
Computer programmers	23	2.2	8.5
Engineering technicians	21	2.0	19.7
All other occupations	9	0.9	20.4

Telecommunications equipment mechanics, installers, and repairers install, repair, and maintain the array of increasingly complex and sophisticated communications equipment. For example, *central office equipment installers* or *equipment installation technicians* set up, rearrange, and remove the complex switching and dialing equipment used in central offices. They may also solve network-related problems and program equipment to provide special features.

Station installers and repairers, sometimes called *telephone installers* or *service technicians*, install, service, and repair telephone systems and other communications equipment on customers' property. When customers move or request new types of service, installers relocate telephones or make changes in existing equipment. They assemble equipment and install wiring. They also connect telephones to outside service wires and sometimes must climb poles or ladders to make these connections.

Administrative support workers perform a variety of duties. *Communications equipment operators*, including *central office operators*, *directory assistance operators*, and *switchboard operators*, make telephone connections; assist customers with specialized services such as reverse-charge calls; and provide telephone number assistance.

Excluding operators, other *administrative support* occupations make up over one-fourth of all telecommunications employment. *Customer service representatives* help customers understand the new and varied types of services offered by telecommunications providers. Some customer service representatives are also expected to sell services and may work on a commission basis. Other administrative support workers include *adjusters, investigators, and collectors*; *records processing occupations*; *secretaries*; *general office clerks*; and *office and administrative support supervisors and managers*. These workers perform a variety of duties including keeping service records, compiling and sending bills to customers, and preparing statistical and other company reports.

Over 9 percent of the industry's employees are professional workers. Many of these are scientific and technical personnel such as *engineers* and *computer systems analysts, engineers, and scientists*. Engineers plan cable and microwave routes, central office and PBX equipment installations, the expansion of existing structures, and solve other engineering problems. Some engineers also engage in research and development of new equipment. *Computer engineers* who work with software, known as *software engineers*, design, develop, test, and debug software products, such as computer-assisted engineering programs for schematic cabling projects, modeling programs for cellular and satellite systems, and programs for telephone options, such as voice mail, electronic mail, and call waiting. *Telecommunications specialists* design voice and data communications systems, helping to integrate communications equipment with computer networks. They work closely with clients, who may not understand sophisticated communications systems, and design systems that meet their customers' needs. Telecommunications specialists coordinate the installation of these systems and may provide follow up maintenance and training. In addition, the industry employs many other managerial, professional, and technical workers, such as *communication, transportation, and utilities operations managers*; *accountants and auditors*; *human resources managers* and *training and labor relations specialists*; *engineering technicians*; and *computer programmers*.

About 11 percent of the industry's employees are in marketing and sales occupations. These workers sell telecommunications services, such as long distance service, personal answering services, voice mail, electronic mail, and call waiting telephone options.

New occupational specialties have emerged based on the industry's new innovations and technologies. *Laser and fiber optic engineers* conduct research and design gas lasers and related equipment needed to send messages via fiber optic cable transmission. They study the limitations and uses of lasers and fiber optics, find new applications for them, and oversee the building, testing, and operations of the new applications.

Training and Advancement

The telecommunications industry offers employment in jobs requiring a variety of skills and training. Many jobs require a high school education in addition to on-the-job training. Other jobs require particular skills that may take several years of experience to learn completely. For some managerial and professional jobs, employers require a college education.

Line installers are often hired initially as helpers, ground workers, or tree trimmers who clear branches from telephone lines. Because the work entails a lot of climbing, applicants should have stamina and be unafraid of heights. The ability to distinguish colors is necessary because wires and cables are coded by color. Although line installers usually do not complete a formal apprenticeship, they generally receive several years of on-the-job training. Line installers may transfer to other highly skilled jobs, such as engineering assistant, or may move into other kinds of work such as sales. Promotion to crew supervisor, technical staff, or instructor of new employees also is possible.

Most companies prefer to hire telecommunications equipment mechanics, installers, and repairers with postsecondary training in electronics; familiarity with computers is also important. Training sources include 2- and 4- year college programs in electronics or communications, trade schools, and training provided by equipment and software manufacturers. Telecommunications equipment mechanics, installers and repairers may advance to jobs maintaining more sophisticated equipment or to engineering technician positions.

Communications equipment operators should have clear speech and good hearing; computer literacy and typing skills are also important. New operators learn equipment operation and procedures for maximizing efficiency. Instructors monitor both the time and quality of trainees' responses to customer requests. Formal classroom instruction and on-the-job training may last several weeks.

A bachelor's degree in engineering is usually required for entry-level jobs as electrical and electronics engineers. Continuing education is important for these engineers; those who fail to keep up with the rapid changes in technology risk technological obsolescence, which makes them more susceptible to layoffs or, at a minimum, more likely to be passed over for advancement.

While there is no universally accepted way to prepare for a job as a computer professional, most employers place a premium on some formal college education. Computer engineers working with software usually hold a degree in computer science or in software engineering. For systems analyst, programmer-analyst, or database administrator positions, many employers seek applicants who have a bachelor's degree in computer science, information science, or management information systems.

Due to the rapid introduction of new technologies and services, the telephone industry is among the most rapidly changing in the economy. This means workers must keep their job skills up to date. From managers to telephone operators, increased knowledge of both computer hardware and software is of paramount importance. Telecommunications industry employers now look for workers with skills, abilities, and knowledge in the following areas: computer programming and software design; voice telephone technology, known as telephony; laser and fiber optic technology; wireless technology; data compression skills; and sales ability enhanced by interpersonal skills and a knowledge of telecommunications terminology.

Earnings

Average weekly earnings of nonsupervisory workers in telephone communications, the principal sector of the telecommunications industry, were $756 in 1998, significantly higher than average earnings of $442 in private industry. Earnings in selected occupations in telephone communications for 1997 appear in table 2.

Table 2. Median hourly earnings of the largest occupations in telephone communications, 1997

Occupation	Telephone communications	All industries
Communications, transportation and utilities operations managers	$31.13	$24.10
Computer programmers	23.45	22.61
Central office and PBX installers and repairers	20.39	20.06
Telephone and cable television line installers and repairers	19.89	15.32
Station installers and repairers, telephone	18.87	18.71
Sales agents, selected business services	16.56	15.91
Directory assistance operators	14.48	14.33
Customer service representatives, utilities	13.44	12.55
General office clerks	13.06	9.10
Central office operators	12.05	12.07

About 29 percent of employees in the industry are union members or covered by union contracts, compared with 15 percent for all industries. Most telephone employees belong to one of two unions—the Communications Workers of America or the International Brotherhood of Electrical Workers.

Union contracts in most companies determine wage rates, wage increases, and the time needed to advance from one step to the next. According to the Communications Workers of America (CWA), weekly earnings of union craft workers employed by AT&T and the Bell Operating Companies started at an average of $283 in 1998, but increased to $996 a week after 5 years. Telephone operators represented by the union started at an average of $235 a week and averaged $654 a week after 4 years.

Telephone installers and repairers, represented by the International Brotherhood of Electrical Workers, earned approximately $12.60 to $22.50 an hour in 1999. In the same year, equipment installer technicians represented by the union earned approximately $16.70 to $24.80 an hour, and operators earned approximately $10.50 to $17.30 an hour.

Outlook

Employment in the telecommunications industry is expected to increase 23 percent over the 1998-2008 period, faster than the 15 percent projected for all industries combined. Strong growth in both residential and business demand for high-capacity communications will lead to the expansion of telecommunications networks. This expansion will create employment opportunities for individuals with strong technical skills.

Residential demand will increase as technology lowers the price of today's premium services, such as high-speed Internet access and wireless telephone service, bringing them within the price range of more consumers. Demand will also increase as deregulation allows providers to offer combined services, making it easier for households to obtain a wide variety of telecommunications services. Business demand will rise as companies increasingly rely on their telecommunications systems to conduct electronic commerce. In order to remain competitive, businesses will require high-speed access to the Internet for a variety of purposes including purchasing, marketing, sales, and customer service. Some employment loss will result from improved labor-saving technologies, such as self-monitoring equipment, and from layoffs resulting from mergers in the deregulated industry. However, this loss will be more than offset by the employment gain due to the increased demand for telecommunications services.

Technology will continue to transform the industry. The installation and upgrading of fiber optic networks will bring ever-faster communications closer to residential customers. Internet telephony, which transmits voice, video, fax, and electronic mail communications over the World Wide Web, will blur the boundaries between telecommunications providers and Internet service providers. Wireless providers will increase the capacity of their radio networks and introduce portable lightweight devices capable of transmitting voice, data, and video. Undersea cables and orbiting satellites will integrate wireline and wireless customers into a global system of high bandwidth communications. The installation of computerized switching systems designed for digital content will make transmitting data, video, and graphics as easy as making voice telephone calls.

The removal of competitive barriers will increase competition from providers outside the telecommunications industry. Cable TV providers will use their wireline networks to offer customers a combination of services including telephone service, Internet access, and cable TV programming. Electric utilities, which own extensive communications facilities, are entering the telecommunications market and may be joined by communications equipment manufacturers and broadcast TV stations.

Employment growth will differ among the various occupations in the telecommunications industry, largely as a result of technology. Employment of central office and directory assistance operators is expected to decline due to the increasing use of automation. Although telecommunications companies will strive to always provide access to a live operator, improved technologies will reduce the need for their employment. Computer voice recognition technology lessens the need for central office operators, as customers can obtain help with long distance calls from automated systems. This technology, which also enables callers to request numbers from a computer instead of a person,

is expected to reduce the number of directory assistance operators. Their numbers may drop further as the increasing use of the Internet leads customers to use automated directory assistance resources on the Web.

Employment of line installers and repairers is expected to increase as telecommunications providers expand their networks in response to customer demand. New fiber optic networks will be installed and existing ones expanded to provide customers with high-speed access to data, video, and graphics. Businesses will request more wireline installations to provide increased connections to suppliers and customers. Residential customers who are not able to obtain upgrades to their copper wirelines will install additional wirelines in order to use voice and data communications simultaneously.

Employment of telecommunications equipment mechanics, installers, and repairers is also expected to increase. Telecommunications providers will install computerized switching equipment to efficiently route increasing amounts of high bandwidth communications. The lack of individuals with the necessary technical skills will create employment opportunities for qualified applicants. Although newer, reliable technologies will decrease the need for equipment maintenance, this will be offset by the high demand for installation of new equipment.

In addition, employment of engineers and computer professionals is expected to increase. The expansion of communications networks, and the need for telecommunications providers to invest in research and development, will create job opportunities for electrical and electronics engineers. The use of increasingly sophisticated computer technology will increase employment of computer professionals, including computer engineers, computer support specialists, and computer systems analysts. Growth among these occupations will create employment opportunities for engineering, natural science, and computer and information systems managers.

Sources of Additional Information

For more details about employment opportunities, contact your local telephone company or write to:

➤ International Brotherhood of Electrical Workers, Telecommunication Department, 1125 15th St. NW., Washington, DC 20005.

➤ Communications Workers of America, 501 3rd St. NW., Washington, DC 20001.
Internet: **http://www.cwa-union.org**

For more information on the telephone industry, write:

➤ United States Telephone Association, 1401 H St. NW., Suite 600, Washington, DC 20005-2164.
Internet: **http://www.usta.org**

More information about the following occupations in this industry appears in the 2000-01 edition of the *Occupational Outlook Handbook*.

● Communications equipment operators
● Line installers and repairers
● Office clerks, general
● Telecommunications equipment mechanics, installers, and repairers

Trucking and Warehousing

(SIC 42)

SIGNIFICANT POINTS

- Most jobs require no formal education, but truckdrivers must meet qualifications and standards established by State and Federal regulations.

- Truckdrivers hold one-half of all trucking and warehousing jobs.

- Job opportunities are expected to be good for qualified truckdrivers and service technicians.

Nature of the Industry

Firms in the trucking and warehousing industry provide a link between manufacturers and consumers. Businesses, and occasionally individuals, contract with trucking and warehousing companies to pick up, transport, store, and deliver a variety of goods. Increasingly, trucking and warehousing firms provide "logistics services" in addition to traditional transportation, warehousing, and storage services. Logistics services include a range of services related to the distribution of goods, such as inventory control and management, order entry and fulfillment, labeling, light assembly, packaging, and price marking. This industry includes two distinct segments, local and long distance trucking and terminals and public warehousing and storage.

Local and long distance trucking and terminals provide over-the-road transportation of cargo using motor vehicles, such as trucks and tractor trailers. This industry segment is further subdivided based on distance traveled and the type of goods delivered. Local trucking establishments primarily carry goods within a single metropolitan area and its adjacent nonurban areas. Long distance trucking establishments carry goods between distant areas. Courier service establishments handle individual letters and light packages.

Local trucking comprised over 60,000 trucking establishments in 1997. The work of local trucking firms varies depending on the products transported. Produce truckers usually pick up loaded trucks early in the morning and spend the rest of the day delivering produce to many different grocery stores. Lumber truckdrivers, on the other hand, make several trips from the lumber yard to one or more construction sites. Some local truck transportation firms also take on sales and customer relations responsibilities, in addition to delivering the firm's products. Some local trucking firms specialize in local furniture moving, garbage collecting and trash removal, or hauling dirt and debris.

Long-distance trucking firms account for a majority of the jobs in the trucking and warehousing industry. Numbering nearly 50,000 establishments, this sector comprises establishments primarily engaged in providing long-distance trucking between distant areas and sometimes between the United States and Canada and Mexico. These establishments handle a wide variety of commodities, transported in numerous types of equipment—from refrigerated trailers to flatbeds. Included in this industry are establishments operating as truckload (TL) or less than truckload (LTL) carriers.

Truckload carriers move large amounts of goods directly to their destination usually with no stops in between. These long-distance carrier establishments provide full truck movement of freight from the shipment's origin to its destination. The shipment of freight on a truck is characterized as a full single load not combined with other shipments.

Less-than-truckload carriers pick up multiple shipments and bring them to a terminal, where they are unloaded and then reloaded by destination to be carried to distant terminals near the shipments' destination, from where they are delivered. Through a national or regional network of terminals, activities of LTL carriers include local pickup, local sorting and terminal operations, line-haul of freight, destination sorting and terminal operations, and local delivery.

Some goods are carried across country using "intermodal" transportation to save time and money. This can be any combination of truck, train, plane, or ship. Typically, trucks perform at least one leg in the transportation of goods. For example, a tractor-trailer delivers a load of goods to a railroad terminal. The trailer is hoisted onto a train, hauled across country, unloaded from the train, and hauled by truck to the final destination. Goods can be transported at lower cost this way, but they cannot be highly perishable, such as fresh produce, nor have strict delivery time schedules. Trucking still dominates the transportation of perishable and time-sensitive goods.

Courier services establishments deliver letters, parcels, and small packages under 100 pounds, usually within the confines of a metropolitan area. They were one of the fastest growing segments of the industry in the 1980s. (Companies that use aircraft to deliver small items to distant destinations are part of the air transportation industry also included in the *Career Guide*.)

Motor freight transportation terminals are mostly operated by large trucking companies. However, there were nearly 320 independent terminals not affiliated with trucklines in 1997. Many of these independent terminals break down truckloads of produce and other foods into shipments to area wholesalers. Many terminals also offer truck maintenance and repair services.

Public warehousing and storage facilities comprised over 12,000 establishments in 1997. These firms were primarily engaged in operating warehousing and storage facilities for general merchandise and refrigerated goods. They provided facilities to store goods; self-storage mini-warehouses that rent to the general public are also included in this segment of the industry.

Deregulation of interstate trucking in 1980 encouraged many firms to begin providing a wide range of logistical services that complement trucking and warehousing services.

Companies attempted to compete with each other by offering lower rates and unique services for individual customers. This has led to innovations in the distribution process and opened opportunities for customer-oriented services. Logistical services such as computerized inventory information on the location, age, and quantity of goods available can improve the efficiency of relationships between manufacturers and customers. "Just-in-time" shipping, in which trucking companies deliver goods from suppliers just in time for their use, allows recipients to reduce their inventories but requires constant communication and the transferal of accurate information. Packaging, labeling, and repairing manufacturers' products are another service that warehousing establishments use to attract potential customers. The growth of logistics services has blurred the distinction between trucking and warehousing. Many trucking companies have expanded into services encompassing the entire transportation process—including inventory management, materials handling, and warehousing—and are often referred to as "third-party logistics providers."

Working Conditions

In the trucking and warehousing industry in 1998, workers averaged 40.0 hours week, compared to an average of 34.6 hours for all private industries.

The U.S. Department of Transportation governs work hours and other working conditions of truckdrivers engaged in interstate commerce. For example, a long-distance driver generally cannot work more than 60 hours in any 7-day period. Many drivers, particularly on long runs, work close to the maximum time permitted because employers usually compensate them based on the number of miles or hours they drive. Drivers frequently travel at night, on holidays, and weekends to avoid traffic delays and to deliver cargo on time.

Truckdrivers must cope with a variety of working conditions including variable weather and traffic conditions, boredom, and fatigue. Many truckdrivers, however, enjoy the independence and lack of supervision found in long-distance driving. Local truckdrivers often have regular routes or assignments that allow them to return home in the evenings.

Improvements in roads and trucks are reducing stress and increasing the efficiency of long-distance drivers. Many advanced trucks have the capacity to be a mini apartment on wheels. Sleeper cabs are equipped with refrigerators, televisions and beds for the driver's convenience. Included in some of these state-of-the-art vehicles is a satellite link with the company headquarters. Troubleshooting mechanical problems, directions, weather reports, and other important communications can be delivered to the truck from anywhere in the country in a matter of seconds. This keeps the trucker in communication with the dispatcher to discuss delivery schedules and courses of action should there be bad weather or mechanical problems. It also allows the dispatcher to track the location of the truck and monitor fuel consumption and engine performance.

Truck mechanics and service technicians usually work indoors, although they occasionally make repairs on the road. Minor cuts, burns, and bruises are common, but serious accidents can be avoided when the shop is kept clean and orderly and safety practices observed. Mechanics and service technicians handle greasy and dirty parts and may stand or lie in awkward positions to repair vehicles and equipment. They

usually work in well lighted, heated, and ventilated areas, but some shops are drafty and noisy.

Freight, terminal, and warehouse workers usually work indoors, though they may do occasional work on trucks and forklifts outside. Some occasions warrant heavy lifting and other physical labor.

Safety is a major concern of the trucking and warehousing industry. The operation of trucks, lifts, and other technically advanced equipment can be dangerous without proper training and supervision. Efforts are underway to standardize the training programs to make the drivers more efficient and effective truck operators. Truckdrivers already must adhere to federally mandated certifications and regulations. Federal mandates require drivers to submit to drug and alcohol tests as a condition of employment and more employers also require periodic checks while on the job.

In 1997, work-related injuries and illnesses in the trucking and warehousing industry averaged 10.0 per 100 full-time workers, higher than the 7.1-incidence rate for the entire private sector. About 4 out of 5 on-the-job fatalities in the trucking and warehousing industry resulted from motor vehicle accidents.

Employment

The trucking and warehousing industry provided more than 1.7 million wage and salary jobs in 1998. About half of the workers in the industry, 881,000, were truckdrivers. Other operators, fabricators, and laborers numbered 265,000, and another 285,000 workers were in various administrative support occupations. There were 50,000 bus and truck mechanics and diesel engine specialists; 56,000 blue-collar worker supervisors; 114,000 executives, administrators, and managers; and 34,000 marketing and sales workers.

Most employees in the trucking and warehousing industry work in small establishments. Over 3 out of 4 trucking and warehousing establishments employ fewer than 10 workers (chart). Although there are some large national and regional trucking companies, they face constant competition. About 15

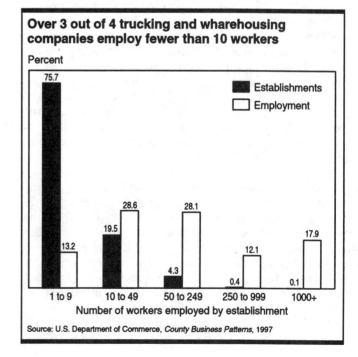

Over 3 out of 4 trucking and wharehousing companies employ fewer than 10 workers

Percent

Legend: ■ Establishments □ Employment

Number of workers employed by establishment	Establishments	Employment
1 to 9	75.7	13.2
10 to 49	19.5	28.6
50 to 249	4.3	28.1
250 to 999	0.4	12.1
1000+	0.1	17.9

Source: U.S. Department of Commerce, *County Business Patterns*, 1997

percent of truckdrivers operate their own business. Although these owner-operators constantly enter the industry each year, intense competition has caused many to eventually fail.

Trucking and warehousing establishments are found throughout the United States, with a slightly higher concentration located in California, New Jersey, and Texas.

Occupations in the Industry

Operators, fabricators, and laborers comprise 66 percent of the jobs in the industry (table 1). *Truckdrivers*, who comprised 51 percent of employment in this industry, transport goods from one location to another. They ensure safe delivery of cargo to a specific destination, often by a designated time. Drivers also perform some minor maintenance work on their vehicles and make routine safety checks.

The length of trips varies according to the merchandise being transported and its final destination. Local drivers provide regular service while other drivers make inter-city and interstate deliveries that take longer and may vary from job to job. The driver's responsibilities and assignments change according to the time spent on the road and the type of payloads transported.

Local drivers usually work more normal schedules and return home at the end of the day. They may deliver goods to stores or homes, or haul away dirt and debris from excavation sites. Many local drivers cover the same routes daily or weekly. Long-distance truckdrivers often are on the road for long stretches of time. Their trips vary from an overnight stay to a week or more. On longer trips, drivers sometimes sleep in bunks in their cabs or share driving with another driver.

Helpers, laborers, and *material movers* help load and unload freight and move it around warehouses and terminals. Often these unskilled employees work together in groups of three or four. They may use conveyor belts, hand trucks, or forklifts to move freight. They may place heavy or bulky items on wooden skids or pallets and have industrial truck and tractor operators move them.

Administrative support workers perform the daily record keeping operations for the trucking and warehousing industry. *Dispatchers* coordinate the movement of freight and trucks. They provide the main communication link that informs the truckdrivers of their assignments, schedules, and routes. Often dispatchers receive new shipping orders on short notice and must juggle drivers' assignments and schedules to accommodate a client. *Shipping, receiving, and traffic clerks* keep records of shipments arriving and leaving. They verify the contents of trucks' cargo against shipping records. They may also pack and move stock. *Billing, cost, and rate clerks* maintain company records of the shipping rates negotiated with customers and shipping charges incurred; they also prepare customer invoices.

Precision production, craft, and *repair* workers generally enter these jobs only after acquiring experience in related jobs or after receiving specialized training. For example, laborers and material movers who demonstrate their dependability and capability for handling responsibility may advance to *blue-collar worker supervisor* jobs. They oversee other workers in the warehouse or terminal. Most *mechanics and service technicians* require special vocational training. Mechanics and service technicians in trucking and warehousing firms perform preventive safety checks as well as routine service and repairs. Mechanics and service technicians sometimes are promoted to parts-manager positions. Parts managers keep the supply of replacement parts needed to repair vehicles. Parts managers monitor the parts inventory using a computerized system, and purchase new parts to replenish supplies. These employees need mechanical knowledge and must be familiar with computers and purchasing procedures.

Marketing and *sales* workers sell trucking and warehousing services to shippers of goods. They meet with prospective buyers, discuss the customer's needs, and suggest appropriate services. Travel may be required, and many analyze sales statistics, prepare reports, and handle some administrative duties.

Executive, administrative, and *managerial* staff provide general direction to the firm. They staff, supervise, and provide safety and other training to workers in the various occupations. They also resolve logistical problems such as forecasting transportation demand, mapping out the most efficient traffic routes, order processing, parts and equipment service support, and transportation of goods to the right place at the right time.

Table 1. Employment of wage and salary workers in trucking and warehousing by occupation, 1998 and projected change, 1998-2008

(Employment in thousands)

Occupation	1998 Employment		1998-2008 Percent change
	Number	Percent	
All occupations	1,745	100.0	11.4
Operators, fabricators, and laborers	1,146	65.7	14.6
Truck drivers	881	50.5	17.8
All other helpers, laborers, and material movers, hand	103	5.9	-7.1
Industrial truck and tractor operators	58	3.3	9.3
Refuse collectors	26	1.5	18.9
Hand packers and packagers	21	1.2	12.7
Administrative support, including clerical	285	16.4	2.1
General office clerks	52	3.0	11.8
Dispatchers	41	2.4	4.5
Office and administrative support supervisors and managers	28	1.6	7.6
Bookkeeping, accounting, and auditing clerks	23	1.3	-11.0
Stock clerks and order fillers	21	1.2	15.6
Secretaries	21	1.2	-13.4
Billing, cost, and rate clerks	20	1.1	-11.8
Shipping, receiving, and traffic clerks	19	1.1	6.3
Precision production, craft, and repair	140	8.1	8.4
Blue-collar worker supervisors	56	3.2	10.5
Bus and truck mechanics and diesel engine specialists	50	2.9	7.2
Machinery mechanics, installers, and repairers	16	0.9	5.9
Executive, administrative, and managerial	114	6.5	6.8
General managers and top executives	53	3.0	6.2
Communication, transportation, and utilities operations managers	26	1.5	8.7
Marketing and sales	34	1.9	9.2
All other occupations	25	1.4	13.7

117

Training and Advancement

Most jobs in the trucking and warehousing industry require only a high school education, although many employers prefer to hire employees with a high school diploma. For the positions requiring higher education, several universities offer "logistics" graduate and undergraduate programs. These programs emphasize the tools necessary to manage the distribution of goods. A growing number of employers recommend some form of formal training either in-house or through trade or union programs. Although, the Federal Government does not mandate these programs, the trend is toward certification and standardized competency.

Whereas many States allow those who are 18 years old to drive trucks within State borders, the U.S. Department of Transportation establishes minimum qualifications for truckdrivers engaged in interstate commerce. Federal Motor Carrier Safety Regulations require truckdrivers to be at least 21 years old, have at least 20/40 vision and good hearing, and be able to read and speak English. They must also have good driving records. In addition, drivers must have a State commercial driver's license, for which they must pass a written examination and a skills test operating the type of vehicle they will be driving. Individual companies often have additional requirements applicants must meet.

Some truckdrivers enter the occupation by attending training schools for truckdrivers. Schools vary greatly in the quality of training they provide, but they are becoming more standardized. Many employers and some States support these programs.

Some large trucking companies have formal training programs that prospective drivers attend. Other companies assign experienced drivers to teach and mentor newer drivers. Local trucking firms often start drivers as truckdriver helpers. As they gain experience and demonstrate their reliability, they receive assignments with greater earnings or preferred work schedules. Because of increased competition for experienced drivers, some larger companies lure these drivers with increased pay and preferred assignments. Some trucking firms hire only experienced drivers.

Some long-distance truckdrivers purchase a truck and go into business for themselves. Although many of these owner-operators are successful, some fail to cover expenses and eventually go out of business. Owner-operators should have good business sense as well as truckdriving experience. Courses in accounting, business, and business mathematics are helpful, and knowledge of truck mechanics can enable owner-operators to perform their own routine maintenance and minor repairs.

Unskilled employees may work as helpers, laborers, and material-movers in their first job. They must be in good physical condition because the work often involves a great deal of physical labor and heavy lifting. They acquire skills on the job and often advance to more skilled jobs in other occupations with which they work closely, such as industrial truck operator, truckdriver, shipping and receiving clerk, or supervisor.

Administrative support jobs in the trucking and warehousing industry require good typing skills and usually some familiarity with computers. Shipping and receiving clerks watch and learn the skills of the trade from more experienced workers while on the job. Stock clerks and truckdrivers often advance to dispatcher positions after becoming familiar with company operations and procedures.

While some diesel mechanics and service technicians learn the trade on the job, most employers prefer to hire graduates of programs in diesel mechanics offered by community and junior colleges or vocational and technical schools. Those with no training often start as helpers to mechanics, doing basic errands and chores such as washing trucks or moving them to different locations. Experience as an automotive mechanic is helpful because many of the skills relate to diesel mechanics. Experienced mechanics and service technicians may advance to shop supervisor or parts manager positions.

For managerial jobs in the trucking and warehousing industry, employers prefer persons with bachelor's degrees in business, marketing, accounting, industrial relations, or economics. Although a few universities offer logistics programs, most managers must learn logistics through extensive training on the job. Good communication, problem solving, and analytical skills are valuable in entry level jobs. Managers hired for entry level logistics positions sometimes advance to top level managerial jobs.

Some college graduates and persons without a college degree enter sales or administrative positions. Marketing and sales workers must be familiar with their firm's products and services and have strong communication skills.

Earnings

Average earnings in the trucking and warehousing industry are higher than the average for all private industry, as shown in table 2. The average wage in the trucking sector of the industry was higher than the average wage in warehousing. Earnings in selected occupations in trucking and warehousing appear in table 3.

Table 2. Average earnings of nonsupervisory workers in trucking and warehousing, 1998

Industry segment	Weekly	Hourly
All private industry	$442	$12.77
Trucking and warehousing	545	13.62
Trucking and courier services, except air	554	13.85
Public warehousing and storage	449	11.16

Most employers compensate truckdrivers with an hourly rate or a rate-per-mile system. Truckdrivers who operate heavy tractor-trailers generally have higher earnings than those who drive light delivery trucks. Benefits, including performance related bonuses, health insurance, and sick and vacation leave are common in the trucking industry.

The major union in the trucking and warehousing industry is the International Brotherhood of Teamsters. About 21 percent of trucking and warehousing workers are union members or are covered by union contracts, compared to 15.4 percent of workers in all industries combined. Some trucking companies use "double breasting" in an attempt to lower labor costs. This involves employing union as well as non-union operating divisions. Other companies use multi-tier wage scales and pay lower wages for new hires. Pay increases after predetermined periods of time and safe driving records.

Table 3. Median hourly earnings of the largest occupations in trucking and warehousing, 1997

Occupation	Trucking and warehousing	All industries
General managers and top executives ...	$24.04	$26.05
First-line supervisors and managers/ supervisors-transportation and material moving machine and vehicle operators	16.46	17.08
Truck drivers, heavy or tractor-trailer	14.09	13.08
Dispatchers, except police, fire and ambulance	13.95	12.26
First-line supervisors and managers/ supervisors-clerical and administrative support workers	13.91	14.26
Bus and truck mechanics and diesel engine specialists	12.43	13.62
Industrial truck and tractor operators	11.43	10.99
Truck drivers, light, including delivery and route workers	10.83	9.38
Refuse and recyclable material collectors	9.93	10.19
General office clerks	9.20	9.10

Outlook

The number of wage and salary jobs in the trucking and warehousing industry is expected to grow 11 percent from 1998 through 2008, compared to projected growth of about 15 percent for all industries combined. Because the industry is large, many job openings will result. A large number of job openings will also result from the need to replace workers who transfer to other industries or retire. Opportunities in this industry should be good for qualified truckdrivers and service technicians.

One of the main factors influencing the growth of the trucking and warehousing industry is the state of the national economy. Growth in the industry parallels economic upswings and downturns. As the national economy grows, production and sales of goods increase, thus increasing the demand for transportation services to move goods from producers to consumers. In a recession, the industry is one of the first to slow down as orders for goods and shipments decline.

Competition in the trucking and warehousing industry is intense, both among trucking companies and, in some long-haul truckload segments, with the railroad industry. In response to the need to increase efficiency and improve customer service, the trucking and warehousing industry is evolving and offering logistical services such as inventory management and "just-in-time" shipping.

Opportunities for qualified truckdrivers are expected to be favorable. In some areas, companies have experienced difficulties recruiting adequately skilled drivers. Truckdriving pays relatively well, but many persons leave the career because of the lengthy periods away from home, long hours of driving, and the negative public image drivers face. Stricter requirements for obtaining—and keeping—a commercial driver's license also make truckdriving less attractive as a career. Opportunities for diesel mechanics and service technicians are also expected to be favorable for applicants with formal postsecondary mechanical training.

Steady growth in the trucking and warehousing industry should prompt an increase in administrative support employment. More dispatchers, stock clerks, and shipping, receiving, and traffic clerks will be needed to support expanded logistical services across the country. However, fewer secretaries, bookkeepers, and file clerks will be needed because computers and other automated equipment will make workers in these occupations more efficient and productive.

Courier and delivery services has been one of the most rapidly growing segments of the industry. Employment is expected to increase about as fast as the industry even as competition from overnight air-courier firms, business use of facsimile (or "fax") machines, and electronic mail (e-mail) moderates growth.

Sources of Additional Information

For additional information about careers and training in the trucking and warehousing industry, write to:

➢ American Trucking Associations, 2200 Mill Rd., Alexandria, VA 22314.
Internet: **http://www.truckline.com**
➢ American Trucking Associations Foundation, 660 Roosevelt Ave., Pawtucket, RI 02860.
➢ International Warehouse Logistics Association, 1300 W. Higgins, Suite 111, Park Ridge, IL 60068.
Internet: **http://www.warehouselogistics.org**
➢ International Association of Refrigerated Warehouses, 7315 Wisconsin Ave., Suite 1200N, Bethesda, MD 20814.
➢ Professional Truck Driver Institute, 2200 Mill Rd., Alexandria, VA 22314, or by calling (703) 838-8842.
Internet: **http://www.ptdia.org**

Detailed information on the following occupations can be found in the 2000-01 *Occupational Outlook Handbook*:

● Diesel mechanics and service technicians
● Dispatchers
● Handlers, equipment cleaners, helpers, and laborers
● Material moving equipment operators
● Manufacturers' and wholesale sales representatives
● Shipping, receiving, and traffic clerks
● Truckdrivers

Department, Clothing, and Accessory Stores

(SIC 53 and 56)

● The industry offers many part-time jobs.

● The total number of wage and salary jobs is projected to increase more slowly than average, but high job turnover will produce a large number of job openings.

Nature of the Industry

Department, clothing, and accessory stores are located throughout the country. Department stores generally carry apparel; home furnishings, such as furniture, floor coverings, curtains, draperies, linens, and major household appliances; and housewares, such as table and kitchen appliances, dishes, and utensils. Different types of merchandise are normally arranged in separate sections or departments under a single management. Department stores commonly provide their own charge accounts, deliver merchandise, and usually have 50 or more employees.

Discount and variety stores carry a wide variety of merchandise, from lawn rakes to dinnerware to motor oil. They emphasize self-service and low prices, and have grown rapidly in recent years, taking much business away from other department, clothing, and accessory stores. Warehouse clubs—which carry a more limited variety of merchandise than department stores, often in bulk quantities—are also included in this industry.

Clothing and accessory stores specialize in men's, women's, or children's clothing and related products, such as ties and shoes. Furriers and custom tailors carrying stocks of materials are also included in this industry. In contrast to department stores, clothing and accessory stores usually are much smaller, may concentrate on a limited type or style of clothing, and employ fewer workers.

Working Conditions

Most employees in department, clothing, and accessory stores work under clean, well-lighted conditions. Many jobs are part time, and employees are on duty during peak selling hours, including nights, weekends, and holidays. Because weekends are busy days in retailing, almost all employees work at least one of these days and have a weekday off. During busy periods, such as Christmas and back-to-school time, longer than normal hours may be scheduled, and the use of vacation time is limited. Buyers and managers may work more than their scheduled 40 hours per week.

Retail salespersons and cashiers often stand for long periods, and stock clerks may perform strenuous tasks such as moving heavy, cumbersome boxes.

The incidence of work-related illnesses and injuries varied greatly among segments of the industry. Workers in general merchandise and apparel and accessory stores had 9.2 and 3.6 cases of injury and illness per 100 full-time workers, respectively, in 1997, compared with an average of 7.1 throughout private industry.

Employment

Department, clothing, and accessory stores had about 3.9 million wage and salary jobs in 1998, making them one of the largest employers in the Nation. Department stores accounted for slightly over half of all jobs in the industry, but only about 7 percent of establishments. In 1997, about two-thirds of workers were employed in department, clothing, and accessory stores with more than 50 workers (chart). An estimated 88,000 self-employed also worked in this industry. In contrast to many industries, this industry employs workers in all sections of the country, from the largest cities to all but the smallest towns.

Many of the industry's workers are young—over 33 percent were under 25 years old in 1998, compared with 15 percent for all industries. More than 34 percent of the workers were employed part time.

Occupations in the Industry

Marketing and sales occupations made up almost two-thirds of workers in the industry in 1998 (table 1). *Retail salespersons*, who comprised 42 percent of employment in this industry, help customers select and purchase merchandise. A salesperson's primary job is to interest customers in the merchandise and to answer any questions customers may have. In order to do this, they may describe the product's various

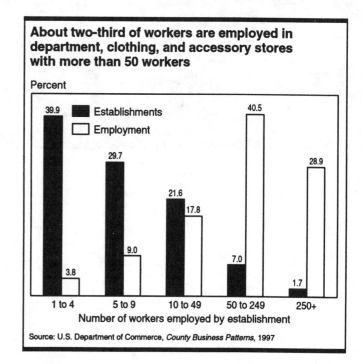

About two-third of workers are employed in department, clothing, and accessory stores with more than 50 workers

Percent

■ Establishments
□ Employment

Number of workers employed by establishment	Establishments	Employment
1 to 4	39.9	3.8
5 to 9	29.7	9.0
10 to 49	21.6	17.8
50 to 249	7.0	40.5
250+	1.7	28.9

Source: U.S. Department of Commerce, *County Business Patterns*, 1997

models, styles, and colors, or demonstrate its use. To sell expensive and complex items, an in-depth knowledge of the products is needed.

In addition to selling, most retail salespersons electronically register the sale on a cash register or terminal, receive cash, checks, and charge payments; and give change and receipts. Depending on the hours they work, they may "open" or "close" their cash registers or terminals. This may include counting the money in the cash register; separating charge slips, coupons, and exchange vouchers; and making deposits at the cash office. Salespersons often are held responsible for the contents of their register, and repeated shortages are cause for dismissal in almost all stores.

Salespersons also may handle returns and exchanges of merchandise, wrap gifts, and keep their work areas neat. In addition, they may help stock shelves or racks, arrange for mailing or delivery of a purchase, mark price tags, take inventory, and prepare displays. They also must be familiar with the store's security practices to help prevent theft of merchandise. *Cashiers* total bills, receive money, make change, fill out charge forms, and give receipts. Retail salespersons and cashiers often have similar duties.

Administrative support occupations make up the next largest group of employees, with about 19 percent of total employment in the industry. *Stock clerks* bring merchandise to the sales floor and stock shelves and racks. They may also mark items with identifying codes or prices so they can be recognized quickly and easily, although many items today arrive pre-ticketed. *Adjustment clerks* investigate and resolve customers' complaints about merchandise, service, billing, or credit ratings. Sometimes they are called customer service representatives or customer complaint clerks. The industry also employs administrative occupations found in most industries, such as general office clerks and bookkeepers.

Executive, administrative, and managerial occupations comprised 5 percent of industry employment. *Department managers* oversee sales workers in a department or section of the store. They set the work schedule, supervise employee performance, and are responsible for the overall sales and profitability of their departments.

Buyers purchase merchandise for resale from wholesalers or manufacturers. Using historical records, market analysis, and their sense of consumer demand, they buy merchandise with the best style, quality, selection, and price. Wrong decisions mean that the store will mark down slow selling merchandise that may have to be sold below cost, causing lost profits. Buyers for larger stores or chains usually buy one classification of merchandise, such as casual menswear or home furnishings; for smaller stores they may buy all the merchandise sold in the store. They also plan and implement sales promotion plans for their merchandise, such as arranging for advertising and ensuring that the merchandise is displayed properly.

Merchandise managers are in charge of a group of buyers and department managers; they plan and supervise the purchase and marketing of merchandise in a broad area, such as women's apparel or appliances. In department store chains, which have many stores, much of the buying and merchandising functions are centralized in one location. Some local managers might decide which merchandise, among that bought centrally, would be best for their own stores. *Department store managers* direct and coordinate the activities in these stores. They may set pricing policies to maintain profitability and notify senior management of concerns or problems. Department store managers usually supervise department managers directly, and indirectly oversee other department store workers.

Because they may be the only manager in smaller stores, *clothing and accessory store managers* combine many of the duties of department managers, department store managers, and buyers. *Retail chain store area supervisors* oversee the activities of clothing and accessory store managers in an area. They hire managers, insure that company policies are carried out, and coordinate sales and promotional activities.

Various other store level occupations in this diversified industry include *interior designers, hairdressers, laborers, food service workers,* and *security personnel.*

Table 1. **Employment of wage and salary workers in department, clothing, and accessory stores by occupation, 1998 and projected change, 1998-2008**

(Employment in thousands)

Occupation	1998 Employment		1998-2008 Percent change
	Number	Percent	
All occupations	3,872	100.0	5.9
Marketing and sales	2,528	65.3	7.9
Salespersons, retail	1,641	42.4	6.6
Cashiers	502	13.0	13.8
Marketing and sales worker supervisors	272	7.0	8.6
Administrative support, including clerical	752	19.4	1.6
Stock clerks and order fillers	331	8.6	4.2
Shipping, receiving and traffic clerks	123	3.2	7.6
Records processing occupations	69	1.8	-14.2
General office clerks	64	1.6	7.8
Adjusters, investigators, and collectors	40	1.0	10.7
Executive, administrative, and managerial	183	4.7	-.3
General managers and top executives	97	2.5	1.1
Management support occupations	30	0.8	0.0
Service	152	3.9	-.4
Food preparation and service occupations	39	1.0	-7.2
Protective service occupations	34	0.9	1.9
Hairdressers, hairstylists, and cosmetologists	33	0.9	8.0
Precision production, craft, and repair	94	2.4	7.8
Mechanics, installers, and repairers	59	1.5	14.8
Operators, fabricators, and laborers	113	2.9	2.8
Helpers, laborers, and material movers, hand	79	2.0	-2.9
Professional specialty	39	1.0	14.8
All other occupations	12	0.3	33.5

Training and Advancement

There are no formal educational requirements for most sales and administrative support jobs; in fact, many people get their first jobs in this industry. A high school education is preferred, especially by larger employers.

Salespersons should enjoy working with people. Among other desirable characteristics are a pleasant personality, a neat appearance, and the ability to communicate clearly. Because of the trend to provide more service, it is becoming increasingly important for salespersons to be knowledgeable about the products and merchandise available. Some employers may conduct a background check—especially for those employees selling high-priced items.

In most small stores, an experienced employee or the manager instructs newly hired sales personnel in making out sales checks and operating the cash register. In larger stores, training programs are more formal and are usually conducted over several days. Some stores conduct periodic training seminars to refresh and improve the customer service and selling skills of their sales workers. Initially, trainees are taught how to make cash, check, and charge sales and eventually are instructed on returns and special orders. Other topics usually included are customer service, security, and store policies and procedures. Depending on the type of product they are selling, they may be given specialized training in their area. For example, those working in cosmetic sales receive instruction on the types of products available and for whom they would be most beneficial.

Some salespersons are hired for a particular department, others are placed after they have completed training. Placement is usually based on where positions are available. There are some salespersons, often called "floaters," who are not assigned to a particular department; instead, they work where needed.

Advancement opportunities for salespersons vary. As those who work full time gain experience and seniority, they usually move to positions of greater responsibility or to positions with potentially higher commissions. Salespersons who are paid on a commission basis—that is, they earn a percentage of the value of what they sell—may advance to selling more expensive items. The most experienced—and highest paid—salespersons sell big-ticket items. This work requires the most knowledge of the product and the greatest talent for persuasion. In some establishments, advancement opportunities are limited because one person, often the owner, is the only manager, but sales experience may be useful in finding a higher level job elsewhere. Retail selling experience is an asset when applying for sales positions with larger retailers or in other kinds of sales, such as motor vehicle, financial services, or wholesale sales.

Traditionally, capable salespersons with good leadership skills, yet without a college degree, could advance to management positions; however, a college education is becoming increasingly important for managerial positions such as department manager, store manager, or buyer. Computer skills are extremely important in all parts of the industry, especially in areas such as inventory control, human resources, sales forecasting, and electronic commerce. Many retailers prefer to hire persons with associate or bachelor's degrees in marketing, merchandising, or business as management trainees or assistant managers. Despite this trend, capable employees without a college degree may still be able to advance to administrative or supervisory work.

Earnings

Hourly earnings of nonsupervisory workers in department, clothing, and accessory stores are well below the average for all workers in private industry. This reflects both the high proportion of part-time and less experienced workers in these stores, and the fact that even experienced workers receive relatively low pay compared with experienced workers in many other industries (table 2). Earnings in selected occupations in department, clothing, and accessory stores appear in table 3.

Table 2. Average weekly and hourly earnings of nonsupervisory workers in department, clothing, and accessory stores, 1998

Industry segment	Weekly	Hourly
All industries	$442	$12.77
General merchandise stores	256	8.59
Department stores	259	8.65
Variety stores	214	7.74
Miscellaneous general merchandise stores	253	8.35
Apparel and accessory stores	226	8.45
Men's and boys' clothing stores	292	10.25
Women's clothing stores	203	8.35
Family clothing stores	227	8.22
Shoe stores	219	8.23

Many employers permit workers to buy merchandise at a discount. Smaller stores usually offer limited employee benefits. In larger stores, benefits are more comparable to those offered by employers in other industries and can include vacation and sick leave, health and life insurance, profit sharing, and pension plans.

Unionization in this industry is limited. Only 3.9 percent of workers were union members or were covered by union contracts, compared with 15.4 percent in all industries.

Table 3. Median hourly earnings of the largest occupations in department, clothing, and accessory stores, 1997

Occupation	General merchandise stores	Apparel and accessory stores	All industries
General managers and top executives	$23.01	$15.27	$26.05
First-line supervisors and managers/supervisors-sales and related workers	10.21	10.76	13.43
General office clerks	8.34	8.05	9.10
Stock clerks-stockroom, warehouse or storage yard	7.48	7.00	8.85
Shipping, receiving, and traffic clerks	7.34	7.72	10.29
Janitors and cleaners, except maids and housekeeping cleaners	7.05	6.36	7.44
Salespersons, retail	6.82	6.33	7.23
Stock clerks, sales floor	6.67	6.31	6.93
Cashiers	6.48	6.29	6.22
Hairdressers, hairstylists, and cosmetologists	5.60	—	7.23

Outlook

Overall, wage and salary jobs in department, apparel, and accessory stores are projected to increase 6 percent over the 1998-2008 period, slower than the average for all industries combined. Slower than average growth is mainly due to the decline in jobs in clothing and accessory store establishments, which itself arises from the increasing popularity among consumers of discount stores and "mega-retailers." Besides stressing low prices, these types of stores also stress self-service, meaning they tend to be less labor-intensive than the traditional retailers. The number of jobs in the department store industry is expected to increase about as fast as the average.

There will continue to be keen competition among retailers, meaning that new stores will continually open and others will close. Alternative retail outlets, such as mail order companies, home shopping, and electronic commerce have carved a niche for themselves in the market, and have taken away customers who usually shop at traditional retail stores. Even large, well-established department stores are subject to mergers, acquisitions, and sometimes bankruptcy. Many retailers are beginning to provide their products through catalogues and the Internet to remain competitive. Some companies are moving towards obtaining goods directly from the manufacturer, bypassing the wholesale level completely, reducing costs, and increasing profits.

Worker productivity is increasing because of technological advances, particularly among clerks, managers, and buyers. For example, computerized systems allow companies to streamline purchasing and reduce the need for buyers. However, because direct customer contact will also remain important, employment of sales workers who interact personally with customers will be less affected by technological advances.

Despite the overall decline in the number of jobs, a large numbers of job openings will result from high job turnover in this large industry. Jobs will be available for young workers, first-time job seekers, persons with limited job experience, senior citizens, and people seeking part-time work, such as those with young children or those who wish to supplement their income from other jobs.

Persons with a college degree or computer skills will be highly sought after for managerial positions in areas such as human resources, data management, logistics, management information systems, and finance.

Sources of Additional Information

General information on careers in retail establishments is available from:

➢ National Retail Federation, 325 7th St. NW., Suite 1100, Washington, DC 20004. Internet: **http://www.nrf.com**
➢ International Council of Shopping Centers, 665 5th Ave, New York, NY 10022. Internet: **http://www.icsc.org**
➢ Retail, Wholesale, and Department Store Union, 30 East 29th St., 4th floor, New York NY 10016.

Information on these occupations may be found in the 2000-01 *Occupational Outlook Handbook*:

- Advertising, marketing, and public relations managers
- Cashiers
- Designers
- Private detectives and investigators
- Purchasing managers, buyers, and purchasing agents
- Retail salespersons
- Retail sales worker supervisors and managers
- Stock clerks

Eating and Drinking Places

SIGNIFICANT POINTS

- Eating and drinking places provide many young people with their first jobs—in 1998, 25 percent of all workers in these establishments were age 16-19, five times the average for all industries.

- Cooks, waiters and waitresses, and other service workers over 3 out of 4 jobs.

- Half of all employees work part-time, more than double the overall average.

- Job opportunities will be plentiful because turnover is high, little or no formal education or previous training is required, and earnings are low.

Nature of the Industry

So fundamental are the services provided by the eating and drinking places industry, that it may be the world's oldest industry. It may also be the world's most widespread and familiar one. In the United States, this industry comprises about 479,000 places of employment in large cities, small towns, and rural areas. These establishments include all types of restaurants, from fast-food to elegant and expensive. They also include drinking places—establishments which primarily sell alcoholic beverages for consumption on the premises.

Restaurants make up the majority of establishments in this industry. The most common is a franchised operation of a nationwide restaurant chain that sells fast food. According to the National Restaurant Association, the fast-food component accounted for more than 1 out of every 3 eating and drinking places in 1998; these establishments have grown steadily from less than 20 percent of the industry in 1970. These restaurants are characterized by their limited menu, lack of waiters and waitresses, and emphasis on self-service. Menu selections usually are prepared by workers with limited cooking skills. Since the food typically is served in disposable, take-out containers that retain the food's warmth, it often is prepared prior to a customer's request. A growing number of fast-food restaurants are providing drive-through and delivery services.

Full-service restaurants, in contrast, offer broader menus with a variety of choices, including appetizers, entreès, salads, side dishes, desserts, and beverages. Waiters and waitresses usually serve meals at a leisurely pace, in comfortable surroundings. Although the number of full-service restaurants that are part of national chains is growing, the typical restaurant is independently owned and locally operated.

Cafeterias open to the general public and those operated under contract by commercial food service companies comprise another major segment of this industry. Like fast-food restaurants, cafeteria menus usually offer a somewhat limited selection, which varies from day to day. Yet like full-service restaurants, their selections may require more culinary skills to prepare. Selections usually are prepared ahead in large quantities and seldom cooked to the customer's order.

Drinking places comprise less than 11 percent of all establishments in this industry. Although considered drinking places, some bars and nightclubs offer patrons limited dining services in addition to alcoholic beverages. In some States,

they also sell packaged alcoholic beverages for consumption off the premises. Establishments selling alcoholic beverages are closely regulated by State and local alcoholic beverage control authorities.

Finally, the eating and drinking places industry includes a wide variety of specialized businesses, such as catering firms, concession stands at sports events, ice cream stores, and even dinner theaters.

Working Conditions

Jobs in eating and drinking places are far more likely to be part-time than those in other industries; about 38 percent of the workers in eating and drinking establishments worked fewer than 35 hours a week in 1998, compared to 15.9 percent in the work force as a whole. Full-time employees often are on the job during evenings, weekends, and holidays. Some employees are required to work split shifts—they work for several hours during one busy period, are off duty for a few hours, and then go back to work during the next busy period. Some employees work rotating shifts on a daily, weekly, or monthly basis.

Although many eating and drinking places have well-designed kitchens and dining areas with state-of-the-art equipment, kitchens usually are noisy, and very hot near stoves, grills, ovens, or steam tables. Dining areas also are noisy when customers are present and servers are waiting on patrons.

Workers directly involved in food preparation and services spend most of their time on their feet. Upper body strength often is needed to lift heavy items, such as trays of dishes or cooking pots. Work during peak dining hours can be very hectic and stressful.

Employees who have direct contact with customers should have a professional and pleasant manner, which may be difficult to maintain over the course of a long shift. Excellent food that is poorly served can result in the failure of a restaurant, while average food served in an outstanding manner often results in success. Therefore, professional hospitality is required from the moment guests enter to the time they leave. According to the American Culinary Institute, a major reason why guests stop patronizing a restaurant is employee indifference to guest service. The average displeased guest will tell 8 to 16 people and 91 percent of unhappy guests will never return.

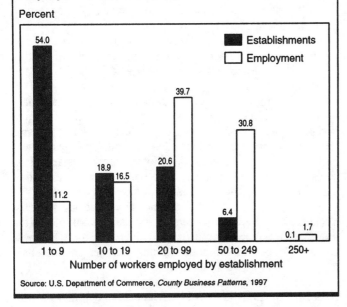

Over half of all eating and drinking establishments employ fewer than 10 people

Percent

Source: U.S. Department of Commerce, *County Business Patterns*, 1997

In 1997, the rate of work-related injuries and illnesses was 6.5 per 100 full-time workers in eating and drinking places, slightly less than the average of 7.1 for the private sector. Work hazards include the possibility of burns from hot equipment, sprained muscles, and wrenched backs from heavy lifting and falls on slippery floors.

Employment

The eating and drinking places industry, with about 7.8 million jobs in 1998, ranks among the Nation's leading employers. Only the educational services and health services industries provide more jobs. Eating and drinking places tend to be small; about 54 percent of the establishments in the industry employ fewer than 10 paid workers (chart). As a result, this industry often is considered attractive to individuals who desire to own and run their own businesses. An estimated 267,000 self-employed people worked in the industry, representing about 3 percent of total employment.

This industry, particularly fast-food establishments, is a leading employer of teenagers—ages 16 through 19—providing first jobs for many new entrants to the labor force. In 1998, nearly 25 percent of all workers in eating and drinking places were teenagers, five times the proportion in all industries (table 1). Almost 45 percent were under age 25, triple the proportion in all industries.

Table 1. Percent distribution of employment in eating and drinking places by age group, 1998

Age group	Eating and drinking places	All industries
Total	100.0	100.0
16-19	24.7	5.4
20-24	19.4	9.5
25-34	23.7	23.8
35-44	17.4	27.5
45-54	9.0	21.0
55-64	4.1	9.8
65 and older	1.6	2.9

Occupations in the Industry

Workers in this industry perform a variety of tasks. They prepare menu items, keep food preparation and service areas clean, wait on and take payment from customers, and provide support services to the establishment. Cooks, waiters and waitresses, and other food preparation and service workers comprise over 3 out 4 jobs (table 2).

Employees in the various food service occupations deal with customers in a dining area or at a service counter. *Waiters* and *waitresses* take customers' orders, serve food and beverages, and prepare itemized checks. In finer restaurants, they may describe chef's specials and suggest wines. In some establishments, they escort customers to their seats, accept payments, and set up and clear tables. In many larger restaurants, however, these tasks are assigned to other workers.

Table 2. Employment of wage and salary workers in eating and drinking places by occupation, 1998 and projected change, 1998-2008

(Employment in thousands)

Occupation	1998 Employment Number	1998 Employment Percent	1998-2008 Percent change
All occupations	7,760	100.0	17.0
Service	6,423	82.8	15.6
Waiters and waitresses	1,677	21.6	19.4
Food counter, fountain, and related workers	1,576	20.3	10.8
Cooks, restaurant	630	8.1	20.7
Food preparation workers	611	7.9	10.8
Cooks, short order and fast food	610	7.9	18.6
Bartenders	270	3.5	-1.5
Dining room and cafeteria attendants and bartenders' helpers	249	3.2	-1.5
Hosts and hostesses, restaurant, lounge, or coffee shop	217	2.8	19.4
Janitors and cleaners	117	1.5	10.8
Cooks, institutional or cafeteria	52	0.7	23.1
Bakers, bread and pastry	41	0.5	23.1
Marketing and sales	521	6.7	31.1
Cashiers	455	5.9	32.8
Executive, administrative, and managerial	450	5.8	19.8
Food service and lodging managers	268	3.5	20.2
General managers and top executives	151	2.0	19.5
Operators, fabricators, and laborers	172	2.2	17.6
Driver/sales workers	74	1.0	10.8
Administrative support, including clerical	126	1.6	19.0
All other occupations	68	0.9	25.8

Other food service occupations include *hosts* and *hostesses,* who welcome customers, show them to their tables, and give them menus. *Bartenders* fill drink orders for waiters and waitresses and orders from customers seated at the bar. *Dining room attendants* and *bartender helpers* assist waiters, waitresses, and bartenders by clearing, cleaning, and setting up tables, as well as keeping service areas stocked with supplies. *Counter attendants* take orders and serve food at counters, cafeteria steam tables, and fast-food counters. Depending on the size and type of establishment, attendants may also operate the cash register.

Workers in the various *food preparation occupations* prepare food in the kitchen. *Institutional cooks* work in the kitchens of schools, hospitals, industrial cafeterias, and other institutions, where they prepare large quantities of a small variety of menu items. *Restaurant cooks* and *chefs* usually prepare a wider selection of dishes for each meal, cooking individual servings to order. *Bread* and *pastry bakers* typically produce small quantities of baked goods for sale or use in the establishment. *Short-order cooks* prepare grilled items and sandwiches in establishments that emphasize fast service. *Specialty fast-food cooks* prepare a limited selection of items in fast-food restaurants, cooking and packaging batches of food that are either prepared to order or kept warm until sold. *Food preparation workers* shred lettuce for salads, cut up food , keep work areas clean, and perform simple cooking tasks under the direction of the chef or head cook. *Dishwashers* clean dishes, glasses, and kitchen accessories by hand or machine.

Managers hire, train, supervise, and discharge these workers in eating and drinking establishments. They also purchase supplies, deal with vendors, keep records, and help whenever an extra worker is needed in the kitchen or dining room. The *executive chef* oversees the kitchen, selects the menu, instructs the food preparation workers, and directs the preparation of food. In fine dining establishments, the *maitre'd* serves as host or hostess while overseeing the dining room. Larger establishments may employ a *general manager*, as well as a number of assistant managers. Many managers are part-owners of the establishments they manage.

Eating and drinking places employ a wide range of other workers, including accountants, advertising and public relations workers, bookkeepers, dietitians, mechanics and other maintenance workers, musicians and other entertainers, personnel workers, and various clerks.

Training and Advancement

Although the skills and experience required by workers in eating and drinking places differ by occupation, many entry-level positions, such as waiter and waitress or food preparation worker, require little or no formal education or previous training. These jobs are most commonly held by young workers; for many, this is their first job. On-the-job training, typically under the close supervision of an experienced employee or manager, often lasts less than a week. Some large chain operations require formal training sessions for new employees and may use video training programs.

Formal training of managers is common. As more restaurants use computers to keep track of sales and inventory, computer training is becoming increasingly integrated into management training programs. In smaller, independent restaurants, assistant managers learn their duties on the job, while most chain-affiliated establishments provide formal programs that introduce new managers to company procedures. Increasingly, establishments use video and satellite TV training programs to educate newly hired staff about quality and daily operational standards. Nationwide restaurant chains often operate their own schools for managers, where people nominated for assistant manager jobs attend training seminars before acquiring additional responsibilities. Eventually, they may advance to general manager of one of the chain's establishments, or even a top management position in a large chain operation.

Completion of postsecondary training in culinary arts, restaurant and food service management, or a related field is increasingly important for advancement in the eating and drinking places industry. Completion of such a program often enables graduates to start as trainee chefs or assistant managers. Management programs last from 18 months to 4 years; upon completion, a bachelor's degree is awarded. Programs are available through junior and community colleges, 4-year colleges and universities, trade schools, hotel or restaurant associations, and trade unions. The Armed Forces are another source of training and experience in food service work.

Training for chefs has changed radically in the past 10 years, as chefs assume greater leadership and managerial roles in the industry. Today most culinary programs offer more business courses along with computer training to better prepare chefs to manage a large operation.

Promotion opportunities in eating and drinking places vary by occupation and the size of individual establishments. Similar to other industries, larger establishments and organizations usually offer better advancement opportunities. As beginners gain experience and basic skills, those who choose to pursue careers in eating and drinking places transfer to other jobs that require greater skill and offer higher earnings. Many workers earn progressively larger incomes as they gain experience by switching to jobs in other establishments offering higher compensation or requiring greater service skills and managerial responsibilities. For example, waiters and waitresses may transfer to jobs in more expensive or busier restaurants that offer higher tips.

Advancement opportunities are better for food preparation workers, particularly for those who work in full-service restaurants. Starting as unskilled food preparation workers, some advance to cook jobs as they pick up skills in the kitchen, and from those jobs to more challenging chef positions. As chefs improve their culinary skills, their opportunities for professional recognition and higher earnings improve.

Many managers of eating and drinking places obtain their positions through hard work and experience. Chefs often advance to executive chef positions, and food service workers often are promoted to *maitre'd* or other managerial jobs. Many managers of fast-food restaurants have advanced from the ranks of hourly workers. Managers with access to the necessary capital may even open their own eating and drinking places.

Earnings

Earnings in eating and drinking places usually are much lower than the average for all industries (table 3). These low earnings are supplemented for many workers, however, by tips from customers. Waiters, waitresses, and bartenders, for example, often derive the majority of their earnings from tips, which depend on menu prices and the volume of customers served. In some establishments, workers who receive tips share a portion of their gratuities with other workers in the dining room and kitchen.

Table 3. Average earnings of nonsupervisory workers in eating and drinking places, 1998[1]

Industry segment	Weekly	Hourly
All private industry	$442	$12.77
Eating and drinking places	162	6.35

[1] Money payments only; tips not included.

Workers' earnings vary by occupation and by location, type, and size of the establishment. Usually, skilled workers, such as chefs, have the highest wages, and workers who receive tips, the lowest. Many workers in the industry earn the Federal minimum wage of $5.15 an hour or less, if tips are included as a substantial part of earnings. A number of employers provide free or discounted meals and uniforms to full- and part-time employees. Earnings in the largest occupations employed in eating and drinking places appear in table 4.

Table 4. Median hourly earnings of the largest occupations in eating and drinking places, 1997

Occupation	Eating and drinking places	All industries
Food service and lodging managers	$12.01	$12.18
Cooks, restaurant	7.39	7.54
Hosts or hostesses, restaurant, lounge, or coffee shop	5.98	6.11
Food preparation workers	5.88	6.42
Bartenders	5.84	5.94
Cashiers	5.71	6.22
Combined food preparation and service workers	5.69	5.72
Cooks, fast food	5.69	5.70
Dining room and cafeteria attendants and bartender helpers	5.63	5.73
Waiters and waitresses	5.57	5.59

Unionization is not widespread in the eating and drinking places industry. Only 1.6 percent of all employees are union members or are covered by union contracts, compared to 15.4 percent for all industries.

Outlook

Job opportunities in eating and drinking places should be plentiful. Wage and salary jobs in eating and drinking places are expected to increase by 17 percent over the 1998-2008 period, somewhat faster than the 15 percent growth projected for all industries combined. In addition to employment growth, vast numbers of job openings will stem from replacement needs in this large industry, as experienced workers find other jobs or stop working. This high job turnover reflects the large number of young, part-time workers in this industry. Thus, numerous jobs will be available for people with limited job skills, first-time job seekers, senior citizens, and those seeking part-time work.

Increases in population, personal incomes, leisure time, and dual-income families will contribute to job growth. With a growing proportion of the population concentrated in the older age groups, moderately-priced restaurants offering table service that appeal to families should be the fastest growing segment of the eating and drinking places industry; fine dining establishments, which appeal to affluent, often older, customers, should grow as the 45-and-older population increases rapidly. Limited-service and fast-food restaurants that appeal to younger diners should increase more slowly than in the past. Contracting out of institutional food services in schools, hospitals, and company cafeterias should shift jobs to firms specializing in these services. Also, an aging population should increase the demand for managerial and food service workers in nursing homes and assisted-living facilities through the year 2008. Some of the increased demand for food services will be met through more self-service facilities such as salad bars, untended meal stations, and automated beverage stations.

Occupational projections reflect different rates of growth among the various segments of the eating and drinking places industry (table 2). For example, rapid job growth is projected for skilled cooks and chefs, while relatively slow growth is projected for unskilled food preparation workers and food counter, fountain, and related workers. Those who qualify—either through experience or formal culinary training—for skilled cook, chef, and baker positions should be in demand. The number of bartender jobs is expected to decline as the consumption of alcoholic beverages outside the home continues to decline in volume and people shift from mixed drinks to beer and wine. The greatest number of job openings will be in the largest occupations—waiters and waitresses, and food counter, fountain, and related workers.

Employment of salaried managers is projected to grow as a result of rapid growth of chain and franchised establishments. Graduates of college hospitality programs should have especially good opportunities, particularly those with good computer skills who can design spreadsheets. The growing dominance of chain-affiliated eating and drinking places should also enhance managers' opportunities for advancement into general manager positions and corporate administrative jobs. Employment of self-employed managers of independent eating and drinking places is expected to increase more slowly.

Sources of Additional Information

For additional information about careers and training in the eating and drinking places industry, write to:

➤ National Restaurant Association, 1200 17th St. NW., Washington, DC 20036.
➤ The American Culinary Federation, P.O. Box 3466, St. Augustine, FL 32085.

For a list of educational programs in the eating and drinking industry, write to:

➤ Council on Hotel, Restaurant, and Institutional Education, 1200 17th St. NW., Washington, DC 20036-3097.

Information on vocational education courses for food preparation and service careers may be obtained from your State or local director of vocational education or superintendent of schools.

Information on these, and other occupations, found in eating and drinking places appears in the 2000-01 *Occupational Outlook Handbook*:

- Cashiers
- Chefs, cooks, and other kitchen workers
- Food and beverage service occupations
- Restaurant and food service managers

Grocery Stores

SIGNIFICANT POINTS

- Numerous job openings—many of them part time—should be available due to the industry's large size and high rate of turnover.

- Cashiers and stock clerks account for over half of all jobs.

- The retail food industry will seek college graduates to fill most new management positions.

Nature of the Industry

Grocery stores, also known as supermarkets, are familiar to everyone. They sell an array of fresh and preserved foods, primarily for preparation and consumption at home. Increasingly, they also sell prepared food for takeout meals, such as hot entrees and salads. Stores range in size from supermarkets, which may employ hundreds of workers and sell numerous food and nonfood items, to convenience stores, with small staffs and limited selections. (Specialty grocery stores—meat, seafood, and vegetable markets; fruit, candy, health, and dietetic food stores; and bakeries, for example—are not covered in this section. Also excluded are eating and drinking establishments that sell foods and beverages for consumption on the premises, which are discussed elsewhere in the *Career Guide*.)

Grocery stores are found everywhere, although the size of the establishment and range of goods and services offered varies. Traditionally, inner-city stores are small and offer a limited selection, although larger stores are now being built in many urban areas; suburban stores tend to be large supermarkets with a diverse stock. Many supermarkets include several specialty departments that offer the products and services of bakeries, delicatessens, pharmacies, or florist shops. Household goods, health and beauty care items, automotive supplies, greeting cards, and clothing also are among the growing range of nonfood items sold. Some of the largest supermarkets even house cafeterias or food courts, and a few feature convenience stores. In addition, grocery stores increasingly offer basic banking services, such as personal check cashing, money orders, and automatic teller machines; postal services, such as mail boxes and postage stamps; on-site film processing; dry cleaning; video rentals; and catering services.

Working Conditions

Working conditions in most grocery stores are pleasant, with clean, well-lighted, climate-controlled surroundings. Work can be hectic, however, and dealing with customers sometimes can be stressful.

Grocery stores are open to the public many hours each day, so workers are needed for early morning, late night, weekend, and holiday work. With employees working fewer than 30 hours a week, on average, these jobs are particularly attractive to workers who have other family or school responsibilities or another job.

Most grocery store workers wear some sort of clothing, such as a jacket or apron, that identifies them as store employees and keeps their personal clothing clean. Health and safety regulations require some workers, such as those who work in the delicatessen or meat departments, to wear head coverings, safety glasses, or gloves.

In 1997, cases of work-related injury and illness averaged 9.6 per 100 full-time workers in grocery stores, compared to 7.1 per 100 full-time workers in the entire private sector. Some injuries occur while transporting or stocking goods. Butchers and meat, poultry, and fish cutters, as well as cashiers working with computer scanners or traditional cash registers, may be vulnerable to cumulative trauma and other repetitive motion injuries.

Employment

Grocery stores ranked among the largest industries in 1998, providing just under 3.1 million wage and salary jobs. Over 32 percent of all grocery store employees work part time and the average workweek is less than 30 hours. An estimated 93,000 self-employed workers also worked in grocery stores, mostly in smaller establishments.

In 1997, about 131,000 grocery stores operated throughout the Nation. Most grocery stores are small; over 60 percent employ fewer than 10 workers. Most jobs, however, are found in the largest stores. About two-thirds of workers were employed in grocery stores with more than 50 workers (chart).

Many grocery store workers are young, with persons 16 to 24 years old holding 35 percent of the jobs. This reflects the large number of jobs in this industry open to young workers who have little experience.

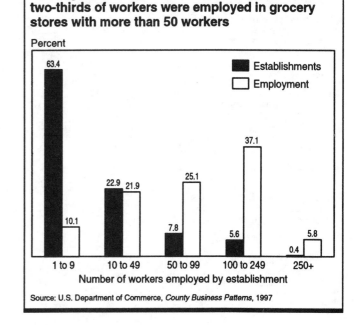

Although most establishments are small, about two-thirds of workers were employed in grocery stores with more than 50 workers

Percent

Number of workers	Establishments	Employment
1 to 9	63.4	10.1
10 to 49	22.9	21.9
50 to 99	7.8	25.1
100 to 249	5.6	37.1
250+	0.4	5.8

Number of workers employed by establishment

Source: U.S. Department of Commerce, *County Business Patterns*, 1997

Occupations in the Industry

Grocery store workers perform a variety of tasks. These include stocking shelves on the sales floor; preparing food and other goods; assisting customers in locating, purchasing, and understanding the content and uses of various items; and providing support services to the establishment. If the store is part of a chain, then many important tasks are done at a centralized corporate headquarters. They include marketing and promotion, inventory control and management, and financing. However, over half of all grocery store employees are cashiers or stocks clerks.

Cashiers, sometimes called checkers, comprise the largest occupation in grocery stores, accounting for about 3 of every 10 workers (table 1). They scan the items being purchased by customers, total the amount due, and produce a cash register receipt that shows the quantity and price of the items. In most supermarkets, the cashier passes the universal product code on the item's label across a computer scanner that identifies the item and its price, which is automatically relayed to the cash register. In other grocery stores, the cashier reads a hand-stamped price on the item and keys that price directly into the cash register. Cashiers then place items in bags for customers; accept cash, personal check, credit card, or an electronic debit card in payment; and make change. When cashiers are not needed to check out customers, they sometimes assist other workers.

Stock clerks comprise the second largest occupation in grocery stores, accounting for 2 of every 10 workers. They fill the shelves with merchandise and arrange displays to attract customers' attention. In stores without computer scanning equipment, stock clerks may have to manually mark prices on individual items and count stock for inventory control.

Table 1. Employment of wage and salary workers in grocery stores by occupation, 1998 and projected change, 1998-2008

(Employment in thousands)

Occupation	1998 Employment Number	1998 Employment Percent	1998-2008 Percent change
All occupations	3,066	100.0	5.7
Marketing and sales	1,313	42.8	11.5
Cashiers	976	31.8	12.0
Marketing and sales worker supervisors	195	6.4	13.0
Retail salespersons	104	3.4	6.6
Administrative support, including clerical	807	26.3	-10.2
Stock clerks and order fillers	669	21.8	-12.3
Bookkeeping, accounting, and auditing clerks	42	1.4	-10.8
General office clerks	31	1.0	10.6
Service	393	12.8	19.6
Food preparation workers	133	4.3	20.5
Food counter, fountain, and related workers	116	3.8	31.5
Bakers, bread and pastry	64	2.1	23.4
Janitors and cleaners	24	0.8	-1.4
Operators, fabricators, and laborers	285	9.3	10.0
Hand packers and packagers	225	7.3	9.6
Precision production, craft, and repair	131	4.3	-10.2
Butchers and meatcutters	115	3.7	-12.3
Executive, administrative, and managerial	110	3.6	4.8
General managers and top executives	74	2.4	6.4
Management support occupations	16	0.5	3.0
All other occupations	27	0.9	31.2

Many office clerical workers, such as *secretaries*, *general office clerks*, and *bookkeeping, accounting, and auditing clerks*, type, file, and maintain the records necessary to keep grocery stores running smoothly. *Hand packers and packagers*, also known as courtesy clerks or baggers, perform a variety of simple tasks, such as bagging groceries, loading parcels in customers' cars, and returning unpurchased merchandise from the checkout counter to shelves.

Butchers and *meat, poultry, and fish cutters* prepare meat, poultry, and fish for purchase by cutting up and trimming carcasses and large sections into consumer-sized pieces, which they package, weigh, price, and place on display. They also prepare ground meat from other cuts and fill customers' special orders. Butchers and meat, poultry, and fish cutters also may prepare ready-to-heat foods by filleting or cutting meat, poultry or fish into bite-sized pieces, preparing and adding vegetables, or applying sauces or breading.

Some specialty workers prepare food for sale in the grocery store and work in kitchens that may not be located in the store. *Bakers* produce breads, rolls, cakes, cookies, and other baked goods. *Food preparation workers* make salads—such as coleslaw or potato, macaroni, or chicken salad—and other entrees, and they prepare ready-to-heat foods—such as burritos, marinated chicken breasts, or chicken stir-fry—for sale in the delicatessen or in the gourmet food or meat department. Other food preparation workers arrange party platters or prepare various vegetables and fruits that are sold at the salad bar.

In supermarkets that serve food and beverages for consumption on the premises, *food counter workers* take orders and serve customers at counters. They may prepare short order items, such as salads or sandwiches, to be taken out and consumed elsewhere. *Janitors* and *cleaners* keep the stores clean and orderly.

In the warehouses and stockrooms of large supermarkets, *freight, stock,* and *material movers* move stock and goods in storage and deliver them to the sales floor; they also help load and unload delivery trucks.

Department managers direct the grocery, produce, meat, and other specialty departments, supervising mostly entry level employees. Department managers train employees and schedule their hours; oversee ordering, inspection, pricing, and inventory of goods; monitor sales activity; and make reports to store managers. *Store managers* are responsible for the efficient and profitable operation of grocery stores. Working through their department managers, store managers may assist in setting store policy, hire and train employees, develop merchandising plans, maintain good customer and community relations, address customer complaints, and monitor the store's profits or losses.

Purchasing managers plan and direct the activities of *buyers*, who purchase goods for resale to consumers. Purchasing managers and buyers must thoroughly understand grocery store foods and other items, and they must select the best suppliers and maintain good relationships with them. Purchasing managers and buyers evaluate their store's sales reports to determine what products are in demand and plan purchases according to their budget.

Because of the expansion of the industry to meet the consumers' desire for "one-stop shopping," grocery stores have begun to employ a wide array of workers to help meet that need. For example, *marketing managers* forecast sales and develop a marketing plan based on demographic trends, sales data, community needs, and consumer feedback. *Consumer affairs specialists* provide information to help consumers choose among the many food and nonfood products, and develop nutrition education programs. *Pharmacists* fill customers' drug prescriptions and advise them on over-the-counter medicines. *Computer programmers* and *computer systems analysts* develop management information systems. *Inspectors, testers,* and *graders* assess whether products and facilities meet quality, health, and safety standards. *Human resources* and *training specialists* are responsible for making sure that employees maintain and, if necessary, improve their skill levels.

Training and Advancement

Most grocery store jobs are entry level and can be learned in a short time. Employers generally prefer high school graduates for occupations such as cashier, stock clerk, or counter worker. In large supermarket chains, prospective employees are matched with available jobs, hours, and locations, and they are sent to a specific store for on-the-job training. Many cashiers are trained in a few days, with some stores offering formal classroom training to familiarize workers with the equipment they will work with. Meatcutters and bakers are more skilled. Trade schools and industry associations offer training for these jobs, but the skills also can be learned on the job.

Graduates of technical institutes, junior and community colleges, and colleges and universities that offer programs in food marketing, food management, and supermarket management are increasingly being sought after. Many supermarket chains seek graduates of these programs, or of bachelor's or master's degree programs in business administration, to enter various professional positions or management training programs in areas such as logistics, replenishment, food safety, human resources, and strategic planning. Management trainees start as assistant or department manager and, depending on experience and performance, may advance to positions of greater responsibility. It is not unusual for managers to supervise a large number of employees early in their careers.

Courtesy clerks sometimes advance to work as service clerks in the delicatessen or bakery, stock clerks, or perhaps cashiers. Sometimes workers rotate assignments in a supermarket; for example, a cashier might occasionally wrap meat. Union contracts, however, may have strict occupational definitions in some stores, making movement among departments difficult.

Entry level workers may advance to management positions, depending on experience and performance. Grocery store management has become increasingly complex and technical. Managers of some large supermarkets are responsible for millions of dollars in yearly revenue and hundreds of employees. They use computers to manage budgets, schedule work, track and order products, price goods, manage shelf space, and assess product profitability. Many stores that promote from within have established tracks by which workers move from department to department, gaining broad experience, until they are considered ready for an entry-level management position. Opportunities for advancement to management jobs exist in both large supermarket chains and in small, independent grocery stores.

Grocery store jobs call for various personal attributes. Almost all workers must be in good physical condition.

Because managers, cashiers, stock clerks, and other workers on the sales floor constantly deal with the public, a neat appearance and a pleasant, businesslike manner are important. Cashiers and stock clerks must be able to do repetitive work accurately while under pressure. Cashiers need basic arithmetic skills, good hand-eye coordination, and manual dexterity. Stock clerks, especially, must be in good physical condition because of the lifting, crouching, and climbing they do. For managers, good communication skills, and the ability to solve problems quickly and perform well under pressure, are important.

Earnings

Average weekly earnings in grocery stores are considerably lower than the average for all industries, reflecting the large proportion of entry level, part-time jobs. In 1998, nonsupervisory workers in grocery stores averaged $276 a week, compared to $442 a week for all workers in the private sector. Earnings in selected occupations in grocery stores appear in table 2.

Managers receive a salary and often a bonus based on store or department performance. Managers in highly profitable stores generally earn more than those in less profitable stores.

Full-time workers generally receive typical benefits, such as paid vacations, sick leave, and health and life insurance. Part-time workers who are not unionized may receive few benefits. Unionized part-time workers sometimes receive partial benefits. Grocery store employees may receive a discount on purchases.

About one-fourth of all employees in grocery stores belong to a union or are covered by a union contract. Workers in chain stores are more likely to be unionized or covered by contracts than workers in independent grocery stores. In independent stores, wages often are determined by job title, and increases are tied to length of job service. The United Food and Commercial Workers International Union is the primary union representing grocery store workers.

Table 2. Median hourly earnings of the largest occupations in grocery stores, 1997

Occupation	Grocery stores	All industries
General managers and top executives	$17.67	$26.05
First line supervisors and manager/ supervisors-sales and related occupations	11.95	13.43
Butchers and meat cutters	10.90	15.57
Bakers, bread and pastry	8.09	7.96
Food preparation workers	7.20	6.42
Stock clerks, sales floor	7.08	6.93
Combined food preparation and service workers	6.80	5.72
Salespersons, retail	6.78	7.23
Cashiers	6.32	6.22
Hand packers and packagers	5.65	6.90

Outlook

Employment in grocery stores is expected to rise about 6 percent by the year 2008, compared to the 15 percent rate of growth projected for all industries combined. Many additional job openings will arise from the need to replace workers who transfer to jobs in other industries, retire, or stop working for other reasons. Replacement needs are particularly significant due to the industry's large size and the high rate of turnover among cashiers and other workers who do not choose to pursue grocery industry careers.

Employment will grow as the population increases and as more grocery stores offer a wider array of goods and services that include prescription drugs, flowers, liquor, and carryout food, as well as banking, postal, and catering services. In addition, grocery stores are adding and enhancing delicatessens, bakeries, and meat and seafood departments to counter the trend toward eating away from home. This expansion is expected to create many new jobs.

Some technological advances—such as computer scanning cash registers and automated warehouse equipment—have boosted productivity, but these innovations are not expected to severely threaten employment levels. In fact, past technological improvements like scanners and electronic data interchange are expected to improve opportunities in areas such as category management and distribution. Increasing competition from large discount department stores will encourage the industry to continue to improve its efficiency by adopting new technologies and procedures and by reducing redundancies, especially in the supply lines. However, many tasks, such as stocking shelves on the sales floor or accepting payment from customers, cannot be performed effectively by machines. In addition, many consumers have demonstrated their strong desire for personal services. For example, consumers want managers to answer questions about store policy and services; they want cashiers and courtesy clerks to answer questions, bag goods, or help them bring groceries to their cars; and they want workers in specialty departments to advise them on their purchases and fill personal orders by providing special cuts of meat, fish, or poultry.

Projected growth for some grocery store occupations differs from the slower than average growth projected for the industry as a whole. Employment of bakers and food preparation workers is expected to grow faster than average because of the popularity of fresh baked breads and pastries, carryout food, and catering services. Employment of retail sales worker supervisors and managers is expected to grow as fast as average as new service departments and stores are built. A decline in employment of butchers and meatcutters is expected as more meat cutting and processing shifts from the retail store to the manufacturing plant.

Electronic shopping currently is gaining in popularity across the country. Its impact on the industry could be significant within the near future for both perishable and nonperishable goods, depending on how fast consumers adopt the new technology.

Sources of Additional Information

For information on job opportunities in grocery stores, contact individual stores, the local office of the State employment service, or:

➤ United Food and Commercial Workers International Union, Education Office, 1775 K St. NW., Washington, DC 20006-1502. Internet: **http://www.ufcw.org**

General information on careers in retail establishments is available from:

➤ National Retail Federation, 325 7th Street, NW., Suite 1100, Washington, DC 20004.
Internet: **http://www.nrf.com**

Information on most occupations in grocery stores, including the following, appears in the 2000-01 *Occupational Outlook Handbook*:

- Advertising, marketing, and public relations managers
- Butchers and meat, poultry, and fish cutters
- Cashiers
- Chefs, cooks, and other kitchen workers
- Handlers, equipment cleaners, helpers, and labors
- Pharmacists
- Pharmacy technicians and assistants
- Purchasing managers, buyers, and purchasing agents
- Retail salespersons
- Stock clerks

Motor Vehicle Dealers

SIGNIFICANT POINTS

- Most jobs in motor vehicle dealerships offer above average earnings, but only require 2 years of postsecondary training or less.

- Motor vehicle dealerships are expected to decline in number but increase in size as consolidation continues in the industry.

- Employment growth is expected to be average but very sensitive to downturns in the economy.

Nature of the Industry

Serving America's fascination with automobiles are the Nation's new and used motor vehicle dealers. They are the bridge between automobile manufacturers and the consumer.

A full-service motor vehicle dealership provides service for its customers in four general departments: New vehicle sales, used vehicle sales, aftermarket sales, and service. These departments employ a wide range of occupations including managerial, administrative support, sales, and mechanic and repairer occupations. In addition to full-service dealerships, some motor vehicle dealers specialize in used vehicle sales only.

The *new vehicle sales department* in full-service dealerships accounts for the majority of total sales, making it the cornerstone and life blood of the dealership. Although the profit margins on new-car sales are quite small in comparison to other departments, these sales spawn additional revenue from more profitable departments of the dealership. By putting a new car on the street, the dealership can count on aftermarket additions to the car, a new repair and service customer, and future used car trade-ins.

Sales of new cars, trucks, and vans depend on changing consumer tastes, popularity of the manufacturers' vehicle models, and the intensity of competition with other dealers. The business cycle greatly affects automobile sales—when the Nation's economy is declining, car buyers may postpone purchases of new vehicles and conversely, when it is growing and consumers feel more financially secure, vehicle sales increase.

Car and truck leasing is included in the new car sales department. Leasing services have grown in recent years to accommodate changing purchasing habits of consumers. As vehicles have become more costly, growing numbers of consumers are unable or reluctant to make the long-term investment entailed by the purchase of a new car or truck. Leasing provides an alternative to high initial investment costs while typically maintaining lower monthly payments.

The *used vehicle sales department* sells trade-ins and former rental and leased cars, trucks, and vans. Because new vehicles prices continue to increase faster than used car prices, used vehicles have become more popular. Also, innovative technology has increased the durability and longevity of new cars, resulting in higher quality used cars. In recent years, the sale of used vehicles has become a major source of profits for many dealers in the wake of decreasing margins for new vehicles.

In economic downturns, the demand for used cars often increases as sales of new vehicles decline.

The *aftermarket sales department* sells additional services and merchandise after the new-vehicle sales worker has closed a deal. Aftermarket sales workers sell service contracts and insurance to new and used car buyers and arrange financing for their purchase. Representatives offer extended warranties and additional services such as under-coat sealant and environmental paint protection packages to increase the revenue generated for each vehicle sold.

The *service department* usually has the smallest share of the average dealership's total sales, but generally is the dealer's greatest source of profits. It provides automotive repair services and sells accessories and replacement parts. Most service only cars and small trucks, but a small number service large trucks, buses, and tractor-trailers. Some of the larger dealerships also have body shops to do collision repair and painting. The work of the service department has a major influence on customers' satisfaction and willingness to purchase future vehicles from the dealership. The revenue from the service department of the dealership typically offsets the costs of running the shop. In some cases, service department revenue is used to pay for dealership overhead.

As is the case in the used vehicle department of a traditional full-service dealership, stand alone *used vehicle dealers* sell trade-ins and former rental and leased vehicles. These dealers range from small, one location stores to large, nationwide superstores. Each one capitalizes on the increased demand for used vehicles and relatively large profits for previously owned cars, trucks, and vans. Some of the larger stores offer low-hassle sales on large inventories of these popular vehicles. These dealers typically contract out warranty and other service-related work to other dealers or satellite service facilities. Growth in leasing agreements and rental companies will continue to provide quality vehicles to these dealers, thus providing for future employment growth in the used vehicle market.

Working Conditions

Persons in motor vehicle dealerships work longer hours than in most other industries. About 85 percent worked full time in 1998; nearly 45 percent worked more than 40 hours a week. To satisfy customer service needs, many dealers provide evening and weekend service. The 5-day, 40-hour week is usually the exception, rather than the rule, in this industry.

Most automobile salespersons and administrative workers spend their time in dealer showrooms. Individual offices are a rarity. Most office space is shared by multiple users and may be cramped and sparsely equipped. The competitive nature of selling is stressful to automotive sales workers, as they try to meet company sales quotas and personal earnings goals. Turnover in automotive sales jobs is relatively high.

Service technicians and automotive body repairers generally work indoors in well ventilated and lighted repair shops. However, some shops are drafty and noisy. Technicians and repairers frequently work with dirty and greasy parts, and in awkward positions. They often lift heavy parts and tools. Minor cuts, burns, and bruises are common, but serious accidents are avoided when the shop is kept clean and orderly and safety practices are observed. Despite hazards, precautions taken by dealers to avoid and prevent injuries have kept the workplace relatively safe. In 1997, there were 7.3 cases of work-related injuries and illnesses per 100 full-time workers in the new and used motor vehicle dealers industry, close to the national average of 7.1 cases. Separately, stand alone used motor vehicle dealers reported only 1.8 cases of work-related injuries and illnesses per 100 full-time workers—well below the national average.

Employment

Motor vehicle dealers provided about 1.1 million wage and salary jobs in 1998. An additional 51,000 self-employed persons worked in this industry. Sales workers, service technicians, and repairers shared two-thirds of industry employment. The remaining third were executive and managerial, administrative support, and operator and laborer positions.

Workers in motor vehicle dealerships tend to be somewhat older than those in other retail trade industries. The median age of workers in dealerships was 38, with 26 percent between the ages of 35-44.

Since 1950, the trend in this industry has been toward consolidation. Franchised dealers have decreased in number while

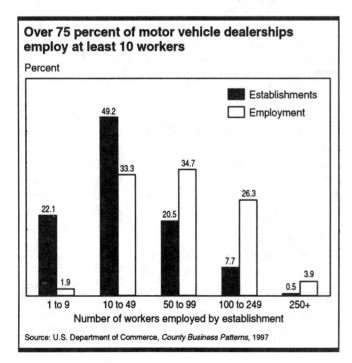

Over 75 percent of motor vehicle dealerships employ at least 10 workers

Source: U.S. Department of Commerce, *County Business Patterns*, 1997

their sales volume has increased. Having larger dealerships means offering more services at typically lower costs to the dealership and the customer. Over 75 percent of motor vehicle dealerships employ at least 10 workers, compared to about 32 percent for retail trade establishments in general. Dealerships with 10 or more workers employ about 98 percent of the workers in the industry, whereas such establishments account for fewer than 85 percent of all retail trade employment (chart). On average, motor vehicle dealers employ nearly 45 employees per establishment, compared to an average of 14 employees in all retail businesses.

Occupations in the Industry

The number of workers employed by motor vehicle dealers varies significantly depending on dealership size, location, makes handled, and distribution of sales among departments. Table 1 indicates that the majority of workers in this industry are sales workers, automotive mechanics and service technicians, or administrative support personnel.

Marketing and *sales occupations* are among the most important occupations in the dealership. Their success in selling vehicles and services determines the success of the dealership. *Automotive sales workers* usually are the first to greet customers and determine their interests through a series of questions. They explain and demonstrate the car's features in the showroom and on the road and negotiate the terms and price of the sale. A high school diploma usually is the minimum educational requirement for beginning sales workers, however, many managers prefer candidates who have a college education. They must be tactful, well groomed, and able to express themselves well. Their success in sales depends upon their ability to win the respect and trust of prospective customers. Employers view ambition, personal integrity, and common sense as the most important traits for prospective employees.

Automotive repair and *service occupations* are another integral part of dealerships. Employers look for persons with mechanical and technical aptitude and knowledge of how automobiles work to fill entry level jobs. Good reading and basic math skills are also required to study technical manuals and keep abreast of new technology and learn new service and repair techniques. Nearly all employers require a high school diploma and computer literacy. Due to the increasingly complex technology in today's new automobiles, most employers regard the successful completion of a formal postsecondary training program for automotive mechanics and service technicians as the best preparation for trainee positions. These programs give dealers well trained, certified employees who are more valuable to prospective employers.

Motor vehicle dealers devote a large share of their workers, facilities, and equipment to maintenance and repair services. *Automotive mechanics and service technicians* fix automobiles and light trucks with gasoline engines, such as vans and pickups. *Automotive body repairers* straighten bent body parts, remove dents, and replace crumpled parts that are beyond repair. In support of the service and repair department, *automotive parts counter workers* supply vehicle parts to technicians and repairers. They also sell replacement parts and accessories to the public.

Administrative support workers handle the paperwork of motor vehicle dealers. *Bookkeeping, accounting,* and *auditing clerks; billing, cost,* and *rate clerks; general office clerks;* and *secretaries* prepare reports on daily operations, inventory, and accounts receivable. In addition, they gather, process, and record information; operate telephone switchboards; and perform other administrative support and clerical duties. Dealership *office managers* organize, supervise, and coordinate administrative operations. Many office managers also are responsible for collecting and analyzing information on each department's financial performance.

Vehicle washers and *equipment cleaners* prepare new and used cars for display in the showroom or parking lot and for delivery to customers. They may wash and wax vehicles by hand and perform simple services like changing a tire or battery.

Truckdrivers operate customer service vans to transport customers to and from the dealership. Drivers also operate light delivery trucks to pick up and deliver automotive parts, and tow trucks to bring in damaged vehicles. They also drive new automobiles between preparation areas and consumer delivery areas.

Executive, administrative, and *managerial* jobs often are filled by promoting workers with years of related experience. For example, in automotive service departments, most managers have experience as mechanics and service technicians, and most sales managers start as automotive sales workers. *Shop managers* usually are among the most experienced mechanics and service technicians. They supervise and train other mechanics and technicians to make sure that service work is performed properly. *Parts managers* run the parts department and keep the automotive parts inventory. They display and promote sales of parts and accessories, and deal with garages and other repair shops seeking to purchase parts. *Service managers* oversee the entire service department and are responsible for the department's reputation, efficiency, and profitability. Increasingly, service departments use computers to increase productivity by scheduling customer appointments, trouble-shooting technical problems, and improving service workflow. This results in increased customer satisfaction.

Service advisors handle the administrative and customer relations part of the service department. They greet customers, listen to their description of problems or service desired, write repair orders, and estimate the cost and time needed to do the repair. They also handle customer complaints, contact customers when technicians discover new problems while doing the work, and explain to customers the work performed and the charges being billed.

Sales managers hire, train, and supervise the dealership's sales force. They are the lead negotiators in all transactions between sales workers and customers. Most advance to their positions after success as sales workers. They review market analyses to determine consumer needs, estimate volume potential for various models, and develop sales campaigns to accomplish dealership goals.

General managers are in charge of all the dealership's operations. They need extensive business and management skills, usually acquired through experience as a manager in one or more of the dealership departments. Dealership performance and profitability are ultimately up to them. General managers sometimes have an ownership interest in the dealership.

Table 1. Employment of wage and salary workers in motor vehicle dealers by occupation, 1998 and projected change, 1998-2008

(Employment in thousands)

Occupation	1998 Employment Number	1998 Employment Percent	1998-2008 Percent change
All occupations	1,145	100.0	11.6
Marketing and sales	410	35.8	10.7
Retail salespersons	238	20.8	11.4
Marketing and sales worker supervisors	71	6.2	26.0
Cashiers	14	1.2	3.4
Parts salespersons	62	5.4	-8.4
Precision production, craft, and repair	322	28.1	14.1
Automotive mechanics and service technicians	203	17.7	14.5
Automotive body and related repairers	49	4.2	14.5
Blue-collar worker supervisors	49	4.3	14.5
Administrative support, including clerical	179	15.7	8.4
General office clerks	50	4.4	26.1
Bookkeeping, accounting, and auditing clerks	39	3.4	-6.8
Office and administrative support supervisors and managers	25	2.2	11.3
Secretaries	15	1.3	-8.8
Stock clerks and order fillers	14	1.2	14.5
Billing, cost, and rate clerks	11	1.0	3.1
Operators, fabricators, and laborers	142	12.4	13.9
Cleaners of vehicles and equipment	69	6.1	14.5
All other helpers, laborers, and material movers, hand	35	3.1	14.5
Truckdrivers	26	2.3	13.5
Executive, administrative, and managerial	73	6.4	10.8
General managers and top executives	49	4.3	11.1
Management support occupations	9	0.8	10.2
Service	16	1.4	4.1
Janitors and cleaners	13	1.1	3.1

Training and Advancement

Requirements for many jobs may vary from dealer to dealer. To find out exactly what you need to qualify for a specific job, ask the dealer or manager in charge. The majority of positions do not require postsecondary education—more than half of those employed have not received any formal education past high school. In today's competitive job market, however, nearly all dealers demand a high school diploma. Courses in automotive mechanics are important for service jobs, as well as a basic background in business, electronics, mathematics, computers, and science. Sales workers require strong communication skills to deal with the public because they represent the dealership.

Most new sales workers receive extensive on-the-job training beginning with mentoring from sales managers and experienced sales workers. In large dealerships, beginners receive several days of classroom training to learn the models for sale, how to approach prospective customers, negotiation techniques, and ways to close sales. In addition, manufacturers furnish training manuals and other informational materials for sales workers. Managers continually guide and train sales workers, both on the job and at periodic sales meetings.

Service technicians and repairers may begin as apprentices or trainees, helpers, or lubrication workers. They work under close supervision of experienced technicians and service managers. Even though beginners may be able to perform routine service tasks and make simple repairs after a few months on the job, they usually need 1 to 2 years of experience to acquire enough skills to become a certified mechanic and service technician.

Automotive technology is rapidly increasing in sophistication, and dealerships increasingly prefer to hire graduates of postsecondary mechanic training programs for trainee positions. Graduates of such programs often earn promotion to service technician after only a few months on the job. Most community and junior colleges and vocational and technical schools offer postsecondary automotive training programs leading to an associate's degree in auto mechanics or auto body repair. They generally provide intense career preparation through a combination of classroom instruction and hands-on practice.

In addition, various automotive manufacturers and their participating dealers sponsor 2-year associate degree programs at community and junior colleges across the Nation. Students in these programs typically spend alternate 10 to 12 week periods attending classes full time and working full time in the service departments of sponsoring dealers. Dealers increasingly send experienced mechanics and technicians to factory training centers to receive special training in the repair of components, such as electronic fuel injection or air-conditioning. Factory representatives often come to shops to conduct short training sessions.

Years of experience in sales, service, or administration are needed to advance to managerial positions in dealerships. Persons with 4-year college degrees in business administration and marketing increasingly are preferred for some managerial jobs, particularly by dealerships that are larger, more competitive, and more efficient. Motor vehicle manufacturers offer management training classes and seminars, in addition to sponsoring 2-year automotive mechanic training programs.

Earnings

Average weekly earnings of nonsupervisory workers at full-service motor vehicle dealerships were $561 in 1998, higher than the average for retail trade, as well as for all private industry (table 2). Earnings vary depending on occupation, experience, and the dealer's geographic location and size. Earnings in selected occupations in motor vehicle dealers appear in table 3.

Table 2. Average earnings of nonsupervisory workers in motor vehicle dealers, 1998

Industry segment	Weekly	Hourly
All private industry	$ 442	$ 12.77
Total retail trade	255	8.75
New and used car dealers	561	15.21

Most automotive sales workers are paid on a commission-only basis. Commission systems vary, but dealers often guarantee new salespersons a modest salary for the first few months until they learn how to sell cars. Many dealers also pay experienced, commissioned sales workers a modest weekly or monthly salary to compensate for the unstable nature of sales. Dealerships, especially larger ones, also pay bonuses and have special incentive programs for exceeding sales quotas. With increasing customer service requirements, some dealerships and manufacturers have adopted a non-commissioned sales force paid entirely by salary in order to reduce the reputation of cut-throat sales people. In addition, many automotive mechanics and service technicians receive a commission related to the labor cost charged to the customer. Their earnings depend on the amount of work available and completed.

Relatively few workers in motor vehicle dealerships are union members or are covered by union contracts, 3.2 percent compared to 15.4 percent of all workers in private industry.

Table 3. Median hourly earnings of the largest occupations in motor vehicle dealers, 1997

Occupation	New and used car dealers	Used car dealer	All industries
General managers and top executives	$38.14	$19.57	$26.05
First-line supervisors and managers/supervisors- sales and related workers	24.07	16.63	13.43
First-line supervisors and managers/supervisors- mechanics, installers, and repairers	18.01	—	18.17
Salespersons, retail	15.08	12.83	7.23
Automotive mechanics	15.03	10.69	12.84
Automotive body and related repairers	14.15	—	12.95
Salespersons, parts	12.24	—	10.41
Bookkeeping, accounting, and auditing clerks	10.22	—	10.80
General office clerks	8.32	—	9.10
Vehicle washers and equipment cleaners	7.27	6.88	6.77

Outlook

Wage and salary jobs in motor vehicle dealerships are projected to increase 12 percent over the 1998-2008 period, compared to projected growth of about 15 percent for all industries combined. Growth in the automobile industry strongly reflects consumer confidence and purchasing habits. The structure of dealerships, strength of the Nation's economy, and trends in consumer preferences will influence the employment outlook for this industry.

Over the 1998-2008 period, population growth will increase demand for motor vehicles and employment in motor vehicle dealerships. Growth of the labor force and increasing numbers of families in which both spouses need vehicles to commute to work will contribute to increased car sales and employment in this industry. As personal incomes continue to grow, increasing numbers of persons will be able to afford the luxury of owning multiple vehicles, which also should increase sales. However, the penchant for the public to keep their cars for many more years than in the past may have a dampening effect on motor vehicle sales.

Employment growth will also be slowed as the industry continues to become more competitive, cost efficient, and responsive to consumer demand. Although there has been a slowdown in the number of dealership consolidations since 1993, the industry is expected to experience further dealership consolidations in an effort to achieve greater financial and operational efficiency and flexibility. Individual dealers increasingly will represent more than one manufacturer. In addition, greater emphasis will be placed on after-sales services, such as financing and vehicle service and repair. For larger dealerships, this will also include on-site body repair facilities.

Opportunities in the service and repair sectors of this industry should be plentiful, especially for persons who complete formal automotive mechanic training. The growing complexity of automotive technology increasingly requires highly trained mechanics and service technicians to service cars. Most persons who enter service and repair occupations may expect steady work because changes in economic conditions have little effect on this part of the dealership's business.

Opportunities for sales positions will depend to a large extent on the state of the economy, which will continue to play a dominant role in motor vehicle sales. Replacement needs will be a greater source of job openings than overall dealership expansion. The high turnover of sales jobs, characteristic of this industry, will ensure many job openings for sales workers in motor vehicle dealerships. In addition, as consumers' expectations and demands continue to increase, dealerships will seek more highly educated salespersons. Persons who have a college degree and previous sales experience should have the best opportunities. If alternative sales techniques and compensation systems, such as using salaried non-commissioned sales professionals, become more common, the greater income stability may lead to less turnover of sales jobs.

Opportunities in managerial occupations will be best for persons with college degrees. The steady decline in the number of dealerships will slow the growth of managerial jobs.

Sources of Additional Information

For more information about work opportunities, contact local motor vehicle dealers or the local offices of the State employment service. State employment service offices also may have information about training programs.

For additional information about careers and training in the motor vehicle dealers industry, write to:

➤ National Automotive Dealers Association, 8400 Westpark Dr., McLean, VA 22102.

Information on certified automotive mechanic and service technician training programs is available from:

➤ National Automotive Technicians Education Foundation, 13505 Dulles Technology Dr., Herndon, VA 20171-3421. Internet: **http://www.natef.org**
➤ SkillsUSA-VICA, P.O. Box 3000, 1401 James Monroe Hwy., Leesburg, VA 22075. Telephone (toll free): 1-800-321-VICA. Internet: **http://www.skillsusa.org**

More information on the following occupations may be found in the 2000-01 *Occupational Outlook Handbook:*

● Advertising, marketing, and public relations managers
● Automotive body repairers
● Automotive mechanics and service technicians
● Blue-collar worker supervisors
● Retail salespersons
● Retail sales worker supervisors and managers

Wholesale Trade

(SIC 50, 51)

SIGNIFICANT POINTS

- Most workplaces are small, employing fewer than 10 workers.

- Seven out of 10 workers are in clerical, sales, or operator and laborer occupations.

- The industry is becoming increasingly automated and will require a technically trained workforce.

Nature of the Industry

When consumers purchase goods, they usually buy them from a retail establishment such as a supermarket, department store, gas station, or hardware store. When businesses, governments, or institutions—such as universities or hospitals—need to purchase equipment, office supplies, goods for resale, or any other items, they normally buy them from wholesale trade establishments.

Wholesale trade firms are essential to the economy. They buy large lots of goods, usually from manufacturers, and sell them in smaller quantities to businesses, governments, other wholesalers, or institutional customers. They make the transfer of goods efficient by acting as intermediaries in the process of bringing goods from the manufacturer to the final customer. In so doing, they fill three vital roles in the economy: They provide businesses a nearby source of goods made by many different manufacturers; they provide manufacturers with a manageable number of customers, while allowing their products to reach a large number of users; and they allow manufacturers, businesses, institutions, and governments to devote minimal time and resources to transactions.

There are three types of wholesale trade firms. *Merchant wholesalers*, more commonly known as wholesaler-distributors, purchase goods from manufacturers in large quantities, store them, and then sell them to retailers, manufacturers, other wholesalers, or other customers. They are by far the most common type of wholesaling business, comprising over 90 percent of the firms in the industry.

Sales branch offices of manufacturing operations are local offices of manufacturers. They market their companies' products and coordinate distribution directly from the producer to the buyer. Often, they do not handle stock during a sale.

Wholesale brokers, or *agents*, coordinate the sale of goods from one party to another—usually from manufacturers to retailers. They seldom take title or handle goods in the process.

Only firms that sell most of their wares to businesses, institutions, and governments are considered part of wholesale trade. As a marketing ploy, many retailers that sell mostly to the general public present themselves as wholesalers. For example, "wholesale" price clubs, factory outlets, and other organizations are retail establishments, even though they sell their goods to the public at "wholesale" prices.

The size and scope of firms in the wholesale trade industry vary greatly. They sell any and every type of goods for many purposes. Customers buy goods to use in making other products, such as a bicycle manufacturer that purchases steel tubing, wire cables, and paint; for use in the course of daily operations, such as a government agency that buys office furniture, paper clips, or computers; or for resale to the public, such as a department store that purchases socks, flatware, or televisions. Wholesalers may offer only a few items for sale, perhaps all made by one manufacturer, or they may offer thousands of items produced by hundreds of different manufacturers. Wholesalers may only sell a narrow range of goods, such as very specialized machine tools, or a broad range of goods, such as all the supplies necessary to open a new store, including shelving, light fixtures, wall paper, floor coverings, signs, cash registers, accounting ledgers, and perhaps even some merchandise for resale.

Besides selling and moving goods to their customers, wholesaler-distributors have now begun to provide other services to clients, such as extending credit or providing financing; providing marketing services, like advertising and promotion; and, perhaps most importantly, offering technical or logistical advice and installation and repair services. After customers buy equipment, such as cash registers, copiers, computer workstations, or various types of industrial machinery, assistance is often needed to integrate the products into the customers' workplace. Wholesale trade firms often employ workers who visit customers, install or repair equipment, train users, troubleshoot problems, or advise on how to use the equipment most efficiently.

Working Conditions

Working conditions and physical demands of wholesale trade jobs vary greatly. Moving stock and heavy equipment can be strenuous; but freight, stock, and material handlers may be aided by forklifts in large warehouses. Workers in some automated warehouses use computer-controlled storage and retrieval systems that further reduce labor requirements. Employees in refrigerated meat warehouses work in a cold environment, and those in chemical warehouses often wear protective clothing to avoid harm from toxic chemicals. Outside sales workers are away from the office for much of the work day, and may spend a considerable amount of time traveling. Alternatively, most management, administrative support, and marketing staff work in offices.

Overall, work in wholesale trade is relatively safe. In 1997, there were 6.5 work-related injuries or illnesses per 100 full-time workers, less than the 7.1 incidence rate for the entire private sector. Not all wholesale trade sectors are equally safe, however. Occupational injury and illness rates were considerably higher than the national average for wholesale trade workers who dealt with lumber and construction materials (10.7 per 100 workers); metals and minerals (12.6); groceries (10.6); and beer, wine, and distilled beverages (12.5).

Most workers put in long shifts, particularly during peak times, and others, such as produce wholesalers, work unusual hours. These workers must be on the job early in the morning to receive shipments of vegetables and fruits, and they must be ready to deliver goods to local grocers at dawn.

Employment
Wholesale trade accounted for about 6.8 million wage and salary jobs in 1998, about 5 percent of all jobs in the economy. Firms that employed 10 or more workers provided about 83 percent of the jobs in wholesale trade; nevertheless, roughly 7 out of 10 establishments in the industry are small, employing fewer than 10 workers (chart). Although some large firms employ many workers, when compared to other industries, wholesale trade is characterized by a large number of relatively small establishments. Wholesale trade workers are spread fairly evenly throughout the country, have relatively low union membership, and are more likely to work full-time than workers in most other industries.

Occupations in the Industry
Many occupations are involved in wholesale trade, but not all are employed in every type of wholesale trade firm. For example, manufacturers' sales branch offices do not employ *wholesale buyers*, because they do not purchase goods for resale; and brokers employ few *stock clerks* or *truckdrivers*, because they keep little stock. Merchant wholesalers—by far the largest part of the industry—employ workers in most of the occupations that appear in table 1.

The activities of merchant wholesaling firms commonly center on storing, selling, and transporting goods. As a result, the three largest occupational groups in the industry are *administrative support* workers, many of whom work in inventory management; *sales* and *marketing* workers; and *operators, fabricators,* and *laborers*, most of whom are truckdrivers and material movers. In 1998, more than 7 out of 10 wholesale trade workers were concentrated in these three groups.

Most administrative support workers need to have at least a high school degree, and some related experience or additional schooling is an asset. Like most industries, many *secretaries* and *accounting, bookkeeping,* and *general office clerks* are employed in wholesale trade. Most other administrative support workers are needed to control inventory. *Shipping* and *receiving clerks* check the contents of all shipments, verifying condition, quantity, and sometimes, shipping costs. They may use computer terminals or bar code scanners and in small firms may pack and unpack goods. *Order fillers* or *order clerks* handle order requests from customers or from the firm's regional branch offices in the case of a large, decentralized wholesaler. These workers take phone orders, check the goods, and route them on to the warehouse for packing and shipment. Often, they must be able to answer customer inquiries about products and monitor inventory levels or record sales for the accounting department. *Stock clerks* code or price goods and store them in the appropriate warehouse sections. They also retrieve from stock the appropriate type and quantity of goods ordered by customers. In some cases, they may also perform tasks similar to shipping and receiving clerks.

Like administrative support workers, many marketing and sales workers need no postsecondary training; but many employers seek applicants with prior sales experience. Generally, workers in marketing and sales occupations try to interest customers and assist them in purchasing a wholesale firm's goods. There are three primary types of sales people in wholesale firms, and their duties vary considerably.

Counter sales workers wait on customers who come to the firm to make a purchase. These workers must be knowledgeable about product lines and able to use computer terminals to check on the availability of particular goods in inventory.

Inside sales workers usually are more experienced and more knowledgeable about specific products, prices, and the lead times required for delivery. Like order clerks, they take phone orders but may also solicit new business over the phone.

Outside sales workers, also called *wholesale sales representatives*, are the most skilled workers and the largest single occupation in wholesale trade. They travel to customers' places of business—whether manufacturers, retailers, or institutions—to maintain current customers or to secure new ones. They make presentations to buyers and management or may demonstrate items to production supervisors. Sales representatives must be very knowledgeable about product operation, prices, maintenance needs, and capabilities and must be thoroughly familiar with customers' needs and business goals, to suggest how customers can use products to their greatest advantage. For example, sometimes sales representatives advise manufacturers on how to use a new piece of equipment to make production more efficient or may train workers to use the equipment. In the case of complex equipment, sales representatives may need a great deal of highly technical knowledge. For this reason, some outside sales workers need to have postsecondary technical education, prior to starting work; some even have engineering degrees.

Sales managers monitor and coordinate the work of the sales staff and often do outside sales work themselves. In small firms, owners and top executives may engage in some selling activity.

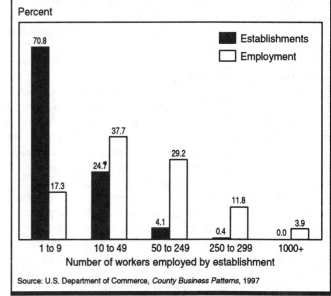

About 7 out of 10 wholesale trade establishments are small, employing fewer than 10 workers

Percent

Legend: ■ Establishments □ Employment

Number of workers employed by establishment	Establishments	Employment
1 to 9	70.8	17.3
10 to 49	24.7	37.7
50 to 249	4.1	29.2
250 to 299	0.4	11.8
1000+	0.0	3.9

Source: U.S. Department of Commerce, *County Business Patterns*, 1997

Operators, fabricators, and laborers move stock around the warehouse, pack and load goods for shipment, and transport goods to buyers. *Freight* and *material movers* manually move goods to or from storage and help load delivery trucks. *Hand packers* and *packagers* also prepare items for shipment.

Industrial truck and *tractor operators* use forklifts and tractors with trailers to transport goods within the warehouse, to outdoor storage facilities, or to trucks for loading. *Truckdrivers* transport goods between the wholesaler and the purchaser or between distant warehouses. Drivers of medium and heavy trucks need a State Commercial Driver's License (CDL).

Drivers/sales workers deliver goods to customers, unload goods, set up retail displays, and take orders for future deliveries. They are responsible for maintaining customer confidence and keeping clients well-stocked. Sometimes these workers visit prospective clients, in hopes of generating new business.

Executive and managerial workers direct the operations of firms and include *general managers* and *top executives*, as well as *middle managers*, who supervise workers and ensure that operations meet standards and goals set by top management. Managers also often have some sales responsibilities and may have ownership interest in smaller firms.

Two large management support occupations are *wholesale buyers* and *purchasing managers*. Wholesale buyers purchase goods from manufacturers for resale, based on price and what they think customers want. Purchasing managers coordinate the activities of buyers and determine what types and quantities of goods to purchase.

Mechanics, installers, and *repairers* set up, service, and repair equipment sold by wholesalers. For these jobs, firms usually hire workers with maintenance and repair experience or mechanically inclined individuals who can be trained on the job. Supervising warehouse workers—such as clerks, material movers, and truckdrivers—and seeing that standards of efficiency are maintained is the work of *blue-collar worker supervisors*.

Electronics technicians and *technologists* set up and adjust complex equipment, such as electronic automated guided vehicles, which automatically transport goods throughout a warehouse. These workers often have formal technical training, such as a 2-year associate degree.

Training and Advancement

Although some workers need a college degree, most jobs in wholesale trade can be entered without education beyond high school. New workers usually receive training after they begin work—for instance, in operation of inventory management databases, on-line purchasing systems, or electronic data interchange systems. Technological advances and market forces are rapidly altering this industry. Even workers in small firms need to keep informed about new selling techniques, management methodologies, and information systems. In addition, these technological advances affect the necessary skill requirements for occupations across the entire industry—from warehouse workers to truckdrivers to those in management. As a result, numerous firms devote significant resources to worker training.

Currently, many firms offer on the job training. However, as providing training is becoming more costly and complex, the industry is increasingly using third party training organizations and trade associations to reduce this burden. For productivity reasons, many companies make their employees responsible for more than one function and cross-train them by familiarizing them with many aspects of the company.

Table 1. Wage and salary employment in wholesale trade by occupation, 1998 and projected change, 1998-2008

(Employment in thousands)

Occupation	1998 Employment Number	Percent	1998-2008 Percent change
All occupations	6,831	100.0	7.3
Administrative support, including clerical	1,801	26.4	3.8
Stock clerks and order fillers	452	6.6	11.8
General office clerks	208	3.1	12.5
Shipping, receiving and traffic clerks	183	2.7	-3.5
Bookkeeping, accounting, and auditing clerks	181	2.7	-9.3
Secretaries	135	2.0	-11.2
Office and administrative support supervisors and managers	133	2.0	16.4
Order clerks	118	1.7	1.0
Adjusters, investigators, and collectors	74	1.1	21.4
Marketing and sales	1,602	23.5	4.4
All other sales and related workers	959	14.0	2.2
Marketing and sales worker supervisors	226	3.3	11.5
Retail salespersons	206	3.0	8.7
Parts salespersons	123	1.8	-2.4
Operators, fabricators, and laborers	1,407	20.6	11.6
Truck drivers, light and heavy	479	7.0	23.6
Freight, stock, and material movers, hand	214	3.1	-5.6
Hand workers, including assemblers and fabricators	162	2.4	13.4
Drivers/sales workers	111	1.6	2.3
Machine setters, set-up operators, operators, and tenders	110	1.6	15.8
Hand packers and packagers	77	1.1	-9.0
Industrial truck and tractor operators	66	1.0	14.9
Executive, administrative, and managerial	843	12.3	7.0
General managers and top executives	395	5.8	8.2
Buyers and purchasing agents	77	1.1	3.1
Purchasing managers	50	0.7	1.3
Precision production, craft, and repair	664	9.7	7.6
Vehicle and mobile equipment mechanics and repairers	146	2.1	3.5
Blue-collar worker supervisors	135	2.0	11.0
Machinery mechanics, installers, and repairers	84	1.2	-4.2
Other mechanics, installers, and repairers	74	1.1	13.5
Professional specialty	199	2.9	30.3
Computer systems analysts, engineers, and scientists	74	1.1	55.7
Technicians and related support	145	2.1	8.1
Agricultural, forestry, fishing, and related	95	1.4	15.2
Service	76	1.1	-.8

142

Wholesale trade has historically offered good advancement opportunities from the lowest skilled jobs up through management positions. For example, unskilled workers can start in the warehouse or stock room. After they become familiar with the products and procedures of the firm, workers may be promoted to counter sales or even to inside sales positions. Others may be trained to install, service, and repair the products sold by the firm. Eventually, workers may advance to outside sales positions or to managerial positions. Wholesale trade firms often emphasize promotion from within, especially in the numerous small businesses in the industry. Even in some of the largest firms, it is not uncommon to find top executives who began as part-time warehouse help.

As the wholesale trade industry changes in the coming years, advancement opportunities could become more limited. Market forces, new technologies, and changing management techniques are placing increasing demands on managers, so it will become more difficult to promote less-educated workers from within. Currently, several large firms in this industry have formal management training programs that train college graduates for management positions; and the number of these programs will probably grow. There are also a growing number of university programs providing students with both business and technical training.

In addition to advancement opportunities within a firm, there are also opportunities for self-employment. For example, because brokers match buyers with sellers and never actually own goods, those with the proper connections can establish wholesale brokerage businesses with only a small investment—perhaps working out of their home. Moreover, establishing a merchant wholesaling business can be easier than establishing many other kinds of businesses. Wholesalers who get exclusive distribution rights to popular items can become profitable quickly; although merchant wholesaling firms usually require a substantial investment, obtaining rights to a successful product can be the foundation of a successful new business.

Earnings

Nonsupervisory wage and salary workers in wholesale trade averaged $538 a week in 1998, higher than the average of $442 a week for the entire workforce. Earnings varied greatly between wholesale trade sectors. For example, in the sector with the highest earnings—professional and commercial equipment—workers averaged $687 a week; but in the sector with the lowest earnings—farm-product raw materials—workers made $342 a week. Earnings in selected occupations in wholesale trade appear in table 2.

Part of the earnings of some workers is based on performance, especially for outside sales workers who frequently receive commissions on their sales. Although many sales workers receive a base salary in addition to commission, some receive compensation based solely on sales revenue. Performance-based compensation may become more common among other occupations, as wholesaling firms attempt to offer more competitive compensation packages.

Like earnings, benefits vary widely from firm to firm. Some small firms offer few benefits. Benefits in larger firms include life insurance, partially or fully paid health insurance, and a pension. Other benefits may include profit sharing, savings or investment plans, and fully or partially paid dental insurance.

Less than 7 percent of workers in the wholesale trade industry are union members or are represented by unions, compared to 15 percent of the entire workforce.

Table 2. Median hourly earnings of the largest occupations in wholesale trade, 1997

Occupation	Wholesale trade-durable goods	Wholesale trade-nondurable goods	All industries
General managers and top executives	$31.68	$29.79	$26.05
First-line supervisors and managers/supervisors-sales and related workers	24.74	18.28	13.43
Sales representatives, scientific and related products and services, except retail	20.07	19.26	20.07
Sales representatives, except retail and scientific and related products and services	17.19	16.01	16.54
Truck drivers, heavy or tractor-trailer	11.72	12.80	13.08
Salespersons, retail	11.58	9.57	7.23
Salespersons, parts	11.25	—	10.41
General office clerks	9.30	9.00	9.10
Order fillers, wholesale and retail sales	9.21	9.03	8.82
Truck drivers, light, including delivery and route workers	8.53	10.06	9.38

Outlook

Wage and salary jobs in wholesale trade are projected to grow about 7 percent through the year 2008, slower than the 15 percent rate of growth projected for all industries combined. Industry trends will change the composition and nature of much wholesale trade employment. Consolidation of the industry into larger firms and the spread of new technology should slow growth in some occupations. However, many new jobs will be created in other fields, as firms provide a growing array of support services. In addition, these trends will change the roles of many other workers.

Heightened competition and pressure to lower operating costs should continue to force distributors to merge with, or acquire, other firms. The resulting consolidation of wholesale trade among fewer, larger firms will reduce demands for some workers, as merged companies eliminate duplicated staff.

Consolidation and greater competition among wholesale trade firms will lead more firms to expand their customer services, increasing demands for related workers. Adjustment clerks and sales workers will advance to many of these new customer service and marketing jobs. New workers with the necessary education and training may be needed for financial, logistical, technical, or advertising positions.

Wholesale trade will undoubtedly feel the effects of electronic commerce and new technology. Few jobs will be left untouched by technological innovations, and demand for some occupations will decline considerably, as computer systems dramatically improve worker productivity. The two largest occupational groups in wholesale trade, administrative support and marketing and sales occupations, will be the most affected.

Employment in administrative support occupations will grow more slowly than most other wholesale trade occupations. Advanced computer systems will enable much of the record-keeping, ordering, and processing in wholesaling to be automated. Use of computerized labels with bar codes will allow stock clerks with scanners to immediately record locations, quantities, and types of goods in a computerized inventory management system. Customers frequently order goods electronically through the Internet, extranets, or other special systems, or go to wholesalers' warehouses and place orders on computerized purchasing systems. Increasingly, bills are paid through electronic funds transfers. Therefore, fewer bookkeeping, accounting, and auditing clerks will be needed, as fewer paper transactions are conducted. Despite this new technology, some administrative support workers will still be needed to oversee the process and make adjustments when problems occur. These workers will need to be proficient with new computerized systems, and their jobs will be very different from those of today's clerks.

The work of sales workers will also change, both as the selling process becomes more automated and as customer service becomes more important. As customers increasingly purchase goods electronically, more of the selling will fall upon inside sales workers. They will field calls, track customers' inventory needs using on-line computer systems, solicit new business by phone or the Internet, and assist buyers with computerized purchases. However, more of outside sales workers' responsibilities will be complex customer service work. They will still visit customers to solicit new business and maintain good relations, to aid with installation and maintenance, and to advise on the most efficient use of purchases. Although the duties of sales workers will change, their importance will not. Increasingly, they will tailor inventory and distribution systems to individual customer's needs.

Sources of additional information

For information about job opportunities in wholesale trade, contact local firms.

For a list of colleges and universities with industrial distribution programs, contact:

➤ Industrial Distribution Association, 3 Corporate Square, Suite 201, Atlanta, GA 30329. Internet: **http://www.ida-assoc.org**

For information on food industry trends contact:

➤ Food Distributors International, 201 Park Washington Ct., Falls Church, VA 22046. Internet: **http://www.fdi.org**

Information on careers in the wholesale trade industry is available from:

➤ Retail, Wholesale, and Department Store Union, 30 East 29th St., 4th floor, New York, NY 10016.

Information on many of the key occupations in wholesale trade may be found in the 2000-01 *Occupational Outlook Handbook*:

- Bookkeeping, accounting, and auditing clerks
- Computer, automated teller, and office machine repairers
- Farm equipment mechanics
- Manufacturers' and wholesale sales representatives
- Order clerks
- Purchasing managers, buyers, and purchasing agents
- Shipping, receiving, and traffic clerks
- Stock clerks
- Truckdrivers

Finance and Insurance

Banking

- Administrative support and clerical workers comprise almost 7 out of 10 jobs; tellers account for 1 out of 4 jobs.

- Banking employment is projected to grow only slightly as mergers and automation make banks more efficient.

- Projected employment varies by occupation. Tellers will decline, while growth is expected for loan officers, customer service representatives, and securities and financial services sales representatives.

- Despite declining employment, job openings for tellers arising from replacement needs should be plentiful because turnover is high and the occupation is large; best opportunities will be for part-time tellers.

Nature of the Industry

Banks safeguard money and valuables, and provide loans, credit, and payment services, such as checking accounts, money orders, and cashier's checks. As the banking industry is slowly deregulated, banks are also beginning to offer more investment and insurance products that they were once prohibited from selling. Although other "nonbank" financial companies increasingly provide many of the same depository and payment services, a major difference between banks and other financial institutions is that deposits in banks are insured by the Federal Deposit Insurance Corporation. This ensures that depositors will get their money back, up to a stated limit, if a bank should fail.

There are several types of banks, also called depository institutions, which differ in the number of services they provide and the clientele they serve. *Commercial banks*, which dominate this industry, offer a full range of services for individuals, businesses, and governments. These banks come in a wide range of sizes from large "money center" banks to regional and community banks. Money center banks are often located in major financial centers and are usually involved in international lending and foreign currency, in addition to the more typical banking services. Regional banks usually are concentrated in a geographical area and their numerous branches and Automated Teller Machine (ATM) locations appeal to individuals. Community banks are based locally and offer more personal attention that small businesses prefer.

Savings banks and *savings and loan associations*, also known as thrift institutions, are the second largest group of depository institutions. They were first established to make it easier for people to buy homes, but now mostly cater to the savings and lending needs of individuals.

Credit unions are also considered banks. Most credit unions are formed by people with a common bond, such as people who work for the same company or belong to the same labor union or church. Their members pool their savings. When a member needs money, he or she may borrow from the credit union, often at a lower interest rate than from other financial institutions.

Federal Reserve banks are Government agencies that perform many financial services for the Government. Their chief responsibilities are to regulate the banking industry and to control the Nation's money supply—the total quantity of money in the country, including cash and bank deposits. Federal Reserve banks also perform a variety of services for other banks. For example, they make emergency loans to banks that are short of cash and clear checks that are drawn and paid out by different banks.

Interest on loans is the principal source of revenue for most banks, making their various lending departments critical to their success. The commercial lending department loans money to companies to start or expand a business or purchase inventory and capital equipment. The consumer lending department handles student loans, credit cards, and loans for home improvements, debt consolidation, and automobile purchases. Finally the mortgage lending department loans money to individuals and businesses to purchase real estate.

The money to lend comes primarily from deposits in checking and savings accounts, certificates of deposit, money market accounts, and other deposit accounts that consumers and businesses set up with the bank. These deposits often earn interest for the owner, and with accounts that offer checking, they provide an easy method for making payments safely without using cash.

The bank's trust department performs a number of other services. For example, the trust department may act as executor and administrator of a will, assembling and distributing assets to the beneficiaries. It may also serve as guardian of assets for minors or incompetent people. One of the department's most important functions is to manage assets entrusted to it, such as a pension fund or endowment fund, and to distribute the proceeds. Some trust departments also act as stock transfer agents for corporations. As agents, they record the transfer of ownership of stock. They also distribute dividend checks, annual reports and other mailings to stockholders.

Technology is having a major impact on the banking industry. For example, many routine bank services that once required a teller, such as making a withdrawal or deposit, are now available through ATMs that allow people to access their accounts 24-hours a day. Also, direct deposit allows companies and governments to electronically transfer payments into various accounts. Further, debit cards and "smart cards" instantaneously deduct money from your account when you swipe the card across a machine at a store's cash register. Finally, electronic banking by phone or computer allows you to pay bills and transfer money from one account to another.

Other fundamental changes are occurring in the industry as banks diversify their services to become more competitive. Many banks now offer financial planning and asset management services to their customers as well as brokerage and insurance services, often through a subsidiary or third party. And others are beginning to provide investment banking services that involve raising money for companies and governments through the issuance of stocks and bonds; this is usually done through a subsidiary. As deregulation continues and competition in this sector grows, the nature of the banking industry will continue to undergo even more significant changes.

Working Conditions

The average workweek in banking was 36 hours in 1998, although wide variations exist by occupation. Tellers increasingly work part-time, while managers and officers often put in 50 hours per week or more.

Variations also exist based on where the employee works. Employees in a typical branch work weekdays, some evenings if the bank is open late, and Saturday mornings. Hours may be longer for workers in bank branches located in grocery stores and shopping malls, which are open most evenings and weekends. Branch office jobs, particularly teller positions, require continual communication with customers, repetitive tasks, and a high level of attention to security. Tellers must also stand for long periods of time in a confined space.

To improve customer service and provide greater access to bank personnel, banks are establishing centralized phone centers, staffed mainly by customer service representatives. Employees of phone centers spend most of their time answering phone calls from customers and must be available to work evening and weekend shifts.

Clerical employees may work in large processing facilities, or in the banks' headquarters, or in other administrative offices. Most clerical staff work a standard 40-hour week; some may work overtime. Those clerks located in the processing facilities may work evening shifts.

Commercial and mortgage loan officers often work out of the office, visiting clients, checking out loan applications, and soliciting new business. Loan officers may be required to travel, if a client is out-of-town, or to work evenings, if that is the only time a client can meet. Financial service sales representatives may also visit clients in the evenings and on weekends to go over the client's financial needs.

The remaining employees located primarily at the headquarters or other administrative office usually work in comfortable surroundings and put in a standard workweek. In general, banks are relatively safe places to work. In 1997, cases of work-related injury and illness averaged 1.8 per 100 full-time workers, among the lowest in the private sector, where the rate was 7.1.

Employment

The banking industry employed over 2 million wage and salary workers in 1998, making it the largest industry in the finance, insurance, and real estate sector of the economy. More than 7 out of 10 jobs were in commercial banks; the remainder were concentrated in savings and loan associations and credit unions (table 1).

Table 1. Percent of employment in banking by type of institution, 1998

Establishment	Percent
Depository institutions	100.0
Commercial banks	71.5
Savings institutions	12.9
Credit unions	8.8
Banking and closely related functions, nec	6.7

In 1997, nearly 95 percent of the approximately 115,000 establishments in banking employed fewer than 50 workers (chart). However, these small establishments, mostly bank branch offices, employed only half of all employees. The other half worked in establishments with 50 or more workers. Banks are found everywhere in the United States, but most bank employees work in heavily populated States such as New York, California, Illinois, Pennsylvania, and Texas.

Occupations in the Industry

Clerical and administrative support positions account for about 7 out of 10 jobs in the banking industry (table 2). *Bank tellers*, the largest individual banking occupation, provide routine financial services to the public. They handle customers' deposits and withdrawals, change money, sell money orders and travelers checks, and accept payment for loans and utility bills. *New accounts clerks*, also called customer service representatives, help customers open and close accounts and fill out forms to apply for banking services. They are knowledgeable about a broad array of bank services and must be able to

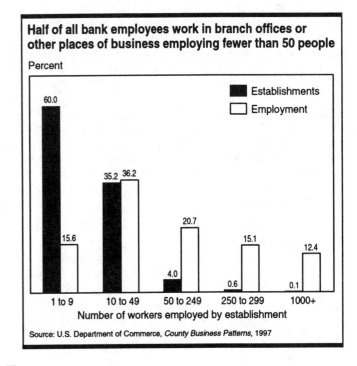

Half of all bank employees work in branch offices or other places of business employing fewer than 50 people

Percent

Legend: ■ Establishments □ Employment

- 1 to 9: 60.0 / 15.6
- 10 to 49: 35.2 / 36.2
- 50 to 249: 4.0 / 20.7
- 250 to 299: 0.6 / 15.1
- 1000+: 0.1 / 12.4

Number of workers employed by establishment

Source: U.S. Department of Commerce, *County Business Patterns*, 1997

sell those services to potential clients. Tellers are increasingly being trained to perform many functions of customer service representatives.

Loan and *credit clerks* assemble and prepare paperwork, process applications, and complete the documentation after the loan or line of credit has been approved. They also verify applications for completeness. Many *general office clerks* and *bookkeeping, accounting, and auditing clerks* are employed to maintain financial records, enter data, and process the thousands of deposit slips, checks, and other documents that banks handle daily. Banks also employ many secretaries, typists, receptionists, computer operators, and other clerical workers. *Clerical supervisors* and *managers* oversee the activities and training of workers in the various administrative support occupations.

Executive, administrative, and managerial occupations account for about 25 percent of employment in the banking industry. *Financial managers* direct bank branches and departments, resolve customers' problems, ensure that standards of service are maintained, and administer the institutions' operations and investments. *Loan officers* evaluate loan applications, determine an applicant's ability to pay back a loan, and recommend approval of loans. They usually specialize in commercial, consumer, or mortgage lending. When loans become delinquent, loan officers, or *loan counselors*, may advise borrowers on the management of their finances or take action to collect outstanding amounts. Loan officers also play a major role in bringing in new business and spend much of their time developing relationships with potential customers. *Trust officers* manage a variety of assets for other people or organizations that were placed in trust with the bank, including pension funds, school endowments, or a company's profit sharing plan. They also act as executors of estates upon a person's death. Trust officers also may work as accountants, lawyers, and investment managers.

Securities and financial services sales representatives, who make up the majority of marketing and sales positions in banks, sell complex banking services. They contact potential customers to explain their services and to ascertain the customer's banking and other financial needs. They may also discuss services such as deposit accounts, lines of credit, sales or inventory financing, certificates of deposit, cash management, or investment services. These sales representatives also solicit businesses to participate in consumer credit card programs. At most small and medium-size banks, however, branch managers and commercial loan officers are responsible for marketing the bank's financial services.

Other occupations used widely by banks to maintain financial records and ensure the bank's compliance with State and Federal regulations are *accountants and auditors*, and *lawyers*. In addition, *computer systems analysts* are needed to maintain and upgrade the bank's computer systems and to implement the bank's entry into the world of electronic banking and paperless transactions.

Training and Advancement

Bank tellers and other clerks usually need only a high school education. Most banks seek people who have good basic math and communication skills, enjoy public contact, and feel comfortable handling large amounts of money. Through a combination of formal classroom instruction and on-the-job training under the guidance of an experienced worker, tellers learn the procedures, rules, and regulations that govern their jobs. Banks encourage upward mobility by providing access to higher education and other sources of additional training.

Table 2. Employment of wage and salary workers in banking by occupation, 1998 and projected change, 1998-2008

(Employment in thousands)

Occupation	1998 Employment Number	1998 Employment Percent	1998-2008 Percent change
All occupations	2,042	100.0	2.8
Administrative support, including clerical	1,351	66.2	-3.1
Bank tellers	542	26.5	-6.4
Office and administrative support supervisors and managers	139	6.8	17.9
New account clerks, banking	97	4.8	13.9
Loan and credit clerks	87	4.3	5.1
General office clerks	86	4.2	-28.5
Bookkeeping, accounting, and auditing clerks	62	3.0	-9.2
Secretaries	52	2.6	-10.5
Adjustment clerks	43	2.1	21.3
Duplicating, mail, and other office machine operators	27	1.3	-28.3
Bill and account collectors	25	1.2	11.1
Executive, administrative, and managerial	503	24.6	10.6
Loan officers and counselors	116	5.7	12.8
Financial managers	97	4.8	7.2
General managers and top executives	67	3.3	7.9
Accountants and auditors	31	1.5	4.7
Marketing and sales	77	3.8	29.0
Securities, commodities, and financial services sales representatives	38	1.9	45.4
Professional specialty	67	3.3	34.4
Computer systems analysts, engineers, and scientists	45	2.2	48.8
Service	24	1.2	4.4
All other occupations	21	1.0	0.0

Tellers and clerks prepare for positions with more responsibilities by taking courses accredited by the American Institute of Banking, an educational affiliate of the American Bankers Association, and the Institute of Financial Education. These organizations have several hundred chapters in cities across the country and numerous study groups in small communities. Most banks use the facilities of these organizations, which assist local banks in conducting cooperative training programs or developing independent programs. Some community colleges also offer courses for employed tellers and those seeking to become tellers. Taking these courses can give applicants an advantage over other jobseekers.

Some banks have their own training programs, which result in teller certification. Experienced tellers qualify for certification by taking required courses and passing examinations. Experienced tellers and clerks may advance to head teller, new accounts clerk, or customer service representative. Outstanding tellers who have had some college or specialized training offered by the banking industry are sometimes promoted to managerial positions.

Workers in executive, administrative, and managerial banking jobs usually have at least a college degree. A bachelor's degree in business administration or a liberal arts degree with business administration courses is suitable preparation, as is a bachelor's degree in any field followed by a Master of Business Administration (MBA) degree. Many financial management positions are filled by promoting experienced, technically skilled professional personnel—for example, accountants, auditors, budget analysts, credit analysts, insurance analysts, or securities analysts—or accounting or related department supervisors in large banks.

Financial services sales representatives usually need a college degree; a major or courses in finance, accounting, economics, marketing, or related fields serve as excellent preparation. Experience in sales is also very helpful. These workers learn on the job under the supervision of bank officers. Sales representatives selling securities need to be licensed by the National Association of Securities Dealers.

Advancement to higher-level executive, administrative, managerial, and professional positions may be accelerated by special study. Banks often provide opportunities for workers to broaden their knowledge and skills, and they encourage employees to take classes offered by the AIB and IFE as well as courses at local colleges and universities. In addition, financial management and banking associations, often in cooperation with colleges and universities, sponsor numerous national or local training programs. Each of their schools deal with a different phase of financial management and banking, such as accounting management, budget management, corporate cash management, financial analysis, international banking, and data processing systems procedures and management. Employers also sponsor seminars and conferences and provide textbooks and other educational materials. Many employers pay all or part of the costs for those who successfully complete courses.

In recent years, the banking field has been revolutionized by technological improvements in computer and data processing equipment. Knowledge of their application is vital to upgrade managerial skills and to enhance advancement opportunities.

Earnings

Earnings of nonsupervisory bank employees averaged $384 a week in 1998, compared to $512 for all workers in finance, insurance, and real estate industries, and $442 for workers throughout the private sector. Relatively low pay in the banking industry reflects the high proportion of low-paying clerical jobs.

Earnings in the banking industry vary significantly by occupation. Earnings in the largest occupations in banking appear in table 3.

Based on a 1998 salary survey by Robert Half International—a staffing services firm specializing in accounting and finance—annual salaries of professional and managerial employees in banks with assets of $1 billion or higher ranged from around $35,000 to $215,000 (table 4).

Table 3. Median hourly earnings of the largest occupations in banking, 1997

Occupation	Banking	All industries
General managers and top executives	$31.64	$26.05
Financial managers	21.54	25.19
Loan officers and counselors	16.29	16.25
First-line supervisors and managers/ supervisors-clerical and administrative support workers	13.22	14.26
Secretaries, except legal and medical	11.21	11.00
Loan and credit clerks	9.92	10.36
New accounts clerks	9.79	9.85
Bookkeeping, accounting, and auditing clerks	9.62	10.80
General office clerks	9.60	9.10
Tellers	7.97	7.99

Table 4. Annual salary range for selected occupations in banking, 1998

Occupation	Salary range
Senior vice-president/head of lending	$200,000-215,000
Lending division head/lender	95,000-133,500
Marketing director	73,000-98,000
Loan workout officer	60,000-82,000
Asset/liability investment manager	59,000-81,000
Commercial real estate mortgage lender	46,000-74,000
Loan review officer	48,000-59,500
Branch manager	38,000-50,000
Employee benefits trust officer	38,000-48,000
Consumer loan officer	35,000-49,000

Source: Robert Half International

In general, greater responsibilities result in a higher salary. Experience, length of service, and, especially, the location and size of the bank also are important. In addition to typical benefits, equity sharing and performance-based pay increasingly are part of compensation packages for some bank employees. As in other industries, part-time workers do not enjoy the same benefits as full-time workers.

Very few workers in the banking industry are unionized—only 1.8 percent are union members or are covered by union contracts, compared to 15.4 percent of workers throughout private industry.

Outlook

Employment in the banking industry is expected to increase 3 percent between 1998 and 2008, compared to the 15 percent growth projected for the economy as a whole. Much of the increase; however, will occur in credit unions and small regional banks and savings institutions, with little to no growth projected for the large commercial banks. This projected growth reverses a trend of declining employment. The downsizing and cost cutting that has been taking place in this industry since the early 1990s is expected to slow and banks will begin hiring again and putting more emphasis on retaining employees. The mergers and acquisitions that led to significantly fewer banks are expected to continue, but result in fewer layoffs than in the past, because more of the mergers will occur between banks across geographical areas rather than within geographical areas, which results in fewer branch closings. Also, as banks diversify and begin offering new financial products, they will hire additional people with experience and skills to sell these new products.

Advances in technology are expected to significantly affect future employment. Computer specialists will benefit from this trend, as banks hire additional workers to make more of their services available electronically and through the Internet. The overall effect of automation on employment is expected to be negative, however. Employment of tellers is projected to decline, as ATMs become able to provide additional services, such as account changes and applications for loans and credit cards. Employment of clerical staff, in general, also will be adversely affected by the growing use of direct deposit of payroll checks, debit and "smart" cards, and automated bill paying through phones and computers. Moreover, as banking services become more automated and the industry strives for paperless transactions, the number of clerical employees who process the large volume of paper will decline substantially. Due to the large number of clerical workers and their high turnover, however, job opportunities are still expected to be plentiful, especially for part-time positions.

A number of occupations are expected to grow significantly over the next 10 years. Employment increases can be expected for customer service representatives, who will assume many functions of the traditional teller in addition to their other duties. Customer service representatives will also staff a growing number of phone centers. Loan officers, who develop new business for banks and evaluate loan applications, will also be in great demand, provided that the economy and demand for loans remains strong. Banks will also hire more trust officers to administer the estates of an aging population. Finally, employment in

human resources departments is expected to grow, as the need to train employees about new bank services and new regulations becomes more urgent.

Banks will also place greater emphasis on hiring people with marketing, sales, and financial skills as they try to redefine themselves as a "one-stop-shop" for financial services. The employment of securities and financial services sales representatives is expected to double over the next ten years as these workers are needed to sell the increasing variety of bank products and services. Those with a financial planning background are expected to fare even better.

Sources of Additional Information
For information about careers in the banking industry, contact:

➢ American Bankers Association, 1120 Connecticut Ave. NW, Washington, DC 20036. Internet: **http://www.aba.com**

Information about careers with the Federal Reserve System is available from the website or human resources department of the Federal Reserve Bank in which you are interested.

Information on the many occupations in banking, including the following, may be found in the 2000-01 *Occupational Outlook Handbook*:

- Accountants and auditors
- Adjusters, investigators, and collectors
- Bank tellers
- Bookkeeping, accounting, and auditing clerks
- Computer engineers and scientists
- Computer systems analysts
- Credit and loan authorizers, checkers, and clerks
- Financial managers
- Loan officers
- New accounts clerks
- Securities, commodities, and financial services sales representatives

Insurance

SIGNIFICANT POINTS

- Administrative support occupations, including clerical, account for 4 out of 10 jobs; executives, administrators, managerial, and sales workers make up most of the remaining jobs.

- Clerical jobs usually require a high school diploma, while employers prefer college graduates for sales, managerial, and professional jobs.

- Employment opportunities will be favorable despite limited job growth caused by corporate downsizing, computerization, and changes in business practices.

Nature of the Industry

The insurance industry provides protection against financial losses resulting from a variety of perils. By purchasing insurance policies, individuals and businesses can receive reimbursement for losses due to car accidents, theft of property, fire and storm damage, medical expenses, and loss of income due to disability or death. The insurance industry is mainly comprised of *insurance carriers*, or *"insurers,"* and *insurance agents* and *brokers*. In general, insurance carriers are large companies that provide insurance and assume the risks covered by the policy. Agents and brokers sell insurance policies for the carriers, and work either for themselves or for relatively small firms.

Insurance carriers offer a variety of insurance policies. *Life insurance* policies provide financial protection to beneficiaries—usually spouses and dependent children—upon the death of the insured. *Disability insurance* provides income if a person is unable to work, and *health insurance* pays the expenses resulting from accidents and sickness. *Annuities* (contracts that provide a periodic income at regular intervals for a specified period of time) provide a steady income during retirement for the remainder of one's life. *Property-casualty insurance* protects against loss or damage to property resulting from hazards such as fire and theft. *Liability insurance* shields policyholders from financial responsibility for injuries to others or damage to other people's property. Most policies, such as automobile and homeowner's insurance, bought by consumers, combine both property-casualty and liability coverage. Companies that write this kind of insurance are called property-casualty carriers.

Some insurance policies cover groups of people, ranging from a few individuals to thousands. These policies usually are issued to employers for the benefit of their employees. Among the most common policies are group life and health plans. Insurance carriers also write a variety of specialized types of insurance, such as real estate title insurance and employee surety and fidelity bonding. In addition to underwriting policies, some carriers manage pension funds.

Insurance agents and brokers act as intermediaries between policyholders and insurance carriers. In addition to selling policies, agents and brokers assist clients in submitting their claims to carriers after a loss occurs. Many agents and brokers are independent and are free to market their policies through a variety of insurance carriers. Other agents may work exclusively for one insurance carrier, selling only that carrier's policies. These "exclusive" agents may be employed by the insurance carriers they represent. Like many agents, insurance brokers do not represent any particular insurance carrier. They are retained primarily by clients with special insurance needs to approach and negotiate insurance contracts with carriers on the client's behalf.

The insurance industry also includes a number of independent organizations that provide a wide array of insurance-related services to carriers and their clients. One such service is the processing of medical claims forms for medical practitioners. Other services include loss prevention and risk management. Also, carriers hire independent claims adjusters to investigate accidents and claims for property damage and assign a dollar estimate to the claim.

Other organizations are formed by groups of insurance companies to perform functions that would result in a duplication of effort if each company carried them out individually. For example, rating bureaus are supported by insurance companies to provide loss statistics which the companies use to set their rates. Information institutes produce and distribute relevant statistics and educational materials to teachers and schools on the different lines of insurance, and prepare news releases concerning developments of general interest to the public. This segment of the industry is also supported by numerous educational institutions that grant certifications and designations to insurance industry employees as well as provide a source of continuing education that is required by many state licensing bureaus.

Working Conditions

Many workers in the insurance industry, especially those in administrative support positions, work a 5-day, 40-hour week. Those in executive and managerial occupations may often put in more than 40 hours. Many sales workers and claims adjusters work irregular hours outside of office settings. Often, sales staff and adjusters arrange their own hours, scheduling evening and weekend appointments for the convenience of clients.

Sales personnel, including agents and brokers, often visit prospective and existing customers' homes and places of business to market new products and provide services. Claims adjusters frequently leave the office to inspect damaged property.

A small but increasing number of insurance employees spend most of their time on the telephone working in call-centers, answering questions and providing information to prospective clients or current policyholders. These jobs may include selling insurance, taking claims information, or answering medical questions. Because these centers operate 24 hours a day, 7 days a week, they involve working evening and weekend shifts. The irregular business hours in the insurance industry provide some workers with the opportunity for part-time work. Part-time employees make up 8.8 percent of the workforce.

As would be expected in an industry dominated by office and sales employees, the incidence of occupational injuries and illnesses among insurance workers is low. An average of only 2.2 cases per 100 full-time workers was reported in 1997 in the insurance carriers segment, and 1.3 in the agents and brokers segment, compared with an average of 7.1 for all private industry.

Employment

The insurance industry, including both insurance carriers and agents and brokers, employed about 2.3 million wage and salary workers in 1998. Insurance carriers provided nearly 7 out of 10 jobs in the insurance industry; insurance agents, brokers, and providers of other insurance-related services held about 3 out of 10 jobs. In addition, there were about 150,000 self-employed workers in 1998, most of whom were insurance agents or brokers.

Insurance carriers are mostly large employers, as shown in the chart above. Over half of their employment is in establishments with 250 or more employees and 80 percent is in establishments with 50 or more workers. Conversely, small establishments dominate the agents and brokers segment of the industry with nearly all employing fewer than 50 workers (see chart below). Approximately 40 percent work in establishments with fewer than 10 employees, and another 30 percent work in establishments with 10 to 49 employees.

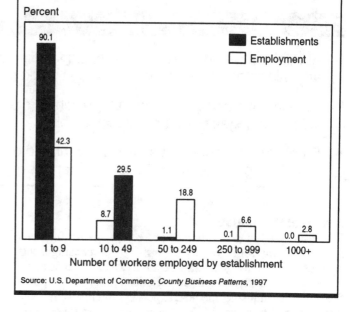

Nearly all insurance agencies employ fewer than 50 workers

Source: U.S. Department of Commerce, *County Business Patterns*, 1997

Insurance carriers' home and regional offices are commonly located near large urban centers. Insurance workers who deal directly with the public—sales personnel and claims adjusters—are located throughout the country. Almost all insurance agents and brokers work out of local company offices or independent agencies. Many claims adjusters work for independent firms located in small cities and towns throughout the country.

Occupations in the Industry

More than 4 in 10 insurance workers are in administrative support jobs found in every industry, including jobs such as secretaries, typists, word processors, bookkeepers, and other clerical workers (table 1). Many administrative support positions in the insurance industry, however, require skills and knowledge unique to the industry.

Insurance policy processing clerks, for example, process insurance policy applications, changes, and cancellations. Clerks usually work at computer terminals. They review applications for completeness, compile data on policy changes, and verify the accuracy of insurance company records. Over half of all policy processing clerks work in insurance agencies and are usually referred to as customer service representatives. These workers are taking on increased responsibilities in insurance offices, such as handling most of the continuing contact with clients.

Insurance adjusters, examiners, and *investigators* decide whether claims are covered by the customer's policy, confirm payment, and, when necessary, investigate the circumstances surrounding a claim. *Claims adjusters* work for property and liability insurance carriers or for independent adjusting firms. They plan and schedule the work required to process claims, which includes interviewing the claimant and witnesses, consulting police and hospital records, and inspecting property damage to determine the extent of the insurance company's liability.

In life and health insurance carriers, the counterpart of the claims adjuster is the *claims examiner*, who investigates

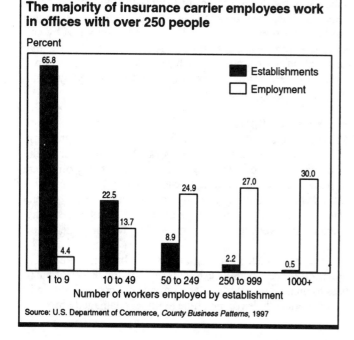

The majority of insurance carrier employees work in offices with over 250 people

Source: U.S. Department of Commerce, *County Business Patterns*, 1997

questionable claims or those exceeding a designated amount. Examiners check claim applications for completeness and accuracy, interview medical specialists, and consult policy files to verify information on a claim. Claims adjusters and examiners rely heavily on *insurance claims clerks*, who obtain and record claims information from customers and from claims adjusters and examiners.

About 3 in 10 insurance workers have an executive, administrative, or managerial job. *Sales managers* constitute the majority of managers in carriers' local sales offices and in the agents and brokers segment. They sell insurance products, work with clients, and supervise staff. Other managers who work in home offices are in charge of departments such as actuarial calculations, policy issuance, accounting, and investments.

Risk managers assess various risks faced by insurance companies. They develop risk policies by analyzing historical data regarding workplace injuries, automobile accidents, natural hazards, and conditions which may result in catastrophic physical and financial loss. For example, they might recommend that a factory add safety equipment, that a house be built to withstand environmental catastrophes, or that incentives be implemented to encourage automobile owners to install air bags in their cars. Because these standards can greatly reduce the probability of loss, risk managers are increasingly important to both insurance companies and the insured.

Another important executive, administrative, and managerial occupation in insurance is *underwriter*. These professionals evaluate insurance applications to determine the risk involved in issuing a policy. They decide whether to accept or reject the application and determine the appropriate premium rate for each policy.

Claims examiners in property and casualty insurance review settled claims to determine whether payments and settlements have been made in accordance with company practices and procedures. They ensure adjusters have followed proper methods when investigating claims. Examiners may consult with lawyers on claims requiring legal action.

About 15 percent of wage and salary employees are sales staff, who sell policies to individuals and businesses. Insurance sales workers include *insurance agents* and *brokers*, also known as producers. Insurance sales workers can be further classified into three categories: Exclusive agents—sometimes called captive agents—independent agents, and brokers. *Insurance agents* may work as exclusive agents selling for one company or as independent agents selling for several companies. Through regular contact with clients, agents are able to update coverage, assist with claims, ensure customer satisfaction, and obtain referrals. *Insurance brokers* represent the client or the insured. Agents and brokers may sell many types of insurance: Life, annuities, property-casualty, health, or disability. Also, many insurance agents and brokers are involved in "cross-selling" or "total account development," which means that besides insurance, some agents have become licensed to sell mutual funds, annuities, and other securities. These agents usually find their own customers and ensure that policies they sell meet the specific needs of their policyholders.

The insurance industry employs relatively few people in professional specialty occupations; however, these professionals are essential to insurance companies. For example, lawyers representing insurance companies are needed to defend clients who are sued, especially when potentially large claims are involved. They also review regulations and policy contracts. Nurses and other medical professionals advise clients on wellness issues and on medical procedures covered by their managed care plan. *Systems analysts* and *computer scientists* are needed to analyze, design, develop and program the systems that support the day to day operations of the insurance company.

Actuaries represent a relatively small proportion of insurance employment, but they are vital to the industry's profitability. Actuaries study the probability of an insured loss and determine premium rates. They must set rates so there is a high probability that premiums paid by customers will cover claims, but not so high that their company loses business to competitors.

Table 1. Employment of wage and salary workers in the insurance industry by occupation, 1998 and projected change, 1998-2008

(Employment in thousands)

Occupation	1998 Employment Number	1998 Employment Percent	1998-2008 Percent change
All occupations	2,344	100.0	9.9
Administrative support, including clerical	993	42.4	4.8
Insurance policy processing clerks	165	7.1	8.2
General office clerks	120	5.1	5.3
Insurance claims clerks	108	4.6	11.4
Office and administrative support supervisors and managers	105	4.5	9.7
Secretaries	102	4.4	-7.3
Adjustment clerks	66	2.8	31.7
Bookkeeping, accounting, and auditing clerks	54	2.3	-7.7
Receptionists and information clerks	49	2.1	14.3
File clerks	27	1.2	-10.8
Word processors and typists	24	1.0	-28.2
Data entry keyers	22	0.9	-8.2
Executive, administrative, and managerial	709	30.2	12.6
Insurance adjusters, examiners, and investigators	162	6.9	21.7
General managers and top executives	106	4.5	9.0
Insurance underwriters	88	3.8	.5
Claims examiners, property and casualty insurance	47	2.0	12.1
Accountants and auditors	39	1.7	13.6
Financial managers	26	1.1	4.0
Marketing and sales	349	14.9	7.3
Insurance sales workers	259	11.0	6.2
Marketing and sales worker supervisors	44	1.9	10.1
Professional specialty	182	7.8	35.5
Computer systems analysts, engineers, and scientists	93	4.0	53.1
Technicians and related support	84	3.6	5.3
Computer programmers	37	1.6	-14.5
Legal assistants and technicians, except clerical	31	1.3	23.3
All other occupations	28	1.2	5.2

Training and Advancement

Many jobs in the insurance industry, especially in clerical occupations, require no more than a high school diploma. For others, including sales jobs and some managerial and professional jobs, employers prefer to hire workers with a college education. When specialized training is required, it usually is obtained on the job or through independent study during work or after-work hours.

Graduation from high school or business school is adequate preparation for most beginning administrative support jobs. Courses in word processing and business math are assets, and the ability to operate computers is essential. These and other special skills also help beginners advance to higher-paying positions. On-the-job training usually is provided for clerical jobs unique to insurance, such as policy processing or claims clerks.

Executive, administrative, and professional jobs require the same college training as similar jobs in other industries. Managerial positions usually are filled by promoting college-educated employees within the company. For beginning underwriting jobs, many insurance companies prefer college graduates who have a degree in business administration or a related field. However, some companies prefer to hire liberal arts graduates at a lower cost and send them to company schools and to outside institutes for professional training. For actuarial jobs, companies prefer candidates to have degrees in actuarial science, mathematics, or statistics. Actuaries must pass a series of national examinations to become fully qualified. Completion of all the exams takes from 5 to 10 years. Some of the exams may be taken while in college, but most require extensive home study.

Although some employers hire high school graduates with potential or proven sales ability for entry-level sales positions, most employers prefer to hire college graduates. All insurance agents and brokers must obtain a license in the States in which they plan to sell insurance. In most States, licenses are issued only to applicants who complete specified courses and pass written examinations covering insurance fundamentals and State insurance laws. New agents receive training from their employer either at work or at the insurance company's home office. Sometimes, entry-level employees attend company-sponsored classes to prepare for examinations. Others study on their own and, as on-the-job training, accompany experienced agents when they meet with prospective clients.

Advancement opportunities are relatively good in the insurance industry. Clerical workers can advance to higher paying claims adjusting positions and entry-level underwriting jobs. Sales workers may advance by handling greater numbers of accounts and more complex commercial insurance policies. Having a Master's Degree helps advancement into higher levels of management. Many insurance companies expect their employees to take continuing education courses to improve their professionalism and their knowledge of the industry.

Earnings

Weekly earnings of nonsupervisory workers in the insurance carriers' segment of the industry averaged $649 in 1998, considerably higher than the average of $442 for all private industry. Earnings for the largest occupations in insurance for 1997 appear in table 2.

Table 2. Median hourly earnings of the largest occupations in insurance, 1997

Occupation	Insurance carriers	Insurance agents, brokers, and service	All industries
General managers and top executives	$40.72	$37.75	$26.05
Insurance underwriters	19.07	15.46	17.80
First-line supervisors and supervisor-mangers-clerical and administrative support workers	18.49	14.91	14.26
Insurance adjusters, examiners, and investigators	18.34	16.90	17.96
Sales agents and placers, insurance	15.64	15.95	15.75
Secretaries, except legal and medical	13.01	10.51	11.00
Insurance claims clerks	12.19	10.94	11.27
Adjustment clerks	11.61	11.87	10.43
Insurance policy processing clerks	11.56	10.97	11.23
General office clerks	9.98	8.55	9.10

Most independent agents, who own their own business, are paid by commission only. Sales workers who are employees of an agency may be paid by salary only, salary plus commission, or salary plus bonus. An agent's earnings usually increase rapidly with experience. Many agencies also pay an agent's expenses for automobiles and transportation, travel to conventions, and continuing education.

Insurance carriers offer attractive benefits packages, as is often the case with benefits in large companies. Yearly bonuses, retirement investment plans, insurance, and paid vacation often are standard. Insurance agencies, which are generally smaller, offer less extensive benefits.

Unionization is not widespread in the insurance industry. In 1998, 3.3 percent of all insurance workers were union members or were covered by union contracts, compared to 15.4 percent of workers throughout private industry.

Outlook

Employment in the insurance industry is projected to increase 10 percent between 1998 and 2008, more slowly than the 15 percent average for all industries combined. While demand for insurance is expected to rise, job growth will be limited by downsizing, computerization, and a trend towards direct mail and telephone sales. Nevertheless, thousands of openings are expected to arise in this large industry to replace those who leave and to accommodate the industry's push into the broader financial services field.

Population growth will stimulate demand for all types of insurance, but particularly auto and homeowners. It will also create demand for businesses to service its needs, and these businesses will also need insurance. As the population ages, more people are expected to buy health and long-term care insurance as well as annuities and other types of pension products sold by insurance sales agents. Also, laws to help people purchase health insurance, should boost demand. And large liability awards are motivating many individuals and businesses to purchase liability policies to cover lawsuits brought by people claiming damage or injury by a particular person or product.

Productivity gains caused by the greater use of computers will limit the growth of certain professional, clerical, and sales jobs. For example, the use of underwriting software that automatically analyzes and rates insurance applications will lead to slower than average employment growth for underwriters. Also, computers that are linked directly to the insurance carriers have greatly facilitated communications between agencies and insurance carriers, making the agency and its employees, primarily policy processing clerks, much more productive and subject to slower than average growth. Job growth for sales agents will also be limited by the increased use of direct marketing by insurance carriers, who will centralize sales activities in a growing number of telephone service centers.

Employment of claims professionals, especially in the property and casualty and health fields, will grow faster than average as companies strive for better customer service. These jobs are less easily automated because they require contact with policyholders and actual inspection of damaged property or consultation with a physician. Especially in the faster growing parts of the country, claims adjusters and examiners will be in great demand. In addition, many property and casualty and health insurance companies are setting up 24-hour call-in centers for clients to report claims or to ask health-related questions. This will create a demand for claims clerks to process the information generated from the calls. It will

also create a growing demand for health care professionals familiar with medical terminology.

Sources of Additional Information

General information on employment opportunities in the insurance industry may be obtained from the human resources departments of major insurance companies or from insurance agencies in local communities.

Other information on careers in insurance is available from:

➤ Life Insurance Marketing and Research Association, P.O. Box 208, Hartford, CT 16141-0208.
   Internet: **http://www.limra.com**
➤ Insurance Information Institute, 110 William St., New York, NY 10034.
   Internet: **http://www.iii.org**
➤ The American Institute for Chartered Property and Casualty Underwriters, and the Insurance Institute of America, 720 Providence Rd., P.O. Box 3016, Malvern, PA 19355-0716.
   Internet: **http://www.aicpcu.org**
➤ Health Insurance Association of America, 555 13th St. NW., Suite 600 East, Washington, DC 20004.
   Internet: **http://www.hiaa.org**

Information on the following insurance occupations may be found in the 2000-01 *Occupational Outlook Handbook*:

- Actuaries
- Adjusters, investigators, and collectors
- Insurance sales agents
- Insurance underwriters

Securities and Commodities

- Securities sales representatives and executive, administrative, and managerial workers, who generally have a college degree, account for about half of all jobs in the industry; the rest are mainly clerical.

- Increasing investment in securities and commodities along with the growing need for investment advice, is projected to produce rapid employment growth.

- The potential for high earnings means keen competition for securities sales representative positions—particularly in larger firms.

Nature of the Industry

The securities and commodities industry has been at the forefront of an investment boom in recent years, as investors have spent vast amounts of money buying stocks, bonds, mutual funds, commodity futures, and other financial products. Especially throughout the latter half of the 1990s, the industry has been adding large numbers of workers to facilitate the growing purchase and sale of securities and commodities.

The industry is made up of a variety of firms and organizations that bring together buyers and sellers of securities and commodities, manage investments, and offer financial advice. Brokerage firms are the most numerous, employing nearly 8 out of 10 people in the industry. In these firms, investors place their buy and sell orders for a particular security or commodity by phone, online, or through a broker. The firm fills the order in one of two ways. If the stock or commodity is sold on an exchange, such as the New York Stock Exchange, the firm will send the order electronically to the company's floor broker at the exchange, who will post the order and execute the trade by finding a seller or buyer for the security or commodity at the best price for the client. Alternatively, if the stock is not listed on an exchange, the firm can contact a dealer through a dealer network, such as Nasdaq, who trades in that security and stands ready to buy or sell it at any time. Large investors can access an "electronic communications network," or ECN, which bypasses the exchanges and dealer networks and matches buy and sell orders through the computer, eliminating the middleman.

Investors who do not have time to research investments on their own, will likely rely on a full-service broker who has access to a wide range of reports and analyses from the company's large staff of financial analysts. These analysts research companies and make recommendations on which investments are best for people with different savings and investment needs.

Brokerage firms also provide investment banking services. Investment banking involves buying initial stock or bond offerings from private companies or from Federal, State, and local governments, and in turn selling them to investors for a potential profit. This service can be risky, especially when it involves a new company selling stock to the public for the first time. Investment bankers must try to determine the value of the company based on a number of factors, including projected growth and sales, and decide what price investors are willing to pay for the new stock. Investment bankers also advise businesses on merger and acquisition strategies and may arrange for the transfer of ownership.

A relatively small number of professionals in the industry work in the exchanges, where the actual trading of securities and commodities takes place. Computers and their applications have made brokers in the exchanges much more productive and capable of handling ever increasing volumes of trades.

Companies that specialize in providing investment advice and portfolio management are also included in this industry. These companies range from very large mutual fund management companies to self-employed financial planners. They also include managers of pension funds, commodity pools, trust funds, and other investment accounts.

Firms in this industry offer a number of other services, many of which you can also obtain from other financial service providers. Cash management accounts that many brokerage firms offer, for instance, are similar to checking accounts in that they allow account holders to deposit money into a money market fund and then write checks, take out margin loans, or use a debit card. Some brokerage firms offer mortgages and other types of loans and lines of credit. Also, they may offer trust services, help businesses set up benefit plans for their employees, and sell annuities and other life insurance products.

Employment in each of the segments of the securities and commodities industry is directly affected by the activity of the stock and futures markets and the sales levels of financial products. Because these factors are determined largely by the strength of the economy, the industry prospers during good times, but is more adversely affected by downturns than many other industries.

Working Conditions

Most people in this industry work in comfortable offices; however long hours, including evenings and weekends, are common. Even when not working, professionals in this industry must keep abreast of events that may affect the markets in which they specialize. The average workweek for this industry is 39 hours, with most professionals working substantially longer. Opportunities for part-time work are limited—only 7.4 percent work part-time. In 1997, the industry had only 0.7 injuries and illnesses per 100 full-time workers. Working conditions varry by occupation.

Security sales representatives who deal mostly with individual investors and small businesses often work in branch offices of regional or national brokerage firms or for a small brokerage or financial planning firm. New sales representatives work long hours, mostly soliciting customers. During the day, they are on the phone continually to prospective customers, while at night they may attempt to generate new business by giving classes or seminars or attending community functions. New sales representatives also spend many hours studying for a variety of tests to qualify them to sell other investment products, such as commodities or insurance. Although established representatives work more regular hours, all representatives meet with clients in the evenings and on weekends, as needed.

Sales representatives who actually perform the buying and selling of securities and commodities may have one of the most hectic jobs of any profession. Often called traders, market makers, dealers, or floor brokers, they work on the floors of exchanges or at a computer that is linked to other traders. They not only take orders from clients and try to get the best price for them, they must constantly keep an eye on market activity and stay in touch with other traders and brokers to know what prices are being offered.

Jobs in investment banking, including those of financial managers, analysts, or assistants, generally require the longest hours—often 70-80 hours per week—in addition to extensive travel. In this area, there is a great deal of pressure to meet deadlines and acquire new business. Researchers, financial analysts, and investment managers working for brokerage and mutual fund firms also work long hours, researching and evaluating companies and their markets. Frequent travel to visit companies is common.

Financial planners work in offices or out of their homes. Most work regular business hours, but many accommodate clients by visiting them at their homes in the evenings or on weekends. Administrative support workers usually work a 40-hour week, but overtime may be necessary during times of heavy trading.

Employment

The securities and commodities industry employed 644,700 wage and salary workers in 1998. An additional 102,000 workers were self-employed. With their large network of retail sales representatives located in branch offices throughout the country, the large nationally-known brokerage companies employ the majority of workers in this industry (see chart). The headquarters of many of these firms, where most executives and administrative support personnel are employed, are located in New York City. Many people are also employed by mutual fund management companies and smaller regional brokerage firms. A relatively small number work at securities or commodity exchanges—primarily the New York Stock Exchange, the Chicago Board of Trade, the Chicago Mercantile Exchange, and a number of regional exchanges.

Occupations in the Industry

Securities, commodities, and financial services sales representatives make up the single largest occupation in this industry (table 1). Although the occupation includes a variety of job titles and activities, all involve placing orders or buying and selling securities, commodities, or other financial services.

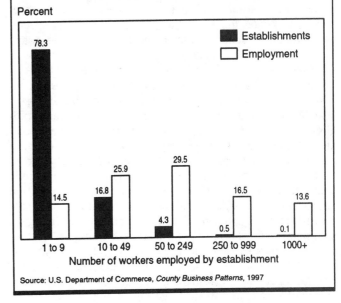

Ninety-five percent of establishments in securities and commodities employ fewer than 50 people

Percent

Source: U.S. Department of Commerce, *County Business Patterns*, 1997

The most common sales representatives deal directly with the public and are often called retail brokers, account executives, registered representatives, or financial consultants. Securities brokers typically buy and sell stocks, bonds, mutual funds, and other financial services, while commodity brokers deal primarily with futures contracts on metals, energy supplies, agricultural products, and financial instruments.

When a client places an order for one of these items, brokers relay the order through the firm's computers to the floor of the exchange or to a dealer. Upon confirmation of the trade, the broker notifies clients of the final price. As part of their job, brokers often provide advice to clients about possible investments, taking into consideration the client's financial situation, tolerance for risk, and savings needs. Because sales is one of their major responsibilities, brokers also spend a considerable amount of time soliciting new business.

A small number of sales representatives deal exclusively with large investors, such as insurance companies, pension funds, and mutual funds. They are typically called institutional representatives or institutional brokers and provide many of the same services as a retail broker, but on a larger scale.

Sales representatives, referred to as *traders, market makers, and floor brokers*, actually make the trades on the exchange floor or over the computer. They match buyers and sellers of a particular security or commodity, sometimes using their own or their firm's money to close the deal.

Financial planners, also included among sales representatives, provide advice to both individuals and businesses on a broad range of financial subjects, such as investments, retirement planning, tax management, and employee benefits. They may take a comprehensive approach to the client's financial needs or just address a specific issue. Planners may also buy and sell financial products, such as stocks, bonds, mutual funds, and insurance for their clients.

Keeping track of transactions and paperwork constitutes a large portion of the work in this industry, which is why its largest occupational group is administrative support, including clerical, workers. *Brokerage clerks,* the largest occupation in this category, handle much of the day-to-day operations within a brokerage firm. The largest group of clerks, called sales assistants, take calls from clients, write up order tickets and enter them into the computer, handle the paperwork for new accounts, inform clients of stock prices, and perform other tasks as needed. Some sales assistants obtain licenses to sell securities. This allows them to call brokers' clients with recommendations from the broker on specific investments. Other brokerage clerks may compute transfer taxes and dividends and keep daily records of transactions and holdings. At some companies, a number of brokerage clerk positions are considered entry level with promotion potential to securities sales representative jobs or other higher level jobs.

Executive, administrative, and managerial occupations make up 25 percent of total employment, a larger proportion than in most industries. This category includes accountants and auditors, who prepare the firm's financial statements; general managers, who run the business; and a myriad of other people with expertise in finance and investment policy.

Financial analysts generally work in the research and investment banking departments. They review financial statements of companies, evaluate economic and market trends, and make recommendations concerning the potential profits from investments in specific companies. They may also attempt to determine fair market values for companies wishing to trade their stocks publicly or those involved in mergers or acquisitions. Analysts in large firms usually specialize in a certain industry sector, like transportation or utilities, or in a market, such as government financing.

Financial managers are employed throughout the industry, preparing financial documents for the regulatory authorities or directing a firm's investment policies. In many departments, managers act as senior advisors and oversee teams of junior analysts or brokers while continuing to be actively involved in working out deals with clients.

Portfolio managers and *commodity trading advisors* are responsible for making investment decisions for clients with large sums of money to invest. These clients include mutual funds, pension funds, trust funds, commodity pools, and high net-worth individuals. Portfolio managers must know the investment goals of the client and ensure that the investments they make meet those goals.

Training and Advancement

This industry has one of the most highly educated and skilled workforces of any industry, and the requirements for entry are high—even brokerage clerks often have a college degree. The most successful workers at all levels have an aptitude for numbers and a very keen interest in investing. In addition, most people in this industry are required to be licensed by the National Association of Securities Dealers (NASD) before they can sell securities or recommend specific investments. To be licensed, brokers and assistants must pass an examination that reflects their knowledge of investments. Various licenses are available for different investment products. However, the one most brokers and broker's assistants receive is the "Series 7" license, which requires a passing score on the General Securities Registered Representative Examination administered by the NASD. Since 1995, the NASD has also required all registered persons to undergo a continuing education program every 3 years

in order to retain their licenses. Classes consist of computer-based training in regulatory matters and training on new investment products.

Table 1. Employment of wage and salary workers in securities and commodities by occupation, 1998 and projected change, 1998-2008

(Employment in thousands)

Occupation	1998 Employment		1998-2008 Percent change
	Number	Percent	
All occupation	645	100.0	39.6
Administrative support, including clerical	212	32.9	26.6
Brokerage clerks	60	9.4	28.0
Secretaries	39	6.0	12.8
General office clerks	22	3.4	42.0
Office and administrative support supervisors and managers	21	3.2	38.1
Receptionists and information clerks	11	1.7	42.1
Bookkeeping, accounting, and auditing clerks	8	1.3	16.6
Marketing and sales	199	30.9	38.5
Securities, commodities, and financial services sales workers	164	25.5	38.8
Marketing and sales worker supervisors	10	1.5	40.4
Executive, administrative, and managerial	163	25.3	51.2
General managers and top executives	34	5.3	39.2
Financial managers	23	3.6	43.2
Accountants and auditors	14	2.2	37.1
Professional specialty	47	7.3	68.7
Computer systems analysts, engineers, and scientists	23	3.6	99.0
Technicians and related support	15	2.3	20.2
Computer programmers	12	1.8	9.9
All other occupations	8	1.3	41.1

A number of professionals in this industry begin their careers as brokerage clerks. Depending on the actual job, brokerage clerks can be high school or college graduates. Positions dealing with the public, such as brokers or sales assistants, and those dealing with more complicated financial records, are increasingly held by college graduates. In addition, these jobs require good organizational ability, phone skills, and attention to detail. A Series 7 brokerage license can make a clerk more valuable to the broker because it gives the assistant the ability to answer more of a client's questions and to pass along securities recommendations from the broker. Clerks may be promoted to sales representative positions or other professional positions. Some of the larger firms have training programs, especially for their college graduates, to provide clerks with the skills needed for advancement.

A college education, although not essential, is increasingly important for securities and commodities futures sales representatives because it helps them to understand economic conditions and trends. In fact, the overwhelming majority of entrants to this occupation are college graduates. Still, many employers consider personal qualities and skills more important than academic training. Employers seek applicants with good communication skills, a professional appearance, and a strong desire to succeed. Securities and commodities sales workers must meet Federal and State licensing requirements, which generally include passing an examination, passing a background investigation, and, in some cases, furnishing a personal bond. Most of the large brokerage firms provide formal classroom training for new brokers that can last a couple weeks to several months. Smaller firms usually rely on informal on-the-job training.

Although there are no specific licensure requirements to be a financial planner, most planners must be knowledgeable about economic trends, finance, budgeting, and accounting. Therefore, a college education is important. Financial planners must possess excellent communication and interpersonal skills to be able to explain complicated issues to their clients. Many financial planners earn a Certified Financial Planning (CFP) designation issued by the CFP Board of Standards in Denver, Colorado, or a Chartered Financial Consultant (ChFC) designation offered by the American College in Bryn Mawr, Pennsylvania. To receive these designations, a person must complete a series of exams on insurance, investments, tax planning, employee benefits, and retirement and estate planning; have the required experience in related jobs; and in the case of the CFP, must abide by the rules and regulations issued by the Board of Standards. It may take from 2 to 3 years of study to complete these programs.

Entry level analyst and other managerial support positions usually are filled by college graduates who have majored in business administration, marketing, economics, accounting, industrial relations, or finance. Many of the large companies have management training programs for college graduates in which trainees work for brief periods in various departments to get a broad picture of the industry before they are assigned to a particular department. Those working as financial analysts are encouraged to obtain the Chartered Financial Analyst designation sponsored by the Association of Investment Management and Research. To qualify, they must pass a series of rigorous essay exams requiring an extensive knowledge of many areas, including accounting, economics, and securities.

Advancement opportunities vary in the securities and commodities industry by occupation. To advance into the managerial ranks or to get some of the more lucrative and prestigious jobs on Wall Street, a master's degree is becoming increasingly essential. In investment banking, for example, most firms select the top candidates from the Nation's most prestigious business schools. However, because many business schools only accept master's degree candidates with some job experience, many securities firms hire analysts with a bachelor's degree and give them the experience they need, assuming that they will eventually obtain their master's degree.

The principal form of advancement for securities and commodity futures sales representatives is an increase in the number and size of the accounts they handle. Although beginners usually service the accounts of individual investors, a select few may eventually handle very large institutional accounts. Administrative support workers such as brokerage clerks may advance to sales representative positions or to other professional positions. Financial analysts may advance to positions in management, where they may manage investment portfolios or negotiate investment banking deals.

Earnings

Most workers in the securities and commodities industry are paid a salary on an annual or weekly basis. In 1998, the average weekly earnings of nonsupervisory workers in the security and commodity services industry were $800, compared to $442 in all industries combined. Earnings in 1997 for the largest occupations in the securities and commodities industry are in table 2.

Table 2. Median hourly earnings of the largest occupations in securities and commodities, 1997.

Occupation	Securities and Commodities	All industries
General managers and top executives	over $60.01	$26.05
Financial managers	45.74	25.19
Computer programmers	27.62	22.61
Sales agents, securities, commodities, and financial services	25.20	22.20
Financial analysts, statistical	24.90	24.68
Accountants and auditors	20.52	17.66
First-line supervisors and managers/ supervisors-clerical and administrative support workers	18.04	14.26
Transit clerks	14.53	8.02
Brokerage clerks	12.86	12.80
General office clerks	10.94	9.10

Earnings of securities and commodities futures sales workers, especially those working for full-service brokerage firms, depend in large part on commissions from the sale or purchase of stocks, bonds, and other securities or futures contracts. Commission earnings are likely to be lower when there is a slump in market activity. Earnings can also be based on the amount of assets a broker or portfolio manager has under management; with the broker or portfolio manager receiving a small percentage of the assets.

For many in this industry, a large part of their earnings come from annual bonuses based on the success of the firm. Profit sharing and stock options are also common. Salaried employees are more likely to receive typical benefits, such as paid vacations, sick leave, and pension plans, than self-employed workers.

Outlook

Employment in the securities and commodities industry is projected to rise 40 percent from 1998 to 2008, much faster than the 15 percent expected for all industries in the economy. Job growth will be fueled primarily by the increasing levels of investment in securities and commodities in the global marketplace. As long as interest rates remain low and the stock market performs adequately, people will continue to seek higher rates of return by investing in stocks, mutual funds, and other investments. In addition to the many new job openings stemming from this growth, a large number of openings will arise as people retire or leave the industry for other reasons.

Several trends bode well for the industry through the next decade. For instance, baby boomers are in the middle of their peak savings years and the government is helping to fuel the savings boom by creating a number of tax-favorable retirement plans, such as the 401(k) and, most recently, the Roth IRA. These plans have been one of the major causes of huge inflows of money into the stock market and into mutual funds, and this trend towards saving for retirement is expected to continue.

Also, although online trading will grow and reduce the need for direct contact with an actual broker, the number of securities sales representatives is still expected to grow much faster than average, as many people will still be willing to pay for the advice a full service representative can offer. Employment of financial planners will grow for the same reason. As the number of self-directed retirement plans increases and as the number and complexity of investments rises, individuals will require more help in managing their money. Competition for securities sales representative jobs, though, is usually keen because the job attracts a large number of qualified applicants. Job opportunities for sales representatives should be best for mature individuals with successful work experience.

Another factor contributing to projected employment growth is the "globalization" of securities and commodities markets—the expansion of traditional exchange and trading boundaries into new markets in foreign countries. This, in turn, has provided an expanding array of investment opportunities and access to markets where new financial products are now available to domestic investors. These new products and markets encourage trading and prompt firms to hire more workers.

The need for skilled financial management, stemming from the demands of global markets and increasingly complex financial products, will result in faster than average employment growth for financial managers and analysts and other managerial and administrative workers. In addition, rapid growth among high-technology industries will create a demand for analysts in the investment banking field to assist new high-technology companies in raising money. However, competition for entry level analyst positions is typically intense, as the number of applicants usually far exceeds the number of vacancies.

Due to advances in telecommunications and computer technology, the securities and commodities industry has become highly automated. This automation is expected to cause employment of computer scientists, computer engineers, and systems analysts, although currently relatively small in number, to more than double. On the other hand, automation has resulted in computerized recordkeeping of transactions, more productive administrative support staffs, and enhanced communications among foreign firms. Accordingly, employment of brokerage clerks will not grow as rapidly as the securities and commodities industry as a whole, and employment of secretaries and bookkeeping, accounting, and auditing clerks is projected to grow more slowly than the average for this industry.

Sources of Additional Information

For general information on the securities industry, contact:

➢ Securities Industry Association, 120 Broadway, New York, NY 10271. Internet: **http://www.sia.com**

Detailed information on many key occupations in the securities and commodities industry, including the following, may be found in the 2000-01 *Occupational Outlook Handbook*:

- Brokerage clerks
- Financial managers
- Office clerks, general
- Securities, commodities, and financial services sales representatives

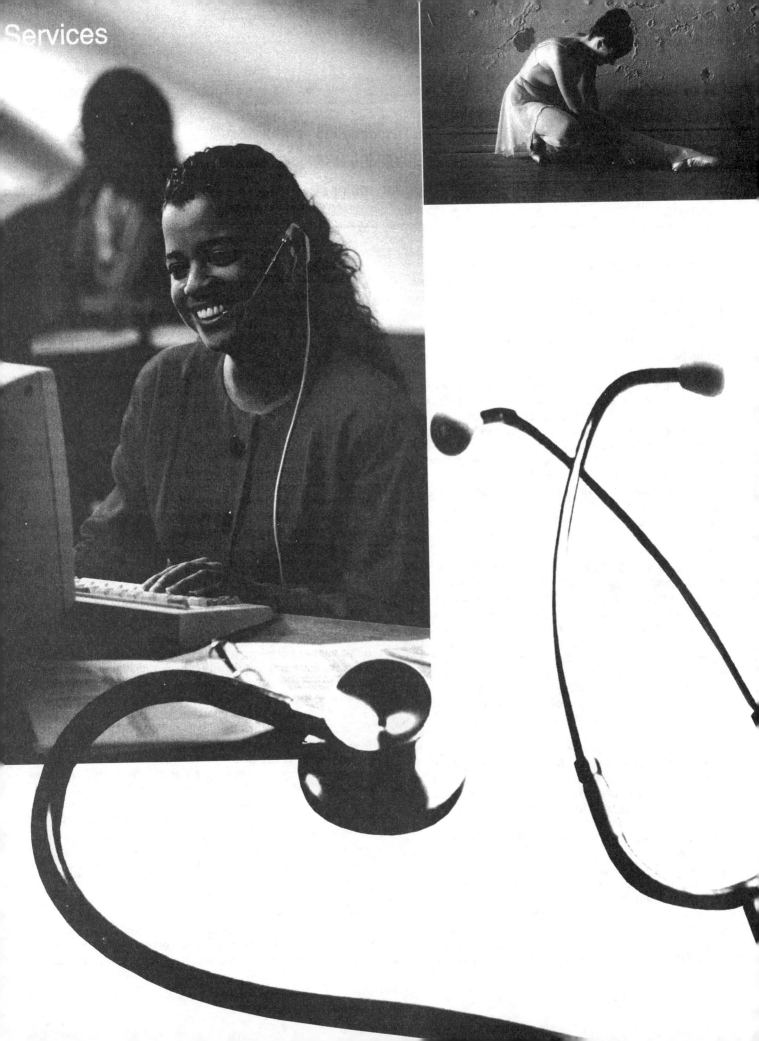

Advertising

(SIC 731)

SIGNIFICANT POINTS

- Employment is concentrated in large cities, especially New York City.

- Competition is keen for glamourous, high-paying professional positions.

- Layoffs are common when accounts are lost, major clients cut advertising budgets, or agencies merge.

Nature of the Industry

Firms in the advertising industry prepare advertisements for other companies and organizations and might also arrange to place them in print, broadcast, interactive, and other media. This industry also includes firms that sell advertising space for publications, radio, television, and the Internet. Divisions of companies that produce and place their own advertising are not considered part of this industry.

Companies often look to advertising as a way of increasing sales. Most companies do not have the staff with the necessary skills or experience to create effective advertisements; furthermore, many advertising campaigns are temporary, so employers would have difficulty maintaining their own advertising staff. Instead, companies commonly solicit bids from ad agencies to develop advertising for them. Next, ad agencies offering their services to the company often make presentations. If an agency wins the account, the real work begins. Various departments within the agency—such as creative, production, media, and research—work together to meet the client's goal of increasing sales.

There are over 21,000 advertising establishments in the United States. About 6 out of 10 write copy and prepare artwork, graphics, and other creative work, and then place the resulting ads in periodicals, newspapers, radio, television, or other advertising media. Within the industry, only these full-service establishments are known as *advertising agencies*. Many of the largest agencies are international, with a substantial proportion of their revenue coming from abroad.

About 3 out of 10 advertising firms specialize in a particular market niche. Some companies produce and solicit outdoor advertising, such as billboards and electric displays. Buses, subways, taxis, airports and bus terminals also frequently carry ads. A small number of firms produce aerial advertising, while others distribute circulars, handbills, and free samples.

Groups within agencies have been created to serve their clients' electronic advertising needs on the Internet. The Internet is a medium that fosters rapid growth of advertising and commercial activities. Advertisements often link users from one website to the company's or product's website where information such as new product announcements, contests, and product catalogs appear.

Some firms are not involved in the creation of ads at all; instead, they sell advertising time or space on radio and television stations or in publications. Because these firms do not produce advertising, their staffs are mostly sales workers.

In an effort to attract and maintain clients, advertising agencies are diversifying their services, offering advertising as well as sales, marketing, public relations, and interactive media services. Advertising firms have found that highly creative work is particularly suitable for outsourcing, resulting in a better product and increasing the firm's profitability.

Working Conditions

Most advertising employees work in comfortable offices; however, long hours, including evenings and weekends, are common. Opportunities for part-time work are limited; in 1998, 9.7 percent worked part-time, compared to 15.9 percent of all workers.

Advertising work is fast-paced and exciting, but it also can be stressful. Being creative on a tight schedule can be emotionally draining. In addition, frequent meetings with clients and media representatives may involve substantial travel. Among all full-time advertising workers, almost one-quarter work 50 or more hours per week.

Employment

The advertising industry employed 268,000 workers in 1998. Although advertising firms are located throughout the country, they are concentrated in the largest cities: New York with the most firms, Chicago, and Los Angeles. Other top cities are Detroit, San Francisco, Minneapolis, Boston, and Dallas. Firms vary in size, ranging from one-person shops to international agencies employing thousands of workers. About 4 of 5 advertising firms employ fewer than 10 employees, somewhat higher than the proportion for all industries combined (chart).

The small size of the average advertising firm demonstrates the opportunities for self-employment. It is relatively easy to open a small ad agency; in fact, many successful agencies began as one- or two-person operations. In 1998, 15 percent of all advertising workers were self-employed, compared to 9 percent of workers in all industries combined.

The median age of advertising workers is about 36, compared to nearly 39 for all workers. About 59 percent of advertising employees are 25 to 44 years of age, compared to 51 percent of all workers in the economy. Very few advertising workers are below the age of 20, which reflects the need for postsecondary training or work experience.

Occupations in the Industry

In advertising, managers and executives, professionals, sales workers, and administrative support workers account for 9 of every 10 jobs (table 1). Employees have varied responsibilities

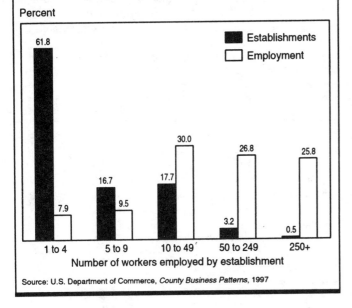

About 4 out of 5 advertising firms employ fewer than 10 employees

Percent

Legend: ■ Establishments ☐ Employment

Number of workers employed by establishment	Establishments	Employment
1 to 4	61.8	7.9
5 to 9	16.7	9.5
10 to 49	17.7	30.0
50 to 249	3.2	26.8
250+	0.5	25.8

Source: U.S. Department of Commerce, *County Business Patterns*, 1997

in agencies with only a few workers, and the specific job duties of each worker are often difficult to distinguish. Workers in relatively large firms specialize more, and therefore, the distinctions among occupations are more apparent.

Advertising agencies have five categories of jobs—account management, creative, media, research, and support services and administration. Account management links the agency and the client. It represents the agency to the client as well as the client to the agency. Account management brings business to the agency and is ultimately responsible for the quality of the advertisement. Account management workers carefully monitor the activities of the other areas to ensure that everything runs smoothly. *Account managers* and their assistants analyze competitive activity and consumer trends, report client billing, forecast agency income, and combine the talents of the creative, media, and research areas.

Working with the marketing idea that account management obtains from the client, the creative department brings the idea to life. Here, staff work together to transform a blank piece of paper into an advertisement. As the idea takes shape, *copywriters* and their assistants write the words of ads—both the written part of print ads as well as the scripts of radio and television spots. *Art directors* and their assistants develop the visual concepts and designs of advertisements. They prepare paste-ups and layouts for print ads and television storyboards, a cartoon style summary of how an advertisement will appear. They also oversee the filming of television commercials and photo sessions. Once completed, the ad is shown to the client. At this point, the job of the creative department could be over; however, based on the client's response, it is likely that the creative department staff will have to modify their ideas or develop an entirely different approach.

The *media department* is responsible for placing advertisements in the right place at the right time, so they will reach the desired audience for the least amount of money. *Media planners* gather information on the public's viewing and reading habits, and evaluate editorial content and programming to determine the potential use of media such as newspapers, magazines, radio, television, or the Internet. The media staff calculate the numbers and types of people reached by different media, and how often they are reached. *Media buyers* track the media space and times available for purchase, negotiate and purchase time and space for ads, and make sure ads appear exactly as scheduled. Additionally, they calculate rates, usage, and budgets.

Table 1. Employment of wage and salary workers in advertising by occupation, 1998 and projected change, 1998-2008

(Employment in thousands)

Occupation	1998 Employment Number	1998 Employment Percent	1998-2008 Percent change
All occupations	268	100.0	20.5
Executive, administrative, and managerial	71	26.3	25.8
Advertising, marketing, promotions, public relations, and sales managers	24	9.0	37.0
General managers and top executives	18	6.7	20.9
Financial managers	5	1.8	17.2
Buyers and purchasing agents	4	1.6	24.5
Accountants and auditors	4	1.4	17.1
Administrative support, including clerical	62	23.1	12.1
Secretaries, stenographers, and typists	10	3.7	-1.6
General office clerks	9	3.4	25.7
Bookkeeping, accounting, and auditing clerks	8	2.9	1.4
Office and administrative support supervisors and managers	8	2.8	21.1
Receptionists and information clerks	6	2.2	24.4
Production, planning, and expediting clerks	6	2.1	11.4
Professional specialty	61	22.6	27.4
Artists and commercial artists	23	8.7	16.3
Writers and editors, including technical writers	9	3.2	24.5
Actors, directors, and producers	5	1.8	37.0
Public relations specialists	5	1.7	26.9
Computer engineers and scientists	4	1.3	63.4
Systems analysts	3	1.0	86.8
Marketing and sales	49	18.4	15.2
All other sales and related workers	36	13.6	12.1
Models, demonstrators, and product promoters	7	2.5	23.6
Marketing and sales worker supervisors	6	2.2	24.5
Operators, fabricators, and laborers	12	4.4	20.1
Hand packers and packagers	3	1.2	24.5
Truck drivers	3	1.2	17.8
Precision, production, craft, and repair	9	3.5	24.4
Painters and paperhangers	3	1.3	24.5
All other occupations	4	1.6	11.2

Workers in the *research department* try to understand the wants, desires, motivations, and ideals of consumers, in order to produce and place the most effective advertising in the most

163

effective media. *Research executives* compile data, monitor the progress of internal and external research, develop research tools, and interpret and provide explanations of the data gathered. Research executives often specialize in specific research areas and perform supervisory duties.

Media salespeople sell air time on radio and television, and page space in the print media. They work in firms representing radio stations, television stations, and publications.

Support services and *administration* includes jobs ranging from janitors to administrative assistants to accountants and vary widely among agencies.

Training and Advancement

Most entry-level professional and managerial positions in the advertising industry require a bachelor's degree, preferably with broad liberal arts exposure. Beginners usually enter the industry in the account management or media department. Occasionally entry-level positions are available in the market research or creative departments of an agency, but these positions usually require some experience.

Completing an advertising-related internship while in school provides a definite advantage when applying for an entry-level position. In addition to an internship, courses in marketing, psychology, accounting, statistics, and creative design can help prepare potential entrants for this field.

Assistant account executive, the entry-level account management position in most firms, requires a bachelor's degree in marketing or advertising. At some agencies, a master's degree in business administration may be required.

Bachelor's degrees are not required for entry-level positions in the creative department. Assistant art directors usually need at least a 2-year degree from an art or design school. Although advantageous, assistant copywriters do not need a degree, but they must demonstrate superior communication skills and abilities.

Assistant media planner or assistant media buyer are also good entry-level positions, but almost always require a bachelor's degree, preferably with a major in marketing or advertising. Experienced applicants who possess at least a master's degree usually fill research positions. Often they have a background in marketing or statistics and years of experience. Requirements for support services and administrative positions depend on the job and vary from firm to firm.

Employees in the advertising industry should have good people skills, common sense, creativity, communication skills, and problem-solving ability. New media, such as the Internet, are creating new opportunities to market products, but also the need for additional training for those already employed. Keeping pace with technology and incorporating it are fundamental to success in the industry. Besides staying abreast of new technology, advertisers must keep in tune with the changing values, cultures, and fashions of the Nation.

Success in progressively responsible staff assignments usually leads to advancement to supervisory positions. As workers climb the organizational ladder, broad vision and planning skills become extremely important. Another way to get to the top in this industry is to open one's own firm. In spite of the difficulty and high failure rate, many find starting their own business personally and financially rewarding. When self-employed, advancement takes the form of increasing the size and strength of the company.

Earnings

In 1998, nonsupervisory workers in advertising averaged $647 a week—significantly higher than the $442 a week for all nonsupervisory workers in private industry. Earnings of workers in selected occupations in advertising appear in table 2.

Table 2. Median hourly earnings of the largest occupations in advertising, 1997

Occupation	Advertising	All industries
General managers and top executives ...	$45.53	$26.05
Marketing, advertising, and public relations managers	26.11	25.61
Writers and editors	18.31	15.69
Artists and related workers	16.74	14.89
Sales agents, advertising	15.68	14.16
First-line supervisors and managers/supervisors-clerical and administrative support workers ...	15.17	14.26
Secretaries, except legal and medical	11.89	11.00
Bookkeeping, accounting, and auditing clerks	11.54	10.80
General office clerks	9.23	9.10
Demonstrators and promoters	7.95	7.65

Outlook

Employment in the advertising industry is projected to grow 21 percent over the 1998-2008 period, faster than the average for all industries. Besides job openings created as an expanding economy generates more products and services to advertise, job openings will also arise as workers transfer to other jobs or stop working. Increased demand for advertising services will also stem from growth in the number and types of media outlets used to reach consumers. Opportunities will be good for people skilled in preparing material for presentation on the Internet.

Employment growth may be tempered by the increased use of more efficient technologies that could replace some workers. Competition for jobs will be keen because the glamour of the industry traditionally attracts many more job seekers than there are job openings. Employment also may be adversely affected if legislation further restricts advertising for specific products such as alcoholic beverages or via specific media such as billboards.

Sources of Additional Information

For information about careers or training contact:

➤ American Association of Advertising Agencies, 405 Lexington Ave., New York, NY 10174.
Internet: **http://www.aaaa.org**
➤ American Advertising Federation, 1101 Vermont Ave., NW., Suite 500, Washington, DC 20005.
Internet: **http://www.aaf.org**

Information on these occupations can be found in the 2000-01 *Occupational Outlook Handbook*:

● Advertising, marketing, and public relations managers
● Models, demonstrators, and product promoters
● Services sales representatives
● Visual artists
● Writers and editors, including technical writers

Amusement and Recreation Services

SIGNIFICANT POINTS

- Over 40 percent of all workers have no formal education beyond high school.

- Employment growth, along with high turnover, should create numerous job opportunities.

- Earnings are relatively low, reflecting the large number of part-time and seasonal jobs.

Nature of the Industry

As leisure time and personal incomes have grown across the Nation, so has the amusement and recreation services industry. This industry is made up of about 99,000 establishments, ranging from theme parks to fitness centers. Practically any activity that occupies a person's leisure time, excluding motion pictures and videotape rentals, is part of the amusement and recreation services industry. The diverse range of activities offered by this industry can be categorized into three broad groups—sports, performing arts, and amusement including gaming.

Sports. This sector includes professional sports, as well as establishments providing sports facilities and services to amateurs. Commercial sports clubs are made up of establishments that operate professional and amateur athletic clubs and promote athletic events. Every possible type of sport can be found in these establishments, including baseball, basketball, boxing, football, ice hockey, soccer, wrestling, and even auto racing. Professional and amateur companies involved with sports promotion also are part of this sector, as are sports establishments where gambling is allowed, such as auto, dog, and horse racetracks.

Also included in this segment of the industry are physical fitness facilities that feature exercise and weight loss programs, gyms, health clubs, and day spas. These establishments also frequently offer aerobic dance, yoga, and exercise classes. Other amusement and recreation businesses include bowling centers that rent lanes and equipment for tenpin and duckpin bowling.

These facilities may be open to the public or offered on a membership basis. Sports and recreation clubs open only to members and their guests include some golf, yacht, tennis, racquetball, hunt, and gun clubs. Public golf courses, unlike private clubs, offer facilities to the general public on a fee basis.

Performing arts. A variety of businesses and groups involved in live theatrical and musical performances are included in this segment. Theatrical production companies, for example, coordinate all aspects of producing a play or theater event, including employing actors and actresses. Agents represent actors and assist them in finding jobs. Booking agencies line up performance engagements for theatrical groups. Costume design management companies design costumes for productions. Also included are lighting and stage crews that handle the technical aspects of productions.

Performers of live musical entertainment include popular music artists, dance bands, orchestras, jazz musicians, and rock-and-roll bands. Orchestras range from major professional orchestras with million dollar budgets to community orchestras, often with part-time schedules. Also in this segment are dance studios, schools, and halls, which provide places for professional and amateur dancers to practice, perform, and learn. The majority of these dance troupes perform ballet or modern dance.

Amusement. A wide variety of establishments provide amusement for a growing number of customers. Some of these businesses provide video game, pinball, and gaming machines to amusement parks, arcades, and casinos. Casinos and other gaming establishments that offer off-track betting are a rapidly growing part of this sector. Also included in this segment are amusement and theme parks, which range in size from local carnivals to multi-acre parks. These establishments may have mechanical rides, shows, and refreshment stands. Other amusement and recreation services include day camps, fireworks display services, go-cart rentals, rodeos, riding stables, waterslides, skating rinks, ski lifts, and establishments offering rental sporting goods.

Working Conditions

Jobs in amusement and recreation services are more likely to be part time than those in other industries. In fact, the average worker in the amusement and recreation industry worked a 27-hour workweek in 1998. Entertainers, actors, and musicians were most likely to work part time, due to the large number of performers competing for a limited number of positions. The majority of performers are unable to support themselves in this profession alone and are forced to supplement their income through other jobs.

Many types of amusement and recreation establishments dramatically increase employment during the summer and either scale back employment during the winter or close down completely. Workers may be required to work nights and holidays, because most establishments are busiest during major holidays. Some jobs require extensive travel. Music and dance troupes, for example, frequently tour or travel to major metropolitan areas across the country, in hopes of attracting large audiences.

Many in this industry work outdoors, whereas others may work in hot, crowded, or noisy conditions. Some jobs, such as those at fitness facilities or in amusement parks, involve some manual labor tasks and, thus, require physical strength and stamina. Also, athletes, dancers, and many other performers must be in particularly good physical condition. Many jobs include customer service responsibilities, so employees must be able to work well with the public.

In 1998, cases of work-related illness and injury averaged 8.1 for every 100 full-time workers, higher than the average of 7.1 for the entire private sector. Risks of injury are high in some jobs, especially for athletes. Although most injuries are minor, including sprains and muscle pulls, they may prevent an employee from working for a period of time.

Employment

The amusement and recreation services industry provided about 1.6 million jobs in 1998. Miscellaneous amusement and recreation services—which includes amusement parks, coin-operated amusement devices, public golf courses, membership sports and recreation clubs, and physical fitness facilities—accounted for 3 out of 4 jobs (table 1).

Table 1. Employment in amusement and recreation services by segment, 1998

(Employment in thousands)

Industry segment	Employment
Amusement and recreation services	1,601
Miscellaneous amusement and recreation services	1,189
Producers, orchestras, and entertainers	176
Commercial sports	127
Bowling centers	82
Dance studios, schools, and halls	27

Although most establishments in the amusement and recreation industry are small, over half of all jobs were in establishments that employ more than 50 workers (chart).

The amusement and recreation services industry is characterized by a large number of seasonal and part-time positions and workers who are younger than the average for all industries. The majority of workers are under the age of 35. Many

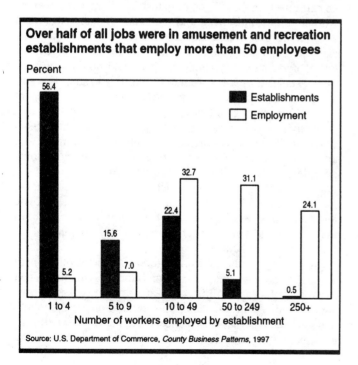

Over half of all jobs were in amusement and recreation establishments that employ more than 50 employees

Percent

Source: U.S. Department of Commerce, *County Business Patterns*, 1997

businesses in the industry increase hiring during the summer, often employing high school- and college-age workers

Occupations in the Industry

About 44 percent of workers in the industry are employed in service occupations (table 2). *Amusement and recreation attendants*, the largest occupation in amusement and recreation services, perform a variety of duties depending on where they are employed. Common duties include setting up games, handing out sports equipment, providing caddy services for golfers, collecting money, and operating amusement park rides.

Other service workers include *waiters* and *waitresses*, who serve food in entertainment establishments; *food counter and fountain workers,* who serve and sometimes prepare food for patrons; and *bartenders,* who mix and serve drinks in amusement establishments.

Personal, buildings, and grounds service occupations include *houseworkers*, *janitors*, and *general cleaning crews*, who clean up after shows or sporting events and are responsible for the daily cleaning and upkeep of facilities. *Landscaping, groundskeeping, nursery, greenhouse, and lawn service workers* care for athletic fields and golf courses. These workers maintain artificial and natural turf fields, mark boundaries, and paint team logos. They also mow, water, and fertilize natural athletic fields and vacuum and disinfect synthetic fields. Protective service occupations include *security guards*, who patrol the property and guard against theft, vandalism, and illegal entry. At sporting events, guards maintain order and direct patrons to various facilities.

Professional specialty occupations account for 17 percent of all jobs in this industry. One of the most well-known, *athletes,* perform in a variety of sports. Professional athletes compete in events for compensation, either through salaries or prize money. Organizations such as the Women's National Basketball Association (WNBA) and the National Football League (NFL) sanction events for professionals. Few athletes are able to make it to the professional level, where high salaries are common. In some professional sports, minor leagues offer lower salaries with a chance to develop skills through competition before advancing to major league play.

Coaches, *athletic trainers*, and *fitness instructors* train athletes to perform at their highest level. Often they are experienced athletes who have retired and are able to provide insight from their own experiences to players. *Referees* and *umpires*, even in professional sports, usually work part time and often have other full-time jobs. For example, many professional sport referees and umpires officiate at amateur games, as well.

Musicians may play musical instruments, sing, compose, arrange music, or conduct groups in instrumental or vocal performances. The specific skills and responsibilities of musicians vary widely by type of instrument, size of ensemble, and style of music. For example, musicians can play jazz, classical, or popular music, either alone or in groups, ranging from small rock bands to large symphony orchestras.

Actors entertain and communicate with people through their interpretation of dramatic and other roles. They can belong to a variety of performing groups, ranging from community theater shows and local dinner theaters to full-scale Broadway productions. *Dancers* express ideas, stories, rhythm, and sound with their bodies through different types of dance, including ballet, modern dance, tap, and jazz. Dancers usually perform in a

166

troupe, although some perform solo. Many become teachers when their performing careers end. *Directors* interpret plays or scripts and give directions to actors and dancers. They conduct rehearsals, audition cast members, and approve choreography. *Producers* select plays or scripts, arrange financing, and decide on the size and content of the production and its budget. They also hire directors, principal members of the cast and production staff members, and negotiate contracts with personnel.

Recreation workers plan, organize, and direct activities. They generally are employed by organizations such as schools; theme parks, and other tourist attractions; or health, sports, and other recreational clubs. Recreation workers schedule organized events to structure leisure time. These programs are oriented toward activities, such as sports and fitness or arts and crafts.

About 12 percent of all jobs in this industry are in marketing and sales occupations. The largest of these, *cashiers*, often use a cash register to receive money and give change to customers. *Counter and rental clerks* check out rental equipment to customers, receive orders for service, and handle cash transactions.

About 7 percent of industry employment is in administrative support occupations. *Information clerks*, one of the larger occupations in this category, answer questions and provide general information to patrons. Other large occupations in this group include *general office clerks* and *secretaries*.

Executive, administrative, and managerial occupations make up 7 percent of employment in this industry. Managerial duties in the performing arts include marketing, business management, event booking, fundraising, and public outreach. *Recreation supervisors* and *park superintendents* oversee personnel, budgets, grounds and facility maintenance, and land and wildlife resources. Some common administrative jobs in sports are *tournament director, health club manager,* and *sports program director*.

Precision production, craft, and repair occupations make up 4 percent of industry employment. *General utility maintenance repairers* are the largest occupation in this group.

Training and Advancement

Around half of all workers in the amusement and recreation industry have no formal education beyond high school. In the case of performing artists or athletes, talent and years of training are more important than education. However, upper-level management jobs usually require a college degree.

Most of these service jobs require little or no previous training or education beyond high school. Many companies hire young, unskilled workers, such as students, to perform low-paying, seasonal jobs. Amusement parks prefer workers who are at least 17 years old. Employers look for people with good interpersonal skills to work with the public.

In physical fitness facilities, aerobic and instructional exercise teachers must be certified to perform cardiopulmonary resuscitation (CPR) and often must be certified by the Aerobics and Fitness Association of America. Sometimes fitness workers become health club managers or owners. To advance to a management position, a degree in physical education, sports medicine, or exercise physiology is useful. Certification from a professional organization also is beneficial. This involves knowledge of CPR, experience as an instructor at a health club, and passing written and oral exams, covering a variety of areas, including anatomy, nutrition, and fitness testing.

Table 2. Employment of wage and salary workers in amusement and recreation services by occupation, 1998 and projected change, 1998-2008

(Employment in thousands)

Occupation	1998 Employment Number	Percent	1998-2008 Percent change
All occupations	1,601	100.0	31.7
Service	700	43.7	25.9
Amusement and recreation attendants	191	11.9	39.1
Waiters and waitresses	88	5.5	-11.0
Janitors and cleaners, including maids and housekeeping cleaners	50	3.1	25.0
Food counter, fountain, and related workers	50	3.1	25.1
Bartenders	38	2.4	20.1
Guards	36	2.3	27.6
Ushers, lobby attendants, and ticket takers	28	1.8	26.3
Cooks, restaurant	27	1.7	8.6
Food preparation workers	25	1.5	29.2
Child-care workers	21	1.3	40.2
Dining room and cafeteria attendants and bar helpers	17	1.1	28.9
Cooks, short order and fast food	16	1.0	32.1
Professional specialty	271	17.0	35.6
Instructors and coaches, sports and physical training	120	7.5	44.6
Musicians, singers, and related workers	38	2.4	18.5
Athletes, coaches, umpires, and related workers	20	1.3	25.0
Actors, directors, and producers	16	1.0	18.5
Adult and vocational education teachers	17	1.0	24.4
Recreation workers	15	1.0	45.4
Marketing and sales	193	12.1	44.4
Cashiers	69	4.3	32.6
Counter and rental clerks	52	3.2	58.2
Marketing and sales worker supervisors	31	2.0	50.8
Administrative support, including clerical	108	6.8	28.3
General office clerks	22	1.4	41.0
Bookkeeping, accounting, and auditing clerks	20	1.2	14.5
Receptionists and information clerks	20	1.2	42.7
Secretaries	18	1.1	12.4
Executive, administrative, and managerial	108	6.8	32.9
General managers and top executives	46	2.9	35.9
Agriculture, forestry, fishing, and related	105	6.6	44.8
Laborers, landscaping and groundskeeping	91	5.7	45.5
Precision production, craft, and repair	67	4.2	18.7
Maintenance repairers, general utility	35	2.2	1.2
Operators, fabricators, and laborers	40	2.5	37.1
Helpers, laborers, and material movers, hand	25	1.5	34.0
All other occupations	8	0.5	39.9

In the arts, employment in professional specialty occupations usually requires a great deal of talent. There are many highly talented performers, creating intense competition for every opening. Performers such as musicians, dancers, actors, and actresses often study their professions most of their lives, taking private lessons and spending hours practicing. Usually, performers have completed some college or related study. Musicians, dancers, and actors often go on to become teachers, requiring the completion of at least a bachelor's degree. Musicians who complete a graduate degree in music sometimes move on to a career as a conductor. Dancers often become choreographers, and actors can advance into producer and director jobs.

Almost all arts administrators have completed 4 years of college, and the majority possess a master's degree or a doctorate. Experience in marketing and business is helpful because promoting events is a large part of the job.

Entry-level supervisory or professional jobs in recreation sometimes require completion of a 2-year associate degree in parks and recreation at a junior college. Completing a 4-year bachelor's degree in this field is necessary for high-level supervisory positions. Students can specialize in such areas as aquatics, therapeutic recreation, aging and leisure, and environmental studies. Those who obtain graduate degrees in the field and have years of experience can usually obtain administrative or university teaching positions. The National Recreation and Parks Association certifies individuals who meet eligibility requirements for professional and technical jobs. Certified Leisure Professionals must pass an exam; earn a bachelor's degree with a major in recreation, park resources, or leisure services; and have at least 2 years of relevant full-time experience.

Earnings

Earnings in amusement and recreation services generally are low, reflecting the large number of part-time and seasonal jobs. Nonsupervisory workers in amusement and recreation services averaged $258 a week in 1998, compared to $442 throughout private industry.

Earnings vary according to occupation and segment of the industry. For example, some professional athletes earn millions, but competition for these positions is intense, and most athletes are unable to even reach the minor leagues. Many service workers make the minimum wage or a little more. Many actors go long periods with little or no income from acting, so they are forced to work at second jobs. Earnings in selected occupations in amusement and recreation services in 1997 appear in table 3.

Because many amusement and theme parks dramatically increase employment during vacation periods, employment for a number of jobs in the industry is seasonal. Theme parks, for example, frequently hire young workers, often students, for summer employment. Also, many sports are not played all year, so athletes and people in the service jobs associated with those sports are often seasonally employed.

Employers in some segments of this industry offer benefits not available in other industries. For instance, benefits for workers in some theme parks include free passes to the park, transportation to and from work, housing, scholarships, and discounts on park merchandise.

Although unions are not common in most segments of this industry, they are important in the performing arts sector.

Virtually all actors, actresses, and performers are members of a union. Consequently, earnings of most performers are determined by union contracts that specify minimum salary rates and working conditions.

Table 3. Median hourly earnings of the largest occupations in amusement and recreation services, 1997

Occupation	Amusement and recreation services	All industries
General managers and top executives ...	$18.24	$26.05
Instructors and coaches, sports and physical training	9.80	10.15
Guards and watch guards	7.72	7.57
Laborers, landscaping and groundskeeping	7.48	8.08
Cashiers	6.80	6.22
Bartenders	6.56	5.94
Counter and rental clerks	6.35	6.67
Combined food preparation and service workers	5.94	5.72
Amusement and recreation attendants ...	5.77	5.88
Waiters and waitresses	5.75	5.59

Outlook

Wage and salary jobs in amusement and recreation services are projected to increase 32 percent over the 1998-2008 period, more than double the rate of growth projected for the entire economy. Growing participation in amusement and recreation—reflecting increasing incomes, leisure time, and awareness of the health benefits of physical fitness—will provide a large market for establishments providing amusement and recreational facilities and services.

Changing demographics of the Nation will also have a major impact on industry employment. For example, amusement and recreation services are expected to increasingly target the growing elderly population. Consequently, employment opportunities may be better in those establishments, such as cruise ships and golf courses, which serve active adults between 50 and 75 years old. Continued growth in hospital and hotel fitness centers and instructional exercise programs, especially those designed and marketed for retirees, should also lead to more job openings. Growth is also expected in those amusement and recreation services, such as health spas and fitness centers, that cater to younger adults in their 20s and 30s with steadily rising incomes.

In addition to these increases, employment in the performing arts will grow rapidly, along with demand for entertainment from a growing population. However, the supply of workers in this sector will also rise, because of the appeal of these jobs, insuring continued intense competition. Additionally, amusement and theme parks should experience steady growth and offer many seasonal and part-time job opportunities.

The amusement and recreation services industry has relied heavily on workers under the age of 25 to fill seasonal and unskilled positions. Although the pool of these workers will grow in coming years, opportunities should be good for young, seasonal, part-time, and unskilled workers. In addition, the industry is expected to hire a growing number of workers in other age groups.

Sources of Additional Information

For additional information about careers and training in the amusement and recreation services industry, write to:

➤ National Recreation and Parks Association, 22377 Belmont Ridge Rd., Ashburn, VA 20148.
Internet: **http://www.nrpa.org**

Information on the following occupations employed in amusement and recreation services may be found in the 2000-01 *Occupational Outlook Handbook*:

- Actors, directors, and producers
- Adult and vocational education teachers
- Dancers and choreographers
- Landscaping, groundskeeping, nursery, greenhouse, and lawn service occupations
- Guards
- Musicians, singers, and related workers
- Recreation workers

Child-Care Services

- Preschool teachers, teacher assistants, and child-care workers account for more than 7 out of 10 wage and salary jobs.

- Training requirements for most jobs are minimal, but range from a high school diploma or less for child-care workers to a college degree for some teachers and directors.

- Job openings should be numerous because of rapid employment growth coupled with high turnover—reflecting few benefits, low pay, and occasionally stressful working conditions.

Nature of the Industry

Child-care needs are met in many different ways. Care in a child's home, care in an organized child-care facility, and care in a provider's home are all prevalent arrangements for pre-school-age children. Older children may receive child-care services when they are not in school, generally through before- and after-school programs or during breaks. With the increasing number of women in the workforce, child-care services has become one of the most talked about, and fastest growing, industries in the U.S. economy. Obtaining afford-able, quality child care, especially for children under age 5, is a major concern for many parents.

This industry consists of establishments that provide paid care for infants, prekindergarten or preschool children, or older children in after-school programs. Formal child-care centers include nursery schools, preschool centers, Head Start centers, and group day care centers. Self-employed workers in this industry often provide care from their home for a fee. This industry does not include occasional babysitters or persons who provide unpaid care in their homes for the children of relatives or friends. (Social services, except child care is covered in a separate *Career Guide* statement.)

The for-profit sector of this industry includes centers that operate independently or are part of a local or national chain, whereas nonprofit child-care organizations include religious institutions, YMCA's, colleges, employers, public schools, social service agencies, and State and Federal Government agencies. For-profit establishments have grown rapidly in response to demand for child-care services. Within the nonprofit sector there has been strong growth in Head Start, the Federally funded child-care program designed to provide disadvantaged children with social, educational, and health services.

Child care shifted in the past from unpaid to paid caregivers, particularly child-care centers. Center-based care has in-creased, substituting for unpaid care by relatives, as fewer families have access to relatives who were willing or able to keep their children.

Some employers offer child-care benefits to employees. They recognize the lack of child-care benefits as a barrier to the employment of qualified women, and that positive results come in the form of increased employee morale and reduced absenteeism. Some employers sponsor child-care centers in or near the workplace; others offer direct financial assistance, vouchers, or discounts for child care, after-school or sick child-care services, or a dependent care option in a flexible benefits plan.

Working Conditions

Watching children grow, enjoy learning, and gain new skills can be very rewarding. Preschool teachers and child-care workers often improve their own communication, learning, and other personal skills by working with children. The work is never routine; each day is marked by new activities and challenges. However, child care can be physically and emotionally taxing, as workers constantly stand, walk, bend, stoop, and lift to attend to each child's interests and problems. They must be constantly alert, anticipate and prevent trouble, deal effectively with disruptive children, and provide fair but firm discipline. However, this is a relatively safe industry; in 1997, child-care services had an injury and illness rate of 3.0 per 100 full-time workers, compared to a rate of 7.1 throughout private industry.

The hours of child-care workers vary. Many centers are open 12 or more hours a day and cannot close until all the children are picked up by their parents or guardians. Unscheduled overtime, traffic jams, and other types of emergencies can cause parents or guardians to be late. About 3 out of 10 full-time employees in the child-care services industry work more than 40 hours per week. Self-employed workers tend to work longer hours than their salaried counterparts. The industry also offers many opportunities for part-time work—around 30 percent of all employees work part-time.

Many child-care workers are faced with stressful conditions, low pay, and few benefits. Turnover in the occupation is high.

Employment

About 605,000 workers held wage and salary jobs in child-care establishments in 1998. An additional 536,000 self-employed persons worked in the industry; most of the self-employed were family child-care providers, and some were self-employed managers of child-care centers. Employment estimates understate the total number of people working in this industry because family child-care homes run by relatives often are not counted, and because many other family child-care providers operate without a license to avoid the burden of licensing and taxation.

Jobs in child care are found across the country, mirroring the distribution of the population. Child-care operations vary in size, from the self-employed person caring for a few children in a private home to the large corporate-sponsored center employing a large staff. More than 2 out of 10 wage and salary jobs are located in establishments with fewer than 10 employees. Nearly all have fewer than 50 (chart).

Opportunities for self-employment in this industry are among the best in the economy. Nearly half of all workers are self-employed, compared to less than 1 out of 10 throughout industry. This reflects the ease of entering the child-care business.

The median age of child-care providers is 36, compared to 39 for all workers. More than 21 percent of all care providers are 24 years of age or younger (table 1). About 8 percent of these workers are below the age of 20, reflecting the minimal training requirements for many child-care positions.

Table 1. Percent distribution of employment in child-care services by age group, 1998

Age	Child-care services	All industries
Total	100.0	100.0
16-19	7.9	5.4
20-24	13.5	9.5
25-34	25.3	23.9
35-44	26.7	27.5
45-54	16.2	21.0
55-64	7.9	9.8
65 and older	2.5	2.9

Occupations in the Industry

There is far less occupational diversity in the child-care services industry than in most other industries. Three occupations—*preschool teachers, teacher assistants,* and *child-care workers*—account for nearly 75 percent of all wage and salary jobs (table 2).

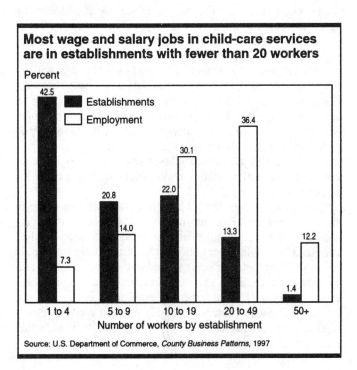

Most wage and salary jobs in child-care services are in establishments with fewer than 20 workers

Percent

■ Establishments
□ Employment

	1 to 4	5 to 9	10 to 19	20 to 49	50+
Establishments	42.5	20.8	22.0	13.3	1.4
Employment	7.3	14.0	30.1	36.4	12.2

Number of workers by establishment

Source: U.S. Department of Commerce, *County Business Patterns*, 1997

Table 2. Employment of wage and salary workers in child-care facilities by occupation, 1998 and projected change, 1998-2008

(Employment in thousands)

Occupation	1998 Employment Number	1998 Employment Percent	1998-2008 Percent change
All occupations	605	100.0	32.3
Professional specialty	237	39.2	34.7
Teachers, preschool	193	31.9	33.3
Teachers, kindergarten	11	1.8	40.7
Social workers....................................	7	1.2	40.7
Teachers, elementary school	7	1.2	40.7
Service	209	34.6	36.7
Child-care workers	174	28.8	38.5
Cooks, institution or cafeteria	14	2.3	26.6
Janitors and cleaners, including maids and housekeeping cleaners	9	1.4	26.6
Food preparation workers	6	1.1	26.6
Administrative support, including clerical	99	16.3	15.0
Teacher assistants	79	13.1	12.6
Executive, administrative, and managerial	48	8.0	36.0
General managers and top executives	17	2.8	36.6
Education administrators	17	2.7	40.7
Operators, fabricators, and laborers ...	8	1.3	39.0
Busdrivers	7	1.1	40.7
All other occupations	3	0.5	35.5

Preschool teachers comprise the largest occupation in the child-care industry, accounting for about 32 percent of wage and salary jobs. They teach pupils basic physical, mental, and developmental skills in public or private schools. *Teacher assistants* account for 13 percent of employment. They give teachers more time for teaching by assuming a variety of tasks. For example, they may record grades, set up and dismantle equipment, or prepare instructional materials.

Child-care workers account for about 29 percent of wage and salary jobs. Large proportions of the self-employed who keep children in their homes also are child-care workers. In a home setting, they are known as *family child-care providers*. Regardless of the setting, these workers feed, diaper, comfort, and play with infants. When dealing with older preschoolers, they attend to the children's basic needs and organize activities that stimulate physical, emotional, intellectual, and social development.

Managers, who account for about 8 percent of wage and salary workers, establish overall objectives and standards for their center and provide day-to-day supervision of their staff. They bear overall responsibility for program development as well as for marketing, budgeting, staffing, and all other administrative tasks.

In addition to the above occupations, child-care centers also employ a variety of *administrative support personnel, cleaners, cooks,* and *busdrivers*.

Training and Advancement

Most States do not impose training requirements for family child-care providers. However, many local governments offer training and require family child-care providers to obtain

OUACHITA TECHNICAL COLLEGE

licenses. Home safety inspections and criminal background checks are usually required of an applicant. In the case of child-care centers, however, staffing requirements are imposed primarily by the States and by insurers. Although requirements vary, in most cases a minimum age of 18 is required for teachers, and a 21-year minimum age for directors or officers. In some States, assistants may work at 16, and in several States, at age 14.

Most States have established minimum educational or training requirements. Training requirements are most stringent for directors, less so for teachers, and minimal for child-care workers and teacher assistants. In many centers, directors must have a college degree, often with experience in child care and specific training in early childhood development. Teachers must have a high school diploma and, in many cases, a combination of college education and experience. Assistants and child-care workers usually need a high school diploma, but it is not always a requirement.

Many States also mandate other types of training for staff members, such as health and first aid, fire safety, and child abuse detection and prevention. In nearly all States, licensing regulations require criminal record checks for all child-care staff. This screening requirement protects children from abuse and reduces liability risks, making insurance more available and affordable.

State governments also have established requirements for other child-care center personnel involved in food preparation, transportation of children, provision of medical services, and other services. Most States have defined minimum staff-to-children ratios. These vary depending on the State and the age of the children involved.

Earnings

In 1998, hourly earnings of nonsupervisory workers in the child-care services industry averaged $7.89, much less than the average of $12.77 for all industries combined. On a weekly basis, earnings in child-care services averaged $237 in 1998, barely more than half the average of $442 for all industries. Weekly earnings, in part, reflect hours worked— salaried workers in child-care services averaged 30 hours a week, compared to about 35 throughout private industry. Earnings in selected occupations in child-care services in 1997 appear in table 3.

Employee benefits often are minimal as well. A substantial number of child-care centers offer no health care benefits to any teaching staff. Reduced child care fees for workers' children, however, is a common benefit. Wage levels, employee benefits, and resulting turnover depends in part on the type of child-care center. Nonprofit and religiously affiliated centers generally pay higher wages and offer more generous benefits than for-profit establishments.

Only about 4 percent of all workers in child-care services are union members or are covered by union contracts, compared to 15.4 percent of all workers in private industry.

Outlook

Wage and salary jobs in the child-care services industry are projected to grow 32 percent over the 1998-2008 period, more than double the rate of growth projected for the entire economy. In addition to openings created by rapid employment growth, an unusually large number of job openings will result each year from the need to replace experienced workers who leave the industry. Turnover is very high, reflecting the low wages and relatively meager benefits. Rapid growth coupled with high turnover should create excellent employment opportunities.

Table 3. Median hourly earnings of the largest occupations in child-care services, 1997

Occupation	Child-care services	All industries
General managers and top executives ...	$12.55	$26.05
Education administrators	12.02	28.02
Social workers, except medical and psychiatric.....................................	10.82	14.01
Teachers, elementary school	9.63	—
Teachers, kindergarten	8.61	—
Teachers, preschool	7.54	8.03
Cooks, institution or cafeteria.................	6.62	7.51
Teacher aides and educational assistants, clerical	6.51	7.13
Janitors and cleaners, except maids and housekeeping cleaners	6.44	7.44
Child care workers	5.96	6.48

The rising demand for child-care services reflects demographic trends. Over the 1986-96 period, the population of women of childbearing age (widely considered to be age 15 to 44) increased by over 2 million, accompanied by a rise in their labor force participation. The interplay of these forces increased very rapidly the number of women in the labor force with children young enough to require child care. These demographic changes are projected to slow over the 1998-2008 period, and projected employment growth in the child-care services industry—while rapid—represents a slowdown from the previous 10 years. The number of women of childbearing age is expected to grow very slowly and the number of children under age 5 will decline during this period before rising to just above 1998 levels.

Nevertheless, the demand for child care services will remain high. As the labor force participation of women between the ages of 16 and 44 increases, more parents of preschool and school-age children will seek suitable daycare arrangements. More child-care centers will be needed if more parents enroll their children in nursery school or preschool programs. School-age children, who generally require child care only before and after school, increasingly are being cared for in centers.

Center-based care should continue to expand its share of the industry as government increases its involvement in promoting and funding child-care services. Increased funding for Head Start and other national child-care programs would result in more children being served in centers. Another factor that could result in more children being cared for in centers is the greater involvement of employers in funding and operating daycare centers. Recently enacted welfare reform legislation requiring more welfare recipients to work could also contribute to demand for child-care services.

Sources of Additional Information

For additional information about careers and training in the child-care services industry, write to:

➤ National Association for the Education of Young Children, 1509 16th St. NW., Washington, DC 20036. Internet: **http://www.naeyc.org**
➤ Center for the Child Care Workforce, 733 15th St. NW., Suite 1037, Washington, DC 20005. Internet: **http://www.ccw.org**

Detailed information on the following key occupations in the child-care services industry appears in the 2000-2001 *Occupational Outlook Handbook*:

● Preschool teachers and child-care workers
● Teacher assistants

Computer and Data Processing Services

SIGNIFICANT POINTS

- Employment is projected to grow 117 percent between 1998 and 2008, making this the fastest growing industry.

- Job opportunities will be excellent for most workers; the best prospects will be found in the professional and technical occupations, reflecting continuing demand for higher level skills to keep up with changes in technology.

- Computer systems analysts, engineers, and scientists and computer programmers comprise over 4 out of 10 employees in the industry.

Nature of the Industry

All organizations today rely on computer and information technology to conduct business and operate more efficiently. Often, however, these establishments do not have the resources to effectively implement new technologies or satisfy their changing needs. When this happens, they turn to the computer and data processing services industry to meet their specialized needs on a contract or customer basis. Firms may enlist the services of one of almost 106,000 establishments in the computer and data processing services industry for help with a particular project or problem, such as setting up a secure Web site or ensuring Year 2000 compliance. Or, they may choose to "outsource" one or more activities, such as management of their entire data center or help desk support, to a computer and data processing services firm.

Services provided by this industry include prepackaged software; customized computer programming services and applications and systems software design; data processing, preparation, and information retrieval services, including on-line databases and Internet services; integrated systems design and development and management of databases; on-site computer facilities management; rental, leasing, and repair of computers and peripheral equipment; and a variety of specialized consulting services. Computer training contractors, however, are grouped with educational services, and establishments that manufacture and sell computer equipment are included with electronic equipment manufacturing. Telecommunications services are also classified separately.

Software and professional services offered within this industry include prepackaged software, custom programming, integrated systems design, and other specialized consulting. Prepackaged software establishments develop operating system software as well as word processing and spreadsheet packages, games and graphics packages, and Internet-related software tools such as search engines and Web browsers—the software that permits browsing, retrieval, and viewing of content from the World Wide Web. Some may install the software package on a user's system and customize it to their specific needs. Programming service firms may be hired to code large programs or to get new systems up and running. Programming service firms also may update or reengineer existing systems. With the growth of the Internet and Intranets, which link people and computers within an orga-

nization, and the expansion of electronic commerce, some service companies specialize in developing and maintaining Web sites and corporate Intranets for client companies. These firms or consultants also provide assistance at various stages of development, from design and content to administration and site security. Integrated systems design firms develop and market new computer hardware and software systems, integrate new software into existing systems, or open systems to an entire organization. These firms design sophisticated computer networks, assist with upgrades or conversions, and engage in continual maintenance. They help clients select the right hardware and software products for a particular project, develop, install, and implement the system, and train their users. Other firms also offer consulting services throughout the entire process.

Information services include data preparation and processing services, as well as information retrieval services. Usually, information is collected from the client's databases, processed, and passed to other online subscribers, to contracted users, or back to the client. Establishments in these sectors may provide payroll processing, credit reporting, data entry services, and optical scanning services, as well as the leasing of computer time. Establishments in these sectors also include the growing number of Internet service providers. These companies provide access to end users of the Internet who usually subscribe for a set fee.

Hardware services for computers and other data processing equipment include facilities management and operation, rental and leasing, maintenance and repair of computers and peripheral equipment. Such services usually are offered on the customer's site, though in the case of maintenance and repair work, equipment may be taken to repair shops and replacements left for temporary use. Miscellaneous services establishments include database development firms engaged in building and maintaining databases of critical information. Miscellaneous services also include disk and diskette conversions, hardware requirements analysis, and computer consultants operating on a contract or fee basis.

Working Conditions

Most workers in this industry work in clean, quiet offices. Those in facilities management or maintenance and repair may work in computer operations centers or repair shops. Given the technology available today, however, more work can be done from remote locations using modems, fax machines, e-mail, and even the Internet. For example, data entry keyers, word processors, and secretaries may work from home with their home computers linked directly to computers at a data processing service firm. Though they often relocate to a customer's place of business while working on a project, programmers and consultants may actually perform work from locations off site. Even technical support personnel can tap into a customer's computer remotely in order to identify and fix problems.

About 6.8 percent of the workers in computer and data processing services firms work part time, compared to 15.9 percent of workers throughout all industries. For some professionals or technical specialists, evening or weekend work may be necessary to meet deadlines or solve problems. Professionals working for large establishments may have less freedom in planning their schedule than consultants for very small firms whose work may be more varied.

Data entry keyers and others who work at video terminals for extended periods of time may experience musculoskeletal strain, eye problems, stress, or repetitive motion illnesses, such as carpal tunnel syndrome.

Employment

Employment in computer and data processing services grew by more than 900,000 jobs from 1988 to 1998. In 1998, there were about 1.6 million wage and salary jobs, and an additional 216,000 self-employed workers, making it one of the largest industries in the economy. Most self-employed workers are independent consultants. Since the late 1980s, employment has grown most rapidly in the computer programming services and prepackaged software segments of the industry. From 1988 to 1998, about 245,000 jobs were created in programming services and another 166,000 in prepackaged software.

While it has both large and small firms, the average establishment in this industry is relatively small; approximately 80

percent of establishments employed fewer than 10 workers. The majority of jobs, however, are found in establishments that employ 50 or more workers (chart). Many small establishments in this industry are startup firms that hope to capitalize on a market niche.

There are significantly fewer very young and older workers in computer and data processing establishments (table 1). The scarcity of very young workers is tied to the time required to acquire the educational and training requirements needed to qualify for many jobs in this industry. The lack of older workers reflects the industry's explosive growth in employment since the early 1980s. This huge increase in employment afforded thousands of opportunities to younger workers possessing the newest technological skills. Sufficient time has not passed for these workers to reach age 55 or older; this industry's workforce remains younger than most.

Table 1. Percent distribution of employment in computer and data processing services by age group, 1998

Age group	Computer and data processing services	All industries
Total	100.0	100.0
16-19	1.6	5.4
20-24	8.2	9.5
25-34	35.2	23.8
35-44	32.2	27.5
45-54	17.0	21.0
55-64	5.1	9.8
65 and older	0.6	2.9

Occupations in the Industry

Providing a wide array of information services to clients requires a diverse and well-educated workforce. The majority of workers in computer and data processing services are managers; professional specialists, such as computer systems analysts, engineers, and scientists; and technicians, such as computer programmers (table 2). Together, these occupational groups accounted for 70 percent of the jobs in the industry, reflecting the emphasis on high level skills and creativity. By 2008, the employment share of professional specialty occupations is expected to be even greater, while the employment share of administrative support jobs, currently accounting for 18 percent of industry employment, is projected to fall.

Programmers write, test, and maintain the detailed instructions, called programs or software, that computers must follow to perform their functions. These programs tell the computer what to do, such as which information to identify and access, how to process it, and what equipment to use. Programmers write these commands by breaking down each step into a logical series, converting specifications into a language the computer understands. While many still work with traditional programming languages like COBOL, object-oriented programming languages, such as C++ and Java, computer-aided software engineering (CASE) tools, and artificial intelligence shells are now being used to create and maintain programs. These languages and tools allow portions of code to be reused in programs that require similar routines. Many programmers also customize a package to clients' specific needs or create better packages.

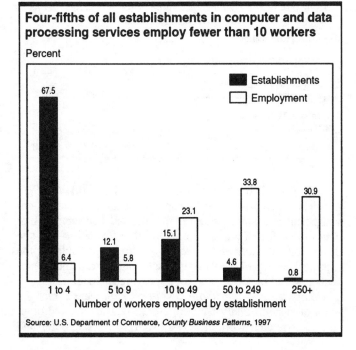

Four-fifths of all establishments in computer and data processing services employ fewer than 10 workers

Percent

■ Establishments
□ Employment

	1 to 4	5 to 9	10 to 49	50 to 249	250+
Establishments	67.5	12.1	15.1	4.6	0.8
Employment	6.4	5.8	23.1	33.8	30.9

Number of workers employed by establishment

Source: U.S. Department of Commerce, *County Business Patterns*, 1997

Computer engineers design and develop new software and hardware. Although programmers write and support programs in new languages, much design and development work is now the responsibility of *software engineers* or *software developers*. These professionals develop software systems for control and automation in manufacturing, business, and other areas. They research, design, and test operating system software, compilers—software that converts programs for faster processing—and network distribution software. Software engineers working in applications development analyze users' needs and design, create, and modify general computer applications software or specialized utility programs. *Hardware engineers*, on the other hand, usually design, develop, and test computer hardware and supervise production—for example, assembly of computer chips.

Other professionals involved in analyzing and solving problems include *systems analysts*, who study business, scientific, or engineering data processing problems and design new flows of information. Computers need to be connected to each other and to a control server to allow communication among users, thus enhancing use of their computing power. Systems analysts tie together hardware and software to give an organization the maximum benefit from its investment in machines, personnel, and business processes. To do this, they may design entirely new systems or add a single new software application to harness more of the computer's power. They use data modeling, structured analysis, information engineering, and other methods. Systems analysts prepare charts for programmers to follow for proper coding of machines and also perform cost-benefit analyses for management to evaluate the system. They ensure that the system performs to its specifications and test it thoroughly.

Database administrators determine ways to organize and store data and work with database management systems software. They set up computer databases and test and coordinate changes to them. Because they also may be responsible for design implementation and system security, database administrators often plan and coordinate security measures.

Computer support specialists provide technical assistance, support, and advice to customers and users. This group of occupations includes workers with a variety of titles, such as *technical support specialists*, *help desk technicians*, and *customer service representatives*. These are the troubleshooters responsible for interpreting problems and providing technical support. They answer phone calls, use automated diagnostic programs, and resolve recurrent problems.

Other computer scientists include a wide range of related professionals who specialize in operation, analysis, education, application, or design of a particular piece of the system. Many are involved in the design, testing, and evaluation of network systems such as LAN, WAN, Internet, and other data communications systems. Growing specialty occupations reflect an emphasis on client-server applications and end-user support; however, occupational titles shift rapidly to reflect new developments in technology. *Network* or *computer systems administrators*, or *network specialists*, for example, design, install, and support an organization's local area network (LAN), wide area network (WAN), network segment, or Internet system. They maintain network hardware and software, analyze problems, and monitor the network to ensure availability to system users. Administrators also may plan, coordinate, and implement network security measures. In some organizations,

computer security specialists are responsible for the organization's information security.

Table 2. Employment of wage and salary workers in computer and data processing services by occupation, 1998 and projected change, 1998-2008

(Employment in thousands)

Occupation	1998 Employment Number	1998 Employment Percent	1998-2008 Percent change
All occupations	1,599	100.0	117.1
Professional specialty	560	35.0	186.8
Systems analysts	141	8.8	187.6
Computer engineers	122	7.6	214.9
Computer support specialists	113	7.0	222.3
Writers and editors, including technical writers	21	1.3	97.0
Electrical and electronics engineers	21	1.3	124.6
Database administrators	20	1.2	238.8
Operations research analysts	15	1.0	55.6
Administrative support	291	18.2	62.7
Data entry keyers, except composing	41	2.6	57.6
Computer operators	37	2.3	-21.6
Secretaries	30	1.9	57.0
Office and administrative support supervisors and managers	28	1.8	91.5
General office clerks	25	1.6	98.8
Bookkeeping, accounting, and auditing clerks	22	1.4	60.4
Receptionists and information clerks	20	1.3	96.7
Executive, managerial, and administrative	286	17.9	94.5
General managers and top executives	73	4.6	91.2
Engineering, natural science, and computer and information systems managers	33	2.1	136.4
Financial managers	16	1.0	66.9
Accountants and auditors	16	1.0	85.1
Technicians and related support	280	17.5	79.1
Computer programmers	243	15.2	76.7
Engineering technicians	33	2.1	97.0
Marketing and sales	108	6.8	81.3
Precision production, craft, and repair	43	2.7	82.1
Data processing equipment repairers	23	1.5	77.3
Operators, fabricators, and laborers	25	1.6	93.5
All other occupations	6	0.4	78.0

Growth of the Internet and expansion of the World Wide Web have generated a variety of occupations relating to design, development, and maintenance of Web sites and their servers. *Web developers*, for example, are responsible for day-to-day site design and creation while *webmasters* are responsible for the technical aspects of the Web site, including performance issues such as speed of access, and for approving site content.

Computer and information systems managers direct the work of systems analysts, computer programmers, and other computer-related workers. They analyze the computer and information needs of their organization and determine personnel and equipment requirements. These managers plan and coordinate activities such as the installation and upgrading of hardware and software; programming and systems design; the development of computer networks; and the implementation of Internet and Intranet sites.

Traditionally, the role of *computer operators* has been to ensure that computer systems run as efficiently as possible. Depending upon the size of the computer installation, they may work with mainframes, minicomputers, or networks of personal computers. They oversee regular operations and solve problems that surface within the system. Peripheral equipment, such as printers and tape drives, and the console of the computer itself must be correctly accessed and controlled. As errors arise, operators respond by resetting controls or terminating the run. In some establishments, they keep logs of malfunctions, suggest new equipment, or supervise and train other operators or peripheral equipment operators.

Data entry keyers transfer information from audio or printed forms to a computer system. Many also manipulate or edit existing data or proofread entries to an existing database. Increasingly, data are entered into computer systems at the point of origin, such as in the case of automatic teller machines and sophisticated optical character readers, which scan a document and copy the information to the computer.

Data processing equipment repairers, also known as *computer repairers*, maintain mainframe and personal computers, printers, and other peripheral equipment. They install new equipment for clients, do preventive maintenance, and correct emergency problems. Workers may also install operating software and peripheral equipment, checking that all components are configured to correctly function together. Repairers may work in both repair shops and customer locations. When equipment breaks down, many repairers travel to customers' workplaces or other locations to make the necessary repairs. As the amount of computer equipment increases, more installation, maintenance, and repair work will become necessary.

A number of other workers in this industry are in marketing and sales occupations. These workers are responsible for promoting and selling the products and services provided by the various sectors of this industry.

Training and Advancement

Occupations in the computer and data processing services industry require varying levels of education. The level of education and type of training required depend on employers' needs. One factor affecting these needs is changes in technology. As demonstrated by the current demand for workers with skills related to the Internet or World Wide Web, employers often scramble to find workers capable of implementing "hot" new technologies. Another factor driving employers' needs is the time frame in which a project must be completed.

Entry level positions such as data entry keyers generally need a high school diploma. Most data entry positions are entry level and are awarded to those applicants with the greatest keyboarding speed and some business education. Computer operators may need some postsecondary education or training. Some computer operator positions may require an associate degree or even a bachelor's degree. More commonly, however, a high school diploma, previous experience with an operating system, and familiarity with the latest technologies

are the minimum requirements. Completion of vocational training also is an asset.

Computer programmers commonly hold a bachelor's degree; however, there are no universal educational requirements. Some hold a degree in computer science, mathematics, or information systems while others have taken special courses in computer programming to supplement their study in fields such as accounting, inventory control, or other areas of business. Because employers' needs are so varied, a 2-year degree or certificate may be sufficient for some positions so long as applicants possess the right technical skills.

Most computer systems analysts, engineers, and scientists, on the other hand, usually have a bachelor's or higher degree and work experience. Many hold advanced degrees in technical fields or a master's degree in business administration with a concentration in information systems and are specialists in their fields. For systems analyst, programmer-analyst, or even database administrator positions, many employers seek applicants who have a bachelor's degree in computer science, information science, or management information systems (MIS). Computer hardware engineers generally need a bachelor's degree in computer engineering or electrical engineering, whereas software engineers are more likely to hold a degree in computer science. However, computer support specialists generally need only an associate degree in a computer-related field, as well as significant hands-on experience with computers.

The size of the firm and the local demand for workers also may influence training requirements for specific jobs. Smaller firms may be willing to train informally on the job, whereas larger organizations may pay for formal training or higher education. With more formal education, employees may advance to completely different jobs within the industry. Education or training in a specialty area may provide new opportunities for the worker and allow the establishment to offer new services.

As technology becomes more sophisticated and complex, employers in all areas demand a higher level of skill and expertise. Technical or professional certification is a way employers ensure competency or quality. Many product vendors or software firms offer certification and may require it of individuals who work with their products. Many computer professionals also voluntarily obtain some type of technical or professional certification in their field.

The computer and data processing services industry offers advancement opportunities for all workers who keep up with changing technology. Beginning data entry keyers may move to project leader, and then to first-line supervisor of other keyers or to office manager. This advancement may result from work experience or from continued training and education.

Computer operators may begin on small computer installations or supervise one aspect of operations. They may move to larger systems that run a greater number of jobs and require more complex problem-solving skills. They also may advance to become operations analysts, or move into computer operations management. These employees apply available computing power to business situations, and they research and suggest upgrades or modifications to the operation of the computer system. Some operators may even become system supervisors. Because they work closely with computer operating languages and systems, computer operators may gain the necessary experience to become programmers or customer support liaisons within their specialty. Many also seek formal education to advance to emerging occupations, such as operations analysts or network administrators.

Entry level computer programmers usually start working with an experienced programmer updating existing code, generating lines of one portion of a larger program, or writing relatively simple programs. They then advance to more difficult programming and may become project supervisors, or move into higher management positions within the organization. Many programmers who work closely with systems analysts advance to systems analyst positions.

Systems analysts may begin working with experienced analysts or may only deal with small systems or one aspect of a system. They also may move into supervisory positions as they gain further education or work experience. Systems analysts, who work with one type of system, or one aspect or application of a system, can become specialty consultants or move into management positions. Computer engineers and scientists may also advance into project leadership positions or management positions. Technical support specialists may advance by developing expertise in an area that leads to other opportunities. For example, those responsible for network support may advance into network administration or network security.

Consulting is an attractive option for experienced workers, especially programmers and systems analysts who do not wish to advance to management positions, or who would rather continue to work with hands-on applications or in a particular specialty. They may market their services on their own under contract as specialized consultants or with an organization that provides consulting services to outside clients. Many of the largest firms today have subsidiaries that offer specialized services to the host company and to outside clients.

Many experienced workers also have opportunities to move into sales positions as they gain knowledge of specific products. Data entry keyers, for example, may represent an organization in contracting with clients to ensure proper completion of a data entry project. Computer programmers who adapt prepackaged software for accounting organizations may use their specialized knowledge to sell such products to similar firms.

Earnings

Employees in the computer and data processing services industry generally command higher earnings than the national average. This reflects the concentration of professionals and specialists who are often highly compensated for their specialized skills or expertise. Given the pace at which technology advances in this industry, earnings can be driven by demand for specific skills or experience. Workers in segments of the industry that offer only professional services have even higher average earnings because there are fewer less skilled, lower paid workers in these segments. Earnings in selected occupations in computer and data processing services appear in table 3.

As one might expect, education and experience influence earnings as well. For example, annual earnings of computer engineers ranged from less than $37,150 for the lowest 10 percent to more than $92,850 for the highest 10 percent in 1998. Managers usually earn more because they have been on the job longer and are more experienced than their staffs,

but their salaries too can vary by level and experience. Earnings also are affected by other factors such as size, location, and type of establishment, hours and responsibilities of the employee, and level of sales.

Table 3. Median hourly earnings of the largest occupations in computer and data processing services, 1997

Occupation	Computer and data processing services	All industries
General managers and top executives ...	$43.56	$26.05
Engineering, mathematical, and data processing managers	36.90	34.94
Marketing, advertising, and public relations managers	29.21	25.61
Computer engineers	27.28	28.07
Systems analysts, electronic data processing	24.53	23.82
Computer programmers	23.50	22.61
Computer support specialists	17.43	17.24
Secretaries, except legal and medical	12.15	11.00
Computer operators, except peripheral equipment	11.66	11.64
Data entry keyers, except composing	8.39	8.91

Unionization is rare in the computer and data processing services industry; less than 2 percent of all workers are union members or are covered by union contracts, compared to 15.4 percent of workers throughout private industry.

Outlook

The computer and data processing services industry has grown dramatically in recent years and employment is expected to grow about 117 percent by the year 2008, making this the fastest growing industry in the U.S. economy (chart). Given the rate at which the computer and data processing services industry is expected to grow and the increasing complexity of technology available, job opportunities will be excellent for most workers in this industry. The best job opportunities will be created in the professional and technical occupations, reflecting their rapid growth and continuing demand for higher level skills to keep up with changes in technology.

An increasing reliance on information technology and falling prices of computers and related hardware mean that individuals and organizations will continue to turn to computer and data processing service firms to maximize the return on their investments in equipment and to fulfill their growing computing needs. Such needs include the expansion of electronic commerce, an increased reliance on the Internet, faster and more efficient internal and external communication, and the development of new technologies and applications. With increasing global competition and rising costs, organizations must be able to obtain and manage the latest information in order to make business decisions.

Within the industry, projected growth varies by sector. Among the fastest growing sectors should be client-server applications, consulting and integration services, prepackaged software, and end-user support. The demand for networking

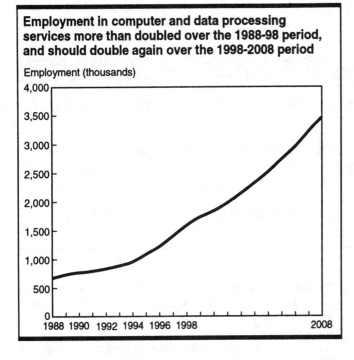

Employment in computer and data processing services more than doubled over the 1988-98 period, and should double again over the 1998-2008 period

Employment (thousands)

and the need to integrate new technologies will drive the demand for consulting and integration. Advances in software technology and expanding Internet usage will increase the need for software support and services. Prepackaged software has historically grown very rapidly and will continue to grow as individuals and establishments try to capitalize on the latest improvements. And, as more computing power is made available to the individual user, demand for support services should spur growth in areas such as help-desk outsourcing.

New growth areas will continue to arise from rapidly evolving technologies and business forces. The rate at which the Internet and in particular the World Wide Web have expanded demonstrates the potential effects of yet unknown technological developments and the tremendous room for growth. The expansion of the Internet and the proliferation of World Wide Web sites have created a demand for a wide variety of new products and related services including Internet and Web software, on-line services, Internet design services, web site development, and a range of specialized consulting. Yet the way the Internet is used is constantly changing, and so are the products, services, and personnel required to support new applications. Expanding electronic commerce, for example, has changed the way companies transact business, enabling markets to expand and an increasing array of services to be provided to customers. Demand for an even wider array of services should increase as companies continue to expand their capabilities, integrate new technologies, and develop new applications.

Given the increasingly widespread use of information technologies and overall rate of growth expected for the entire industry, most occupations should experience very rapid growth, though some much faster than others. As firms continue to install sophisticated computer networks, set up Internet and Intranet sites, and engage in electronic commerce, the most rapid growth will occur among computer systems analysts, engineers, and scientists. Rapid growth is also expected among electrical and electronics engineers and computer and information systems managers. Employment of data processing equipment repairers also will grow rapidly due to increasing dependence of business and residential customers on computers and sophisticated office machines.

Employment of programmers should grow faster than the average for all occupations, but more slowly than other occupations, as the proportion of programmers decreases in relation to other types of computer professionals. Employment of administrative support occupations, including data entry keyers, is also expected to grow more slowly than the rest of the industry, while employment of computer and peripheral equipment operators is expected to decline. As client-server environments and automation continue to increase productivity, automated operating packages and robotic equipment should continue to reduce the need for such workers.

Sources of Additional Information

Information regarding certification of computer professionals is available from:

➢ Institute for Certification of Computing Professionals (ICCP), 2200 E. Devon Ave., Suite 268, Des Plaines, IL 60018. Internet: **http://www.iccp.org**

Further information about computer careers is available from:

➢ Association for Computing Machinery (ACM), 1515 Broadway, New York, NY 10036.
Internet: **http://www.acm.org**
➢ Institute of Electrical and Electronics Engineers—United States of America, 1828 L St. NW., Suite 1202, Washington, DC 20036. Internet: **http://www.ieee.org**

Information on the following occupations can be found in the 2000-01 *Occupational Outlook Handbook*:

● Computer, automated teller, and office machine repairers
● Computer operators
● Computer programmers
● Computer systems analysts, engineers, and scientists
● Engineering, natural science, and computer and information systems managers
● Operations research analysts
● Word processors, typists, and data entry keyers

Educational Services

SIGNIFICANT POINTS

- With about 1 in 4 Americans enrolled in educational institutions, educational services is one of the largest industries with over 11 million jobs.

- Most managerial and professional specialty positions—which account for more than 6 out of every 10 jobs—require at least a bachelor's degree, and some require a master's or doctoral degree.

- The number of job openings for teachers should increase substantially due to expected increases in enrollments and retirements.

Nature of the Industry

Education is an important part of life. The type and level of education that an individual attains often influences such important aspects of life as occupational choice and earnings potential. Lifelong learning is important to acquire new knowledge and upgrade skills, particularly in this age of rapid technological and economic changes.

Educational services are provided in cities, suburbs, small towns, and rural areas throughout the Nation. The industry includes a variety of institutions that offered academic instruction, technical instruction, and other educational and training services to about 67 million students in 1998. Most students are enrolled in elementary and secondary schools, and institutions of higher learning. Of these, about 86 percent were enrolled in public schools and 14 percent were enrolled in private schools.

School attendance is compulsory, usually until age 16 to 18, in all 50 States and the District of Columbia, so elementary and secondary schools are the most numerous of all educational establishments, making up 37 percent of the educational services industry in 1997. Elementary and secondary schools provide academic courses, ordinarily for kindergarten through grade 12, in public schools, parochial schools, boarding and other private schools, and military academies. Some secondary schools provide a mixture of academic and technical instruction.

Higher education institutions accounted for about 8 percent of all educational establishments in 1997, and provide academic or technical courses or both in colleges, universities, professional schools, community or junior colleges, and technical institutes. Universities offer bachelor's, master's, and doctoral degrees, while colleges generally offer only the bachelor's degree. Professional schools offer graduate degrees in fields such as law, medicine, business administration, and engineering. The undergraduate bachelor's degree typically requires four years of study, while graduate degrees require additional years of study. Community colleges and technical institutes offer associate degrees, certificates, or diplomas, typically involving two years of study or less.

Establishments that make up the remainder of the educational services industry include libraries; vocational schools, such as data processing, business, secretarial, commercial art, practical nursing, and correspondence schools; and institutions providing a variety of specialized training and services, such as student exchange programs, curriculum development, and charm, drama, language, music, reading, modeling, and survival schools.

In recent decades, the Nation has focused attention on the educational system because of the growing importance of producing a trained and educated workforce. Government, private industry, and numerous research organizations have become involved in improving the quality of education. For example, businesses often donate instructional equipment, lend personnel for teaching and mentoring, host work-site visits, and provide job shadowing and internship opportunities. Businesses also collaborate with educators to develop curriculums that will provide students with the skills they need to cope with new technology in the workplace.

Secondary schools, in addition to preparing students for higher education, also prepare the large number of students who do not attend college for the transition from school to work. School-to-work programs integrate academic subjects with vocational classes providing skills specific to an occupation or discipline and teach problem solving, communication, and teamwork skills. Programs providing students with marketable skills include cooperative education, tech-prep, and youth apprenticeship programs. Youth apprenticeship programs, although relatively small in number, provide students with occupational skill training by working under the supervision of a mentor. Tech-prep programs begin in high school and continue through 2 years of postsecondary training, usually leading to an associate degree or certificate. Technical vocational education programs at the community college level have grown as employers have increasingly demanded higher levels of education from their employees. While most vocational programs focus on technical skills training—such as those skills needed in manufacturing, health services, or automotive repair—more programs are offering training for service sector jobs, including financial services, hospitality and culinary jobs, and child care.

Many school districts have enacted reforms in response to declining student test scores, concerns that students would not be prepared to enter the workforce, or other reasons. The methods and goals of school reform vary by locale and the results achieved have been mixed over the years. In recent years, the average number of high school credits earned in mathematics, science, and foreign languages has risen; the high school dropout rate has fallen; and the proportion of women in the labor force with 4 or more years of college has risen. However, many problems remain. American students at the elementary and secondary levels continue to lag behind their peers in some other countries in mathematics and science, and Scholastic Assessment Test scores have risen only marginally. Although the difference in high school graduation rates between blacks and whites has decreased in recent years, graduation rates for Hispanics remain far behind. Social and economic problems continue to affect schools and students—for example, the quality of education in many schools with high minority enrollments and high poverty rates does not measure up to that in schools in other districts. Study of mathematics, science, and foreign languages has increased among high school students, but some employers still complain that many entry-level workers lack the basic writing, math, and computer skills necessary to perform in the workplace. In addition, some school districts are experiencing funding problems under tight government budgets, sometimes forcing them to restrict or eliminate some services.

Working Conditions

In educational institutions with a traditional school year schedule, most workers—including teachers, teacher assistants, library workers, school counselors, cooks, and food preparation workers—work about 10 months a year. Some workers take jobs related to or outside of education during their summer break, and others pursue personal interests. Education administrators, administrative support and clerical workers, and janitors often work the entire year. Night and weekend work is common for adult education teachers, college faculty, and college library workers. Part-time work is common for school busdrivers, adult education teachers, college faculty, teacher assistants, and some library workers. School busdrivers often work a split shift, driving one or two routes in the morning and afternoon; drivers who are assigned field trips, athletic and other extracurricular activities, or midday kindergarten routes work additional hours during or after school.

Seeing students develop and enjoy learning can be very rewarding for teachers. Dealing with unmotivated students, however, requires patience and understanding. College faculty and adult education teachers instruct older students, who tend to be highly motivated. These instructors generally do not encounter the behavioral and social problems sometimes found when teaching younger kindergarten, elementary, and secondary school students. Many teachers spend significant time outside of school preparing for class, doing administrative tasks, conducting research, writing articles and books, and pursuing advanced degrees.

Library workers who work at video display terminals for extended periods may experience headaches, eyestrain, or musculoskeletal strain. In general, however, educational services is a relatively safe industry. There were 2.9 cases of occupational injury and illness per 100 full-time workers in private educational establishments in 1997, compared with 7.1 in all industries combined.

Employment

Educational services was the largest industry in the economy in 1998, providing jobs for nearly 11.2 million workers—about 11 million wage and salary workers, and 155,000 self-employed

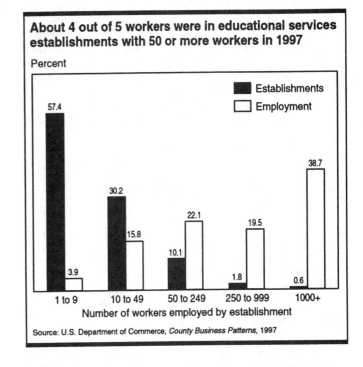

About 4 out of 5 workers were in educational services establishments with 50 or more workers in 1997

Percent

Source: U.S. Department of Commerce, *County Business Patterns*, 1997

workers. About 57 percent of private educational establishments had 1 to 9 workers. However, 4 out of 5 jobs were in private establishments with 50 or more workers (chart).

Employees in educational services were older than average, with 42 percent over age 45, compared to 34 percent of employees in all industries combined (table 1).

Table 1. Percent distribution of employment in educational services by age group, 1998

Age group	Educational services	All industries
Total	100.0	100.0
16-24	10.4	14.9
25-34	19.6	23.9
35-44	25.6	27.5
45-54	29.2	21.0
55-64	12.6	9.8
65 and older	0.3	2.9

Occupations in the Industry

Workers in this industry take part in all aspects of education, from teaching and counseling students to driving school buses and serving cafeteria lunches. Although most occupations are professional, the industry employs many administrative support, managerial, service, and other workers (table 2).

Teachers account for almost half of all workers in the educational services industry. Their duties depend on the age group and subject they teach and on the type of institution in which they work. Teachers should have a sincere interest in helping students and the ability to inspire respect, trust, and confidence. Strong speaking and writing skills, inquiring and analytical minds, and a desire to pursue and disseminate knowledge are vital for teachers. (*Preschool workers*, who nurture and teach children younger than 5 years old, are discussed in the *Career Guide* statement on child-care services.)

Kindergarten and *elementary school teachers* play a critical role in the early development of children. They usually

181

instruct one class in a variety of subjects, introducing the children to mathematics, language, science, and social studies. They use games, artwork, music, computers, and other tools to teach basic skills. Kindergarten and elementary teachers also may supervise extracurricular activities after school.

Table 2. Employment of wage and salary workers in educational services by occupation, 1998 and projected change, 1998-2008

(Employment in thousands)

Occupation	1998 Employment		1998-2008 Percent change
	Number	Percent	
All occupations	11,175	100.0	15.3
Professional specialty	6,133	54.9	17.7
Teachers, elementary school	1,677	15.0	11.5
Teachers, secondary school	1,425	12.8	22.6
College and university faculty	863	7.7	22.6
Teachers, special education	402	3.6	33.7
Adult and vocational education teachers	268	2.4	14.1
Teachers, preschool and kindergarten	226	2.0	11.5
Instructors and coaches, sports and physical training	138	1.2	11.5
Counselors	129	1.2	22.6
Health assessment and treating occupations	127	1.1	36.9
Librarians, professional	98	0.9	.3
Administrative support, including clerical	2,210	19.8	19.9
Teacher assistants	1026	9.2	33.7
Secretaries	459	4.1	10.9
General office clerks	209	1.9	12.5
Records processing occupations	164	1.5	9.3
Service	1,238	11.1	.4
Janitors and cleaners, including maids and housekeeping cleaners	489	4.4	.3
Cooks, institution or cafeteria	178	1.6	-10.8
Food preparation workers	170	1.5	.3
Executive, administrative, and managerial	742	6.6	11.5
Education administrators	367	3.3	11.5
Management support occupations ...	140	1.3	15.1
Operators, fabricators, and laborers	367	3.3	9.8
Bus drivers, school	318	2.8	11.5
Precision production, craft, and repair	226	2.0	15.7
Maintenance repairers, general utility	99	0.9	21.5
Technicians and related support	174	1.6	10.9
All other occupations	85	0.8	9.7

Secondary school teachers help students delve more deeply into subjects introduced in elementary school. Secondary school teachers specialize in a specific subject, such as English, Spanish, mathematics, history, or biology. They also may help students deal with academic problems and choose courses, colleges, and careers.

Special education teachers work with students—from toddlers to those in their early 20s—who have a variety of disabilities. Most special education teachers are found at the elementary, middle, and secondary school level. Special education teachers design and modify instruction to meet a student's special needs. These teachers also work with students who have other special instructional needs, including those who are gifted and talented.

College and *university faculty* generally are organized into departments or divisions, based on subject or field. Faculty teach and advise college students and perform a significant part of our Nation's research. They also consult with government, business, nonprofit, and community organizations. They prepare lectures, exercises, and laboratory experiments; grade exams and papers; and advise and work with students individually. Faculty keep abreast of developments in their field by reading current literature, talking with colleagues, and participating in professional conferences. They also do their own research to expand knowledge in their field, often publishing their findings in scholarly journals, books, and electronic media.

Adult education teachers work mainly in four areas—adult vocational-technical education, adult remedial education, adult continuing education, and prebaccalaureate training. Adult education teachers in vocational-technical education provide instruction for occupations that do not require a college degree, such as welder, cosmetologist, or dental hygienist. These teachers may also help people update their job skills or adapt to technological advances. Adult remedial education teachers provide instruction in basic education courses for school dropouts. Adult education teachers in junior or community colleges prepare students for a 4-year degree program, teaching classes for credit that can be applied towards that degree. Other adult education teachers teach courses that students take for personal enrichment, such as cooking or dancing.

Education administrators provide vision, direction, leadership, and day-to-day management of educational activities in schools, colleges and universities, businesses, correctional institutions, museums, and job training and community service organizations. They set educational standards and goals and aid in establishing the policies and procedures to carry them out. They develop academic programs; monitor students' educational progress; hire, train, motivate, and evaluate teachers and other staff; manage guidance and other student services; administer recordkeeping; prepare budgets; and handle relations with staff, parents, current and prospective students, employers, and the community.

School and college counselors—who work at the elementary, middle, secondary, and postsecondary school levels—help students evaluate their abilities, talents, and interests so that the student can develop realistic academic and career options. They also help students understand and deal with their social, behavioral, and personal problems. Secondary school counselors use interviews, counseling sessions, tests, or other methods when advising and evaluating students. They advise on college majors, admission requirements, entrance exams, and on trade, technical school, and apprenticeship programs. Elementary school counselors do more social and personal counseling and less vocational and academic counseling than secondary school counselors. School counselors work with students individually, in small groups, or with entire classes.

Librarians assist people in finding information and using it effectively in their scholastic, personal, and professional pursuits. They manage staff and develop and direct information programs and systems for the public as well as oversee the selection and organization of library materials. Librarians may supervise *library technicians*—who help librarians acquire, prepare, and organize material; direct library users to standard references; and retrieve information from computer data bases—and *library assistants* and *bookmobile drivers*—who check out and receive library materials, collect overdue fines, and shelve materials.

Teacher assistants, also called teacher aides or instructional aides, provide instructional and clerical support for classroom teachers, allowing teachers more time for lesson planning and teaching. Teacher assistants tutor and assist children in learning class material using the teacher's lesson plans, providing students with individualized attention. Assistants also aid and supervise students in the cafeteria, schoolyard, school discipline center, or on field trips. They record grades, set up equipment, and prepare materials for instruction.

School busdrivers transport students to and from school and related events.

The educational services industry employs many other workers who are found in a wide range of industries. For example, *secretaries*, *general office clerks*, and other *administrative support* and *clerical workers* account for about 1 out of 10 jobs in educational services.

Many State and local school systems are engaged in efforts to restructure the learning environment. This is resulting in increased responsibilities, and the need for additional skills, among some occupations in the educational services industry. For example, teachers are more involved in developing curricula and multiple instructional approaches in the classroom, including the use of computers and other technologies. Teachers also are more involved in matters outside the classroom, such as management of the school budget and parent and community relations. Similarly, principals are assuming more responsibility for management of their schools, taking less direction from higher-level education administrators such as school superintendents. In addition, principals are taking a more active role in working with the community. In response to the growing number of dual-income and single parent families and teenage parents, principals are setting up before- and after-school child-care programs and family research centers. They also are establishing programs to combat the increase in crime, drug and alcohol abuse, and violence.

Training and Advancement
The educational services industry employs some of the most highly educated workers in the labor force. College and university faculty generally need a doctoral degree for full-time, tenure-track employment, but sometimes can teach with a master's degree, particularly at 2-year colleges. Most faculty members are hired as instructors or assistant professors and may advance to associate professor and full professor. Some faculty advance to administrative and managerial positions, such as department chairperson, dean, or president.

Elementary and secondary school teachers must have a bachelor's degree and complete an approved teaching training program, with a prescribed number of subject and education credits and supervised practice teaching. All States require public school teachers to be licensed; licensure requirements vary by State. Many States offer alternate licensure programs for people who have bachelor's degrees in the subject they will teach, but lack the necessary education courses required for a regular license. Alternative licensure programs were originally designed to ease teacher shortages in certain subjects, such as math and science. However, the programs have expanded to

attract other people into teaching, including recent college graduates and mid-career changers. With additional education or certification, teachers may become school librarians, reading specialists, curriculum specialists, or guidance counselors. Some teachers advance to administrative or supervisory positions—such as department chairperson, assistant principal, or principal—but the number of these jobs is limited. In some school systems, highly qualified, experienced elementary and secondary school teachers can become senior or mentor teachers, with higher pay and additional responsibilities.

Adult education teachers normally need work or other experience in their field—and a license or certificate when required by the field—for full professional status. Most States and the District of Columbia require adult education teachers to have a bachelor's degree and some States also require teacher certification.

School counselors generally need a master's degree in a counseling specialty or a related field. All States require school counselors to hold State school counseling certification; however, certification varies from State to State. Some States require public school counselors to have both counseling and teaching certificates. Depending on the State, a master's degree in counseling and 2 to 5 years of teaching experience may be required for a counseling certificate. Experienced school counselors may advance to a larger school; become directors or supervisors of counseling, guidance, or student personnel services; or, with further graduate education, become counseling psychologists or school administrators.

Training requirements for education administrators depend on where they work. Principals, assistant principals, and school administrators usually have held a teaching or related job before entering administration, and they generally need a master's or doctoral degree in education administration or educational supervision, as well as State teacher certification. Academic deans usually have a doctorate in their specialty. Education administrators may advance up an administrative ladder or transfer to larger schools or school systems. They also may become superintendent of a school system or president of an educational institution.

Training requirements for teacher assistants range from a high school diploma to some college training. Districts that assign teaching responsibilities to teacher assistants usually have higher training requirements than those that do not. Teacher assistants who obtain a bachelor's degree, usually in education, may become certified teachers.

Librarians normally need a master's degree in library science. Many States require school librarians to be licensed as teachers and have courses in library science. Experienced librarians may advance to administrative positions, such as department head, library director, or chief information officer. Training requirements for library technicians range from a high school diploma to specialized postsecondary training; a high school diploma is sufficient for library assistants. Library workers can advance—from assistant, to technician, to librarian—with experience and the required formal education. School busdrivers, who need a commercial driver's license, have limited opportunities for advancement; some become supervisors or dispatchers.

Earnings
Earnings of occupations concentrated in the educational services industry—education administrators, teachers, counse-

lors, and librarians—are significantly higher than the average for all occupations, reflecting their older age and higher level of educational attainment. Among teachers, earnings increase with higher educational attainment and more years of service. College and university faculty earn the most, followed by secondary and elementary school teachers. Educational services employees who work the traditional school year can earn additional money during the summer in jobs related to or outside of education. Earnings in selected occupations in educational services appear in table 3.

Table 3. Median hourly earnings of the largest occupations in educational services, 1997

Occupation	Educational services	All industries
Education administrators	$29.12	$28.02
Teachers, special education	17.63	—
Teachers, secondary school	17.61	—
Teachers, elementary school	16.81	—
Secretaries, except legal and medical	10.76	11.00
Janitors and cleaners, except maid and housekeeping cleaners	9.16	7.44
General office clerks	9.10	9.10
Bus drivers, school	8.58	8.80
Teacher aides, paraprofessional	7.51	7.51

Almost 50 percent of workers in the educational services industry—the largest number being in elementary and secondary schools—are union members or are covered by union contracts, compared to only 15.4 percent of workers in all industries combined. The American Federation of Teachers and the National Education Association are the largest unions representing teachers and other school personnel.

Outlook

Employment in the educational services industry is projected to increase by 15 percent over the 1998-2008 period, the same as the rate of growth projected for all industries combined. In addition to employment growth, the need to replace experienced workers who find jobs in other industries or stop working will create many job openings. Due to the large size of this industry, the number of jobs arising from replacement needs is particularly significant. On the other hand, the number of individuals competing for kindergarten, elementary, and secondary school teaching positions also may increase in response to alternate certification programs, increased salaries, and greater teacher involvement in school policies and programs. Prestigious occupations such as education administrators and college faculty will continue to attract a large number of applicants for available positions.

Several important factors will shape the outlook for the industry. Enrollment growth at the secondary and postsecondary level over the 1998-2008 period should spur employment growth in educational services. At the postsecondary level, in addition to growth in domestic enrollment, enrollment of foreign students has been growing rapidly. Enrollment of special education students has been rising significantly over the last 20 years, and growth is expected to continue. In addition, teacher retirements are projected to create many new job openings in the industry.

Concerns that the future workforce may not meet employers' needs are leading educational institutions and employers to work together in developing programs to train students for jobs of the future. Initiatives include enhanced programs in reading, writing, and mathematics; emphasis on skills traditionally required only of managers, such as communications, decision making, and problem solving; and increased focus on technical and computer skills. Such emphasis on marketable skills should increase the importance of postsecondary education, and could spur employment growth in the educational services industry.

Projected employment growth varies by occupation. The number of special education teachers is expected to grow the fastest, spurred by growing enrollment of special education students, increased emphasis on inclusion of disabled students into general education classrooms, and the effort to reach students with problems at a young age. The number of teacher assistants also will grow much faster than average as many assist special education teachers; as school reforms call for more individual attention to students; and as the number of students who speak English as a second language rises.

Occupations expected to grow faster than average include secondary school teachers, college and university faculty, and counselors. Average growth is projected for school bus drivers, sports and physical fitness instructors and coaches, adult education teachers, elementary school teachers, and preschool and kindergarten teachers. Little or no growth is expected for librarians. Projected growth reflects demographic changes, enrollment increases, government legislation affecting education, expanded responsibilities of workers, and efforts to improve the quality of education.

Despite an expected increase in education expenditures, budget constraints at all levels of government may place restrictions on educational services, particularly in light of the rapidly escalating cost of college tuition and special education and other services. Cuts in funding could affect student services—such as school busing, educational materials, and extracurricular activities—and employment of administrative, instructional, and support staff. Budget considerations also will affect attempts to expand school programs, such as increasing the number of counselors and teacher assistants in elementary schools.

Sources of Additional Information

Information on unions and education-related issues can be obtained from:

➤ American Federation of Teachers, 555 New Jersey Ave. NW., Washington, DC 20001.
➤ National Education Association, 1201 16th St. NW., Washington, DC 20036.

Information on most occupations in the educational services industry, including the following, appears in the 2000-01 *Occupational Outlook Handbook.*

- Adult education teachers
- Busdrivers
- College and university faculty
- Counselors
- Education administrators
- Librarians
- Library assistants and bookmobile drivers
- Library technicians
- School teachers—kindergarten, elementary, and secondary
- Special education teachers
- Teacher assistants

Health Services

- Health services is one of the largest industries in the country, with about 11.3 million jobs, including the self-employed.

- About 14 percent of all wage and salary jobs created between 1998 and 2008 will be in health services.

- Twelve out of 30 occupations projected to grow the fastest are concentrated in health services.

- Most jobs require less than 4 years of college education.

Nature of the Industry

Combining medical technology and the human touch, the health services industry administers care around the clock, responding to the needs of millions of people—from newborns to the critically ill.

More than 460,000 establishments make up the health services industry; all vary greatly in terms of size, staffing, and organization. Two-thirds of all private health services establishments are offices of physicians or dentists. Although hospitals comprise less than 2 percent of all private health services establishments, they employ nearly 40 percent of all workers (table 1). When government hospitals are included, the proportion rises to almost half the workers in the industry.

Table 1. Percent distribution of wage and salary employment and establishments in private health services, 1997

Establishment type	Establishments	Employment
Total, health services	100.0	100.0
Hospitals, private	1.6	39.6
Offices of physicians and osteopaths..........................	41.8	18.5
Nursing and personal care facilities ..	4.3	18.1
Home health care services	3.3	7.3
Offices of dentists.............................	23.8	6.5
Offices of other health practitioners ..	18.7	4.5
Health and allied services, not elsewhere classified	3.1	3.4
Medical and dental laboratories	3.4	2.0

The health services industry includes small-town physicians with private practices who employ only one medical assistant, as well as busy inner city hospitals that provide thousands of diverse jobs. Over half of all non-hospital health services establishments employ fewer than 5 workers (see chart). On the other hand, almost two-thirds of hospital employees were in establishments with over 1,000 workers (see chart on next page).

The health services industry is made up of the following eight segments:

Hospitals. Hospitals provide complete health care, ranging from diagnostic services to surgery and continuous nursing care. Some hospitals specialize in treatment of the mentally ill, cancer patients, or children. Hospital-based care may be on an inpatient (overnight) or outpatient basis. The mix of workers needed varies, depending on the size, geographic location, goals, philosophy, funding, organization, and management style of the institution. As hospitals work to improve their efficiency, care continues to shift from an inpatient to outpatient basis whenever possible. Many hospitals have also expanded into long-term and home health care services, providing a continuum of care for the communities they serve.

Nursing and personal care facilities. Nursing facilities provide inpatient nursing, rehabilitation, and health-related personal care to those who need continuous health care, but do not require hospital services. Nursing aides provide the vast majority of direct care. Other facilities, such as convalescent homes, help patients who need less assistance. A growing segment within personal care is assisted living facilities. These facilities house the elderly in a home-like, independent setting and provide care appropriate to each resident's level of need.

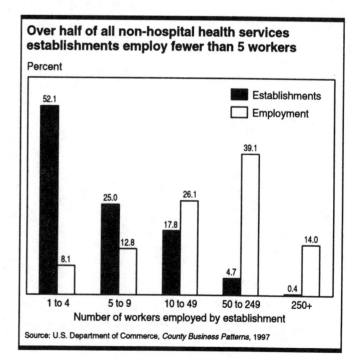

Over half of all non-hospital health services establishments employ fewer than 5 workers

Percent

- Establishments
- Employment

	1 to 4	5 to 9	10 to 49	50 to 249	250+
Establishments	52.1	25.0	17.8	4.7	0.4
Employment	8.1	12.8	26.1	39.1	14.0

Number of workers employed by establishment

Source: U.S. Department of Commerce, *County Business Patterns,* 1997

Unlike other segments of the health services industry, almost two-thirds of hospital employees work in establishments with 1,000 or more workers

Percent

■ Establishments
☐ Employment

Number of workers employed by establishment	Establishments	Employment
1 to 9	2.8	0.0
10 to 49	3.5	0.1
50 to 249	33.5	6.7
250 to 999	37.7	27.6
1000+	22.5	65.5

Source: U.S. Department of Commerce, *County Business Patterns*, 1997

Offices and clinics of physicians, including osteopaths. Doctors of medicine and osteopathy practice alone and in groups of practitioners who have the same or different specialties. Group practice has become the recent trend, including clinics, free standing emergency care centers, and ambulatory surgical centers. Physicians are more likely now to work as salaried employees of group medical practices, clinics, or health care networks than in the past.

Home health care services. Skilled nursing or medical care is sometimes provided in the home, under a physician's supervision. Home health care services are provided mainly to the elderly. The development of in-home medical technologies, substantial cost savings, and patients' preference for care in the home have helped make this once small segment of the industry one of the fastest growing in the U.S. economy.

Offices and clinics of dentists. Almost 1 out of every 4 health care establishments is a dentist's office. Most employ only a few workers who provide general or specialized dental care, including dental surgery.

Offices and clinics of other health practitioners. This segment includes offices of chiropractors, optometrists, and podiatrists, as well as occupational and physical therapists, psychologists, audiologists, speech-language pathologists, dietitians, and other miscellaneous health practitioners. Demand for services in this industry is related to the ability of patients to pay, either directly or through health insurance. Hospitals and nursing facilities may contract out for these services. This industry also includes alternative medicine practitioners, such as acupuncturists, hypnotists, and naturopaths. Demand for these services has grown with public awareness of the professions.

Health and allied services, not elsewhere classified. Among the diverse establishments in this group are kidney dialysis centers, outpatient facilities such as drug treatment clinics and rehabilitation centers, and other miscellaneous establishments such as blood banks and providers of childbirth preparation classes.

Medical and dental laboratories. Medical laboratories provide professional analytic or diagnostic services to the medical profession or directly to patients following a physician's prescription. Workers analyze blood, take x rays, or perform other clinical tests. In dental laboratories, workers make dentures, artificial teeth, and orthodontic appliances. Medical and dental laboratories provide the fewest number of jobs in health services.

Technological advances have made many new procedures and methods of diagnosis and treatment possible. For example, information technology continues to improve care and efficiency with devices such as hand held computers that record notes on each patient. Information on vital signs and orders for tests are then transferred to a main database, eliminating paper and reducing record keeping errors. Clinical developments such as organ transplants, less invasive surgical techniques, skin grafts, and gene therapy for cancer treatment continue to increase longevity and improve the quality of life for many Americans, as well as redistribute the demand for health care workers. Advances in medical technology have improved the survival rates of trauma victims and the severely ill, who then need extensive care from therapists and social workers, among other support personnel.

Cost containment in the health care industry is important as shown by the growing emphasis on providing services on an outpatient, ambulatory basis; limiting unnecessary or low priority services; and stressing preventive care that reduces the eventual cost of undiagnosed, untreated medical conditions. Enrollment in managed health care programs—predominantly Health Maintenance Organizations (HMO's), Preferred Provider Organizations (PPO's), and hybrid plans such as Point-of-Service (POS) programs—continues to grow. These prepaid plans provide comprehensive coverage to members and control health insurance costs by emphasizing preventive care. A growing phenomenon in the health services industry is the formation of Integrated Delivery Systems (IDS) where two or more segments of the industry are combined to increase efficiency through the streamlining of primarily financial and managerial functions. According to a 1998 Deloitte & Touche Survey, only 34 percent of surveyed hospitals expect to be stand-alone, independent facilities in 2003, as compared to 58 percent in 1998. These changes will continue to reshape not only the nature of the health services workforce, but also the manner in which health services are provided.

Working Conditions

Nonsupervisory workers in private health services averaged 33.1 hours per week in 1998, compared to 34.6 for all private industry. Hours varied somewhat among the different segments of the industry. Workers in home health care averaged only 29.0 hours per week; those in nursing and personal care facilities worked 32.6 hours; and hospital workers averaged 35.0 hours.

Many workers in the health services industry are on part-time schedules. Part-time workers comprised 15.9 percent of the workforce as a whole in 1998, but accounted for 35.6 percent of workers in offices of dentists and 19.6 percent of those in offices of physicians. Students, parents with young children, dual jobholders, and older workers make up much of the part-time workforce.

Many health services establishments operate around the clock and need staff at all hours. Shift work is common in some occupations, such as registered nurses. Many health service workers hold more than one job; particularly registered nurses, health technologists and technicians, and nursing aides.

In 1997, the incidence rate for occupational injury and illness in hospitals was 10.0 cases per 100 full-time workers, compared to an average of 7.1 for the private sector. Nursing and personal care facilities had a much higher rate, 16.2. Health care workers involved in direct patient care must take precautions to guard against back strain from lifting patients and equipment, exposure to radiation and caustic chemicals, and infectious diseases such as AIDS, tuberculosis, and hepatitis. Home care personnel who make house calls are exposed to the possibility of being injured in highway accidents, all types of overexertion when assisting patients, and falls inside and outside homes. Mechanical lifting devices, found in institutional settings, are seldom available in patients' homes.

Employment

The health services industry provided over 10.8 million wage and salary jobs in 1998. Almost one-half of all health services jobs were in hospitals; another one-third were in either nursing and personal care facilities or offices of physicians. About 92 percent worked in the private sector; the remainder worked in State and local government hospitals.

In addition to wage and salary workers, an estimated 446,000 workers in the industry were self-employed in 1998. Of these, about 70 percent were in offices of physicians, dentists, and other health practitioners. Health services jobs are found throughout the country, but are concentrated in large States, specifically California, New York, Florida, Texas, and Pennsylvania.

Workers in this industry tend to be older than workers in other industries, especially in occupations requiring higher levels of education and training, because they are more likely to stay in such occupations for a number of years.

Occupations in the Industry

Health services firms employ workers in professional specialty and service occupations in about equal numbers. Together, these two occupational groups cover nearly 3 out of 5 jobs in the industry. The next largest share of jobs is in administrative support occupations, followed by technicians and related support occupations. Executive, administrative, and managerial occupations account for only 6 percent of employment. Other occupations in health services comprise only 1 percent of the total (table 2).

Professional specialty occupations, such as *physicians, registered nurses, social workers,* and *therapists,* mostly require a bachelor's degree in a specialized field or higher education in a specific health field, although registered nurses also enter through associate degree or diploma programs. Respiratory therapists often do not need a bachelor's degree, but this degree or a higher one is the most significant source of training for all other therapist occupations. Professional workers often have high levels of responsibility and complex duties. They may supervise other workers or conduct research, as well as provide services.

Service occupations attract many workers with little or no specialized education or training. This group includes *nursing and psychiatric aides, food preparation and service occupations, janitors and cleaners, dental* and *medical assistants,* and *personal care and home health aides.* Service workers may advance to higher-level positions or to new occupations, with experience and, in some cases, further education and training.

Technicians and related support occupations include many fast growing health occupations, such as *health information technicians* and *dental hygienists.* These workers may operate technical equipment and assist health practitioners and other professional workers. Graduates of 1- or 2-year training programs often fill these positions; these jobs usually require specific formal training beyond high school, but less than 4 years of college.

Most jobs in health services provide clinical services, but there also are many in occupations with other functions as well. Numerous workers in executive, administrative, and managerial occupations and marketing and administrative support jobs keep organizations running smoothly. Although many *health services managers* have a background in a clinical specialty or training in health services administration, many enter these jobs with a general business education.

Each segment of the health services industry employs a different mix of health-related occupations and other workers.

Hospitals. Hospitals employ workers with all levels of education and training to provide a wider variety of services than other segments of the health services industry. About 1 in 4 hospital workers is a registered nurse. Hospitals also employ many physicians, therapists, and social workers. About 2 in 10 jobs is in a service occupation, such as *nursing aide, psychiatric aide, food preparation and service worker,* or *janitor.* Hospitals also employ large numbers of health technicians, administrative support workers, craft workers, and operatives.

Nursing and personal care facilities. Almost two-thirds of all nursing facility jobs are in service occupations, primarily *nursing aides.* Professional specialty and administrative support occupations are a much smaller percentage of nursing facility employment than for other parts of the health services industry. Federal law requires nursing facilities to have licensed personnel on hand 24 hours a day, and to maintain an appropriate level of care.

Table 2. Employment of wage and salary workers in health services by occupation, 1998, and projected change, 1998-2008

(Employment in thousands)

Occupation	1998 Employment Number	1998 Employment Percent	1998-2008 Percent change
All occupations	10,829	100.0	25.7
Professional specialty	3,195	29.5	27.4
Registered nurses	1,734	16.0	21.6
Physicians	412	3.8	35.3
Social workers	157	1.5	47.4
Physical therapists	109	1.0	34.5
Respiratory therapists	84	0.8	43.0
Dentists	80	0.7	18.9
Physician assistants	60	0.6	52.0
Pharmacists	54	0.5	11.5
Occupational therapists	49	0.5	30.3
Computer systems analysts, engineers, and scientists	41	0.4	62.3
Speech-language pathologists and audiologists	39	0.4	37.3
Dietitians and nutritionists	29	0.3	20.1
Service	3,011	27.8	29.7
Nursing aides and psychiatric aides	1,064	9.8	23.8
Personal care and home health aides	368	3.4	74.5
Janitors and cleaners, including maids and housekeeping cleaners	333	3.1	7.3
Medical assistants	246	2.3	58.8
Dental assistants	222	2.1	43.4
Food preparation workers	132	1.2	3.4
Food and beverage service occupations	92	0.9	6.9
Physical therapy assistants and aides	79	0.7	44.7
Guards	41	0.4	-1.7
Pharmacy assistants	34	0.3	11.6
Administrative support	2,030	18.8	18.2
General office clerks	280	2.6	30.1
Receptionists and information clerks	376	3.5	15.2
Medical secretaries	210	1.9	12.5
Office and administrative support supervisors and managers	174	1.6	30.2
Secretaries, except legal and medical	173	1.6	15.9
Billing, cost, and rate clerks	113	1.1	34.7
Bookkeeping, accounting, and auditing clerks	95	0.9	8.8
Technicians and related support	1,707	15.8	26.9
Licensed practical nurses	567	5.2	19.2
Clinical laboratory technologists and technicians	277	2.6	17.4
Radiologic technologists and technicians	160	1.5	19.8
Dental hygienists	140	1.3	41.3
Medical records and health information technicians	81	0.8	48.2
Surgical technologists	54	0.5	41.8
Psychiatric technicians	50	0.5	4.3
Emergency medical technicians	35	0.3	37.6
Dispensing opticians	34	0.3	22.8
Executive, administrative, and managerial	597	5.5	27.4
Health services managers	175	1.6	36.1
General managers and top executives	90	0.8	31.3
Precision production, craft, and repair	152	1.4	3.7
Dental lab technicians, precision	34	0.3	-1.8
All other occupations	136	1.3	13.4

Offices and clinics of physicians, including osteopaths. Many of the jobs in offices of physicians are in professional specialty occupations, primarily physicians and registered nurses. Even more jobs, however, are in administrative support occupations, such as *receptionists* and *medical secretaries*, who comprise almost two-fifths of the workers in physicians' offices.

Home health care services. More than half of the jobs in home health care are in service occupations, mostly *personal care and home health aides.* Nursing and therapist jobs also account for substantial shares of employment in this industry.

Offices and clinics of dentists. About one-third of the jobs in this segment are in service occupations, mostly *dental assistants.* The typical staffing pattern in dentists' offices consists of one professional with a support staff of *dental hygienists* and *dental assistants.* Larger practices are more likely to employ office managers and administrative support workers, as well as *dental laboratory technicians.*

Offices and clinics of other health practitioners. As in offices of physicians, many jobs are in administrative support occupations. About 1 in 6 jobs in this segment were for physical therapists, occupational therapists, or speech-language pathologists and audiologists.

Medical and dental laboratories. Technician and related support workers account for almost twice the proportion of jobs in this segment as in the total health services industry. These workers are mostly *clinical laboratory technologists and technicians* and *radiologic technologists.* This segment also has the smallest percentage of professional specialty workers of any segment of the health services industry. Many jobs also are in precision production, craft, and repair occupations—most notably, *dental laboratory technicians.*

Health and allied services, not elsewhere classified. This segment employs the highest percentage of professional specialty workers, many of whom are *social workers, social and human services assistants, registered nurses,* and *therapists.*

Training and Advancement

A variety of programs after high school provide specialized training for jobs in health services. Students preparing for health careers can enter programs leading to a certificate or a degree at the associate, baccalaureate, professional, or graduate levels. Two-year programs resulting in certificates or associate degrees are the minimum standard credential for occupations such as *dental hygienist* or *radiologic technologist.* Most *therapists* and *social workers* have at least a bachelor's degree; *physicians, optometrists,* and *podiatrists* have additional education and training beyond college. Persons considering careers in health care should have a strong desire to help others, genuine concern for the welfare of patients and clients, and an ability to deal with diverse people and stressful situations.

The health services industry provides many job opportunities for people without specialized training beyond high school. In fact, 56 percent of the workers in nursing and personal care facilities have a high school diploma or less, as do 24 percent of the workers in hospitals.

Some health services establishments provide on-the-job or classroom training, as well as continuing education. For example, in all certified nursing facilities, nursing aides must complete a State-approved training and competency evaluation program and participate in at least 12 hours of in-service education annually. Hospitals are more likely than other segments of the industry to have the resources and incentive to provide training programs and advancement opportunities to their employees. In other segments, staffing patterns tend to be more fixed and the variety of positions and advancement opportunities more limited. Larger establishments usually offer a greater range of opportunities.

Some hospitals provide training or tuition assistance in return for a promise to work for a particular length of time in the hospital after graduation. Many nursing facilities have similar programs. Some hospitals have cross-training programs that train their workers—through formal college programs, continuing education, or in-house training—to perform functions outside their specialties.

Health specialists with clinical expertise can advance to department head positions or even higher level management jobs. Health services managers can advance to more responsible positions, all the way up to chief executive officer.

Earnings

Average earnings of nonsupervisory workers in health services are slightly higher than the average for all private industry, with hospital workers earning considerably more than the average, and those in nursing and personal care facilities and home health care services earning considerably less (table 3). Average earnings often are higher in hospitals because their percentage of jobs requiring higher levels of education and training is greater than in other segments. Segments of the industry with lower earnings employ a large number of part-time service workers.

Table 3. Average earnings and hours of nonsupervisory workers in private health services by segment of industry, 1998

Industry segment	Earnings Weekly	Hourly	Weekly hours
Total, private industry	$442	$12.77	34.6
Health services	454	13.72	33.1
Hospitals, private	541	15.46	35.0
Offices of physicians	470	14.28	32.9
Offices of dentists	399	14.15	28.2
Offices of other health practitioners	397	13.13	30.2
Home health care services	334	11.50	29.0
Nursing and personal care facilities	318	9.76	32.6

As in most industries, professionals and managers typically earn more than other workers. Earnings in individual health services occupations vary as widely as their duties, level of education and training, and amount of responsibility (table 4). Some establishments offer tuition reimbursement, paid training, child day care services, and flexible work hours. Health care establishments that must be staffed around the clock to care for patients and handle emergencies often pay premiums for overtime and weekend work, holidays, late shifts, and when on-call. Bonuses and profit-sharing payments also may add to earnings.

Earnings vary not only by type of establishment and occupation, but also by size. Salaries are often higher in larger hospitals and group practices. Geographic location also can affect earnings.

Table 4. Median hourly earnings of the largest occupations in health services, 1997

Occupation	Health services	All industries
Registered nurses	$18.84	$18.88
Licensed practical nurses	12.34	12.46
Dental assistants	10.59	10.62
Medical assistants	9.71	9.71
Receptionists and information clerks	9.19	8.69
General office clerks	9.05	9.10
Home health aides	7.94	7.75
Nursing aides, orderlies, and attendants	7.70	7.76
Maids and housekeeping cleaners	7.16	6.74

Unionization is more common in hospitals, although most segments of the health services industry are not heavily unionized. In 1998, 14.9 percent of hospital workers and 10.7 percent of workers in nursing and personal care facilities were members of unions or covered by union contracts, compared to 15.4 percent of all workers in private industry.

Outlook

Employment in the health services industry is projected to increase 26 percent through 2008, compared to an average of 15 percent for all industries (table 5). Employment growth is expected to add about 2.8 million new jobs—14 percent of all wage and salary jobs added to the economy over the 1998-2008 period. Projected rates of employment growth for the various segments of this industry range from 8 percent in hospitals, the largest and slowest growing industry segment, to 80 percent in the much smaller home health care services.

Table 5. Employment of wage and salary workers in health services by segment of industry, 1998, and projected change, 1998-2008

(Employment in thousands)

Industry	1998 Employment	1998-2008 Percent change
All industries	128,008	15.3
Health services	10,829	25.7
Hospitals, public and private	4,909	7.7
Nursing and personal care facilities	1,762	25.6
Offices of physicians	1,853	41.2
Home health care services	672	80.5
Offices of dentists	646	29.9
Offices of other health practitioners	450	42.8
Health and allied services, not elsewhere classified	339	64.9
Medical and dental laboratories	199	24.5

Employment in health services will continue to grow for a number of reasons. The elderly population, a group with much greater than average health care needs, will grow faster than the total population between 1998 and 2008, increasing the demand for health services, especially for home health care and nursing and personal care. As the baby boom generation ages, the incidence of stroke and heart disease will increase. Advances in medical technology will continue to improve the survival rate of severely ill and injured patients, who will then need extensive therapy. New technologies often lower the cost of treatment and diagnosis, but also enable identification and treatment of conditions not previously treatable. In addition, medical group practices and health networks will become larger and more complex, and will need more managerial and support workers.

Employment growth in the hospital segment will be the slowest within the health services industry, as it consolidates to control costs and as clinics and other alternate care sites become more common. Hospitals will provide more outpatient care, rely less on inpatient care, and streamline health care delivery operations. Job opportunities, however, will remain plentiful because hospitals employ a large number of people. The demand for dental care will increase due to population growth, greater retention of natural teeth by the middle-aged and older persons, and greater awareness of the importance of dental care and ability to pay for services. Rapid growth in other health services segments will mainly result from the aging of the population, new medical technologies, and the subsequent increase in demand for all types of health services. Also contributing to industry growth will be the shift from inpatient to less expensive outpatient care, made possible by technological improvements and Americans' increasing awareness and emphasis on all aspects of health. Various combinations of all these factors will assure robust growth in this massive, diverse industry.

The fastest growth is expected for workers in occupations concentrated outside the inpatient hospital sector, such as *medical assistants* and *personal care and home health aides*. Because of cost pressures, many health care facilities will adjust their staffing patterns to lower bottom-line labor costs. Where patient care demands and outside regulations allow, health care facilities will substitute lower-paid providers and

cross-train their workforce. Many facilities have cut the number of middle managers, while simultaneously creating new managerial positions as they diversify. Because traditional inpatient hospital positions are no longer the only option for many future health care workers, they must be flexible and forward-looking (chart).

Besides job openings due to employment growth, additional openings will result as workers leave the labor force or transfer to other occupations. Occupations with the most replacement openings are usually large with high turnover due to low pay and status, poor benefits, low training requirements, and a high proportion of young and part-time workers. Many are service occupations, such as nursing aides. Occupations with relatively few replacement openings, on the other hand, are those with high pay and status, lengthy training requirements, and a high proportion of full-time workers, such as physicians.

For some executive, administrative, and managerial occupations, rapid growth will be countered by restructuring to reduce administrative costs and streamline operations. The effects of office automation and other technological changes will slow employment growth in administrative support occupations, but because the employment base is large, replacement needs will still create substantial numbers of job openings. Slower growing service occupations will also have job openings due to replacement needs.

Many of the occupations projected to grow the fastest are concentrated in the health services industry. By 2008, employment in all industries of personal care and home health aides is projected to increase by 58 percent, medical assistants by 58 percent, physician assistants by 48 percent, and health information technicians by 44 percent.

Technological changes, such as increased laboratory automation, will also affect the demand for some occupations. For example, the use of robotics in blood analysis may limit growth of clinical laboratory technologists and technicians, although the nature of health care precludes wholesale productivity gains in many instances.

Although workers at all levels of education and training will continue to be in demand, in many cases it may be easier for job seekers with health-specific training to obtain jobs and advance. Specialized clinical training is a requirement for many jobs in health services and is an asset even for many administrative jobs that do not specifically require it.

Sources of Additional Information
For referrals to hospital human resources departments about local opportunities in health care careers, write to:

➢ American Hospital Association/American Society for Hospital Human Resources Administrators, One North Franklin, Chicago, IL 60606.

For information on educational programs for allied health occupations from the *Health Professions Education Directory*, contact:

➢ American Medical Association, 515 North State St., Chicago, IL 60610. Internet: **http://www.ama-assn.org**

There is also a wealth of information on health careers and job opportunities available on the Internet from schools, associations, and employers.

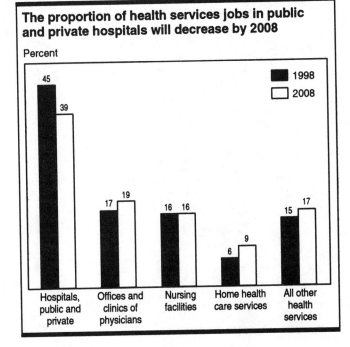

The proportion of health services jobs in public and private hospitals will decrease by 2008

Information on these occupations may be found in the 2000-01 *Occupational Outlook Handbook*.

- Cardiovascular technologists and technicians
- Chiropractors
- Clinical laboratory technologists and technicians
- Dental assistants
- Dental hygienists
- Dental laboratory technicians
- Dentists
- Dietitians and nutritionists
- Electroneurodiagnostic technologists
- Emergency medical technicians and paramedics
- Health information technicians
- Health services managers
- Licensed practical nurses
- Medical assistants
- Medical secretaries
- Nuclear medicine technologists
- Nursing and psychiatric aides
- Occupational therapists
- Ophthalmic laboratory technicians
- Opticians, dispensing
- Optometrists
- Personal care and home health aides
- Pharmacists
- Pharmacy technicians and assistants
- Physical therapists
- Physician assistants
- Physicians
- Podiatrists
- Psychologists
- Radiologic technologists
- Receptionists and information clerks
- Recreational therapists
- Registered nurses
- Respiratory therapists
- Social and human service assistants
- Social workers
- Speech-language pathologists and audiologists
- Surgical technologists
- Veterinarians

Hotels and Other Lodging Places

(SIC 70)

SIGNIFICANT POINTS

- Service and clerical jobs, most of which do not require postsecondary training, account for nearly 3 out of 4 jobs.

- Hotels employ many young workers and others in part-time and seasonal jobs.

- Average earnings are lower than in most other industries.

Nature of the Industry

Hotels and lodging places are as diverse as the many families and business travelers they accommodate. The industry includes all types of lodging, from upscale hotels to camp grounds. Other accommodations included in this category are motels, destination spas, inns, and boarding houses. In fact, over 59,000 establishments provided overnight accommodations to suit many different needs and budgets in 1997.

Establishments vary greatly in size and in the services they provide. *Hotels* and *motels* make up the majority of establishments and tend to provide more services than other lodging places. They consist of three basic types—*commercial*, *resort*, and *residential*. Most hotels and motels are *commercial* properties that cater mainly to business people, tourists, and other travelers who need accommodations for a brief stay. Commercial hotels and motels usually are located in cities or suburban areas and operate year round. Larger properties offer a variety of services for their guests, including coffee shops, restaurants, and cocktail lounges with live entertainment. Some even provide gift shops, newsstands, barber and beauty shops, laundry and valet services, theater and airline counters, swimming pools, and fitness centers and health spas.

Larger hotels and motels often have banquet rooms, exhibit halls, and spacious ballrooms to accommodate conventions, business meetings, wedding receptions, and other social gatherings. Conventions and business meetings are major sources of revenue for these hotels and motels.

Conference hotels, are fully self-contained entities specifically designed for meetings. They provide physical and recreational facilities for meetings in addition to state of the art audiovisual and technical equipment.

Resort hotels and *motels* offer luxurious surroundings with a variety of recreational facilities like swimming pools, golf courses, tennis courts, game rooms, and health spas, as well as planned social activities and entertainment. Resorts are located primarily in vacation destinations near mountains, the seashore, or other attractions. As a result, the business of many resorts fluctuates with the season. Some resort hotels and motels provide additional convention and conference facilities to encourage customers to combine business with pleasure. During their off season, they solicit conventions, sales meetings, and incentive tours to fill their otherwise empty rooms.

Residential hotels provide living quarters for permanent and semi-permanent residents. They combine the comfort of apartment living with the convenience of hotel services. Many have dining rooms and restaurants that are also open to the general public.

In addition to hotels and motels, *inns, campgrounds,* and *destination spas* provide lodging for overnight guests. *Inns* vary greatly in size, appearance, type of operation, and cost. Some inns are very large and provide services similar to those found in hotels, and others are quite small and often run by families. Their appeal is quaintness, unusual service, and decor. *Campgrounds,* including *trailer and recreational vehicle (RV) parks,* cater to people who enjoy recreational camping at moderate prices. Some campgrounds provide service stations, general stores, shower and toilet facilities, and coin-operated laundries. Although some are designed for overnight travelers only, others are for vacationers who stay longer. *Destination spas* offer an all-inclusive package with lodging, food, and spa programs included for a single fee. Most destination spas are small, with under 80 guestrooms.

In recent years, hotels, motels, camps, and RV parks affiliated with national chains have been growing rapidly. To the traveler, familiar chain establishments represent dependability and quality at predictable rates. Many chains are owned by national corporations, although others are independently-owned, but affiliated with a chain through a franchise agreement.

Increased competition and greater traveler sophistication have induced the chains to provide lodging to serve a variety of customer budgets and accommodation preferences. In general, these lodging places may be grouped into properties that offer luxury, all-suite, moderately priced, and economy accommodations. The number of "limited service" properties—economy lodging without lobbies, restaurants, lounges, and meeting rooms—has been growing. These properties are not as costly to build and operate. They appeal to budget-conscious family vacationers and travelers who are willing to sacrifice amenities for lower room prices.

All-suite facilities, especially popular with business travelers, offer a living room and a bedroom. These accommodations are aimed at travelers who require lodging for extended stays, families traveling with children, and business people needing to conduct small meetings without the expense of renting an additional room.

Increased competition has spurred many independently-owned and operated hotels and other lodging places to join national or international reservation systems, which allow travelers to make multiple reservations for lodging, airlines, and car rentals with one telephone call. Nearly all hotel chains operate on-line reservation systems through the Internet. For now, these Internet systems are complementing more established reservation systems; however, in the future a high percentage of lodging reservations will be made through the Internet.

Working Conditions

Work in hotels and other lodging places can be hectic, particularly for those providing check-in and checkout services. Hotel desk clerks must quickly, accurately, and cordially process large numbers of sometimes impatient and irate guests. Hotel managers often experience pressure and stress when coordinating a wide range of events such as conventions, business meetings, and social gatherings. Further, large groups of tourists can present unusual problems requiring extra work and long hours.

Because hotels are open around the clock, employees frequently work varying shifts. Employees who work the late shift generally receive additional compensation. Although managers who live in the hotel usually have regular work schedules, they may be called at any time in the event of an emergency. Those who are self-employed tend to work long hours and often live at the establishment.

Food preparation and food service workers in hotels must withstand the strain of working during busy periods and being on their feet for many hours. Kitchen workers lift heavy pots and kettles and work near hot ovens and grills. Job hazards include slips and falls, cuts, and burns, but injuries are seldom serious. Food service workers often carry heavy trays of food, dishes, and glassware. Many of these workers work part-time, including evenings, weekends, and holidays.

In 1998, work-related injuries and illnesses averaged 8.4 for every 100 full-time workers in hotels and other lodging places, compared to 7.1 for workers throughout private industry. Work hazards include burns from hot equipment, sprained muscles and wrenched backs from heavy lifting, and falls on wet floors.

Employment

Hotels and other lodging places provided almost 1.8 million wage and salary jobs in 1998. In addition, there were about 61,000 self-employed workers in the industry, who were found mostly in lodging places other than hotels and motels, such as inns, campgrounds, and destination spas.

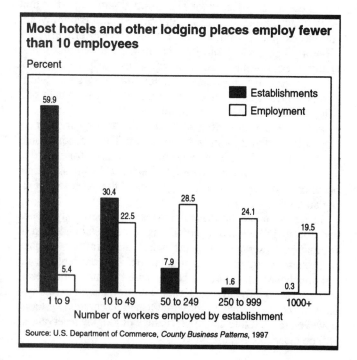

Most hotels and other lodging places employ fewer than 10 employees

Source: U.S. Department of Commerce, *County Business Patterns*, 1997

Employment in the hotel and motel industry is concentrated in densely populated cities and resort areas. Compared to establishments in other industries, hotels, motels, and other lodging places tend to be small. Over 90 percent employed fewer than 50 people; about 60 percent employ fewer than 10 workers (see chart). As a result, lodging establishments offer opportunities for those who are interested in owning and running their own business. Although establishments tend to be small, most jobs are in large hotels and motels with over 50 employees.

Many of the industry's workers are young because the industry provides first jobs to many new entrants to the labor force. About 20 percent of the workers were younger than age 25, compared to about 15 percent across all industries (table 1).

Table 1. Percent distribution of employment in hotels and other lodging places by age group, 1998

Age group	Hotels and motels	All industries
Total	100.0	100.0
16-19	6.9	5.4
20-24	13.4	9.5
25-34	24.5	23.9
35-44	26.0	27.5
45-54	16.4	21.0
55-64	9.2	9.8
65 and older	3.7	2.9

Occupations in the Industry

The vast majority of the workers in this industry—over 3 out of 4 in 1998—were employed in service and administrative support occupations (table 2). Workers in these occupations usually learn their skills on the job. Postsecondary education is not required for most entry-level positions; however, college training may be helpful for advancement in some of these occupations. For many clerical and service occupations, personality traits and special abilities may be more important than formal schooling. Traits most important for success in the hotel and motel industry are good communication skills; the ability to get along with people in stressful situations; a neat, clean appearance; and a pleasant manner.

Service occupations, by far the largest occupational group, account for 63 percent of the industry's employment. Most service jobs are in housekeeping and building service occupations—including maids, housekeepers, janitors, linen room attendants, and laundry workers—and in food preparation and service jobs—including chefs and cooks, waiters and waitresses, bartenders, food counter workers, and various kitchen workers.

Workers in *cleaning* and *housekeeping occupations* ensure that the lodging facility is clean and in good condition for the comfort and safety of guests. *Maids* and *housekeepers* clean lobbies, halls, guest rooms, and bathrooms. They make sure guests not only have clean rooms, but all the necessary furnishings and supplies. They change sheets and towels, vacuum carpets, dust furniture, empty waste-baskets, and mop bathroom floors. In large hotels, the housekeeping staff may include assistant housekeepers, floor supervisors, housekeepers, and executive housekeepers. *Janitors* help with the cleaning of the facility and perform minor maintenance work. They may fix leaky faucets, do some painting and carpentry, see that heating and air-conditioning equipment works properly, empty trash, mow lawns, and exterminate insects and rodents.

Table 2. Employment of wage and salary workers in hotels and other lodging places by occupation, 1998 and projected change, 1998-2008

(Employment in thousands)

Occupation	1998 Employment Number	1998 Employment Percent	1998-2008 Percent change
All occupations	1,776	100.0	17.6
Service	1,120	63.1	15.6
Janitors and cleaners, including maids and housekeeping cleaners	425	24.0	18.1
Waiters and waitresses	167	9.4	2.3
Cooks, restaurant	68	3.8	12.2
Amusement and recreation attendants	51	2.9	27.9
Dining room and cafeteria attendants and bar helpers	49	2.8	5.6
Food preparation workers	48	2.7	17.8
Food counter, fountain, and related workers	40	2.3	44.7
Bartenders	40	2.3	5.7
Institutional cleaning supervisors	32	1.8	12.8
Baggage porters and bellhops	28	1.6	16.9
Guards	27	1.5	16.9
Hosts and hostesses, restaurant, lounge, or coffee shop	25	1.4	15.4
Administrative support, including clerical	273	15.4	15.7
Hotel, motel, and resort desk clerks	155	8.7	13.8
Bookkeeping, accounting, and auditing clerks	22	1.3	6.9
Office and administrative support supervisors and managers	24	1.3	26.8
Executive, managerial, and administrative	124	7.0	19.8
Food service and lodging managers	39	2.2	6.4
General managers and top executives	31	1.7	26.2
Management support occupations	17	1.0	27.0
Precision production, craft and repair	81	4.6	21.7
Maintenance repairers, general utility	59	3.3	18.7
Marketing and sales	72	4.0	26.8
Cashiers	36	2.0	22.7
Operators, fabricators, and laborers	48	2.7	35.4
Laundry and drycleaning machine operators and tenders	27	1.5	38.1
Professional specialty	34	1.9	30.3
Agriculture, forestry, fishing and related	20	1.1	27.7
Laborers, landscaping and groundskeeping	19	1.1	27.6
All other occupations	3	0.2	27.7

Workers in the various *food service* occupations deal with customers in the dining room or at a service counter. *Waiters* and *waitresses* take customers' orders, serve meals, and prepare checks. In restaurants, they may describe chef's specials and suggest appropriate wines. In small establishments, they often set tables, escort guests to their seats, accept payments, and clear tables. They may also deliver room service orders to guests. In large restaurants, some of these tasks are assigned to other workers.

Hosts and *hostesses* welcome guests, show them to their tables, and give them menus. *Bartenders* fill beverage orders that waiters and waitresses take from the customers at tables and seated at the bar. *Dining room attendants* and *bar helpers* assist waiters, waitresses, and bartenders by clearing, cleaning, and setting up tables, and by keeping the serving areas stocked with linens, tableware, and other supplies. *Counter, fountain,* and *cafeteria workers* take orders, assemble, and serve food at fast food counters and cafeteria steam tables. They also may operate the cash register.

Workers in the various *food preparation* occupations prepare food in the kitchen. Beginners may advance to more skilled food preparation jobs with experience or specialized culinary training. *Food preparation workers* shred lettuce for salads, cut up food for cooking, and perform simple cooking under the direction of the chef or head cook. *Cooks and chefs* generally prepare a wide selection of dishes, often cooking individual servings to order. Large hotels employ cooks who specialize in the preparation of many different kinds of food. They may have such titles as salad chef, roast chef, sauce chef, or dessert chef. Chef positions generally are attained after years of experience and sometimes formal training, including apprenticeships. Large establishments also have *chief stewards* and *assistant stewards* who plan menus, purchase food, and supervise various kitchen personnel.

Many full-service hotels employ a uniformed staff to assist arriving and departing guests. *Bellhops* and *baggage porters* carry bags and escort guests to their rooms. *Door-keepers* help guests into and out of their cars or taxis, summon taxis, and carry baggage into the hotel lobby.

Administrative support positions account for about 15 percent of the jobs in hotels and other lodging places. Hotel desk clerks, secretaries, bookkeeping and accounting clerks, and telephone operators see to it that all operations of the front office are carried out smoothly. The majority of these workers are *hotel desk clerks*. They process reservations and guests' registration and checkout, monitor arrivals and departures, handle complaints, and receive and forward mail. The duties of hotel desk clerks depend on the size of the facility. In small lodging places one clerk or a manager may do everything. In large hotels, the duties are divided among several types of clerks. Although hotel desk clerks sometimes are hired from the outside, openings usually are filled by promoting other hotel employees such as bellhops and porters, credit clerks, and other administrative support workers.

Hospitality workers arrange special services for guests, such as city tours, theater tickets, baby sitting, personal maid service, or hotel reservations in other cities. Hotel *public relations workers* are usually executive assistants to top management. They must be completely familiar with all hotel operations and policies and act as spokespersons for the hotel. They may handle press, community, and consumer relations, and prepare radio or television announcements as well as newspaper and magazine articles. Some hotels combine the public relations functions with advertising or sales. *Advertising workers* design and coordinate advertising campaigns and oversee the production of promotional literature.

Hotels and motels employ many different types of *managers* to direct and coordinate the activities of the front office, kitchen, dining rooms, and the various hotel departments, such as housekeeping, accounting, personnel, purchasing, publicity, sales, and maintenance. Managers make decisions on room rates, establish credit policy, and have ultimate responsibility for resolving problems. In small hotels or inns, the manager also may perform much of the front office clerical work. In the smallest hotels and motels, the owners—sometimes a family team—do all the work necessary to operate the business.

General managers in large hotels often have several assistant managers, each responsible for a phase of operations. For example, *food* and *beverage managers* oversee restaurants, lounges, and catering operations. Large hotels and conference centers also employ *public relations* and *sales managers* to promote their image as well as to bring in business. Large hotels have many different sales managers, including convention managers, merchandise managers, foreign sales managers, and tour and agency managers. They often travel around the country selling their meeting, banquet, and convention facilities.

Hotels employ a variety of workers found in many other industries. Among these are cashiers, accountants, personnel workers, entertainers, recreation workers, and maintenance workers, such as stationary engineers, plumbers, and painters. Still others include guards and security officers, barbers, cosmetologists, valets, gardeners, and parking attendants.

Training and Advancement

Although the skills and experience needed by workers in this industry depend on the specific occupation, most entry-level jobs require little or no previous training. Basic tasks usually can be learned in a short time. Almost all workers in the hotel and motel industry undergo on-the-job training which usually is provided under the supervision of an experienced employee or manager. Some large chain operations have formal training sessions for new employees, and others have video training programs.

Hotel operations are becoming increasingly complex, with a greater emphasis being placed on specialized training. Therefore, the demand for people with special skills obtained in colleges, junior colleges, technical institutes, vocational schools, and high schools is increasing. Vocational courses and apprenticeship programs in food preparation, catering, and hotel and restaurant management, offered through restaurant associations and trade unions, provide training opportunities. Programs range in length from a few months to several years. Nearly 200 community and junior colleges offer 2-year degree programs in hotel and restaurant management. The Armed Forces also offer experience and training in food service.

Traditionally, many hotels filled first-level manager positions by promoting administrative support and service workers—particularly those with good communication skills, a solid educational background, tact, loyalty, and a capacity to endure hard work and long hours. People with these qualities still advance to manager jobs, but more recently lodging chains have primarily been hiring persons with 4-year college degrees in the liberal arts or other fields and starting them in trainee or junior management positions. Bachelor's and master's degree programs in hotel and restaurant management provide the strongest background for a career as a

hotel manager, with nearly 150 colleges and universities offering programs. Graduates of these programs are highly sought by employers in this industry. New graduates often go through on-the-job training programs before being given much responsibility. Eventually, they may advance to a top management position in a large chain operation.

Upper management positions, such as general manager, food and beverage manager, front office manager, or sales manager, generally require considerable formal training and job experience. Some department managers, such as comptrollers, purchasing managers, executive housekeepers, and executive chefs, generally require some specialized training and extensive on-the-job experience. To advance to positions with more responsibilities, managers frequently change employers or relocate to a chain property in another area.

For administrative support and service workers, advancement opportunities in the hotel industry vary widely. Some workers, such as housekeepers and janitors, generally have few opportunities for advancement. In large properties, however, some janitors may advance to supervisory positions. Hotel desk clerks, hospitality workers, and chefs, sometimes advance to managerial positions. Promotional opportunities from the front office often are greater than from any other department, because one has an excellent opportunity to learn the overall operation from this vantage point. Front office jobs are excellent entry-level jobs and can serve as a stepping stone to jobs in hospitality, public relations, advertising, sales, and management.

Advancement opportunities for chefs and cooks are better than those for most other service occupations. Cooks often advance to chef or to supervisory and management positions, such as executive chef, restaurant manager, or food and beverage manager. Some transfer to jobs in clubs, go into business for themselves, or become instructors of culinary arts.

Earnings

Earnings in hotels, motels, and other lodging places generally are much lower than the average for all industries. In 1998, average earnings for all nonsupervisory workers in hotels and motels were $8.92 an hour, or $279 a week, compared to $12.77 an hour, or $442 a week, for workers throughout private industry. Many workers in this industry earn the Federal minimum wage of $5.15 an hour. Some States have laws which establish a higher minimum wage. Federal laws, however, allow employers to pay below the minimum wage when an employee is expected to receive tips.

Food and beverage service workers as well as hosts and hostesses, doorkeepers, housekeepers, and bellhops and baggage porters derive their earnings from a combination of hourly earnings and customer tips. Waiters and waitresses often derive the majority of their earnings from tips, which vary greatly depending on menu prices and the volume of customers served. Many employers also provide free meals and furnish uniforms. Food service personnel may receive extra pay for banquets and other special occasions. In general, workers with the greatest skills, such as restaurant cooks, have the highest earnings, and workers who receive tips have the lowest. Earnings in the largest occupations in hotels and other lodging places appear in table 3.

Salaries of hotel managers and assistants are dependent upon the size and sales volume of the establishment and their specific duties and responsibilities. Managers may earn bonuses ranging up to 20 percent of their basic salary. In addition, they and their families may be furnished with lodging, meals, parking, laundry, and other services. Some hotels offer profit-sharing plans, tuition reimbursement, and other benefits to their employees.

About 10.6 percent of the workers in hotels and other lodging places are union members or are covered by union contracts, compared to 15.4 percent of workers in all industries combined.

Table 3. Median hourly earnings of the largest occupations in hotels and other lodging services, 1997

Occupation	Hotels and other lodging services	All industries
Cooks, restaurant	$8.69	$7.54
Maintenance repairers, general utility	8.19	10.89
Janitors and cleaners, except maids and housekeeping cleaners	7.37	7.44
Hotel desk clerks	7.05	7.05
Food preparation workers	7.01	6.42
Bartenders	6.65	5.94
Maids and housekeeping cleaners	6.37	6.74
Dining room and cafeteria attendants and bartender helpers	6.10	5.73
Amusement and recreation attendants	5.80	5.88
Waiters and waitresses	5.66	5.59

Outlook

Employment in hotels, motels, and other lodging places is expected to increase 18 percent over the 1998-2008 period, faster than the 15 percent growth projected for all industries combined. Job growth reflects rising personal income, an increase in the number of two-income families, continued low-cost airfares, emphasis on leisure-time activities, and growth of foreign tourism in the United States. In addition, special packages for short vacations and weekend travel should stimulate employment growth and, as more States allow some form of gambling, the hotel industry will increasingly invest in gaming, further fueling job growth.

Job opportunities should be concentrated in the largest hotel occupations, such as chefs and cooks, hotel desk clerks, and janitors and cleaners, including housekeepers. Many of these openings will arise in full-service hotels and resorts and spas. Because all-suite properties and budget hotels and motels do not have restaurants, dining rooms, lounges, or kitchens, these limited-service establishments offer a narrower range of employment opportunities for workers in the industry.

Employment outlook varies by occupation. Employment of hotel desk clerks is expected to grow rapidly as some of these workers assume responsibilities previously reserved for managers. However, the spread of computer technology will cause employment of other clerical workers—bookkeeping, accounting, and auditing clerks and secretaries, for example—to grow more slowly than the industry as a whole.

Employment of hotel managers and assistants is also expected to increase more slowly than the overall hotel industry due to the growth of economy-class establishments with fewer departments to manage. However, the trend toward chain-affiliated lodging places should provide managers with opportunities for advancement into general manager positions and corporate administrative jobs. Opportunities should be more limited for self-employed managers or owners of small lodging places.

Job turnover is relatively high in this industry, particularly in lodging places, other than hotels and motels. To attract and retain workers, the lodging industry is placing more emphasis on hiring and training. Nevertheless, many young workers and others are only looking for seasonal or part-time work, not a career. Therefore, job opportunities exist for first-time job seekers and people with a wider range of experience and skills, including those with limited skills.

Sources of Additional Information

For information on hospitality careers write to:

➢ Council on Hotel, Restaurant, and Institutional Education, 1200 17th St. NW., Washington, DC 20036-3097.
➢ The American Hotel and Motel Association, Information Center, Suite 600, 1201 New York Ave. NW., Washington, DC 20005.

General information on food and beverage service jobs is available from:

➢ National Restaurant Association, 1200 17th St. NW., Washington, DC 20036-3097.

Information about housekeeper and janitorial jobs may be obtained from a local State employment service office or from:

➢ Service Employees International Union, 1313 L St. NW., Washington, DC 20005.

Information on housekeeping management may be obtained from:

➢ National Executive Housekeepers Association, Inc., 1001 Eastwind Dr., Suite 301, Westerville, OH 43081. Phone: (800) 200-6342.

For information on the American Culinary Federation's apprenticeship and certification programs for cooks, write to:

➢ American Culinary Federation, P.O. Box 3466, St. Augustine, FL 32085.

Detailed information on the following occupations employed in hotels and other lodging places may by found in the 2000-01 *Occupational Outlook Handbook*:

● Chefs, cooks, and other kitchen workers
● Food and beverage service occupations
● Guards
● Hotel managers and assistants
● Janitors and cleaners and institutional cleaning supervisors
● Restaurant and food service managers

Management and Public Relations Services

(SIC 874)

SIGNIFICANT POINTS

- The management and public relations services industry is projected to be one of the fastest growing through the year 2008.

- Nearly one-fourth of all workers are self-employed.

- About 70 percent of workers have a bachelor's degree or higher; nearly half of all jobs are in managerial and professional occupations.

- This industry is one of the highest paying.

Nature of the Industry

Widespread management and public relations services firms influence how businesses, governments, and institutions make decisions, and in so doing, affect the lives of every American. Often working behind the scenes, these firms have a variety of functions. For example, a management consulting team recommends that a pharmaceutical company take a brand of pain reliever off the market. A construction management firm oversees the building of a new airport. A facilities support services firm manages the daily operations of a local hospital. A traffic consultant concludes that a major highway should be widened. Or a public relations firm issues a press release that is printed in newspapers across the country.

Firms in management and public relations services offer one or more resources that clients cannot provide themselves. Usually this resource is expertise—in the form of knowledge, experience, special skills, or creativity—but sometimes the resource is time or personnel that the client cannot spare. Clients are large and small, private-sector, for-profit firms; bodies of State, local, or the Federal Government; institutions, such as hospitals, universities, unions, and trade groups; and foreign governments or businesses.

The management and public relations services industry is diverse. In general, firms in management or other business consulting offer operational advice, those in public relations services advise and implement public exposure strategies, and firms in management or facility support services furnish administrative services. Management services and management consulting were by far the largest sectors, together accounting for most of the industry's revenue. The facilitiy support, business consulting, and public relations segments brought in the remaining revenue.

Management consulting firms advise on almost any aspect of corporate operations, including marketing; finance; corporate strategy and organization; manufacturing and technology; information systems and data processing; and human resources, benefits, and compensation. Depending on the nature of clients' problems and needs, management consulting firms might advise how to best enter a new market or increase the clients' share in an existing market. They might suggest how to get the most out of a computer network or which department or subsidiary should be sold, shut down, or merged. They might recommend how to adhere to Federal environmental regulations or when to issue a new public offering of stock. Occasionally, management consulting firms also help implement their advice.

Management consulting has grown rapidly over the past several decades, as businesses increasingly use consulting services. Using consultants is advantageous, because these experts are experienced, well trained, and abreast of the latest technologies, government regulations, and management and production techniques. In addition, consultants are cost efficient, because they can be hired temporarily and can objectively perform their duties, free of the influence of company politics.

Miscellaneous business consulting firms offer a variety of services similar to those of management consultants, but the former primarily offer technical expertise or advise clients on non-management issues. For example, an economic consultant might be hired to help a business project future product sales, or a traffic consultant might be retained to advise a city government on how much a proposed new tunnel would alleviate traffic congestion. This group includes sociological research firms, architectural consultants, educational consulting firms, city planners, and many others. In fact, there are highly specialized consultants with expertise in almost every business and government-related activity.

Public relations firms help secure favorable public exposure for their clients, advise them in the case of a sudden public crisis, and design strategies to help them attain a certain public image. Toward these ends, public relations firms analyze public or internal sentiment about clients; establish relationships with the media; write speeches and coach clients for interviews; issue press releases; and organize client-sponsored publicity events, such as contests, concerts, exhibits, symposia, and sporting and charity events. Clients of public relations firms include all types of business, institution, trade and public interest groups, and even some high profile individuals.

Lobbying firms, a special type of public relations firms, differ somewhat. Instead of attempting to secure favorable public opinion about their clients, they attempt to influence legislators in favor of their clients' special interests. Lobbyists often work for large businesses, industry trade organizations, unions, or public interest groups.

Management services and facility support services firms are similar but differ in one important respect. Management services firms administer other firms' properties, businesses, or projects and provide management personnel but not operating staff. In contrast, facility support services firms provide both management and staff. For example, a common type of management service is construction management. A corporation, real estate developer, or group of investors might hire a construction management firm to oversee a construction project to ensure that it is completed within certain time and cost constraints. The construction management firm prepares estimates of building costs and a project schedule; coordinates the work of designers, contractors, workers, and suppliers; and inspects the work as it progresses, to ensure that it conforms to plans, budget, quality standards, and the completion schedule. However, the construction management firm employs none of the construction workers, designers, or contractors; it only coordinates and administers the process.

Facility support services firms, on the other hand, might administer and staff various services at airports, correctional facilities, military installations, universities, hospitals, or corporate research and development complexes. Unlike management services firms, facility support services firms employ all of the workers necessary to run these facilities—managers, guards, maintenance and custodial staff, groundskeepers, and other workers.

Entry-level positions within the management and public relations industry start with very little responsibility. Striving for and displaying quality work results in more responsibility.

The vast majority of firms in the management and public relations services industry are small, primarily because new firms, particularly the consulting and public relations segments, can easily enter the industry. Licensing, certification, and large capital outlays seldom are necessary to become a management or business consultant, public relations specialist, or construction manager; and the work can be quite lucrative for those with the right education, experience, and contacts. As a result, many wage and salary workers in management and public relations services eventually leave established firms to go into business for themselves. In addition, after developing specialized expertise, people working in other industries often start their own consulting businesses; and some experienced workers perform consulting work after retiring.

Working Conditions

For most employees, working conditions in management and public relations services are similar to those for most office workers operating in a teamwork environment. The work is rarely hazardous, except in a few cases—such as for facility support workers contracted to run correctional institutions or construction management workers who must inspect construction sites. In 1998, the industry had only 2.5 injuries and illnesses per 100 full-time workers, compared to an average of 7.1 throughout private industry.

Most firms encourage employees to attend employer-paid time-management classes. This helps reduce the stress sometimes associated with working under strict time constraints. Also, with today's hectic lifestyle, many firms in this industry offer or provide health facilities or clubs for employees to maintain good health.

Not all employees in this industry work under identical conditions. In 1998, workers in the industry averaged 36.2 hours per week, a little above the national average. However, some must work long hours in stressful environments, as is often the case with lobbyists, consultants, construction man-

agers, and public relations writers, who frequently must meet hurried deadlines. Workers whose services are billed hourly—such as many business and management consultants and public relations specialists—are often under pressure to manage their time very carefully. Occasionally, some weekend work is also necessary, depending upon the job that's being performed. In addition, the increasing globalization of the marketplace compels some executives and consultants to travel extensively or live away from home for extended periods.

Employment

The management and public relations services industry had about 1 million wage and salary workers in 1998, and about 299,000 were self-employed. Management services and management consulting firms were the largest employers in the industry, accounting for nearly 79 percent of wage and salary jobs. Miscellaneous business consulting and facility support services made up 18 percent and public relations services, 3 percent.

The vast majority of establishments in this industry were fairly small, employing fewer than 5 workers (chart). Self-employed individuals operated many of these small firms. Despite the prevalence of small firms and self-employed workers, large firms tend to dominate the industry. Nearly 60 percent of jobs are found in only about 3 percent of the establishments, and some of the largest firms in the industry employ several thousand people.

Although employees in this industry work in all parts of the country, many workers are concentrated near large urban centers.

Occupations in the Industry

Although management and public relations services are fairly specialized, a variety of occupations are found in this industry (table 1). Some of these occupations, such as *public relations specialists* and *publicity writers*, are specific to only one segment of the industry whereas others, such as *bookkeeping, accounting,* and *auditing clerks* or *general managers,* can be found throughout the industry.

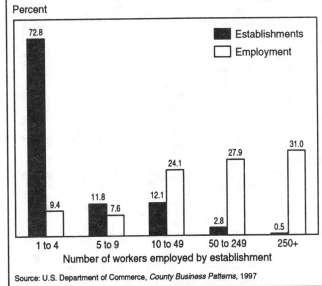

Three-fourths of establishments in management and public relations employ fewer than 5 people

Percent

Source: U.S. Department of Commerce, *County Business Patterns*, 1997

199

Table 1. Employment of wage and salary workers in management and public relations services by occupation, 1996 and projected change, 1998-2008

(Employment in thousands)

Occupation	1998 Employment Number	1998 Employment Percent	1998-2008 Percent change
All occupations	1,034	100.0	45.1
Executive, administrative, and managerial	298	28.9	47.3
General managers and top executives	73	7.1	41.3
Advertising, marketing, promotions, public relations and sales managers	22	2.1	60.2
Administrative services managers	21	2.0	65.7
Accountants and auditors	21	2.0	82.5
Financial managers	20	1.9	37.1
Management analysts	20	1.9	39.7
Administrative support, including clerical	251	24.3	30.6
Secretaries	44	4.2	16.2
General office clerks	35	3.4	47.0
Office and administrative support supervisors and managers	29	2.9	41.6
Bookkeeping, accounting, and auditing clerks	22	2.1	18.6
Receptionists and information clerks	18	1.7	45.4
Material recording, scheduling, dispatching, and distributing occupations	12	1.2	36.5
Data entry keyers	10	1.0	16.5
Professional specialty	188	18.2	67.4
Engineers	34	3.3	54.6
Computer support specialists	15	1.5	96.6
Systems analysts	13	1.3	118.4
Social scientists	13	1.3	38.8
Public relations specialists	11	1.1	48.4
Physical scientists	11	1.1	68.6
Teachers, librarians, and counselors	10	1.0	183.9
Regstered nurses	10	1.0	45.6
Technicians and related support	73	7.1	35.7
Computer programmers	26	2.5	24.1
Health technicians and technologists	20	1.9	45.6
Engineering technicians	13	1.3	45.6
Service	66	6.4	42.1
Protective service occupations	18	1.7	72.7
Janitors and cleaners, including maids and housekeeping cleaners	16	1.6	31.1
Food preparation and service occupations	11	1.1	18.2
Marketing and sales	61	5.9	45.1
Precision production, craft, and repair	53	5.1	40.5
Mechanics, installers, and repairers	18	1.7	38.6
Construction trades	16	1.6	40.1
Operators, fabricators, and laborers	36	3.5	42.6
Helpers, laborers, and material movers, hand	20	1.9	40.1
All other occupations	7	0.7	45.5

Compared to other industries, a relatively high proportion of workers in the industry are highly educated. Over 70 percent of those in management and public relations services have a bachelor's degree or higher, compared to one-quarter of the workers throughout the rest of the economy. Certain jobs may have stringent entry requirements. For example, some management consulting firms only hire workers who have a master's degree in business administration (MBA). Other positions can only be attained after many years of related experience.

In management and public relations services, workers in *executive, administrative,* and *managerial* occupations and *administrative support* occupations make up 53 percent of employment. These same occupations account for 29 percent of workers across the entire economy. These workers comprise a disproportionate share of jobs in this industry because they not only manage and administer their own firms, but often manage clients' businesses or properties as well. For example, office management services and facilities support firms might need only a handful of managers, bookkeepers, and secretaries to handle their own affairs, but need many more to administer each office or facility it contracts to manage.

General managers and *top executives,* the largest managerial occupation in the industry, includes both the highest level managers—such as chief executive officers and vice presidents—and many middle managers with duties too diverse to classify elsewhere. Managers at the top shape company policy, often with the help of other executives or a board of directors. They oversee all activities of the firm, coordinate duties of subordinate executives and managers, and often bear ultimate responsibility for a firm's performance. At the middle manager level, they may oversee the activities of one department or, when working for a management services firm, all the activities of one or more establishments, properties, or construction ventures. These jobs are found throughout the industry, but they are particularly concentrated in the management services and facility support services segments.

Management analysts, also called *management consultants,* are the highest profile employees in the management consulting industry. Their work is quite varied, depending on the nature of the project and the client's needs. In general, consultants study and analyze business-related problems, synthesizing information from many sources, and recommend solutions. Suggested solutions can range from overhauling a client's computer systems, offering early retirement incentives to middle managers, switching health plans, improving just-in-time inventory systems, hiring public relations firms, or selling troublesome parts of businesses. Because of the varied nature of these jobs, firms hire workers with diverse backgrounds, such as engineering, finance, actuarial science, chemistry, and business. Many firms require consultants to have MBA's, whereas others hire workers who have bachelor's degrees only. Many workers have experience in other industries, prior to entering management consulting work.

Construction managers work almost exclusively for construction management firms in the industry. In construction industries, the term "construction manager" is sometimes used to refer to the jobs of constructors, construction superintendent, general construction manager, project supervisor, and any number of contractors. In the management services segment of this industry, construction managers are highly trained or experienced workers who control the entire construction process. Through precise scheduling and cost estimation techniques, these managers oversee projects to insure they are completed on time and at a reasonable cost. Their work requires a thorough understanding of the construction process. As a result, most construction managers have an extensive educational background—in subjects such as architecture, engineering, construction technology, law, and business administration—as well as many years of related construction experience before entering this occupation.

Facility managers coordinate the physical workplace with the people and work of an organization. While specific tasks assigned to facility managers vary substantially, depending on the organization, responsibilities can be categorized as operations and maintenance; real estate; project planning and management; communication; finance; quality assessment; facility function; and human and environmental factors. Facility managers suggest and oversee renovation projects for a variety of reasons, ranging from improving efficiency to ensuring that facilities meet government regulations and environmental, health, and security standards. In addition, the facility manager continually monitors a facility to ensure that it remains safe, secure, and well maintained. Often, the facility manager directs maintenance, grounds, and custodial staff.

Other executive, administrative, and managerial occupations include *financial managers*, who prepare financial statements and assess the financial health of firms. Often, they must have at least a bachelor's degree in accounting or finance. As one might expect, most *marketing, advertising,* and *public relations managers* in the industry are employed in public relations firms where they manage publicity campaigns and supervise *public relations specialists* and *publicity writers*, discussed below. *Administrative services managers* typically administer a firms' support services, overseeing secretaries, data entry keyers, bookkeepers, and other clerical staff. In the management services industry, they also often supervise a clients' clerical and support staff. *Accountants* and *auditors* monitor firms' financial transactions and often report to financial managers.

Administrative support positions in management and public relations services resemble those in other industries. Management and facility support services firms often staff clients' businesses, so administrative support workers are needed in large numbers. Particularly numerous are *secretaries*—the single largest occupation in the industry—*general office clerks*, and *bookkeeping, accounting,* and *auditing clerks*, who record and classify financial data. The industry also employs many *clerical supervisors* and *managers*, who oversee the support staff, often reporting to administrative services managers.

One of the industry's largest professional specialty occupations is *public relations specialists* and *publicity writers*, almost all of whom work in the public relations segment of the industry. Under the guidance of public relations managers, these workers design, implement, and analyze public relations strategies and materials. They write press releases, contact people in the media, encourage their clients to sponsor special events, prepare clients for interviews or crises, and advise them on how to achieve a desired public image. In almost all cases, workers in these jobs must have strong writing skills and a bachelor's degree; applicants with degrees in communications, journalism, English, or business and prior job experience are preferred.

Designers in this industry are mostly either *industrial designers* or *interior designers*. Industrial designers create or improve designs of manufactured items, usually with the goal of making a product more efficient or aesthetically pleasing. Most of these workers are employed by management or business consulting firms. Interior designers plan and furnish offices or other commercial establishments, keeping in mind the functional and aesthetic needs of the client. Many interior designers in the industry work for facility support services firms.

Systems analysts, computer scientists, and *computer engineers* design new computer systems or redesign old systems for new applications. For example, a systems analyst from a management consulting firm might be hired by a wholesale firm to implement an online inventory database. In the consulting segments of this industry, systems analysts, computer scientists, and computer engineers are sometimes referred to simply as "consultants."

Compared to the primary occupational groups discussed above, the industry has relatively few jobs in service occupations or technicians and related support occupations. The most common service occupations are *janitors and cleaners*, who keep offices and other facilities clean and orderly, and *food preparation and service workers,* who prepare and serve meals in business or institutional cafeterias. These occupations are found throughout the industry, but many food preparation and service workers are employed in facilities support services firms.

Technicians and related support occupations include *computer programmers*, who write programs and create software—often in close conjunction with systems analysts—and *engineering technicians*, who aid engineers in research and development. Like systems analysts and engineers, persons in these occupations work primarily in the business and management consulting segments of the industry.

Management and public relations service firms do not produce any goods; and as a result, employ relatively few workers in sales and production occupations. Marketing and sales occupations; precision production, craft, and repair occupations; and the remaining occupational groups make up only about 15 percent of industry employment.

Training and Advancement

Training and advancement opportunities vary widely within management and public relations services, but most jobs in the industry are similar in three respects. First, clients usually hire management and public relations firms based on the expertise of their staffs, so proper training of employees is vital to the success of firms. Second, although a bachelor's degree or higher is generally preferred by employers, most jobs require also extensive on-the-job training or related experience. Third, advancement opportunities are best for workers with the highest levels of education.

The management and public relations services industry offers excellent opportunities for self-employment. Because capital requirements are low, highly experienced workers can start their own businesses fairly easily and cheaply; and every year, thousands of workers in this industry go into business for themselves. Some of these workers come from established management and public relations services firms, whereas others leave industry, government, or academic jobs to start their own businesses.

Most organizations need prospective employees to possess a variety of skills. To a large extent, a degree is only one desired qualification. Workers must also possess a proven analytical and problem solving ability; excellent written and verbal communications skills; experience in a particular specialty; assertiveness and motivation; a strong attention to detail; and a willingness to work long hours, if necessary.

Whereas very few universities or colleges offer formal programs of study in management consulting, many fields provide a suitable background. These include most areas of business and management, as well as computer and information sciences and engineering. Management consulting firms also provide extensive training on the job. The method and extent of training can vary, based on the type of consulting and the nature of the firm. Information systems, industrial production, and other highly technical consulting requires particularly extensive formal training; but training for other types of consulting work is often less rigorous.

There are management and leadership classes and seminars available throughout the United States; some are hosted by volunteer senior executives and management experts, representing a variety of businesses and industries. Some large firms invest a great deal of time and money in training programs, educating new hires in formal classroom settings over several weeks or even months, and some even have separate training facilities. Small firms often combine formal and on-the-job training.

Most management consulting firms have two entry-level positions. Workers who hold bachelor's degrees usually start as research associates; those with graduate degrees usually begin work as consultants. Successful workers progress through the ranks from research associate to consultant, management consultant, senior consultant, junior partner, and after many years, to senior partner. In some firms, however, it is very difficult for research associates to progress to the next level without further education. As a result, many management consulting firms offer tuition assistantships, grants, or reimbursement plans, so workers can attain the MBA or another degree.

In business consulting firms, workers usually have extensive formal education, such as a master's or doctoral degree, in a relevant field. Additionally, few start in business consulting firms without some prior experience. Often, they have worked as university or college professors or as researchers in government or private industry. New entrants normally begin as research assistants and work under experienced consultants, until they are able to carry out projects independently.

In public relations, employers prefer applicants with degrees in communications, journalism, English, or business. Some 4-year colleges and universities have begun to offer a concentration in public relations. Because there is keen competition for entry-level public relations jobs, workers are encouraged to gain experience through internships, co-op programs, or one of the formal public relations programs offered across the country. However, these programs are not available everywhere, so most public relations workers get the bulk of their training on the job. At some firms, this training consists of formal classroom education; but in most cases, workers train under the guidance of senior account executives or other experienced workers, gradually familiarizing themselves with public relations work. Entry level workers often start as research or account assistants and may be promoted to account executive, account supervisor, vice president, and executive vice president.

Voluntary accreditation programs for public relations specialists and management consultants, respectively, are offered by the Public Relations Society of America and the Institute of Management Consultants. Both programs are recognized marks of competency in the profession and require that workers be employed in the field for several years.

Almost all workers in management services and facility support services receive on-the-job training and the remainder usually have prior work experience in a related field. Most managerial and supervisory workers gain experience informally, overseeing a few workers or part of a project under the close supervision of a senior manager. Although it is less common, some large firms offer formal management training.

Workers who advance to high-level managerial or supervisory jobs in management services or facility support services firms usually have an extensive educational background. For example, a worker with an electrical engineering degree might start work in a construction management firm as a field inspector and advance quickly. On the other hand, a worker without such a degree, but with many years of construction experience, might also hold the position of field inspector. However, the latter employee will be at a disadvantage for further advancement. Frequently, the highly technical nature of work in these firms makes it difficult for less educated workers to advance.

Earnings

Earnings in management and public relations services typically are considerably higher than the average for the rest of the private sector of the economy. The average earnings of nonsupervisory workers in the industry were significantly higher than the private sector in general. Management and public relations workers' weekly average earnings were $623 in 1998, compared to $442 for workers throughout private industry. Earnings in largest occupations in management and public relations services appear in table 2.

Table 2. Median hourly earnings of the largest occupations in management and public relations services, 1997

Occupation	Management and public relations services	All industries
General managers and top executives ...	$43.95	$26.05
Financial managers	30.17	25.19
Marketing, advertising, and public relations workers	24.59	25.61
Computer programmers	22.32	22.61
Administrative services managers	17.76	20.35
Accountants and auditors	17.34	17.66
First-line supervisors and managers/supervisors-clerical and administrative support workers ...	15.03	14.26
Secretaries, except legal and medical	12.58	11.00
Bookkeeping, accounting, and auditing clerks	12.01	10.80
General office clerks	9.55	9.10

These data do not reflect earnings for self-employed workers, who are often paid very well. Also, both managerial workers and high-level professionals can make considerably more than the industry average. According to a 1997 survey by the Association of Management Consulting Firms, total cash compensation (salary plus bonus/profit sharing) for research associates was $38,900; entry-level consultants, $50,500; management consultants, $69,700; senior consultants, $96,800; junior partners, $151,100; and senior partners, $266,700.

According to a 1998 survey conducted by Abbot, Langer and Associates, the median annual cash compensation for entry-level junior consultants was $40,000; consultants, $51,500; senior consultants, $62,000; principal consultants, $63,100; senior or executive vice president (little or no ownership interest in the firm), $110,000; and senior or executive vice president (ownership interest), $128,500.

In addition to a straight salary, many workers receive additional compensation, such as profit sharing, stock ownership, or performance-based bonuses. In some firms, bonuses can constitute one-third of annual pay.

Less than 2 percent of workers in management and public relations services belong to unions or are covered by union contracts, compared to 15.4 percent of workers throughout private industry.

Outlook

Between 1998 and 2008, wage and salary jobs in the management and public relations services industry are expected to grow by 45 percent—triple the 15 percent growth projected for all industries combined, ranking it among the most rapidly growing industries (chart). Projected job growth can be primarily attributed to the increasing complexity of business. Among other things, today's managers must deal with rapid technological innovations, changes in government regulations, growing environmental concerns, and the continuing reduction of trade barriers resulting in an increasingly global economy. Because it has become difficult to keep abreast of these changes, corporations, institutions, and governments will increasingly need well-trained, well-informed management and public relations services professionals.

Accompanying this changing business environment will be new competitive pressures that will also help spur industry growth. Firms today must produce higher quality goods and services more cheaply, or else lose business to more efficient domestic or foreign competitors. To cut costs, firms increasingly turn to "outsourcing," which means eliminating some in-house staff—such as internal public relations specialists or office managers—and contracting with outside firms to handle these functions. Often, these outside firms are more expensive than in-house workers in the short run; but are advantageous, because they can easily be dismissed, once they are no longer needed. As businesses seek to cut costs over the long term, the practice of outsourcing should become even more common, boosting growth of the management and public relations services industry.

Each segment of the industry will grow at a different rate, for a variety of reasons. The management consulting segment will continue to grow rapidly, as demand for management consulting services increase. But in this maturing market, mergers, acquisitions, and downsizing will become more common, as firms compete by attempting to offer a broader range of consulting services. The resulting consolidation will temper employment growth.

The public relations segment should grow faster than in recent years, due to the growing importance of business media and the corresponding role of public relations. However, the management services and facility support services sectors are being affected by competition from other establishments

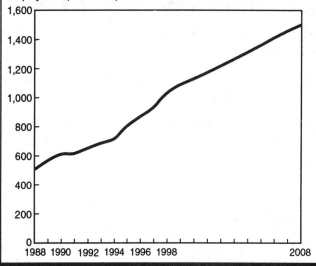

Employment in the management and public relations industry nearly doubled over the 1988-98 period, and is expected to grow by 45 percent over the 1998-2008 period

Employment (thousands)

providing one specialized service, such as janitorial or guard services.

Sources of Additional Information

For more information about career opportunities in management consulting, contact:

➢ ACMF—The Association of Management Consulting Firms, 521 Fifth Ave., New York, NY 10175-3598. Internet: **www.amcf.org**

For a brochure on careers in public relations, contact:

➢ Public Relations Society of America, Inc., 33 Irving Place, New York, NY 10003. Internet: **www.prsa.org**

For further information on career opportunities in construction management, write to:

➢ Construction Management Association of America, 7918 Jones Branch Dr., Suite 540, McLean, VA 22102. Internet: **www.cmaa.org**

Additional information about careers in facility management is available from:

➢ International Facility Management Association, One East Greenway Plaza, Suite 1100, Houston, TX 77046. Internet: **www.ifma.org**

In addition, information on the following occupations found in the management and public relations services industry appears in the 2000-01 *Occupational Outlook Handbook*:

- Administrative services and facility managers
- Advertising, marketing, and public relations managers
- Construction managers
- Designers
- Financial managers
- General managers and top executives
- Management analysts
- Public relations specialists

Motion Picture Production and Distribution

(SIC 781, 782)

SIGNIFICANT POINTS

- Employment is projected to grow rapidly, with keen competition expected for the more glamorous jobs—actors, directors, and producers.

- Although many films are shot on location throughout the United States and abroad, employment is centered in several major cities, particularly New York and Los Angeles.

- Many workers have formal training, but experience, professionalism, talent, and creativity are the most important factors for getting many jobs in this industry.

Nature of the Industry

In its early years, the motion picture industry was synonymous with Hollywood, whose few major studios produced only newsreels and feature films. Over the years, these studios have been joined by several medium-size companies and many small, independent companies that have adapted to changes in the industry created by the advent of television, cable television, videocassette recorders, and the Internet. Today, many films are produced for television and the home video market, including music videos and movies made for television.

Making a movie can be a difficult, yet rewarding experience. However, it is also a very risky one. Although thousands of movies are produced each year, only a small number of these account for most box office receipts. Most films do not make a full return on their investment from domestic box office revenues, so filmmakers rely on profits from other markets, such as broadcast and cable television, videocassette sales and rentals, and foreign distribution. In fact, major film companies are receiving a growing portion of their revenue from abroad. These cost pressures have reduced the number of film production companies—as of mid 1998, seven major studios produced most of the television and movie productions released nationally. Smaller and independent filmmakers are finding it difficult to finance new productions, as large motion picture production companies prefer to support established filmmakers.

In addition to feature films, workers in this industry produce a variety of other types of films. Documentary films—chronicling actual events with real people and using film clips and interviews—have become very popular in recent years. Documentaries offer excellent job and training opportunities for beginners because they do not require the employment of actors and can be made with a small crew and little equipment, which often can be rented. Also, educational films, which vary from "do-it-yourself" projects to exercise films, are growing in popularity. Many film production jobs are also found in advertising agencies that make commercials. Production of these films offers an excellent learning experience for beginning filmmakers.

In addition, many business, industrial, and government films promote an organization's image, provide information on its activities or products, or aid in fund raising or worker training. Some of these films are short enough that they can be released to the public through the Internet. Although many of these films are made by professional film companies, many are also made by in-house audiovisual departments and film staffs of business, industry, or government organizations.

Working Conditions

Most individuals in this industry work in clean, comfortable surroundings. Shooting outside the studio or "on location," however, may require working in adverse weather conditions. Regardless of whether actors and actresses, directors, producers, cinematographers, and camera operators work in the studio or on location, they need stamina to withstand the heat of studio and stage lights, unpleasant and sometimes dangerous conditions on location, long and irregular hours, and travel.

Directors and producers often work under stress as they try to meet schedules, stay within budget, and resolve personnel and production problems. Actors and actresses, directors, producers, cinematographers, and camera operators face the anxiety of rejection and intermittent employment. Writers and editors must deal with criticism and demands to restructure and rewrite their work many times until the producer and director are finally satisfied. All writers must be able to withstand such criticism and disappointment; freelance writers are under the added pressure of always looking for new jobs. In spite of these difficulties, many people find that the glamour and excitement of filmmaking more than compensate for the frequently demanding and uncertain nature of careers in motion pictures.

Unions are very important in this industry. Virtually all film production companies and television networks sign contracts with union locals, mandating the hiring of union workers. When this occurs, nonunion workers can be hired for a short time, after which they must either join the union or be replaced with union workers. Actors who appear in filmed entertainment—including television, commercials, and movies—belong to the Screen Actors Guild, Inc.; those in television generally belong to the American Federation of Television and Radio Artists. Film and television directors belong to the Directors Guild of America. Art directors, cartoonists, editors, costumers, scenic artists, set designers, camera operators, sound technicians, projectionists, and shipping, booking, and other distribution employees belong to the International Alliance of Theatrical Stage Employees and Motion Picture Machine Operators (I.A.T.S.E.), or the United Scenic Artists Association. Opera and stage performers (including Broadway productions), belong to the Actors Equity Association.

Employment

In 1998, there were about 270,000 wage and salary jobs in the motion picture production and distribution industry. Most of the workers were in motion picture production and services. They involved casting, acting, directing, editing, film processing, motion picture and videotape reproduction, and equipment and wardrobe rental. Although seven major studios produce most of the motion pictures released in the United States, many small companies are used as contractors throughout the process. Most motion picture and distribution establishments employ fewer than 10 workers (chart).

Many additional individuals work in the motion picture production and distribution industry on a freelance, contract, or part-time basis, but accurate statistics on their numbers are not available. Many people in the film industry are self-employed, independent contractors. They sell their services to anyone who needs them, often working on productions for many different companies during the year. Competition for these jobs is intense, and many people are unable to earn a living solely from freelance work.

Employment in the production of motion pictures and other films for television is centered in Los Angeles and New York City. Studios are also located in Florida, Texas, and other parts of the country. In addition, many films are shot on location throughout the United States and abroad. In television, most opportunities are at the headquarters of the major networks in New York City, Los Angeles, Atlanta, and, to a lesser extent, Chicago.

Occupations in the Industry

The length of the credits at the end of most feature films gives an idea of the variety of workers involved in producing and distributing films. The motion picture industry employs workers in every major occupational group. Nevertheless, about 2 out of 5 salaried workers held professional and technical jobs and about 14 percent worked in administrative support (table 1).

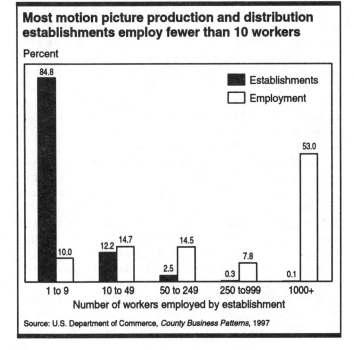

Most motion picture production and distribution establishments employ fewer than 10 workers

Percent

- Establishments
- Employment

Number of workers employed by establishment	Establishments	Employment
1 to 9	84.8	10.0
10 to 49	12.2	14.7
50 to 249	2.5	14.5
250 to 999	0.3	7.8
1000+	0.1	53.0

Source: U.S. Department of Commerce, *County Business Patterns*, 1997

Jobs in the industry can be broadly classified according to the three phases of filmmaking: Preproduction, production, and postproduction. Preproduction is the planning phase. This includes budgeting, casting, finding the right location, set and costume design, set construction, and scheduling. Production is the actual making of the film. The number of people involved in the production phase can vary from a few for a documentary film to hundreds for a feature film. It is during this phase that the actual filming is done. Postproduction activities take place in the editing rooms and recording studios in which the film is shaped into its final form.

Some individuals work in all three phases. *Producers*, for example, are involved in every phase from beginning to end. These workers look for ideas that they believe can be turned into lucrative film projects or television shows. They may see many films, read hundreds of manuscripts, and maintain numerous contacts with literary agents and publishers. Producers are also responsible for all financial aspects of a film, including finding financing for its production. The producer works closely with the director on the selection of script, principal members of the cast, and filming locations, because these decisions greatly affect the cost of a film. Once financing is obtained, the producer works out a detailed budget and sees to it that the production costs stay within that budget. In a large production, the producer also works closely with *production managers* who are in charge of crews, travel, casting, and equipment. For television shows, much of this process requires especially tight deadlines.

Directors translate the script to film and are involved in every stage of production. They may supervise hundreds of people, from scriptwriters to costume and set designers. Directors are in charge of all technical and artistic aspects of the film or television show. They conduct auditions and rehearsals and approve the location, scenery, costumes, choreography, and music. In short, they direct the entire cast and crew during shooting. *Assistant directors* help them with such details as handling extras, transportation of equipment, and arrangements for food and accommodations. Some directors assume multiple roles, such as *director-producer* or *writer-producer-director*. Successful directors must know how to hire the right people and create effective teams.

Preproduction occupations. Before a film or a television program moves into the production phase, it begins with an idea which *scriptwriters* turn into a script. They either develop an original idea or take an existing literary work and adapt it into a screenplay or television pilot (a sample episode of a proposed television series). Scriptwriters work closely with producers and directors. Sometimes they prepare a shooting script that has instructions on shots, camera angles, and lighting. They frequently make changes to reflect the directors' and producers' ideas and desires. The work, therefore, requires not only creativity, but also an ability to write and rewrite many script versions under pressure. Although the work of feature film screenwriters usually ends when the shooting begins, writing for television usually is a continuous process.

Feature film writers usually have many years of experience and work on a free-lance basis. Many start as copywriters in advertising agencies and as writers for educational film companies, government audiovisual departments, or in-house corporate film divisions. These jobs not only serve as a good training ground for beginners but also have greater job security than freelancing.

Art directors design the physical environment of the film or television set to create the mood called for by the script. Television art directors may design elaborate sets for use in situation comedies or commercials. They supervise many different people, including *illustrators*, *scenic designers*, *model makers*, *carpenters*, *painters*, *electricians*, *laborers*, *set decorators*, *costume designers*, and *makeup* and *hairstyling artists*. These positions can provide an entry into the motion picture industry. Many start in these jobs in live theater productions and then move back and forth between the stage, film, and television.

Production occupations. *Actors* and *actresses* entertain and communicate with the audience through their interpretation of dramatic roles. Only a small number achieve recognition in motion pictures or television. Many are cast in supporting roles or as walk-ons. Some start as background performers with no lines to deliver. Also called "extras," these are the people in the background—crowds on the street, working in offices, or dancing at a ball. Others perform stunts, such as driving cars in chase scenes or falling from high places. Although a few actors and actresses find parts in feature films straight out of drama school, most support themselves by working for many years outside of the industry. Most acting jobs are found through an agent. Beginners and lesser known actors and actresses usually register with several agents, who find auditions that may lead to acting assignments.

As the industry changes and becomes more technological, so does the role of the actor. New issues for actors include the use of digital effects using electronic computer-made images and old file footage to create a scene that never really existed. For example, movies now are able to combine various special effect techniques to bring back long-extinct dinosaurs and recreate historical scenes. Computer technology has opened up new opportunities for actors to work in interactive media. Software has advanced to the point that live action film and video can be incorporated into both computer programs and CD-ROM.

Cinematographers, camera operators, and gaffers work together to capture the scenes in the script on film. *Cinematographers* compose the film shots to reflect the mood the director wishes to create. They do not usually operate the camera; instead, they plan and coordinate the actual filming. *Camera operators* handle all camera movements and perform the actual shooting. *Assistant camera operators* check the equipment, load the camera, operate the slate and clapsticks (now electronic), and take care of the equipment. *Commercial camera operators* specialize in shooting commercials. This experience translates easily into documentary work.

Gaffers, or lighting technicians, set up different kinds of lighting needed for filming. They work for the *director of photography*, who plans all lighting needs. Many individuals get started in these occupations by just helping out on sets; they run errands, move things, and help with props.

Sound engineers, recordists, and *boom operators* record dialogue, sounds, music, and special effects during the filming. Sound engineers are the "ears" of the film. They supervise all sound generated during filming. They select microphones and the level of sound from mixers and synthesizers to assure the best sound quality. Recordists help to set up the equipment and are in charge of the individual tape recorders. Boom operators handle long booms with microphones that are moved from one area of the set to another. Because more filming is done on location and the equipment has become compact, lighter, and simpler to operate, one person often performs many of the above functions.

Special effects technicians create the movie "magic." Through their imagination, creativity, and skill, they can create anything required by the script, from talking animals to flaming office buildings and earthquakes. Many begin as stage technicians or scenic designers. They not only need a good imagination, but also must be part carpenter, plumber, electrician, and electronics expert. These workers must be familiar with many ways of achieving a desired special effect because each job requires different skills. Computer skills have become very important in this field. Some areas of television and film production, including animation and visual effects, now rely heavily on computer technology. Although there was a time when elaborate computer animation was restricted to blockbuster movies, much of the 3-dimensional work being generated today is happening in small-to mid-sized companies. Some specialists create "synthespians"—realistic digital humans—which appear mainly in science fiction productions. These digital images are often used when a stunt or scene is too dangerous for an actor.

Postproduction occupations. One of the most important tasks in filmmaking and television production is editing. After the film is shot and processed, *editors* study footage, select the best shots, and assemble them in the most effective way. Their goal is to create dramatic continuity and the right pace for the desired mood. Editors first organize the footage and then structure the sequence of the film by splicing and resplicing the best shots. They must have a good eye and understand the subject of the film and the director's intentions. The ability to work with digital media is also becoming increasingly important. Strong computer skills are mandatory for most jobs. However, few industry-wide standards exist, so companies often look for people with skills in the hardware/software they are currently using.

Assistant editors or *dubbing editors* select the sound track and special sound effects to produce the final combination of sight and sound as it appears on the screen. *Editing room assistants* help with the splicing, patching, rewinding, coding, and storing of the film. Some television networks have *film librarians*, who are responsible for organizing, filing, cataloging, and selecting footage for the film editors. There is no one way of entering the occupation of editor; however, experience as a film librarian, sound editor, or assistant editor—plus talent and perseverance—usually help.

Sound effects editors or *audio recording engineers* perform one of the final jobs in postproduction. They add prerecorded and live sound effects and background music by manipulating various elements of music, dialogue, and background sound to fit the picture. Their work is increasingly computer-driven as electronic equipment replaces conventional tape recording devices. The best way to gain experience in sound editing is through work in radio stations, with music groups, in music videos, or adding audio to Internet sites.

After the film or television show is finished, *marketing personnel* develop the marketing strategy for films. They estimate the demand for the film and the audience to whom it will appeal, develop an advertising plan, and decide where and when to release the film. *Advertising workers* or "unit publicists" write press releases and short biographies of actors, actresses, and directors for newspapers and magazines. They may also set up interviews or television appearances for the stars or director to promote a film. *Sales workers* sell the finished product. Many production companies have their own staff which distributes, leases, and sells their films and made-for-television programs to theater owners and television networks. The best way to enter sales is to start by selling advertising time for television stations.

Table 1. Employment of wage and salary workers in motion picture production and distribution by occupation, 1998 and projected change, 1998-2008

(Employment in thousands)

Occupation	1998 Employment Number	1998 Employment Percent	1998-2008 Percent change
All occupations	270	100.0	16.9
Professional specialty	95	35.2	24.3
Actors, directors and producers	64	23.5	25.6
Artists and commercial artists	7	2.5	26.7
Photographers and camera operators	3	1.1	17.7
Operators, fabricators, and laborers	68	25.3	15.5
Helpers, laborers, and material movers, hand	50	18.5	17.1
Machine setters, setup operators, operators and tenders	8	2.9	3.2
Industrial truck and tractor operators	7	2.6	17.7
Hand workers, including assemblers and fabricators	3	1.0	17.7
Administrative support, including clerical	37	13.7	6.5
Shipping, receiving, and traffic clerks	5	1.7	8.1
Secretaries	5	1.7	-6.4
Production, planning, and expediting clerks	4	1.4	5.2
Office and administrative support supervisors and managers	4	1.4	14.4
General office clerks	3	1.3	18.8
Stock clerks and order fillers	3	1.3	17.7
Financial records processing occupations	3	1.2	-2.4
Executive, managerial, and administrative	27	9.8	13.5
General managers and top executives	9	3.3	14.1
Management support occupations	7	2.5	16.2
Precision production, craft, and repair	20	7.5	13.1
Production occupations, precision	4	1.6	3.5
Mechanics, installers, and repairers	3	1.1	8.3
Marketing and sales	12	4.4	17.4
Technicians and related support	7	2.5	13.2
Broadcast technicians	4	1.4	17.7
Service	4	1.5	6.8

Large film and television studios are headed by a *chief executive officer* (CEO) who is responsible to a board of directors and stockholders. Various managers such as *financial managers* or *business managers*, as well as *accountants* and *lawyers* report to the CEO. Small film companies, and those in business and educational film production, cannot afford to have so many different people managing only one aspect of the business. As a result, they are usually headed by an *owner-producer*, who originates, develops, produces, and distributes films with just a small staff and some freelance workers. These companies offer good training opportunities to beginners because they provide exposure to many phases of film and television production.

Training and Advancement
Formal training can be a great asset to workers in filmmaking and television production, but experience, talent, and creativity are usually the most important factors in getting a job. In almost all areas of film and television production, entry-level workers start at the bottom. Many start out by working on a documentary, business, educational, industrial, or government film, or in the music video industry. This kind of experience can lead to more advanced jobs.

Actors and actresses are usually required to have formal dramatic training or acting experience. Training can be obtained in dramatic arts schools throughout the country, although most schools are located in New York City and Los Angeles. Over 500 colleges and universities offer bachelor's or higher degrees in dramatic and theater arts. Training in singing and dance, experience in modeling, and performing in local and regional theater are especially useful. Many actors begin their career by performing in commercials and as extras. Most professional actors rely on agents or managers to find auditions for them.

There are no specific training requirements for producers and directors. Talent, experience, and business acumen are very important. An ability to deal under stress with many different kinds of people is also essential. Directors and producers come from varied backgrounds. Many start as assistant directors and producers, but actors, writers, film editors, and business managers often enter these jobs. Formal training in directing and producing is available at some colleges and universities. Individuals interested in production management who have a bachelor's degree or 2 years of on-set experience in motion picture or television production may qualify for the Assistant Directors Training Program offered jointly by the Directors Guild of America and motion picture and television companies. Training is given in New York City and Los Angeles. To enroll in this highly competitive program, individuals must take a written exam and go through a series of assessments.

Although many scriptwriters have college degrees, talent and creativity are even more important determinants of success in the industry. Scriptwriters need to develop creative writing skills, a mastery of film language, and a basic understanding of filmmaking. Self-motivation, perseverance, and an ability to take criticism are also valuable.

Editors not only need a formal education, but also apprenticeship training. Many start as copywriters for advertising agencies or as writers for educational and informational film companies. Cinematographers, camera operators, and sound engineers usually have either a college or technical school education, or they go through an apprenticeship program. Computer skills are required for many editing, special effects, and cinematography positions.

In addition to colleges and technical schools, many private institutes offer training programs on various aspects of filmmaking, such as scriptwriting, editing, directing, and acting. For example, the American Film Institute offers training in directing, production, cinematography, screenwriting, and production design.

The educational background of managers and top executives varies widely, depending on their responsibilities. Most managers have a bachelor's degree in liberal arts or business administration. Their majors often are related to the departments they direct. For example, a degree in accounting or finance, or in business administration with an emphasis on accounting or finance, is suitable academic preparation for financial managers.

Employers prefer individuals with an undergraduate degree in marketing, advertising, or business for top-level positions in these departments. Experience in retail and print advertising is also helpful. A high school diploma and retail or telephone sales experience are beneficial for sales jobs.

Promotion opportunities for many jobs are extremely limited because of the narrow scope of duties and skills of the occupations. Thousands of jobs are also temporary, intermittent, part time, or on a contract basis, making advancement difficult. Individual initiative is very important for advancement in these fields.

Scriptwriters usually have had writing experience as freelance writers or editors and writers in other employment settings. As they build a reputation in their career, demand for their screenplays or teleplays increases, and their earnings grow. Some become directors or producers. Editors often begin as editing room assistants; cinematographers usually start as assistant camera operators; and sound recordists often start as boom operators and gradually progress to sound engineer. Computer courses in digital sound and electronic mixing are often important for upward mobility.

General managers may advance to top executive positions such as executive or administrative vice-president in their own firm, or to similar positions in a larger firm. Top-level managers may advance to chief operating officer and CEO. Financial, marketing, and other managers may be promoted to top management positions or may transfer to closely related positions in other industries. Some may start their own businesses.

Earnings

Earnings of workers in the motion picture production and distribution industry vary, depending on education and experience, type of work, union affiliation, and duration of employment. In 1998, average weekly earnings of nonsupervisory workers in motion picture production were $789, compared to $442 for workers in all industries.

Based on a union contract that extends through June 1999, motion picture and television actors and actresses, who are members of Screen Actors Guild, will earn a minimum daily rate of $576, or $2,000 for a 5-day week. They also receive additional compensation for reruns. Annual earnings from acting are low, however, because employment is very irregular. According to the Actors Equity Association, only about 15 percent of the stage actors they represent are employed during any given week. In an entire year, less than half of their membership will receive any income from stage acting. For members who are able to find employment, their average yearly earnings in 1998 were less than $15,000. Many actors and actresses supplement their incomes from acting with other jobs outside the industry. Some well-known

actors get salaries well above the minimums, and of course, earnings of the few top stars are astronomical.

Salaries for directors vary widely. Producers seldom get a set salary; instead, they get a percentage of a show's earnings or ticket sales. Earnings in selected occupations in motion picture production and distribution in 1997 appear in table 2.

Table 2. Median hourly earnings of the largest occupations in motion picture production and services, 1997

Occupation	Motion picture production and services	All industries
General managers and top executives ...	$38.63	$26.05
Artists and related workers	16.89	14.89
Producers, directors, actors, and other entertainers	12.27	—
Industrial truck and tractor operators	9.03	10.99

Outlook

Americans spend billions of dollars every year to be entertained, much of it in this industry. The increasing availability of cable and satellite television has spurred demand for film and videotape production of domestic and foreign television, feature films, home video, and informational, educational, and industrial films. In response to this demand, wage and salary employment in motion picture production and distribution is projected to increase 17 percent over the 1998-2008 period, compared to 15 percent growth projected for all industries combined. In addition to new jobs resulting from growth, many more jobs will arise as workers leave this high-turnover industry.

This growing demand will provide increased employment opportunities for workers in nearly every major occupational group. Among the less glamorous, behind-the-scenes occupations, employment growth is expected for many technicians and helpers, such as gaffers and set construction workers. Job growth is also expected in film reproduction, distribution, and rental, as more large studios turn to this part of the business.

There will also be increased employment opportunities for the more glamorous, higher-paying jobs, such as actors, directors, and producers. As always, however, there will continue to be keen competition for the more visible jobs in the industry because of the number of jobseekers. Relatively few will find regular employment in these jobs.

Sources of Additional Information

For general information on actors, actresses, directors, and producers, contact:

➤ Screen Actors Guild, 5757 Wilshire Blvd., Los Angeles, CA 90036-3600.
➤ American Federation of Television and Radio Artists, Suite 204, 4340 East-West Hwy., Bethesda, MD 20814.

Information on many motion picture production and distribution occupations, including the following, may be found in the 2000-01 *Occupational Outlook Handbook*:

- Actors, directors, and producers
- Artists and commercial artists
- Broadcast and sound technicians
- General managers and top executives
- Photographers and camera operators
- Writers and editors, including technical writers

Personnel Supply Services

(SIC 736)

SIGNIFICANT POINTS

- Personnel supply services ranks among the fastest growing industries in the Nation and among those projected to provide the most new jobs.

- The majority of temporary jobs in the industry only require graduation from high school or the equivalent; some permanent jobs, such as employment interviewer, may require a college education.

- Temporary jobs provide a short-term source of income and may offer flexible schedules.

- Although earnings in the industry vary widely, median earnings are relatively low.

Nature of the Industry

Although many people associate the personnel supply services industry with temporary employment opportunities for clerical workers, the industry provides both temporary and permanent employment to individuals with a wide variety of education and experience. Occupations in the industry range from secretary to computer analyst, and from general laborer to nurse. In addition to temporary jobs in these occupations, permanent positions in the industry include workers such as employment interviewers and marketing representatives who help assign and place workers in jobs.

The personnel supply services industry has two distinct segments: *Employment agencies* that place permanent employees, and *help supply services*—also referred to as temporary and staffing services—that provide employees to other organizations on a contract basis. The typical employment agency has a relatively small permanent staff, usually fewer than 10 workers (see chart below), who interview jobseekers

and try to match their qualifications and skills to those being sought by employers for specific job openings.

In contrast to the smaller employment agencies, almost half of all help supply services firms employ more than 50 workers (see chart on next page). Help supply service firms provide temporary employees to other businesses to support or supplement their workforce in special situations, such as employee absences, temporary skill shortages, and varying seasonal workloads. Temporary workers are employed and paid by the help supply services firm and contracted out to a client at either a prearranged fee or an agreed hourly wage. Some companies choose to use temporary workers full time on an on-going basis rather than employ permanent staff, who typically command greater salaries and benefits. As a result, the overwhelming majority of workers in the help supply services segment of the industry are temporaries; relatively few are permanent staff.

Traditionally, firms that placed permanent employees usually dealt with highly skilled applicants, such as lawyers or accountants, and those placing temporary employees dealt with less skilled workers, such as secretaries or data entry operators. However, temporary help services firms increasingly place workers who have a range of educational backgrounds and work experience because businesses are now turning to temporary employees to fill all types of positions—from clerical to managerial, professional, and technical

Working Conditions

The average annual work week in the personnel supply services industry was about 32.4 hours in 1998, compared to the average of 34.6 hours across all industries. The low average work week reflects the fact that a temporary employee could work 40 or more hours a week on a contract for an extended period and then take a few weeks off from work. Most full-time temporary workers put in 35-40 hours a week, while some work longer hours. Permanent employees in employment agencies usually work a standard 40-hour week, unless seasonal fluctuations require more or fewer hours.

Workers employed as permanent staff of employment agencies or help supply services firms usually work in offices and may meet numerous people daily. Temporaries work in a variety of environments and seldom stay in any one place long enough to settle into a personal workspace or establish close relationships with co-workers. Most assignments are of short

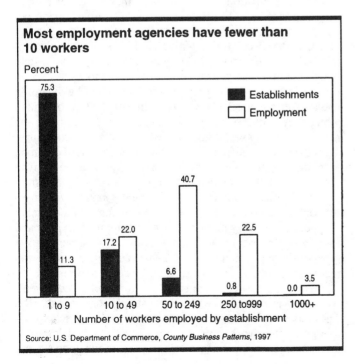

Most employment agencies have fewer than 10 workers

Percent

■ Establishments
□ Employment

	1 to 9	10 to 49	50 to 249	250 to 999	1000+
Establishments	75.3	17.2	6.6	0.8	0.0
Employment	11.3	22.0	40.7	22.5	3.5

Number of workers employed by establishment

Source: U.S. Department of Commerce, *County Business Patterns*, 1997

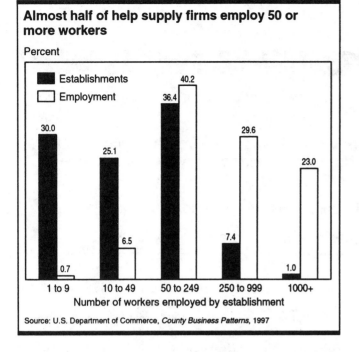

Almost half of help supply firms employ 50 or more workers

Percent

■ Establishments
□ Employment

- 1 to 9: Establishments 30.0, Employment 0.7
- 10 to 49: Establishments 25.1, Employment 6.5
- 50 to 249: Establishments 36.4, Employment 40.2
- 250 to 999: Establishments 7.4, Employment 29.6
- 1000+: Establishments 1.0, Employment 23.0

Number of workers employed by establishment

Source: U.S. Department of Commerce, *County Business Patterns*, 1997

duration because temporaries often are called in to replace a worker who is ill or on vacation or to help with a short-term surge of work. However, assignments of several weeks or longer occasionally may be offered. On each assignment, temporary employees may work for a new supervisor.

Employment as a temporary is attractive to many. The opportunity for a short-term source of income while enjoying flexible schedules and opportunities to take extended leaves of absence is well-suited to students, persons juggling job and family responsibilities, those exploring various careers, and those seeking permanent positions in a chosen career. Firms try to accommodate workers' preferences for particular days or hours of work and for frequency or duration of assignments. Temporary work assignments provide an opportunity to explore first hand a variety of different work settings and employers, to hone skills through practice, and to learn new skills. Nevertheless, many workers in temporary assignments would prefer the stability and greater benefits associated with full-time work.

The annual injury and illness rate for the entire industry was 6.1 cases for every 100 full-time workers in 1997, lower than the rate of 7.1 for the entire private sector. Temporary workers in industrial occupations often perform work that is more strenuous and potentially more dangerous, so they may have a higher rate of injury and illness.

Employment

The personnel supply services industry provided over 3.2 million jobs in 1998, over 2.9 million of them in help supply services firms. Although about 14,000 of the more than 42,000 establishments in the industry are employment agencies, help supply services firms employ over 9 out of 10 industry workers. Employment in help supply services companies has been experiencing dramatic growth, and employment projections indicate continuing rapid growth in personnel supply services.

Employment in the personnel supply services industry is distributed throughout the United States. Workers are somewhat younger than those in other industries—nearly 50 percent of personnel supply services workers are under 35, compared to

39 percent of all workers, reflecting the large number of clerical and other entry-level positions in the industry that require little formal education.

Occupations in the Industry

The personnel supply services industry encompasses many fields, from administrative support occupations to professional and production occupations (table 1). In general, occupations in the industry include the permanent staff of personnel supply service firms, and the occupations supplied as temporary help—health, office, and industrial occupations.

The permanent staff of personnel supply service agencies are responsible for the daily operation of the firm. Most permanent staff jobs require a college degree, with the exception of administrative support occupations. *Managers* ensure that the agency is run effectively, and they often conduct interviews of potential clients and jobseekers. *Employment interviewers* evaluate applicants and attempt to match them with client firms. Most employment interviewers work in the personnel supply services industry. *Marketing* and *sales workers* actively pursue new client firms and recruit qualified workers. Because of fierce competition among agencies, marketing and sales work at times can be quite stressful.

Health occupations generally require the most specialized training of all the temporary jobs. Many of the occupations in this segment require at least 2 or 3 years of college. *Home health aides* usually work in the home of an elderly or ill patient, allowing a patient to stay at home instead of being institutionalized. Becoming a home health aide generally does not require education beyond high school. *Nursing aides* and *orderlies* also seldom need education beyond high school, but employers do prefer previous experience. They assist nurses with patient care in hospitals and nursing homes. *Licensed practical nurses* provide basic bedside care to patients. *Registered nurses* administer medication, tend to patients, and advise patients and family members about procedures and proper care. They usually work in hospitals, but they may be assigned to private duty in patients' homes.

Office occupations in the industry may be either temporary or permanent. Experience in administrative support occupations usually is preferred for these jobs, although some persons take special training to learn skills such as bookkeeping and word processing. *Receptionists* greet visitors, field telephone calls, and perform assorted office functions. *Secretaries* perform a growing range of tasks, such as keyboarding and answering the telephone, depending on the type of firm in which they work. *Medical secretaries* make appointments and need a familiarity with common medical terms and procedures; *legal secretaries* must be familiar with the format of common legal documents. *General office clerks* file documents, type reports, and enter computer data. *File clerks* classify and store office information and records. *Data entry keyers* type information into a computer data base, either through a personal computer or directly into a mainframe computer. *Typists* and *word processors* enter and format drafts of documents using typewriters or computers. *Bookkeepers* compute, classify, and record transactions data for financial records and reports.

Finally, the share of industrial workers employed as temporaries is growing in the personnel supply services industry. These jobs seldom require education beyond high school, although related work experience may be preferred for some jobs. *Freight, stock, and material movers* move goods to and from storage areas either in factories, warehouses, or other businesses. *Hand packers and packagers* wrap, package, inspect, and label materials manually, often keeping records of what has been packed and shipped. *Helpers* and *laborers* perform a variety of mostly unskilled tasks.

Table 1. Employment of wage and salary workers in personnel supply services by occupation, 1998 and projected change, 1998-2008

(Employment in thousands)

Occupation	1998 Employment Number	1998 Employment Percent	1998-2008 Percent change
All occupations	3,230	100.0	43.1
Administrative support, including clerical	1,178	36.5	22.1
General office clerks	231	7.2	-10.2
Secretaries	181	5.6	20.3
Receptionists and information clerks	111	3.4	50.4
Data entry keyers	105	3.2	20.5
Word processors and typists	66	2.1	-5.9
Stock clerks and order fillers	56	1.7	50.6
Bookkeeping, accounting, and auditing clerks	49	1.5	22.6
File clerks	48	1.5	19.1
Office and administrative support supervisors and managers	34	1.1	46.4
Shipping, receiving, and traffic clerks	33	1.0	52.2
Operators, fabricators, and laborers	987	30.6	61.2
All other helpers, laborers, and material movers, hand	263	8.2	50.6
Hand workers, including assemblers and fabricators	230	7.1	51.1
Machine setters, setup operators, operators, and tenders	172	5.3	62.9
Hand packers and packagers	143	4.4	103.3
Freight, stock, and material movers, hand	98	3.0	58.7
Material moving equipment operators	39	1.2	50.6
Truck drivers	34	1.1	48.8
Precision production, craft, and repair	229	7.1	52.0
Inspectors, testers, and graders, precision	49	1.5	74.0
Mechanics, installers, and repairers	34	1.1	32.0
Blue-collar worker supervisors	31	1.0	50.6
Service	229	7.1	44.1
Personal care and home health aides	60	1.9	50.6
Janitors and housekeepers, including maids and housekeeping cleaners	47	1.4	35.5
Nursing aides, orderlies, and attendants	46	1.4	32.0
Food preparation and service occupations	40	1.2	62.7
Professional specialty	158	4.9	60.5
Registered nurses	53	1.6	35.5
Computer engineers and scientists	32	1.0	97.6
Executive, managerial, and administrative	155	4.8	36.5
Employment interviewers, private or public employment service	37	1.2	7.1
Technicians and related support	150	4.6	48.3
Engineering and science technicians and technologists	59	1.8	60.0
Marketing and sales	116	3.6	60.6
All other occupations	28	0.9	50.6

Training and Advancement

The personnel supply services industry offers opportunities in many occupations for workers with a variety of skill levels and experience. The majority of temporary jobs in the industry only require graduation from high school or the equivalent, while some permanent jobs, such as employment interviewer, may require college education. In general, the training requirements of temporary workers mirror those for permanent employees in the economy as a whole. As the industry expands to include various professional occupations, therefore, a growing number of jobs will require professional or advanced degrees.

Many help supply services firms offer skills training to newly-hired employees to make them more marketable. This training often is provided free to the temporary worker and is an economical way to acquire training in important skills such as word processing. Agency training policies vary, so persons considering temporary work should ask firms what training they offer and at what cost.

Advancement as a temporary employee usually takes the form of pay increases or greater choice of jobs. More often, temporaries transfer to full-time jobs with other employers. Turnover among temporaries within help supply firms usually is very high because few choose to work as temporaries for long; many accept offers to work full time for clients for whom they worked as temporaries. Some experienced temporaries may be offered permanent jobs with help supply firms, either as receptionists or in positions screening or training others for temporary jobs.

Permanent staff of employment agencies and help supply services firms are typically employment interviewers, administrative support workers, or managers. The qualifications required of employment interviewers depend partly on the occupations that the employment agency or help supply services firm specializes in placing. For example, agencies that place professionals, such as accountants or nurses, usually employ interviewers with college degrees in similar fields. Agencies specializing in placing administrative support workers, such as secretaries or word processors, are more likely to hire interviewers with less education who have experience in the occupations.

Although permanent staff in administrative support occupations, such as bookkeepers and receptionists, usually do not require formal education beyond high school, related work experience may be needed. Sometimes, staff experienced in administrative support occupations advance to employment interviewer positions. Employment interviewers advance to positions with higher earnings potential in which they interview persons seeking jobs with higher rates of pay. These positions often pay more because many interviewers receive a commission based on the fees paid by clients.

Most managers of employment agencies and help supply services firms have college degrees; an undergraduate degree in personnel management or a related field is the best preparation for these jobs. Employment interviewers often advance to managerial positions, but seldom without a bachelor's degree.

Earnings

In 1998, earnings among nonsupervisory workers in help supply services firms were $10.18 per hour and $330 per week, lower than $12.77 an hour and $442 a week for all private industry.

211

Earnings vary as widely as the range of skills and formal education among workers in personnel supply services. As in other industries, managers and professionals earn more than clerks and laborers. Also, temporaries usually earn less than workers employed as permanent staff, but some experienced temporaries make as much or more than workers in similar occupations in other industries. Earnings in the largest occupations in personnel supply services appear in table 3.

Table 3. Median hourly earnings of the largest occupations in personnel supply services, 1997

Occupation	Personnel supply services	All industries
Registered nurses	$20.67	$18.88
Secretaries, except medical and legal	10.32	11.00
Typists, including word processing	9.73	10.51
Receptionists and information clerks	8.35	8.69
Data entry keyers, except composing	8.11	8.91
General office clerks	8.04	9.10
Home health aides	7.74	7.75
Stock clerks-stockroom, warehouse or storage yard	7.34	8.85
Hand packers and packagers	6.43	6.90

Most permanent workers receive basic benefits; temporary workers usually do not receive such benefits unless they work a minimum number of hours or days per week to qualify for benefit plans. Only 2.8 percent of workers in personnel supply services are union members or are covered by union contracts, compared to around 15 percent of all workers in private industry.

Outlook

Personnel supply services ranks among the fastest growing industries in the Nation and among the industries projected to provide the most new jobs. Wage and salary jobs in the personnel supply services industry are expected to grow 43 percent over the 1998-2008 period, nearly 3 times the 15 percent growth projected for all industries combined. The industry is expected to gain about 1.4 million new jobs over the period.

The growth in demand for temporary employees that has fueled the rapid expansion of the industry is attributable to a number of factors. As competition has grown and businesses have sought new ways to reduce costs and make their staffing patterns more responsive to changes in demand, they have increasingly hired temporary employees to reduce the wage and benefit costs associated with full-time employees. The demand for temporaries also has grown as many large companies discontinued their use of relatively expensive "labor pools," or in-house labor supply services. As governments and other organizations increasingly use temporary workers, demand is expected to continue increasing rapidly. This growth in demand, coupled with significant turnover in these positions, should create plentiful opportunities for persons who seek jobs as temporaries.

Employment agencies also are expected to continue growing, but not as fast as help supply services. Growth in these agencies stems from employers' increasing willingness to allow outside agencies to perform the preliminary screening of candidates and the growing acceptance of executive recruitment services.

Most new jobs will arise in the largest occupational groups in this industry—administrative support occupations and operators, fabricators, and laborers. However, the trend toward specialization also will spur rapid growth among professional workers, including engineers, as well as managers, as government increasingly contracts out management functions. In addition, growth of help supply firms specializing in accounting, legal, and information technology services will provide opportunities for other professional workers within those fields. Marketing and sales representative jobs in temporary help firms are also expected to increase along with competition among these firms for the most qualified workers and the best clients.

Sources of Additional Information

For information concerning employment in help supply services, contact:

➢ The American Staffing Association, 277 S. Washinton St., Suite 200, Alexandria, VA 22314.
Internet: **http://www.natss.org**

For information about employment agencies, contact:

➢ National Association of Personnel Services, 3133 Mt. Vernon Ave., Alexandria, VA 22305.
Internet: **http://napsweb.org**

More information about many occupations in this industry, including the following, appears in the 2000-01 *Occupational Outlook Handbook*:

- Employment interviewers, private or public employment service
- Handlers, equipment cleaners, helpers, and laborers
- Home health and personal care aides
- Office clerks, general
- Receptionists
- Secretaries

Social Services, Except Child-Care

(SIC 83, except 835)

SIGNIFICANT POINTS

- Social services, except child-care, ranks among the fastest growing industries.

- About 2 out of 3 jobs are in professional, technical, and service occupations.

- Human service workers and assistants—the ninth fastest growing occupation—are concentrated in social services.

- Average earnings are low because of the large number of part-time and low-paying service jobs.

Nature of the Industry

Careers in social services appeal to persons with a strong desire to make lives better and easier for others. Workers in this industry usually are good communicators and enjoy interacting with people. Social services workers assist the homeless, housebound, and infirm to cope with circumstances of daily living; counsel troubled and emotionally disturbed individuals; train or retrain the unemployed or underemployed; care for the elderly, and physically and mentally disabled; help the needy obtain financial assistance; and solicit contributions for various social services organizations. About 102,000 establishments in the private sector provided social services in 1998. Thousands of other establishments, mainly in State and local government, provided many additional social services. For information about government social services, see the *Career Guide* statements on Federal Government, and State and local government, excluding education and hospitals.

Social services contain four segments—individual and family services, residential care, job training and vocational rehabilitation services, and miscellaneous social services. (The child-care services industry, including day care and preschool care centers, is covered in a separate *Career Guide* statement.)

Individual and family social services establishments provide counseling and welfare services including refugee, disaster, and temporary relief services. Government offices distribute welfare aid, rent supplements, and food stamps. Some agencies provide adult day care, home-delivered meals, and home health and personal care services. Other services concentrate on children, such as big brother and sister organizations, youth centers, and adoption services. Workers in crisis centers may focus on individual, marriage, child, or family counseling.

Residential care facilities provide around-the-clock social and personal care to children, the elderly, and others who have limited ability to care for themselves. Workers care for residents of alcohol and drug rehabilitation centers, group homes, and halfway houses. Nursing and medical care, however, is not the main focus of establishments providing residential care, as it is in nursing or personal care facilities (see the statement on health services, elsewhere in the *Career Guide*).

Job training and related services establishments train the unemployed, underemployed, disabled, and others with job market disadvantages. Vocational specialists and counselors work with clients to overcome deficient education, job skills, or experience. Often industrial psychologists or career counselors will assess the job skills of a client and, working with both the employer and the client, decide whether the client would be better served by taking additional job training, by being placed in a different job with his or her current skills, or by restructuring the job to accommodate any skill deficiency.

Miscellaneous social services include many different kinds of establishments, such as advocacy groups, antipoverty boards, community development groups, and health and welfare councils. Many miscellaneous social services organizations are concerned with community improvement and social change. They may solicit contributions, administer appropriations, and allocate funds among other agencies engaged in social welfare services.

Working Conditions

Some social services establishments—such as residential care facilities—operate around the clock. Thus evening, weekend, and holiday work is not uncommon. Some establishments may be understaffed, resulting in large caseloads for each worker. Jobs in voluntary, nonprofit agencies often are part time.

Some workers spend a substantial amount of time traveling within the local area. For example, home health and personal care aides routinely visit clients in their homes; social workers and human service workers and assistants also may make home visits. In 1997, the incidence rate for occupational injury and illness in social services varied by industry sector. Compared to the rate of 7.1 per 100 full-time workers for the entire private sector, residential care and job training and related services had higher rates—9.9 and 9.7, respectively. On the other hand, individual and family services and miscellaneous social services had lower than average rates—4.7 and 3.8, respectively.

Employment

Social services provided about 2 million nongovernment wage and salary jobs in 1998. Almost half were in individual and miscellaneous social services (table 1). An estimated 52,000 self-employed persons also worked in the industry.

Table 1. Employment of nongovernment wage and salary workers in social services by detailed industry, 1998

Industry	1998 Employment Number	1998 Employment Percent	1998-2008 Percent change
Total	2,039	100.0	41.1
Individual and miscellaneous social services	923	45.3	32.5
Residential care	747	36.6	56.8
Job training and related services	369	18.1	31.0

In 1997, about 65 percent of social services establishments employed fewer than 10 workers; however, larger establishments accounted for most jobs (chart).

Social services workers are somewhat older than workers in other industries (table 2). About 39 percent were 45 years old or older, compared to 34 percent of all workers. Jobs in social services are concentrated in large States with heavily populated urban areas, such as New York and California.

Table 2. Percent distribution of employment in social services by age group, 1998

Age group	Social services	All industries
Total	100.0	100.0
16-24	12.2	14.9
25-34	24.3	23.9
35-44	24.8	27.5
45-54	21.8	21.0
55-64	11.9	9.8
65 and older	5.1	2.9

Occupations in the Industry

More than one-third of nongovernment social service jobs are in professional and technical occupations (table 3). *Social workers* counsel and assess the needs of clients, refer them to

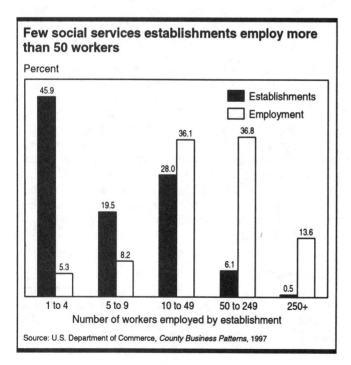

Few social services establishments employ more than 50 workers

Percent

■ Establishments
□ Employment

Number of workers employed by establishment		
1 to 4: 45.9 / 5.3	5 to 9: 19.5 / 8.2	10 to 49: 28.0 / 36.1
50 to 249: 6.1 / 36.8	250+: 0.5 / 13.6	

Source: U.S. Department of Commerce, *County Business Patterns*, 1997

the appropriate sources of help, and monitor their progress. They may specialize in child welfare and family services, mental health, medical social work, school social work, community organization activities, or clinical social work. *Human service workers and assistants* serve in a variety of social and human service delivery settings. Job titles and duties of these workers vary, but they include social service assistant, case management aide, social work assistant, residential counselor, alcoholism or drug abuse counselor, mental health aide, child abuse worker, community outreach worker, and gerontology aide. *Counselors* help people evaluate their interests and abilities and advise and assist them with personal and social problems.

About 3 out of 10 nongovernment jobs in social services are in service occupations. *Residential counselors* develop and coordinate non-medical activities for residents of long-term care and treatment facilities, such as assisted-living housing for the elderly. The social services industry employs over 4 out of 5 residential counselors. *Home health and personal care aides* help elderly, disabled, and ill persons live in their own homes instead of an institution. Although some are employed by public or private agencies, many are self-employed. Persons in *food preparation and service occupations* serve residents at social services institutions. *Nursing and psychiatric aides* help care for physically or mentally ill, injured, disabled, or infirm individuals.

As in most industries, administrative support workers—secretaries and bookkeepers, for example—as well as executives and managers account for many jobs. However, social services employ a much smaller percentage of precision production, craft, and repair, and of marketing and sales jobs, than the economy as a whole.

Certain occupations are more heavily concentrated in some segments of the industry than in others. Individual and miscellaneous social services, for example, employ the greatest numbers of social workers, human service workers and assistants, and home health and personal care aides. Job training and vocational rehabilitation services provide the most jobs for adult education teachers. Nursing and psychiatric aides and food preparation and service workers work mainly in the residential care segment of the industry.

Training and Advancement

Some occupations in social services have very specific entrance requirements. These include most of the professional specialty occupations. Those requiring specific clinical training, such as clinical social workers and psychologists also require appropriate State licensure or certification. Nevertheless, people with a limited background in social services or little education beyond high school can find a job in the industry. Nursing aides and home health and personal care aides are two such occupations. Many establishments provide on-the-job or classroom training, especially for those with limited background or training.

Many employers prefer human service workers and assistants with some related work experience or college courses in human services, social work, or one of the social or behavioral sciences. Other employers prefer a 4-year college degree. A number of employers provide in-service training, such as seminars and workshops.

Entry-level jobs for social workers require a bachelor's degree in social work or in an undergraduate major such as psychology or sociology. However, most agencies require a master's degree in social work or a closely related field. Public agencies and private practice clinics that offer clinical or consultative services require an advanced degree in clinical social work; supervisory, administrative, and staff training positions usually require at least a master's degree.

Table 3. Employment of nongovernment wage and salary workers in social services by occupation, 1998 and projected change, 1998-2008

(Employment in thousands)

Occupation	1998 Employment Number	1998 Employment Percent	1998-2008 Percent change
All occupations	2,039	100.0	41.1
Professional specialty	684	33.6	49.7
Social workers	156	7.6	37.6
Residential counselors	154	7.5	54.1
Human service workers and assistants	130	6.4	73.4
Adult and vocational education teachers	49	2.4	43.6
Registered nurses	31	1.5	41.0
Counselors	28	1.4	43.9
Recreation workers	25	1.2	31.9
Teachers, preschool	22	1.1	36.4
Service	620	30.4	41.8
Home health and personal care aides	246	12.1	46.0
Nursing aides and psychiatric aides	109	5.4	44.4
Janitors and cleaners, including maids and housekeeping cleaners	63	3.1	31.3
Child care workers	51	2.5	54.7
Cooks, institution or cafeteria	28	1.4	37.0
Food preparation workers	23	1.1	26.6
Administrative support, including clerical	252	12.3	26.6
Secretaries	50	2.5	12.3
General office clerks	40	2.0	39.1
Receptionists and information clerks	30	1.5	41.1
Teacher assistants	28	1.4	39.1
Office and administrative support supervisors and managers	27	1.3	34.6
Bookkeeping, accounting, and auditing clerks	26	1.3	14.9
Executive, administrative, and managerial	251	12.3	35.8
General managers and top executives	81	4.0	37.9
Management support occupations	46	2.3	38.2
Administrative services managers	20	1.0	33.0
Operators, fabricators, and laborers	91	4.5	30.1
Motor vehicle operators	37	1.8	32.2
Hand workers, including assemblers and fabricators	30	1.5	32.3
Technicians and related support	58	2.9	45.4
Licensed practical and licensed vocational nurses	24	1.2	42.3
Precision production, craft, and repair	47	2.3	35.8
Maintenance repairers, general utility	21	1.0	35.9
Marketing and sales	27	1.3	31.5
All other occupations	10	0.5	40.6

Volunteering with a student, religious, or charitable organization is a good way for persons to test their interest in social services, and may provide an advantage when applying for jobs in this industry.

Advancement paths vary. For example, some home health and personal care aides get additional training and become licensed practical nurses. Formal education—usually a bachelor's or master's degree in counseling, rehabilitation, social work, or a related field—almost always is necessary for human service workers and assistants to advance. Social workers can advance to supervisor, program manager, assistant director, or executive director of an agency or department. They also may enter private practice and provide psychotherapeutic counseling and other services on a contract basis. Private practice for social workers depends on the affordability of services, including the availability of funding from third parties.

Earnings

Earnings in selected occupations in the four components of the social services, except child care, industry in 1997 appear in table 4. As in most industries, professionals and managers—whose salaries reflect higher education levels, broader experience, and greater responsibility—commonly earn more than other workers in social services.

Table 4. Median hourly earnings of the largest occupations in social services, except child care, 1997

Occupation	Individual and family services	Job training and related services	Residential care	Social services, not elsewhere classified	All industries
General managers and top executives	$19.08	$22.11	$18.55	$22.69	$26.05
Social workers, except medical and psychiatric	12.13	11.37	12.05	12.03	14.01
Secretaries, except legal and medical	9.39	9.51	9.64	10.27	11.00
Human services workers	9.45	8.60	8.12	9.72	9.89
Social workers, medical and psychiatric	13.09	—	12.32	—	14.72
Residential counselors	8.41	8.73	8.63	—	8.57
Nursing aides, orderlies, and attendants	7.17	—	7.20	—	7.76
Home health aides	7.17	—	7.23	—	7.75
Personal and home care aides	6.99	7.29	7.20	—	6.96
Child care workers	6.98	—	7.55	—	6.48

About 10.9 percent of workers in the social services industry were union members or were covered by union contracts in 1998, compared to about 15.4 percent of workers throughout private industry.

Outlook

Job opportunities in social services should be numerous through the year 2008. The number of nongovernment wage

215

and salary jobs is expected to increase 41 percent, compared to only 15 percent for all industries combined. Expected growth rates for the various segments of the industry range from 31 percent in job training and vocational rehabilitation services to 57 percent in residential care over the 1998-2008 period (table 1). In addition to employment growth, many job openings will stem from the need to replace workers who transfer to other occupations or stop working. The greatest number of job openings should arise in large occupations with easy entry, relatively low pay, and high turnover, such as home health and personal care aides.

The expected rapid growth is due to expanding services for the elderly, the mentally and physically disabled, and families in crisis. Older people comprise a rapidly expanding segment of the population and are more likely to need social services than younger age groups. A continuing influx of foreign-born nationals to this country will spur demand for social services, such as relocation, financial, and job training assistance. Businesses are implementing more employee counseling programs. Programs also are increasing for child protective services and special groups, such as adults who were abused as children. The growing emphasis on providing home care services rather than more costly nursing home or hospital care, and on earlier and better integration of the disabled into society also will contribute to employment growth in the social services industry.

Some of the fastest growing occupations in the Nation are concentrated in social services. The number of home health and personal care aides within social services is projected to grow 46 percent by 2008, and human service

workers and assistants, 73 percent, compared to the industry average of 41 percent.

Sources of Additional Information

For additional information about careers in social work, write to:

➢ National Association of Social Workers, 750 First St. NE., Suite 700, Washington, DC 20002.

For information on programs and careers in human services, contact:

➢ Council for Standards in Human Services Education, Northern Essex Community College, 100 Elliott Way, Haverhill, MA 01830

State employment service offices may also be able to provide information on job opportunities in social services.

Information on many occupations in social services, including the following, may be found in the 2000-01 *Occupational Outlook Handbook*:

● Adult education teachers
● Counselors
● Home health and personal care aides
● Nursing and psychiatric aides
● Recreation workers
● Human service workers and assistants
● Social workers

Government

Federal Government, Excluding the Postal Service

- The Federal Government is the Nation's largest employer.

- Almost half of Federal workers held managerial or professional jobs, a rate twice as high as the work force as a whole.

- About 4 out of 5 Federal employees work outside the Washington, D.C. metropolitan area.

- Federal employment is projected to decline slightly due to budgetary constraints, the growing use of private contractors, and the transfer of some functions to State and local governments.

Nature of the Industry

The Federal Government affects Americans in countless ways. It defends Americans from foreign aggression, represents American interests abroad, passes and enforces laws, and administers many different programs and agencies. Americans are particularly aware of the Federal Government when they pay their income taxes each year, but they usually do not consider the government's role when they watch a weather forecast, purchase fresh and uncontaminated groceries, travel by highway or air, or make a deposit at their bank. Workers employed by the Federal Government play a vital role in these and many other aspects of American life. (While career opportunities in the U.S. Postal Service and the Armed Forces are not covered here, both are described in the 2000-01 edition of the *Occupational Outlook Handbook*. See the *Handbook* statements on postal clerks and mail carriers and job opportunities in the Armed Forces.)

The Constitution of the United States divides the Federal Government into the legislative, judicial, and executive branches. The legislative branch is responsible for forming and amending the legal structure of the Nation. Its largest component is Congress, the primary U.S. legislative body, which is made up of the Senate and the House of Representatives. This body includes senators, representatives, their staffs, and various support workers. The legislative branch employs only about one percent of Federal workers, nearly all of whom work in the Washington, D.C. area.

The judicial branch is responsible for interpreting the laws the legislative branch enacts. The Supreme Court, the Nation's definitive judicial body, makes the highest rulings. Its decisions usually follow an appeal of a decision made by the one of the regional Courts of Appeal, which hear cases appealed from U. S. District Courts, the Court of Appeals for the Federal Circuit, or State Supreme Courts. U. S. District Courts are located in each State and are the first to hear most cases under Federal jurisdiction. The judicial branch employs about the same number of people as the legislative branch, but its offices and employees are dispersed throughout the country.

Of the three branches, the executive branch has the widest range of responsibilities. Consequently, it employed about 98 percent of all Federal civilian employees (excluding postal workers) in 1998. The executive branch is composed of the Executive Office of the President, 14 executive cabinet departments, and over 90 independent agencies, each of which has clearly defined duties. The Executive Office of the President is composed of several offices and councils that aid the President in policy decisions. These include the Office of Management and Budget, which oversees the administration of the Federal budget; the National Security Council, which advises the President on matters of national defense; and the Council of Economic Advisers, which makes economic policy recommendations.

Each of the 14 executive cabinet departments administers programs that oversee an element of American life. They are referred to as cabinet departments because the highest departmental official of each, the Secretary, is a member of the President's cabinet. Each, listed by employment size, is described below (table 1).

- *Defense:* Manages the military forces that protect our country and its interests, including the Departments of the Army, Navy, Air Force, and a number of smaller agencies. The civilian workforce employed by the Department of Defense performs various support activities, such as payroll and public relations.
- *Veterans Affairs:* Administers programs to aid U.S. veterans and their families, runs the veterans' hospital system, and operates our national cemeteries.
- *Treasury:* Regulates banks and other financial institutions, administers the public debt, prints currency, and carries out law enforcement in a wide range of areas, including counterfeiting, tax, and customs violations.
- *Agriculture:* Promotes U.S. agriculture domestically and internationally and sets standards governing quality, quantity, and labeling of food sold in the U.S.
- *Justice:* Enforces Federal laws, prosecutes cases in Federal courts, and runs Federal prisons.
- *Interior:* Manages Federal lands including the national parks and forests, runs hydroelectric power systems, and promotes conservation of natural resources.
- *Transportation:* Sets national transportation policy, runs the Coast Guard except in time of war, plans and funds the construction of highways and mass transit systems, and regulates railroad, aviation, and maritime operations.
- *Health and Human Services:* Sponsors medical research, approves use of new drugs and medical devices, runs the Public Health Service, and administers the Social Security and Medicaid programs.

- *Commerce:* Forecasts the weather, charts the oceans, regulates patents and trademarks, conducts the census, compiles statistics, and promotes U.S. economic growth by encouraging international trade.
- *State:* Oversees the Nation's embassies and consulates, issues passports, monitors U.S. interests abroad, and represents the U.S. before international organizations.
- *Energy:* Coordinates the national use and provision of energy, oversees the production and disposal of nuclear weapons, and plans for future energy needs.
- *Labor:* Enforces laws guaranteeing fair pay, workplace safety, and equal job opportunity; administers unemployment insurance; regulates pension funds; and collects economic data in the Bureau of Labor Statistics.
- *Housing and Urban Development:* Funds public housing projects, enforces equal housing laws, and insures and finances mortgages.
- *Education:* Provides scholarships, student loans, and aid to schools.

Table 1. Federal Government executive branch civilian employment, March 1999

(In thousands)

	United States	Washington, DC area
Total	2,737	322
Executive departments		
Defense, total	832	86
Army	260	25
Navy	255	35
Air Force	182	6
Other	135	20
Veterans Affairs	262	8
Treasury	160	22
Health and Human Services	129	30
Agriculture	109	13
Justice	96	21
Interior	78	10
Transportation	67	10
Commerce	37	20
State	9	7
Energy	20	7
Labor	17	6
Housing and Urban Development	13	3
Education	5	3
Independent agencies		
National Aeronautic and Space Administration	24	6
Federal Deposit Insurance Corporation	20	4
General Services Administration	20	7
Tennessee Valley Authority	19	0
Environmental Protection Agency	18	6

Source: U.S. Office of Personnel Management

Numerous independent agencies perform tasks that fall between the jurisdictions of the executive departments or that are more efficiently executed by an autonomous agency. Some smaller, but well known independent agencies include the Peace Corps, the Securities and Exchange Commission, and the Federal Communications Commission. Although the majority of these agencies are fairly small, employing fewer than 1,000 workers (many employ fewer than 100 workers), some are quite large. The largest independent agencies are:

- *National Aeronautics and Space Administration:* Oversees aviation research and conducts exploration and research beyond the Earth's atmosphere.
- *Environmental Protection Agency:* Runs programs to control and reduce pollution of the Nation's water, air, and lands.
- *General Services Administration:* Manages and protects Federal Government property and records.
- *Tennessee Valley Authority:* Operates the hydroelectric power system in the Tennessee river valley.

Working Conditions

Due to the wide range of Federal jobs, most of the working conditions found in the private sector are also found in the Federal Government. Most white-collar employees work in office buildings, hospitals, or laboratories, and most of the blue-collar workforce can be found in warehouses, shipyards, military bases, construction sites, national parks, and national forests. Work environments vary from comfortable and relaxed to hazardous and stressful, such as those experienced by law enforcement officers, astronauts, and air traffic controllers.

The vast majority of Federal employees work full time, often on flexible or "flexitime" schedules, which allow workers more control over their work schedules. Some agencies also have "flexiplace" programs, which allow selected workers to perform some job duties at home or from regional centers.

Some Federal workers spend much of their time away from the offices in which they are based. Inspectors and compliance officers, for example, often visit businesses and work sites to ensure laws and regulations are obeyed. Some Federal workers frequently travel long distances, spending days or weeks away from home. Auditors, for example, may spend weeks at a time in distant locations.

Employment

In 1998, the Federal Government employed about 1.8 million civilian workers, or about 2 percent of the Nation's workforce. Although the Federal Government employs workers in every major occupational group, workers are not employed in the same proportions in which they are employed throughout the economy as a whole (table 2). The analytical and technical nature of many government duties translates into a much higher proportion of professionals and technicians in the Federal Government, compared with most industries. Conversely, the Government sells very little, so it employs relatively few sales workers.

Even though most Federal departments and agencies are based in the Washington, DC area, only about 16 percent of all Federal employees worked in the vicinity of the Nation's Capital in 1998. In addition to Federal employees working throughout the United States, about 3 percent are assigned overseas, mostly in embassies or defense installations.

Occupations in the Industry

Although the Federal Government employed workers in almost every occupation in 1998, about 71 percent of Federal workers were employed in professional specialty, administrative support, and executive, administrative, and managerial occupations (table 3). Professional specialty occupations comprise about 31 percent of Federal employ-ment. The largest group of these workers are engineers, such as *chemical, civil, aeronautical, industrial, electrical, mechanical,* and *nuclear engineers.* These professionals are found in every department of the executive branch, but they most commonly work in the Department of Defense, the National Aeronautic and Space Administration, and the Department of Transportation. In general, they solve prob-lems and provide advice on technical programs, such as building highway bridges or implementing agency-wide computer systems.

Table 2. Percent distribution of employment in the Federal Gov-ernment and the total for all industries by major occupational group, 1998

Occupational group	Federal Government	All industries
Total	100.0	100.0
Professional specialty	30.8	13.9
Administrative support, including clerical	22.5	18.7
Executive, administrative, and managerial	17.6	9.9
Precision production, craft, and repair	9.2	10.7
Technicians and related support	8.3	3.8
Service	6.8	16.5
Operators, fabricators, and laborers	3.2	14.0
Marketing and sales	0.7	10.4
Agriculture, forestry, fishing, and related	0.7	2.1

Other professional specialty workers include *computer en-gineers, computer scientists,* and *systems analysts,* who are employed throughout government. They write computer pro-grams, analyze problems related to data processing, and keep computer systems running smoothly. Also in this group are health professionals, such as *registered nurses* and *physicians,* most of whom are employed by the Department of Veterans Affairs (VA) in one of the many VA hospitals. Other profes-sionals included *life scientists,* such as *biologists, foresters* and *conservation scientists,* who research problems dealing with life processes, and *physical scientists,* such as *geologists, me-teorologists,* and *physicists,* who examine the state of the earth and research physical phenomena. The Department of Agri-culture employs the vast majority of life scientists, but physi-cal scientists are distributed throughout government.

Executive, administrative, and managerial workers, who comprise about 18 percent of Federal employment, are pri-marily responsible for overseeing operations. *Legislators,* for example, are responsible for passing and amending laws. Managerial workers include a broad range of officials who, at the highest levels, may head Federal agencies or programs, such as *general managers* and *top executives. Middle manag-ers,* on the other hand, usually oversee one activity or aspect of a program.

Other executive, administrative, and managerial workers provide management support. *Accountants* and *auditors* pre-pare and analyze financial reports, review and record rev-enues and expenditures, and investigate operations for fraud and inefficiency. *Inspectors* and *compliance officers* enforce Federal regulations governing everything from aircraft to food. *Tax examiners* determine and collect taxes. Manage-ment support workers also include *purchasing agents,* who handle Federal purchases of supplies, and *management ana-lysts,* who study government operations and systems and suggest improvements.

Over 1 Federal worker in 5 is in administrative support. These employees aid management staff with administrative duties. Administrative support workers in the Federal Gov-ernment include *secretaries, bookkeepers, receptionists, switchboard operators,* and *accounting, auditing, stock, traf-fic, shipping,* and *receiving clerks.*

Technicians make up about 8 percent of the Federal workforce. They may aid professionals in research, analysis, or law enforcement. Often their tasks and skills are quite spe-cialized, as with *air traffic controllers.* Also, *engineering tech-nicians,* who may work either directly with engineers or by them-selves, are commonly found in Federal employment. Other tech-nician occupations include *health technicians,* such as *dental hygienists* and *radiologists,* who have specialized health ser-vice jobs, and *legal assistants,* who aid judges and attorneys.

Compared to the economy as a whole, service workers are relatively scarce in the Federal Government. Nearly half of all Federal workers in these occupations are *firefighters, law enforcement agents and officers,* and *correctional officers.* These workers protect the public from crime, oversee Federal prisons, and stand ready to intervene in emergencies.

Over half of the Federally employed precision production, craft, and repair occupations were mechanics, such as *vehicle* and *mobile equipment mechanics,* who fix and maintain all types of motor vehicles, aircraft, and heavy equipment, and *electrical and electronic equipment operators.* Other preci-sion production workers are skilled in construction trades, such as *painters, plumbers,* and *electricians.*

The Federal Government employs few workers in *fabrica-tor, operator,* and *laborer occupations; agriculture, forestry, fishing,* and *related occupations;* or *marketing* and *sales oc-cupations.*

Training and Advancement
Training and educational requirements in the Federal Govern-ment mirror those in the private sector for most major occupa-tional groups. Almost all professional specialty jobs, for example, require a 4-year college degree. Some, such as *engineers, physi-cians* and *life* and *physical scientists,* require a bachelor's or higher degree in a specific field of study. Also, because managers are usually promoted from professional occupations, most have at least a bachelor's degree. Administrative support workers in the government usually only need a high school diploma, though any further training or experience, such as a junior college degree, or at least 2 years of relevant work experience, is an asset. As in the private sector, most technicians are required to have some voca-tional training or extensive work experience; many have 2-year associate degrees. Most Federal jobs in other occupations re-quire no more than a high school degree, although most depart-ments and agencies prefer workers with vocational training or previous experience.

In general, each Federal department or agency determines its own training requirements and offers workers opportunities to improve job skills or become qualified to advance to other jobs. These may include technical or skills training, tuition as-sistance or reimbursement, fellowship programs, and execu-tive leadership and management training programs, seminars, and workshops. This training may be offered on the job, by another agency, or at local colleges and universities.

Table 3. Employment in the Federal Government, excluding the Postal Service, by occupation, 1998 and projected change, 1998-2008

(In thousands)

Occupation	1998 Employment Number	1998 Employment Percent	1998-2008 Percent change
All occupations	1,819	100.0	-9.0
Professional specialty	561	30.8	-0.4
Engineers	90	5.0	-12.2
Systems analysts	54	3.0	31.8
Registered nurses	46	2.5	-1.8
Physicians	45	2.5	-3.4
Life scientists	38	2.1	5.8
Teachers, librarians, and counselors	32	1.8	12.2
Physical scientists	31	1.7	-4.1
Judges, magistrates, and other judicial workers	31	1.7	0.9
Lawyers	26	1.4	24.3
Social scientists	25	1.4	-7.5
Administrative support, including clerical	410	22.5	-16.2
Other clerical and administrative support workers	180	9.9	-4.4
Secretaries	63	3.5	-25.0
Office clerks, general	54	3.0	-7.6
Bookkeeping, accounting, and auditing clerks	36	2.0	-9.8
Office and administrative support supervisors and managers	30	1.7	-6.0
Stock clerks and order fillers	25	1.4	-29.7
Welfare eligibility workers and interviewers	23	1.3	-26.3
Computer operators	21	1.2	-42.9
Executive, administrative, and managerial	321	17.7	-5.3
Inspectors and compliance officers, except construction	53	2.9	3.8
Accountants and auditors	51	2.8	-26.6
Management analysts	37	2.1	13.8
Buyers and purchasing agents	33	1.8	-3.4
Managerial and administrative occupations	28	1.5	-7.9
Tax examiners, collectors, and revenue agents	27	1.5	-0.2
Human resources, training, and labor relations specialists	25	1.3	4.5
Precision production, craft, and repair	168	9.2	-17.2
Mechanics, installers, and repairers	89	4.9	-13.4
Construction trades	32	1.8	-16.8
Blue-collar worker supervisors	25	1.4	-29.7
Technicians and related support	151	8.3	-13.0
Health technicians and technologists	41	2.3	-11.5
Engineering technicians	39	2.1	-20.9
Air traffic controllers and airplane dispatchers	25	1.4	-3.4
Service	125	6.8	7.1
Police and detectives	42	2.3	9.7
Health service occupations	22	1.2	-12.1
Operators, fabricators, and laborers	58	3.2	2.3
Helpers, laborers, and material movers, hand	26	1.4	-50.2
Transportation and material moving machine and vehicle operators	18	1.0	-25.0
All other occupations	26	1.4	-12.3

Advancement in the Federal Government is commonly based on a system of occupational pay levels, or "grades." Workers enter the Federal civil service at the starting grade for an occupation and begin a "career ladder" of promotions until they reach the full-performance grade for that occupation. This system provides for a limited number of non-competitive promotions which usually are awarded at regular intervals, assuming job performance is satisfactory. Although these promotions do not occur more than once a year, they sometimes are awarded in the form of 2-grade increases. The exact pay grades associated with a job's career track depend upon the occupation. For example, the pay grades in the career track for an attorney are significantly higher than those associated with a secretary.

Once workers reach the full-performance level of the career track, they must compete for subsequent promotions, and advancement becomes more difficult. At this point, promotions occur as vacancies arise, and they are based solely on merit.

The top managers in the Federal civil service belong to the Senior Executive Service (SES), the highest positions Federal workers can reach without being specifically nominated by the President and confirmed by the U.S. Senate. Only a relative few workers attain SES positions, and competition is intense. Because it is the headquarters for most Federal agencies, opportunities to advance to upper level managerial and supervisory jobs are best in the Washington, D.C. metropolitan area.

Table 4. Federal Government General Schedule pay rates, 1999

GS level	Entrance level	Step increase	Maximum level
1	$ 13,362	$ varies	$ 16,718
2	15,023	varies	18,907
3	16,392	546	21,306
4	18,401	613	23,918
5	20,588	686	26,762
6	22,948	765	29,833
7	25,501	850	33,151
8	28,242	941	36,711
9	31,195	1,040	40,555
10	34,353	1,145	44,658
11	37,744	1,258	49,066
12	45,236	1,508	58,808
13	53,793	1,793	69,930
14	63,567	2,119	82,638
15	74,773	2,492	97,201

SOURCE: U.S. Office of Personnel Management

Earnings

There are several pay systems governing the salary rates of Federal civilian employees. In 1999, the majority of Federal workers were paid under the General Schedule (GS). The General Schedule, shown in table 4, has 15 grades of pay for civilian white-collar and service workers, and smaller within-grade step increases that occur based on length of service and quality of performance. Workers in localities with high costs of living are paid as much as an additional 12 percent, and some hard-to-fill occupations are paid more as an incentive. In general, this schedule is amended every January to reflect changes in the cost of living.

In 1999, the average worker paid under the General Schedule earned $46,600; the average full-time, professional worker earned $61,600. Patent administrators had the highest average earnings of $99,000 (table 5), while some administrative support workers started at salaries less than $14,000.

Table 5. Average annual salaries in the Federal Government in selected occupations, 1999

Occupation	Salary
All occupations	$46,580
Patent administrator	98,900
Astronomer	81,310
Attorney	77,740
Financial manager	73,350
Economist	67,790
Computer scientist	66,510
Chemist	64,230
Electrical engineer	63,590
Statistician	62,840
Microbiologist	62,570
Architect	62,180
Podiatrist	61,960
Personnel manager	59,060
Accountant	58,190
Chaplain	57,330
Ecologist	57,130
Librarian	56,370
Intelligence agent	54,210
Physical therapist	51,370
Forester	51,010
Social worker	50,230
Botanist	48,770
Nurse	46,950
Engineering technician	46,230
Law clerk	41,810
Border patrol agent	40,200
Computer operator	34,220
Secretary	30,230
Police officer	29,990
Medical technician	27,820
Nursing assistant	24,990
Mail and file clerk	23,740
Telephone operator	23,560

SOURCE: U.S. Office of Personnel Management

The Federal Government hires employees in an occupational specialty with a career ladder. Typically, workers without a high school diploma who are hired as a clerks start at GS-1, and high school graduates with no additional training hired at the same job start at GS-2 or 3. Entrants with some technical training or experience who are hired as technicians may start at GS-4. Those with a bachelor's degree are generally hired in professional occupations, such as economist, with a career ladder that starts at GS-5 or 7, depending on academic achievement. Entrants with a master's degree or Ph.D. may start at GS-9. Individuals with professional degrees may be hired at the GS-11 or 12 level.

New employees almost always start at the first step of a grade; however, if the position in question is difficult to fill, entrants may receive somewhat higher pay or special rates. Almost all physician and engineer positions, for example, fall into this category.

Nonsupervisory Federal workers usually receive periodic step increases within their grade if they are performing their job satisfactorily. In addition to these within-grade longevity increases, Federal workers are awarded bonuses for excellent job performance.

Workers who advance to managerial or supervisory positions are paid under the General Schedule pay system and may receive within-grade longevity increases, bonuses, and promotions to higher GS levels. Managers at the highest levels belong to the Senior Executive Service, or SES, and their bonus provisions are even more performance-based.

The Wage Board schedule is used to pay most Federal workers in craft, repair, operative, and laborer jobs. This schedule sets Federal wages so they are comparable to prevailing regional wage rates for similar types of jobs. As a result, wage rates paid under the Wage Board schedule can vary significantly from one locality to another.

In addition to base pay and bonuses, Federal employees may receive incentive awards. These one-time awards, ranging from $25 to $25,000, are bestowed for a significant suggestion, a special act or service, or sustained high job performance. Some workers also may receive "premium" pay, which is granted when the employee must work overtime, on holidays, at night, or under hazardous conditions.

Benefits are an important part of Federal employee compensation. Federal employees may choose from a number of health plans and life insurance options; premium payments for these policies are partially offset by the government. In addition, workers hired after January 1, 1984 participate in the Federal Employee Retirement System (FERS), a three-tiered retirement plan including Social Security, a pension plan, and an optional Thrift Savings Plan. Worker participation in the Thrift Savings Plan is voluntary, but any contributions made are tax-deferred, and, up to a point, matched by the Federal Government. In addition to other benefits, some Federal agencies provide public transit subsidies in an effort to encourage employee use of public transportation.

Federal employees receive both vacation and sick leave. They earn 13 days of vacation leave a year for the first 3 years, 20 days a year for the next 12 years, and 26 days a year after their fifteenth year of service. Workers also receive 13 days of sick leave a year, which may be accumulated indefinitely. About 60 percent of all Federal civilian employees are represented by unions through their bargaining units, although a smaller percentage of these employees actually belong to a union.

Outlook

Employment in the Federal Government is projected to decline by 9 percent through the year 2008, while the economy as a whole is expected to grow 15 percent over the 1998-2008 period, in comparison. The projected reduction in Federal jobs reflects governmental cost-cutting, the growing use of private contractors, and continuing devolution—the practice of turning over the development, implementation, and management of some programs of the Federal government to State and local governments. As a result, keen competition is expected for many Federal positions, especially during times of economic uncertainty when workers seek the stability of Federal employment. In general, Federal employment is considered to be relatively stable because it is not affected by cyclical fluctuations in the economy, as are employment levels in many construction, manufacturing, and other private sector industries.

Because of its public nature, the factors that influence Federal Government staffing levels are unique. The Congress and

President determine the Government's payroll budget prior to each fiscal year, which runs from October 1 through September 30 of the following year. Each Presidential administration and Congress have different public policy priorities, resulting in increasing levels of Federal employment in some programs and declines in others. The effect of these priorities in recent years has been a decline in Department of Defense civilian employment, which equals about 40 percent of Federal civilian employment. Although this decline is expected to level off over the next decade, the emphasis on reduced government payrolls will lead to decreases in employment in many other agencies.

Much of this decline will be carried out through attrition—simply not replacing workers who retire or leave the Federal Government for other reasons. Layoffs, called "reductions in force", have occurred in the past, but they are uncommon and usually affect relatively few workers. In spite of attrition and declining employment, there still will be numerous employment opportunities in many agencies due to the need to replace workers who leave the workforce, retire, or accept employment elsewhere. Furthermore, some occupations, especially professional, technical, and managerial occupations, will be in demand even as employment in other occupations is being reduced.

The distribution of Federal employment will continue to shift toward a higher proportion of professional, technical, and managerial workers, as employment declines will be most rapid in blue-collar and clerical occupations. Employment among blue-collar workers is expected to decline as many of their functions are contracted out to private companies. In addition to the outsourcing of their duties, employment of administrative support and clerical workers in the Federal Government also will be adversely affected by the growing use of office automation.

Sources of Additional Information

Information on acquiring a job with the Federal Government may be obtained from the Office of Personnel Management through a telephone-based system. Consult your telephone directory under U.S. Government for a local number or call (912) 757-3000; TDD (912) 744-2299. That number is not tollfree and charges may result. Information is also available from their Internet site: **http://www.usajobs.opm.gov**

The duties of Federal Government workers in various occupations are similar to those of their private sector counterparts. Further information on the specific occupations discussed in this statement can be found in the 2000-01 edition of the *Occupational Outlook Handbook*.

State and Local Government, Excluding Education and Hospitals

SIGNIFICANT POINTS

- An excellent economy has led to budget surpluses in many State and local governments, allowing for increased spending on programs and employment.

- State government has a larger percentage of executive and professional specialty occupations, while local government employs a higher share of service and production workers.

Nature of the Industry

State and local governments provide vital services to their constituents, such as transportation, public safety, health care, education, utilities, and courts. Excluding the education and hospital sectors, State and local governments employ about 7.2 million workers, placing them among the largest employers in the economy. Almost two-thirds of these employees work for local governments, such as counties, cities, special districts, and towns. (Jobs of State and local government employees who work in education are described in the *Career Guide* statement on *Educational Services;* those employed in hospitals are covered in the *Health Services* statement.)

In addition to the 50 State governments, there are about 87,000 local governments, according to the Bureau of the Census. These include counties; municipalities, including villages, towns, and cities; townships; special districts; and school districts. Of the local governmental units, about 3,000 were county governments; 19,400 were municipal governments; 16,600 were townships; 13,700 were school districts; and 34,700 were special districts. Illinois had the most local government units, with over 6,800; Hawaii had the fewest, with 19.

In many areas of the country, citizens are served by more than one local government unit. For example, most States have *counties,* which may contain various municipalities such as cites or towns, but which also often include unincorporated rural areas. *Townships,* which do not exist in some States, may or may not contain municipalities and often consist of suburban or rural areas. Supplementing these forms of local government, *special district* government bodies are independent, limited purpose governmental units that usually perform a single function or activity. For example, a large percentage of special districts manage the use of natural resources. Some provide drainage and flood control, irrigation, and soil and water conservation services.

The Council of State Governments reports that State and local governments' responsibilities were augmented in the 1990s through "devolution," the practice through which the Federal Government turns over to State and local governments the development, implementation, and management of programs. Welfare reform typifies devolution in practice, with States receiving considerable leeway to devise programs that meet their needs as a result of the 1996 Congressional reform act that provided block grants to States. As the relationship between levels of government continues to change in the coming decade, so will the nature of services provided by State and local governments.

Working Conditions

Working conditions vary by occupation and, in some instances, by size and location of the State or local government. For example, chief executives in small jurisdictions may work less than 20 hours a week; in larger jurisdictions they often work more than 40 hours per week. Chief executives in large jurisdictions work full time year round, as do most county and city managers. Most State legislators work full time only when in session, usually for a few months a year, and work part time the rest of the year. Local elected officials in some small jurisdictions work part time.

Firefighters' hours are longer and vary more widely than those of most workers. Many professional firefighters are on duty for several days in a row, working over 50 hours a week. They often eat and sleep at the fire station. Following this long shift, they are then off for several days in a row or for the entire next week. In addition to irregular hours, firefighting can involve the risk of death or injury. Some local fire districts also use the services of volunteer firefighters, who tend to work shorter, regularly scheduled shifts.

Law enforcement work is also potentially dangerous. The injury and fatality rates among law officers are higher than in many occupations, reflecting risks taken in apprehending suspected criminals and responding to various emergency situations such as traffic accidents. Most police and detectives work 40 hours a week, with paid overtime when they testify in court or work on an investigation. Because police protection must be provided around the clock, some officers work weekends, holidays, and nights. Many officers are subject to call any time their services are needed and are expected to intervene whenever they observe a crime, even if off duty.

Most driver/operator jobs in public transit systems are stressful and fatiguing because they involve dealing with passengers, tight schedules, and heavy traffic. Bus drivers and subway operators with regular routes generally have consistent weekly work schedules. Those who do not have regular schedules may be on-call and must be prepared to report for work on short notice. To accommodate commuters, many operators work "split shifts," for example, 6 a.m. to 10 a.m. and 3 p.m. to 7 p.m., with time off in between.

A number of other State and local government jobs also require weekend or night work. Because electricity, gas, and water are produced and used continuously throughout each day, for example, split, weekend, and night shifts are common for utility workers. Also, some social services workers are on the job evenings, weekends, and holidays, such as those who work in residential care facilities, which must be staffed 24 hours a day.

Employment

State and local governments, excluding education and hospitals, employed about 7.2 million people in 1998. Local government employed the largest number of workers, accounting for 2 out of every 3 (table 1).

Table 1. Wage and salary employment in State and local governments, excluding education and hospitals, 1998

(Employment in thousands)

Jurisdiction	Employment	Percent
State and local	7,152	100.00
Local	4,804	67.2
State	2,348	32.8

Occupations in the Industry

Service occupations comprised the largest share of employment in State and local governments, accounting for almost 29 percent of all jobs (table 2). Of these, protective service occupations and firefighters were the largest occupations. Administrative support occupations accounted for about 20 percent of employment, and professional specialty and managerial occupations accounted for 16 and 13 percent, respectively.

Local governments had a smaller share of managerial and professional specialty occupations than State governments. Local governments, on the other hand, had a larger share of service occupations, particularly firefighting and law enforcement occupations (see chart).

State and local governments employ people in occupations that are found in nearly every industry in the economy, including managers, engineers, computer occupations, secretaries, and technicians. Certain occupations, however, are mainly or exclusively found in governments, such as government chief executives and legislators, tax examiners, urban and regional planners, judges, magistrates, police officers, and deputy sheriffs.

Chief executives and legislators establish government policy and develop laws, rules, and regulations. They are elected or appointed officials who either preside over units of government or make laws. Chief executives include governors, lieutenant governors, mayors, and city managers. Legislators include State senators and representatives, county commissioners, and city council members.

Inspectors and *compliance officers* enforce a wide range of laws, regulations, policies, and procedures designed to protect the public. They enforce regulations covering health, safety, food and restaurant cleanliness and licensing, and standards of weights and measures in commerce. *Tax examiners, collectors,* and *revenue agents* determine tax liability and collect past-due taxes from individuals or businesses.

Urban and *regional planners* draft plans and recommend programs for the development and use of resources like land and water. They also propose construction of physical facilities like schools and roads under the authority of cities, counties, and metropolitan areas. Planners devise strategies outlining the best use of community land and identify where residential, commercial, recreational, and other types of development should be located.

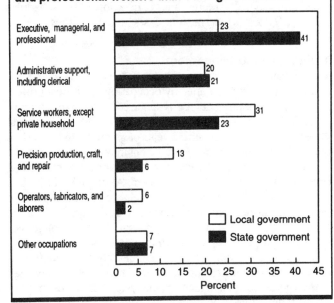

Local governments employ fewer executive, managerial, and professional workers than State governments

Judges arbitrate, advise, and administer justice in a court of law. They oversee legal processes in courts and apply the law to resolve civil disputes and determine guilt in criminal cases. *Magistrates* resolve criminal cases not involving penitentiary sentences and civil cases involving damages below a sum specified by State law.

Social workers counsel and assess the needs of clients, refer them to the appropriate sources of help, and monitor their progress. *Welfare eligibility workers* and *interviewers* interview and investigate applicants and recipients to determine eligibility to receive, or continue receiving, welfare and other types of social assistance. *Human services workers'* duties vary with specific job titles. These workers include social service technicians, case management aides, social work assistants, residential counselors, alcoholism or drug abuse counselors, mental health technicians, child abuse workers, community outreach workers, and gerontology aides.

Court clerks prepare dockets of cases to be called, secure information for judges, and contact witnesses, lawyers, and attorneys to obtain information for the court. *Municipal clerks* draft agendas for town or city councils, record minutes of council meetings, answer official correspondence, keep fiscal records and accounts, and prepare reports on civic needs.

Firefighters control and extinguish fires, assist with emergency medical treatment, and assist in recovery from natural disasters such as earthquakes and tornadoes. *Fire inspectors* inspect public buildings for conditions that might present a fire hazard.

Police officers and *detectives* have duties that range from controlling traffic to preventing and investigating crimes. They maintain order; enforce laws and ordinances; issue traffic summonses; investigate accidents; give evidence in court; and apprehend, arrest, and process prisoners. State and local *correctional officers* guard inmates in jails, prisons, or juvenile detention institutions. *Sheriffs* and *deputy sheriffs* enforce the law on the county level and may serve legal documents for the court system. *Bailiffs* keep order in courts.

Busdrivers and *subway car operators* pick up and deliver passengers at prearranged stops throughout their assigned routes. Operators may collect fares, answer questions about schedules and transfer points, and in some cases announce stops.

Training and Advancement

The education level and experience needed for workers in State and local government varies by occupation. For most professional jobs, a college degree is required. To obtain an entry level urban or regional planning position most State and local government agencies require 2 years of graduate study in urban and regional planning or the equivalent in work experience. To become a judge, particularly a State trial or appellate court judge, one usually is required to be a lawyer. About half of all State judges are appointed and the other half are elected in partisan or nonpartisan elections. Most State and local judges serve fixed terms, ranging from 4 or 6 years for limited jurisdiction judges to 14 years for some appellate court judges.

A master's degree in public administration is widely recommended, but not required, for city managers. They may gain experience as management analysts or assistants in government departments working with councils and mayors. After several years, they may be hired to manage a town or a small city and eventually become manager of larger cities.

Voters elect most chief executives and legislators, so local support is very important. Volunteer work and community services are valuable ways to establish vital community support. Those elected to these positions come from a variety of backgrounds, but must conform to age, residency, and citizenship regulations. Advancement opportunities for most elected public officials are limited to other offices in the jurisdictions in which they live. For example, a local council member may run for mayor or for a position in State government, and State legislators may decide to run for governor or Congress.

Most applicants for firefighting jobs must have a high school education or its equivalent and pass a civil service examination. In addition, they need to pass a medical examination and tests of strength, physical stamina, coordination, and agility. Experience as a volunteer firefighter or as a firefighter in the Armed Forces is helpful, as is completion of community college courses in fire science. Recruits study firefighting techniques, fire prevention, local building codes, emergency procedures, and the proper use of rescue equipment. Firefighters may be promoted depending on written examination results and job performance.

Bus drivers must comply with Federal regulations that require drivers who operate vehicles designed to transport 16 or more passengers to obtain a commercial driver's license from the State in which they live. To qualify for a commercial driver's license, applicants must pass a written test on rules and regulations and demonstrate they can operate a commercial vehicle safely. For subway and streetcar operator jobs, applicants with a high school education have the best chance. In some cities, prospective subway operators are required to work as busdrivers for a specified period of time. Successful applicants are generally in good health, possess good communication skills, and are able to make quick, sound judgments. Because busdrivers and subway operators deal with passengers, they need an even temperament and emotional stability. Driving in heavy, fast-moving, or stop-and-go traffic and dealing with passengers can be stressful.

Table 2. Employment of wage and salary workers in State and local government, excluding education and hospitals, by occupation, 1998 and projected change, 1998-2008

(Employment in thousands)

Occupation	1998 Employment Number	1998 Employment Percent	1998-2008 Percent change
All occupations	7,152	100.0	11.8
Service	2,043	28.6	19.5
Police patrol officers	431	6.0	32.1
Correctional officers	361	5.0	37.9
Fire fighters	228	3.2	5.5
Cleaning and building service occupations, except private household	124	1.7	1.7
Personal service occupations	104	1.5	10.4
Police and detective supervisors	102	1.4	13.3
Sheriffs and deputy sheriffs	91	1.3	34.2
Nursing aides, orderlies, and attendants	71	1.0	10.8
Administrative support, including clerical	1,445	20.2	1.6
Office clerks, general	281	3.9	18.1
Secretaries	197	2.8	-10.8
Word processors and typists	111	1.6	-31.2
Office and administrative support supervisors and managers	103	1.4	7.7
Bookkeeping, accounting, and auditing clerks	85	1.2	-9.7
Dispatchers, police, fire, and ambulance	77	1.1	6.0
Adjusters, investigators, and collectors	76	1.1	-3.0
Professional specialty	1,134	15.9	18.7
Social workers	219	3.1	35.2
Teachers, librarians, and counselors	128	1.8	10.6
Recreation workers	109	1.5	11.9
Lawyers and judicial workers	105	1.5	10.0
Social and human service assistants	84	1.2	21.3
Engineers	75	1.1	10.6
Registered nurses	82	1.1	10.3
Executive, administrative, and managerial	936	13.1	8.4
Inspectors and compliance officers, except construction	84	1.2	12.1
Government chief executives and legislators	79	1.1	2.8
General managers and top executives	76	1.1	7.6
Accountants and auditors	78	1.1	3.2
Precision production, craft, and repair	757	10.6	8.0
Highway maintenance workers	143	2.0	11.2
Blue-collar worker supervisors	109	1.5	11.1
Maintenance repairers, general utility	89	1.2	-10.2
Water and liquid waste treatment plant and system operators	80	1.1	12.0
Construction equipment operators	75	1.1	11.2
Operators, fabricators, and laborers	358	5.0	8.2
Helpers, laborers, and material movers, hand	166	2.3	8.4
Motor vehicle operators	140	2.0	7.0
Technicians and related support	316	4.4	7.3
Health technicians and technologists	133	1.9	9.1
Technicians, except health and engineering and science	94	1.3	5.6
Engineering and science technicians and technologists	55	0.8	10.1
Agriculture, forestry, fishing, and related	116	1.6	11.5
Laborers, landscaping and groundskeeping	79	1.1	11.7
All other occupations	47	0.7	9.5

226

Police departments in most areas require applicants to be U.S. citizens of good character, at least 20 years old, and able to meet rigorous physical and mental standards. Police departments increasingly encourage applicants to take college courses, and some require a college degree. Many community and junior colleges, as well as colleges and universities, offer programs in law enforcement or administration of justice. Officers usually attend a local or regional police academy program, which includes classroom instruction in constitutional law and civil rights, State laws and local ordinances, and accident investigation. They also receive training in patrol, traffic control, using firearms, self-defense, first aid, and emergency management. Promotions for police officers are highly influenced by scores on a written civil service examination and subsequent performance evaluations by their superiors.

Earnings

Earnings vary by occupation, size of the State or locality, and region of the country. As in most industries, professionals and managers earn more than other workers. Earnings in the occupations having the largest in employment State and local government appear in table 3.

Table 3. Median hourly earnings of the largest occupations in State and local government, 1997

Occupation	State government	Local government	All industries
Police patrol officers	$15.76	$17.65	$17.68
Social workers, except medical and psychiatric	14.80	15.44	14.01
Fire fighters	14.14	15.10	14.73
Correction officers and jailers	13.14	14.27	16.63
Sheriffs and deputy sheriffs	—	13.10	13.11
Secretaries, except legal and medical	11.21	11.50	11.00
Highway maintenance workers	11.63	11.08	11.24
Typists, including word processing	10.82	10.75	10.51
General office clerks	9.66	9.74	9.10
Recreation workers	—	7.95	7.69

As reported by the International City/County Management Association (ICMA), median annual salaries in 1998 of selected executive and managerial occupations in local government appear in table 4. The ICMA also reported in it's Municipal Year Book for 1998 that according to a 1997 survey, median annual entrance level base salary for firefighters was about $28,000, while the maximum base salary level median was $35,000. According to the same survey, police officers were paid a median entrance salary of $38,100 a year. Earnings vary by region and the size of the police and fire departments. Larger departments generally pay higher salaries.

According to the American Public Transit Association, in early 1999 local transit busdrivers in metropolitan areas with more than 2 million inhabitants were paid an average top hourly wage rate of $17.90 by companies with over 1,000 employees, and $16.00 by those with fewer than 1,000 employees. In smaller metropolitan areas, they had an average top hourly wage rate of $14.70 in areas with between 250,000 and 500,000 residents, and $12.60 in areas with resident populations below 50,000. Generally, drivers can reach the top rate in 3 or 4 years.

According to data from the American Public Transit Association, in early 1999 the top-rate full-time hourly earnings of operators for commuter rail ranged from $17.50 to $28.70; operators for heavy rail from $17.50 to $26.00; and operators for light rail from $13.60 to $21.90. Transit workers in the northeastern United States typically had the highest wages.

Employer-provided benefits—including health and life insurance and retirement benefits—are more common among State and local government employees than among workers in the private sector.

Table 4. Median annual salary for selected executive and managerial occupations in local government, 1998

Occupation	City	County
City manager	$70,000	$76,392
Engineer	59,777	56,623
Information services director	56,989	59,928
Assistant chief administrative officer	56,788	51,723
Chief administrative officer	55,411	56,343
Chief financial officer	55,347	48,892
Economic development /planning director	54,575	48,000
Fire chief	52,645	45,586
Chief law enforcement official	52,407	45,226
Public works director	50,493	56,196
Personnel director	50,543	47,710
Health officer	46,556	49,656
Parks and recreation director	45,960	42,840
Human services director	43,332	54,984
Purchasing director	43,255	40,290
Chief librarian	39,456	40,694
Clerk	36,800	34,626
Treasurer	36,072	34,234
Chief elected officials	5,000	21,011

Source: International City/County Management Association (ICMA)

Outlook

State and local government employment is projected to increase about 12 percent during the 1998-2008 period, slower than the 15 percent growth projected for all sectors of the economy combined. Employment growth will stem from the rising demand for services at the State and local levels. An increasing population and State and local assumption of responsibility for some services previously provided by the Federal Government is fueling the growth of these services. Despite the increased demand for the services of State and local governments, employment growth will be dampened by budgetary constraints due to reductions in Federal aid, especially at the county level, and resistance from citizens to tax increases.

Employment in nearly all major occupational groups is expected to grow in State and local government through the year 2008. For example, demand for most protective service occupations will grow faster than average, spurred by rising demand for law enforcement and correctional officers to oversee the increasing population of convicted offenders. According to the National League of Cities' 1998 survey, over three-fourths of all cities reported that they had increased spending on public safety. Employment of other service workers, production workers, laborers, and operators will grow at a rate slower than average, however, in response to governments' increased tendency to contract out some services. The National League of Cities also reported that cities increased their contracting out of jobs by more than 20 percent in 1998.

Increased demand for services should produce slow growth in employment of motor vehicle operators and helpers, laborers, and material movers through the year 2008. However, rapid increases in demand for some services—such as those for the elderly, mentally impaired, and children—will spur faster than average growth of social and social and human service assistants. Finally, urban and regional planners are expected to experience average growth, as the use of planning is promoted by population growth in city and State government.

Slow growth is projected in executive, administrative, and managerial occupations and administrative support occupations. Employment of government chief executives and legislators will change little through the year 2008 because the number of these positions generally remains fairly stable. Employment change occurs in rare situations, such as when a small town switches from a volunteer chief executive to a manager or paid mayor. Employment in administrative support occupations in State and local government is expected to increase very little and employment in many occupations is projected to decline, as the increasing use of personal computers by professionals and managers continues to reduce the need for secretaries, typists, word processors, and data entry operators.

Sources of Additional Information

Individuals interested in working for State or local government agencies should contact the appropriate agencies. City, county, and State personnel and human resources departments, and local offices of State employment services have applications and additional information.

Other information about careers in government is available from:

➤ The Council of State Governments, P.O. Box 11910, Research Park Drive, Lexington, KY 40578-1910. Internet: **http://www.csg.org**
➤ International City Management Association (ICMA), 777 North Capital NE., Suite 500, Washington, DC 20002. Internet: **http://www.icma.org**
➤ International Personnel Management Association, 1617 Duke Street, Alexandria, VA. Internet: **http://www.ipma-hr.org**
➤ National Association of Counties, 440 First Street NW., Suite 800, Washington, DC 20001. Internet: **http://www.naco.org**
➤ National Association of State Personnel Executives, P.O. Box 11910, Iron Works Pike, Lexington, KY 40578-1910. Internet: **http://www.statesnews.org/naspe/rolesnfn.html**
➤ National League of Cities, 1301 Pennsylvania Avenue, NW., Washington, DC 20004. Internet: **http://www.nlc.org**

Information on many occupations commonly employed by State and local government may be found in the 2000-01 *Occupational Outlook Handbook*:

● Correctional officers
● Firefighting occupations
● Government chief executives and legislators
● Lawyers and judicial workers
● Police and detectives
● Social and human service assistants
● Urban and regional planners

Sources of State and Local Job Outlook Information

State and local job market and career information is available from State employment security agencies. These agencies develop detailed information about local labor markets, such as current and projected employment by occupation and industry, characteristics of the work force, and changes in State and local area economic activity. Listed below are addresses and telephone numbers of the directors of research and analysis in these agencies and, in most cases, Internet addresses of these agencies.

Alabama
Chief, Labor Market Information, Alabama Department of Industrial Relations, 649 Monroe St., Room 422, Montgomery, AL 36130. Phone: (334) 242-8800. Internet: **http://www.dir.state.al.us/lmi**

Alaska
Chief, Research and Analysis, Alaska Department of Labor, P.O. Box 25501, Juneau, AK 99802-5501. Phone: (907) 465-4500. Internet: **http://www.labor.state.ak.us**

Arizona
Research Administrator, Arizona Department of Economic Security, P.O. Box 6123, Site Code 733A, Phoenix, AZ 85005. Phone: (602) 542-3871. Internet: **http://www.de.state.az.us/links/economic/webpage/page6.html**

Arkansas
Labor Market Information Director, Arkansas Employment Security Department, P.O. Box 2981, Little Rock, AR 72203-2981. Phone: (501)682-3159. Internet: **http://www.state.ar.us/esd**

California
Chief, Labor Market Information Division, California Employment Development Department, P.O. Box 826880, MIC 57, Sacramento, CA 94280-0001. Phone: (916) 262-2160.
Internet: **http://www.calmis.cahwnet.gov**

Colorado
Director, Labor Market Information, Colorado Department of Labor and Employment, 1515 Arapahoe St., Tower 2, Suite 400, Denver, CO 80202-2117. Phone: (303) 620-4977. Internet: **http://lmi.cdle.state.co.us**

Connecticut
Director, Office of Research and Information, Connecticut Labor Department, 200 Folly Brook Blvd., Wethersfield, CT 06109-1114. Phone: (860) 263-6255. Internet: **http://www.ctdol.state.ct.us/lmi/index.htm**

Delaware
Labor Market Information Director, Delaware Department of Labor, 4425 N. Market St., Wilmington, DE 19802. Phone: (302) 761-8060. Internet: **http://www.oolmi.net**

District of Columbia
Chief of Labor Market Information, District of Columbia Department of Employment Services, 500 C St. NW., Room 201, Washington, DC 20001. Phone: (202) 724-7214.

Florida
Chief, Bureau of Labor Market and Performance Information, Florida Department of Labor and Employment Security, 2012 Capitol Circle SE., Hartman Bldg., Suite 200, Tallahassee, FL 32399-2151. Phone: (850) 488-1048. Internet: **http://lmi.floridajobs.org**

Georgia
Director, Labor Market Information, Georgia Department of Labor, 148 International Boulevard NE., Atlanta, GA 30303-1751. Phone: (404) 656-3177. Internet: **http://www.dol.state.ga.us/lmi**

Guam
Administrator, Department of Labor, Guam Employment Services, P.O. Box 9970, Tamuning, Guam 96931. Phone: (671) 475-0111.
Internet: **http://gu.jobsearch.org**

Hawaii
Chief, Research and Statistics Office, Hawaii Department of Labor and Industrial Relations, 830 Punchbowl St., Room 304, Honolulu, HI 96813. Phone: (808) 586-8999. Internet: **http://dlir.state.hi.us**

Idaho
Bureau Chief, Research and Analysis, Idaho Department of Labor, 317 Main St., Boise, ID 83735-0001. Phone: (208) 334-6170.
Internet: **http://www.sde.state.id.us/cis**

Illinois
Economic Information and Analysis Manager, Illinois Department of Employment Security, 401 South State St., Suite 743, Chicago, IL 60605. Phone: (312) 793.-2316.
Internet: **http://www.ioicc.state.il.us/LMI/default.htm**

Indiana
Director, Labor Market Information, Indiana Department of Workforce Development, Indiana Government Center, South , E211, 10 North Senate Ave., Indianapolis, IN 46204-2277. Phone: (317) 232-7460.
Internet: **http://www.dwd.state.in.us**

Iowa
Division Administrator, Research and Information Services, Iowa Workforce Development, 1000 East Grand Ave., Des Moines, IA 50319-0209. Phone: (515) 2 81-6647. Internet: **http://www.state.ia.us/iwd**

Kansas
Chief, Kansas Department of Human Resources, 401 SW Topeka Blvd., Topeka, KS 66603-3182. Phone: (785) 296-5058.
Internet: **http://entkdhr.ink.org/cgi-dir/newjob.cgi**

Kentucky
Manager, LMI Branch, Division of Administration/Financial Mngt, Kentucky Department of Employment Services, 275 East Main St., Suite 2-C, Frankfort, KY 40621. Phone: (502) 564-7976.
Internet: **http://www.des.state.ky.us/agencies/wforce/des/lmi/lmi.htm**

Louisiana
Director, Research and Statistics Division, Louisiana Department of Labor, P.O. Box 94094, Baton Rouge, LA 70804-9094. Phone: (225) 342-3140. Internet: **http://www.ldol.state.la.us/lmipage.htm**

Maine
Director, Labor Market Information Services, Maine Department of Labor, 20 Union St., Augusta, ME 04330. Phone: (207) 287-2271.
Internet: **http://www.state.me.us/labor/lmis/frdef.htm**

Maryland
Director, Office of Labor Market Analysis and Information, Maryland Department of Labor, Licensing and Regulations, 1100 North Eutaw St., Room 601, Baltimore, MD 21201. Phone: (410) 767-2250.
Internet: **http://www.dllr.state.md.us/lmi/index.htm**

Massachusetts
Labor Market Information and Research Director, Massachusetts Division of Employment and Training, 19 Staniford St., 5th Floor, Boston, MA 02114. Phone: (617) 626-6560. Internet: **http://www.detma.org/lmiinfo.htmb**

Michigan
Director, Office of Labor Market Information, Michigan Jobs Commission, Employment Service Agency, 7310 Woodward Ave., Room 520, Detroit, MI 48202. Phone: (313) 872-5904.
Internet: **http://www.michlmi.org**

Minnesota
Director, BLS Programs, Research and Statistical Office, Minnesota Department of Economic Security, 390 North Robert St., St. Paul, MN 55104. Phone: (612) 296-4087.
Internet: **http://www.des.state.mn.us/lmi/careers**

Mississippi
Labor Market Information Director, Mississippi Employment Security Commission, P.O. Box 1699, Jackson, MS 39215-1699. Phone: (601) 961-7424. Internet: **http://208.137.131.31/lmi/index.html**

Missouri
Chief Administrator, Research and Analysis, Missouri Department of Labor and Industrial Relations, 421 East Dunkin St., P.O. Box 59, Jefferson City, MO 65104-0059. Phone: (573) 751-3637.
Internet: **http://www.works.state.mo.us/lmi**

Montana
Director, Office of Research and Analysis, Montana Department of Labor and Industry, P.O. Box 1728, Helena, MT 59624-1728. Phone: (406) 444-2430; within Montana at (800) 633-0229; outside Montana at (800) 541-3904. Internet: **http://rad.dli.state.mt.us**

Nebraska
Labor Market Information Administrator, Nebraska Department of Labor, 550 South 16th St., Lincoln, NE 68509-4600. Phone: (402) 471-9964.
Internet: **http://www.dol.state.ne.us/nelmi.htm**

Nevada
Chief, DETR, Bureau of Research and Analysis, Information Development and Processing Division, 500 East Third St., Carson City, NV 89713-0001. Phone: (775) 687-4550, ext. 228.
Internet: **http://www.state.nv.us/detr/lmi/index.htm**

New Hampshire
Director, Economic and Labor Market Information Bureau, New Hampshire Department of Employment Security, 32 South Main St., Concord, NH 03301. Phone: (603) 228-4123.
Internet: **http://www.nhworks.state.nh.us/LMIpage.htm**

New Jersey
Assistant Commissioner, Labor Planning and Analysis, New Jersey Department of Labor, P.O. Box 56, 5th Floor, Trenton, NJ 08625-0056.
Phone: (609) 292-2643. Internet: **http://www.state.nj.us/labor/lra/**

New Mexico
Chief, Economic Research and Analysis Bureau, New Mexico Department of Labor, 401 Broadway Blvd. NE, P.O. Box 1928, Albuquerque, NM 87103. Phone: (505) 841-8645.
Internet: **http://www3.state.nm.us/dol/dol_lmif.html**

New York
Director, Division of Research and Statistics, New York Department of Labor, State Office Building Campus, Room 400, Albany, NY 12240.
Phone: (518) 457-6369.
Internet: **http://www.labor.state.ny.us/html/atool/lmiatool.htm**

North Carolina
Director, Labor Market Information, North Carolina Employment Security Commission, P.O. Box 25903, Raleigh, NC 27611. Phone: (919) 733-2936. Internet: **http://www.esc.state.nc.us**

North Dakota
Program Support Area Manager, North Dakota Job Service, 1000 East Divide Ave., P.O. Box 5507, Bismarck, ND 58506-5507. Phone: (701) 328-2868. Internet: **http://www.state.nd.us/jsnd/lmi.htm**

Ohio
Director, Ohio Bureau of Employment Services, Labor Market Information Division, 145 South Front St., P.O. Box 1618, Columbus, OH 43216-1618. Phone: (614) 752-9494. Internet: **http://lmi.state.oh.us**

Oklahoma
Director, Labor Market Information, Oklahoma Employment Security Commission, 2401 North Lincoln, Will Rogers Memorial Office Bldg., Oklahoma City, OK 73105. Phone: (405) 525-7265.
Internet: **http://www.oesc.state.ok.us/lmi/default.htm**

Oregon
Labor Market Information Director, Oregon Employment Department, 875 Union St. NE., Salem, OR 97311. Phone: (503) 947-1212.
Internet: **http://olmis.emp.state.or.us**

Pennsylvania
Director, Bureau of Research and Statistics, Pennsylvania Department of Labor and Industry, 7th and Forester Streets, Room 101, Harrisburg, PA 17120-0001. Phone: (717) 787-3266. Internet: **http://www.lmi.state.pa.us**

Puerto Rico
Director, Research and Statistics Division, Puerto Rico Bureau of Employment Security, 505 Munoz Rivera Ave., 20th Floor, Hato Rey, PR 00918. Phone: (787) 754-5385.

Rhode Island
Director, Labor Market Information, Rhode Island Department of Employment and Training, 101 Friendship St., Providence, RI 02903-3740. Phone: (401) 222-3730.
Internet: **http://www.det.state.ri.us/web1dev/lmi/rioicchm.html**

South Carolina
Director, Labor Market Information, South Carolina Employment Security Commission, 610 Hampton St., P.O. Box 995, Columbia, SC 29202.
Phone: (803) 737-2660. Internet: **http://www.sces.org/lmi/index.htm**

South Dakota
Director, Labor Market Center, South Dakota Department of Labor, P.O. Box 4730, Aberdeen, SD 57402-4730. Phone: (605) 626-2314.
Internet: **http://www.state.sd.us/dol/lmic/index.htm**

Tennessee
Director, Research and Statistics Division, Tennessee Department of Employment Security, 500 James Robertson Pkwy., Davy Crockett Tower, 11th Floor, Nashville, TN 37245-1000. Phone: (615) 741-2284.
Internet: **http://www.state.tn.us/empsec/lmi.htm**

Texas
Director of Labor Market Information, Texas Workforce Commission, 9001 North IH-35, Suite 103A, Austin, TX 78778. Phone: (512) 491-4802. Internet: **http://www.twc.state.tx.us/lmi/lmi.html**

Utah
Director, Labor Market Information, Utah Department of Workforce Services, 140 East 300 South, P.O. Box 45249, Salt Lake City, UT 84145-0249. Phone: (801) 526-9401. Internet: **http://www.dws.state.ut.us**

Vermont
Chief, Research and Analysis, Vermont Department of Employment and Training, 5 Green Mountain Dr., P.O. Box 488, Montpelier, VT 05601-0488. Phone: (802) 828-4153. Internet: **http://www.det.state.vt.us**

Virgin Islands
Chief, Bureau of Labor Statistics, Virgin Islands Department of Labor, 53A and 54B Kronprindsens Gade, Charlotte Amalie, St. Thomas, VI 00820. Phone: (340) 776-3700.

Virginia
Director, Economic Information and Services Division, Virginia Employment Commission, 703 East Main St., P.O. Box 1358, Richmond, VA 23218-1358. Phone: (804) 786-7496.
Internet: **http://www.vec.state.va.us/lbrmkt/lmi.htm**

Washington
Director, Labor Market and Economic Analysis, Employment Security Division, Mail Stop 6000—P.O. Box 9046, Olympia, WA 98507-9046. Phone: (360) 438-4804. Internet: **http://www.wa.gov/esd/lmea**

West Virginia
Director, Research, Information and Analysis, West Virginia Bureau of Employment Programs, 112 California Ave., Charleston, WV 25305-0112.

Phone: (304) 558-2660.
Internet: **http://www.state.wv.us/bep/lmi/default.htm**

Wisconsin
Chief, LMI Data Development, Wisconsin Department of Workforce Development, 201 East Washington Ave., Room 2214, Madison, WI 53702. Phone: (608) 266-2930.
Internet: **http://www.dwd.state.si.us/dwelmi**

Wyoming
Manager, Research and Planning, Division of Administration, Wyoming Department of Employment, P.O. Box 2760, Casper, WY 82602-2760. Phone: (307) 473-3801. Internet: **http://wydoe.state.wy.us**

*U.S. Government Printing Office: 2000 — 463-328

Here Are Just Some of Our Products!

JIST publishes hundreds of books, videos, software products, and other items. Some of our best-selling career and educational reference books and software are presented here, followed by an order form. You can also order these books through any bookstore or Internet bookseller's site.

Check out JIST's Web site at www.jist.com for tables of contents and free chapters on these and other products.

Occupational Outlook Handbook, 2000-2001 Edition

U.S. Department of Labor

We will meet or beat ANY price on the OOH!

The *Occupational Outlook Handbook* is the most widely used career exploration resource. This is a quality reprint of the government's *OOH,* only at a less-expensive price. It describes 250 jobs–jobs held by almost 90 percent of the U.S. workforce–making it ideal for students, counselors, teachers, librarians, and job seekers. Job descriptions cover the nature of the work, working conditions, training, job outlook, and earnings. Well-written narrative with many charts and photos. New edition every two years.

ISBN 1-56370-676-8 / Order Code LP-J6768 / **$18.95** Softcover
ISBN 1-56370-677-6 / Order Code LP-J6776 / **$22.95** Hardcover

*The O*NET Dictionary of Occupational Titles*™

Based on data from the U.S. Department of Labor
Compiled by J. Michael Farr and LaVerne L. Ludden, Ed.D.,
with database work by Paul Mangin

JIST is the first publisher to use the Department of Labor's new O*NET data, which was developed to replace the *Dictionary of Occupational Titles.* This reference includes descriptions of all 1,100 jobs in the O*NET database and is the only printed source of this information!

ISBN 1-56370-510-9 / Order Code LP-J5109 / **$39.95** Softcover
ISBN 1-56370-509-5 / Order Code LP-J5095 / **$49.95** Hardcover

JIST Order and Catalog Request Form

Purchase Order #: _____ (Required by some organizations)

Billing Information

Organization Name: _____

Accounting Contact: _____

Street Address: _____

_____

_____

City, State, Zip: _____

Phone Number: ( ) _____

Shipping Information with Street Address (If Different from Above)

Organization Name: _____

Contact: _____

Street Address: (We *cannot* ship to P.O. boxes) _____

_____

_____

City, State, Zip: _____

Phone Number: ( ) _____

> Please copy this form if you
> need more lines for your order.

Phone: 1-800-648-JIST
Fax: 1-800-JIST-FAX
World Wide Web Address:
http://www.jist.com

Credit Card Purchases: VISA_____ MC_____ AMEX_____

Card Number: _____

Exp. Date: _____

Name As on Card: _____

Signature: _____

Quantity	Order Code	Product Title	Unit Price	Total
	———	Free JIST Catalog	Free	———

jist
Publishing

8902 Otis Avenue
Indianapolis, IN 46216

Shipping / Handling / Insurance Fees

In the continental U.S. add 7% of subtotal:
- Minimum amount charged = $4.00
- Maximum amount charged = $100.00
- FREE shipping and handling on any prepaid orders over $40.00

Above pricing is for regular ground shipment only. For rush or special delivery, call JIST Customer Service at 1-800-648-JIST for the correct shipping fee.

Outside the continental U.S. call JIST Customer Service at 1-800-648-JIST for an estimate of these fees.

Payment in U.S. funds only!

Subtotal	
+5% Sales Tax *Indiana Residents*	
+Shipping / Handling / Ins. (See left)	
TOTAL	

JIST thanks you for your order!